The Adventures of Wu

The Adventures of Wu

The Life Cycle of a Peking Man

Volumes I and II

By H. Y. LOWE

盧興源

With an Introduction by
Derk Bodde

PRINCETON UNIVERSITY PRESS
PRINCETON, NEW JERSEY

Published by Princeton University Press,
41 William Street, Princeton, New Jersey 08540
In the United Kingdom: Princeton University Press,
Guildford, Surrey
Introduction and index copyright © 1983
by Princeton University Press

LCC 82-48568
ISBN 0-691-06552-7
ISBN 0-691-01400-0 pbk.

Printed in the United States of America by
Princeton University Press, Princeton, New Jersey

This one-volume edition consists of a photo-offset
facsimile of Volumes I and II of *The Adventures of Wu*
by H. Y. Lowe, originally published by
The Peking Chronicle Press in 1940 and 1941.
The pagination of the text is identical
to that of the original edition.

First Princeton Paperback printing, 1983

ORIGINAL PUBLISHER'S NOTE

This is the first volume of "The Adventures of Wu," the life cycle of a Peking man which ran so successfully for almost a year in THE PEKING CHRONICLE. There was originally no intention to issue these series in book form but so persistent and frequent have been the requests to do so that the pressure of public opinion was finally yielded to.

The series have been thoroughly revised and rewritten and will be published complete in two volumes. The second book will appear in the autumn.

The appearance of the present book has been delayed due to the fact that it had to be written, set up, printed and bound in between the publication of a daily newspaper. Under these circumstances the publisher has done the best he could and it is hoped that this little volume and its forthcoming companion will meet with the approval of the public.

An index to both volumes is being prepared and will be included in Volume II. The table of contents in this book has been made as comprehensive as was thought desirable and the main subject matter of each page is indicated.

Constructive criticism and suggestions for improvements will be welcome and may be addressed to The Editor, THE PEKING CHRONICLE, 2 Mei Cha Hutung, Peking.

[1940]

CONTENTS

CONTENTS

CONTENTS

CONTENTS

CONTENTS

INTRODUCTION

This book is the story of a Chinese boy named Wu, but in a larger sense it is also the story of one of the world's great cities, Peking. The book begins with the birth of the hero in Peking early in the present century, continues with his upbringing and education, and ends with his marriage, all in Peking. Converted into the temporal framework of a city as old as Peking, this span of somewhat over twenty years corresponds very roughly, perhaps, to half a year or slightly more than that in the life of such a city. For Peking this particular half year was of exceptional importance because it marked the conclusion of an ancient way of life before the city, at mid-century, abruptly began that metamorphosis which has made it what it is today.

In the course of narrating young Wu's upbringing, the book tells us a great deal about day-to-day life in old Peking: the festivals celebrated by Wu, his family and friends, the foods they ate, the games they played, the teahouses, fairs, temples or rural places they visited. Its focus is not, however, solely on the pleasures of life, for it also tells how people sometimes sickened, died and were buried in Peking. We shall read more below about how the book came to be written, who its author is or was, and what it tells us. First, however, let us examine the city that provides its setting.

THE CITY

Peking stands near the northwestern rim of the great North China plain, some ninety-five miles from the sea. Its position just south of the fortieth parallel places it on the same latitude or nearly the same latitude as several other noted cities around the world: Philadelphia, Madrid, Naples, Ankara, and Samarkand. Beyond the miles of flat terrain surrounding Peking rise the silhouettes of the Western Hills on its western horizon. And not far beyond these silhouettes, where the hills become mountains, China's Great Wall snakes its way across some eighteen hundred miles of mountain, steppe and desert from the China Sea to Central Asia.

Peking's name, made up of two Chinese words that mean "Northern Capital," stands in apposition to that of another well-known city, Nanking or "Southern Capital." Other spellings also exist for Peking, such as Pei-ching or Beijing, but of them all, Peking is the oldest, best known, and the one regularly used in this book.

Peking's history, under several earlier names, goes back nearly three thousand years to a time when it was the capital of a small principality, long before a united Chinese empire yet existed. Only much later, under the rule of the alien Mongols (1280-1367), did the city become capital of all China, and thereby simultaneously the world metropolis of a Mongol empire extending from the Yellow Sea to the Danube. Even then Peking was still not called Peking. This name was given it in 1421, more than half a century after the expulsion of the Mongols, at the same time that the capital was returned to it after having been at Nanking during the intervening years.

Thereafter Peking retained both its name and political status until the end of the empire in 1911, as well as during a good part of the republican period that followed. During the years of 1928-37 and 1945-49, however, when the city was controlled by the Kuomintang (Nationalist) government of Chiang Kai-shek, it was officially renamed Peiping, "Northern Peace," while Nanking again became the capital. But from 1949 onward, when the People's Republic of China was established, Peking has regained both its old name and its status as capital.

Of the countless Westerners who over the centuries have lengthily sojourned in China and thereby acquired the status of "old China hands," one of the earliest and probably still the best known today is Marco Polo. For seventeen years (1275-

92) he lived and travelled in China in the service of the Mongol emperor Khubilai, before returning to his native Venice. Assuredly he knew much about the future Peking, which he termed Cambaluc, a word derived from Khanbaligh, "City of the Khan," itself a name probably of Central Asian Turkish origin. Here is part of what he says about the city:[1]

> As regards the size of this city you must know that it has a compass of 24 miles, for each side of it hath a length of 6 miles, and it is four-square. And it is all walled round with walls of earth which have a thickness of full ten paces at bottom, and a height of more than 10 paces. . . . And they are provided throughout with loop-holed battlements. . . . There are 12 gates and over each gate there is a great and handsome palace. . . . In those palaces are vast halls in which are kept the arms of the city garrison.
>
> The streets are so straight and wide that you can see right along them from end to end and from one gate to the other. And up and down the city there are beautiful palaces, and many great and fine hostelries, and fine houses in great numbers. All the plots of ground on which the houses of the city are built are four-square, and laid out with straight lines; all the plots being occupied by great and spacious palaces, with courts and gardens of proportionate size. . . . Each square plot is emcompassed by handsome streets for traffic; and thus the whole city is arranged in squares just like a chess-board, and disposed in a manner so perfect and masterly that it is impossible to give a description that should do it justice. . . .

Despite the long time interval, there are evident similarities between Marco Polo's thirteenth-century Cambaluc and Peking of the early twentieth century. Like Cambaluc, Peking was a quadrangle whose moated city walls, each facing one of the four compass points, sharply divided the hustle-bustle of some one million inhabitants within from the quiet open fields of rural China outside.

Within the walls, a gridiron of major avenues and interspersed smaller streets crossed the city from north to south and east to west. Networks of still lesser lanes and alleys, not always so precisely oriented, intersected these thoroughfares. Fronting all of them were the white or grey plastered walls (often windowless) and red or dark wooden gates (often closed) of palace and temple enclosures, mansions and ordinary houses. Shops, by contrast, had windows and doors open to the street, and facades whose wooden frames were sometimes elaborately painted and carved. All buildings, whether shops or otherwise, were usually small and limited to a single storey, and all were oriented to face the south, direction of the life-giving sun. Behind the somewhat drab exteriors of most, their rooms were arranged around one or several receding courtyards, usually invisible from the street and embellished by trees and greenery. Finally, at the very center of the city—and therefore, symbolically, at the very center of the cosmos—stood (and still stands) the vast assemblage of imperial palace buildings known as the Forbidden City. This was separated from the remainder of the city by its own four-square wall and moat.

But old Peking was much more than a complex of streets, walls and buildings conforming to a cosmic pattern. It also represented an ancient way of life, full of color, variety and refinement for those with the modest wherewithal needed to enjoy it, but sometimes harsh and bitter for others lacking it. Sitting in my courtyard, as I often did as a student in the 1930s, I could hear, from the streets beyond the walls of the compound, the distinctive calls or other signals of itinerant food or cloth vendors, barbers or knife sharpeners, and many more. Or, from overhead,

[1] See Henry Yule, tr., *The Book of Ser Marco Polo*, 3rd ed., revised by Henri Cordier (2 vols.; London: John Murray, 1921), I, 374-375. For a more detailed but less flowing version, see A. C. Moule and Paul Pelliot, *Marco Polo, the Description of the World* (2 vols.; London: George Routledge & Sons, 1938), I, 212-213.

I could hear the soft aeolian hums of a flock of pigeons wheeling in the sky. The sounds came from the tiny bamboo whistles attached to the tails of these birds by their owners.

On the larger streets outside, a few cars, buses or trams might be seen. Much more common, however, were two-wheeled carts and pushcarts as well as one-wheeled barrows, all pulled or pushed by horses, donkeys or human beings. Sometimes their loads included humans or squealing pigs as well as inanimate objects. From a coal mine in the Western Hills came occasional files of plodding camels, large blocks of coal piled around their double Bactrian humps. Men trotted along the dusty streets, shouldering heavy loads slung from the ends of jouncing poles. And everywhere, of course, were the pedestrians, bicyclists and man-drawn rickshaws. The Chinese appropriately called the latter *yang ch'e*, "foreign vehicles"— a lasting reminder that the earliest rickshaws had been imported from Japan, where they had been allegedly invented by a nineteenth-century American missionary.

By visiting certain parks at the appropriate seasons, one could see extraordinarily diversified displays of peonies or chrysanthemums. Over one hundred varieties of the latter have been recorded in Chinese writings, with such fanciful names as "snow-covered azure mountain," "evening sun on a duck's back," or "silver tiger-whiskers." At other specified times—particularly in spring—large crowds visited temple festivals and fairs within the city or made longer pilgrimages to other temples in the Western Hills.

All this and much more still flourished in Peking of the 1930s, declined somewhat during the Sino-Japanese War of 1937-45, and then virtually disappeared during the years following the establishment of the People's Republic of China in Peking in 1949. Most devastating of many physical changes since 1949 has been demolition of the city walls which had shaped Peking and given it so much meaning and beauty. Within these former walls, many avenues have been widened and the low buildings once flanking them have been replaced by huge, often towering, structures, sometimes garishly colored and sometimes already looking dilapidated. Among them are examples of "Stalinesque Gothic" architecture, standing as mute reminders of an era of Sino-Soviet friendship otherwise almost forgotten.

Freed from the constraints of the city walls, the avenues now push their way for many miles into the surrounding countryside, bringing with them factories, apartment buildings, and much else, by which the once open fields have been effectively obliterated. And with this urban sprawl has also come urban smog, as well as a Peking population explosion to five, six, or who knows how many millions. Psychologically, too, the changes have been equally sweeping even though less immediately apparent. In short, except within the Forbidden City or at a very few other places, it is difficult for those few who still remember Peking as it once was to recognize it in the present megalopolis. Granted that the extremes of wealth and poverty have been greatly reduced since 1949, when, for example, beggars were often seen at certain frequented places in the city. One may nevertheless still rightly question whether all these changes were really necessary or desirable in order to effect this undoubted improvement.

* * *

Peking has inspired the writing of scores of books in addition to this one. Here I wish to mention seven others because, in my opinion, each effectively portrays some important aspects of the old city. All are in English, all illustrated, but only a few are still in print.

1. *Peking and the Pekingese During the First Year of the British Embassy at Peking*. By D. F. Rennie. London: John Murray, 1865. 2 vols. Pp. xix, 351 and x, 332.
   A remarkably perceptive and sympathetic account (especially for its time)

of a Peking as yet untouched by foreign influences. The author, then the physician at the British Embassy, kept a diary (March 22, 1861-April 15, 1862) covering the first year of this and the French Embassy in Peking.

2. *Annual Customs and Festivals in Peking, as Recorded in the Yen-ching sui-shih-chi*. By Tun Li-ch'en. Tr. and anot. by Derk Bodde. Peiping: Henri Vetch, 1936. 2nd ed. with new added introduction. Hong Kong: Hong Kong University Press, 1965. Pp. xxii, 147.

The author, a Manchu, wrote this charming account in Chinese in 1900. Much of what he records was still to be seen in Peking of the 1930s.

3. *The Pageant of Peking*. Photographs by Donald Mennie. Introduction by Putnam Weale (pseud. for Bertram L. Simpson). Shanghai: A. S. Watson, 1920; further printings in 1921 and 1922. Pp. 40; 66 mounted plates.

These superb large photographs, bound within a beautiful blue silk cover, provide the finest pictorial record known to me of old Peking and its environs. The historical introduction is pleasantly written but unscholarly and not always reliable.

4. *In Search of Old Peking*. By L. C. Arlington and William Lewisohn. Peiping: Henri Vetch, 1935. Pp. vi, 382.

By far the best guidebook, filled with information that is detailed, accurate, unsentimental, and comprehensive. Numerous maps and plans.

5. *Rickshaw, the Novel Lo-t'o Hsiang Tzu*. By Lao She (pseud. of Shu Ch'ing-ch'un, 1899-1966). Tr. by Jean M. James. Honolulu: University Press of Hawaii, 1979. Pp. ix, 249.

A powerful novel of the lives of the poor in pre-1937 Peking, valuable as a counterbalance to the rosier portrayals in the other books here listed. This translation is faithful to the original, whereas that by Evan King (New York: Reynal & Hitchcock, 1945) makes serious changes and distortions.

6. *The Years That Were Fat: the Last of Old China*. By George N. Kates. New York: Harper & Bros., 1952. Paperback reprint with new introduction by John K. Fairbank. Cambridge, Mass. and London: The M.I.T. Press, 1967. Pp. 268.

A unique account of Peking during its last golden years, 1933-41, by a cosmopolitan American who made himself part of the Chinese environment and lived as a Confucian gentleman.

7. *Peking Diary, a Year of Revolution*. By Derk Bodde. New York: Henry Schuman, 1950, and London: Jonathan Cape, 1951. Paperback reprint with new foreword, Greenwich, Conn.: Fawcett Premier Books, 1967 (photos in original deleted). Hardback reprint. New York: Octagon Books, 1976. Pp. xxi, 292.

A day-to-day account (August 21, 1948-August 25, 1949) of the final five months of Chiang Kai-shek's Kuomintang rule of Peking and the subsequent first seven months of Mao Tse-tung's Communist rule. This was the year of irreversible transition from old to new Peking, old to new China.

The Book

Despite its title, *The Adventures of Wu* is by no means a book primarily intended for children. Rather, it is a factual account for everyone of the traditional way of life in old Peking as it still existed during the first half of this century. Many books have been written on the sights of Peking and many on Peking festivals. Why then this republication of a book that at first sight looks like one more of the same? The answer is that *The Adventures of Wu*, though saying much about monuments and festivals, is a good deal more than just another Peking guidebook or festival book. Under the device of tracing the life of a son of the fictional Wu family from birth to marriage, it gives an amazingly comprehensive yet detailed picture of the beliefs and practices of a very traditionally-minded, lower middle-class Peking family (the boy's father is a bank cashier). The topics it treats are manifold: the mores of birth, death and marriage; nursery rhymes, children's games, and traditional education; the flowers, animals and foods of Peking; street entertainers and popular recreations; medical beliefs, birthday celebrations, and ancestor worship; hunting and fishing, and a great deal more.

Admittedly, the book is a distillation and idealization of the past in the sense that it is difficult to imagine that any single family, even one as traditional as the Wu family, could possibly have believed and practiced *everything* described in the book. Yet it is wholly believable in the sense that what it describes could all be found somewhere or sometime in Peking during the early decades of this century.

Although the author's approach is charmingly informal and makes no pretence at profound scholarship, the certainty of his knowledge is evident on every page. He and we are fortunate that, as a native of Peking, he is able to see his subject from the inside, yet as a cultured man with obvious understanding of the outside world, he is also able to view it objectively. The English he uses is sometimes quaint but always clear and effective, and his exposition is enormously helped by the many vivid pen sketches that also come from his hand.

Originally, this book appeared as separate installments in the English-language *Peking Chronicle* in 1939-40. These proved so popular that, with some revision, they were then republished in the form of two volumes in 1940-41. These were the dark days of Japanese occupation, not long before Pearl Harbor fused the Sino-Japanese War and World War II into one. The book, as a result, achieved only a modest circulation, so that copies of the original edition are excessively rare today. In the United States, for example, only four institutions are recorded in *The National Union Catalog* as possessing the work. They are Cornell University (its Wasson Collection), the Field Museum of Natural History (Chicago), the University of Utah, and Bluffton College (Bluffton, Ohio).

By great good fortune my father, a long-term resident of Peking until wartime internment by the Japanese at Wei-hsien, Shantung, had purchased copies of *The Adventures of Wu*. It is very gratifying that now, some four decades later, one of these copies has made it possible for Princeton University Press to produce the present reincarnation.

I had originally sent the copy to my friend and publisher, Henri Vetch. This unusually gifted Frenchman, well-known among foreign circles in China, had successively been a seller and publisher of books in Peking in the 1930s and '40s, then director of Hong Kong University Press, and finally, following retirement, again a publisher of books under his own name in Hong Kong. It was during this third stage that I sent him the copy of *Adventures* which he was on the point of republishing when he died in 1978. To his widow, Mme. Elena Vetch, I am deeply indebted for returning the copy to me with permission to publish it elsewhere, and sending me at the same time an index to the book upon which she herself had been working at the time of his death. This I have now considerably further revised for final publication.

The original publisher, in his "Publisher's Note" at the beginning of Volume I, had promised there would be an index at the end of Volume II, but for understandable reasons it never materialized. The new Index, beginning at Volume II, page 227, constitutes an important addition to the book, because it provides ready access to an abundance of diverse topics that would otherwise be buried in the text. Although the author of *Adventures* succeeded rather well in romanizing Chinese words according to the standard Wade-Giles system, he nevertheless left a fair number of romanization errors in the text, and these have now all been corrected throughout the Index. For technical details, see the statement that introduces the Index. Other than the addition of this Index and of the present Introduction, as well as the printing within a single cover of what had originally been two separate volumes, this new Princeton edition is an exact reproduction of the original.

The author of *The Adventures of Wu*, H. Y. Lowe, remains a man of considerable mystery. We know that in 1942 the Peking Chronicle Press published a second book by him, *Stories from Chinese Drama*, which provides useful synopses of several hundred plays. By good fortune, we also know the Chinese characters and correct romanization of H. Y. Lowe's name. They are Lu Hsing-yüan 盧興源 [2]

Aside from this, we have very little further information. Inquiries made by me to no less than nine different persons, most of them residents of Peking when Lowe's (or Lu's) books were published, have yielded only one positive but meager reply. It comes from Professor Emeritus Hellmut Wilhelm of the University of Washington (Seattle), who was able to pass on to me information culled from a friend who had known Lowe. The information states merely that Lowe had had many children and had worked hard to give them an education. Remarks in Lowe's own book (Foreword and Volume I, pp. 2, 99 and elsewhere) indicate that he was a native of Peking, that he consulted books in English, Chinese and Japanese when writing his own book, and that possibly he had some slight personal familiarity with certain habits of life in the United States. It is barely conceivable, therefore, that he may once have been a student in Japan and/or Britain or America. With these meager hints we have to stop. Perhaps, now that the new edition is published, some reader may still write in at this late hour to say who the mysterious Mr. Lowe really was.

In a book originally published in the form of newspaper installments, it is not surprising that the chronology of its hero's life should be vague and contradictory. The book provides no dates for young Wu's birth and marriage, with which it begins and ends. From oblique references, however, we may surmise that the author perhaps thought of young Wu as being born somewhere around 1915 or not too long thereafter, and of marrying not long before 1939, when the book began to be serialized.

There is no need to speculate further. Instead, we should read the book simply as an account of how traditional people in Peking—those belonging to a secure though scarcely sumptuous level—continued to live and think during those last two or three decades (roughly from the mid 1910s to the late 1930s) when life in the ancient city was still relatively unmodernized. To that now tiny and rapidly diminishing circle of people who personally witnessed this way of life, it is hoped that the book will bring back nostalgic memories. To that vastly larger public that has never experienced the old China, it is hoped that the book will provide a

---

[2] This information comes from T. L. Yuan, *China in Western Literature* (New Haven: Far Eastern Publications, Yale University, 1958), under his listings of the two Lowe books, pp. 257, 418, 436.

sympathetic portrayal of what life was like in one of the world's most refined and beloved cultural centers, before war and revolution irrevocably changed the face of China.

March, 1982
Philadelphia

DERK BODDE
Professor Emeritus of Chinese Studies
University of Pennsylvania

FOREWORD

Since my school days I have often been asked by my foreign teachers and friends to explain certain things about the customs and habits of the Chinese people, and it has always been a cause for elation and minor satisfaction when I succeeded in giving the desired information, particularly when some misunderstanding was thus cleared up such as may be represented by the typical remark of "Oh, these Chinese pagans! You can never understand them."

And so when it was made known to me that THE PEKING CHRONICLE was interested in a daily feature describing the everyday life of a typical Chinese family in Peking, I at once decided that here was a chance to inform a goodly number of potential questioners in an interesting and systematic manner.

It was more or less in this spirit that "The Adventures of Wu" was conceived and its preparation started. To me the undertaking was an adventure in itself for I had not had any experience in this line before, and hence there was no idea, indeed, to see it finally in book form. Such an idea was later gradually developed when I had occasion to realize that although volumes have been written along the general lines as pursued in the present work, an authentic, up-to-date account without an abundance of misinterpretations is sadly wanting, not only in so far as accessibility to foreign readers is concerned but also even for the Chinese reading public.

Sections have been devoted to the description of the native life of Peking in certain kinds of books written for Chinese "tourists"—the majority of whom were aspirants for government positions in Peking or candidates for the imperial examinations in the old days—and later on for students and visitors from the provinces who rely solely on them for information, but most of these books are obsolete or even out of print. Such books, like almost all the books foreigners have written about Peking customs, have a way of leaving out certain points in their entity exactly where a thorough-going explanation is an absolute essential for a foreign reader's true appreciation of the situation. The reason for such omission on the part of the writers of these Chinese treatises is not far to seek when we consider that these books were intended not for the visitors and friends from many miles away in foreign countries where people live an entirely different life, but rather for fellow-countrymen from other parts of China where similar customs with minor differences are observed, although in such a vast country as China customs do differ considerably from one place to another. Thus the wall-enclosed Chinese home is still more or less in the same condition of isolation and mysticism as ever, surprising as it may seem, after all these years of contact with foreigners.

This book then, rather than seeking to be exhaustive, has its peculiarity in trying to avoid points which have already been profusely written on, such as the Chinese theatre and the Chinese restaurant, and my intention has always been, as much as possible, to pick up where others left off, explaining and describing things which have not been satisfactorily explained and described before, or even touched upon, judging the value of each item from the point of view of the average foreign observer and trying to answer, so to speak, likely questions from him in a truthful manner.

This book is no fiction and so has no characters or plot worthy of the words, and each section, longer or shorter, can be picked out and read by itself. It has no other motive of any kind than what is mentioned above, and while no attempt has been made to convey the impression that certain customs are most rational and deserve support and preservation, my sympathy has always been with the Peking-*jen* and to be one of whom I am not ashamed, rather the contrary. If this book helps to clear up some puzzles about the life and customs of the Chinese people living in Peking, I shall be very happy indeed.

My thanks are due to many esteemed friends, notably Mr. A. V. Wedekind and Mr. Stephen Wang, for their encouragement, guidance and invaluable assistance in making it possible to publish this work. I am also indebted to the authors of many books on similar subjects in English, Chinese and Japanese to which I had occasion to refer in the preparation of this book.

H. Y. L.

Peking May 1, 1940.

INTRODUCING THE WU FAMILY

WHOEVER has paid a visit to the Lung Fu Ssu fair will remember the narrow lanes branching eastward from the main thoroughfare as one approaches from the south the Four Arches at the junction of the Hata Men, the Chao Yang Men and Pig Streets and the prolongation of the boulevard that leads north to the Tartar City wall. The small lanes look so alike to a stranger that it is difficult for him to distinguish one from the other. Peking is a strange city and will remain strange in spite of the proposed plan for the reorganization of the city. There is no clear demarcation between business quarters and residential districts. Wherever, in days of yore, shops sprang up there were the business quarters; and wherever few of them appeared, there grew the residential districts.

But one of the small lanes, the Li Shih Hutung, the lane of the Mannerly Scholar (an euphemism for Lui Shih Hutung, the Donkey Mart), is at once obvious. Throughout its total length of a third of a mile, from Hata Men Street to South Small Street, there are no more than three shops, or maybe four. Instead it is lined on both sides with the houses of Peking's now defunct Mandarin elite, starting with the official (or private) residence of H. E. Prime Minister Shih Hsu of the Manchu Court before and after the Revolution at the western entrance of the hutung.

I remember, as if it were yesterday, on my way to school during the younger days of the Republic seeing His Excellency coming home at seven o'clock in the morning from his duties after his dawn audience with the Emperor. It was a fine sight, to be seen no more. His carriage, with a mammoth pure white Urumchi horse, and his drivers and mounted valets wearing Court hats with upturned brims of fur decorated with a big red tassel, his folded "document holder"—not a portmanteau— under the arm of the horseman leading the carriage. These linger in the memory.

The entrance to the Shih Mansion on Li Shih Hutung was the back door, and incidentally the stable door, so the whole procession, the carriage bell clanging and horses galloping, turned a 90-degree angle to dash through the back gate into the spacious compound, amidst a cloud of dust. Dust was a characteristic of Peking, particularly that western half of Donkey Mart. For full twenty seconds, I and my schoolmates used to gaze with open mouths at the pomp and gallantry of the spectacle. There was the image of the old man in Mandarin dress, theatrical in effect, with flowing white beard, a foot and half in length, and the calm, serene, opium haggard face, his onetime sparkling eyes taking on a dreary, fatigued look. That was a long time ago, though. Minister Shih Hsu died some twenty years back and I witnessed his elaborate, costly funeral.

*   *   *

A small Chinese gate of rather commonplace construction and design was seen.

In one of the lesser houses on the north side of Donkey Mart, one's attention is drawn to a small Chinese gate of rather commonplace construction and design, unpresuming, ugly and grey—grey like the cat on the backyard fence on a cloudy winter afternoon. But at a second glance one sees that the gate is sprinkled with dashes of colour. The painted beams, the gilded decoration immediately on top of the two-blade door itself, and the bits of red paper representing portions of New Year "spring couplets", all these serve to enliven the general atmosphere. Then there is the small green-lacquered name-board, some four inches wide and ten inches long, nailed upright on the upper right hand corner of the woodwork, bearing in cinnabar red the four Chinese characters Yu Yang Wu Yu—Residence of the Wus from Yu Yang.

During the period of the Warring Kingdoms, or roughly at the time of Confucius, the locality that is now Peking was known as Yu Yang for there was no Peking then. Just as Yedo was old Tokyo, so Yu Yang was old Peking. Scholars of the type of Mr. Wu take great liking in such clever poetizing of things geographic and to those who know Peking intimately nothing like this could ever escape their attention. So it is known that Mr. Wu is a native of Peking, pure and simple, no more no less.

*   *   *

It is worthwhile to make a hurried inspection of the residence of the Wus from Yu Yang for it is, in a general way, typical and therefore representative of the dwellings of the average lower-middle class of Peking's immense Chinese population. Under ordinary circumstances, and even under mildly extraordinary ones, it is not usual to be permitted to look over a Chinese house, for it is "his castle". In the United States for instance, you could easily notice at a glance whether the Smiths are at home or out of town. You can readily see that they are away if the milk bottle and morning paper are still outside and that the curtains are down. Besides when they are at home there is usually some activity noticeable from without. You could almost judge if prosperity is around by the frequent or otherwise changes of those bits of interior decoration perceivable through the sitting room window, or by the colours or texture of the curtains themselves.

But in Peking, and in the greater part of China for that matter, the "devil screen" of solid brickwork is a rubberneck-proof defense work against all and sundry intruding forces—including the neighbours' prying eyes. And Mr. Wu's house is no exception. Mr. Wu is not rich enough to hire a gatekeeper, but his devil screen is reinforced by his old faithful dog "Small Black" (we do not know why he was given such a name, for to all intents and purposes, he was mostly brown in colour and as far as size is concerned he certainly was not small) whose duty it is always to stand by and serve as a mobile devil screen to all outsiders.

The builders, architects and experts of house-designing in China, somehow or other never outgrew their idea about building their houses in the quadrangle principle. The four-sided bungalows of three rooms each surrounding a square courtyard is a project never for a moment out of the mind of every house-planner. Mr. Wu's house is, of course, like everything else, orthodox to the last letter of the word, and the general panoramic view of the house as we enter the gate and pass the devil screen so confirmed our anticipation, that we were somewhat surprised to find a fence of bamboo work segregating the southern rooms from the rest of the square. This fence, we also notice, is thickly covered with an exuberant growth of morning-glories, particularly heavy and pleasing in the central portion of the fence where Mr. Wu's workmen so smartly constructed a moon gate in the bamboo work.

His house was not new, but well kept in repairs, so to speak, for the Wus are quite well-to-do. We can only say that much now, because we are not so well acquainted with Mr. Wu to gain a clear insight of his economic status, much in the same way as we could never with good manners ask a newly made friend how much salary he gets a month. The middle court is beautiful, and yet ugly in that the flowers and plants are arranged in the conventional pattern, and not the least bit of landscape gardening can be said to be effective.

There is no character to the selection of plants and courtyard decorations, you will say. But, no, the Chinese have their own ideas of a scheme of floral decoration. For summer, it provides for pomegranate trees in pairs, two, four, or six flanking a big pottery aquarium in which, it is ordained, goldfish should be kept. A saying goes: "Matshed, fish bowl and pomegranate trees; a fat watch-dog and a fatter slave-girl" as the Chinese describe their proverbial courtyard decorations. Mr. Wu does belong to that school of thought, but he is modernistic enough to discard the slave-girl idea. As to the mat-shed, much as we look, we see only the framework of poles of fir and bamboo and the four discs decorating it, bearing one on each, the four Chinese characters "chi hsing kao chao" (吉星高照) meaning "Lucky stars highly shine". Then, through a brick door in the northeastern part of the yard shaped like a vase, we repair to the backyard where we find the "store-room", generally known to the household as "coal room" but really a counterpart of an "attic", and some more small private quarters.

We hastily beat a retreat from the house. And while thus pulling ourselves away in spite of Mr. Wu's repeated requests

to "come in, sit down and have a
cup of tea," we chose to say farewell
to our host. We were not offended
by the non-appearance of Mrs. Wu,
for we know, not directly from Mr.
Wu, though, that she was now in "a
certain happy state of expectancy",
and that the event was expected
within a day or two.

*   *   *

Mr. Wu went through college
with mediocre marks for modern
education had not long been introduced when he was attending school.
He passed his primary and high
school life in long blue gowns and
so-called horse-jackets and satin
boots, and his regulation school cap
topped his "queued" head in a manner unique in itself and never duplicated anywhere else in the world.
He cut his queue off and entered
college the same year, for that was
in 1911 when the Manchu government was overthrown and when so

Typical Chinese courtyard decorations are a fish bowl, pomegranate trees and a fat watchdog.

many grave steps of modernization were forced, almost unanimously, on the revolution-conscious Chinese. Mr. Wu's father
was an extremist in his time for he allowed young Wu, with full
knowledge of what it meant, to continue his cultural pursuit in
the college of the foreign missionaries. Moreover, the old man
was so intelligent in his "educational program" for his only son
that he gave the latter his unreserved permission to use his own
judgment in selecting his school courses in accordance with his
own likes and dislikes. Mr. Wu majored in economics and then
in chemistry and at last decided on commerce, known as the
Department of Business Training, and graduated in due course
to work in a modern Chinese bank as a junior shroff and later as
understudy cashier. This was as far back as 1915.

In China a marriage was usually arranged by the parents,
especially during Mr. Wu's time. Mr. Wu's father fain would
have left his son remain single until he was able to earn his own
livelihood because, judging from his own experience, a childhood
marriage was decidedly a failure. When Mr. Wu Senior married
he was seventeen and his bride was twenty-two. But old Mrs.
Wu thought otherwise and continued dinning in her husband's
ears the desirability of getting young Mr. Wu a wife. She had
two reasons, one superficial and the other an instinctive one; for
though she argued with her husband that young Mr. Wu needed
a wife to keep him company and to occupy his mind, she was
secretly indulging in the fond dream of "carrying a grandson
around".

Before young Mr. Wu and his wife married, they were cousins.
During the troubled days of 1900, she took refuge in the house
of Mr. Wu when her own home in the western suburbs of Peking

was in great danger of being looted. Not long after she was suggested as Mr. Wu's wife-elect by several friends and well-wishers, particularly the girl's Number Two Aunt who most heartily sponsored the proposition. The ceremony took place a short time later and the young girl became the bride of a high school boy, then the wife of a college student, a junior shroff in a bank, and later an understudy cashier. They were both twenty years old when they married.

Now, young Mr. and Mrs. Wu were not having their first child, for they had had two babies before, but only babies (and girls too) for they did not even grow big enough to have their "milk names" decided. In China girls are not half as welcome or precious as boys and so in neither case was the least bit of celebration made in honour of their arrival. Mr. Wu's mother characteristically said: "Ai Ya! girls are truly like merchandise on which we have to figure a loss! They are just good-for-nothing! I have had no daughter of my own, and that is one of the things for which I feel thrice blessed. If you have daughters you have to watch them so very closely as they grow up. And after marrying them away, you are never certain they will not prove to be a permanent burden to your family. Then, you have no guarantee that their husbands may not want concubines and thereby squander their love on some unworthy harlots. Or you join a richer family, and your attention is constantly taxed to see that your children are not being despised by the husbands and the family. And on the other hand, if your daughter gets a poor husband, how much more attention would be required to see that she does not suffer from poverty? Money, attention, time, energy, and heartache! What a losing proposition! I am glad I had only Kwang Tsung (for that is young Mr. Wu's name) to take care of and I am not half sorry that his two girl babies did not live! Now, here we are with Kwang Tsung's wife an expectant mother. See if we do not get a boy this time! If we do, Heaven be praised, we will stage a celebration that is a celebration!"

Our hero, afterwards to be named Little Bald Head, arrived the third day after his grandmother's remarks.

*　　　*　　　*

There are any number of practical reasons why the Chinese prefer boys to girls and it was not imperative to have quoted old Mrs. Wu's remark to show that a boy was really desired in the family. For more in China than perhaps anywhere else in the world is the tradition deeply rooted that boys will grow up, take wives and carry on the family name, whereas when girls marry they become members of other families. Those who know China at all know of their idea of so-called "familism", and so the lack of male issue creates

Mr. Wu passed his primary and high school life in long blue gowns and so-called horse-jackets.

one of life's greatest disappointments. This is particularly keenly felt during such festivals as the New Year—which, strange to
say, is also the primary annual ancestor worship period.   Confucius listed "having no children" as the greatest of three cases
of negligence of filial duties, but what he really wanted to say
was, apparently, "lack of *male* children".

Old Mrs. Wu certainly did her best to obtain for her only son,
Kwang Tsung, a male child as she had done her part beautifully
in the periodical burning of incense in the courtyard and with
the saying of silent prayers to the Goddess of Children (called in
Chinese, Tse Sun Niang Niang (子孫娘娘) which literally means
the Goddess of Sons and Grandsons !).   Moreover, it was she who
was responsible for young Mrs. Wu's special pilgrimage to the
Tung Yueh Miao (東嶽廟), the Temple of the Sacred Eastern
Mountain, to perform the "baby tying ceremony."   Before young
Mr. Wu's marriage, his mother had been to the same temple to
burn incense and do obeisance before the image of the Old Man
Under the Moon, the patron saint of happy marriages.   It was
quite apparent that her prayers had been bountifully answered.

The "baby tying ceremony", was simple.   After lighting
bundles of incense (otherwise known as joss sticks) and inserting
them in the big burner provided for the purpose, young Mrs. Wu,
in a manner described to her in detail by her neighbourhood
women friends, selected from among the numerous images of babies
in the Hall of the Goddess of Sons and Grandsons, her favourite
and tied a piece of red thread around its neck, while silently
praying that the image come home with her to be born as her son.
Old Mrs. Wu was there during the entire ceremony, watching the
young woman's every movement with great interest.   Her occasional smiles, happy yet serious, showed unconditional approval
of the ceremony.   It was clearly visible from her face alone that
a *boy* was assured there and then.

"The goddess never lets a third prayer be without an answer", said old Mrs. Wu to her husband when she came home.
Old Mr. Wu smiled and said nothing.   He, like his son Kwang
Tsung, did not believe in such things but their sincere desire for
a male child was no different from Mrs. Wu's.

Then there were family meetings as to whether the services
of the same old midwife, Mrs. Ma, should be employed this time
or whether Mrs. Wu should go to the foreign missionary's hospital.
There was an equilibrium of the newer influence and the old in
the family and so the conference was long drawn out.   It was
finally decided that the same old Mrs. Ma should be invited to
give her services in aiding the childbirth.

The next morning old Mrs. Wu consulted her almanac and
found it was definitely a lucky day for such an undertaking as
she planned.   She finished her lunch and repaired herself to Mrs.
Ma's home, not far from her own.   She found the Midwife's house
without trouble.   For the door sign was clearly visible—a wooden
plate about 10 by 14 inches with a piece of red silk attached to
the bottom and suspended from the top of a pole.   On the plate
were written Chinese characters, four on each side.   On one side
it said: *"Ch'ing Cheh K'wai Ma"* (輕車快馬), meaning "Light
cart and speedy horse", and on the other side *"Chi Hsiang Lao
Lao"* (吉祥姥姥), meaning "the Auspicious Grand-Mother-in-

The midwife's sign was clearly visible.

Law", which boils down to an advertising slogan tantamount to "professional efficiency and intimate personal attention". Old Mrs. Wu explained perfunctorily her request to Mrs Ma and received in reply the latter's ceremonial congratulations. She withdrew after having been assured that Mrs. Ma would come to "mark the door" right away.

That afternoon Midwife Ma called. So devoted was she to her duties that she was unusually prompt. Besides the Wu family had always been generous with their fees and they were such nice people, not conceited, always obliging. The "door-marking" or "door-remembering" was more or less another formality. Midwife Ma got a shining silver dollar for her visit.

*   *   *

There had been guesses as to whether the baby to come was to be a boy or a girl ever since young Mrs. Wu's state of expectancy was established and made known to the other members of the family, starting, of course, with old Mrs. Wu. Old Mrs. Wu's presumption that it was going to be a boy had long since lost its status of being a mere hypothesis and had acquired the status of a conviction. She was superstitious, or, let us say, very firm in her belief that the Goddess of Sons and Grandsons was favourably disposed towards the Wu family. But that was not all. For Chinese women have their own versions of obstetrics and certain symptoms and manifestations are readily recognized by them. No highly specialized scientific examination and diagnosis are necessary. They have their own language in describing, for instance, certain motions of the baby in the womb. From these motions, with their respective characteristics, it is possible to judge, but not infallibly, the sex of the coming infant. It was interesting to note that every time the Wu family, in their daily gossipings, touched upon the question or the riddle of the coming baby, there was sure to be observed a round of head-noddings and whispers in the crowd, invariably concluding, however, more and more positively, that it was going to be a boy. So when Midwife Ma came and looked the situation over she made certain predictions in the most expert fashion based on her professional knowledge and experience that at once started the entire family out on the road to celebration.

Midwife Ma commenced her examination by first glancing at young Mrs. Wu's face and then putting her own right thumb and forefinger around the base of the middle fingers of the patient and gradually moving her own finger tips toward the finger tips of the patient, holding her breath and concentrating on the feeling of certain "jumps" and "jerks" along the entire length

of the fingers. She felt the right and then the left middle finger. Meanwhile the room was so quiet in spite of the handful of people around that you could actually have heard a sewing needle drop on the floor. Midwife Ma started to talk. She said, all in one breath:

"*Hsiao tze, hou t'ien hsia wu!*" meaning "it is a boy, some time in the afternoon of the day after tomorrow!"

Then she made further flattering and congratulatory remarks and withdrew from the bedroom of young Mr. Wu and repaired to the parlour.

By feeling the expectant mother's middle finger the midwife was able to say how soon the birth was to take place.

As she and old Mrs. Wu came into the parlour, Midwife Ma, in a very matter-of-fact manner explained to old Mrs. Wu the reasons for her predictions.

"To midwives it is all clear as a picture," said Mrs. Ma. "A girl baby makes the expectant mother look particularly charming during pregnancy, while a boy, on the other hand, makes the mother look off-colour, pale and dryish of skin. And this is as sure as sure can be. Then, like feeling the pulse, we can always tell how soon actual child-birth is to occur by feeling the middle fingers. The more toward the tips of the fingers the 'jumps' move, the sooner the time of birth; until immediately preceding the actual laying-in when the movements will be located almost at the very tips of the fingers."

Then, she made it all the more serious by lowering her voice to a low degree of audibility and added: "Besides, a male baby shows itself in stronger left finger 'pulse' and a female in the right. Don't you see?"

"Oh, Yes? But I have heard differently from that," said old Mrs. Wu. "I have my own reasons for saying it is going to be a boy. For I have faith in the goddess."

When everybody was seated in the parlour, and tea had been served, and the old midwife had received her fee—a silver dollar wrapped in a piece of red paper—she made a move to go. She promised that she would come, as soon as a messenger was sent when signs were apparent that the baby was due to arrive.

"You must be prompt!" said old Mrs. Wu.

"Rest assured, *lao t'ai t'ai*, everything will be just fine! I will arrange to stay home to await the call . . . but I assure you, it will be the day after tomorrow, some time in the afternoon if not later. And remember my prophecy, it is going to be a boy!"

"So be it! Old Buddha be praised!" added old Mrs. Wu.

*   *   *

When it was definitely confirmed that young Mrs. Wu was in the family way, the first outsider that received the news was her Number Two Aunt, who some years before had been so enthusiastic a sponsor of the marriage of young Mrs. Wu, *nee* Ho, and her husband. The news spread fast, and when Number Two

Aunt gets a piece of news it at once becomes public property in the Ho household. This started a series of calls from young Mrs. Wu's mother. She had come on similar missions on two occasions before when the young Wus had their two little daughters who did not live.

In Peking when a young woman is about to give birth to a child it is the mother-in-law's pleasure and responsibility to bring a number of gifts, and the ceremony is commonly known as *ts'ui sheng* (催生), "expediting the birth". Though ordinarily the custom is confined to the first birth of a couple, in the present case it was repeated for the third time for two reasons. First, though this was not the first birth it was considered virtually the first because the previous children did not live. Secondly, in the estima-

A number of gifts were brought to the expectant mother.

tion of many a family only a male child counts at all. Besides, Madame Ho was the type of a woman who had the leisure and means and whim to see that nothing was left undone in so far as ceremonials were concerned. It is all a lot of child's play, we may say, but, nevertheless, it constitutes an opportunity for such relatives "to get in solid" with each other.

So about a week before Midwife Ma's visit, previously related, Madame Ho came to the house of Mr. Wu with bundles and bundles of gifts. Among them may be mentioned a small red satin quilt with beautiful ribbons and laces, a number of blue cloth squares as well as red ones for the baby—which foreigners would call indiscriminately and conveniently "baby's things"—and two suits of small cotton-padded jackets, and a silk piece for wrapping around the baby's loins, as well as a number of soft towels.

She, we presume, must have kept a list of such things in her household utility book, or else a very considerate advisor must have been around to give her tips, for she did not forget to include even the cotton-padded "wind shield" which was to be put up, like a screen, in front of the baby's head to prevent drafts from attacking the baby and giving it a cold. All these, brand new, folded squarely and properly, were wrapped up in a piece of red cloth in one big bundle. She brought also a lot of stores in a variety and quantity exactly as provided for by propriety. These included one hundred fresh eggs of at least one size larger than those usually procurable, some five catties of black sugar and two catties of white sugar. Two big packages of walnut meat and one small package of baked jujubes or dates. One small sack of millet was also brought, as the Ho family owns an immense lot of land in the country near the Western Hills and Madame Ho thought, and old Mrs. Wu agreed, that her millet was of a much better quality and flavour than that which is offered in the grocery stores.

Old Mrs. Wu accepted the entire array of gifts with an expression of thanks. She was sorry, she said, that it caused the Ho family so much trouble, adding that Madame Ho was really doing too much as this was not the first childbirth of her daughter-in-law.   The usual exchange of greetings then followed the presentation of gifts.

The bringing of gifts of such practical use and of an apparently humble nature from the mother-in-law is a custom practiced far and wide throughout China   It should not be construed that it was because the Wu family was not in an equally good position to provide such necessities themselves.   In the Wu family everything had een attended to, including an exact duplicate of everything Madame Ho brought.   Everything was ready and shipshape (or baby shape) thanks to the indefatigable management and careful preparation of old Mrs. Wu herself.   Though no daily bulletins were posted at the door of the Wu house, the glad tidings were eagerly awaited by the entire family as well as by a host of their relatives and well-wishers.

A SON IS BORN

ON the day when our hero, Little Bald Head, came to the Wu household there were all sorts of opportunities to test the strength and capacity for joy of old Mrs. Wu. For it was she who was the conductor of the entire show though young Mrs. Wu and the baby naturally were the central characters of the performance. Midwife Ma's predictions having always proved to be sound in the past, the Wu family held everything ready for the coming event with such great enthusiasm that everybody was at home from early morning on that day—everybody except young Mr. Wu whose sense of duty was so unshakable that nothing could induce him to ask for leave from his work unless it was something very, very important.

Old Mr. Wu, whose everyday program always included a promenade to the vegetable market on Pig Street as a means of morning exercise, did a certain part of the daily shopping and the concurrent duty of airing his pet birds of which he had two. His daily trip was so punctual and according to schedule that it is no exaggeration to say that you could tell precisely how near it was to seven o'clock by observing how far Mr. Wu had passed the Four Arch junction. On this particular morning he was conspicuously absent from the market for he altered his schedule for the day and stayed home, holding himself ready for any urgent errand or something which might happen and need his services. We do not know whether this was of his own free will, or whether it was so ordered by old Mrs. Wu, but the fact remains that he did not show up that morning at his favourite tea shop. Many of his fellow frequenters missed his company that morning and would testify to his absence.

On the other hand, a casual observation found old Mr. Wu holding himself ready for any "emergency", smoking his two-foot pipe and standing in the very center of the inner courtyard, at times gazing at his birds in the cages hanging from the eaves of his room to catch the morning sunshine. The birds, missing the rocking and airing, refused to sing. He smiled as a circle of smoke curled up from the corner of his mouth. His thoughts for the moment could easily be read from his facial expression for they were indicative of an imaginative joy. If he had a grandson to carry around at the morning market and the tea shop, to be admired by all who know him, he thought, how much more fun it would be than carrying the birds and airing *them!*

Two cages hung from the eaves of old Mr. Wu's room to catch the morning sunshine.

His staying home that morning was fully justified for he it was who was asked to go for the midwife toward noon when the first indications of the birth were noticed. Old Mrs. Wu found herself in no position to leave the bedroom for the moment. She was also largely responsible for the preparation and conversion of young Mr. Wu's bedroom into the impromptu maternity ward, which required a personage no less experienced and no less familiar with the locale as well as with the equipment and supply depot than old Mrs. Wu herself. Midwife Ma arrived just in time and the baby was delivered triumphantly.

When young Mr. Wu came home that evening, the first thing that he learned from the emergency maidservant who opened the door for him was a torrent of congratulations, together with the news that a boy had been born by his wife. He rushed into his bedroom, which had just been tidied up, to find his mother and Midwife Ma sitting at the edge of the *k'ang*, or brick bed, and his wife, resting herself in a sleeping posture, and covered with a heavy quilt.

Casting a glance around, he found the window curtains all down and the room warmed by a small stove. Sticks of sandal incense were burning to conceal or combat certain undesirable odours. For the brief fraction of a minute, he forgot all about the baby until the midwife congratulated him saying, "Oh, *ta-yeh*, Big Sir, see what a big fat boy your wife has brought you!"

Young Mr. Wu confirmed her remark as he turned to look at the baby, the upper portion of the body was wrapped in a square of soft silk padded with cotton and then covered up to the shoulders with the red satin quilt with the so-called "wind shield" standing in a curve across the front about five inches from the baby's head. All these, young Mr. Wu noticed, were the pieces brought by Madame Ho, his mother-in-law, some time ago, to "expedite the birth." The baby's big clear eyes were beautiful to look at and as young Mr. Wu bent down to give the baby a scrupulous scrutiny, it burst into a cry of "*Gwala gwala*". Young Wu lifted the quilt a little and in one knowing glance confirmed the news that it was a BOY amid the laughter of all present.

"Why don't you put on his little jacket, mother?" asked Mr. Wu.

"Not now, not until the third day bath has been completed," answered his mother.

*   *   *

The Chinese have a number of petty superstitions for which a sarcastic name is prevalent, they are called *Ma Ma Ta Ch'uan* (媽媽大全) "Old Mother's Encyclopaedia." Such a book, of course, has never been written although there may be found something like a thousand items should an attempt actually be made to list them.

Such "don'ts" and "musts" are handed down by word of mouth from generation to generation principally among the women as occasions arise to invoke such articles. To do them full justice, some of the articles are of no small practical value when the superficial superstitious aspect is first done away with. They are so varied and numerous that they may be said to be a positive testimonial of what the expensive school of experience has taught the immense Chinese population.

To foreigners as a whole, they constitute a labyrinth of mysteries by which a clear understanding of the everyday ways of the Chinese race has been made doubly difficult. But we are not going to discuss them fully here.

For instance when young Mrs. Wu gave birth to the baby, no sooner was the actual lying in process begun than a glass of hot water in which was dissolved some white sugar was offered to her to drink. This is an established custom dating back I do not know how long— nobody does. It could have been easily explained that a little syrup of sugar administered at such a moment was considered good for the mother but nobody can explain with any- thing like reason why a dried shrimp was put in the solution itself (though not to be eaten); and stranger still, this mixture of shrimp flavour and white sugar solution has been given the high-sounding title of *Ting Hsin T'ang* (定心湯) or "Heart Stabilizing Soup!" This custom is universally practiced and we must be satisfied

A glass of hot sugar water with a dried shrimp in it was given to young Mrs. Wu.

that there is some benefit in it to have got where it is. And thus young Mrs. Wu took her "soup".

Then another superstitious rule was observed; who should be the first person admitted to the bedroom after the baby had been properly wrapped up and the room tidied up? It is believed by the Chinese that a certain prudence should be exercised in the case as it is said that the future character and degree of wisdom or even worldly happiness of the baby is in direct proportion to those of the first outsider to come into the bedroom. Old Mrs. Wu had previously arranged to call in the six-year-old son of the next door family, Wang, to come at their invitation to perform the ceremony, known as *Ts'ai Sheng* (踩生), "stepping on the birth". This was because the Wang child had shown signs of cleverness and old Mrs. Wu secretly hoped that her own grand- son would prove to be similarly clever. But in the last minute rush the invitation, previously sanctioned by the boy's own par- ents, had been overlooked. Fortunately no outsider chanced to come in the room until young Mr. Wu came home that evening. It was then that the Wang boy was sent for to look at the baby and thus "step on the birth."

That evening old Mrs. Wu herself went to the main street and bought some sugared cakes and some cakes of egg-mixed dough. These are the only kinds of solid foods to be served to the young nursing mother during most of the month's confine- ment counting from the day of birth. The rest of her menu for at least two weeks can consist of nothing but a thick millet por- ridge profusely mixed with black sugar and hard boiled eggs; cooked in the shell right in the porridge pot and then peeled to serve. The former apparently is a very nourishing food and the latter contains the greatest amount of body building elements though no salt is to be served with the eggs. In the morning, for most of the full thirty days, a goodly sized lot of walnut meat, baked to a golden brown, should be eaten in handfuls and washed down with hot water in which was dissolved white sugar. Then, from time to time, baked jujubes or scorched dates were to be eaten as "between meal snacks". These rules of diet were repeated to young Mrs. Wu, who understood thoroughly already, having had babies before.

*　　　*　　　*

The Chinese language is full of "disguised" expressions and two examples of such euphemisms may here be cited. In referring to somebody having a childbirth, the Chinese either say "*ts'o yueh tze*" (坐月子) or "*ho chow*" (喝粥). Translated word for word this would be "sitting through the month" and "drinking porridge" respectively. Thus you may hear one person asking another. "How soon is your wife going to 'sit through the month'?" and then hear the answer "She is not going to drink porridge for some time yet".

From these two expressions a sidelight can be thrown on the facts that during a childbirth the mother is confined for one whole month in her own bedroom spending most of her time sitting and drinking the millet porridge. And this is, in fact, quite true except that eating hard-boiled eggs should acquire the same footing as drinking porridge. For an average family of medium means, some two hundred to three hundred eggs are to be consumed in the month, all hard-boiled, by the mother alone not counting those given to the midwives either directly or after having been used at the ceremonies on the third day and those given as presents to relatives, neighbours and friends. These last are painted a bright red colour and are welcome gifts to all who receive them as they are a symbol of the coming of similar happy events in the recipient's family.

When young Mrs. Wu had rested a bit, she sat up and received felicitations from all the people in the room. Then her attention was directed to the new-born baby who lay there beside her on the same *k'ang*, warm and comfortable, with but occasional cries. The baby will not need any food until well toward the next day. But she was immediately to get her bowl of hot millet porridge and hard boiled eggs. She got five eggs this first time, since the baby was a boy. Otherwise, had the baby been a girl, she would not have gotten more than one single egg for the first meal! For this custom there are various rationalizations, such as that one single egg denotes the hope that but one girl will be born and no more, and five eggs would mean five boys, but the truth seems to be that a mother who gives birth to a boy well deserves five eggs, while the mother who gives birth to a girl ought to be ashamed of herself and must be content with but one egg. This is another indication of the esteem accorded a boy and ought to be taken as indicating nothing else.

*　　　*　　　*

That evening after Midwife Ma had supper with the Wus, received her fee (four dollars) and departed, a small conference was called at the Wu house requiring all the family members to be present and at which old Mrs. Wu again presided. At this meeting, orders (for they were virtually nothing else) were given that old Mr. Wu should go the next morning to gather some fresh locust twigs to be used for the Third Day Bath, and young Mr. Wu, before going to office, was to make a round of calls on most of the near relatives including his parents-in-law to report the news and to make obeisance to the elder members of the families by kowtowing before each of them, thus announcing that he had lengthened his family "tree" by a new generation.

Old Mrs Wu gave herself the assignment to seek out the old collection of dried catnip plants which she had kept somewhere

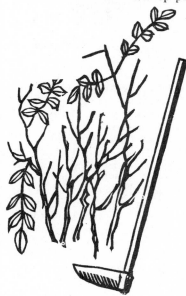

in the family storeroom in the back yard after they were bought and used as door decorations at the last Dragon Boat Festival on the fifth day of the fifth moon. These are also to be used in preparing the bath for the baby on the third day after his birth— and for other purposes too. She was also to prepare the licorice juice and sublimate of alum for the baby's use next morning. For when a baby is born it has no appetite and the instinct for sucking will have to be gradually awakened some twenty-four hours after birth. The Chinese technique is to use a little gadget formed by wrapping up in a small bit of cloth some finely chewed walnut meat and scorched dates mixed with the tincture of licorice (for its sweetening element). As to the alum sublimate, this is to be used the same as talcum powder for its absorbing quality. It is easily made by burning a chunk of alum in the fire.

Old Mrs. Wu sought out the dried catnip plants she had stored away.

It was late when the meeting adjourned. Old Mrs. Wu made another inspection of the "maternity" room, seeing to it that the maidservant was properly attending to the young mother's needs and then went to rest, happy, relieved, eagerly and keenly getting herself ready for receiving the expected callers who were bound to come after learning of the event from young Mr. Wu the next morning. There were to be a lot of congratulations and much receiving of gifts and old Mrs. Wu expected a busy day.

*　　　*　　　*

No matter how we look at it the fact cannot be gainsaid that the Chinese are a practical race. To prove this statement supporting facts are not far to seek, and the bringing of cakes as a present at a childbirth is a case in point. For there are certain hard and fast rules, binding the relatives and more intimate friends to bring gifts to the family in the form of cakes, sugared round ones of fermented dough, and another variety of moulded cakes, very much similar in composition and taste to the foreign sponge cake excepting that the latter are more solid and are assortedly shaped liked a flattened peach, pomegranate, a fan, or a silver ingot. (These cakes contain a goodly percentage of egg and are highly palatable.)

These two kinds of pastries, and nothing else, are to be presented to the nursing mother, and a package of say fifty pieces of the former and some four or five catties of the latter, done up in a straw wrapper—a piece of weaving of dried leaves of the cattail plant decorated with the red advertising leaflet of the shop— would constitute the perfectly acceptable and legitimate present for such an occasion. And this sending of cakes, effected not later than the Third Day Bath ceremony, is an old

The packages were done up in a straw wrapper and decorated with the red advertising leaflet of the shop.

established institution bearing testimony to the highly developed practical-mindedness of the Chinese as a whole. For it is done in such a systematic way as to be adequately comparable to a co-operative system of inter-family mutual assistance.

Any family having accepted such presents are required, in a spirit of reciprocity, to give identically the same gifts back to each family from which such presents have been accepted when there is a childbirth in the latter families. We have never yet seen a case when presents other than these cakes were ever given before the Third Day Bath after a childbirth, and the only way to show preference would be in the quantity of each kind to be given—the sole "most-favoured clause" to this unwritten covenant.

Thus when old Mrs. Wu retired on the night of her grandson's birth, she was fully prepared to expect the visitors the next day and to accept the presents to be brought to the Wu family. If a list of anticipated guests and their respective presents—even to the quantity of each of the two kinds—had been made, the actual results would not have been found to be very much different from the anticipations. As regards the question how the news was made known to outsiders, did we not leave young Mr. Wu being instructed by his mother to report the birth to the relatives?

*   *   *

When evening came the next day and most of the guests had arrived, deposited their presents and departed after viewing the little baby and offering their congratulations by repeated and repeated greetings of "*Ta Hsi, Ta Hsi* . . .", meaning "great happiness", old Mrs. Wu collected all the packages of cakes together and found there were exactly twenty-six packages of cakes of the two categories mentioned previously. When young Wu came home that evening he brought back two more packages of the same stuff—given him by some newly made friends at his office who found they were too busy to come in person. The total was brought up to twenty-eight packages, containing in aggregate some one thousand pieces of the round cakes and no less than seventy catties (or roughly 100 pounds) of "moulded cakes." In view of the great sociability of the Wu family and because they had given a gift package of cakes every time they learned of a childbirth in the circle of their friends, no one in the Wu family was surprised at the immense amount of gifts received.

From out the family storeroom in the back yard, old Mrs. Wu, assisted by the maidservant, brought a huge earthen jar, cleaned it and, opening the parcels one by one, put the entire lot of cakes away to be taken out and consumed as needed.

"They will keep soft and humid here in this jar," said old Mrs. Wu, as she sorted out a small quantity of each kind and bade the servant put them in two red lacquer boxes in young Mrs. Wu's room, easily accessible to the young mother. As previously explained these were to constitute, accompanied by hardboiled eggs and millet porridge, the main portion of the nursing mother's diet for a goodly portion of her confinement.

THE THIRD DAY BATH

CHINESE newborn babies do not get a bath until the third day after birth for it is believed (or has been found out by experience) that it is not advisable to wash the babies before they get a chance to adapt themselves to climatic conditions and environment and until their feeble physique has had a chance to get somewhat "solidified", and that argument seems to be sound sense. The program of things done at the so-called *Hsi San* (洗三), "Washing Third", is a hopeless mess of superstitions mingled with practicalities. It is composed of undertakings both ceremonious and picturesque mixed up with ridiculous nonsense so closely following each other that it is hard to tell where superstitions end and practicalities begin. Since it is such an important phase of Chinese family life we will try to describe it more thoroughly.

In the first place the ceremonies ordain the burning of incense and the offering of the round cakes (such as already described) in front of the paper images of a number of deities at one table and the God and Goddess of the Bed separately on the *k'ang*. At these rites the Chinese have found the most suitable person to officiate is nobody else but the midwife herself! She starts the baby-washing ceremony by arranging the images in the proper places. Then she lights the candles and incense sticks and actually *kowtows* to the deities, concluding the religious services by burning up the paper images and other paper paraphernalia outside in the courtyard. She acts as the sole plenipotentiary at the service and members of the family employing her are strangely banned from the worship.

On a big table, preferably in the hall outside the bedroom but not far from it, is placed a wooden stand about a foot high with two tandem rods holding between their blades a collection of paper images—crude wood block prints of their likenesses, folded to a uniform width and nested together in such a way that only the little squares on the images bearing each of the godly titles are visible, one above the other. In this way a lot of display space is saved. Then three dishes each containing five of the round cakes, are put in a row before the stand on the table. No egg cakes are used as the gods and goddesses are vegetarians. At the edge of the table the incense burner, usually made of wood in the shape of a *To* (斗), or peck measure, is placed in the center and flanked by a pair of candlesticks. From beneath the candlesticks are hung yellow paper money, a string of paper ingots and a string of paper cuttings of a stiff yellow paper called in Chinese *ch'ien ch'ang* (千張), or "thousand pieces", which are supposed to be used, after being burned, as ladders by which the divinities will ascend to heaven. Closely examining the joss papers we find, in order from top to bottom, the following deities:

    (1)   The Family Kitchen God,
    (2)   The Six Minor Gods of the Household,
    (3)   The Goddess of Smallpox,
    (4)   The Goddess of Guidance (for the spirit to find the proper place for incarnation),

(5) The Goddess of Playmates,
(6) The Goddess of Breast Milk,
(7) The Goddess of Child Delivery,
(8) The Goddess of Expediting Birth,
(9) The Goddess of Eyesight,
(10) The Goddess of Sons and Grandsons (for the distribution of offsprings),
(11) The Goddess of Heavenly Angel,
(12) The White-robed Goddess of Mercy for Sending Children,
(13) The God of Heaven and the God of Earth.

It is interesting to note from the above list that at least seven or eight of these deities may be grouped together and considered a mute proof that the Chinese have found themselves so helpless with such problems as pediatrics and child welfare that they have plainly admitted their defeatism by such wholesale deification of everything beyond their intelligence. Another phase of the thing would be that they thus cleverly leave many an important but thorny problem such as birth control (or lack of birth control) and eugenics alone without worrying about it, and lightly pass the responsibilities on to such ridiculous products of their primitive imagination.

*　　　*　　　*

At the religious service preceding the baby washing ceremony, the God and Goddess of the Bed, *K'ang Kung K'ang Mu* (床公床母), occupy a seat of honour right where they belong, namely, on the bed. I am not saying "in the bed" because the Chinese bed—by which I mean that in North China and more especially in Peking—being a solid pile of brickwork with inside conduits for winter heating allows nothing to be "in" it. Here is placed but one piece of the image print standing solitarily against the wall. In front of it tradition dictates a makeshift incense holder in the form of a pint measure, called in Chinese *Sheng* (升), in which, instead of the usual accumulated incense ashes, rice (regular rice from the family rice jar) is used to hold the incense. This incense for the God and Goddess of the Bed (they have a curious assignment of duties befitting those of a watchful baby

amah), it is dictated also, must be but three sticks as compared with the bunch of 52 sticks offered to the multitude of deities on the table. Two dishes of round cakes are also to be offered. The round cakes and the rice in the measure are invisibly earmarked for a special purpose as we will see later and the midwives always cast a casual and yet noticing eye on such offerings.

A great array of paraphernalia to be used in the washing ceremonies was laid out on the bed.

On the heavily mattressed brick bed the female members of the household, excluding the mother who is not allowed to get off the bed for some time yet, co-operating perhaps with the midwife, will put out a great array of paraphernalia to be used at the actual washing ceremony which takes place about noon, or a little later, when the sun's warmth, if available, is at its zenith. Among the things spread out may be noticed a small skein of threads of five colours, a raw egg, a bamboo sieve with a paper pomegranate flower in it, a weight from the steelyard, a brass padlock open and ready to click, a piece of long Chinese onion and a comb. There is also a big dish containing hard-boiled eggs, some dyed red and some yellow and some in their natural colour.

On another part of the bed are put the tiny jackets and cloth squares for the baby, a brand new cake of soap and the alum powder. The center of the bed is occupied by a big flattish basin of brass on the edge of which is spread the piece of red silk which is a gift from the mother's maternal family. A porcelain bowl holding cold water and a spoon is also put near the basin. Also two porcelain dishes one containing thin slices of ginger and some little balls of dried leaves of catnip, about the size of strawberries, and another containing some dried dates and nuts called collectively *Hsi Kuo* (喜果), "fruits of happiness." A pair of scissors and a pair of fire tongs completes the layout.

The preparation and arrangement of all these articles in the Wu family were taken care of by old Mrs. Wu herself who divided her attention between these and also the preparation of the bath itself. No common water is used for the baby-washing, and the baby is to be thoroughly scrubbed in a piping hot bath of water in which locust branches and catnip leaves were literally cooked for many long hours. Mr. Wu senior had no trouble getting enough locust twigs the day before from the neighbour's garden and the catnip plants, which were not in season just then, were, thanks to the foresight of old Mrs. Wu, ready for use stored away in the family attic (Mrs. Wu senior knew just where to lay her fingers on them). The greenish-grey, foaming solution had been kept boiling since early morning and when Midwife Ma arrived to officiate at the bath, the pot of this herbal preparation was boiling briskly on the stove.

There were some visitors on this particular day, notably women including the omnipresent No. 2 Aunt and young Mr. Wu's mother-in-law, Madame Ho. There were also more gift-bearers, bringing the famous round cakes and the moulded cakes, from the neighbourhood. Some of these people had received the news from the "broadcasting" lips of Midwife Ma.

Midwife Ma, having been again perfunctorily invited by old Mr. Wu, presented herself early that morning. She and the other guests, amid exchanges of greetings and congratulatory remarks, sat down to a feast of noodles with a rich, jellied stew, a customary Peking dish for such an occasion—the noodles, made by stretching the dough by hand, are symbolic of the lengthening of the little baby's worldly life, they say.

The event was considered to be of such great significance that even such self-important personages as young Mr. Wu, getting a few hours leave, managed to be present at the ceremony—his paternal feelings apparently, for once, got the better of his sense of duty. His cheerful and noisy presence added the final touch to the fete.

*   *   *

The feast over, the family and friends gathered in the room of young Mrs. Wu to witness the ceremony. It was opened by Midwife Ma, at the suggestion of old Mrs. Wu, by burning incense at the two temporary shrines of the deities. That finished, and after the "joss" papers and other paper objects had been burned in a courtyard bonfire, she went on the bed, occupied the central position, sitting *a la* Laughing Buddha fashion, and requested the guests to please *t'ien p'en* (添盆), namely to "add to the basin".

It would be a sad mistake to infer that this means merely adding water to the basin; it is not that simple. Each guest, as well as every family member, young or old, is required at such a ceremony to take the spoon and pour one spoonful of cold water from a bowl nearby into the brass basin but not until a small sum of money has been put into another bowl resting in the basin itself! At the Third Day Bath ceremony the Midwife's perquisites are legion. All the money deposited by those present is legitimately her "cumshaw" (or tips), and a person who has not a small piece of money ready in his or her palm to drop into the bowl has no business to be around and is present at his or her own risk of embarrassment. In the more prosperous families it is not uncommon for a midwife to receive, besides money, little pieces of jewelry and other trinket gratuities as a result of the ceremony.

No. 2 Aunt started the round of "adding to the basin" by taking a red, a white and a yellow egg from the dish and putting them in the basin, the while expressing a conventional wish: "May the baby grow up to be as beautifully red and white and to possess gold as yellow as these eggs" She then poured a spoonful of water into the basin and expressed another wish; "May he be as fresh as this water!". Then she deposited her tip—a fifty-cent silver piece in the bowl for which Midwife Ma thanked her. In this way the round went on through the relatives, then the neighbours and finally members of the immediate family, from old Mr. Wu down, each put some of the nuts or hard-boiled eggs into the basin as well as some money. Even the maidservant was given a chance to express her kind wishes and deposited ten coppers of her hard-earned cash in the "basin". The biggest contributor was naturally Madame Ho who gave two silver dollars. Midwife Ma collected the money together and, thanking everyone again, pocketed the entire proceeds. (She found on reaching home that the total was four dollars and seventy-five cents in silver and ten coppers).

The basin is then emptied of its accumulated contents of eggs and nuts (these are by law the midwife's perquisite too) and is filled with the locust-branch-and-catnip-leaf bath. As the naked reddish little body is taken out from his bedclothes and passed into the hands of Midwife Ma, she reads a doggerel of conventional kind wishes, something like this :

"Here I knock and knock this basin,
   And I wish that you be blessed with many sisters and brothers"

And the washing, with the prepared solution and soap, ensues. The washing is quite thorough and businesslike and that the bath is hot is proved by the crying of the baby.

"Oh, what a big boy you are, and so heavy, too !" flatters Midwife Ma, as she puts the sublimate of alum on selected places of the baby's body.

The baby was clad in his new jackets and the lower portion of his body was wrapped in pieces of cloth.

The actual bathing is over in three minutes and the baby is then, for the first time, clad in his new jackets while the lower portion of his tiny body is wrapped in cloth pieces. Thus tidied up, he is put on the knees of the squatting midwife. The dressed up little gentleman is the object of another torrent of flattery from every guest.

The bath basin is now removed from the *k'ang*, but the water is not thrown away as it still has certain uses on account of its medical value, but we will omit further details.

After the washing the superstitious aspect of the ceremony begins and this is keenly awaited by the entire assemblage in young Mrs. Wu's bedroom.

* * *

The science of disinfection plays a great part in modern maternity cases and of this the Chinese have their counterpart though only a very faint connection is noticeable. The Chinese have known for centuries that subjecting objects to great heat is the simplest and surest procedure for preventing certain sicknesses (they certainly were unaware of germs). The use of fire as a disinfectant at childbirth at present has degenerated to an almost negligible formality.

If a little imagination is allowed we will admit that it must have been done in a much more thoroughgoing manner in the old days. The primitive "surgical" instruments at a Chinese lying-in operation are the fire tongs and the household scissors. The cutting of the cord from the placenta is done with the domestic scissors and then the fire tongs, or a poker, heated red hot, is applied to the opening of the part of the cord still connected to the baby itself—a highly effective sterilization indeed ! The afterbirth thus separated is buried in an out-of-the-way spot. But what has all this to do with the Third Day Bath ceremony?, it may be asked.

Well, after the baby has been thoroughly washed in the special bath and has been clothed, the little balls of dried catnip leaves are lighted, one by one. The first ball is put on top of the baby's skull and another on the navel where slices of ginger have been placed. This process, lasting for about three minutes, is supposed to be useful in "charming away" any traces of sickness that may be present.

Further, a ball of the same stuff is lighted and put on the scissor blades, another on the fire tongs, another on the window sill, another on the wooden edge of the brick bed and still another on the bedroom threshold. This custom, its true meaning long forgotten, is now more or less a formality but is clearly reminiscent of a faithfully carried out practice in times gone by.

Taking up the five-colour threads, the midwife applies them, loosely twisted, across the back of the infant in the belief that certain hair will be removed in this way, which, if left to stay, would make the baby lean and sickly.   Then rolling a raw egg over the tiny face, the midwife expresses another wish : "May the baby be as smooth and lovely in colour as the raw egg !" Putting down the baby, the midwife shakes the bamboo sieve with the paper pomegranate flower in it over the body and chants for everyone to hear : "What am I doing?   I am sifting the flowers.   The god and goddess will give only a sprinkling of the flowers !"   The Chinese name for smallpox is *hua* (花), a pun on flowers.

Smallpox, until vaccination was introduced some two to three hundred years ago, was supposed to be uncontrollable (It was responsible for a high percentage of infant mortality and still is in the interior).   This "unavoidable" malady, the Chinese believe, is entirely managed by the Goddess of Smallpox.   And thus the Chinese, granting that it is uniformly and indiscriminately distributed to all babies alike and therefore inescapable, comfort themselves by this "sieve" ceremony—praying, as it were, to the goddess to have mercy on this particular baby and bestow on it but a few specks of the "flowers" !

The steelyard weight is now brought into play, being put on the body of the child while the midwife croons :   "The steelyard weight is small in size but it can balance many times its own weight," meaning that for this small child a big future is promised.

Next comes the padlock.   The midwife takes it in her hands and passes it lightly over the baby's mouth, hands and feet, chanting: "*tsueh chin, shou chin, chiao chin*" (嘴緊, 手緊, 脚緊), meaning "Let your mouth be locked fast, as also your hands and feet" (so as not to talk, or do things or go to places which are not approved of by propriety), snapping the lock shut as the words are uttered.

The onion follows.   The midwife lightly taps the baby with it twice and again chants : "With the first tap comes wisdom and with the second tap comes smartness".   The Chinese word for "onion" is *ts'ung* (葱), the same sound as for "wisdom." Hence the onion comes to be used.

While pretending to comb the baby's hair the midwife intones another doggerel.   "As I pass through your hair with this comb, when you grow up you will wear a red Mandarin button on your hat !"   A red button was used by Mandarins of the first rank on top of the hat and so the wish expressed is not difficult to understand.

In orthodox fashion and identical in every detail to the procedure explained above the washing of the Wu baby was faithfully performed in the time-honoured manner.

*   *   *

If the Chinese choose to tap the tiny newborn baby lightly with a piece of onion there can be no objection to it but I do not see any reason why a piece of onion so used should be rendered inedible as the Chinese believe.   For after the ceremony the onion is considered no good and has to be thrown on the roof.

But a superstitious use is found for this perfectly good onion thrown away—a consolation utility—for it is supposed to be instrumental in foretelling the sex of the next baby to be born. As the onion falls on the roof its direction is to be noted. If the root end points to the edge of the eaves, a boy is to come at the next childbirth, and if it lies the other way, a girl is indicated! We do not know what would be the prophecy if the onion should use its own judgment and choose to drop crosswise on the tiles!

The god and goddess of the bed were sent off in a bonfire.

After performing her "jugglery" with the miscellaneous articles as related, the midwife gathers a small quantity of incense ash from the "shrine" of the God and Goddess of the Bed, and, wrapping it in a piece of red paper, she gives the package to the mother who will have it sewed to the end of the new pillow which by now will be used. Before this, the family almanac book, rolled and covered, has been serving as a pillow, as the Chinese feel that since so many godly titles of august divinities are found in the almanac it should be a virtual devil-proof protection against sundry elves and goblins that may lurk in the darkness ready to inflict havoc on the feeble newborn boy.

The time now comes for the God and Goddess of the Bed to be sent off by burning the paper images in another bonfire. Before saying farewell to the deities, the midwife will recite another doggerel. Translated, it says:

"The God and Goddess of the Bed, originally named Lee,
The little baby here of this family I entrust to thee!
Should it fall, or should it tumble (from the bed),
Well, you know what a time I will have with ye!"

In this way the god and goddess receive their commission and then are politely driven off from the scene of their expected duties!

It was while Midwife Ma was performing this portion in the final act of the ceremonies that old Mrs. Wu remarked: "Come to think of it, the God and Goddess of the Bed truly deserve our respect in every way. For you never hear of any family's little infant having been crippled or in any way seriously hurt by falling from the *k'ang*! It is quite high from the floor, too! It is truly marvellous."

* * *

The ceremony, or rather ceremonies, lasted until three o'clock in the afternoon when Midwife Ma departed with a veritable harvest. Besides the money which the various guests had put in the bowl during the "adding to the basin" and her regular fee from the Wu family, she also carried a load of eggs and cakes, those offered to the deities, and a pint of rice from the impromptu incense burner before the God and Goddess of the Bed. All these, as also the barely touched cake of soap, are a midwife's reward for her work.

The midwife's departure also started off the other guests who bade farewell one by one leaving the Wu family to "face realities."

"How is the milk coming?" asked old Mrs. Wu.

"Still very watery", answered her daughter-in-law. "But baby is crying very bitterly and I am afraid he must be terribly hungry !"

"Pu yao chin (that's all right); the breast milk will become denser and denser as the baby grows. It does no harm to starve the baby a little. He is not really hungry yet. We will see how your milk improves. But, by the way, doesn't he cry loudly though ! At the washing ceremony almost everybody favourably remarked on his vocal volume !"

"Oh, yes, how truly wonderful !" put in the proud father, the young Mr. Wu. "They were all very courteous and kind. If they had remarked the other way and said 'See, how weakly the baby wails !', it would not have been very much of a flattery, would it, mother?"

THE FULL MONTH CELEBRATION

ILL health of the mother almost always precedes and follows a childbirth in China for the typical Chinese woman is a weaker person, perhaps, than most of her sisters the world over. The occurrence of sundry sicknesses is so prevalent during such periods that special medical preparations are to be found in the pharmacopoeia, known as the *Kuan Fang Tze* (官方子), "Official Prescriptions". The doses are a mixture of various herbs and other things of a specific quantity each and the juice obtained from boiling these together is taken as a cure-all. These prescriptions are even taken without the mother showing any noticeable symptoms and more or less as a precautionary measure. Those women who do not find such measures necessary are known by their sex as being *Fu Yueh Tze* (服月子), "well adapted to the month's confinement." Such women are usually of an above-the-average physical constitution and young Mrs. Wu belonged to this category.

There was absolutely no trouble at the birth of her son and, to use an old hackneyed expression, mother and child were doing well. She was careful and her mother-in-law's wise counsels being always available this added another factor of protection. And soon the twelfth day after the birth arrived. This twelfth day is, in the Chinese way of things, another occasion for ceremonies.

It may well be admitted that there was a reason for this celebration as the average Chinese, so helpless regarding the physiological and hygienic details of a childbirth, presume that if nothing untoward has happened up to the twelfth day the chances are that nothing untoward will happen in the future and the vigilance is considered over. For the mother it may possess another meaning and that, beginning from the twelfth day, the usual daily rations would be permissible and she would not be so strictly bound to depend for her subsistence on the monotonous diet of millet porridge and hard-boiled eggs.

The twelfth day is also another occasion for gift sending by the mother's family. Propriety requires them to bring in person (if they cannot afford a special footman to carry the gifts in round lacquer boxes balanced from the ends of a pole over his shoulder) a certain quantity of mutton and some wheat flour, two or three heads of cabbage and also a leg of pork. Propriety also requires the nursing mother's own mother, if possible, to come in person and help in making some meat dumplings with the ingredients brought along for the young mother to eat.

A clear soup made from a leg of pork bearing seven little natural marks is considered excellent towards building up a mother's breast milk.

A full meal of these small dumplings is permitted if there is the appetite and there usually is after the period of restricted diet. No vinegar (which is usually served with these dumplings), however, is allowed as it is said to be bad for the mother's teeth. The leg of pork, complete with the foot, bearing seven little natural markings called "seven stars", is to be thoroughly cooked in plain water and the "pork stock" is to be used for cooking some easily digestible dishes as long as the soup lasts. The leg, however, has to be one bearing seven marks like little moles, for such a leg is considered to be good for building up the quality and quantity of the breast milk.

This procedure must be said to be another example of Chinese practical-mindedness for doubtless all mothers wish to see their daughters regain strength rapidly after a childbirth, and so would avail themselves of any opportunity to send their daughters nourishing foods. Since it would hardly be conducive to good manners, with the Chinese family system as it is, for a daughter-in-law to receive gifts of goods from her family expressly for her own benefit alone, a clever camouflage has been found by naming the custom *Nieh Ku Feng-Erh* (捏骨縫兒), the "restoration of body to condition prior to the birth".

The restoration process is not done in actuality but is in the making of the meat dumplings! The dumplings are made by pressing together the edge of a round piece of dough with a stuffing or core of mutton and cabbage, chopped fine and properly seasoned, and shaping it like a half-moon (It tastes very much like the foreign meat pie). By the pressing together of the edges of the dumplings, the pressing of the bodily bone seams, whatever that means in medical science, is symbolized. Meanwhile, a chance for the daughter-in-law to get her food subsidies are thereby guaranteed.

Madame Ho performed the ceremony personally "with great pleasure". The guest and the family then sat together to a feast of the dumplings in a highly congenial spirit. Young Mrs. Wu herself consumed a big plate of the dumplings and heartily enjoyed them.

* * *

The Chinese name, like the English, is divided into two parts; the family name and the personal name. But, unlike the English, the family name is put before, not after, the personal name. Besides the proper name, a Chinese, particularly of the more literary type, will have at least one "courtesy name", and another "fancy name". The fancy name is similar in nature to the foreign *nom de plume*, but is not necessarily a "pen name". Also they are usually more sophisticated than can be imagined. There are "The Old Man of the Chrysanthemum Garden", "The Fisherman at the Clear Stream", "Master of the One Lantern Studio", "The Passing Visitor to the Peach Garden", etc. *ad infinitum*. Besides it is nothing unusual for a Chinese to have five, six or seven names—they don't cost anything and are not expensive to keep. One writer of great fame has used something like thirty-five names. He is still living and may add another thirty-five to his record. Such names, of course, are invented by and given to the person on his own initiative.

Chinese children get their names, naturally, from their parents. They are given a proper name when they become six or seven years old. The name is known as *Ta Ming Tze* ("big name"). Even this name is subject to further changes without notice when the person grows up and takes an official post. Such a change is known as altering the *Hsueh Ming Tze* ("school name") to *Kuan Ming Tze* ("official name"). Such names are usually as high sounding and sagely as it is possible to make them.

Children, before they attain the age when they have proper names, are known and addressed by the family and their playmates by their *Hsiao Ming Erh*, ("small name") which in the *wenli* (classic) style, is known as *Ju Ming*, ("milk name"). Whereas the choosing of an appropriate name for "school" or for "officialdom" may mean pondering for hours over a dictionary and may, for the immense masses of Chinese illiterates, constitute so difficult a problem that no lesser personage than the village schoolmaster can solve it, the giving of the milk name is decidedly an easier job. It is very much like putting the selling price on a piece of rare and authentic curio—you can put any old price you like on it. And similarly if you so decide you may alter it at your own fond pleasure!

But on the other hand the milk name should be possessive of a certain meaning besides the superficial idea it expresses and this may be anything from an ordinary numerical order, a prayer for long life, a wish for a male follower, a chronological registration or a private code. Perhaps it would be clearer by giving a few examples of each kind.

A child born when his or her grandfather or grandmother is sixty years old may be named *Liu Shih-erh*, "Sixty", and a child born to a septuagenarian grandparent may be called *Ch'i Shih-erh*, "Seventy". A child born during the autumn harvest season may be named *Ta Ch'iu-erh*, "Big Autumn", meaning a big harvest. Girls are given such fancy names befitting their sex as *Mei Tze*, "Beautiful One", *Feng Erh*, "Phoenix", *Chin Huan-erh*, "Golden Ringlet", and *Hsiao Yu-tze*, "Small Piece of Jade"! Sometimes, in families where male children are scarce, girls have been named *Ko-erh*, "Enough"—meaning "no more girls are wanted", or *Huan Tze*, "Change to a Boy"!

A child is also often given a milk name in conformity with his physical type, as *P'ang Erh*, "Fat One", *Hei Tze*, "Black One", or *Hsiao To-erh*, "Little Bean", for a tiny under-developed tot! Robust children have been named "Iron Ball", "Iron Egg", or "Stone."

Then, in accordance with the emblem of the animal cycle (the cycle consists of twelve years, each represented by an animal) children are named "Little Cow", "Little Sheep", "Little Horse", "Little Dragon", "Little Tiger", etc. So far, however, no child born in a rat year has been called "Little Rat", nor a snake year baby a "Little Snake"! No "Little Rabbit" either. "Little Pigs" are very common.

Another phenomenon attending the giving of milk names is the way the Chinese fool their gods! They believe that boys are harder to rear because there are always ill elements wanting to do harm to male children and at least a part of these bad spirits are under the jurisdiction of, or responsible to, certain divinities.

To fool the devils the Chinese pierce a boy's ear and insert an earring. The boy is then passed off as a girl

The conception must be either that girls are immune to such malignancy or, to use an old excuse, boys are more precious than girls (I think the latter is the case). A way to fool people has been to give girls' names to boys. And to put something over on the evil spirits, personifications of destructive influences, a "scarce" boy sometimes has one of his ears pierced and an earring inserted. He will then look more like a girl than a boy to the simplebrained devils and thus will be passed as a girl and therefore become immune to molestations. The earring will stay with him his entire lifetime, if possible, in order to "fool all the devils all the time"!

It is also not uncommon to meet a child named *Ko Sheng-erh*, meaning "Left Over from a Dog"! This refers to an old custom any Peking-*jen* of over sixty years of age will recollect. Chinese children dying young were not allowed to be buried in the family graveyard and so, up to the last part of the Manchu dynasty, the practice in Peking was for such dead little bodies (very often not even encoffined) to be collected by a slow-moving ox-cart, maintained by the municipality, and to be buried or thrown out in the outskirts of the city where the corpses were devoured by the wild dogs that haunted such places. A child, therefore, named "Left Over from a Dog" would be safe from all ill influences as he has, nominally, already passed through all the trying periods of a youngster!

*   *   *

The principle on which the Wu child was named is another article of the rules for which an explanation is necessary. Chinese monks or priests are supposed to be beyond the control of the King of Hades and thus children bearing such names as *Ho Shang*—a Buddhist monk, or *Lao Tao*—a Taoist priest, bear also an insurance against untimely death or serious sicknesses. The Chinese believe these calamities are scattered by the respective deities in charge and by naming their children in this manner they would be more leniently treated by the gods—even Chinese gods practice nepotism!

When the Wu family council was in session to decide what should be the milk name of the newcomer to the family, there were a number of suggestions all of which old Mrs. Wu overruled. She was devout Buddhist as we have seen and so that her grandson will "stay" she again sought for help from the Buddha and decided, even before the convening of the family council, that the name should be *Ho Shang*, "Buddhist Monk". A certain measure of opposition was either conquered or withdrawn and old Mrs. Wu emerged triumphant with the name *Ho Shang*. This appelation was soon changed, however, for not long afterwards old Mr. Wu had a sudden brainstorm which was given such attention that the name was altered. He related that an uncle of

his, now dead, used to bear such a milk name.   Since no Chinese
junior must bear the same name as a senior member of the family
it could not under any circumstances be allowed to be carried on
much to the annoyance of old Mrs. Wu.

Finally, thanks to her good humour and resourcefulness, she
advanced an amelioration to her first decision.   She said, "Well,
all Buddhist monks have their heads cleanly shaven, haven't
they?   A clean shaven head looks like a bald one, doesn't it?
Well, hereafter, let's call him *Hsiao T'u-erh*—Little Bald Head!
Is everybody satisfied?"

There was no objection.   The decision was final.

*   *   *

When a Chinese baby is a month old it is an occasion for a
celebration of no small proportions.   The poorest (I do not mean
the destitute) families arrange to have a feast of noodles on such
a day even if it necessitates sending some articles of clothing not
in immediate use to the pawnshop to arrange the financing of the
feast.   In rich families, naturally, much is done.

In families above the well-to-do level these celebrations are
put up for girls and boys alike; whether it is the first or fifth
child makes no difference.   But if the child happens to be the
first one and happens, also, to be a boy, then the celebration
certainly cannot be foregone except if there happens simultaneously to be a mourning in the family.

The occasion is known as *man yueh*, "full month".   To give
a party on such an occasion is known as *pan man yueh*, "doing a
full month".   The guests who come to congratulate are said to
tso man yueh, "make a full month".   There is usually a feast for
all comers and members of the family alike.   If the family can
afford to, or happens to have a rich friend, an entertainment of
some sort will also be in evidence either paid for by the family or
by the rich friend.   Such entertainments may be theatrical or
"vaudeville" in nature, lasting from morning or noon till past
midnight.   The show goes on whether attention is paid to it by the
guests or not.   Much gambling is part of the celebration, too.

Presents are brought by relatives and friends on such a day.
They range in value and variety according to the intimacy of the
friendship in each case, which intimacy, to be perfectly frank,
is translatable into the dollars and cents of a gift's cost. The most
usual procedure is to bring a sum of money in a red envelope, the
sum ranging from as small an amount as forty cents to one, two,
four, ten dollars or more, and to give the recipients theoretically
full liberty to spend the money for any presents they see fit.   The
receivers, in almost all cases, will see no fitter way to spend the
money than to apply it in financing the celebrations!

In an average family there is always a loss, seen when the
balance sheet is prepared after the party is over and all expenses
paid.   To counter-balance this low, however, there will be a long
list of not useful presents of all kinds which, being what may be
called the "conventional gifts", have no commercial value and
besides are not readily convertible into immediately accessible
currency!   These gifts are good only to keep against some future
occasion when they are given back to relatives and friends whenever there is a birth in their respective families.   Attention,

however, must be exercised not to return the original article to a friend from whom it has been received. That would be terrible loss of face! (Loss of face means loss of manners in China.) A duplex or multiplex interchange of gifts should always be given proper attention and the value of each present must be judged by the shrewd eyes of the able housewife. It is bad manners to give a friend a five-dollar present if he has given a two-dollar gift to you before, and *vice versa*.

On the full month celebration day, the baby in whose honour the feast is being staged should be dressed in his holiday best, the hair properly cut or nicely combed, the face cleanly washed and even powdered a little if desired. He must be on exhibit, lying in state as it were, in the bedroom subject to the inspection and admiration of all comers. The same guest would not have been allowed to see the baby and talk to the young mother during the month's confinement if he had not also come and sent gifts before the Third Day Bath Ceremonies. Such people are liable to "stamp off the milk", as the Chinese say, if they should be careless and enter into conversation with the mother. Milk does disappear mysteriously sometimes, somehow.

On the day of the Full Month the maternal grandmother of the child has also a duty, that of "filling the mouth" or *man k'o*

as it is known in Chinese. This consists of her bringing a big basket of steamed breads moulded to bear a Chinese character *hsi*, "happiness", on them. Two of these flat breads, one put on top of another, are to be held by the maternal grandmother while the nursing mother is to bite off one mouthful from both of the two pieces of bread, "filling her mouth to entire capacity".

Two flat pieces of steamed bread are put together and the young mother has to bite off one mouthful.

The intention to stage a celebration was cherished in the minds of the Wus perhaps even before the child was born. It gradually gained momentum as the days rolled by and was encouraged not only by the members of the family and their near kin but also by the intimate friends of old Mr. Wu, particularly his sworn brothers, and by the young fellow-workers of young Mr. Wu at the bank. Most of the last named were what you would call "live wires" and would not have allowed young Mr. Wu his own way even if he had preferred to keep quiet on this occasion. But he did not prefer to keep quiet.

Preparations therefore soon began to be seriously considered and were definitely under way a week before the auspicious day arrived.

*　　　*　　　*

The conventional gifts for respective occasions of celebrations and even of mourning in the established customs of the Chinese people are varied and the unwritten rules governing them are indeed dogmatic if we may use that word to describe them. Of course, China being such a big country it is only natural that

slight variations are noticed in each different locality, particularly as each place has its own special products which may figure
prominently in the conventional gifts.   For instance, the practice
of sending a complete roasted young pig, head, tail and all, as a
gift immediately following a wedding from the bridegroom's
family to that of the bride is indeed very prevalent among the
Cantonese.   Overseas Chinese, who are mostly from the Canton
area, have carried the custom to the far corners of the earth and
it is practised from Singapore to San Francisco (I have seen it
done in many of the Chinatowns in the United States).   Nevertheless such a ceremonial presentation is hardly known to the average
Peking-*jen*.   So we will deal here with those conventional gifts or
kuan li (官禮), "official gifts", which are given at the Full Month
ceremony and are considered proper in Peking.

Such gifts may be classified into three categories: actual
money, clothing for the baby, and ornaments for the baby.

The sending of money is the commonest custom, as we have
already said.   Propriety provides that such a sum of money must
be enclosed in a red envelope about five inches wide and ten
inches long and used length-wise.   A narrow piece of red paper,
the full length of the envelope, should be pasted in the center of
the envelope bearing two Chinese characters *Mi Ching* (彌敬),
(let's call it "Full Month Gift").   Under this is written the
amount of money enclosed as well as the donor's name.   His or
her address, if considered necessary, should be written on the
reverse side of the envelope.   In certain cases a few big characters
indicating a kind wish may also be inscribed on this label in
place of the other details.   Popular phrases are *Ch'ang Ming
Po Sui* (長命百歲), "A Long Life—One Hundred Years", *Fu Shou
Mien Ch'ang* (福壽綿長), "Blessed Life Prolonged", etc.   When
the parties are of greater proportions the amount must be clearly
indicated on the outside of each envelope by the sender.   An
amateur accountant is always invited to take charge of all the
monetary affairs for the duration of the celebration in order to
leave the host and his family free to entertain the guests. Part of
his duty is to list every cash gift and so a prominent marking on
the envelope is essential.

The second category would be clothing or materials for clothing for the baby in whose honour the celebration is being staged.
Formerly such gifts used to be small rolls or brocades, three to
ten feet per piece, of silks of bright colours with appropriate
symbolic designs of good luck.   Such motifs as bats, for *fu* (福 ,
"happiness", and endless knots, for *shou* (壽), "long life", were
considered proper.   Of late, however, the place of such silk rolls
has been taken by little suits of embroidered garments, tiny
shoes and hats of embroidery or fancy needlework, etc., nicely
wrapped or boxed, in red paper preferably, some even glass-cased
to show off to best advantage.

Big pieces of silk of a red colour bearing some auspicious
good luck phrases in gilt-paper Chinese characters also make a
proper and acceptable gift.   These are about eight or ten feet
long and of the natural width of the silk. On the celebration day
they will be hung out to be viewed by all comers.   As such paper
carvings of Chinese characters are only pinned to the material,
felicitations over they can be easily removed and the materials
will retain their intrinsic value. The trouble is, however, as such

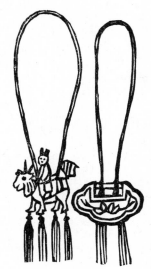

Such gifts of ornaments are as expensive as they are impractical.

silks are bound by tradition to be red in colour, their practical utility is limited. One of these few utilities, it is comforting to say, is to keep them for giving away to others under similar circumstances!

*　　　*　　　*

Of all the gifts sent at a Full Month celebration, the most expensive and yet most impractical kind must be the last category—the ornamental variety.

One of the combinations provided by propriety is a set of jewelry for the infant—a pair of bracelets and a "locket" of silver suspended from a red silken cord and decorated with tassels which is to be worn as a necklace. Although some of these "lockets" may be in the shape of a divine boy riding a unicorn, or a flower basket or some other popular motifs like five bats around a long-life character, others may actually resemble in shape and design a regular Chinese lock, the idea being to lock the boy to this world to prevent him from "fading out". Such locks closely resemble real ones in shape or design but not in construction or utility.

Another gift set would include four little silver trinkets, each weighing about five grams, the facsimiles of a peck measure, a pint measure, a bell and a seal. The first two would indicate abundance of foods or grains and the seal may be an emblem of "authority", but no handy meaning can easily be found for the bell. Such little things are worn from a fine silk string tied around the boy's wrist in the same way as a bracelet. Sometimes in the course of the boy's growth the silk string may be bitten apart or worn out and the little trinkets will be swallowed during an unguarded moment and do mischief in the little belly!

Still another combination includes a figure or a set of figures some three inches high made by hammering with a die and finely chasing or engraving a flat piece of silver plate and then thinly plating it with gold. The Long-life God (God of Longevity) with the famous big forehead is usually indispensable in such a combination. More spendthrift givers may even give the entire troupe of eight Chinese Immortals as well as the *Lao Shou Hsing* (老壽星), as the Long-life God is known in Chinese, although four small plaques of silver, square or octagonal in shape, each bearing one of a four-character phrase of good wishes would form a perfectly agreeable combination with the Long-life God. All such ornaments are mounted in a brocade or quasi-brocade box which would give a casual observer the idea that the box is worth more than its contents!

It is hardly fair to say that it is an absolute waste of money to send such gifts. For although they may appear at first glance to be a lot of useless "junk", on closer examination you will see that little holes are made around the edge of each piece by which it can be sewn on to a hat if there happens to be a hat.   In fact that is really what they are intended for.

An average well-to-do family would receive something like twenty to thirty of such ornament sets and it would require that baby change his hat or at least its ornaments about twice every month to give a fair chance of display to each set for a duration of two weeks.   Any child above three years of age would protest desperately against wearing any hat with such ornaments!

To do full justice to the practical-minded Chinese this custom of sending ornaments at least at one period in history was quite understandable.   For in olden times such things used to be made of solid silver and silver being then the legal tender for all transactions the gifts were instantly convertible and the melted metal was put back into circulation.   In such cases nothing but the workmanship would have to be forfeited.   But of late the metallic contents of these ornaments have long been destandardized, and it is safe to say that at least half of these ornaments are entirely brass in composition.   They cost a lot to buy, but would be worth next to nothing if you wished to sell them.   To use my old phrase they will be good only as gifts to others on the proper occasions.

*   *   *

One evening not long before Little Bald Head was due to have his Full Month celebration, old Mr. Wu happened to dig up from the old family archives a record book of pinkish paper (it had once been as red as a Flanders Poppy) in which were listed the various gifts received when young Mr. Wu was himself a month old.   After perusing it carefully from cover to cover with a smile of satisfaction on his face he brought it to his wife and asked her, "Say, do you recognize this?"

Old Mrs. Wu lifted her head from a piece of sewing and recognized the book, "Oh, very good!" she exclaimed.

*   *   *

One of the initial steps in the preparation of the Full Month celebration consists of printing invitations and making a list of people to be invited.   On this work old Mr. Wu immediately started to busy himself after hunting out from the family files the record of gifts received at young Mr. Wu's Full Month ceremony.   Though the record was more than twenty years old, it served as a rather dependable basis for drawing up a list for the current occasion.

There were some one hundred and twenty entries in the old book.   Of these entries, representing roughly the same number of families, some had to be deleted as they were out of date due to various reasons.   And to the new list made had to be added a number of new entries, including young Mr. Wu's newly-made friends and a few of his former schoolmates with whom friendship had been maintained.

The new complete list was then examined jointly by young Mr. Wu and his father, each checking off certain families to whom it was not enough nor appropriate to send a mere invitation and for whom a personal call was considered by tradition to be the only fitting and proper procedure on this occasion.   They soon settled all the problems and a separate list was supplied to each of the three "delegates" who were to take care of these perfunctory calls. Old Mr. Wu had the longest list, 24 families; old Mrs. Wu, 17 families; and young Mr. Wu merely 4. Young Mr. Wu, being a young man in the early stage of a career, was always busy at the bank and his time was valuable and so as far as it could be helped no family chores fell to his lot.

The invitation was then drafted and given to the little printing shop around the corner. It was to be printed by the lithograph method on crimson paper with envelopes to match. The size of the "card" was some five inches by ten inches. The wording, translated, read as follows:

"The twelfth day of this current month being the day on which our little grandson will be a month old, we are arranging a happy feast and respectfully request the presence of your entire family.

"Wu Shih-jen and son, Kwang Tsung, do their obeisance.

"The feast will be held at our humble home on Donkey Mart."

One hundred invitations were printed and ninety-two were mailed.

The next item to be considered was who should be called upon to supply the feast itself and on this point the family was divided in its opinion. Young Mr. Wu's idea was to give the order to some fashionable restaurant in Peking and have them supply the entire feast, using a portable kitchen and employing some of the restaurant's own waiters for the day. His father, on the other hand, being of the old school, was of the opinion that a jobber should be called to take care of the matter and have the cooking done on the spot which is another time-honoured custom among old Peking people. In this he was supported by his wife, old Mrs. Wu.

It was finally decided to call in the feast jobber, Chef Chow who, after hearing their rough plans, submitted tentative menus for approval. A few minor changes were made by old Mrs. Wu, who did it more from a vain desire to show off her wide knowledge than anything else. The morning feast, or luncheon, would consist of four courses of four dishes each, topped with three main dishes of what may be termed *pièces de resistance;* the whole menu, including nuts and fruits, being popularly known as *kuo hsi* (果席) or "fruit feast". The supper was to be of a different kind and much less elaborate. The main dish was to be *lu mien* (滷麵), "noodles with jellied stew" (noodles have a symbolic meaning of "long life" and are indispensable at such a feast). There were ordered eighteen "tables" of the former and ten of the latter. The wines were to be supplied by the Wu family and treated apart from the contract. The prices were agreed upon and even the smallest detail was clearly understood between the high contracting parties. The contract also provided that the cooking was to the done in the Wu house, in the back yard where a temporary kitchen was to be established for the day.

"We do not propose to use the round table to seat ten people as it would be hardly fair to our guests. We still prefer the *kuan tso-erh* (官座兒)," old Mrs. Wu declared:

"Yes, *Lao T'ai T'ai* (Old Lady) always wants to do things in the old orthodox manner!" complimented the "feast contractor".

In case you are not familiar with the term, a *kuan tso-erh*, or "official seat", is a square table to seat six people only, two on each of three sides and the fourth side left open for the convenience of the waiter and the host who is required to come to offer thanks during a feast to the guests in person. The advantage of this arrangement is that in this way the seats of honour, the two middle ones, are clearly shown, whereas guests will be seated in a more "democratic" fashion with the "honour seat principle" entirely discarded if a round table is used.

When the intention of the Wus to stage a celebration in honour of their new baby became known, a few of young Mr. Wu's associates at the office decided to contribute and to present them with a group of singing girls at the feast, and they began to sound the Wus' opinion on the matter. These young songstresses, known in Chinese as *ch'ang ta ku ti* (唱大鼓的), or "big drum singers," were very much in vogue as an entertainment then; they are less now. Young girls with special training recite in a singing style stories from the historical romances or from folklore and are accompanied on a stringed instrument, somewhat like the foreign banjo, played by a male musician, while the girls also beat time on a drum about ten inches in diameter. Young Mr. Wu, not being familiar with such things, did not give an immediate answer but promised to refer the offer to his parents. His parents flatly turned down the proposal and politely refused their friends' suggestion.

Nor did old Mr. Wu's idea of an entertainment get passed at the family council. What he proposed was *tsa shua erh* (雜耍兒), "miscellaneous funs," a sort of "vaudeville" show, consisting 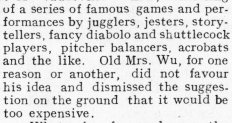 of a series of famous games and performances by jugglers, jesters, storytellers, fancy diabolo and shuttlecock players, pitcher balancers, acrobats and the like. Old Mrs. Wu, for one reason or another, did not favour his idea and dismissed the suggestion on the ground that it would be too expensive.

The shadow show figures are first carved from transparent donkey skin and then properly coloured

What she favoured was the shadow show called *ying hsi* (影戲), in Chinese. No sooner was this mentioned than everybody, not excluding young Mr. Wu's wife who was standing nearby, agreed that a shadow show would be excellent.

"Didn't we have the shadow show here when Little Bald Head's father was a month old?" Old Mrs. Wu asked.

"Of course we had", said her husband. "Funny I never thought of it. We will get the same company. It will be reasonable in cost, too. And all the neighbourhood children will swarm into our courtyard to enjoy the fun!"

*   *   *

The shadow show originated in Luanchow, the present Tangshan district of Hopei province. It still bears the name *Luanchow Ying Hsi* (灤州影戲), and dates back for hundreds of years to at least the Ming Dynasty. Briefly described, the show consists of the clever manipulations of a number of figures carved from semi-transparent donkey skin and the throwing of their shadows (with colours, as the figures are almost transparent) on a paper screen with the light from a big burner or lamp. The figures are made in sections and the trunks, the heads and the limbs, are joined loosely together by threads. They are attached to the ends of wires mounted on little rods.

The magically dexterous fingers of the performers move the figures near the screen with marvellous skill and the shadows thrown,

The showman manipulates the figures with great dexterity.

viewed from the "front" of the screen are so lifelike in effect that it is no exaggeration to say that they give an impression similar to the foreign animated cartoons. The movements of the characters are synchronized with the singing or talking of their parts by performers who read from their scripts behind the screen, accompanied by music supplied by a small orchestra and somewhat similar to the regular stage music.

This kind of shadow show has occupied a special position as a family entertainment because certain pieces in the repertoire are of a decidedly high moral level, touching at times on family ethics and preaching certain domestic sermons that make them all the more agreeable to the women. Comedies and burlesques abound, too. And as the actors or directors or performers (whatever they may properly be called) often give to the scenario their own interpretation of the theme, introducing supernumerary characters and interpolating dialogue and songs and mixing the same with bits of current satire, quips and jokes, they make the shadow shows particularly acceptable and a highly desirable entertainment for "home consumption".

On account of the reasons stated, the shadow show, to old Peking people, has closely associated itself with a birthday party or a Full Month celebration like the present case. It is not expensive, and certainly not extravagant. Its place in the mind of entertainment-conscious Chinese families has been deep-rooted.

The Wus decided to do as the family had done for generations. Old Mr. Wu arranged the details with the shadow show company, the proprietor of which at once recognized him as an old patron for in the course of years, as an old "Peking hand", he had spoken highly of the company and in certain cases actually landed them contracts. The show at the Wu residence was to start at noon on the day of celebration and end about midnight. It was to cost the sum of eight silver dollars.

A man from the company was to come early in the morning on the proper day to erect the "stage."

*   *   *

Although the actual celebration day was the 12th day of the 9th moon, the activities definitely started on the tenth of the month. The Wu family had their own mat shed the framework of which was kept in condition all the year round though the matting was put up only during the summer months. For the Full Month Day fete the matting and some decorative touches were to be put up for which the mat shed shop was summoned. For birthday parties the decorative glass panes should bear the character *Shou* (壽), "long life", in red, and for a funeral the same character in blue. For a ceremony like the present one, red *Hsi* (喜), "happiness", characters should be the motifs—the same as at a wedding feast.

The work was finished in no time and the complete courtyard, besides the various rooms in the house, was ready to be thrown open to all guests who would come to offer their congratulations. The guests naturally being expected to come during meal times, additional furniture was rented and was laid out in the proper manner in the courtyard. The backyard, by the next evening, had become fully occupied by the cooks who made it their temporary headquarters. The preparatory stages of the culinary enterprises soon began, accompanied by the indispensable noises. The place was literally humming with activity.

Early the next morning the head of the shadow show company presented himself. He consulted the household about the erection of the stage. The proper place was soon found to be the central part of the main courtyard, with the stage facing the main parlour on the north side. He assembled a number of tables and massed them in a big "U" formation and from the corners he put up bamboo poles and had the spot rounded up with pieces of blue cloth, the front being overhung with hangings of embroideries surrounding a screen some four feet wide and three feet high of white rice paper.

His "properties" soon came, trunks of donkey skin figures and the musical equipment consisting of stringed instruments, drums, cymbals, trumpets, gongs, castanets, and so forth. Then there also came the collection of scenarios from which the players would actually read their lines during the performances from behind the screen. Such details were unknown to members of the audience except to the more inquisitive ones, who might intrude "back stage" to discover the technique.

The Wu family rose early the morning of the twelfth and had their entire house fixed up and ready for the reception. The amateur bookkeeper for the day was found in the capable person of old Mr. Wu's sworn brother, Chao, who appeared on the scene not long after dawn and put up his impromptu accounts division in one of the side rooms where he was supplied with the various appliances not excepting that omnipotent Chinese abacus. He was given a cash box and some loose change for petty expenses, the big record book of red paper, brush pen and inkstone and the like. Opening the record book, he discovered that the first entry had already been made, of silks and jewelry from Madame Ho, the maternal grandmother.   She never failed to score the No. 1 entry on such occasions!

The doors to the various rooms were then decorated with gay-coloured pieces of silk, and the entire interior of the mat shed was profusely touched up with squares of red paper bearing on each the big Chinese character "happiness".

The guests soon began to come in by twos and threes, the men in their "Sunday best" and the women and children gaily dressed and ornamented, faces thickly powdered and heavily rouged.   Men, women and children alike, however, invariably wore a smile (the type known as a "million dollar smile") as they in turn did obeisance to the old Wu couple and made bows to the young parents.   For some time nothing but the giggles and the exchange of greetings could be heard in the parlour.   The cooks and the professional master of ceremonies contributed their due share of noise and the children brought by the guests were responsible for another share of commotion.

There were also the children from the neighbourhood who did not know anything else about the entire affair except that since they had seen the shadow show men carry their things to this compound, they at once, by virtue of their instinct, concluded that here was a free show for all to see.   The news spread to their sisters and brothers and they began soon to come in earnest.   The courtyard was literally crowded with them by the time the show actually started about noon.

*   *   *

One of the things old Mrs. Wu liked about any feast was the courtesy (even if affected) shown by the guests asking each other to assume a seat of a more "honourable" position.   At a dinner or luncheon, as the guests are not provided with seating arrangements beforehand, there is no way to foretell who will come and sit where and with whom.   Etiquette calls for great prudence in seating a group of six guests at a table and such courteous bargaining may take easily ten minutes. Chinese guests are not requested to arrive at a certain hour and, as the feast is supposed to last the whole day, guests arrive and depart as they please.   Fortunately nature and human habits combine to create a workable formula.   Guests arrive, see the host and hostess, deliver their presents, find an acquaintance in the assemblage in the courtyard and talk "about the weather", or strike up a new friendship if there happen to be no friends in the gathering, and then wait for their turn or seek their turn to sit at the feast and, finishing that, either stay for the entertainment if there is one or leave.   At least 60 per cent. of the guests will leave after the feast as they come expressly to "drink the happy wine".   When guests are invited, they are supposed to have been asked to do exactly that.   The phrase is *ch'ing ho hsi chiu* (請 喝 喜 酒), "invitation to drink happy wine".

"Happy wine drinking" guests usually arrive around meal time and so the Chinese way is to hire additional tables and chairs to take care of the "peak".   At the Wus' ceremonial feast no fewer than seven tables were kept going at one time by noon. There were four in the main courtyard, seating gentlemen guests and two tables in the parlour where women and children sat and then one additional table in the southern rooms where young Mr.

Wu wanted to have his personal friends, the younger set, sit together by themselves.

The feast was of the *kuo hsi* (果席), or "fruit feast", category and was not a very costly affair and in keeping with family life. Some guests actually felt disappointed to find no bird's nest or shark's fins. Such guests (excuse me for saying so) apparently either did not know much about Peking family life, or had only rich and extravagant

Old Mrs. Wu liked to have high-legged dishes at feasts.

friends being extravagant themselves.

The feast started with "four dry fruits", salted almond kernels, watermelon seeds, candied walnut meat, fried hazelnut meat. The next to come were "four confectioneries", jellied crab apples, honeyed apricots, honeyed lotus seeds and green preserved plums. (These were, like four dessert dishes, added to the menu after the contract was concluded with Chef Chow,—old Mrs. Wu would always do something like that!) Then "four fresh fruits", apples, pears, grapes and bananas. Then "four cold meats", jellyfish and shrimps, preserved eggs, slices of duck with yeast, and sausage. Next, "four meat dishes", freshwater shrimps in stew, carp in sour and sweet sauce, kidneys in fancy cuttings, and sea cucumbers. "Four desserts" followed: steamed dumplings, fried cakes, steamed lama pastry, and little steamed puddings with assorted cores. Then came the three *pièces de resistance*, roasted ham in red sauce, stewed Peking duck, and a sweet dish of lotus seed tea with slices of lily bulbs.

Everybody liked the feast very much and told the Wu family so and old Mrs. Wu, who liked nothing better than flattery, was not disappointed.

"I am glad you have enjoyed it", she said to the guests. "See, I like the old fashion of having the parties right in your home and not in a restaurant. To be in keeping with my old ideas, I have had the cooks use the old type high-legged dishes. I think they are lovely".

To be perfectly frank, her feast was a success, in so far as the selection and appointments were concerned.

*   *   *

While the feast was on the shadow show people got everything ready and the big glass burner of sesamum oil, suspended from a pole over the chief showman's head, was also lighted. The adjustments were made so as to get the proper distance and angle to throw the shadows on the screen properly. A musical selection served as prelude and the show started immediately with a piece from popular folklore, appertaining to the birth of a high-born child predestined to be an accomplished scholar and a successful court dignitary. The boy was supposed to have been sent by the goddesses and to have descended to earth riding a unicorn—a legendary animal, a combination of dragon and buffalo. This was the special feature in keeping with the occasion of the celebration and was over in about seven minutes.

The program for the day was not pre-arranged or specified by the hosts and the audience was allowed, or requested, in the usual manner to choose their own favourite pieces for which privilege the time-honoured usage is for the person who chooses a piece to give a little "wine money". In China all tips are "wine money", just like they are "tea money" (*chadai*) in Japan.

The entire repertoire is listed, name by name, on an elongated piece of bamboo plate, lacquered white and bent in a slight curve with one end somewhat narrower than the other. This is a facsimile of the ancient scepter of authority borne respectfully with both hands by high officials during imperial audiences—the original ones were made of ivory. The chief showman produced the repertoire and gave it to old Mr. Wu to pass around to the guests for their selection. "Please bestow on us your commands," Showman Li smilingly added.

The scepter-like piece was then passed around, the highlights on which showed among other things the following:

"The Fine Steed with Red Manes" (or "Lady Precious Stream," as it is known to Londoners and New Yorkers).

"Madame Wang Ch'un Ao and Her Son," complete with "The Double Diploma Honour".

"Hu Ti Reviles the King of Hell" and "The Visit through the Eighteen Departments of ortures".

"Temple Societies and Games Demonstrated".

"The Gold Mountain Monastery" or "The Legend of the White Snake and the Green Snake".

"Eight Immortals Traverse the Seas".

"The Conflagration of the Bamboo Grove", and so on.

Part of the guests not familiar with the shadow show were somewhat surprised at the wide range of plays presentable and which certainly did not seem possible with the comparatively small group of "operatives" in the company. There were listed between seventy and eighty plays, from one-act monologues to lengthy historical dramas such as the Three Kingdoms plays, the performance of which would take four or even five hours in the Chinese theatre.

Quite a few of the guests named their pieces and waited their turn to see them enacted.

The Wu family had also their own selections. Old Mrs. Wu selected a piece known as "The Quarrel between Mother and Daughter" and her husband chose "The Donkey Driver's Follies". As to Madame Ho's young son, he had his chance too and ordered "Patching the broken Jar" or "the Hill of Hundred Grasses". "Passing the Night in the Flower Pavilion", a love romance, was selected by one of young Mr. Wu's "younger set" friends. This man being young Mr. Wu's best friend at the bank his selection was performed first as he had to hurry back to the office.

A lot of agitation took place in the parlour where the women were gathered and the result was that the play, "The Little Bald Head's Adventures in the Bridal Chamber", was asked to be enacted without fail. Nobody knew who actually motivated this selection. Old Mrs. Wu might have named it herself.

* * *

The Full Month celebration for Little Bald Head was a tremendous success. There were, suffice it to say, more guests than were anticipated and the gifts received were many and bounteous. Most of the gentleman guests left in the late afternoon but a greater part of the women stayed until after supper. The show did not stop until the small hours of the morning.

It is needless to say that the Wu family took fully three days to rest. They then attended to the "thanking" of the guests, either by a printed card bearing their names and the big Chinese character *hsieh* (謝), meaning "thanks", or by paying personal calls to see that the guests "had not been inconvenienced". This latter form of expressing thanks is known as *tao fa* (道乏), or "acknowledge the infliction", meaning that the hosts fully understand that their invitation had been an imposition on their friends' good nature.

THE VISIT TO THE GRANDPARENTS

THE Wu child fared very well from the day of his birth and by the time the date of the Hundred Days Ceremony arrived he had grown fat, strong and robust and as cheerful as few other babies of his age could have been. His mother's breast milk was good, the care taken was thorough in every respect and nutrition was in perfectly good order. In roughly three months he had

He would have served nicely for baby food advertisements.

grown up to be a typical baby that could challenge any medical test. His picture would have made a fine advertisement for any milk food or for any baby's patent tablets!

On the hundredth day after a birth there are more formalities. This again necessitated the bringing of gifts from Madame Ho, the maternal grandmother. This time in the traditional manner, these were a smoked chicken from the town's most famous delicatessen store and a couple of live shrimps and another leg of pork. The occasion is known as *po lu erh* (百露兒). Translated word for word, this would be "a hundred dews", meaning etymologically "having passed one hundred dewy nights"!

The tongue of the chicken is to be pulled out and applied by the maternal grandmother lightly with a few strokes across the baby's mouth, suggesting that the boy was to develop a good and clever (a pun for chicken, *chi*) tongue. The Chinese proverb has it that "a fine man grows a good tongue and a fine horse grows strong legs", and this shows how important a part the tongue plays in the Chinese conception of a person's valuable assets. (It does not necessarily follow that the boy grows up to be a great linguist though!)

Then the two live shrimps are taken ceremoniously from a dish and flourished in the same manner about the baby's lips, expressing thereby a hope that the baby will grow up to be as active and lively as the shrimps! The leg of pork is for the making of some clear broth with some of which the baby's face is to be washed in order that he will develop a white and velvety skin. The actual washing, of course, is nothing more than the dipping of a plug of cotton in the soup and smearing it lightly over the baby's face! All these procedures were attended to most faithfully. The occasion was also the day for a feast of noodles.

A touch of Buddhist influence was also added to the ceremony by old Mrs. Wu. She, in compliance with a custom handed down from time immemorial, caused some little steamed muffins to be prepared and strung on a piece of thread like a string of beads. The string of muffins was then hung on the neck of Little Wu, and the baby, muffins and all, was taken out into the street. The neighbourhood children were summoned and each was given one muffin from the string until they were all gone. This is an evolution, apparently, from the Buddhist theory of the retribution of deeds. The Christian says "as a man sows, so shall he reap"; the Buddhist says "he takes what he gives and suffers what he does". The giving away of muffins symbolizes all giving, and from this, arranged by the invisible gods, the donor expects sooner or later to get back something. From such a small detail certain angles of the philosophy of life of the Chinese can well be perceived.

The birth of Little Bald Head, from the very beginning, was considered by old Mrs. Wu to have been an act of blessing from the Goddess of Sons and Grandsons more than anything else. And it was therefore her unshakable belief that the boy came not as the little fat cherub which it was to all eyes but as a little doll from the Hall of the Goddess of Sons and Grandsons in the Temple of the Sacred Eastern Mountain. On the neck of such a doll, among the multitude of dolls in that place, young Mrs. Wu, supervised by her mother-in-law, had tied a piece of red string and had thus virtually "dragged" it into her household. And then this idea began to trouble her. She began to reflect.

Without the slightest inkling of the foreign saying "Whosoever God loves dies young," she began to recall various cases of particularly lovely children who died a sudden death or suffered from mysterious diseases that eventually killed them at a tender age. She also remembered how relatives and friends consoling the families so bereaved would explain, in the regular Chinese manner, that the children in question had not actually been their own offspring but merely little dolls from the Goddess of Sons and Grandsons who had secretly run away from the goddess and got themselves incarnated in this world. Moreover, she had heard it said that borrowed babies from the goddess were wont to run back at the most undesirable moments unless the loans were squared up at an early date. All such misfortunes had come because, it was said, having taken a baby from the goddess they neglected to return an effigy in its place. These thoughts urged her to act and act promptly she did.

Old Mrs. Wu did not consult her husband this time nor her son for that matter. Her husband had his own ideas about such things, which were considered queer by his wife. As to young Mr. Wu, he never refused to allow her to do as she pleased as long as it meant no bigger harm than the small expenditure of money. He thought that his mother probably needed something that he had learned was "faith" and besides she would need a walk from time to time anyway. A promenade would do her good, he thought.

The next 15th day of the moon, a proper day for offering sacrifices, having arrived she betook herself that morning most devotedly to the Temple of the Sacred Eastern Mountain which is located outside of Ch'ao Yang Men on the main highway

The effigy of a baby when burnt cancels the loan of a newborn child.

and not quite a mile from the Wu house on Donkey Mart. At the main entrance to the Temple, where there is a big incense store, she purchased one *feng*, five bundles of incense of 52 sticks each, of incense of the highest grade obtainable at five big coppers per *feng* higher than the regular quality. From a nearby stall she purchased the paper effigy of a boy about sixteen or eighteen inches high. Being illiterate herself, she had the stall-keeper put on the name "Wu, the Little Bald Head" on the tag dangling from the effigy's hand. Then, thus well equipped, she repaired to the Hall of the Goddess of Sons and Grandsons. Assisted by the temple steward, she lighted the incense, bundle after bundle, and kneeling down, she kowtowed three times, said her prayers and gave thanks, delivering the paper effigy to the steward. She insisted that the effigy be burned in her presence. In this manner whatever she had borrowed from the goddess was properly returned. She was pleased and went home with a heart immeasurably lighter than when she came.

It was when she got home that she explained what she had done.

"I have returned the 'doll' for Little Bald Head", she said, "and there need be no fear now. The goddess will cancel the item from her books of loans of babies and Little Bald Head will not have to go back now".

Recounting the details of her trip and describing the paper effigy she had bought and offered up, she related that she saw to it that it was actually burned before her eyes. "The temple assistants would not burn the effigies if you trusted them to do that and would forget all about it. They actually would keep them for resale for which clever arrangement they are well organized with the effigy stall men at the temple gates," she explained.

*   *   *

One evening after supper the entire Wu family, excepting old Mr. Wu, were gathered in the bedroom of young Mr. Wu for their usual after-supper chat. And their conversation invariably, as if by a set rule, began to center around the fat Little Bald Head as it was old Mrs. Wu's custom to make the daily rounds of the "nursery" to see how her grandson was getting along. Then they hit upon an interesting thing to do, it was to tell the baby's fortune from the family almanac in which a large section is devoted to this feature.

The Chinese believe that the year, the month, the day and the hour at which a child is born have their respective significance and these combined in their various ways represent a framework upon which the entire pattern of luck or ill-luck, fortune or misfortune, are woven. These things are supposed to carry such a great meaning with their kaleidoscopic combinations that every important step in the person's life, the matrimonial arrangements, and indeed even his death and the funeral itself are predestined by the four time factors of the birth. The force is so strong that it is considered inescapable whatever Fate says it has in store for one.

There are certain specialists in China who try to fathom the unfathomable and according to what they declare their art (or should it be called a "science?") is infallible. There are others, of course, who do not believe such things can be possible and prefer to plod along the best they know how but such people are comparatively few who are not tempted to pry into the unknown to see if Fortune has anything nice awaiting them. And to the majority the Wu family naturally belonged.

They soon found the family almanac and the book was opened at the page which contained the method for telling a person's fortune by the time factors. The calculation immediately began.

They found that the year was that of the "rooster" and that accounted for 1.6 ounces weight of "significance." That he was born on the second eighth moon (it happened to be a Lunar leap year which added one full month instead of the one day for February in the Solar system) accounted for 1.5 ounces. The 12th day accounted for 1.8 ounces, and the hour, between 5 and 6 o'clock in the afternoon, or "monkey" time, accounted for 0.8 ounces. Thus the total was 5.7 ounces, which was a good weight, according to the almanac. The maximum weight is 7 ounces and the minimum is 2.1 ounces and so Little Bald Head was way "above the average," so to speak. Looking further they found the predictions, which were as follows:

"The Star of Fame shines through this man's Future,
And his position will be of high rank whatever he'll
        venture;
His stomach filled entirely with literary embroidery,
And to his family he will bring reputation and glory."

At these lines, as they were read aloud sarcastically by young Mr. Wu and listened to intently by all present, they rejoiced and clapped their hands.

"Oh, Little Bald Head! His stomach is going to be filled with literary embroidery, eh? And he will bring reputation and glory to the Wu family! Just think of it!" exclaimed the young father.

"Do not laugh about it!" said his mother. "Such things were all the result of years of study by the sages and should not be looked upon with contempt. By the way, come to think of it, read to me, Kwang Tsung, what it says for your father. I always enjoy hearing it read. What was his total weight? Oh, yes, 4.4 ounces. Find it."

Young Mr. Wu found the column instantly. For any person whose time factors add up to 4.4 ounces it has the following to say:

"This life, it is bounteously blessed with happiness
        and wealth,
And great peace and comfort, and then best of health;
A virtuous wife, clever sons and grandsons to him
        belong,
A good nature, a fine character and his body strong."

At this moment, old Mr. Wu happened to enter the room. Having heard the hilarious laughter, he decided to investigate. He heard the reading, shook his head and withdrew.

*   *   *

A newborn baby in China makes his maiden trip to the outside world with a certain amount of formality, and tradition and practicality have found no more proper place for him to go to than the maternal grandparents' house. This in Peking is known as *nuo sao wo-erh* (挪騷窩兒), or "moving away from the odorous spot". It is true that a newborn baby does not travel light; he does not need a ticket to travel but his baggage is excessive. If the baby does not happen to have enough and to spare of his mother's breast milk it is necessary for him also to carry around his tin of milk-food, his mixer and feeder, or their Chinese equivalents.

His changes of clothes being necessarily frequent, his additional wardrobe is naturally large. Such being the case, perhaps the maternal grandparents' house would be the only family willing and prepared to board the guest at all. Of course, it is understood that the mother is to travel with him as a member of his retinue. It also means a lot of trouble and expense for the mother's family. To start with, the young proud mother has to be feted. Then a gala time is sure to follow. If it is conveniently possible for some young woman to take charge of the baby at home, the schedule should also include going to the theatre for the married daughter and dining outside. Indeed such pleasures become at times actually boring and a real burden to the maternal family. No wonder old Mrs. Wu deemed it a blessing that she had no female children to rear.

Ever since Madame Ho and her family attended the Full Month Ceremony for their grandson, the occasion of the baby's coming visit to the Ho family had been looked forward to with much fond anticipation. They went specially to invite the "party," but no definite date was promised by the Wu family. Old Mrs. Wu reasoned that since the "doll" had not yet been returned to the goddess, Little Bald Head was a sort of an "unregistered guest" and as such no publicity should be allowed. In reality, however, it may be presumed that the baby was too precious to be missed or taken away from their midst for any duration of time, meaning, in a word, that they had not yet begun to get tired of the novelty! Madame Ho insisted otherwise.

"If you will not allow the mother and child to come over to our house just now 'to move away from the odorous spot,' I cannot, of course, object," said Madame Ho. "But there is a custom, perhaps you have forgotten, that if the baby does not pay a visit to the maternal grandparents before he is fully a hundred days old, then it will be a bad omen to do so afterwards, and the curse would not be off until the baby grows up to be tall enough to ring the brass knockers on the door himself, and that would be a long time to come."

Now that the "doll," or paper effigy, had been offered up there was no objection to get the baby a-travelling.

They soon got Little Bald Head dressed up having put on him his most exquisitely embroidered red satin jacket, a Full Month gift, and green silk trousers tied at the ankles with beautiful ribbons. A big "tiger" hat and "tiger" shoes completed his ensemble. A red brocade cape with white rabbit fur collar was the overall garment. His face was cleanly washed and a mark of rouge was put on between his eyebrows. The finest silver locket with the prettiest silk cord was selected from the many gift pieces and thrown around his neck. (The baby was so fat that there was no neck visible.)

The mule cart sent by the Ho family soon arrived with Madame Ho herself who came to welcome them, and they, after a hurried conversation, rode off, for the Ho estate in the Western Hills near the former Imperial Hunting Park. There, commanded by old Mrs. Wu and sanctioned previously by young Mr. Wu, the mother and child were to stay for six days as the Ho family's *chiao k'e* (嬌客), "tender guests."

Before leaving, a little touch of black dust was put on the baby's nose by the Wu family and even after the passengers were all aboard the mule cart, there were heard repeated instructions to the young mother that they remember to put a touch of white powder on baby's nose when he returned home. Both Madame Ho and young Mrs. Wu promised to do so without fail.

This is another custom peculiar to Peking. The meaning in the practice is that as the baby leaves the paternal family "black and lean" and comes home from the maternal family "white and fat," there is no question that he was well taken care of and properly nourished during his first outing.

*   *   *

Seriously speaking, some of the Chinese superstitions are not without their merits in reality. Since the Chinese, not unlike many other peoples, are not fully possessive of a generous measure of scientifically sound commonsense that make them fully prepared to cope with all emergencies, it is just as well for them to be bound by sundry precautionary rules of blind belief. Such rules may not be really harmful and at times are responsible in the long run for warding off a lot of trouble and nipping them in the bud. For instance, the Chinese nursing mother is advised to be very careful not to do certain things which may cause the breast milk to disappear. It would be very sensible to say that all emotional shocks should be avoided. Unfortunately, no such generalization· has been discovered and the Chinese still have their cautions in a more or less "itemized" manner.

The Wu child and his mother went to stay at Madame Ho's estate for a six-day vacation and it was during this period that young Mrs. Wu suddenly lost her breast milk. Toward the fourth day of their visit, the milk began to get thinner and watery, until by the time they were due to come home only a very poor stream of milk was available and this caused them to come home in a noticeably dejected frame of mind. It happened that there was a funeral in the Ho neighbourhood. The woman who died was one who was dear to young Mrs. Wu. The sad news gave her a shock. The grief, somewhat repressed, caused her milk to disappear entirely without her being aware of the reason.

The baby came home with his nose properly powdered white as dictated by tradition but it was apparent that he was not "white and fat" as had been expected.

A lot of anxiety was caused in the Wu household by this mishap. The entire family was agitated. The baby, too, was restless and kept crying from hunger. The family council was called for an urgent meeting.

Young Mr. Wu suggested getting a wet nurse, some poor woman from the country east of Peking who makes it a business to be a wet nurse to a rich family. He thought that this was the logical thing to do.

Old Mrs. Wu objected. "We do not wish to employ a wet nurse, as long as it is possible not to do so," said she. "A wet nurse is hard to shake off as she would expect to be kept in our employ even long after the baby has grown big enough to do without her. Such a servant may become absolutely uncontrollable by virtue of her affected intimacy and relationship with the baby. Using such special circumstances to coerce us for better and better treatment and still not satisfied, she would go on strike and leave the baby "high and dry" without thinking the least of the baby's welfare. And in our presence she may pretend to be very tender and careful in feeding and looking after the baby in a general way, but once away from our eyes she would treat him with horrible indifference. The proverb says you cannot paste a piece of pork onto the body of a sheep. Besides, a wet nurse will expect to "grow" with the child and become his guardian-nurse at the same scale of wages. It would be all right if she really liked the child, but the fact is that it is not so. I have seen such nurses spank little children in the street when away from their parents and threatening more spanking should the children report it to their parents! No, we must think of some other way."

"How much does a wet nurse cost a month, anyway?" young Mr. Wu asked.

The wet nurse is given a set of silver jewelry when she has been employed for a year.

"The wet nurse is not satisfied with monthly wages. The usual custom is like this. The nurse's wages are about three times that of a regular maid-servant. She is supposed to have the same food as the mistress and her family. When she first comes, she is to be supplied with all her personal clothes and bedding. She, of course, will expect better gratuities at the festivals and at the new year than the other servants. When she has been in the service a year, we must buy her a set of silver jewelry, composed of pins and things worn in the hair and bracelets and earrings and finger rings. When she has been in the family another year, such jewelry will have to be plated with leaf gold at our expense. Then if there is no serious mistake on her part, she cannot be discharged unless a piece of land has been bought for her in her home district, or a sum of money enough for such a purpose is paid in its place." old Mrs. Wu explained.

"Since that is the case", said young Mr. Wu, "it seems to me we are just about in for it, are we not?"

"No, not necessarily," said his mother. "I just asked your wife and she said the milk did not disappear entirely. And so I expect some medicine will most probably help."

*   *   *

Madame Ho was no less anxious than the Wu family about her daughter's breast milk on which her grandson's welfare depended so much. She was particularly concerned because the "disappearance" took place while the young mother was supposed to have been under her attention during a sojourn to her family. She did not return to her home when she accompanied the mother and child back to the city but stayed with the Wu family for another day, being anxious to see conditions improve. She left the day after without seeing any improvement.

Old Mr. Wu was the least agitated of all because he had his own way of looking at things. He thought that since there are substitutes for human milk available, they could at least fall back on them. He suggested to his wife and bought for the baby some steamed rice-powder, called in Chinese *kao kan mien-erh* (糕乾麵兒), or "dry cake powder." Then, at the recommendation of a tea-house companion of his, he made a trip to the Eastern Willow Tree Well Street, and there at a monopolistic milling establishment purchased another kind of rice-flour, known as *lao mi mien-erh* (老米麵兒), or "old rice flour." These two brands have been, it is true, China's own Lactogen and Klim for centuries and have fed and saved perhaps millions of Chinese babies. Either stuff, being previously seasoned, is to be cooked into a thick paste and literally smeared in "fingerfuls" into the baby's mouth. Some say that a certain fungus (considered to be of a curative value), ground into a fine powder is mixed in the flour, but this seems unlikely, considering the flour's inexpensiveness.

The fat baby, hungry like a young wolf cub, sucking and sucking hastily and heartily at the finger laden with the cooked dough was a most pathetic sight. Moreover, the food was apparently not satisfying and the baby kept on crying and crying for more.

Old Mrs. Wu, witnessing the heartrending sight, concluded that such a solution was decidedly unsatisfactory and something must indeed be done before the baby was definitely "in the sick bed."

As the news spread in the neighbourhood, there soon began to appear sympathizers from next door and the door after next. A lot of

The hungry baby eagerly sucked the dough-covered finger.

advice was soon forthcoming. Among which were some *p'ien fang erh* (偏方兒), or "unrecognized prescriptions," which have been tried and found to be of great help in re-obtaining the milk.

One woman said that the ears of a wild hare should be put between two pieces of rooftiles and baked into ashes and the ashes taken by the mother would do the trick. Another advanced the theory that incense should be burned at the shrine of the goddess who would certainly not fail to mend matters. Old Mrs. Wu felt influenced by the latter suggestion at once but as to the former she chose rather to sound out the young mother's opinion and willingness to take the "medicine" before doing anything on the project. She was not herself "sold" on the idea.

Young Mrs. Wu, however anxious for her son's welfare, did

not seem to like the idea of the "scorched rabbit-ear policy."
(We don't blame her!) . She did not say that directly, though, but
asked her mother-in-law in a circumlocutory manner to please see
if there was not some other way out of her difficulty.

Not long afterward another preparation was suggested as a
very effective remedy and highly recommended for trial by old
Midwife Ma, the undisputed authority on such matters. The concoction was simple. It consisted of pounding two live crabs (a
female and a male) into a fine pulp, adding water and cooking
the pulp into a soup in which were to be put two pouched eggs.
The mother was to eat the soup and the eggs and then, as Midwife Ma put it, "you watch the milk flow like an artesian well!"
Young Mrs. Wu liked this idea much better than the other.

Old Mr. Wu rushed to the market and bought the crabs. In
thirty minutes the concoction was ready to serve. Young Mrs.
Wu took it without any particular disgust.

That same evening the milk began to flow freely. Little Bald
Head was re-assured of his daily fare, and the entire Wu family
was relieved. Old Mrs. Wu told her daughter-in-law that she
actually felt ten years younger as she was saved from much
headache.

THE FIRST YEAR PASSES

ALMOST as soon as an "unrecognized prescription" of eggs cooked in the soup of crab pulp was administered to young Mrs. Wu her breast milk reappeared and a calamitous crisis was fortunately avoided.

This probably impressed young Mrs. Wu with the importance of taking still greater care of both herself and the baby. As no stone was left unturned to see that Little Bald Head obtained "the best that he deserved" of everything, he made excellent progress in personal habits as well as bodily growth. A Chinese aphorism for judging the proper infant development says: "Three, turns; six, sits; and eight crawls," which means, paraphrased, when a healthily developed child is three months old, he or she should be able to turn the tiny body without outside help; a six-month-old one should be able to sit steady; and an eight-month-old should crawl about freely. This scale is found to be so true that it has become a well-known household saying. Any infant failing in these tests is considered mal-nutritioned or under-developed. Needless to say, the Wu child lived up to the standard.

The time soon arrived to give the child his first vaccination. And the old method was favoured by the family.

The so-called old method of vaccination is not really an old native art in China but, it is safe to say, is the original form of some early European method introduced into China most probably by the early missionaries. Like everything else in China there is always a tendency on the part of the average Chinese mind to let well alone. Any new method introduced and found "quite serviceable" would stay where it was and it is harder to add further improvements to it than it was to pioneer the original method, because, it should always be borne in mind, the Chinese are a practical race. A new method is adopted because there is an acute need or a genuine desire for such a thing. If that is obtained, everything is settled. Why bother to improve on it. In other words, it has to be something very badly needed to be noticed by the Chinese—a necessity, never a luxury!

According to the old methods of vaccination, unlike the modern practice which provides that "any day is a vaccination day," only the fourth moon (about May of the solar calendar) is the proper time. The belief is that since spring is such a favourable season for the growth of all flowers it ought to be, as well, the proper time for vaccination as vaccination is known as *chung hua-erh*(種花兒), "flower-planting", in China. The children have lighter clothing by then and the weather is warmer and it is not a bad time for such a purpose either. To explain the foregoing it may not be out-of-place to add that the amount of clothing a Chinese wears is in direct proportion to the cold of the weather. No central heating or any heating that is worthy of the word is to be found in the majority of Chinese houses. A plump child wearing three thick cotton-padded garments one over the other is not very handy for a surgical operation, indeed.

Not being inclined to run the risk of smallpox, the Wu family soon decided to have the baby vaccinated and as a preliminary formality a blind fortune-teller, one of those roaming the streets with a guiding stick and carrying a single cymbal knocked by a little wooden hammer as announcer, was summoned for his opinion on the matter. He very wisely advised that the boy was quite favourably prepared for the undertaking. The blind sooth-sayer further suggested that since the boy's life was of the "wood" pattern, he should best be vaccinated on a day of strong "water" element which would be a suitable combination for the growth of the "flower." He naturally based his calculations on the Five Elements Principle (Fire, Water, Wood, Metal and Earth). He further advised that a day should best be selected in the period between the day of *Mang Chung* (芒種), "Sowing Festival", and the Summer Solstice, which is a superfluous re-commendation, comparable to telling a man to be sure to open his mouth when eating something!

*   *   *

Not far from Donkey Mart, right on the main thoroughfare leading west from the Four Arches Junction called Pig Street, is a small temple facing north and known by the name of Ti Tsang An (地藏菴), or the God of Hell's Nunnery. The temple ought to have its name changed to something else at the first opportunity as no nuns have been seen living there in years. A great portion of the temple grounds has been rented to various organ-izations, business and otherwise, and it is here that every Spring some Chinese practitioners gather to dispense their vaccination services, á la ancient manner. A yellow poster, familiar to all Peking residents, with wood block printing of the Chinese char-acters, *Shih Chung Niu To* (施種牛痘), or "Free Planting of Cows Vaccine," appears punctually. each year pasted on every wall corner in the neighbourhood of the station advertised, calling to every child-rearing family to have their babies registered for the "planting" of the "flowers."

The old method also ordains that the vaccination be done only once, when the baby is about a year old and the child so treated is considered to be immune to smallpox for life. Contam-inations or inoculations are given three in a row on each of the two tiny upper arms. The serum used is obtained directly from the cows, and preserved in tiny bottles. The doctor dons no white operation gown and there are no nurses to assist. His equipment is simple and requires no trays or racks to contain it nor an auto-clave to sterilize it. It consists of nothing more than a crude instrument, a steel facsimile of a small double-edged sword, fold-ed like a boy scout's jackknife when not in use. The knife may be used for forty or fifty operations daily and there is no bother about disinfecting it, not even a frequent wiping or cleaning of the instrument has been noticed.

The parent registers the baby's name and awaits his turn to get the vaccination. The "doctor" carves three small crosses on each baby's arm with the small sword applying from his midget bottle particles of the precious fluid on the "wounds," and the operation is over. The parent, usually the mother, will see to it that the little jacket sleeves do not interfere with the wounds; this she usually does by inserting a piece of red (nothing but red) string through the sleeves and tying them high above the elbow at the armpits. The child is to return for examination after the

A piece of red string is used to tie the jacket sleeve under the armpit clear from the vaccination spots.

seventh day. The service, advertised as "free," costs twenty to forty cents.

Little Bald Head went with his mother and grandmother and his "flowers" were planted without anything worse than a lot of hearty crying—the process must have been painful. A red jacket, single, was previously sewn by his loving mother especially for the occasion. Old Mrs. Wu, true to her tradition, again burnt incense and craved the protection of the goddesses, for which occasion she made another pilgrimage to the temple.

During the six or seven days ensuing foods supposed to have a "fermenting" property were given to the mother and in small quantities to the child, consisting of fresh black dates as it would then be assured that the "flowers" would be well fermented, meaning that the reaction would be medically satisfactory, or positive, if that is the proper word. From hearsay old Mr. Wu understood that a cooked pig's snout would be the most effective "fermenter." The suggestion was not accepted as his wife insisted that since other foods were available, there was no need to resort to such a special victual. "Let those who can ill afford fresh mushrooms eat that stuff!" old Mrs. Wu stated.

Little Bald Head stood the trial very nicely and was not any the worse in spite of the experience. A little fever was noted but his reaction was very good, the swelling and reddening were satisfactory and by the seventh day scabs formed themselves and these fell off one after another. The second visit to the "doctor" was duly carried out as a formality as a repeat process was hardly needed.

That Little Bald Head had his vaccination in a smooth-sailing manner and that no inconvenience was experienced was the reason for much rejoicing in the family. Old Mrs. Wu, in due course, thanked the Goddess of Smallpox in a fitting manner.

*   *   *

There is a Chinese proverb which says "A man has seven fathers and eight mothers," which would indicate by what a great network of family relationship he is bound. And this incidentally would also show what a great multitude of duties he has to perform, as the supreme social relationship in China, as well as Japan if not in the entire Orient, is that of "familism" and filial piety.

It would not be easy to list all of the "fathers" and "mothers," considering the fact that any person of the same age as the father would be the son's "uncle" or "aunt," and in China "uncles" and "aunts" are known as "uncle-fathers" and "aunt-mothers." To these should be added the parents and parents-in-law. Besides, a schoolboy's teacher and the teacher's wife are also known at "teacher-father" and "teacher-mother", and they consequently are included in the list. There is one more mother than fathers as the Chinese have been a polygamous race and, believe it or not, the father's concubines also acquire automatically a motherly status and come to be called *Yi Mu* (姨母)!

There is another variety of parents which would be somewhat similar in nature to the foreign godfather and godmother or perhaps the adopted father and adopted mother but really different from either. This kind is known as *yi fu* (義父) and *yi mu* (義母), or "father-in-faith" and "mother-in-faith" in classical terminology, but commonly known as *kĭn lao·erh* (乾老兒) and *kan ma* (乾媽) respectively. Translated, they are the "dry old one" and the "dry mother." Why and how such parents are "adopted" makes interesting reading.

The blind fortune-teller having advised rather wisely about Little Bald Head's vaccination was also informative about the peculiar life pattern of our little hero. He proceeded to give an exhaustive analysis of the design on which his life was cast, as controlled by the birth time factors. The blind man must have developed a sixth sense for he soon sized up the situation and very sagaciously talked old Mrs. Wu into believing his arguments. He explained himself in the most convincing manner.

He told old Mrs. Wu that since the baby's life was on the wood pattern, he ought not to have been born on a day of fire but such was exactly the day he was born on. For the five elements are known to be mutually related and the combinations may be either beneficial and constructive or else hostile and destructive to each other. Water helps Wood, but is harmful to Fire. Metal would form a good combination with Earth but does not agree with Fire. That the combination of Wood and Fire did not do any harm to the child was clearly indicative of how strong a life the baby had. The baby's life was therefore destined to be of a very solitary kind as no brother or sister immediately preceeding or succeeding his birth could be expected to live. (At this old Mrs. Wu nodded her head in full agreement as this reminded her of the two granddaughters who had died so young). In such a case it would be highly desirable to have the baby get at least one father-in-faith and mother-in-faith, the more the better, for fear that the harmful elements in the baby's life would tend to cause either or both of his parents to sicken or even to die!

"The first emperor Chu Hung-wu of the Ming Dynasty," the blind man quoted as historical reference, "was of a great 'life pattern,' and he was orphaned at an early age, though he later inaugurated the Ming Dynasty that ruled China for three hundred years. When he became big enough for it he called his father

A blind fortune-teller is fully capable of advising on such matters as the selection of "parents-in-faith".

'Daddy' and his father died instantly, he called his mother 'Mamma' and his mother succumbed, too. This is a popularly known example of what a solitary life may mean."

Old Mrs. Wu's face became decidedly grave at these words. She asked, "Judging from what you have said it seems our baby is bound to cause a lot of misfortune in the family, is that right?"

"No, no, certainly not," said the blind man, "for if you will just do as I have said, that is, get for him some nominal 'parents,' then the destructive influence will be gotten rid of. Moreover, if you will take care to see that his nominal parents, or parents-in-faith (particularly the father), are of the Water or Earth pattern then the evil would be converted into a benevolent and not obstructive influence, as they would mutually be of help as I have said. Remember also, that children of such time factors are invariably destined to be great personages, either of immense wealth or else of no mediocre official rank if he pursues a governmental occupation."

What a deep impression the blind man's arguments made on old Mrs. Wu may well be adjudged by the fact that she deposited in his hand one extra twenty-cent piece besides the agreed fee for the services he had rendered.

*   *   *

The Wu family proceeded to select some nominal parents for Little Bald Head.

There were any number of people of similar age as the young Wu couple among their friends and relatives and not a few who would be willing and glad to be thus honoured. But not all of them possessed the suitable life pattern factors that would answer the bill. They at last found a proper couple in the family of a great friend of old Mr. Wu. Old Mrs. Wu started negotiations by mentioning the facts and their intentions to the young couple, Mr. and Mrs. Chao, through their father and forthwith secured their welcomed approbation.

The Wu family were glad as not all Chinese are so receptive of such a request. There is a superstition that if a family "adopts" some baby from another family, it is liable to cause one of their own babies bad luck or even death. The explanation is that since a person is destined prior to his birth to have so many or so few children or no children at all, it is therefore against the will of the divinities to so change the lot of any human being. It would be a very poor bargain indeed if a man gets a son-in-faith and loses one of his own children in his place! So the selection of an accommodating couple was not so easy as it might be presumed. Mr. and Mrs. Chao apparently were of another frame of mind and were the sort of people who, we would say, were "always thinking of the other fellow."

Many gifts are required for the ceremony of formalizing "parents-in-faith".

It would be quite sinful to infer that the Chao couple just happened to be ignorant of the inadvisability and possible evil consequences of acting as parents-in-faith.

There was then another ceremonial rite for the adoption.

The Wu family bought a hat and a pair of shoes for Mr. Chao and a set of hair pins and also shoes for his wife, supposed to come from the young baby himself as initiation presents. In return the baby was given many gifts, too, consisting in the traditional manner of a teakwood rice bowl (its unbreakability is a good omen) and a pair of ivory chopsticks. He was also given a suit of clothes, a hat and a pair of small shoes. As may be easily seen from the Chinese symbolic point of view there was already shown in the new relationship parental love and filial respect.

On an auspicious day, selected by the indispensable family almanac, the new "parents-in-faith" were respectfully invited by the Wu family to a feast. A pair of pantaloons of red cloth of immense proportions was especially prepared in the Wu house and the ceremony took place there.

Young Mrs. Chao was requested to sit on the edge of the brick bed wearing, on top of her regular clothing, the big and loose pair of red pantaloons. The baby was carried ceremoniously from the bed and deposited into the red pantaloons by young Mrs. Wu herself and immediately after another woman was asked to receive the baby together with the red pantaloons which were taken off at the same moment. This, as is easily perceived, would be indicative of the baby's having actually been given birth to by Mrs. Chao, his "mother-in-faith!"

Then the baby was made to kowtow, or knock his head, three times on the ground before his new parents, recognizing them as his father and mother. Thus the rites were completed.

"There will be no locking ceremony," said Mrs. Chao, "and so we have not prepared the silver lock and chain."

"Quite right," said the happy grandmother, "We have no use for it as Little Bald Head is getting his parents-in-faith for an entirely different reason from that which would necessitate a lock."

It was understood that children who get nominal parents because of a fear of short life require the new parents to bring a silver lock attached to a silver chain. The lock, in the ceremony, is to be snapped shut by the new mother, "locking the child to this world." Such a lock, or necklace, may be required to be worn as a charm all the time, or at least on birthdays and during long distance travels. It is further provided by Chinese superstition that the lock is to be opened by the "parents-in-faith" themselves at the son's wedding, marking the consummation of their custodianship.

*　　　*　　　*

Master Average Chinese Child gets very few toys or playthings which may be worthy of the name, and the more decent toys are the privilege of the children of the "born with a silver spoon in the mouth" type whose rich and prosperous parents can afford such things. It is quite true to say that the more expensive toys are more often bought as gifts for other families' children than for a man's own sons or daughters. If you will observe but casually, for instance, at a temple fair or a bazaar,

A "running horse lantern" delighted Little Bald Head.

which are usually the toy hunting
children's paradise, you will see that
the majority of the toys are made
for the double purpose of serving
first as a plaything and then as an
eatable—-representative of which are
the candy figures and the fancy-
shaped cakes made of pea-flour
dough.

There are of course playthings
which are nothing but playthings,
but such are generally of a very
flimsy and highly inexpensive variety. They have to be cheap to get
where they are. The crude mud
dolls, the balls of coloured paper,
the little whistles made of bamboo,
the little horns made from cast-away
bits of otherwise useless tin, the little cocks made with the core
of the cornstalk (or is it the kaoliang stalk?) and bits of chicken
feather...they are all priced suitably to exploit the very poor
spending money allowance of average Chinese children. They
retail, delivered at the little customers' door with inspection
privileges, at about 2 big coppers each (about 12/100 of a U.S.
cent) at the maximum. How such a business organization of
manufacturing, merchandising and distribution can pay its overhead expenses and declare a dividend for the shareholders after
all jobbers and retailmen are satisfied is a mystery beyond the
sphere of imagination of the world's cleverest economic brain
trust.

There are on the other hand the expensive toys, particularly
the imported kind of Japanese origin (this is nothing to be surprised at as Japanese mechanized and celluloid toys are exported
to all countries in the world and are on sale from Rotterdam to
Rio, admired and welcomed by all) but these, as I have said, are
for the upper ten thousand and are principally bought and given
as gifts between friends. The giving and exchanging of such toys
in a somewhat Christmas-like spirit lasts throughout the year
among the rich Chinese in Peking. Part of such giving, it must be
admitted, bears a diplomatic significance.

Little Bald Head's sources of supply were legion. For young
Mr. Wu himself was that sort of a person who, in spite of his
adult age, was still fortunate (or unfortunate) enough to find joy
in handling children's "treasures." He was so enthusiastic about
his son that he actually bought his son a tricycle when his son
was exactly eleven months old! He had only four odd years to
wait until the boy would be in a position to put the machine to
any practical use!

The baby's grandparents bought toys for him too. As the
baby lay flat on the brick bed his grandfather provided him with
a big glass bowl in which were kept some goldfish from the family
aquarium. Watching the moving fish was oftentimes the remedy
for many a bitter fit of crying. This novelty had to be reluctant-
ly eliminated afterwards when he became old enough to sit up, as
he would knock on the bowl as he watched the fish and get his
sleeves all wet and the water would splash onto the mattress.

Madame Ho brought him toys too. She brought a big paper lantern in the design of a red fish and also a so-called *tso ma teng* (走馬燈), or "running horse lantern." This latter contained in a decorative framework a paper disc with bent notches on the edge and fixed on an axis resting at the end of a wire on a piece of glass. A lighted candle produces a current of hot air which propels the disc and carries around the paper figures pasted on projecting wires from the rotating axis. The effect is that of an endless procession.

The baby gazed at the lighted lanterns with his mouth wide open and waved his tiny arms in the fashion of a four-week-old chick testing its new grown wings as he was carried about, being utterly perplexed by the big masses of colour and the moving objects of the lantern which he could not understand. He represented one of the features of domestic bliss in the Wu family.

*   *   *

The standard scale for judging a baby's stages of physical growth, incorporated in a proverbial saying, has already been introduced and we have also noted that Little Bald Head's developments coincided beautifully with the specifications. Another step further and we found him being able to walk by himself when he was about a year old, though his gait was of necessity not devoid of some swaying and tottering: "A baby should start walking before being a year old" is a familiar saying in China. The fact that he was the only child in the family and therefore much handled by his parents and grandparents was also responsible for the exercises which were so instrumental in building up his physique.

At last at the suggestion of a woman from the neighbourhood, a superstitious final touch was added to the process, a ritual called the "cutting of the foot-entangling ropes" was performed and the child began to gain a steady carriage.

The young mother was asked to lead the tottering baby and the grandmother followed immediately behind, holding a meat chopper in her hand. As the little tot walked forward the old woman pretended to chop three times on the ground between the two little legs every time the baby made a step, cutting invisible entanglements. The mother, as arranged, was to ask her mother-in-law what on earth she was doing. The latter was to answer, "I am cutting the foot-entangling ropes of our baby."

If we were to let the above suffice and give no further explanation, it would never be possible to fully appreciate the significance of this performance.

It has been the practice in China for generations to tie one or more

The "cutting" of invisible foot-entangling ropes is supposed to improve a baby's gait.

ropes about the ankles of a dead person before the corpse is encoffined. This is a preventive against the possible "resurrection" of the corpse. Dead bodies had been known suddenly to return to life, though for a short while only and in a harmful and most terrorizing manner. Examples of such happenings have been recorded in such books as the *Liao Chai Chih Yi* (聊齋誌異), the English translation of which, "Strange Stories from a Chinese Studio" by Herbert Giles, is available.

Such animated corpses were known to be in the habit of chasing human beings and if caught by the corpse the victims would be choked to death. As the spirits of the dead are supposed to be reincarnated into the world again and again, newborn babies are supposed to carry forward into the new page of their lives the ropes for holding down a possible animated corpse in a previous existence. Such ropes, unless cut, would be responsible for a poor walking gait in an infant until he has grown up perhaps to be able to do the cutting for himself in his subconscious mind!

It makes altogether no difference whether we believe in such things or not, just as it brought up no pros or cons from such people as young Mr. Wu and his father. There was at least one person, however, who definitely noticed an improvement in the boy's pedestrianism and believed it to be the result of the ropes having been cut. That one person was our old Mrs. Wu.

Nevertheless, the fact that Little Bald Head grew up to have nice straight legs could not but also be attributed to the perseverance and steadfastness of his grandmother for it was she who insisted on keeping the baby's legs tightly wrapped together with a piece of cloth and tied with a strong ribbon until he was fully one hundred days old. And this in spite of the baby's clearly manifested objections. If things had been left to the soft-hearted young mother, Little Bald Head might have developed the world's ugliest pair of bow legs !

*   *   *

On the day a baby is a year old, another lot of things is done in the house. A Chinese baby is considered a year old as soon as he or she is born. After that the age is counted according to the calendar year and not by the actual number of days that have elapsed. On the day when a baby is actually a year old, his age is two. If a baby is born, for example, on December 31, 1938, he would be considered three years of age on January 1, 1940.

On such a day—a baby's first birthday let us say—Propriety provides that a perambulator should be brought for the baby by the mother's maternal family, besides another array of wearing apparel and the like. In so far as clothing was concerned, Little Bald Head was never in want. In fact he had more than was necessary; a great part was given by his grandmother, Madame Ho, and included some things from the hands of young Mrs. Wu's "kid" sister, who was very well taught on such household subjects. She had indeed become an expert in the designing and execution of baby's accessories, such as bibs, aprons, shoes, hats and the "wind shield" which her mother had brought to the Wu family before Little Bald Head was born.

A typical Chinese girl should possess four main accomplishments: Virtue, Deeds, Words and Work. Of the last mentioned,

Madame Ho's young daughter was assuredly *au fait*, thanks to the tutoring of her mother and her own cleverness and industry. As to the vehicular possessions of the Wu child, his father had bought a beautiful, foreign-made perambulator not long after he was vaccinated. The weather getting warmer and warmer, the little heir was seen out in his "chariot", airing on many a bright and sunny afternoon with his grandmother as the attending "matron." When Madame Ho, following traditional dictation, brought him the little rattan and bamboo affair with the gay cloth awnings and cast iron wheels at the first birthday celebration of our little hero that put him in the proud "two-car" class. We must also remember the tricycle his father had bought him. This they had to store away for some time in the backyard family attic.

On that particular day the family saw to it that he was given to eat some of the Chinese fried doughnuts, known as *yu cha-kwei* (油炸燴), which are part of the daily breakfast foods of almost all the urban families of North China. These, if taken on this day, are supposed to have a peculiar property in helping the baby acquire promptly a pair of strong legs. The meaning would not be far to seek if we remember the fact that these doughnuts, if made in larger and thicker rings of elongated shape, are also known by the fantastic name of *hei-han-t'ueh* (黑漢腿), "Black Ruffian's Legs!"

In the afternoon the entire family gathered to witness the so-called *chua-chow-erh* (抓週兒), or "the grabbing test on the occasion of a baby's first birthday." Various articles were assembled and spread out purposely in a listless manner on the bed. Such articles were present as a Chinese brush pen, a book, an inkstone, workman's tools, playthings and eatables, cosmetics and many an unexpected gadget. The baby was then set before the large array of things and was watched with keen interest as to what particular article he would pick up upon the nature and implied meaning of which a general idea of his future character and pattern of life, his career and behaviour, his habits and hobbies could be observed, It has been the fond purpose of parents to observe their baby's own meaningless and yet meaningful choice and watch later on for the presence or absence of signs for the prediction's materialization.

Little Bald Head dashed forward and, using both his hands, snatched up his father's abacus.

The meaning, whatever it was, as interpreted by each individual present at the "test," was considered good and promising.

"Not so bad at all," said old Mr. Wu, who was manifestly pleased with the choice.

"If Little Bald Head has his future career shaped around the abacus, it would be very gratifying," commented the old man.

He went on.

"The other day I read a story about one of China's great men of the Sung Dynasty. Ts'ao Pin was his name. When he was a year old, his family spread out an array of toys and miniatures of various things for the test and what do you think he took? His left hand grabbed the *ke* (戈) or the warrior's long spear and his right hand grasped the *to* (豆), the sacrificial vessel used at the state worship of Heaven and Earth! And that was not all. For after a pause, he took up another article from the lot of things spread out before him—a jade seal, symbolic of great authority! And he did not even cast a single glance at the various toys and foods!

Such is the way of a great man, for he grew up to be a famous statesman. This happening is recorded in the authentic official history of the Sung Dynasty."

"Let us try again," suggested young Mr. Wu.

"You cannot do that, my son," objected his father. "That would not be proper, just as our lot is cast for life only once!"

*   *   *

A Chinese household proverb has it that if you expect a child to be healthy you must allow him 30 per cent of hunger and the same percentage of cold, *Yao teh hsiao erh an, hsui tai san fen chi yu han*. (要得小兒安須帶三分饑與寒), for it has been learnt from experience that a child usually gets indisposed through the faults of the parents who give him too much to eat and too much to wear. Indigestion and non-exposure, individually or jointly, are responsible for a great part of children's sicknesses.

But there is another category of indisposition to which Chinese children are particularly liable and this, a proper name failing to be found, could be classified as "nerves." The Chinese expression is *hsia cho la* (嚇着啦) or "frightened." A sudden fall or tumble may cause a fit of nerves. Or it may be a great cracking or booming noise. Or a fight or quarrel in the house. Such a "fright" may serve as the fuse to a bombardment by a long line of sicknesses, with indigestion and sleeplessness heading the list. In some particularly unfortunate cases it has been known to give rise to fits or violent convulsions. For all minor cases of this kind a first-aid treatment is to hurry and snatch up a pinch of dust from the ground exactly where the accident took place and forthwith smear the dust on the frightened child's head, right in the center of the skull. This peculiar therapeutic demonstration is very widely known and easily observed.

Another treatment of such sickness would be for the child's mother to knock three times on the upper door frame at twelve o'clock noon with a kitchen ladle, usually made of the half sphere of a cocoanut shell attached to a bamboo handle, accompanying the knocking with the calling out aloud of the child's "milk-name" and following with a call to come home, meanwhile getting either the child himself or an adult proxy nearby to answer that he has done so. Three daily performances of this calling of the "scattered spirits" usually do the trick.

If the trouble should take a graver turn a religious rite will be performed right in the sick child's bedroom, nightly for three consecutive days. If this still fails to give the desired effect then it must be agreed that the trouble has been something other than the "frightened" kind and the services of a doctor or a "witch" are therefore desirable.

One day, Little Bald Head, following his usual perambulator excursions in the care of his grandmother, suddenly became unwell, refused to eat and kept on crying. He was feverish and restless. The trouble was traced to a "fright" which allegedly he must have sustained as there was a dog fight near his perambulator when their "Little Black" attacked a neighbour's Pekingese. Experienced old Mrs. Wu did not take long to realize that he must have lost his "spirits" and that the Divine Chaser should be prevailed upon to use his influence in regaining them.

She had the servant go to the grocery store and get three sheets of the paper images of *Pai Ma Hsien Feng* (白馬先逢), or "Prompt Meeter on the White Horse," and gave instructions for young Mrs. Wu to perform the proper rites for three days at midnight. The latter had the paper images cut up with a pair of scissors where the legs of the horse were, getting ready the four legs of the horse for active service. When everybody had gone to bed, she put up a small table near the bed, set the joss paper on a frame and burned three sticks of incense before it, kowtowing as pre-scribed. She also offered a cup of cold water to the divine horse. When the incense was exhausted, she burned the paper and sent the chaser on his way to look for and arrest the lost soul.

Three days later Little Bald Head became hale and hearty again. This was strong evidence to old Mrs. Wu that the divinity on horseback had succeeded in apprehending the lost spirit and had restored it to the child.

This reminds us of the foreign medical credo that time is the best cure for nerve troubles. It also reminds us of the statement of a famous physician that to cure a cold by medicine takes four-teen days and without medical care it will be gone in two weeks.

*   *   *

Regular adult food is gradually introduced to Chinese babies as they grow. In most cases, especially when the mother's milk happens to be of a poor quality and therefore not satisfactory to the instinctive desire for food which is noticeable almost all the waking hours in babies, children begin to be given common foods by the sixth or seventh month and even as early as the fifth month. It would seem to be quite correct to give them certain foods, such as thoroughly cooked rice porridge or noodles or macaroni overdone till they resemble photographic paste in appearance, in anticipa-tion of the pending change of diet which is usually unavoidable as due to certain reasons the mother's breast milk will discontinue to be available.

Some families are so progenically productive that children are obliged, whether they like it or not, to change their feeding habits drastically about a year after birth, some even earlier than that. Little Bald Head was an exception, for though his first teeth came when he was eight months old (another point in favour of his healthy growth) and after that he was given regular foods from time to time, his mother's milk continued to be enjoyed. This com-bination diet was naturally conducive to fine physical develop-ment. That he became used to foods other than his mother's milk had a by-effect in that he became less fixed to his mother.

During fine days, after his own and his grandmother's after-noon siesta, his habitual program included daily outings with his grandmother in his own little push-cart. His grandfather, in the course of time, also developed a grandson-mania for he could hardly find the same satisfaction and enjoyment as heretofore in his daily visit to the tea house without carrying the little cherub with him. Of course the fact that the child was so smart-looking and playful that he was the object of verbal volleys of flattery wherever he was shown added automatically to the zest of old Mr. Wu. For people would ask the old man (I am sure at least half of them did that purposely just to tease the old grandpa), as to who the little gentleman was that he was carrying about, and to hear him answer in his typical self-important fashion, *Wo sun tsa*, meaning "My grandson", with an emphasis on the second syllable. One of the persistent chronic teasers was Old Chao the No. Four, whose extra-sized bird cage with his prize lark was his emblem and trade mark.

But there were several little things which he was always cautioned by his over-prudent wife not to do. One of the things was that he should under no circumstances take the baby inside a Buddhist temple because the baby must not be seen by the divinities in there. Old Mr. Wu did exactly as he was told as he feared that the boy might be frightened by the ugly faces of some of the mud figures of demons and ghosts found there.

Another thing was for him to see that no matter how friendly Little Bald Head might become with some other babies he should not come too near such babies, nor be hand in hand with another small child for fear, as the Chinese superstitious rationalization has it, that that might cause both of the children to become dumb as Little Wu had not yet developed his talking faculties. Besides the foregoing he must not give him chewed foods even if the baby should demonstrate his appetite by crying.

Old Mr. Wu was as trustworthy a person to take the baby around as anyone could be expected to be and he was never tired of this duty and pleasure combined. Nor was the tea-shop the only place he would take the boy for there were some old friends living in the neighbourhood and he would either be invited in or just happened to drop in himself with the baby in his arms. Each time when they went to a new family the baby was sure to receive a little sum of money from the family visited as a "commencement" gift, wrapped up in a tiny packet of red paper and tied on a long loop made with a little skein of white cotton thread and thrown around his neck much in the same fashion as the famous locket.

All these little sums were intended as contributions toward the baby's candy and toy fund. It might be asked why it is, since red is the colour of happiness and white of mourning in China, that white cotton thread is used on such an occasion. The answer would be that the colour signifies white hair, conveying a wish that the baby may grow to such an age as to have hair of that colour. Of course, white thread is usually much more handy in a house than red thread! There is no doubt about that.

Old Mrs. Wu saw to it that all such small sums of money were carefully deposited in the little pottery bank specially bought for the purpose. When a large sum had been accumulated the bank would be smashed and the contents would be used to buy the baby wearing apparel, as they were representative of the good wishes of all friends.

*   *   *

Chinese windows are made of frames of latticed woodwork over which is pasted white bamboo paper. This method has been used for we do not know how many centuries but certainly not before the Han Dynasty (206 B.C. — 219 A.D.) for it is clearly chronicled in history that paper was invented by Ts'ai Lun in this dynasty. In China the paper is pasted from within and in Manchuria it is pasted from without. To verify the difference

Poking holes in window paper is taken as a definite sign that baby will soon begin to talk.

does not require skeptical readers to go to Mukden for in Peking, in the Forbidden City palaces, there are halls for ancestral worship and imperial wedding ceremonies where this practice is observed in typical Manchurian manner—the paper is pasted onto the frame from without. In the Wu house the windows were mostly fitted with rather large panes of clear glass but in the characteristic manner the glass was surrounded with a band of wooden lattices superimposed with white paper. The effect, as we saw during our inspection trip earlier, was very pleasing. It was well that they did use this combination design for else our Little Bald Head would have found it hard to select an opportune moment to start talking.

One day Little Bald Head was tottering around on his broad brick bed and moving along crosswise, like the crab, with his hands resting on the brick work of the window sill called in Peking the *ch'uang t'ai erh* (窗臺兒), or "window terrace," and he was seen to stick his tiny fingers through the window paper. And as his fingers were in the habit of going into his mouth for excursions, a typical thing with all Chinese babies known in Peking colloquialism as "sucking the ten ounces of honey," his fingers were wet with saliva and so in no time a group of tiny holes were made in the paper. Discovering this his young mother became angry and she scolded him and quickly moving the child away was going to give him a sound spanking.

Old Mrs. Wu heard the commotion and betook herself to the scene and stopped her daughter saying: "Do nòt beat him! All children do that. For after poking these little holes through the window paper he will start to talk!"

That evening the happening was reported to young Mr. Wu as the first thing he saw when he came home was the patched-up window paper. The young mother had temporarily fixed up the holes as there was no proper paper handy in the house and the paper used by all experienced Peking families was the kind known as "Korean paper", famous for its silk content and its durability. Young Mr. Wu was not to be satisfied with anything so fantastic as saying that poking through window paper made a child start his function of speech. He soon realized the fact that when a child becomes active and naughty enough to poke little holes in window paper with his tiny fingers for fun, it is just about time for him to start babbling his own unintelligible jargon.

The first words the child learned to utter, as the family observed, was the word "Mama," that sound which is the simplest and the easiest. The premier utterances were thrilling to the young mother as well as to the other members of the family. The next word of the child's vocabulary was "Papa" with which he soon learned daily to "lisp the sire's return."

Before long he had acquired a workable vocabulary for his own little sphere of activity. As typical of all Chinese children his other first words were "Bo bo" which means "cake" or anything eatable. *"T'ang"* or "candy" and *"Wo yao"* which means "I want," and so on. Besides these and some others he became capable of uttering a lot of unintelligible sounds accompanied by all sorts of gesturings and phonetic question marks and exclamation points!

One thing displeased his grandmother very much and that was, in spite of all the daily efforts, she failed to succeed until long afterward in teaching Little Bald Head to call her *"Nai nai"* or "Grandma!" She had to give up in disgust. "He is duller than a parrot," she commented.

*   *   *

There is a theory or belief in China that a person's sons and daughters represent the reincarnations of creditors and/or debtors of unliquidated responsibilities in a former existence. This hypothesis and great tinge of Buddhist influence has often been used as a warning to people not to get involved in monetary obligations which are not within their means to fulfill. Such debts may not always be of a financial nature, as very often it may be a debt of tears, of heartaches or other torments and injustices, which, in the imaginative mind of the Chinese, reflect bitterly in the supposed reincarnated life.

A Chinese beneficiary is often heard to say: "Oh, I am so grateful to you. I will always remember to repay your kindness. If there is no chance in this lifetime, I will certainly be a horse or a dog in my next life in order to repay you." It is indeed quite true to say that the skeleton of "heavenly retribution" and even of entire Buddhism is founded on this presupposition. It amounts to the same thing as "an eye for an eye and a tooth for a tooth" only it is extended "on bail" for an infinite or lifetime moratorium.

To demonstrate this formula strange tales have been told by many a religious-minded Chinese writer. In one story, and a famous one too, it says that a man whose wife was about to give birth to a baby had a dream in which he saw an old acquaintance of his who had been dead for many years come into his house. This old acquaintance accosted him and said, "You owed me forty thousand cash and I have come to collect," and so saying made his way to his wife's private chamber.

The man woke up with a cold sweat running down his spine as he well remembered that he had actually been indebted to that same man that same sum before he died. No sooner had his shudder abated than the announcement was made that his wife had just then given birth to a boy. The man at once concluded that since this baby was nothing but a disguise for that old acquaintance who had come to square up an old account with him no future was to be expected of the baby. He secretly put away the sum of forty thousand cash from which he took out from time to time amounts to pay for everything the upbringing of the child required. The baby later got sick and died. When his funeral expenses were paid, he added up his record and found, lo and behold, that exactly forty thousand cash had been spent and the last of the money put away was expended.

Such is the way the Chinese look at their children particularly when there is an unfilial sign or some unexpected and unwilling expenditures because of a son or a daughter. Another interpretation of the theory would be the invoking of this formula when a dearly loved child is lost by death by the parents consoling and comforting themselves with the idea that the child was really just a "bill collecting devil", or *t'ao chai kwei* (討債鬼), anyway. Sour grapes, in other words!

The Wu family was just such a typical family. More so was this the case with old Mrs. Wu than with anybody else in the house. The fact that of the half-dozen or so children that she had had only young Mr. Wu himself matured is an incident or a fact that had always reminded her of the old theory.

As Little Bald Head began to develop little by little his faculty of speech, he became the target of all sorts of silly "yes or no" questions and which the child answered either one way or the other just as he chanced to find it convenient in the imitation of the words (or rather sounds). He naturally did not know the difference or indeed the graveness of any of the questions. Before long there developed a regular catechism, to rehearse which was much fun for the family. And one of these silly and yet philosophical questions thrusted mercilessly at him was whether he was a *yao chang ti* (要賬的) or a *huan chang ti* (還賬的), a bill collector or bill payer. To the great satisfaction of all, his answer was always that he was a *huan chang ti*!

It is to be understood that only a *huan chang ti* baby could ever be expected to grow up to bring glory and good name to the family. No wonder Little Bald Head's answer was so encouraging to hear.

A DOCTOR IS CONSULTED

"**N**O flower can stay in full bloom for one hundred days, nor can a person expect to be well for a thousand days continuously," says a Chinese proverb. Even such a sturdy and robust "big boy" as Little Bald Head was not entirely sickness-proof. He became sick.

He was hot with fever and his eyes were red and watery. His nose ran profusely. He refused to eat and looked bad. He was sleepy and fastidious.

Even experienced old Mrs. Wu lost confidence in herself as to what was the matter with Little Bald Head. She wisely decided to take him to a Chinese doctor.

There were several doctors in the neighbourhood to any of whom they might go, but it was exactly on account of the fact that there were several doctors instead of but one to go to that they became perplexed as to who should be the best one to consult.

There was Chang with his preposterously big signboard with the shiny brass trimmings (a marvellous evidence of what his servant's elbow-grease and Brasso could jointly accomplish) bearing the not very diffident inscription of *"chuan chih nan fu hsiao erh nei wai ke k'e yi nan ta cheng"* (專治男婦小兒內外各科疑難大症) which would translate most conservatively as: "Specialist for curing men's and women's and children's dubious and difficult cases of great proportions in internal, external, as well as other divisions of sicknesses." The sign had caused old Mr. Wu a laugh every time he passed the doctor's door and noticed it. (He got as big a "kick" out of pondering over the lines as he did from scanning Tu Fu's best poems.)

There were in evidence also many wooden tablets, literally tiers of them, hanging on the doctor's walls, supposed to be gifts from grateful ex-patients endorsing Chang as a fine doctor, who had cured people of dangerous diseases. These tablets, some three feet high and five feet wide, beautifully varnished in assorted colours, bore inscriptions mainly of four-character phrases such as: "Truly a Miraculous Doctor," "He Called Back a Departed Soul," "Medical Theories Deep and Thorough," ' Has Saved My Entire Family," "Nation's Champion for Seasonal Diseases," "Today's Pien Ch'ueh"—referring to a famous physician of the Spring and Autumn period (about 10th century B. C.). Although these served very well in conveying a convincing impression to patients from distant parts of the city, they had no effect whatever on our Wu family. For Chang was a childhood friend of old Mr. Wu and just how far his medical research extended was an

Many a Chinese doctor takes a great liking to boastfully worded signboards outside his door.

open secret of which old Mr. Wu knew all the inside "dope." In friendship and not in commemoration of a therapeutic feat, old Mr. Wu had a hand in sending at least four of the tablets now hanging at the doctor's door alleging professional successes! He knew, besides, almost half of the people whose names appeared as donors of tablets well enough to guess that they had also presented them in the advertising campaign they had fostered in the earlier days of his practice. As friend to friend, old Mr. Wu had given him aid in everything except a request for a consultation much less his patronage. A Chinese saying has it: "A monk from a distant land reads the best sutras." A doctor, to be trusted and confided in, must be one who lives a long way from his patient!

"How about Uncle Chang?" suggested young Mr. Wu, for Chang had always been "Uncle Chang" to him, never "Doctor Chang."

"Nothing doing," said his father, shaking his head in the most disapprobating manner. "He would be all right to look over a 'peaceful pulse.' He probably will do no harm to Little Bald Head, but he will not do him any good."

"*Hsiao Hai-erh* Li (小孩兒李) (or "baby doctor Li") then, whose advertisement is in the daily paper?" young Mr. Wu made another proposal.

"Not him either. I have heard too much about *Hsiao Hai-erh* Li to want to go to him. His father used to be pretty good, but he is dead now. The son learned absolutely nothing from him and only got the goodwill as legacy." Old Mr. Wu apparently did not trust the so-called *shih-yi's* (世醫) or "doctors by inheritance."

"Let us keep calm," said old Mrs. Wu. "I have just looked him over carefully again and I have reasons to believe that his case is one of spring measles and as such it is nothing to be over-apprehensive about, though it is rather serious. What we want to do now is to check my diagnosis first. For, you seem to have all forgotten, did not Kwang Tsung have annual attacks of the measles in the early summer when he was a child? I do not remember very clearly now what his symptoms were then, but it looks as though Little Bald Head is suffering from the same complaint."

"Yes, so I recollect now," said old Mr. Wu. "Still we want to get some advice and give him some proper medicine for the weather lately has not been quite right and we do not want to complicate matters."

*　　　*　　　*

Unlike foreign medical men who are usually contented with and proud of their professional standing, physicians in China try to pose as philosophical scholars besides healers. They have a propensity to be known also as poets, calligraphical artists or "theoretical politicians," if there is such a term. Other points for which doctors sometimes strive to be famous is amateur seal-carving and painting of the so-called literati school, and the like.

The consultation office of the so-called "famous" Chinese doctor looks not unlike that of his European or American cousin in that it is lined with shelves and shelves of books, sometimes labeled and perhaps catalogued as in a regular library. The difference is in the fact that if you glance casually at the bookshelves of a foreign medical man, the chances are that you will find most of the books are of the professional kind, with titles in long Latin or

Greek words which laymen find hard to decipher. On the other hand, the Chinese doctor's book shelves may contain a collection of anything from treatises on ancient bronze mirrors, "complete works" of some T'ang Dynasty poet, notes on the cultivation of garden orchids, etc. which would not have the slightest bearing, if any, on his professional career. It would be a dangerous matter, indeed, for a doctor to mis-appropriate his energy and actually to delve into such sundry interests as these books represent, and fortunately the truth is not so. For he does not go beyond just "storing" such books as a hobby, and of purposely conveying an erroneous impression to his clientele that this man of medicine is also a sentimental poet and a refined scholar of "genteel elegance."

Of the "true" medical men, there are not many who concentrate on nothing else but administering carefully to the sick. Their residences may not be marked with a colourful "shop-front", nor may their offices be masterpieces of the art of interior decoration. Such doctors do not get the custom of the spendthrift elite for whom getting sick and consulting a doctor is a refinement and luxury of life, though their grateful following may be quite large.

Old Mr. Wu knew better than to go to any doctor except the proper one, and of the ones he respected he chose Dr. Li to examine his little grandson. Dr. Li lived not far from the Donkey Mart, in a small lane known by the charming name of Tung Hua T'ing, or Eastern Flower Pavilion.

Thickly and warmly wrapped in a cotton-padded cape of red satin, the boy was conveyed in his mother's arms by a hooded rickshaw to Dr. Li's house, followed by another rickshaw which carried old Mrs. Wu, as the latter could not very well suffer herself to be so nonchalant as to stay home. Old Mr. Wu had himself preceded the "ambulance" and had arrived at Dr. Li's an hour earlier to arrange the registration in order to save the baby the wait for his turn.

The registration consisted mainly of paying the fee and surcharge known as *men mo* (門脈) and *hao chin* (號金) respectively. The former, which translates as "door pulse," or "fee for feeling the pulse at the doctor's own door," is the doctor's own remuneration, and the latter, "number money," is a perquisite of the doctor's servant Dr. Li's rickshaw man was also in charge of the registration desk. In the mornings, his duty it was to take care of the registration, acting as an usher and cashier combined, and in the afternoons he pulled his master around for outside visitations to "private patients." This in Peking, and in all China too for that matter, is known as *ch'u ma* (出馬), or "outing the horse;" the fees received are known as *ma ch'ien* (馬錢) or "horse money", both of which remind us of the 18th century doctor of England or America, who was expected any snowy or stormy night to run to his stable, saddle his horse and carrying his medicine chest and instrument box ride out "into the cold" in response to an urgent call ten or fifteen miles away.

The consultation fee was forty cents and the registration fee ten coppers. The list price for "outing the horse" was four dollars "within city limits."

*　　　　*　　　　*

Doctor Li took the child's wrist and felt his pulse with three fingers.

The Chinese doctor depends for his diagnosis on four points: "Viewing, Listening, Asking and Cutting," the last means feeling the pulse. He first sizes up the situation by noticing the general appearance of the patient and then listens attentively to the complaints which are bound to be stated by the patient without asking. This proving not enough for his purpose, he asks further questions about the condition or discomforts of the patient. After that his judgment about the case is about ready, and the feeling of the pulse serves as a "check up." The technique consists of resting the patient's wrist, first the left and then the right, on a miniature pillow and the doctor takes the pulse by placing three of his own fingers lightly over the blood vessels.

In so far as it appears to the laymen, the pulse is significant to modern medical men only in its frequency and perhaps strength, variations in which are evidence of a person's indisposition. Not so with the Chinese doctor, who advocates that the pulse is an all-round evidence of a patient's disorder—a good doctor can locate the trouble at the proper spot by merely feeling the pulse. They have special terms to describe certain characteristic motions or states of the pulse which, to them, is divided into three parts: the *ch'ih* (尺) or "foot," the *ts'uen* (寸) or "inch" and *kuan* (關) or "joint." Some pulses are noticed as "floating," others "numerous" and others "sunk." Some are "too strong," others "too big," still others "voluminous," the difference in the feeling is very minute and is known only to the profession.

Without hesitation Dr. Li told the Wu family that the boy was suffering from measles, which were due to appear in another day or so. He felt the boy's pulse by holding his tiny wrist and nodded his head. Forthwith, he pulled out a sheet of paper, plain note paper and not the top-heavy kind, over-printed like a shipping company's advertising letterhead as is the habit with other Peking Chinese doctors. He wrote out his diagnosis and then the prescription which consisted of twelve kinds of medicinal herbs. Some of these were: dried mulberry leaves gathered after frost, peppermint leaves, bitter almond kernels, the downy seeds of dandelions, fine shavings of bamboo, dried wheat-sprouts, etc., each marked with the weight required, 1/5 or 1/10 of an ounce, etc.—the doses being necessarily small for such an infant. The last or thirteenth item, listed by itself, was a so called *yao yin tze* (藥引子), or "guide medicine," which in the present case was 1/20 of an ounce of the hairy roots of the water rush. (Other "guide medicines" usually prescribed in Chinese medicine are "three slices of ginger," "five big red dates," "rooted head of an onion cut off an inch from tip," and the like.) All these herbs were to be boiled thoroughly in a sand vessel and the bitter brown-coloured juice given to the child to drink.

"Do you think his condition is very serious?" asked the anxious young mother.

"No, far from it!" answered the quiet but interested physician.

"So I thought," put in the wise grandmother. "All children get the measles. They come out of the intestines and are a sign of children's food-poison finding a chance to scatter out, and it is indicative of proper physical growth, too. Only let it develop by itself—much like boating down a mountain stream. In four or five days he will be all right." Old Mrs. Wu's profound knowledge of pediatrics found a healthy chance to scatter, too, this time.

"Only see that the baby gets plenty of water to drink—give him hot water and the measles will come out with the sweat. Give him no fruits or anything raw or cold. Do not let him catch cold. If measles do not appear tomorrow, come back to me, and I will write out another prescription for him to take. Otherwise give him a repeat. Nothing serious. Rest assured." Thus the doctor gave them further instructions.

They wrapped up the child again and left.

The family quartet parted at the door as the old man went to obtain the medicine from the native apothecary and the others went straight home.

"Let me see how you have folded the prescription," asked old Mrs. Wu. "Yes, that is right. Never fold a prescription with the writing inside, as it is an omen that the sickness will be prolonged," she added as an explanation. She always looked out for such details.

*   *   *

While Little Bald Head, carried in his mother's arms, was sent home in the hooded rickshaw accompanied by his grandmother, old Mr. Wu, the grandfather, went to the drugstore to have the prescription filled. He made his way direct to Ch'ien Men Street where Peking's most dependable pharmacists have their shops.

The Chinese pharmacists are an interesting people, and their business is conducted in such a mysterious way that it has been hard for even a Peking-*jen* to understand it. The shops are usually prominent with their gaudy, gilded appearance and with the most elaborate carvings decorating the shop front. The interiors, particularly in recent years, have become entirely out of harmony with the serious nature of their trade, being so expensively furnished and painted that it would seem that they are the only people who were not hit by the depression. Their sign is composed of blocks of wood carvings, some square and others triangular in shape, representing the folded and opened Chinese plasters with the black disc in the center standing for the mysterious black stuff which passes as a curative ointment, more often than not of an omnipotent nature.

Each string of such universal trade marks starts with a lotus leaf at the top and finishes at the bottom with a pair of gold fish carvings. The signboards themselves are interesting in that besides the center one bearing the shop's name, they carry four-character phrases of some poetical or historical allusion, rather than stating right out what the shop is and what it offers. Some of the typical ones translate: "The Apricot Forest is Warm with Spring;" "The Water at the Orange Well is Fragrant." Another advertising equipment for such stores is often a narrow perpendicular sign, sometimes a foot and a half wide but twenty

The Chinese drug store sign is a string of wood replicas of plasters with a lotus leaf at the top and a pair of fish at the bottom.

odd feet high, which they proudly call *ch'ung t'ien chao p'ai* (冲天招牌), or "sky-scraping signboards." These bear a many character sentence invariably emphasizing the genuine quality and the careful selection of their wares, and last but not least the much-desired cleanliness. They further claim that their goods are procured by special purchasing agents in such remote provinces as Yunnan, Szechuan, Kwangsi and Kweichow. The geographical reference is quite permissible in the case of some ten or fifteen varieties of medicines or spices which they carry as a side-line (Chinese drug stores do not sell cosmetics, perfumes or ice cream). There must be something like a thousand kinds of herbs alone which are used as ingredients for preparing the many medicinal concoctions in China. Among these may be counted quite a few little groups which are various parts of the same plant, or else the same part of the same plant only cured differently. The leaves of one plant may be good for one sickness but the roots absolutely a poison for the same malady. All these drugs or herbs are put in "wallfuls" of small drawers the combined multitudinous appearance of which remind an observer of the letter boxes at the general post office. Each of these drawers is labeled prominently for quick identification. As one drawer is required to do the double duty of holding two or three kinds of herbs, the marker has developed ways of economizing on the use of characters making each serve two uses, first horizontal and then vertical, like in a cross word puzzle, the center space being reserved for the ring pull.

Besides things from the vegetable kingdom, many varieties of which are greens in pots, the wares are also composed of dried insects such as scorpions, centipedes, silkworms, etc. as well as the shedded skins of snakes, cicadas and the like, also live insects and reptiles and certain kinds of fossilized shells, etc. (one kind of which is known under the fancy trade name of "dragon's teeth"). It is no exaggeration to say that the general storeroom must be not very different from the curator's office of an amalgamated botanical, geological and biological museum. The various bundles and packages hanging from the ceiling and collecting dust are indeed amazing to say the least.

Old Mr. Wu appeared at the counter of exactly such a store.

He produced the prescription and gave it to the clerk who spread it out on the counter and put a foot-long hardwood paper weight on its edge. He snatched up a little steel-yard, called *teng tze* (戥子), and started the assembling. The clerk looked up an item at a time and hunted out the stuff from each drawer; weighing the proper amount, he deposited it on a small square of paper.

The prescription not being complicated, the preparation was ready in ten minutes. Then each item was wrapped up and the small packages were then piled one on top of the other and again wrapped up as a typical package in the shape of a topless pyramid.

Manipulating, more or less as a formality, the counting box or abacus, the clerk found the proper price to charge and forthwith had it marked out in code words on the prescription. He neatly folded the prescription and put it on top of the small bundle which was then fastened with a small string.

The prescription cost twenty-three cents to fill.

*　　*　　*

Price standardization laws find a Chinese druggist's the hardest place for their enforcement. Here cost accounting is the hardest problem and profit-figuring the easiest. I am saying this with the fullest measure of respect for the pharmaceutical trade as a whole, but when you think of the fact that a Chinese druggist offers a fifty per cent reduction on Sundays and other holidays like the birthday of the God of Medicine, etc., and still can run his business on a profitable basis, it is easy to imagine what his usual profit percentage must be like. The cost accounting is hard because his merchandise is bought in hundreds of catties in some cases and then retailed in such infinitesimal quantities as 1/10 of an ounce or even a fraction of that; the best way, indeed, would be to leave out the cost accounting entirely,

The theory may be advanced that druggists have to figure on a higher percentage of profit in view of the wide range of goods they have to stock, the uncertain market demand they have to contend with and also stock depreciation and waste, but when it is noted that each prescription is marked in a code word as to the amount charged as an insurance against any ridiculous price variations in case of a repeat and that identically the same prescription may cost ten cents today and forty cents the next morning, or, indeed, fifteen cents at the hands of clerk A and fifty-five at the hands of clerk B at the same time, the pricing habits of the firm must indeed be said to be very strange.

Psychologists say that human nature takes on an offensive attitude as a defensive measure and makes a person pretend to be friendly just when he is instinctively most hostile. When we take the big, almost indispensable honest-to-goodness tablet on display at a Chinese druggist's, reading *T'ung So Wu Ch'i* (童叟無欺) or "No cheating even of children and the aged," and apply their peculiar merchandising methods beside it, we cannot fail to get an impression that the not-always-right psychological expert sometimes does "say a mouthful"!

Old Mr. Wu was the type of person who knows all the secrets (at least the How's if not the Why's of them) but he was not the type who would ask the clerk to first calculate the cost and then give the order to fill the prescription (as some shrewd shoppers usually do), not because he was of a very forgiving tendency but truly because of another psychological background in his own habits of thought. He believed that for a child, or anybody else in a family, to actually get sick and to be obliged to patronize the druggist is "an ill wind that blows nobody good," and "what cannot be cured must be endured." And such being the case, it was considered

no use trying to save any straggling
pennies haggling with a druggist's
attendant.

Besides, in his mind was the old
Chinese motto which says the poor
eat the medicines and the rich pay
the cost, meaning there is, philan-
thropically speaking, an excusable
reason why druggists may be allowed
to charge a different scale of prices
for each of the social or economical
strata of customers with a tolerably
clear conscience. This, though it
may seem rather funny as a commercial attitude, nevertheless, is
the customary way of thinking of the average ailing Chinese.

The bundle containing the packages of herbs was opened and the
contents were slipped into a
sand bowl to boil.

*   *   *

Old Mr. Wu went home with the preparation. The bundle of
packages of herbs was opened and slipped into a sand bowl to
boil. Old Mrs. Wu saw to it that the little illustrated explanatory
slips of each herb were carefully put away for young Mr. Wu when
he came home to read to her what the medicine was and what it
was good for, so that she would be able to check over whether the
doctor was right in recommending such a prescription. She felt,
it may be guessed, that by doing so she would be in a better
position to cope with the doctor at the next visit with a "do-not-
fool-the-expert" sort of gesture.

"Do not make a fool of yourself," said old Mr. Wu when he
noticed what his wife was doing, "because you cannot trust the
explanations on this advertising stuff. I used to feel the same
way as you do, but you will find it absolutely annoying because
the merits given for each herb are diagonally contradictory to
each other by themselves and in nine cases out of ten, you will
find they are horribly misleading."

"It is fun anyway," old Mrs. Wu gave as her compromising
answer.

Half an hour later, the medicine was ready for Little Bald
Head to take and they expected a hard time administering it for
the medicine was truly bitter. A Chinese proverb says "a bitter
medicine is a good medicine". Children never like good medicines
anyway.

*   *   *

If my description of the Chinese doctor and Chinese pharma-
cist has given an impression that in my judgment they are
absolutely a lot of nonsense and do not amount to anything, I
must, indeed, quickly correct such an impression. For side by side
with the introduction, almost aggressive and overwhelming in
effect, of modern medical practice into China the study of Chinese
medical and therapeutical sciences has been engaging the attention of a great number of learned scholars from many a scientifically advanced country. I have found by contact with medical
men, both Chinese and foreign as well as foreign-trained Chinese,
that some of the ailments foreign doctors consider to be incurable
are almost nothing to be alarmed about in the eyes of Chinese

physicians. The more carefully we consider the question, the less we are prepared to form a definite opinion whether or not Chinese doctors should come in for a lot of deserving credit for what they have accomplished, beginning with the appearance of China's first pharmacopoeia popularly attributed to the legendary sage Shen Nung, some three thousand years before Christ was born.

This Shen Nung was China's first farmer as his name, the Divine Farmer, indicates and is famed for having tasted "hundreds" of herbs and plants. It is said that from the discoveries which he made by personally tasting each species of vegetables and watching their effect on himself, he was able to teach people how and with which herbs to cure their sicknesses. There is no catch in it either, for this is recorded in the authentic pre-historic history of China and is stated in the textbook of every school child in China as an actual fact. Granting that China's flora was the same then as now (there is no reason to doubt it was not) it would be necessary either to admit that he was of a unique physical constitution or else draw the conclusion that he just did not happen to run into a genuine poisonous specimen for, otherwise, it would be difficult to reason how he managed to survive to tell the story.

The medicine was soon ready for Little Bald Head, and in order that the bitter fluid be administered to him with the least resistance, it was proposed and adopted to have the sugar bowl handy and each small spoonful of medicine was immediately followed by a big mouthful of sugar. The medicine was very bitter yet not quite as bitter as the child's crying. He refused to take it but his weak point was found in his typically Chinese sweet tooth. He took about two-thirds of the small cupful of the stuff until he could stand absolutely no more as was evidenced by an obstinate refusal to open his mouth any longer. Everyone in the room was at his or her wits' end.

Old Mrs. Wu saved the situation by suggesting a little rest.

"We had better stop here as I fear the child will vomit what he has already swallowed if we force him," suggested the young mother.

"That is quite all right. Even if he does vomit, it does not mean that the medicine is wasted for the medicine can be thrown out but the taste cannot," said old Mrs. Wu, quoting another Chinese maxim.

The measles began to show themselves that very afternoon, just as Dr. Li had predicted, particularly in the regions of the "five hearts" by which the Chinese refer to the breast, the two palms, and the two soles of the feet. They were red and marked with irruptions which gave the child a slightly swollen appearance. Following the doctor's advice, a repeat of the medicine was administered the next day.

Now that the measles had actually appeared, the Wus were calmed as the symptoms proved that the child had exactly the same sickness his father used to have in his childhood. They did not even bother to return to the doctor for further advice. They knew that measles would take three days to come out and three more days to vanish. When they vanished the sickness was over. And all they had to do was to give less food to the boy but plenty of water to drink, besides taking good care of him in a general way.

After about a week's confinement and dieting on a vegetarian principle, Little Bald Head became his former self again.

* * *

The Chinese people have a practice of "looking at a sick person" as an act of courtesy, the same as the Japanese, which they call by the special term of *"byoki mimai"*. This consists of formal visits characterized by certain kinds of presents, mostly of various tonic or luxurious foods, etc., and the expression of a great number of regrets, suggestions and recommendations as to where a good doctor may be had, what special treatment, in the experience of the callers, has been found to be good for just that particular kind of sickness, and so forth. Such calls are often accompanied by a unique sort of arguments and debates on such related topics as the respective merits and demerits of Chinese and foreign physicians, conversations which not infrequently last long hours. Where the patient is not in a position to receive such calls, some other attending family member is obliged to answer questions which at times become absolutely boring.

The sympathetic relatives and friends are so "wise" in everything that it is hard to visualize how in the world they can be so ignorant, to say the least, as to deliberately rob the patient of his valuable rest. Their persistent affected interest in the condition of the patient and their disturbing presence cannot be daunted even by outspoken threats of possible contagion. In fact, such a warning has been found to have exactly the opposite of the desired effect, for it gives them argumentative reasons to stay longer. "We are such good friends," they will say, "that my intimate interest in his welfare far outbalances the fear of contamination." Such is "good form" in China. No wonder modern hospitals make a rule to discourage such visitors to patients. Fortunately, being a mere child, Little Bald Head was not bothered with the polite intruders although there was many a well-meaning "friend in need."

The most interesting part of the activities surrounding the somewhat serious event was the almost farcical doings of the grandmother. For just as young Mrs. Wu was sitting out that critical night of the child's first nasty day and everyone else was tossing about in his or her bed, being keyed up with great anxiety, old Mrs. Wu was seen performing a religious ceremony on her own free, faithful will. Though she had confidence in the doctor, whom she had not yet consulted, she preferred to depend at least in an equal measure

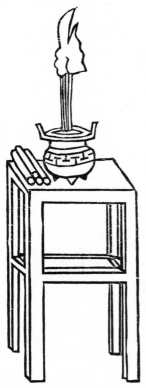

Bundles of incense sticks were burned by Mrs. Wu at an impromptu altar in the courtyard.

on her goddess as a safety factor.   Safety first being her creed, old Mrs. Wu took no chances.

She had bought five bundles of incense sticks and waited till "all the stars were out," that is toward midnight, to move a small tea table out into the center of the courtyard near the spot where the goldfish bowl was.   ringing her best incense burner from the shrine of the family Kitchen God and setting it solemnly on the tea table, she proceeded to burn the incense sticks bundle after bundle.   As each bundle was lighted, she was observed quietly and respectfully to kneel down and kowtow three times in the four directions, praying to the various "passing" deities to show mercy to her grandchild who was so unwell. After this she lighted the fifth bundle and again knelt down and did her obeisance, this time to the most benevolent and responsive goddess in the Miao Feng Shan (妙峯山) whose temple is some thirty or more miles to the northwest of Peking on one of the lofty spots in the heart of the Western Hills.   She prayed to the goddess to save her grandson, in return for which blessing she promised to pay a pilgrimage to her temple during the next open season in the fourth moon of the lunar calendar.

To all intents and purposes, the goddess responded bounteously to her prayers.

THE MIAO FENG SHAN PILGRIMAGE

THE Temple of the Goddess of Azure Clouds, situated on the summit of the Miao Feng Shan, the Mystic Peak, is the most important of sacred spots to the immense following of devout Buddhists of Peking and, indeed, also of Tientsin and the neighbouring districts. It is comparable to the T'ai Shan of Shantung province in religious esteem though not in natural or scenic grandeur. To this temple thousands and thousands of pilgrims, men and women, young and old, literally toil their way during the open season either to beg for an all-year long-term protection or, full of gratitude because their former prayers had been answered, to burn incense as a way of showing their religious feeling.

The principal hall in the temple is the one dedicated to the goddess herself, whose image occupies the center space and who, according to popular legend, is the deified daughter of Tung Yueh Ta Ti (東嶽大帝), or the Great Kingly God of the Eastern Mountain (T'ai Shan). She is also known as the Yu Nui Niang Niang (玉女娘娘), or Goddess of the Jade Damsel. A commonly accepted explanation has been that she is really only a transformation of the Goddess of Mercy, Kuan Yin (觀音) herself, symbolizing "Great Compassion and Great Mercy," for she it is who answers the prayers of all people, particularly of women and children during times of great distress and saves them from imminent destruction and hardships. Her title is surmounted with the two characters, ling kan (靈感) which would translate as "reactional sensitivity."

The miracles credited to the goddess of Miao Feng Shan are so many that they have become a household word to all Peking families. She was found to be the most responsive of all deities and has never failed to reward even the humblest believer. It has been alleged that sick people, so weak as being forced to make the pilgrimage on sticks or crutches, have found their ailments entirely eradicated by religious fervour and faith so that they returned home with such renewed energy that no supports were any longer necessary. In the Miao Feng Shan shrine we find an oriental counterpart to Aimee McPherson's Four-Square Gospel Church, known if I remember correctly, by the name of Angelus Temple in Los Angeles.

Nor were the miracles of the goddess limited to cases of sickness for with suggestions clearly indicated on printed forms, she advises what to do and decides the course of action for many a doubt-ridden man. She does reveal the future, people say, and tells each individual case how to take advantage of his destiny. Other things in which the goddess has helped her great following have been the improvement of business profits, avoidance of disharmony between husband and wife, and particularly the solution of the offspring problem by sending petitioners high-born babies. Of the many people whom I had occasion to question on what made them so zealous believers in the great power of the goddess and what prompted them to perform the annual pilgrimage, only one admitted that besides a religious rite, the trip was also an opportunity for an excursion and for some exercise and "there are many *jeh nao* (熱鬧), or sights, to see."

Not having been imbued with the craze of twentieth century "tourism," old Mrs. Wu was not interested in her planned pilgrimage as a sight-seeing trip. All she felt was that she was duty bound to redeem her pledge made that star lit night when young Little Bald Head was so distressingly sick with the measles.

When her proposal was made to the family the next season, something like a year after the boy's sickness, it met with unreserved approval. Even old Mr. Wu himself, that "sacrilegious renegade," favoured the project which approval was not a matter of usual course. He really did not believe as his wife did, in the merits of such an undertaking but, automatically, out of his orthodox "familism" anything calculated to be to the good of the Wu family need fear of no objection from him. According to him she was performing one of her inherent duties to the Wus' ancestors in the interests of their future generations. Of these Little Bald Head was the symbol.

*   *   *

I need not acquaint my readers with the fact that the Chinese, as a race, are not well known for their genius of or inclination to organization or collective discipline, but there is one apparent exception and that is when it comes to religious fervour. And of this aspect one outstanding example would be the various "mountain societies" whose good work is in evidence all along the road leading to the Miao Feng Shan Temple of the goddess during the open season from the first to the fifteenth of the fourth moon. The societies are so efficient in their work and so well organized that any member or even non-member in the enormous multitude of pilgrims need not feel lonely or estranged unless he purposely keeps away from their activities. Besides cutting down substantially the expenses of such trips for pilgrims and therefore making the undertaking accessible to the rich as well as the poor, they give all sorts of facilities and accommodations to the devout travellers, actually supplying them free of charge with food, drink and lodging. Some of these activities are indicated by the names of the societies.

These societies establish temporary mat sheds all the way along the different routes leading to the sacred precincts where they offer to the hungry and thirsty pilgrims free millet porridge, free steamed breads and free tea, all prepared on the spot and served "piping" hot, besides a place to rest and enjoy the much demanded hospitality extended to the "wayfarers in a strange land." These mat sheds, the contributions of the mat shed guild, are beautifully but solemnly beflagged with all kinds of banners inscribed with the names of their respective owner organizations and a motto advocating "collective practice of virtue and universal religious comradeship." These sheds are veritable oases in the desert.

One group of such sheds, believe it or not, confine their good work to nothing but free shoe repairs. The service is the pilgrim's for the asking and his shoes are quickly repaired "while he waits," with no charge made. Chinese shoes, particularly the kind suitable for mountaineering, are made of native cloth, the upper part as well as the sole. They are sewn together with hemp string and as they often wear out at the wrong moments the free repair service, offered as a token of devotion and fellowship by the cobblers'

The mountain society's yellow posters are a familiar sight in Peking and indicate that the person on whose house wall they are posted is a member of a Miao Feng Shan pilgrim organization.

guild, is indeed much appreciated.

In all these places, the pilgrim is free to avail himself of all services offered upon identifying himself as a *bona fide* pilgrim. And this is easy, as what Miao Feng Shan pilgrim does not wear a pseudo-turban by tying a big square of orange-yellow cloth around his or her head, or would refuse to kowtow to the altars occupying the center of each of the many "service stations?" One more kind of such temple societies, sponsored by a group of "virtue practisers" from the port city of Tientsin, donates a "street lamp" service, bringing the required equipment, kerosene and all, with them each year. As the main causeways up and down the hills are narrow, rocky and dangerously steep in a good many places, their enterprise fills a keenly felt need for the pilgrims who travel by day as well as by night, being prompted by religious zeal to attain the summit of the hill as soon as possible.

The headmen of such temple societies are usually venerable elderly gentlemen who carry a small triangular flag as their emblem bearing the name of the society to which they belong. They are the foundation members of the *hui* (會) and are the heaviest contributors either in money or in time and attention. They are known as *lao tu kwan* (老都管), or "old superintendents." One of these superintendents of a certain tea society was an old man of seventy years by the name of Ch'uan, an old Manchu or "bannerman" as his name indicates. Mr. Ch'uan lived about four doors to the east of the Wu family and was old Mr. Wu's friend of many years' standing.

Old Mr. Wu approached him in his wife's behalf and told him of her intention. He expressed great delight in the matter. Old Mr. Wu further offered through Mr. Ch'uan a small contribution of "incense money" as an initiation fee for his membership in the society. A few days later, the society's people came with a big yellow poster, printed by wood block and giving a prospectus of the society's activities, outlining therein also their itinerary for the forthcoming trip to Miao Feng Shan, besides acknowledging the receipt of Mr. Wu's donation. Explaining their intention to the Wu family they had the big poster pasted onto their wall near the door, amid the sounding of big bronze gongs, correctly known as *hao* (號), four in number, each carried by a society member.

Such posters are seen in great number on Peking house walls during the spring months, giving silent proof of the strength of pilgrimage-conscious inhabitants. They are easily identified by the popular motifs of the "art" portions; the peaches (for "long life") and persimmons and jade scepter (for "everything desired").

*   *   *

The activities of the various temple societies are many and diverse and besides the ones mentioned previously there are also such as the *hsien hua lao hui* (獻花老會), "The Old Society for the Presentation of Artificial Flowers," with their immense flower baskets in full view in the Hall of the Goddess at Miao Feng Shan; the *ch'iao lu lao hui* (巧爐老會), "The Old Society of the Ingenious Incense Burner," whose specialty is the free repair of Chinaware that may chance to be broken in the various tea and porridge depots during the pilgrim season; and the *p'an hsiang lao hui* (盤香老會), which conducts free distribution of incense sticks besides making a large-scale offering of them in their own mat shed. Another society, called *jan teng lao hui* (燃燈老會), distributes free paper lanterns and candles for the benefit of nocturnal pilgrims. The *pai hsi lao hui* (拜蓆老會), or the society for the free supply of straw mats for ceremonial uses, is also gratefully utilized by the tired pilgrims in the various stations for sitting or sleeping on. All these are donations by the guilds of the various trades represented.

All the foregoing are known as *wen hui* (文會), which may be translated as "civilian societies," and which stand in relativity with the *wu hui* (武會) or "militant societies." The *wu hui* are organized or sponsored by groups of people who are more or less the sportsman type and their activities consist of various shows and entertainments, mostly of the theatrical or acrobatic varieties, as a gesture of devotion to the goddess as well as a demonstration for the benefit of the pilgrims.

The heyday of the various *wu hui* was toward the end of the Manchu Dynasty, no doubt in consequence of the moral effect of the encouragement given by the late Empress Dowager Ts'u Hsi who spent $50,000,000 to construct the world-renowned Summer Palace as a birthday present to herself. She unprecedentedly bestowed on the various *hui* the favour of her royal inspection. The original motifs of decorations in commemoration of the natal celebration of the "Old Buddha," as the Empress loved to hear herself called, carrying the designs of the imperial five-clawed dragons and the slogan phrase *wan shou wu chiang* (萬壽無疆), meaning "Endless Long Life of Ten Thousand Years (sic)", are still in evidence, reminiscent of Her Majesty's imperial patronage!

The various games and shows of the temple societies are comparable to the variety performances or perhaps to foreign vaudeville, the only difference being that each society has its own specialty which the name of the society clearly indicates. There are the Bamboo Flagpole Balancers, Fancy Cymbals, Fancy Kettledrums, Treasure Chests, Lions, Road Openers (players of the "fork", a warring weapon), and Five Tiger Rod, Weight Lifters, Stilted Dancers (otherwise known as Singers of Rice-planting Songs) and some others. The modern addition to them are the Fancy Bicycle Riders. There are various competitive groups in each of the different localities which they pretend to represent vying with each other in the elaborateness of luxurious appointments of equipment, skill of performance, as well as the number of active players and the size of the cheering audience attracted.

Not being willing to submit to a competitive organization, there is bound to be a lot of hard discipline and indiscriminate spending of money and, indeed, of regretful waste of time during the training periods. When it is taken into consideration that a good portion of the pioneering partakers were of Manchu families who were regularly paid by the now defunct Manchu government and virtually encouraged to be idle, it is a surprise that such non-profit and economically non-productive follies could be carried on at all. The general motto of such zealous devotees has been *hao ts'ai mai lien* (耗財買臉), meaning "squandering of money for the purchase of 'face'," which is absolutely correct in so far as the money squandering portion of it is concerned.

Of course, the fundamental aims, expressed or understood, of the societies were an expression of gratitude to the almighty goddess, a demonstration of the members' faith and their desire to see the cause of the goddess glorified and aggrandized. But the performances of all the parties being obliged by the various free service stations on the way to do their stunts at every stop was certainly responsible for a great measure of action and noise particularly as most are with musical accompaniments of the typical Chinese kind. Here is the notorious noise and din besides the conscientious cheering of the crowds of bystanders, mostly pilgrims. It must be admitted that some or most of the stunts are quite difficult and often really deserve a good cheering crowd. The general effect on the fatigued pilgrims is very stimulating and as such it adds in a good measure to the atmosphere that makes the Miao Feng Shan temple pilgrimage one of the highlights of native Peking life.

Old Mrs. Wu, on the pilgrimage in the interest and on behalf of her grandson Little Bald Head, was to see much of the various temple society performances as a by-product of her trip of religious devotion. Frankly speaking, she was looking forward to just such an experience.

*   *   *

Though the pilgrimage to Miao Feng Shan was to take only three days for old Mrs. Wu, there were as many preparations and inquiries made as if old Mrs. Wu were going on a world tour. Chinese women in her time did not go out much. Indeed, it was true that most Chinese women, and some men too for that matter, might spend their entire lifetime without having gone through all of the sixteen gates of the Peking wall. This may sound like nonsense but any checkup with the true Peking-*jen* will confirm my statement.

The intention of such a trip for the old lady being a novelty, it was soon known to the neighbours and friends who made all sorts of suggestions as to how and what to do in the holy precincts as well as on the way. "Old Superintendent" Ch'uan of the Tea Society was not without his recommendations either. According to his idea, old Mrs. Wu ought to travel with his party in one of their specially chartered open carts in the middle of the Society's procession to the village of Pei An Ho at the foot of the hill and make the balance of the trip up and down the hill on foot. For to

him, a typical devotee, the trip should be as frugal and self-deny-
ing as possible as a sincere tribute to the faith. But old Mrs. Wu,
though younger in years than Mr. Ch'uan, found herself physically not up to it and she had to refuse his suggestion with sincere
regrets.

There was much negotiation about everything.

It was just when she was utterly at a loss in deciding on the
details and was so desperate that she had actually begun to think
that after all the best thing to do perhaps was to put off the trip
another year, that it was announced Madame Ho, young Mrs. Wu's
mother, had come. She had learned of old Mrs. Wu's intentions
and, being an experienced hand at it, she had come to offer her
good offices. Old Mrs. Wu was very glad to see her.

The drawing up of the itinerary, with the wise counsel and
inexhaustible wealth of experience of Madame Ho at her disposal,
proved simple and the details were soon worked out.

According to Madame Ho, old Mrs. Wu should leave (the day
they later decided on was the eighth day of the fourth moon as
the family almanac dictated that this was a very lucky day for
such a venture) after lunch and proceed by rickshaw to the Hsi
Chih Men where Madame Ho's private mule cart of 1900 vintage,
with driver attending, would meet and convey her to the Ho
estate in the Hsiang Shan village beyond the Jade Fountain Hills
where she was to be the guest of honour of the Ho family. The
incense burning mission was to start in earnest early the next
morning by mule cart to the village of Pei An Ho, at the foot of
the Miao Feng Shan, where she would arrive about ten o'clock the
same morning. At that point the typical bamboo and rattan
chair, borne by four mountain climbing men, was to be rented for
the trip to the Temple of the Goddess. Old Mrs. Wu was to proceed to the Hall of the Goddess, burn the incense, spend some time
looking around and then return in the waiting chair to the
village of Pei An Ho.

The whole trip in the hills was to take about seven hours.
She was also required (according to the judgment of Madame Ho)
to buy souvenirs at some spots and also at the temple entrance.
The private mule cart of the Hos would be waiting for her at the
village, all ready to "sail", making immediate connection with the
chair to bring her back to the Ho estate for the night. She was to
come home the next morning by "mule cart express" with an
option for a prolonged stay at the Ho estate if she liked. The details were so carefully worked out and expenses estimated that
the itinerary, as a whole, had nothing to lose even if put side by
side with any of Cook's suggested tours, the only difference being
that no mention was made by Madame Ho about the advisability
of carrying her funds in travellers checks which were cashable
everywhere during the trip!

Madame Ho expressed her regret that because of very important affairs, she was not able to go with old Mrs. Wu but if old
Mrs. Wu liked, she would send her daughter to accompany her as
the young girl had once been to the Miao Feng Shan and might be
of help.

"That would be too much trouble but I thank you just the
same," answered old Mrs. Wu, "but how about your woman servant, Liu Ma? She is a native of the Miao Feng Shan neighbourhood, I seem to remember, is she not?"

"That is right, she will make a fine guide and your lady-in-waiting, would she not? She will be glad to go, I am sure," Madame Ho declared.

*   *   *

There were certain things on which old Mr. Wu and his wife found it hard to agree though on general principles he was quite willing to meet his wife more than half way and the pilgrimage to the Miao Feng Shan was an example. For though old Mr. Wu could not be said to be entirely opposed to the project for reasons explained before, he would not suffer himself to go with his wife on the trip for all the world in spite of the fact that such a desirability was intimated directly and indirectly to him. Like all human beings, old Mr. Wu had his own idiosyncrasies and one of them was that he found it difficult to kowtow to any image. If he refused to fulfil this condition he might as well not go, according to his wife. Whatever indecision remained in the matter was expelled when Madame Ho called and offered a full measure of assistance. With this attention provided old Mr. Wu found there was no need for him to go.

The day to start old Mrs. Wu on her sacred mission soon arrived, it was the eighth day of the fourth moon. The weather was ideal. Old Mrs. Wu's things were all fixed up, including bundles of incense which the had specially purchased from a famous store on main street. She did not want to buy the incense at the temple though there were temporary stalls there and all along the way up to the main temple entrance, as told her by Madame Ho, for she wanted to be sure to get the "grade A" kind from a dependable shop. This she discovered to her sad disillusionment was really to no end, except for the "effect" on the peace of her religious mind.

Old Mr. Wu escorted her as far as the Hsi Chih Men and after seeing his wife board the mule cart of Madame Ho he turned back home. In an hour and a half old Mrs. Wu arrived at the Ho estate in the country, amid the full-forced welcome at the gate.

An early start was made the next morning. The roads were thick with pilgrims and some of the "early bird" ones were already "homeward going their weary way." These could be easily identified from the characteristic souvenirs they invariably carried. Most of them had long sticks made from peach trees with the rich mahogany-coloured outer skin still shiny and fresh, or fans and hats and other novelties made of wheat stalks, dyed and woven into fancy patterns, and all of them, men and women alike, wearing on their hats or orange-yellow cloth turbans red velvety decorations of some auspicious symbols with lucky bats predominating.

"There do not seem to be many *hui* people this year, Liu Ma?" old Mrs. Wu asked her "valet", the maidservant temporarily loaned by the Ho family.

"Yes, there are," Liu Ma answered. "But they have all gone ahead and must now be busy in the hills as the principal day for the *wu hui* (militant societies) is the eighth day, that was yesterday. As to the other organizations, we have been watching the processions in the outskirts of our village since the end of last month. For all of them must get to the scene before the general rush of pilgrims in order to be ready to render the desired services."

"But we will miss all the fun then, will we not?"

"No, Wu T'ai T'ai, we will meet the various shows on their way back from the temple tomorrow in so far as the *wu hai* are concerned. As to the tea and porridge sheds, they will not close until the fifteenth of the month and we will see them at their best. The various sports societies choose the eighth day for their presentation to the goddess because it is a *hao jih tze* (好日子) or a 'good day'. It has never rained on the eighth of the fourth moon."

"Of course not," explained the religion-wise old Mrs. Wu. "For it is the day on which Buddha Cakyamuni himself was enlightened after a long meditation under the Bodhi tree. It is called the *Fo Tao Jih*, (佛道日) or the 'Day of Buddha's Enlightenment'. By the way, did you observe a vegetarian diet yesterday?"

"Oh yes, the Ho family observe all fasting days and we servants follow suit," answered Liu Ma.

*   *   *

The Chinese have a well known maxim embodying an attitude of distrust and, indeed, hatred towards all transportation and subjoining enterprises as a whole which I cannot afford to give here nor muster enough courage to translate for the benefit of my foreign readers for it is too harshly worded. And of all the various ramifications of the transportation business, in so far as difficulty in dealing with them is concerned, mountain chairs are the limit. No matter how hard you bargain with the carriers and how systematic a business mind you may boast of possessing, your unwritten contracts with these people never seem to cover everything. And no time limits, however clearly understood between the high contracting parties, can be expected to be used as a basis for making payments on the contract!

I remember seeing an American gentleman arguing with the bearers at a journey's end on the dependability of his Elgin watch which he held in his hand in support of his attempt at a correct fulfilment of a payment contract. He was all heated up with the argument, explaining loudly to the gathering crowd what a famous timepiece his was and how utterly unreasonable it was for the bearers to allege that his watch was not keeping correct time. Poor fellow! He should never have carried a timepiece to begin with on such an excursion.

For the chair people have in long years of experience learned that any one who has the time and money to come to Miao Feng Shan or any other mountain or seaside resort must be crazy; for judging from their point of view it is a sinful waste of good money. Besides, such people being in a so-called "holiday spirit" (which means "insanity" to the chair people) and therefore frequently in no mood to argue the bearers never fail to get the better of the customers either by hook or by crook. If they fail, once in a hundred times, to get satisfaction by argumentation and debate and purposeful misunderstanding of terms, they usually have a special trick to fall back on and that is by flattering you and literally begging you for an "unreasonable" extra ten or twenty-cent piece. In flattery the customer's weak point is often found.

But old Mrs. Wu had nothing to worry about as Madame Ho's mule cart driver, an old servant in the house, and the maidservant Liu Ma, a native of the district, knew things too well for old Mrs. Wu to be uncomfortable. In a few minutes time she and the servant woman were safely seated in a couple of the "mountain climbing tigers" as such chairs are locally called and were well on their way. It being a little cooler in the hills, old Mrs. Wu had put on an extra coat on the insistence of Madame Ho.

The first sight they saw was a young woman pilgrim; so devot and sincere that she knelt down and made a kowtow after every three steps all the way from the foot of the hill to the Temple and Hall of the Goddess of Azure Clouds. Further on they saw another devotee who had clad himself entirely in red and had his hands and legs chained in exactly the same fashion as a prisoner of olden times. From his neck hung a heavy iron chain from which dangled an iron lock some ten inches across. And every step he made, which was made rather clumsy due to his heavy burden, he followed with kneeling and knocking his forehead on the hard rock path. The poor fellow looked so callous to the apparent discomfort that it would seem he was insensitive or immune to pain.

Of the plain "kowtow and walk" variety, old Mrs. Wu counted some fifteen examples on the trip uphill. Of the other kind she saw but two. One of them actually had a horse saddle tied on his back besides other items of extra-costume similar to those already described above and judging from his countenance and the number of friends and servants attending him this particular pilgrim was apparently from a well-to-do family.

Old Mrs. Wu had heard so much about these worshippers and having previously been informed by the Ho family what she was liable to see, she was not astonished, though she could hardly find a reason to sympathize with such self-inflicted tortures.

It is said that these acts of devotion are the fulfilment of pledges made to the goddess during a parent's or a husband's critical sickness, or great life-and-death misfortunes in which the goddess, answering a prayer, had effected the desired change. The type with a horse saddle on his back usually has something awful on his mind or on his record, that bothers him so terribly that nothing short of leading, in a mimicry fashion at least for a day, the life of a beast of burden would wash away the sin. These people do not make open confessions, and bystanders have to make their own guesses as to their reasons. The usual term accorded such tortures is *sheh shen* (捨身), "bodily sacrifice." In the T'ai mountains in the province of Shantung there is a place called *sheh shen yah* (捨身崖), or the "Precipice for Bodily Sacrifice," from which every year some grateful pilgrim or pilgrims will jump and dash out their brains on the gorges many feet below. A special police force, it is said, has to be stationed there during pilgrimage periods to stop such lunatic attempts.

*   *   *

The distance from the foot of Miao Feng Shan to the very summit of the hill where the temple of the goddess is located is a strenuous climb, indeed, as old Mrs. Wu had a chance to verify for herself, and she was glad that she had not come on foot with the members of the tea organization of which her husband's friend, Mr. Ch'uan, was one of the promoters. Three different roads lead to the main shrine and the one taken by old Mrs. Wu's party was the shortest and the steepest. The distance is said to be about forty Chinese *li* or about thirteen English miles. The various temple societies maintain their mat sheds at an average distance of two or three miles from each other.

Most of the places are rather elaborate affairs with the scroll portrait of the goddess occupying a paper shrine in the central position. Inside the shed there are banners, hanging from the ceilings, of multi-coloured embroidery, facsimiles of the conventional Buddhist canopies, the emblem of protection. An oblong table is in front of the altar on which is put the incense burner in the center flanked by a pair of flower vases besides food offerings. A bronze gong in the shape of a semi-sphere is also provided on which a *hui* member knocks regularly to keep time for the kowtowing pilgrims. These pilgrims are invited by other members at the door of the shed to come in and first to kneel down on a mat spread before the altar table to do obeisance and then to make themselves at home, resting and sipping the hot tea on the seats close by.

Outside, there are also teams of members who sing in a drawling manner certain phrases in chorus calling upon the passing pilgrims to drop in and enjoy their hospitality. Inside, monstrous-sized candles are kept lighted all the time and bundles of incense burn briskly with flames fully two feet high. The singing of the members, led by the "choir-master", and the beating of the gong mingled with the typical noise of the tide of humanity echoing and re-echoing in the mountains is audible within a radius of a mile, heartening the devotees forward on their worthy and meritorious journey.

On big tables tea pots and tea cups are spread out. Tea is already poured into the array of cups and the pilgrim is free to drink to his heart's content. One of the *lao tu kuan*, or "Old Superintendents", has the special duty of earnestly requesting the guests to please not waste the precious water as it is very hard to procure in such mountainous regions. Donkeys are used, he explains, to carry the water in little flattish buckets from the nearest village many *li* away at the foot of the hill. Each donkey carries two buckets which contain no more than half a little jarful of water each trip and he points to little earthen container near the stove which could hardly hold twenty gallons.

The various tea stations have also itinerant parties who see to it that the body of sacrificing pilgrims are given special service by solemnly escorting them from station to station, carrying tea for their need at any moment.

According to them such people deserve the highest degree of respect being so devoted to the faith.

*   *   *

The human noise, the echoing of bronze bells and gongs, the keepers of temporary incense stands and souvenir stalls hawking their wares and the tall flag pole with the big apricot-coloured banner at the temple gate were the first impressions made on old Mrs. Wu. The sight of the temple refreshed her after the mixture of feelings with which she was literally saturated *en route*, and with the help of the maidservant she alighted from the chair.

Inside the temple the precincts were so crowded that it was not without trouble that she and the servant managed to keep in close touch with each other. She had imagined that she would be able to kneel down respectfully and pray to the goddess leisurely, expressing her gratitude in a fitting manner but there was absolutely no room for her to do so, the halls being so densely packed with pilgrims.   Nor was she able to burn her specially selected "Grade A" incense, inserting each bundle in the burner on the altar table as she did at the Temple of the Sacred Eastern Mountain.   Here was no place for high-minded old Mrs. Wu to do things in her own refined and lady-like manner.   The great majority of the pilgrims, she observed, knelt down where they happened to find kneeling room in the courtyard and kowtowed in the direction of the main shrine after throwing the incense sticks, paper wrappings and all, directly into the big iron brazier in the open courtyard which was some six feet wide and ten feet long and in which a continuous bonfire was kept flaming and smoking skyward by the immense quantity of incense sticks fed into the fire. She waited and waited, but the crowd got thicker and thicker. She had to satisfy herself by doing as the others did—throwing all her incense into the big iron burner and doing her obeisance from a distance.

*   *   *

Nowhere in the world are omens taken so seriously as in China and in the Miao Feng Shan Temple this universal weakness of the people was exploited to the limit by the keepers of souvenir stalls who sold ornaments in the shape of bats, and so forth, made of scarlet chenille of which stuff every pilgrim on the devotional trip is a potential buyer.   The Chinese character for "bat" is *fu* indentical in sound with that for "blessing," and the word for "red" is *hung*, the same as for "big."   The shrewd stall-keepers ask the pilgrims to buy their wares by requesting them to carry home a "red bat" which sounds exactly like a "big blessing".   And what pilgrim does not fancy himself carrying home a "big blessing" from the goddess on such a trip?   And naturally the merchants obtain the lion's share of the pilgrim souvenir trade.

Next come the peach wood stick sellers who also do a great amount of business as the majority of travellers are quite tired and certainly need a stout walking cane to help them in coming down the hill.   Besides, since ancient times, peach wood has been known to possess certain exorcistic properties against all evil influences and this would be a catchword enough with which to make a sale if the prospective customer could not be moved to buy a stick for any other reason.

Old Mrs. Wu bought some of the chenille flowers and stuck them in her hair in the same manner the other pilgrims did and of the peach sticks she bought four, for peach trees growing wild in that region the sticks, about the size of a regular walking cane only somewhat longer as a rule, are "dirt cheap."   Besides these, she loaded herself up with a number of wheat stalk articles, fans, baskets, hats, and a kind of a decorative spiral object known as a "dragon" but looking surprisingly like a foreign sign of plenty, the cornucopia.

Soon they were seated in their chairs and ready for the return trip.   By then the various *wu hui* or "militant societies", who had made their ceremonial starts before old Mrs. Wu arrived at the Temple, were on their way homeward too.   Comfortably

seated in the chair and her sacred mission having been successfully fulfilled, she now prepared herself for a "joy ride" and
sight-seeing. She had not seen much of the temple society shows
before.

The first of the shows they saw was the Lions. She had seen
this kind before and so the experience was not entirely novel to
her.

The lions are conventional in design and shape but quite
different in appearance from the real African variety, resembling
almost the Pekingese dog. The heads, some three feet across, are
made of papier-mâché with big bulging eyes, grotesque teeth and
big shaggy ears. A belt is put around the neck with big brass
bells attached, each ten inches in diameter, which clang away as
the show goes on. The body is made of a long piece of yellow or
blue cloth ridged with green or orange silken hair and with a big
bushy tail of matching colour. Two men make a team for a single
lion. Each of the men wears a pair of trousers made of cloth of a
matching colour with the body, and "decorated" with hair and
claws, etc., in the "form" of the lion's legs. The "headman" puts
the lion's head over his own, supporting it, probably, with his
hands and the "tailman" takes care of the other end. Thus prepared, the pair of lions containing four people in their huge
bodies will go into their act. There are all sorts of lifelike antics
in various movements, jumping, running, walking, now rolling on
their backs, now scratching violently at a supposedly present flea.
All the time each lion parallels the movements of the other in
perfect harmony directed by the "master." They even make a
dash for the hillocks nearby or scramble up a steep incline or play
with an "embroidered ball," showing off the best of their art to
the hearty cheering of the crowd. The Lions are often requested
to stop and perform at a tea or porridge society station, the
gathering place of society and non-society pilgrims alike.

*   *   *

Each of the various troupes of temple society shows have a
lot of equipment to carry about with them during their performing trips, including the various costumes and "properties", besides miscellaneous articles such as pigments and brushes for
painting the faces of the warrior-type characters, and so forth.
This equipment is invariably contained in round wooden boxes,

Two men make a
team for the lion
show, the "head-
man" and the
"tailman".

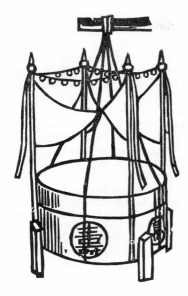

The temple society's equipment is carried in boxes decorated with little flags and bells.

usually eight in number, and carried by four liveried labourers, two boxes to each man, from the ends of a pole carried over the shoulder. The boxes are decorated with four little flag-poles, each bearing small triangular flags joined together. Then from the tops of the little poles, strings of little brass bells are suspended. In the parading procession these men, in spite of the burdens carried, walk with a certain conventional "poetry of motion" and the four-man group keep such a harmony of step that by their swaying and swinging, the tiny bells themselves tinkle with a rhythm that is a feature all by itself.

The flags bear Chinese characters, representing the name of the society to which the equipment belongs as well as some other phrases of four characters each, either mottoes of the society or the special slogan bespeaking an equivalent of "By Appointment to Her Late Imperial Majesty the Empress Dowager Ts'u Hsi," a reminder of their society's bygone splendour. The colour scheme of the flags of some of the societies has yellow predominating, others blue. It is understood that only those shows which have been favoured with imperial patronage during the late Manchu dynasty are entitled to fly banners of this colour. Such equipment boxes are usually not very big, only about eighteen inches high and thirty inches or so across, but those for the Lion society are necessarily much wider and higher as the bulkiness of the costumes and the immense lion heads have to have big boxes to contain them.

*　　*　　*

The next show that old Mrs. Wu and her servant, riding in the swift-going muntain chairs, caught up with was the *Chung Fan Hui* (中幡會), or Fancy Flagpole Balancers. The crowd around the performing group was particularly big and old Mrs. Wu had to work hard to get to a vantage point for a full view of what was going on.

The main attraction of the society is an immense bamboo pole some thirty feet from tip to tip and fully eight or nine inches in diameter at the bottom and tapering to the size of a pencil at the top. The full natural length of a big bamboo is utilized to make the holy flagmast which is supposed to be a temple banner *de luxe*. The pole is decorated at the top with three little umbrella shaped canopies with additional little flags branching out on each side. The pole, during the performance, is kept erect and is not to touch the ground. It is not held tightly in the hands of the players who show the utmost dexterity in juggling the monstrous affair. The great cloth piece of yellow, draping half of the pole and inscribed with a religious phrase in boldface black Chinese

The female impersonator in the stilt dance beats a brass gong as part of the musical accompaniment.

characters, adds colour to the show but also, it must be admitted, is an additional difficulty as it catches the mountain breeze on its broad surface. As a matter of fact, the men's performance is truly worthy of a great measure of admiration and applause.

The performers balanced it, as old Mrs. Wu saw, with effortless grace on the palm of a hand, then on the tip of a finger, then they tossed the immense pole into the air for another man to catch and balance on his forehead where a small felt cushion had been fixed. At critical moments when the long banner swung alarmingly over the spectators' heads it provided the biggest thrills, but in each case a tragedy was avoided by the clever stunts of these amateur showmen who were devout members of the society. If practice does make perfect then the amount of practice put in by the flagpole balancers must be considerable. The flagpole must easily weigh a hundred pounds and it would be a great sacrilegious blunder, as we may be sure, to miss the "center of gravity" and let it fall to the ground! It is the most rigid test of the balance of the nerve system, for a mishap may mean a human skull or two smashed beyond repair!

All these bold performers have the favour of the goddess on their side and therefore they need fear nothing. So why worry? Just have faith!

*   *   *

The *Kao Ch'iao Hui* (高跷會), or "Stilt Dancing" as it is generally known to foreigners, is a very popular show in North China and Manchuria alike. Being more or less a peasant recreation, it is not particularly "local colour" in Peking life but in so far as the luxury of appointment and the fullness of repertoire are concerned Peking boasts of the best. The stilts are made of strong wood and are four feet or more in height with cogs for the feet. The upper portion of the stilts is tied with strong bandages to the outer sides of the legs from the knee down.

The proper full-force troupe should contain twelve stilt dancers, each dressed in a different costume and being a distinctly different character. The twelve original parts are two drummers, two gong-beaters, the old fisherman, his wife, the woodcutter, the quack doctor and medicine pedlar, the old hermit monk, the country squire, his young and pretty wife, and their little son, named *Hsiao Erh-Ke* (小二哥) (pronounced like *hsiao erg*), or "Little Brother No. Two."

Some new characters have been added from time to time as "extras". The drummers are male characters, their drums, cylindrical in shape and struck with two sticks are suspended from the shoulder on a belt, hanging at the hips, and looking not unlike an Arabian waterpedlar in a nightmare! Two other female impersonators, thickly powdered and outrageously rouged, carry the little brass disc gongs which are struck with small pieces of wood. These simple musical instruments provide the interludes between chapters of the songs as well as the timing during the parades, besides announcing their impending arrival with the typical "march."

The performers walk rather fast on the stilts which allow them the advantage of having extra-lengthened legs as it were. They have certain special stunts, too, such as throwing themselves flat on the ground with their legs parted in opposite directions while keeping the upper part of their bodies erect, and forthwith resuming their original standing position with no outside help. Their singing pieces sometimes are long drawn-out affairs, some are of historical and rural or folklore origins, some sing solo and others in chorus. Representative pieces are "The Dialogue between the Fisherman and the Wood-cutter," "The Romance of the White Snake, the Green Snake and their Joint Sweetheart, the Scholar Hsu Hsien," etc.

Old Mrs. Wu found them performing the play "Farewell at the Ten-mile Pavilion," from the famous old dramatic masterpiece known as *Hsi Hsiang Chi* (西廂記), or "Romance of the Western Chamber." (This play has been translated into English in its original form.) The famous beauty Ying Ying, or Oriole-Oriole, was seeing her young husband Chang Chun Jui off on his journey to the capital to attend the Imperial examinations. The Little Harp Boy, the scholar's servant, and the Scarlet Maid, Oriole-Oriole's charming young *valet de chambre*, who had played such an important part carrying messages back and forth between her mistress and Scholar Chang in their pre-marriage days, were both in evidence. The various parts sung by the stilt actors, accompanied by the beating of drums and gong , were so well accomplished that the immense crowd of pilgrims and others were held spellbound throughout the duration of the lengthy performance. Old Mrs. Wu and Liu Ma stood through the entire play and then, remounting the chairs, proceeded on their way.

"We did not see the *kang tze* (槓子) or trapeze acrobats. Do they not come too?" old Mrs. Wu asked her servant.

"Yes, they come, of course, but the roads here are not suitable for them as their trapeze equipment, erected and ready at all times, is mounted on an open mule cart. Or perhaps they have chosen the southern route *via* the San Chia Tien village where the road is better."

"Is that so? I did not know that," old Mrs. Wu remarked.

*   *   *

On that pilgrimage to the Miao Feng Shan Temple of the Goddess of Azure Clouds, old Mrs. Wu had a fine opportunity of inspecting at close quarters Peking's temple society shows. The various society processions, after ceremonials at the sacred precincts, had preceded them from the temple on the trip down hill but as each show was stopped at every one of the many free tea and porridge stations for a demonstration, old Mrs. Wu was able to catch up with many a party of performing groups of devotees.

The fourth group she saw was the Five Tiger Rod, in which a group of athletes performed a close fight in mimicry, each with a different weapon accompanied by drums and cymbals of deep intonations. It seems the story is based on the legend of Chao K'wang Yin, who later became the first emperor of the Sung Dynasty (A.D. 960-1276). The time was when he ran away from his home town after he had murdered somebody in the red light district. Hungry and desperate, the fleeing law-breaker chanced to pass through an orchard, where the ripening red dates biased his sense of possession. He poached the dates, was stopped by a young woman, whereupon he gave her a sound beating. The woman's husband and his four brothers, all of whom were of the regular bully type, the Five Tigers, came up to settle with him. A close fight ensued. Young Chao, unsubdued, was found to be a good match for the single, double and multiplex offensives. Surprised, the Five Tigers called a truce. It was then discovered that the Five Tigers of the Tung family were nobody else but his uncles on' his mother's side and the woman he beat up was one of his aunts. Peace was soon established.

There are no singing parts in this show and all the characters are of the "warrior" type as on the stage, having their faces painted in many colours, and seem to be fighting in earnest the hardest way they know how. But actually it is nothing but a gymnastic or acrobatic demonstration, characterized by great dexterity and fine "teamwork," contributing a showy effect.

There were also other shows old Mrs. Wu met with as she went on but because she was anxious to get home, she did not stop long to give each party its due inspection. Late in the afternoon they arrived at the Pai An Ho village.

The chair bearers were paid to their satisfaction and old Mrs. Wu and the servant were soon transferred to the Ho family's mule cart. The trip to the Jade Fountain was long and monotonous and they soon struck up a conversation.

"What other *wu hui* have you seen before, Wu *T'ai T'ai*?" Liu Ma asked.

"Not many, only the *K'ai Lu Hui* (開路會) with the fancy playing of the branched weapon called *ch'a* (叉), and one or two others. As you know we city women are not allowed so much liberty as you country people. Since I started to learn needlework (by which she meant when she attained a marriageable age) I had not been allowed to go out. All that I have seen of things like temple society shows was either when I was a mere child or only in passing glances which we girls used to make, surreptitiously peeping from closed doors or from the gauzed windows of the mule cart on the streets. Moreover we had always been taught that the *hui* people are not all good people," explained old Mrs. Wu. Young women from reputable families, it is true, never attended such functions.

"There are certain rules about the societies requiring them to do only as provided for by these rules. For instance, did you see the big flagpole of the *Chung Fan Hui*? Well, if the procession should ever pass an arch (known as *pailou* in Peking), the rules say they must toss the great pole vertically up over the arch and catch it neatly as it drops down straight on the other side!"

"No, I have never heard of that. But I do know that when the Lions pass a stream, they are required to perform the trick of drinking water." Old Mrs. Wu did not have to admit complete ignorance either.

CHINESE NURSERY RHYMES

THE pilgrimage of old Mrs. Wu was soon brought to a triumphant end and arriving home she found her grandson glad to see her back. It gave her immense pleasure to hear that ever since she left, the child had constantly been inquiring as to where his grandmother had gone and when she would be back. There was a close companionship between her and him and so they had missed each other very much. Old Mrs. Wu was glad of it.

* * *

The child soon developed into a very smart and talkative youngster. He was not quite four years old but his memory was marvellous for his age, being well cultivated. In the course of time, thanks to the old woman's tutorship, he had learned to recite a number of Chinese nursery rhymes of which there are a good many. The learning and repeating of these provided fun for both the child and the family members.

Little Bald Head had no trouble memorizing such short ones as "*Ma Ssu Yah-erh's* Tea Shop," which reads:

"*Ma Ssu Yah-erh*, (馬四眼兒)
K'ai ch'a kuan-erh, (開茶舘兒)
Yi ke ch'a hu (一個茶壺)
Lia ch'a wan-erh" (倆茶碗兒)

which translates as:

"Ma, the be-spectacled,
Opens a tea shop;
He has but one teapot
And two cups available."

Another one that he liked very much was about the "Small Boy Who Fell Down the Temple Steps." It goes as follows:

"A little, little boy,
Went up the temple steps;
He fell flat on the ground,
And a lost cash he found.
With this, he bought oil;
With this, he bought salt;
He used the rest getting himself a wife,
And the balance he spent for a happy new year."

There was also the one about a "Small Boy Craving a Wife;" which runs:

"A little, little boy,
Sits on the door step.
He weeps, weeps bitterly,
For he wants a wife.
'Wants a wife, but what for'
'To make me rice, to make me vegetables,
To make me trousers, to make me socks,
To light the lamp, to talk with me,
To blow out the lamp, and keep me from loneliness
Next morning, she will also comb and make my little queue!' "

But there were also some longer ones which he finally conquered after some effort. One of them was the "Yellow Dog."

"Yellow Dog, Yellow Dog, watch my home,
For I am going to the South Garden to gather some
　　plum flowers.
Not a single flower have I gathered,
When relatives and friends arrive at my home.
In my home the wife makes the best noodles,
That twirl and whirl in the cooking pot.
The father-in-law he gets one bowl,
The mother-in-law she gets one bowl,
Under the kitchen-board I hide another bowl.
The cat comes around and breaks the bowl,
The dog comes and licks the bowl,
The little mouse comes and mends the bowl."

There are also little songs peculiar to girls. Of these an example is the "Pedlar."

"Little Pedlar Brother,
Please stop for a moment.
Give me some blue steel needles,
Also heavy threads for making shoes;
Of vat-dyed black cloth, give me eight pieces;
For Father-in-law, two pairs;
For Mother-in-law, two pairs;
Husband he gets two pairs; and I two pairs;
Oh, what a big face you have, my girl!"

*　　　*　　　*

As Little Bald Head learned so fast, his grandmother's stock
of old nursery rhymes was soon exhausted. There were some
songs which old Mrs. Wu did not like to teach her grandson as
they were too tragic in tone or because they contained matters too
difficult for the little child to understand. Some songs contained
phrases beyond the intelligence of the little child and his questions not having been answered to his own full satisfaction, he
naturally lost interest in memorizing such songs. The Chinese
nursery rhymes are often heavily tinted with social, and more
particularly, family problems, such as the miserable life of a
daughter at the hand of her stepmother, or the unbeloved young
daughter-in-law. So deep and touching in meaning and expression
are they that they cease to be a juvenile delight. It is, indeed, true
that they may be said to represent a distinctive branch of folklore
literature all by themselves. Such simple and catchy English
verses as "Little Jack Horner, sat in a corner...." or "When
Jack is a very good boy, he shall have cakes and a custard....."
find no counterpart in China.

Before long old Mrs. Wu hit upon an interesting substitute.

"Now let me give you a riddle to answer," said old Mrs. Wu,
and proceeded to tell Little Bald Head what a riddle was and
how it was to be solved. Little Bald Head understood; he would
try.

"Now what is this animal,
'From the south there comes a crowd of big black rascals,
Each of them has a pair of big black fans,
Each step they walk, they fan their fans and growl,
Oh, Omita Buddha, what a hot day.'"

Little Bald Head thought seriously for a moment. Promptly his answer came.

"Pigs!"

"Very good. Now hear this one; it is about four things.

'Having one leg, it grows from the earth,

Having two legs, it crows at the five hourly watches,

Three legs, it stands in front of the Buddha's shrine,

Four legs, it runs about and bores holes in the walls'."

Nor was our little hero puzzled by this one. For one by one the answers came. The one-legged was the mushroom. The two-legged, the rooster. The three-legged, the incense burner. The four-legged, the rat.

Another one that she gave him to solve was the "four fruits."

"The first sister, how red and lovely;

The second sister, she twists her tiny mouth;

The third sister, she grins and shows her pretty teeth;

The fourth sister, she is full of tears!"

The answers to these are: the apple, the peach, the pomegranate and the grape.

And also the one about the "four animals," Little Bald Head was given to solve.

"The first one glides uphill smoothly,

The second one rolls downhill like an embroidered ball,

The third one shakes its head and knocks the watch-man's wooden rattle,

The fourth one washes its face, but does not comb its hair!"

This one proved to be very hard to solve. Old Mrs. Wu had to give the answers. They are the snake, the hedgehog, the woodpecker and the domestic cat respectively.

*　　　*　　　*

Making and solving riddles or conundrums is a highly developed literary pursuit in China and is the universal hobby of all learned scholars. They are known as *teng mi* (燈迷), or "lantern riddles," on account of the fact that originally they were written on strips of paper and hung up on a paper lantern for the public to solve—a very interesting out-door pastime for talented "men of letters." The lanterns were necessary as the meetings were almost always nocturnal. The riddle clubs' meetings are still observable in Peking's side streets and quiet lanes during hot summer evenings. Very often they compose riddles by quotations from famous poems as the question, called *mien* (面) or "face," and using the sub-title in a Chinese story book, or a sentence from the classics, or a popular proverb, or the name of a famous play or an actor, as the answer, called *li* (裡) or "lining." They are very difficult for a beginner, and provide more fun and brain-twisting than a combination of the foreign conundrums mixed with the hardest of cross-word puzzles. Of late the tendency is to move the meetings indoors and make the entire year eligible for these games as against only the summer evenings, a practice of former generations.

*　　　*　　　*

Like all children, Chinese children find it great fun to listen to fairy tales. Strange as it may seem, the story of the Big Bad Wolf has its almost exact equivalent in Chinese folklore. There is also a story which may be named "Why the hinder part of the monkey is red," comparable to the foreign tale (from Grimm?) "Why the tail of the fox has a white tip." There has, however, been no Chinese Hans Christian Anderson that could be compared with that great genius. There is no Jack and the Beanstalk, or Little Snow White, or Cinderella, nor even a Momo Taro, the Japanese demon-subduer who jumped out from the old washerwoman's big peach, all of which and many others besides, translated, find in Chinese children an eager audience. The Chinese may boast of great literary achievements in a good many things but in so far as pure fairy tales are concerned, any attempt toward collecting a reasonable number of them should better be dropped as soon as possible in order that disillusionment and despair may be avoided. There are, in the modern libraries, I admit, volumes of stuff supposed to be fairy tales from the Chinese, mystic narrations from the seas of Old Cathay but, to me, as a native Peking-*jen* great enjoyment has been experienced in reading these fairy tales which seem to come from anywhere but China—they sound so strange! There are, of course, the parables which some of the ancient Chinese philosophers like Chuang Tze or Lieh Tze took a fancy in using to bring out the high lights of their treatises. They may come to be called "fables," being decidedly not appreciated by the infantile mind.

A popular children's tale, known to almost all Peking youngsters, is the story of the simpleton, the indispensable central character of a good many similar stories. Little Bald Head soon learned it by heart.

"Once upon a time there lived a simpleton and his wife. The simpleton was so true to his name that he was unable to make even the barest living for himself and his wife. As a result, in spite of his inherited riches, he soon became very poor. At last there was nothing left in his possession but five horses.

"One day his wife told him to try and see what he could do with the five horses. 'You must learn to do some business in order to save both of us from starvation,' said his wife. He agreed and led the five horses away.

"On the road he met a man with six sheep. He offered to barter his five horses for the six sheep, as he thought that after all six was one more than five. The exchange was soon made.

"Further on he met another man with seven rabbits. He thought that seven was more than six, so he asked the man if he would be willing to barter with him for the six sheep. Of course, he was not disappointed.

"Satisfied, he went further and met a man with a basket full of chickens. There must be some eight or ten of them, he calculated to himself. So at his own proposal, another exchange was made.

"Carrying the basket of chickens, he went forward. Rain was threatening, the clouds were gathering overhead. Being quite far from home, he did not know what to do. Suddenly he saw a man walking with a broken umbrella under his arm. He soon made an exchange of his basket of chickens for the umbrella.

"The rain was soon over. He was hungry. In a close-by restaurant, steamed meat puddings, hot and fresh, were just then ready. He went inside and filled up his stomach with the delicious meat puddings.

"When his meal was over, the waiter asked him for money of which, of course, he had none. The waiter became

angry and boxed his ear repeatedly.
A compromise was soon arranged by
passers-by by which the waiter accepted the broken umbrella in lieu of
cash 'for value received.'

"At the end of his first business
day the simpleton went home with
empty hands."

*   *   *

Little Bald Head, the darling of
every member of the Wu family, was
the "life of the party" in the house
for he, in every meaning of the word,
was a GOOD boy. Not only to his
parents and grandparents was he the
object of much affection but also to
all the neighbours and friends of the
Wu family. He was active but not
naughty, quiet and thoughtful but
never timid, a welcome little guest
wherever he went.

His mind was as well developed
as his body. He provided companionship for all the family, particularly for his grey-haired grandfather, old Mr. Wu, whom he constantly kept busy either with his
playthings or his clever conversation. The old man was devoted

Little Bald Head, at six, was a
welcome young guest everywhere he went. Thoughtful and
bright he had the makings of a
poet.

to him. He was soon a big boy and accompanied his grandfather on his daily walks and went visiting and sightseeing
sometimes. On Sundays when young Mr. Wu did not go to work
he almost monopolized Little Bald Head's activities in which he
found recreation and one of life's highest encouragements. But
like all ambitious fathers, young Mr. Wu wished to give his son
the best environment within his power and he was often found to
be hammering into the little brain things which in his opinion
would provide a foundation for the school days soon to come.

He told his son about table manners. That he should use his
chopsticks with only the right hand. He told him to always address a person properly, calling "Father", "Mother" "Grandfather", "Grandmother", etc., respectively when he wanted to
talk to anybody. His father also told him stories of famous Chinese children of ancient times who became big people. The story
of young Ssu Ma Kuang breaking a water jar with a stone in
order to save from drowning a playmate who had fallen in was
among the first tales told him. Little Bald Head thoroughly
absorbed such stories for he was now six years old. He was tall
and handsome and could easily pass for seven. Other stories he
was told included the one about the courteous Kung Jung.

"Long ago there was a boy whose name was Kung Jung. He
was barely four years old at the time of this anecdote. One day
he and his brothers were eating some pears. The pears were put
together on a tray. Little Kung was told to select one for himself
from the lot. Little Kung took the smallest one from the tray.

Asked why he did not take a big one, Kung said that since he was a small boy he should take a small pear."

On another occasion, young Mr. Wu told his son the story of the boy, Huang Hsiang. "Huang was nine years old," he related. "But he was a very good boy. He loved his father very much. During the summer time he used to fan the pillow and mats for his father in order to cool them during his sleep. In the winter time he would go into his father's bed before bedtime in order to warm the bedclothes for his parent."

Young Mr. Wu became so enthusiastic about his son that, if we could have analyzed his habits of thought, it would have been seen that young Mr. Wu was apparently pinning very high hopes on his son. For he told him also about Lo Pin Wang, the T'ang Dynasty poet.

"When Lo Pin Wang was seven years old," the story began, "he was watching some geese on a pond with his father. His father, a poet himself, asked the young boy to compose a poem on the geese, whereupon the youngster submitted a nice little poem without much time wasted. His famous Ode to the Geese was:

"Geese, Geese, Geese,
Bending your neck and singing with your head
    skyward;
Your white feathers brush on the green water,
Your red feet stir the blue waves".

"This was his *shih* (詩) or poem", said young Mr. Wu after repeating the verse from memory.

"Oh, but father, what is a *shih*," asked Little Bald Head.

"A *shih* is something like a song that is very nice to hear", explained young Mr. Wu.

"That is easy. This year I am six; next year I will be seven and will also write a *shih*".

"Oh, do not make me laugh, Little Bald Head!" his father exclaimed.

*   *   *

If the foundation of the national life of some countries may be said to be built on the word Liberty or Loyalty, a corresponding word for the four hundred million Chinese would no doubt be *Hsiao* (孝) or Filial Piety. It is the one single thread that strings together all the beads of virtues in this part of the world.

To Little Bald Head, like to all Chinese youngsters, this highest of all virtues was early taught. The first lesson is for a child to be obedient to his parents, to listen to the commands of father and mother and as these are also duty-bound and directly responsible to their own parents the natural corollary is that he is to listen to the words of his grandfather and grandmother too. If a child does not love his parents when young, it is said, he can never be expected to obey his teacher at school. He will not be submissive as a subordinate to his superiors, nor as a minister to the emperor, nor as a human being can he be expected to be reverent to Heaven and Earth, the greatest providers of mankind. There are five "honourable ones", Heaven, Earth, Emperor, Parents and Teacher, and a man's relationships to them all is founded on the theory of filial piety. For this is the Chinese social philosophy, the balancer of the universe. There is no substitute.

And as was usual, young Mr. Wu taught his son to be filial, "becoming or befitting a son or a daughter" as the dictionary says, for there is hardly a fully proper word with which to translate the Chinese word *hsiao*. After teaching his son to be a good boy by naming some historically famous boys of the past, he also in the same spirit bought for him the pictures of the Twenty-Four Cases of Filial Piety—the *erh shih ssu hsiao* (二十四孝). This is a household word to all Chinese, for what Chinese brought up in the orthodox fashion cannot name at least ten of the twenty-four anecdotes which are so famous?

By way of examples, there is the ancient Shun (another emperor-to-be) who loved his unreasonable and hard-to-please father so much that as he tilled the field with the help of a tame elephant, even the humble sparrows became so moved by his great virtue that instead of eating away the seeds he sowed, they actually volunteered to help cover up the seeds. Or the old Lao Lai Tze, a septuagenarian who, in order to arouse a smile from his even more aged parents, is said to have put on the flower-patterned clothes and manipulated a little drum with a long handle which only three-year-old children would show any desire for, rolling himself on the ground without the slightest thought as to the chances of getting his flower-patterned clothes all soiled and messed up.

Then there is also Wang Hsiang, whose mother liked fish so much. At one time winter was at its worst; the ice in the river was good and thick. The market being so far distant or he was so hard up that necessity, the mother of all inventions, inspired him to devise a clever and inexpensive way of lying bare-backed on the ice to melt it and a pair of big carps, so the story goes, jumped out from this man-made ice hole.

Another story is about a boy and his mother who apparently did not live after Benjamin Franklin discovered what was electricity and was therefore afraid of the thunder. The boy was observed to hurry to his mother's grave, after her death, every time there was a rainstorm to keep his dead mother company and to shed bitter tears.

Huang Hsiang, introduced before, has also been listed among the twenty-four "star" boys for he risked malaria by presenting his body as a browsing ground for clouds of mosquitoes in order that his father would not suffer from his old complaint of chronic insomnia.

Another boy, during a famine, was described as gathering wild mulberries to save his mother and himself from lack of material for metabolism. He even took the time, in complete disregard of his roaring stomach (we can imagine), to sort out the ripe ones for his mother, keeping the green ones for himself. And so forth and so forth.

Yes, Chinese boys are expected to do many things their foreign brethren either do not have to do or would not do at all.

For, exceptions allowed, all Chinese love their parents; there is no doubt about that. For does not a proverb say: "A filial man begets filial sons, and a disobedient man disobedient offspring"? This is a secure investment and the prospects of remuneration are sound, and Oriental justice at that. Tit for tat, in other words.

FAMOUS FLOWERS OF PEKING

COMING to think of it, Peking people are the most resourceful and painstaking people in the world in so far as eating problems and their associated "fine arts" are concerned. Peking people pay more attention to palatal satisfaction than perhaps Confucius did himself. Confucius, in his famous book "Lun Yu" (論語) or "The Analects", referred again and again to the question of eating, to which subject, indeed, a goodly portion of his chapter on living (I refer to that famous Section Ten, known as *Hsiang Tang* (鄉黨) or "Among Fellowtownsmen") was devoted. He emphatically said that he would object to eating anything unless the ginger had not been removed during the preparation of the various dishes. Nor would he eat anything that had not been cut geometrically straight. In other words, he would much rather cut out the fruit salad or dessert course if he could not get the machine-sliced and machine-holed "Dole" brand of Hawaiian pineapples for example. He would not drink anything from the retail wine merchant but insisted on the "bottled in bond" variety, nor would he eat the assorted cold meats from the corner sausage factory if he was not hopeless of getting some meat cooked in his home. He would shout at the headwaiter and make a scene if the latter brought him something that was not right in colour or was off in smell, or the seasoning of which was not exactly right, or was without the proper sauce (this is exactly the word he used) or if the chef had happened unfortunately to lose the knack of his art out of sheer joy at the sage's patronage. If you feel that I am misquoting the august master or deliberately misrepresenting our great sage, all you need do to get the facts straight is to look into the original book any time you have a chance.

Alas, as we look at Peking people from many an angle, we cannot help lamenting how the Confucian ways of life, as a whole, have been badly neglected. However, we must say that at least one thing has certainly been observed. He had said that "he would not eat anything except when it was in season". Peking people eat many things as a "seasonal touch", not knowing they are doing exactly as Confucius liked to do. Some of these foods are not eaten as a necessity but rather as a luxury. They are consumed as a "poetic gesture" as well as an indication that the existence and timely appearance of the things have not escaped notice. Such families like the Wu family—the "leisured class" —are privileged to enjoy these refinements handed down for generations and of this kind of "poetic atmosphere" Little Bald Head naturally had his due share.

The elm tree grows seeds before it grows leaves in late spring. These seeds are equipped with the flat green "wing" originally bestowed by Mother Nature as a convenience in the propagation of its kind. The seeds are known in Peking as *yu-ch'ien-erh* (榆錢兒), or "elm cash", for they are round in shape and about half an inch in diameter, of a beautiful jade green colour with the seed itself occupying a hermetically sealed center. They are gathered when tender, mixed with flour dough and baked into cakes, called "Elm-Cash-Cakes." The practice has become a regular vogue in Peking as baskets of the stuff at the vegetable markets during their annual appearance bears witness.

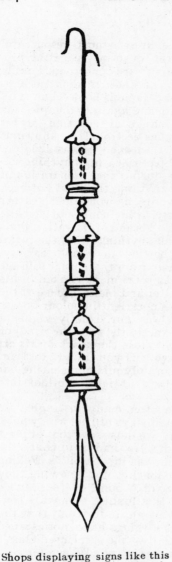

Shops displaying signs like this one offer delicious fresh wisteria or rose petal cakes in season.

The Wu family did not have to buy these seeds as there was a big elm tree right in their backyard which every year yielded literally barrels of such seeds. The Wus made the cakes at least once or twice a year and while they lasted consumed them with great enthusiasm, though, to be frank, they are as flat and tasteless as a tallow candle.

"When we eat the Elm Cash Cake, we must remember that the elm tree is a godsend to famine-stricken people, for its bark constitutes a substitute during periods of acute grain shortage", old Mr. Wu used to say. "We ought to be thankful we do not have to peel our trees, but we want to experience at least an inkling of such things. Every time I taste the Elm Cash Cakes, I get a better appetite for my next regular meal".

*   *   *

If I understand my English reasonably well when an American gentleman finds a statement untrue or unreliable or meaningless, he says it "should be taken with a pinch of salt". Not so the Chinese; they feel that if anything is as uninteresting as all that why should they extend it the great favour of swallowing it? But anything that is beautiful or fragrant has to be careful for the Chinese would soon devise a scheme to "edibilize" it and actually eat it.

We have noted how the winged seeds of the elms have come to be eaten by the Chinese and may draw our own conclusions that it is but the development from something of a famine-time makeshift. But such a rule will not always apply. For two of the early summer delights of Peking gourmets are cakes prepared with the petals of the wistaria flower and the fragrant rose.

On Peking's main streets there are any number of old-fashioned pastry shops, the kind which display the sign of a string of gilt-lacquered wooden plaques each bearing a fancy name for their masterpieces. And in early summer they put up a special sign-board, announcing the annual debut of cakes with the core of honey mixed with fresh petals of wistaria or with fresh rose flowers. They do not cost outrageously high and the "cultured" old Peking-*jen* would be reminded by the sign to come in and get a couple of dozens of each kind while they are in season.

The wistarias, before they are in full bloom, are gathered in clusters and the petals removed. Once they are in full bloom the flavour would be no more. The other parts, such as the stamens, the pistils and the calixes are discarded. Then these petals are mixed with honey and sugar. The mixture is used as the core for little round cakes some three inches in diameter and baked to retail at about three cents each.

The rose petal cakes are prepared in the same manner, except that while the wistaria kind are sold only about two weeks in every year during the flowering season, the rose kind is procurable all the year round, the rose petals being preserved in a syrup besides being available from bushes from the middle of May to perhaps the middle of June. To be fair to these cakes they do taste very nice and are certainly not to be missed.

Peking families, including the Wu family, have their own recipes for these delicacies. For besides getting those from the shops, they also cooked their own. They used the same petals and the same sugar but added to the mixture little cubes of fresh lard and prepared the cakes in their own kitchen. The wistaria flowers not being found in their own garden, they always appreciated them as a gift from a neighbour who never failed to remember distributing clusters of the flowers every year for he had a big tree whose intertwining branches covered a big framework shading two-thirds of his courtyard. As to roses, they bought them easily from street vendors at so much per fifty or a hundred flowers. This type of flower pedlars are a distinct group from the florists and the roses are kept in a basket refrigerated by chunks of ice.

Speaking of wistarias and roses as items of delicacy, how much satisfaction and also economic value are being lost each year, from the Chinese gourmet's point of view, as millions admire the beauty and fragrance of these blossoms everywhere in the world, and nobody ever thinks of converting them into a cooking ingredient except the comparatively few Peking Chinese. What a waste of raw material!

*　　　*　　　*

Flower-viewing in spring is one of the few popular pleasures of Peking's aesthetics. Barring a few cases, the majority of the opportunities are so easily accessible to all people, rich and poor alike, that it is one of the main inexpensive attractions of the capital. To neglect the call on Peking flowers is one of the gravest injustices a person can do to Peking for which there is no excuse. To have no time would make the flimsiest alibi because the season is not a short one but extends for weeks, starting from late February until the end of May when, to quote a T'ang Dynasty poet, "The blossoming of the climbing rose puts the finale on the flower season". Nor is it good to say that since the flowers to be seen are more or less common varieties there is no meaning in going every year, for you are not expected to discover some new specimens of plant life nor to check yourself on the identification of each kind and try to give its Latin scientific name as if you were writing a thesis for a degree in botany.

All you need do to be a typical *Lao Pei Ching* (老北京) or "Old Peking" is to go where you are supposed to go, as tradition dictates, and admire the flowers, the kind for which the place in question is famous either doing so outspokenly or by silent approval. Sit down and try to think up some old lines of Chinese poetry that would be tolerably appropriate to the occasion, or better still write a piece or two yourself. Do not use a fountain pen or bond paper. Ask the host (usually the abbot of some Temple) for some old Chinese *hsuan* (宣) paper and a brush pen, and freshly ground Chinese ink on a Sung Dynasty inkstone. Or else, organize a tea or wine party and hold it at the foot of the famous blossoms or, failing everything else, linger at least thirty minutes or so at the place, trying to look poetical, appreciative and tuned up sharp for some immeasurable pleasure and communicate with nature (whatever that means). In reality, however, between you and me, all this is unnecessary. All you have to do is to see the flowers, for it is flower-viewing that you are doing, like the Japanese *hanami*.

Old Mr. Wu, during his younger days, used to go with his schoolmates every year to such famed places as the Black Dragon Pool near the Warm Springs some sixty *li* or twenty miles away in the heart of the Western Hills to see the apricot trees in bloom. They, Wu and his friends, used to go out there on donkeys, and sat among the full blossoming trees and enjoyed something stronger than water and actually composed some poems. But his zeal had abated as his age advanced though the happy memory was still dear to his old heart.

But there were places within easy reach of the Wu family, such as the Summer Palace, half way between their home and the Ho estate, young Mrs. Wu's maternal home, where people had by then begun to be allowed access to the famous gardens to see the magnificent magnolia in bloom. Another place to go was Fa Yuan Ssu, or the Temple of the Origin of Doctrine, where people went to see the famous white cloves. There are so many trees of this kind in the temple courtyards that the grandiloquent name of "Fragrant Sea of Snow" has been given to them by a certain aristocratic patron of the temple.

Another place to go to would be the Ch'ung Chiao Ssu, or the Temple of the Consecrated Teaching, another mossy, time-worn and weather-beaten old monastery—the rendezvous of the group of scholars who self-proclaimedly represent Peking's intelligentsia during the week or ten days when the temple's famous tree peonies are in bloom.

Then there are other places where Peking people go to see the lotus flowers, or the red maple leaves, or the blossoms of the rush while these are in season. All these add to the colour of Peking life. The proper thing, as I said, is to go. If you do not get any specially pleasant experience or inspiration you at least get the satisfaction that you have given such and such a famous flower your personal inspection.

*   *   *

Following the example set by the so-called cultured class of Peking people, old Mr. Wu decided to make another visit to the Temple of Consecrated Teaching, Ch'ung Chiao Ssu, famous for the tree peonies its monks have been raising as a hobby for many years. It was early in May and the flowers were in full bloom. He decided to take Little Bald Head along.

There is no doubt that the Ch'ung Chiao Ssu is an old temple though it does not look its age for unlike most old temples in Peking it has been kept in reasonable repair. Its lengthy history is vouched for by an old stone monument in the front yard the writing on which has been almost obliterated by the elements and is beyond legibility. The stone was erected, as the inscription purports to tell, in commemoration of some repair work carried out in the certain year of Chia Ching (嘉靖), during the Ming Dynasty. (This should not be confused with Chia Ch'ing (嘉慶), a Ch'ing emperor.) The reign of Emperor Chia Ching began in the year 1522 A.D., thirty years after Columbus discovered America. Exactly how long the temple had stood before this repair work was done is unknown. But to prove that the temple is an old one, the above mentioned facts should suffice.

To get to the temple, which is roughly speaking close to the southwestern corner inside the walls of the Outer or Chinese City of Peking, the flower-viewers turn to the south from Kwang An Men Street and go along Cow Street on which is a famous Mosque, indicating an Islam colony in the neighbourhood. At the end of Cow Street there are open fields. Still continuing a due south course, the Temple is reached by the visitors at the rear.

The peonies are planted almost all over the premises, and each group is marked with little wooden tags bearing its respective fancy name such as Golden Dragon, Lotus Dress, Pink Ice Pond, etc., but the star specimens are in some side yards behind the main temple halls. There are the green ones and the so-called black ones. While the former is quite correctly named as the petals are decidedly a pretty green, the latter is a misnomer, for the colour is a dark purple. In order to keep the flowers as much as possible from fading quickly, the monks have put up mat sheds to combat nature so that late visitors will not be disappointed. Some of the peonies are said to be over two hundred years old but they are still going strong and they have a pedigree which the temple people will trace for the benefit of interested visitors. When at their best the flowers measure seven or even eight inches in diameter. The trees seem rather dwarfed in comparison being only three feet or so in height.

The temple is also famous as possessing a treasured heirloom in the form of an ancient picture of an old monk standing against a venerable pine tree and looking at a blossoming apricot tree at the side of a brook. This picture is said to be by an old monk and a former abbot of the temple in the beginning of the Ch'ing Dynasty. The picture became such a well known art object that all famous visitors, such as artists, scholars and others, have been in the habit of asking to see the picture. After inspecting it, they would ask for pen and ink and write lines of poems on the picture to express their inspired sentiments in commemoration of the occasion. The fashion thus started was followed by all scholars. The picture not being large the monks have been adding to it as time went on, making it an endless scroll in order to accommodate Peking's thousands of poetic geniuses. In three hundred years, the scroll is said to have reached the fabulous length of over three hundred feet!

Anybody who wishes to autograph this picture, so to speak, may do so if he will kindly pay a little incense money and anybody who wishes to use the temple's guest rooms for a party may also do so against a donation. Visitors may be guided about the premises and obtain some tea to quench their thirst. Contributions of money constitute a meritous act and one which is certainly appreciated in the name of Buddha. For, other things excepted, do not the monks need the money to take care of the flowers for the public?

*   *   *

There are two classes of peonies, namely, the common peony and the tree peony. They are both perennials but, scientifically speaking, the former is a "herb" while the latter is a "shrub." In other words, the former has a green or grassy stem and the latter a woody stem. There are other ways of distinguishing the two varieties but to laymen the above-mentioned characteristics are the most conspicuous. It is the latter kind that thousands of Peking-*jen* flock to the Ch'ung Chiao Ssu to see, although Peking is famous for both varieties.

The Chinese have a good many ways to symbolize character types by certain plants and they do sometimes also "say it with flowers". There has so far not been noticed a Chinese set of flower "codes". For instance, the tree peony has been called the "King of all Flowers", with the sub-title of "Empire's Colour and Heaven's Fragrance" superimposed. It is the *fu kwei hua* (富貴花), or the Flower of Wealth and High Rank. The lotus or water lily has been likened to the "superior man", also as the Chinese orchid is likened to the "kingly way", and so forth.

But the common peony, called in Chinese *shao yao* (芍藥)— the Chinese name for tree peony is *mu t'an* (牡丹)—though of an almost equally lovely appearance and quite comparable in colours, is decidedly much less esteemed than its cousin the tree variety. Being popularly priced to suit everybody's purse, the common peony has been democratized. Flowering branches each with a ready-to-bloom bud are tied most unceremonially together into bundles and offered for sale—a commodity of the mass production category, so to speak. For ten cents you get a bunch comprising eight or ten magnificent flowers.

The most popular place in Peking and which is easily accessible to all residents to see peonies is the famous Central Park where they make their annual debut with great numerical strength. But people usually do not care to humble themselves for such a visit. Street pedlars carry the peonies from house to house in much the same way as they do the ordinary kitchen vegetables. When the flowers are in season it is an interesting experience to hear hawkers crying their unique wares from one lane to another. The flowers sold are raised in the village of Fengtai not far to the southwest of Peking in virtual plantations and are cut and distributed wholesale at the vegetable mart, strange to say.

Living up to the name of a typical Peking family, the Wus put the seasonal touch into their home by getting these inexpensive and yet highly aesthetic additional decorations. Old Mrs. Wu bought plenty of the flowers to fill each one of the vases in the various rooms, just as she did regularly with the other cut flowers beginning with the branches of mountain peaches in early spring. For such are the environs in which children in typical Chinese families of the well-to-do class are brought up. Of these Little Bald Head is an example.

The market price of the common peonies is a joke. The florists' guild in Peking, if they are wise and alert and economically well advised, ought to call a meeting of all peony growers and pass a legislation to limit the growing of the flowers and thereby enhance the market value of their product. The flowers are well worth a better price than what they have been in the habit of getting. The trouble is, though, that the florists are most probably not ready for the suggestion. It is no use to tell them that mountains of good coffee are being burnt in Brazil for a similar purpose.

Farm-boys occupy their free spring days with selling tadpoles and little fish in the city.

*　　　*　　　*

One springtime novelty which Peking children like Little Bald Head take a matter-of-course delight in is a kind of little creature, known in Chinese as *ha ma ku to-erh* (哈媽骨朵兒) "buds of frogs", or in plain English, tadpoles.

The little farm boys who find themselves, or are found by their family, to be idling away their existence during the early spring days usually make it the side line of a lucrative pursuance to peddle these little live objects through the winding byways of Peking, crying aloud their wares with a typical chanting tune which heralds the advent of warm spring days. Such a premature businessman is usually the proud possessor of a wooden tub some two feet or so in diameter carried from the end of a long stick over his young shoulder and balanced on the other end by a basket or something else. A little home-made holed spoon is the only other item of equipment. The proud little fellow feeling the first touch of the wheel of commercial life and with the prospect of good profits ahead though necessarily in small proportions is the autocratic managing director of his establishment which is sponsored, perhaps, by a single trustee, his father or older brother. He manages his business in a way to suit his own whims, charging anything he likes as to price,—more tadpoles to one customer for a copper and less to another at the same price. His eyes dance with glee as every prospective buyer calls him to halt and purchases from him a copper or two coppers' worth of the merchandise which he gets for the catching from a brook or a pond near his father's farm where the water is thick with them. His business is run on a most profitable basis and contains besides a goodly measure of pleasure for himself, for what boy does not enjoy spending his time out of doors on a warm spring day at the riverside face to face with Mother Nature?

Nor are the tadpoles the only wares he has to offer. For he carries also in a separate partition of his little tub the small newly hatched fish, something between a little less and a little more than an inch in length, known by their ridiculously disproportionately large eyes as *ta yen tse-erh* (大眼賊兒) or the "big eyed thieves"! In spite of their thievish big eyes, however, they are a lot of "poor fish", for they apparently over-confided in their big eyes and are obliged to pay highly for their one mistake in life! During his search for the stock-in-trade, the little business-man also keeps his eyes open for a kind of fresh-water univalve known as *tien lo ssu* (田螺絲), or "field shellfish." If he can get hold of these he is in luck for they command a high price in the urban market.

The tadpoles are not bought for amusement only. They are sup-posed to possess certain elements of medicinal value and to be a good remedy or preventive for excessive "heat" in the human sys-tem and at least half of the purchasers use them for this purpose after getting their due share of pleasure watching the wriggling objects in a basin or a glass jar. The directions for medicinal use are simple: Get a copper's worth of tadpoles and swallow them alive, water and all! The majority of the "addicts" do not even trouble to replace the water, which, it is easily understood, must be direct from the country brook or from the moats outside Peking's walls.

The field shellfish are also said to be good for children if pounded to a pulp and eaten in the proper manner. Whether city-dwellers discovered these virtues first and then exploited the country boys to work out their scheme afterwards, or whether the innocent-looking farm boys started the ball rolling by pulling a dirty one on their city cousins in creating a demand for their wares by direct propaganda, nobody can tell. But the fact remains that one way or the other, the poor tadpoles are the only victims to any appreciable extent!

Little Bald Head was made the proud owner of a pot of these tadpoles and was hopeful of seeing them converted into little frogs, dropping their tails, as his grandfather explained, at the first peal of thunder in the year. In a few days he actually noticed their little hind legs in the offing. Thinking what an interesting addition they would be if he put them in the family goldfish aquarium, he did so without asking for advice from anybody who ought to have known better.

The next morning he went to see how much his tadpoles had grown. He found that they had disappeared. They had made agreeable goldfish food.

THREE PICTURESQUE TEMPLES

THE Tung Yueh Miao or the Temple of the Sacred Eastern Mountain is one of the chief monasteries in Peking and is frequented by devout worshippers in vast numbers. It is situated in the eastern gate of Ch'ao Yang Men, the Gate of the Morning Sun. This temple is open to receive incense burning pilgrims on the first and fifteenth of each lunar calendar moon. But throughout the latter half of the third moon, its precincts are thrown open to all pilgrims, particularly as some special rites sponsored by various temple societies (a distinct variation from the Miao Feng Shan type) are performed on certain days during this fortnight.

The Tung Yueh Miao stands unique among the dozens of temples in Peking, as it is a temple dedicated to a mixture of Buddhist and Taoist faith though technically it is a Taoist institution. The two faiths are thoroughly amalgamated here and it is just the place where a general idea of the Polytheistic aspect of the Chinese religious mind may be obtained. Strange as it may seem, there are no special ceremonial halls dedicated to such purely Buddhist deities as the Goddess of Mercy or Cakyamuni or even that popular symbolism of optimism, the Laughing Buddha himself. The principal shrine is that of the God of the Sacred Eastern Mountain, whose permanent headquarters, so to speak, is found at the top of the famous T'ai Shan in the district of T'ai-an in the province of Shantung.

But, on the other hand, there may be found a god for almost every purpose, a deity for every aspect of human life and activity. There are the God of War, the God of Literature, the God of Medicine, the God of Wealth, the God of Handicraft and the God of Marriage (otherwise known as the Old Man Under the Moon). Some deities are personified as feminine, the Goddess of Sons and Grandsons, the Goddess of Sight, etc. In these goddesses old Mrs. Wu had unshakeable belief.

And these are not all. All round the main courtyard in the temple and lined up on the four sides are seen the shrines of seventy-two (some say seventy-six) departmentalized branches of the administration of the next world, each a full-sized shrine with full-sized images of the various gods in charge. They, as a system, represent the zenith of the Chinese capacity for religious or mythological imagination. By these various gods the machinery of "heavenly retribution", rewarding the good and punishing the evil, and sundry other ramifications of religio-governmental functions are visualized. Departments and divisions are found here, each of the various bureaux being represented by separate groups of images graphically demonstrating the dispensing of justice under the directorship of a godly image occupying the central position in the respective rooms, or offices, flanked by his coterie or clerical staff, as it were. Signboards and explanations, reminding surprisingly of the working regulations of a regular government office, displayed for the benefit of the governed, give the worshippers an idea of what is supposed to be going on in each department. The images are masterpieces of the image-craft and each department head has characteristics and facial expression all his own. Some bear such a kindly and joyous expression that you could get a fine Santa Claus by throwing a red robe with a fur collar over his shoulders, others would "scare stiff" any enraged elephant or the fiercest man-eating crocodile from the darkest African jungle.

Pilgrims like old Mrs. Wu are seen during the open days doing obeisance at all the main halls and burning incense before the images. The biggest crowds are naturally seen at the door of the God of Wealth and also before the Old Man Under the Moon, but a straggling few, fearing that respect should be shown to all divinities alike and not daring to risk displeasing an inadvertently left out dignitary, have a habit of lighting big bundles of incense sticks and inserting a uniform three sticks in the incense burner before each of the seventy odd bureaux in the courtyard. This practice is known as *san ssu* (散司), "interdepartmental distributions".

Such is the religious psychology of the Chinese people. There has been no questioning by the believers; the system has apparently been acceptable.

*   *   *

Organizations to glorify or assist in the religious activities at the Tung Yueh Miao are many and each of them has its peculiar division of work. Representative of these are the *Tan Ch'en Hui* (撣塵會), or "Society for Dusting the Images," the *Fang Sheng Hui* (放生會), or "Life Liberation Society," and, perhaps, the *Tze Chih Hui* (字紙會), or "Society for the Reverence of Paper Bearing Chinese Characters." Each of these societies has its particular "convention" day during the latter part of the Chinese third moon when the entire temple is thrown open to the religion-wise frequenters.

The Dusting Society is a group of volunteer workers who carry out the spring cleaning in the holy premises. They donate dust pans, brooms, feather dusters, in short, all the equipment needed for carrying out the campaign of the once-every-year cleaning of the various temple halls. Of course there are professional temple janitors part of whose job it is to tidy up the hall or halls in their charge, sweeping up the debris of paper wrappings of incense sticks, etc., and keeping the incense burners from looking littered after every pilgrim rush.

The fact is that there are far too many shrines in this pantheon of images of assorted sizes and variegated shapes and it is well-nigh impossible to keep the place reasonably free from dust. Besides, most of the smaller halls are not even screened, and the famous Peking dust is freely admitted, particularly during dust-storms. The amateur house-cleaning squads therefore fill a crying need.

The *Fang Sheng Hui* has its specialty in the encouragement and sponsoring of the sparing of animal life as a meritorious religious function. Centering on the Buddhist idea of reincarnation of souls, they advocate, nay, they promote the practice of releasing captured birds, fish, etc., who are considered companions of human beings created by the Almighty to be free and equal. Bringing the theory a step further, we are told that by setting free and thereby saving from peril such animals we might unknowingly spare from the cruelty of death a former friend or even a relative who has been transformed into a bird or a beast by the invisible but invincible wheel of transmigration.

At the Tung Yueh Miao beadtelling devotees may be seen buying from bird sellers (whose trade, it may be inferred, the belief has actually created) cages and cages of sparrows, sometimes hundreds of them, and even magpies and crows and after paying the price, opening up the cages. They watch with immense satisfaction the feathered beneficiaries dashing for liberty and the patrons slowly chant a Buddhist prayer that they may be spared from being caught again by the tricky bird catchers!

Paid labourers carry large yellow bags and collect scraps of character-bearing paper from the streets.

The Society for the Reverence of Paper Bearing Chinese Characters seems also to require a little explanation. Though at least one Chinese diplomatic genius of modern times has been quoted as having declared to the world at large before an important international gathering that China has "abolished" (sic) illiteracy, a goodly proportion of the four hundred million still cannot read or write. In China, more than anywhere else, knowledge is power—and a knowledge of reading and writing is double power. Hence, even scraps of paper bearing Chinese ideographs are considered to be objects of reverence be they a torn up draft copy of an important document or a printed wrapper for the basest kind of merchandise. To demonstrate such reverence is a gesture of respect to the God of Literature who will shower blessings on such people as a reward, perhaps arranging the possibility of permitting the family of the devotee in question to carry on as a "reading" family or making a "reading" family of a "non-reading" family, and so forth. Paid labourers in the society's employ may be seen from time to time on the streets carrying a big bag made of yellow cloth, bearing their dogmatic motto in Chinese characters, picking up scraps of character-bearing paper and when a sufficient quantity has been gathered, burning them in a bonfire—the most honourable manner of destroying anything. It is for the purpose of propagating this doctrine that the organization in question came into existence.

*   *   *

All these religious side lights, merits or demerits, have their corresponding bearing on the cultivation of a child's character and upon the upbringing of Chinese children like Little Bald Head of the Wu family.

*   *   *

One of the Taoist dogmatic principles is the sparing of animal life in so far as it is within human power to do so. This is why Taoists are supposed to be the most ardent advocates of vegetarianism, although not a few Taoist priests have found the temptation of palatal enjoyment of meaty fares far too strong to resist. Taoists are theoretically such sparers of life that an example of conventionalized "couplet" proverbs decorating their temple pillars reads: "When sweeping the ground, we see to it that we do not destroy ants; in order to spare moths from burning themselves, we put a screen around our candle lights". And in order to popularize the theory of "Live and let live", cautions have been advanced that all such sparing of life, like all other deeds of merit or demerit, are clearly and eagerly observed by the almighty supervisors in heaven.

It is a Taoist belief that the gods are so watchful of everything happening on earth, no matter how minute the matter may be, that a complete regiment of combination detectives and book-keepers are constantly on the alert, recording every human activity in an endless number of day books and posting each item later in the ledgers. Their X-ray eyes are all-penetrating and omnipresent and it is useless for human beings to expect to do anything without it being noticed and registered and harder still to get away with it. The debits and credits are so clearly registered in the books that after death each person will be required to answer every charge during the judgment and make good faults by suffering tortures in the various departments of hell or by other fitting penalties in a future life.

Actions that please the gods are, of course, also justly recorded, permitting the persons concerned as a result to enjoy a fuller life or better circumstances and opportunities in their next incarnation. Though we do not know what is the unit of accounting used, or more graphically what mediums or currencies are used in the world above our heads, we are told that the entries in the two bookkeeping columns cancel each other exactly in the same manner as in a bank statement. It is the symbolization of this theory that monstrous-sized wooden abacuses some five or six feet wide are hung on the walls of the famous Tung Yueh Miao to warn the ever-erring people.

Moreover, it is believed that retributions do not have to wait for another incarnation and stories are told that even the humble insects have a way of repaying any protection given them in this world.

A Chinese scholar, resting after a diligent research into the classics, a story goes, was watching a group of ants marooned in a gathering pool of rain water outside his studio. He picked up a piece of bamboo and made a bridge with it for the ants to crawl to safety. The event was soon forgotten. Many years afterward he was attending the imperial examinations in Peking and was writing an essay as part of the literary competition. As you probably already know, Chinese characters are made up of strokes and dots, much like the dots on the i's and j's in English. The leaving out of a dot on a Chinese character requiring it would constitute a blunder of such great significance during an imperial examination that it renders an otherwise promising piece of composition absolutely unacceptable for imperial perusal and therefore makes it a laughing-stock for all scholars in the land besides disqualifying it in spite of all the possible merits of the entry. As the scholar busied himself with his work, he noticed a small black ant persistently distracting his attention from his work. He took the ant off the examination paper but it came back again and again and deliberately stopped at a certain spot on his sheet of writing every time.

His attention was soon drawn to the spot and exactly there he found he had left out a dot. He added the dot and saved his essay from being barred and thus won a degree at the examination.

Nor are Chinese the only people given to this formula of thought, for we find a counterpart in Japanese folklore in the story of Urajima Taro and the Turtle. Urajima saved a turtle from torture at the hands of a group of mischievous children and released it into the sea; later he was welcomed at the palace of the Dragon Princess who gave him royal entertainment and bounteous gifts.

Stories like the above were told to Little Bald Head as he became big enough to appreciate the points or the morals in them. And he grew to be as tender-hearted and kindly to all animal life as could be expected.

*   *   *

As if to serve as extensions to the Tung Yueh Miao, there are further to the east on the same main road the Temple of the Ninth Heaven and the Temple of the Eighteen Hells. These have their open seasons simultaneously with their neighbour institution though few people are seen at these two lesser temples, especially as the Temple of the Ninth Heaven is in a most pitiful state of disrepair.

The Temple of the Ninth Heaven has several big halls the last one of which, the innermost one, houses a magnificent piece of art work, a sort of "mural imagecraft", depicting scenes from the Buddhist Heavens. Figures are seen all along the walls against a background supposed to represent clusters of clouds. But this splendid panorama of paradise is to be seen no more as human neglect and other major forces have jointly wrought destruction, rendered all the more devastating, it may be imagined, by the foul play of the poverty-stricken priests themselves if not by the equally poverty-stricken neighbours who most probably had their respective parts in making such a thorough-going job of it.

But there were still to be seen, at least until a few years ago, the statues of the God of Thunder and the Goddess of Lightning, standing intact near the temple entrance. If these statues could talk, they would have much to say about the temple's destruction, having been the eye-witnesses of each stage of the temple's history.

The God of Thunder is a peculiar type of an image and stands alone as a characteristic kind of presentation for it is very grotesquely conceived, having been given a face black as tar and a most demoralizing pair of eyes perched above a regular beak, like that of an eagle's, serving as mouth besides having been given a pair of wings like those of a bat. The Chinese certainly paint their devil as black as he is said to be and surprisingly enough, he does take on an appearance much like the foreign conceived devil and is equally air-minded as his foreign distant cousin though differently positioned.

In the way of equipment the God of Thunder is represented as holding a sort of a heavyweight chisel in his left hand and in his right hand a big hammer, ready to strike forcefully on the chisel. When he strikes the chisel with his hammer, like a carpenter does, he produces peals of thunder.

The Goddess of Lightning, on the other hand, is a very

pretty young lady, wearing an agreeable ensemble of pink blouse and a long, sweeping skirt of a beautiful shade of aquamarine. In each of her hands she holds a mirror by a loop behind it. The mirrors are of a round kind like those the professor of archaeology has in his private collection of bronzes. The goddess, it is said, when on duty focuses and "de-focuses" these two shiny mirrors and produces what we see as flashes of lightning.

Chinese children from generation to generation have learned from their mothers' lips that thunder and lightning are weapons of the gods with which they mete out severe punishment to evil people on earth. The thunder strikes dead sinners, unfilial sons and unfaithful wives as well as "those children who disobey their parents' commands," while the lightning is directed to shine into dark nooks and corners where sinners take refuge when chased by the peals of thunder. While there is but one kind of thunder there are two kinds of lightning, the red and the white. The red lightning reveals the hiding places of animals that have taken on a human appearance and the white one specializes in human sinners. They work together and make an effective team of dreadful destroying power.

*　　　　*　　　　*

The above explanations were given by old Mrs. Wu when her grandson, Little Bald Head, questioned her during a rainstorm as to what were thunder and lightning.

"The thunder and the lightning are in charge of the God of Thunder, Lei Kung Yeh (雷公爺), and the Goddess of Lightning, Shan Kwang Niang Niang (閃公娘娘) respectively," said the grandmother.

"When you are older", she promised, "I will take you to the Temple of the Ninth Heaven where you will see the images of these two deities."

*　　　　*　　　　*

The Temple of the Eighteen Hells is the name by which a small temple to the east of Tung Yueh Miao is known to the natives of Peking. It is a distinctive example of how Buddhist doctrines have been paraphrased and "made easy" for the uninitiated people. The Buddhist scholars of the more orthodox sect look at it with polite contempt and certainly share the feeling with all enlightened monks. The idea apparently aims at "working from the bottom", catering to the "patronage" of the simpleminded for whom seeing is believing.

For in this temple is shown the aftermath of a human life. Here may be seen a replica of the place where a soul registers upon his arrival at the administrative *yamen* of the next world and the clearing house attached to purgatory where he is shown the balance sheet of his actions during his life. The clever craftsmen have made all images very life-like, showing the dead searching anxiously among the entries for points on which to start an argument or staring with mouth wide open at the red and black figures in the statement of accounts.

Going into the second courtyard, the visitor finds himself literally in a forest of all varieties of tortures conceivable by the human mind and which are practised in the cells of inferno. The various departments in hell are here introduced to the believing or skeptical public.

There is the place where the department head supervises the pulling out of tongues of people whose habits of speech did not please the gods. Next is the place where eyes are hooked out for one reason or another. The place of the Mountain of Knives, the place of the Caldron of Boiling Oil, the place where sinners are made to lie on an iron bed heated red-hot, the place where a human being is inserted between wooden boards and cut into two by a couple of little devils operating an enormous hacksaw, the milling department where sinners are ground to powder or paste or whatever shape they assume after the process. The most pathetic touch is added by the likenesses of dogs licking the blood dripping from bodies being "operated upon" or partitioned.

There is a complete array of these exhibitions and each is explained to the public by a signboard, setting forth the clauses from the Criminal Code of the Underworld with their due penalties as demonstrated by the mud images.

In the Buddhist way of things sinners pay for their follies in this world by various kinds of tortures in the Eighteen Hells, the Oriental counterpart of the Christian purgatory. Some may have to go through several or all the processes according to their records.

Each process is keenly and vividly experienced as the omnipotent force of the creation restores to its original shape what is left from a preceding process, be it a human paste, a human pulp or powder, a limbless torso, or whatever other shape or form it may have been left in.

After having answered all the requirements of the verdict, they are to be reborn as an insect, a bird, a beast, or again a human—a beggar, a pauper, a scholar, a minister, an executive, a generalissimo, or a king. The last category is for people who have glorified themselves by kind deeds in a previous existence. The beasts-to-be are seen in one of the temple departments where skins of various animals are forcefully applied to the protesting criminals. Those who are to be born as humans again will drink a bowl of so-called *mi hung t'ang* (迷魂湯), sense bewildering soup, dispensed by a kindly old lady, known as *Wang Ma Ma* (王媽媽) or Old Mother Wang, so that they will forget everything of the past and not reveal it to the public during their next tenure of reincarnated life.

The Temple of Hells has a great bearing on a child's life, too, for parents are seen here who semi-seriously and semi-humorously explain to the children they have brought along the scenes of tortures and drive home some points of domestic education which they have so far failed to make the child remember by other means.

As a matter of fact since Little Bald Head almost never had to be penalized by his parents for anything serious, there was actually no need for such measures of chastisement for him.

AMUSEMENTS IN SEASON

FAMILY life in Peking is a colourful affair and as such is punctuated at intervals with seasonal touches. These seasonal touches are special fares for the family table, special articles of clothing, special religious observances and devotional exercises. On top of it all, children get special playthings "in season". Some particular items of these will be described.

The season is early summer. To give a general idea of the climatic conditions we can quote a T'ang Dynasty poet, whose poem, "Waking up from an Early Summer Siesta," reads:

"The green plums are sour with their acid juice
    penetrating my teeth;
And the banana plants share their fresh verdure with
    the new gauze on my windows.
As I wake from my lenghty day's nap with an idle
    mind unoccupied by any thoughts,
I watch leisurely the children in the courtyard, try-
    ing to catch the drifting downs of the willows."

It is when everybody feels the same as the poet felt when he wrote these lines that we are suddenly re-acquainted with the sound of the horn announcing that the weed-horn man has arrived at the door.

The weeds, or more exactly the river rushes, are a perennial grass the stems and leaves of which are harvested by the thrifty peasants to be used in a good many ways. In winter time where acres and acres of marshlands with rushes are seen in summer, only barren stretches of bare ground are visible. When spring comes, however, the new shoots of the rushes, like those of the bamboos, pierce the hardened and later moistened surface of the earth in tender spindles. (These rush spindles are a famous delicacy of Peking gourmets, eaten in somewhat the same manner as the foreign asparagus).

When the weather gets warmer, yesterday's spindles become today's young rushes. The resourceful and enterprising rural toy-men gather the young green leaves which are about an inch in width and eight or ten inches long and by clever folding and winding fashion them into horns. They carry the raw material in a basket and the horns are made while the customer waits. It takes about four or five leaves to make one horn and each horn costs about two big coppers. To prevent the leaves from unwinding and the horn from collapsing, the end of the last leaf is pinned secure with a thorn; these thorns are collected from the sour date shrubs growing wild in the country. To add a final *de luxe* effect a tiny triangular flag of paper on a little piece of bamboo is thrown in as added attraction.

The horn-man announces his arrival as he moves along on his itinerant sales campaign by blowing a horn of similar specifications of manufacture as those he sells, but either by chance discovery or by laboratory-tested researches, he finds a way not only to amplify the volume or capacity of his own horn but also to improve the tone-quality to a certain degree by inserting the horn into the mouth of a sand flask, usually made to hold wine, whose bottom has been knocked out. Then demonstrating his latent musical talent, he actually puts a few notes into the otherwise monotonous music by putting the palm of his hand against the opening of the home-made megaphone and alternately closing and opening the tone-chamber as he blows. The result is an adorable piece of advertising for whose gogetting efficiency the world has no equal. It is indeed interesting to notice children who have bought horns being watched by the almost sinister horn-man as they try and invariably fail to imitate the original philharmonic instrument of magic charm and its entrancing notes.

*   *   *

Little Bald Head was never refused or neglected a chance to get a plaything particularly such ones priced as popularly as the horns. He was made the possessor of a magnificent specimen with which he had the jolliest time, blowing it to his heart's content.

He did exactly as Benjamin Franklin did with his whistle; "he went blowing all over the house much pleased with his horn but disturbing all the family." But, there was one thing certain and that was he "certainly did NOT pay too much for his horn."

Being flimsily made, the horns seldom last longer than the patience of any family, Nevertheless, considering the enjoyment children get from them they are worth the price.

*   *   *

Little Bald Head never ran short of toys or playthings to keep his interest alive, in contrast to the average Chinese child. Being the "dearest" in the house, he was constantly given favours not only by the members of the Wu family but also by the Ho family —the maternal family of young Mrs. Wu, as represented by Madame Ho herself who loved him particularly. This is a common phenomenon in China as witnessed by the local expression calling a daughter's child the jo-shang-jo (骨上肉) or "flesh of a piece of flesh".

Another toy source was the child's "parents-in-faith," Mr. and Mrs. Chao. Then there were the itinerant toy-sellers who paraded the streets on regular circuits with various "new numbers."

No sooner had he gotten his money's worth of fun from the weed horn then there struck onto his eardrums the loud call of "See how fat my mules and how warm my carriages are". From this announcement the Peking-jen will know from experience that the beetle-cart man has come.

The little replicas of carts are made from bits of bright-coloured paper pasted onto a framework made from lengths of the core of kaoliang stalks, joined together with pins shaped from bits of bamboo. The hoods and superstructures of paper are supported by little strips of skin from the kaoliang stalks. The tiny carts are gaudy affairs, the over-all length of which (the wheel-base so to speak) is about six inches or so. Examining the carts more carefully the observer will see that the "body" is decorated with certain designs printed with wood block and the wheels are shaped from castoff bits of red cardboard, old wedding invitations, new year greeting cards, etc., conveniently utilized to give that touch of ornate appearance which so effectively strikes a child's fancy. The whole thing is about ten grams in weight.

We will soon know why the vehicles have to be as light 'as possible when we see from where the locomotive power is to generate.

These carts are stored away in a paper box, not quite as big as a wardrobe trunk, on which stands a show case of kaoliang stalks with three or four cross-bars on which a dozen or so of the latest models are on display. Some look like the fast-disappearing old Peking cart, the hooded kind pulled by a mule, and others resemble in appearance an old water wagon with the big wooden tank occupying the greater part of the chassis.

Opening a small door in the side of the box he produces from within a tin can in which are kept the beetles. There is no alternative but to call a spade a spade and these insects are what are known in English, the same as in Chinese, dung beetles! There must be something like a hundred of these apparently harmless black giants, some more than an inch from tip to tip, swarming about in the can. One wonders where the man gets all these beetles. Perhaps he alternates days of cart- selling with days of beetle-collecting among the fertilizer heaps in the country, or else he must have introduced the latest model of hot air incubating endorsed by the Consolidated Beetle Hatchers Association in his establishment!

Selecting a favourite beetle from the can, the little customers point out the fattest ''mule'' and the man deftly ties to it a saddle made of another section of the kaoliang stalk core. A little piece of bamboo with one end thrust into the ''fender'' and the other end into the saddle, the finished piece of merchandise is, thus, in a jiffy, delivered against cash payment.

The beetle is not a willing worker though, for in spite of the fact that he is hopelessly yoked to the cart, he will try to spread out his wings and make attempts to regain his freedom. But this invariably fails and he has to give up trying in the most philosophical manner.

''When you are tired of playing with the beetle-cart unhitch the beetle, saddle and all, and put it in this little jar,'' said old Mrs. Wu, handing her grandson a small covered jar. ''I have put in here some used tea leaves for the beetle to eat and keep alive on. If you take proper care of him, the beetle will be good to play with for a good many days to come.''

*   *   '*

The network of Peking streets aud lanes (called *hutungs*) are the parade grounds of all kinds of pedlars and craftsmen and it is not necessary to exaggerate to show what a colourful and kaleidoscopic feature of the teeming life of such a great metropolis they represent, individually and collectively. As a matter of fact, this is a direct result of the secluded state of the daily life Chinese women, and the children with them, used to lead. For them the idea of a shopping trip or an afternoon spent in town was nothing more than a fond dream. Much less was any thought given to spending any appreciable length of time in a public place like a bazaar or a place of community amusements until things began to change in comparatively recent years.

Here, then, was the clear manifestation of the economic force which, when the buyers refused to come to the sellers drove the sellers to mobilize themselves and come to the buyers. Here it did not have to be Realsilk stockings or life insurance or expensive editions of the Holy Bible to deserve house to house canvassing. The field of the Chinese itinerant pedlars is wide and varied as so many of the things or services Chinese housewives and children need or might need are hawked at the doors. As a whole the pedlars are a great regiment of commercial effectives and are jointly responsible for a great percentage of the annual business turnover. Chinese houses being invariably walled-in affairs, the shrewd *mai-maijen* (businessmen) have devised means to have their advertising "audibilized" by either crying out the names of their wares or by special kinds of sound instruments, by listening to which prospective customers can identify their tradesmen without having to come out for a look. All the foregoing, of course, is but an explanation of the

The monkey is trained to don one mask after another to amuse the patrons.

principle and practice of this enormous system. But it is for a few particular kinds of sounds that children strain their ears listening for and trying to pick up, and of these examples have been given in the weed-horn and the beetle-cart sellers.

Then there is the monkey "circus" man who announces his arrival by beating a big brass gong, and the man with the performing mice whose announcing instrument is a musical horn with which he plays familiar tunes as he trudges along. The Punch and Judy show man announces his arrival beating alternately a small and a large gong. He carries his entire paraphernalia from the ends of a pole across his shoulder. All these and some others provide the inmates of a Chinese house with their respective kinds of entertainment for the consideration the equivalent of a dime or a nickel in local currency.

*   *   *

The monkey "circus" that Little Bald Head and his family saw one day was typical of the many "troupes", usually consisting of two men with a trained monkey, a Pekingese dog and a sheep. All these animals have learned to perform, under constant threats of hearty whippings, at the hand of their masters. They listen to the beating of the gongs with their characteristic groups of strokes and one by one perform a series of various tricks. There are the masks and little caps which the monkey, wearing a red jacket, will take out from the box in which they are kept and don them one after another, each time stalking about erect for the patrons to view and laugh at. The monkey will then imitate the wheelbarrow man and the rickshaw puller or play on a swing suspended from the top of a bamboo pole. All equipment the company carries about on its daily rounds. After the dog has performed some tricks, notably running through bamboo circles in different manners, the final piece is presented in which the monkey rides the sheep around the courtyard in the manner of jockey and racing pony.

The mouse show's equipment is unique and consists of many a queer object, including a miniature rope ladder.

All this may seem very crude and not much to marvel at but it does constitute a pleasant variation from the Chinese housewife's unending program of domestic duties and household drudgeries.

The performing mice is also a native show of the northern cities of China, particularly Peking, to which city all the various entertainers from the surrounding districts flock to get a side income during seasons when they are not being profitably and productively employed with farm work. The best time to review Peking's variety shows is during the Chinese New Year, when slack farm work is coupled beautifully in an economic synchronization with the loosened purse-strings of the holiday-spirited urban people. I have been told that most of these showmen come from the same district. Having had to go so far as to question a few unwilling and unaccommodating individuals among them I have not been able to verify this statement and so would not vouch for it as a fact. It makes no difference, anyway. But here they are, appearing and disappearing mysteriously like the robins or the migrating woodpeckers.

The man of the mouse show carries a squarish wooden box on a belt suspended from his shoulder. From the box rises a wooden pole some two feet high on which are mounted the various "properties" for the performance. There are the wooden pagoda, the hollow wooden peach, the little water bucket, the dangling fish, the wooden melon, etc., as well as the hanging rope-ladder made of strings and little sticks of bamboo. (If anybody doubts the etymological origin of the English word "ratlin", which means, of course, the rope work of an old time windjammer, he may wish to refer to this item of dependable Chinese information.) The little white mice, hardly more than two inches from tip to tip, with cherry-red eyes and the cutest little tail you ever saw, are kept three or four in number in a small wooden box in which bits of cotton keep them comfortably warm.

*   *   *

The man, after concluding a verbal contract of the price, is invited to come into the courtyard. Before he starts his show, he asks if there is a cat in the house. If there is he will request the family to please shut it up in a safe place. He would not enjoy seeing his star performer coming to such a grief! Then opening a tiny box the little white mice are taken out one after another to go through the various acts of the show. The man recites certain folklore anecdotes in brief sentences which correspond loosely with each of the acts in order to add "life" to the program as the mice climb around going through the hole in wooden objects bored for the purpose. The entire program lasts about fifteen minutes on an average and costs five cents to witness.

At the conclusion of the show old Mrs.Wu remarked to the family who had gathered to watch the mice (Little Bald Head included) that the itinerant bear show had not been seen by her for a good many years. The bear show is much more interesting than the little mice for the clumsy black beast is taught to perform tricks in its own awkward way that are much more amusing. The bear turns summersaults forward and backward or balances his heavy body on his head. It plays with a big wooden sword with a long handle and balances heavy sticks with heavy stone disks secured to the two ends. It is made to mimic a prisoner wearing the heavy wooden pillory but reserving growlingly to itself the right to protest. The climax of the show is reached when the bear is made to play the country medicine man, ringing the circular iron rattle on a "thumb" as it stands erect on his hind legs. The man will poke at the legs of the bear to invoke growls of pain which he pretends to understand and interpret to the bystanders as "My name is Big Black", "I sell plasters". "The cost is two hundred and fifty cash per plaster", etc.

"You watch for the Punch and Judy show man and the Land Boating group when they pass our way and we will get them to perform for us," old Mrs. Wu suggested to her grandson.

He eagerly agreed to keep his eyes open.

*   *   *

Children of Peking families, as we have noticed before, are not a God-forgotten group, considering the variety of toys and entertainments they are so fortunately able to enjoy. Of course it must not be inferred from this that since Peking children have these to amuse themselves with the same must be true of children in other localities in China for there is only one Peking in China—"right underneath the Son of Heaven's feet," as the Chinese say. The special opportunities our hero Little Bald Head had were unique and could not be said to represent the lot of the "great unwashed." One fine afternoon the Wu family successfully negotiated with the passing showman of a puppet entertainment, or Punch and Judy show, to perform in their courtyard.

The showman carried his entire equipment in the typical manner, balanced on his shoulder from the ends of a long pole. The man carried with him not only the various puppets and the many items of stage properties, neatly packed in a many-tiered round box, some three feet or so high, but also the stage and indeed the superstructure that went with it. All was knocked down and folded into a conveniently portable kit—a job that any professional packer would be proud of.

The showman being such a man of skill and versatility, the stage was set up in less than ten minutes after the Wu family had selected the place where he was to perform—against a wall that served as their 'devil screen". The stage was some eighteen inches by twenty-four inches in size and was arranged exactly like that of a typical Chinese theatre with two curtains hung at the two side openings which served as "entrance" and "exit" for the stage characters, with the wood work lacquered in bright colours and the roof and ceilings an exact miniature replica of those of a regular stage. The big carrying pole was used as the sole support of the stage around the "bottom" of which a piece of blue cloth was draped. The stage was mounted high and was some five feet or so from the ground in order to give the showman "standing room". Thus the blue cloth "drapery" concealed not only the performing showman himself but also the cylindrical many-tiered property box which he at once moved inside the cloth "chamber." The beating of the gongs which he had been using as attention-attractors and a short vocal rendition of theatrical music, imitating the original stringed instruments by a little whistle concealed in his mouth, announced that his stage was set. Then a series of short theatricals commenced. Some of them were simple plays of but one or two characters, others were complicated acts necessitating the appearance on the little stage of eight or ten puppets. The movements were cleverly executed by twisting, shaking and other movements of the mechanism of the sticks attached to the puppets. Other puppets as they took sitting postures, the man inserted in a piece of wood board in which had been drilled a number of holes to serve as receptacles.

The puppets were dressed with proper costumes of painted or embroidered gowns and their faces were painted exactly as in "legitimate shows." The eyes of most of the puppets were fitted with movable little eyeballs which gave them a sort of liveliness and expressiveness which added greatly to the fun of the show. By clever and well-studied movements, controlled from beneath, the man entertained his patrons with a variety of features some of them historical dramas and others short farces. All the parts were spoken by the showman in different voices, some broad and flat for the male characters and others a shrill falsetto for the female. All of these were accompanied by music from the two gongs, one large and one small, and the imitation of a fiddle got by blowing the little whistle concealed somewhere in his busy mouth. There are said to be eight lengthy plays performable and as many short ones.

The most interesting short piece was perhaps the one known as "Small Wang and the Tiger". Briefly it is in this wise: A man called Wang Hsiao-erh, or "Small Wang," was a seller of bean curd. On his way home after a successful business day, he had a cup or two too many and while in a not quite sober state was devoured by a tiger. A neighbour witnessed the tragedy and immediately filed his press-copy *via* grapevine cable and the news reached his wife and his son. They quickly armed themselves to the teeth and came to the rescue. They found the stodgy tiger snoring away on the wayside (i.e., along the stage rail). They made a joint surprise attack and killed the tiger. The funniest part then follows when they succeed in pulling Small Wang's body, still intact and none-the-worse for the experience, out from the wide-open mouth of the vicious looking tiger!

All the Wus, young and old alike, had a good time watching the puppet shows.

*   *   *

The Punch and Judy show is a very popular Peking amusement, if somewhat rural in nature, and wherever the man goes he can always count on ready public support and repeated patronage from families with children. Though his "tricks" are by no means uninteresting, he charges very little and hence his income is not very high. But, as a complete business unit, we cannot fail to find that he actually enjoys a very privileged position for being such an all-round businessman and from all phases of his work, the organization, administration, operation and maintenance and from many other points of view his position does come in for a lot of envy and admiration. His overhead is small and his help certainly does not represent an ever-threatening top-heavy sort of a payroll. He fears no labour crisis or trade-unionism. His, it must be admitted, is probably the only kind of a theatre that does not pay exorbitant amusement taxes, to say nothing of contending with expensive rentals of foreign films during exchange upheavals.

Even if you or I do not covet his position that does not mean my statement above is untrue. In some of the points listed as a self-sufficient independent showman sitting on top of the world, the puppet artist's lot is coveted at least by his friend the Land Boater. For unlike the former the boat show man has to arrange his own cast of actors, stars and co-stars, who is to play opposite whom and so forth, and also to bear in mind his two-man orchestra, all of which has to be considered. And so no matter how he shuffles the work, he could not cut down the total number of his troupe to anything less than the staggering figure of three, whereas the Punch and Judy is an honest-to-goodness one-man show.

The boat show man's two assistants seem to be taking up much of his profits, but they also work hard to deserve their earnings as they play the parts of the female impersonator and the clown respectively while the show is on and play the drum and cymbals while marching from street to street advertising their arrival. The fact is, however, that the two assistants are really the showman's brothers or his first cousins who, under the law of "familism", would be his legitimate hangers-on anyway.

The men parade through the streets carrying a sort of a replica of a boat made of pieces of cloth mounted on a bamboo frame and decorated with gay awnings much in the same way as those of a Venetian gondola. It is true that the boat is usually perched on the manager's shoulders with the additional items of properties contained inside while on the "march".

This being a business necessity the august manager does not feel that by this sort of "coolie work" his dignity has been jeopard-

The dry land boat show is of South China origin and some of the songs sung by the performers are very romantic.

ized. The female impersonator parading with his false head-dress decorated with artificial flowers and wearing feminine clothes, with his face thickly powdered and outrageously rouged with the "Sunkist" skin showing underneath the powder and triumphantly drumming his way along means more publicity per-haps than anything a mere Mr. Manager could expect to command.

The spacious courtyard of the Wu family on Donkey Market made a fine playground for the Land Boat company. It was not specially crowded although a group of the neighbourhood chil-dren, having seen the colourful company called in by old Mr. Wu, had followed them into the Wu courtyard, as such a way of shar-ing a neighbour's fun is sanctioned by all good-natured Peking-*jen* as being fitting and proper.

The show started with a few short folk songs, accompanied by the drum and cymbals, which were sung in a sort of dialogue form. There was the comedy of the Henpecked husband and the Song of the *Hsiao Erh Mei Mei* (小二妹妹) or Little Second Sister. The masked dance of the Romance of Willow Jade and the Big-headed Monk, and the crude version of Princess Chao Chun of the Han Dynasty who was given away to a distant region by the Emperor to marry a Mongolian chieftain. In the last mentioned play, the female impersonator rides a papier-mâché horse built on the two-in-one principle, for the horse is cut into two parts with the head and front legs hung from the rider's shoulders in front and the tail portion hung in the same fashion behind. Of course the trotting or running of the horse is done by the rider, with the clown fol-lowing closely behind and whipping the horse occasionally as the two characters recite their parts.

Then the boating commenced. The female impersonator seats "herself" in the pleasure boat, the sides of the boat being held lightly in "her" hand. As the cloth pieces are let down, they conceal the legs of the female impersonator who walks slowly about carrying the boat with him and this gives the impression that the boat is sailing smoothly on a lake, while the clown manipulates a long bamboo stick which suggests an oar. As the pair "float" about in this queer way, they do vividly suggest that the boat is actually shooting forward in the green stretches of a beautiful Soochow or Hangchow lagoon. Meanwhile the theme-piece is per-formed by the responsive singing of certain boat-songs and frolic-some love-ditties by the oarsman to the young lady who is his fare and his sweetheart at first sight.

The show was soon over and the crowd of young neighbour-hood guests withdrew from the scene as the performers thanked the Wus and took their leave after receiving a few coppers for "wine money" aside from the agreed price of thirty big coppers.

HOME GARDENS

IN describing the life of the Wu family in general and that of Little Bald Head in particular, we have had various occasions in the past to refer to that wonderful house hold book, popularly called *Huang Li* (皇曆) or the "Imperial Almanac". This is because the book is the one book, very often the only book in a Chinese home, to which the people almost daily make reference for authority or guidance. This book, it is said, possesses certain benevolent properties which makes it a book "quite all right to read under the lamplight"—a phrase which often appears on its cover. I have often wanted to find a practical explanation for this special remark but have so far failed to satisfy myself. The only reason anywhere near a plausible rationalization may

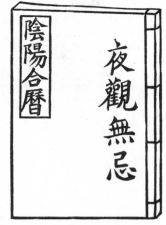

The family almanac often bears an inscription on the cover, meaning "Alright for night reading."

be said to be that since there are so many references to various ous ghosts and goblins in this book, it is feared there might be apprehension on the part of its readers that these phantoms may make mischief at the expense of the readers during the night-tide which is the favourable time for such things to occur. This phrase, conceived by some sagacious salesman, will certainly repel any likely habitual avoidance of perusing the sanctified pages in the evenings.

I might add here that in spite of its deep-rooted position in the every day life of the Chinese people, there are still new discoveries to be made in this wonderful calendar book which are, indeed, so very mysterious and defy any attempt to interpret them as may be evidenced by the fact that so far nobody has succeeded in putting this "best-seller" into a foreign language. It is really a pity that such a monstrous quantity of interesting reading is lost to foreigners.

But, seriously speaking, not all the contents of this book are humbug, for one of the chief purposes of this almanac is to serve as an almost infallible farm calendar.

For the Chinese have found that certain plants have special habits based on the time of planting which is regularized by the various festivals of which every year contains twenty-four. The festivals fall on different dates in the year in different years, and wise men each year make the calculations, put them in the almanac and they are accurate to the minute. An example may be given with the *hu lu* (葫蘆) or "bottle gourd." This is a vine plant of the melon family and is believed to require planting before the Millet Rain festival. If planted later than this, the gourds yielded will lose their bottle shape and grow to be ugly and flat things the shape of a long-handled tomato.

The potted trees of pomegranate and oleander which are so

often seen in a typical Chinese courtyard, like the Wus, are yearly put away during the winter months in storage either with a
florist or in a convenient and sheltered place. The weather becoming warmer these plants are again taken out and placed in
their respective positions in the open. The proper day on which
this is to be done is the festival of *Ch'ing-ming* (清明), "Clear-
bright", or Arbour Day, roughly forty days after the festival
of *Yu-shui*, (雨水) or "Rain-water." This name "Rain-water,"
it must be understood, means, in the circumlocutive fashion
of the Chinese mind, that after this date there will be no
further snowstorms.

In another thirty days or so, the calendar gives one special
day marked in the most matter-of-fact way, *T'u Wang Yung Shih*
(土王用事), which indicates the inauguration of the reign of the
King of the Earth, by which it is interpreted that the earth would
be ready to receive seeds. Thereafter, there will be a period of
some forty-five days for proper profitable planting of everything
until the festival of *Mang-chung* (芒種) which actually means
"Rice-planting." After this particular date there should be no
more "compulsory" planting, according to the Chinese proverb—
Kuo liao mang chung, pu k'e ch'iang chung (過了芒種不可強種)
meaning "The festival of rice planting having passed, it is no use
(or too late) to plant anything". In another two weeks the Summer
Solstice rolls along when the garlic is to be harvested, *Deo volente*.

All these scheduled provisions are apparently of agricultural
origin, considering that the Chinese are such a famous farming
nation. It is but natural that the same observances are firmly
established in the Chinese home life.

Such being the case it is no wonder no Chinese household can
operate without this indispensable source of authority near at
hand.

           *   *   *

Not only did the Wus consult their family almanac in the
preliminary steps of their garden planting but they also checked
up on the life patterns of each person in the family in order to
discover the most suitable persons to do the actual planting.
For if you expect your flowers and plants to flourish you must
have them planted by persons of a *tu* (土) or "earth", life pattern,
failing which the second best ones should be those of a *shui* (水),
or "water", life pattern. Equally acceptable are ones of *mu* (木),
or "wood", life pattern (Little Bald Head, as we have found out
already was of this category). Persons whose life patterns are
formed on the other two of the five elements, namely, fire and
metal, please do not apply for planting.

You will say this is all so much superstition, yet this, it is
sad but true, is not all. For planters have also to look up the
lucky days for such an undertaking, as there are only so many days
scattered at random (!) in every month on which, the almanac
says, it is permissible to dig the ground and for which the terminology is *Tung-t'u* (動土). Excepting these days no Chinese in
his right mind would dare to dig up the earth for the pure and
simple reason that such an act signifies digging a grave for burying a dead person which, of course, is not a particularly charming
omen. It is true, indeed, that not even a dog in a Chinese home
can expect to scratch the earth with impunity.

The first plants that the Wus planted were from seeds. Among these there were several varieties of morning glories, the Chinese name for which is "Cow-leading flower." The Chinese have succeeded in cleverly crossing this into many varieties some of which come under the name of *Ch'in niang-tze* (親娘子), or "Dear Mother's Son!" These were planted beside the bamboo fence that separated the southern rooms from the rest of the main compound and in summer and late autumn the vines yearly covered the entire fence with luxurious growth. This year the Wus also planted a special kind of string bean, which has climbing stalks and a beautiful purplish flower, near the same fence.

The grass jasmine, being a sturdy annual, is found in almost every Chinese family garden.

Beneath the bamboo fence they imbedded a row of the seeds of the so-called Grass Jasmine, a cousin of the American "four o'clock". These bloom in the evenings and are very sturdy annuals.

Finishing the front yard they repaired to the courtyard behind where there was an open space. Part of the yard was shaded by a big elm tree and therefore was no good for flower planting for does not the Chinese proverb say: "Rather be a man under a man than a tree under a tree". The big tree would be harmful to any plant life underneath as it would rob the small plants of their "air", the Chinese say, which, of course, is quite wrong unless the word for "air" be made also concurrently to mean "sunshine".

In the western portion of the same open space they planted a row of "Turning-with-the-sun-lotus" or sunflowers, which grow in the course of the season to such a giant height and yield the big seeds which Chinese children were growing to like as edibles following the example set by their neighbours in Russia.

Another patch of ground was tilled in the proper way and planted with Indian corn seeds in the same manner as many of their friends were in the habit of doing. It all sounds very queer to strangers to Peking, but doesn't fresh corn-on-the-cob from one's own backyard garden taste good? Even Little Bald Head liked them better than those from the street vendors.

* * *

The planting of the various seeds in the courtyard gardens of the Wus did not take long and was duly accomplished. There was no elaborate preparation of the soil with patented chemical fertilizers or scanning of bulky mail-order catalogues and filling up of blank forms for getting the "guaranteed" seeds from any nation-wide distributors. Their seeds did not come in expensively appointed individual bags bearing the pictures of the pedigreed flowers in orthochromatic printings. Most of the seeds they used, as is common with the majority of Chinese amateur gardeners, were collected by them from their previous year's "crops". There was always a fine chance to gather them after they had become

The seed sellers' signs are generally a few gourds and corns·in-the-husk hung high above their stalls.

firm and matured and therefore certain to give good results after replanting. Old Mrs. Wu yearly saw to such things herself and personally gathered the seeds which she put away in tiny packages on which her husband was asked to mark out which was which for easy identification. This last was really quite unnecessary for she had, through years of experience, become quite an expert in her own way and there were not very many species to keep track of. She obtained some new species by exchanging with neighbours and friends—a practice which has become quite popular among Peking families.

There are, of course, the handful of professional seedmen who ply their trade during the spring months at the temple fairs, etc. These people have their own stalls and are a separate group from the regular florists, though they must be somehow or other affiliated with each of them. Wooden trays with partitions, each about two inches square, are filled with all kinds of seeds, each variety in a cell marked with a tag made of bamboo bearing the name of the plant with perhaps a remark as to the colour, etc. They have their signs, too, in the shape of some gourds and Indian corn, complete with husks, which are also available to prospective buyers. Their prices are not unreasonable and the range of selection is wide, as may be witnessed by the rows upon rows of the small squares. Except those plants which propagate by means of bulbs or other parts of the plants, almost all the flower families are represented including, it may be observed, the seeds of string beans and corns testifying to the popularity of these plants as household horticultural sidelines. The seedmen look quite innocent and attend to customers cheerfully as the latter examine the "honeycomb" of holders for some kind of seeds to experiment with. Their patronage is not curtailed in spite of having been cruelly disillusioned before as may be proved by the complaints often heard. Old Mrs. Wu had also been a regular customer and there had been minor cases of misrepresentation in the course of years but she definitely lost confidence in the seed vendors when one year the seeds from one supposed to be of petunias of assorted colours, grew into a magnificent bed of spinach!

Little Bald Head had his noble part in the enterprise, making all the holes in the ground by means of a spade and an iron fire-poker, besides watering each place with a long-necked sprinkler-pot.

But an equally great, if not still greater pleasure, was experienced by the grandfather who watched all with great interest, for it reminded him of the famous lines by Fan Ch'eng Ta, a poet of the Sung Dynasty, which he repeated to himself with a smile of approval:

"Daytime, the farmers weed the grasses from the fields,
    and by night they spin the hemp;
Even the youngsters on the farm are busy at their various
    chores.
The children or grandchildren still not big enough to
    understand weaving or husbandry,
Under the shade of the mulberry trees, they learn first
    to raise watermelons."

*   *   *

There are any number of aristocratic families in Peking who keep their own private hothouse and employ professional horticulturists to take care of their collections of rare and expensive flowers and plants with which they keep the many rooms in their magnificent mansions and the various courtyards supplied with proper floral decorations. The annual upkeep must be very costly but either the satisfaction they get justifies it or it is fostered as a necessity besides being a luxury. Flowers of the expensive varieties make presentable gifts for many occasions and the possession of high-priced species is certainly a sign of prosperity. It is, moreover, a token of a cultured life and refined living Horticulture is said to have a great bearing on the development of character. One of the advantages of studying the famous classic of Shih Ching, or "The Book of Odes," as given by Confucius himself, is the chance to get acquainted with the many names of plants and animals. Few Chinese poets can get along without flowers. Like William Wordsworth who wrote in his "Daffodils": "A poet could not but be gay in such a jocund company", Chinese poets look at flowers as an inexhaustible source of inspiration. Flowers to them stand for beauty, grace, brilliance, elegance and a long train of high-sounding abstract nouns besides being the unprotesting object of all their sentimental expressions. Poets in China are like movie stars in America, they are what every one thinks he or she is material for. Children who cannot expect to be a Shirley Temple at least can buy the brand of tooth paste she is said to endorse. Here you have an expert-eye-view of the psychological background of why so many people in China proclaim flowers to be their hobby.

For these people, the "upper three thousand", there is a floral calendar providing, for instance, that the Mountain-Tea (a variety of sub-tropical hibiscus) be "displayed" (I apologize for failing to find a better and more fitting word) during the first moon of the year together with Water-Nymphs (narcissus), and so forth. It is true that for this group of "classy" connoisseurs, flowers as a hobby mean a great monetary outlay, and this without bringing up these who are duty-bound to carry on the family's good name as amateur growers of the city's best peonies or water lilies or orchids and whose work constitutes an obligation to the ancestors.

But the Wu family was not of this type. They had no special purpose or ambition in their flower-breeding except merely doing as others did. Old Mr. Wu himself, in his bygone days, had been an enthusiastic cultivator of certain kinds of Western-Barbarian-Lotus (dahlias) of which at one time he boasted a great variety in his collection. He dropped the hobby when an extremely cold winter killed his rare specimens. So, as Little Bald Head began to notice flowers, the old man's interest revived, and every time a

flower vendor passed their way it meant two or three additional
plants for them.   The same was true of every trip to the temple
fair near their house on Donkey Mart, where is situated one of
Peking's important flower markets.

There were some plants which the family had always had,
such as the pomegranate trees and oleanders mentioned before.
The oleanders are known by the Chinese name of "Combination-
Bamboo-and-Feach" and are well known as being a poison.   The
Wus also kept some other species from year to year on account of
their medical value. An example might be given with the "Gold-
Silver-Flower" or honeysuckles, the tincture of which is a gentle
laxative.   Clusters of "Jade-Hairpins", or plantain lilies, had
established themselves under the stone steps of the southern rooms,
where it was damp and agreeable for them. These came out every
spring without special attention.   Then right near the house gate,
surmounting the "devil screen" and covering it with thick green
foliage and red berries in autumn, was an old vine the like of
which is known as "Mountain-Climbing-Tiger" (Boston ivy) and
which is a member of the grape family.

These plants formed the permanent skeleton of the Wus'
botanical collection to which were added from time to time various
other "extras" as they made their annual appearances.

*   *   *

Since starting to describe the flowers and plants in the Wu
home, there has occurred to me the possibility that perhaps my
readers may be led to get an impression that our hero, Little Bald
Head, might be visualized as a toiling young "caretaking appren-
tice" in a municipal public garden or a rejuvenescent professor of
biology trying to discover a missing link somewhere in the world's
plant life. If such is the case, I am very sorry.   But I am not
going to skip over this interesting subject.

Peking people are a flower-loving group of humanity and
whatever their purpose or excuse may be makes no difference.
The patronage shown to flowers has been keenly demonstrated
by the imperial families at least since the Han Dynasty if not before.   The great Yehonala Tsu Hsi, the famous Dowager Empress
of the Manchu dynasty, who misruled China for more than half a
century, was perhaps the most outstanding admirer of flowers in
comparatively recent times. Ministers and mandarins, princes
and princesses, it may be imagined, used to vie with each other of
being the proud possessor of prize plants, and gave a great stimulus
to the florists' trade as a whole.   These professionals have received encouragement on top of pecuniary gains, and their "sphere
of influence" has expanded from inside Peking's walls to as far as
the village of Ts'ao Chiao (草橋), outside the Yo An Men, later
to Liu Ts'uen (柳村) and now Fengtai (豐台) and beyond.   In this
fairly vast area at least seventy per cent of the fields are devoted
to the raising of flowers on a mass production scale, expressly to
feed the trade created by the demand of Peking's flower-conscious
population. Directly and indirectly, it feeds a great multitude of
people.   If scientific statistics could be made, Peking's population
must share something like twenty-five flowering plants a year
per capita, besides a few bulbs and cuttings for the vases.

Comparatively few people patronize the florists' shops.   The
itinerant plant and flower vendors carry their stock-in-trade on

their daily rounds from the ends of a pole in identically the same way as many another pedlar. As most of the customers have their own pots, whether of Ch'ien Lung year royal kiln porcelain or ugly inferior-complex affairs of clay (the latter being considered most wholesome for growth, the plants are sold with only a "ball" of mud protecting the roots and providing the nourishment during the transitional period before they are accustomed to a new soil. And it is in this ball of mud, too, that the secret sometimes lies to which the buyer wakes up after noticing a plant that ought to prosper turning "hay-wire" and withering in no time. He discovers that the roots were "faked."

Some of the plants' names are very charming. Pansies of three colours are known in Chinese as "Butterfly Flowers". Pinks are known as "Scissored-Autumn-Silk". Zinnias are "Five-Colour-Lotus" for any and all colours. The pickerel weed is known here as "Phoenix-Eye-Iris." The fuchsias go by the name of "Golden-Bells-Hung-Upside-down." Evening primrose is called "Fragrance-as-Night-Comes." The gladioli are called the "Beauty's Bananas."

In checking up the names of some North China plants, the only name in English which has its Chinese equivalent beat by a long shot is the Bleeding Heart, which in Chinese is called by the clumsy title of "Purse-Peony," For the plant known as touch-me-not, because their seed pots, when ripe, explode in a most unceremonious fashion on being touched, the Chinese name is "Phoenix-Fairy-Flower." It is also known as "Finger-Nail-Grass" for the fresh blossoms of the red ones are used by the native girls for dyeing their finger nails after the blossoms are pounded into a paste and mixed with alum (aluminium oxide). Foreign plants receive Chinese names not by transliteration: tuberoses are christened "Horse-Hoof-Lilies," poinsettias, "First-Rank-Scarlet," flowering cactus is named "Authority-Arrow-and-Water-Lily." A century-plant is an "Iron-Tree" in China, though the Chinese have discounted its century to a mere sixty years— they say it blossoms every sixty years!

*   *   *

Thanks to his careful observation and unusual memory, Little Bald Head soon became flower-wise and could call many a flower "by its first name". Of this his parents and grandparents were naturally very proud.

GAMES FOR CHILDREN

The Wang brothers were the first outside children with whom little Bald Head associated.

CHINESE children are not always destined to lead a life of solitude such as Little Bald Head has apparently been described to be leading, but being the only child in the Wu family he did not have many opportunities to associate with other children for a fuller enjoyment of life. Though his parents and grandparents, in their own pursuance of happiness had been providing pleasant diversions to his otherwise monotonous daily life, he was very often unhappy. Modern kindergartens have only recently been introduced into China and during Little Wu's time they had not yet begun to be popularized. They have not been properly developed even now. There was then only one kindergarten for which a special name had to be coined, *Yu Chih Yuan* (幼稚園) or Children's Garden, or Kindergarten exactly. The Wus, as we have noted before, were not a family of incurable diehards and in spite of the reactionary ideology of the old grandmother would have sent our little hero to the organization named were it not for the fact that the place was a bit too far for comfort from their home on Donkey Mart.

Little Bald Head's young father, proud, ambitious and over-anxious, had by then begun to make preliminary preparations to start his little son out on the road to the Font of Lore, but he was always stopped by his own parents who argued that since the child was so young and his *nao chin* (腦筋) (brain muscles) had not attained the proper stage of development, it was not fitting to overtax them. But as a remedy for his hermit's life he was encouraged to mingle with the neighbourhood children in the daily playtimes which in due course became a regular feature of the child's activities. Even this was not without a due share of opposition from the old grandmother for she had always thought that her grandson, "the luminary pearl on her palm," was a sort of a high born scion and as such should not mingle with the other children of the Toms, Dicks and Harrys, most of whom, in her judgment, were a bunch of nothing but *yeh hai tze* (野孩子), "wild children". But she gradually gave in until the last line was reached—when she absolutely forbade him to play in the company of any female children except those from their relatives.

"Boys and girls should never play together," she said.

"But why, grandmother?" enquired little Wu.

"Because if they do they will have sores on their feet," answered the old lady, repeating an old Chinese superstitious belief.

"Who will have the sores on their feet, the boys or the girls?" persisted little Wu.

"Both," was her ready answer.

Exactly the same reason is given when parents stop girls from playing with boys.

The Chinese keep their male and female children separate when they reach the fateful age of seven years. It is an old custom dating back to misty ancient periods, and being firmly established in the Chinese mind was more of a "historical precedent" than an "imperative command". When co-education was first introduced into Chinese schools, many Peking families actually withdrew their children from public schools altogether—but most of these parents changed their decisions later when they found that it was apparently quite harmless. Of these transitional phenomena, the Wu family stood out as a typical example.

The first outside children that joined Little Bald Head during playtime were the Wang children from next door, one of whom had performed the ceremonial act of "stepping on the birth" of little Wu a few hours after he was born. Following an old tradition, old Mrs. Wu purposely invited the child for he was a very likeable youngster and the grandmother had wished her own grandson to develop like him. This Wang boy was ten years old and three years Little Bald Head's senior. He was attending a school—a sort of a family institution of one class but many grades in the home of the teacher-proprietor, the type which is known as a *ssu shu* (私塾), or a "private school." When he came to the Wu house to "find Little Bald Head to play", he invariably brought along his younger brother, another precocious young five-year-old. This boy went by the milk-name of Erh-fu-tze, or "Second Bliss." They had a sister named Chu-tze, or "Pearl."

Pearl was not allowed to come as the Wangs also held the belief that boys and girls should not play together.

The Wang brothers habitually came to the Wus and after he started to socialize with them Little Bald Head did not have a dull day.

* * *

One of the favourite games that the Wu child and his young friends played and enjoyed thoroughly was *k'o ni ni po po-erh* (搧泥泥餑餑兒), or "moulding clay cakes". Little Wu first learned about this pastime from the Wang children when he was shown the little moulds which they had. Little Bald Head approached his grandfather with the request for similar ones and the next morning he became the proud possessor of a goodly number, some large, some small, and of assorted shapes and designs.

These little moulds are made of reddish clay, the same material

Little reddish moulds made of baked clay are favourites with Peking children to make little figures of earth with.

and process of manufacture being used as in the making of bricks. They are another seasonal toy and the makers offer them for sale at very economical prices—each big copper would buy three or four of the smaller ones. There are also magnificent sets of the moulds at the towering price of twenty-odd coppers a set. The single ones are little figures of houses, temples, pagodas, etc. Some sets contain as many as fifteen or twenty moulds from which clay figures of various groups can be made.

One set, a very popular one, are the figures of Monk T'ang Seng (唐僧) and his coterie, a legendary group of "pilgrims", based on the fiction "Hsi Yu Chi" (西遊記), or "The Trip to the West." Monk T'ang Seng was delegated by the Emperor Hsuan Tsung of the T'ang Dynasty to go to the Western Heaven to procure the sacred editions of the Diamond Sutras. He possessed a miraculous power with which he subdued a number of animal-genii and converted them into his disciples who served as servants on the royal mission. Among these were Sun Hou-erh (孫猴兒), Sun the Monkey, and Chu Pa Chieh (猪八戒), the Pig-headed (not pigheaded) Saint of Eight Abstainments, and the Sand Monk. They also procured a Dragon Horse as the Monk's mount and thus relieved the priest from tedious pedestrianism.

A careful young artisan, with a little care and patience, can shape from these moulds all the figures as well as a big turtle on which the party rode, horse and all, when crossing a wide river supposed to be the famous Indian river, the Ganges. There are also other sets of moulds to make other marvellous masterpieces of "mud-pies."

The clay used is a special kind called Yellow Earth which is from the famous North China loess strata, a very fertile soil formed by the accumulated deposits of fine dust probably blown there by the highland winds from the Gobi Desert of Mongolia. It is possessive of a remarkable adhesive power and so fine in "texture" it is widely used for pottery ware in China. The special kind particularly suitable for making "clay cakes"—in fact for the commercial production of all clay dolls and clay toys—is called *Chiao Ni* (膠泥), or "Glue Earth". For its characteristic properties the name is a good enough description. Children who have special connections get the best "glue earth" for this purpose from the countryside. Most children, however, get their supply *gratis* from the coal shops where their families trade. Incidentally we might add here that without a good supply of this yellow earth no coal shops in Peking can operate, for it is responsible for at least forty per cent of the constituents of the so-called "coal balls", the other sixty percent, according to the coal dealers, is actually whole-bodied coal dust.

The yellow earth or "glue earth" is first pounded into a fine powder and then mixed with water, a little water added at a time, until the proper degree of consistency is reached and then the moulding begins. The children knew nothing about the ambitious schemes of making any "sets" of figures so they merely sped up the production until there were—well, quite many These clay cakes were then put away to dry on the family's washboards before the playing of shop ensued.

*   *   *

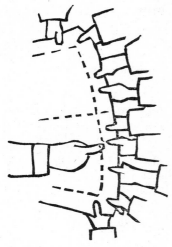

The Chinese way of selecting the first seeker in a game of Hide and Seek.

Playing with yellow clay is passively, if not positively, encouraged by child-rearing families especially in early summer or late spring as it will take out much of the "heat" from the system by contact of the clay or mud with the hot palms of the hands.

If it has not a black tongue, it is not a Chow Chow. If a man does not remember having *ni ni po po-erh*, tell him for me that he had not been a typical Peking boy.

*   *   *

Public playgrounds for children have been only lately introduced to Peking and there are not many in the municipality. Chinese children still gather, during playtime, wherever there are empty lots or wherever a narrow *hutung* suddenly broadens in typical Peking fashion, in the same manner as their fathers and grandfathers had been doing for generations. The ideal hours for such gatherings are the summer evenings, preferably after supper. In summer it is not dark until nearly nine o'clock and for the average Chinese family supper is between six and seven. The walled courtyards being not particularly cool and certainly not breezy, children naturally make an exodus for the streets. Even the stricter parents relax in their disciplinary regulations to keep the children in their compounds and here and there groups are formed in the open and forthwith street playing commences.

The crowds are noisy and, indeed, not without a tinge of "mobbing" tendency, particularly if there happen to be some bigger boys in the crowd. "Camels running around in flocks of sheep", the Chinese call these over-grown children. The practice is not to be eulogized for there is always danger what with the speeding rickshaws and reckless cyclists threading their way in the none-too-well lighted *hutungs*.

*   *   *

Little Bald Head was naturally too "precious" to engage in such games much as his father really would have liked him to join the "gang" of neighbourhood boys (no girls for reasons previously explained) and so the Wus organized their own games in the fairly spacious courtyard on many an interesting evening.

One day they elected to play Hide and Seek.

The Wang boy from next door was the biggest and therefore the chief organizer and he proceeded to select the first "seeker" in the typical Chinese manner. He spread out the front portion of the bottom of his shirt-and-coat and made every boy occupy a place thereon with a hand, putting two fingers each clipped onto the hem of the shirt. There were some eight or nine children in all and the space was almost entirely occupied with tiny fingers.

Then he started counting the "outs". He sang each time:

"Road No. One, Road No. Ten,

Tea and soup, fruits and syrup,
Having money, you eat and drink,
Having no money, out on the road you go!''

With the verse he counted the boys "out" one by one by removing each of the "delegates" of fingers until there was one
single boy left whose finger still clung to his garment. He was the
logical candidate for first seeker. The procedure is very fair and
is very much similar to the American "E Ni, Mi Ni, Mai Ni Mo!
Caught a nigger by the toe.........!" Young Wang held the seeker
tightly in his lap and thus blinded him while the other children
scattered to hide themselves, each one where he thought was
a good place. Soon they were all gone, one of them behind the
"devil screen", another behind the goldfish jar, still another
vanished behind the big elm tree in the back yard and a fourth disappeared somewhere else, each one declaring he was ready by
shouting to that effect. The seeker was then released to try to
find and catch any of the boys he could.

There were some by-laws in this game. One of them was that
"There was to be no 'home', safety zone, or 'night', temporary
truce. Any boy squatting down is a sign that he has gone to sleep
and therefore is not to be pursued until he stands up once more."
Another rule provides that some of the little ones, too young
to be competent "catchers", are exempt from being prospective
"catchees", though they are not excluded from participation.
These little ones are called Hsiao Ts'ai Tieh-erh (小菜碟兒), or
"Little Vegetable Dishes", and are a privileged class with a
special franchise.

The boy caught by the seeker relieves the seeker and the
game begins anew.

There were several hilarious games and the meeting was
broken up at a late hour. After that all was quiet on the Wus'
"western front".

*   *   *

Looking at it from an objective point of view we must admit
that Chinese children, of all children, are perhaps the most poorly
equipped group of playfellows and therefore a remarkable lot, considering the measure of enjoyment and the variety of games they
have with no equipment whatsoever except themselves. Their
parents' poverty, in certain cases, may be counted an important
factor for lack of playthings, as well as the impetus driving the
children to get something out of nothing. It may be imagined
also that some adult mind was responsible for devising their
games. I presume to say this was exactly how these games were
invented although in course of time they have been enjoyed by
the "Haves" and "Have Nots" alike, rich and poor, in Peking
and perhaps in many other places with slight variations. Of this
class of games the Hide and Seek described before is an example.

Another popular amusement is "Beating the Blind Tiger."

A big boy acts as referee and eyewitness. The Blind Tiger is
first selected from among the players by the same method of
gradual "disqualification" as in Hide and Seek. The Tiger is then
blindfolded by the referee's hands and his head thrust against the
referee's chest as an additional precaution, exposing his body to
receive the beating—the agreed points for the beating would be
the upper portions of the thighs. Someone in the crowd gives a

single slap on the leg—the referee sees to it that there is no "mobbing" free-for-all action. Then quickly he resumes his posture and the Tiger is released to try to find out who it was that hit him. If his guess is right, the ex-beater takes his place as next Tiger. In case he guesses wrong, he will carry on for another term. The fun in the game is in the rapid concealing of any telltale manifestations that may betray the "responsible" one, for which clever make-believe way of nonchalant camouflage some Chinese children are remarkable. This game is widely indulged in by bigger children, too.

Little Bald Head played a few rounds of this game and at the suggestion of the grandmother quickly changed to something else. For many of the children in the group were too small to appreciate the sporting aspect of the procedure and were noticeably bored.

Old Mrs. Wu explained to them how to play the *Tien Ko Tze Ming-erh* (點果子名兒), or "Checking the Name of Fruits."

"First you divide into two equal groups. Each group is to have a leader. The two groups then squat down Turkish fashion in two rows about six feet apart, the rows parallelling each other and all the children facing inward. You now agree on what names each is to receive and forthwith the leaders will whisper to each member of his team his temporary name; this, of course, is to be done without "comparing notes" with others, except in order to avoid possible duplication of names. One team will take the names of fruits (this is the "theme center") and the other team will take names of flowers, or birds or anything else. In this way...."

And so saying she proceeded to arrange the two groups in the desired manner. There were ten children altogether and two groups of five each were soon ready. In two more minutes, each of the four members of a team had his name whispered to him. Little Bald Head was the leader of one group and the Wang boy headed the other.

The game started with Little Bald Head's team, as Wang, the leader of the other team, came over and selecting a child, blindfolded him with his hands. Then he gave the order for "Peach" of his own team to come over, strike three light strokes on the child's forehead and return to his own group who clapped their hands to cover up any trace of a clue. The blindfolded boy was asked to guess who this "Peach" had been. His guess was right and so the next boy to be blindfolded was thereby selected.

This is an interesting game though somewhat troublesome in preparation especially as the names have to be changed and given anew after each correct guess. It is a fair one as all the rest of the children are eye witnesses and there is no chance for foul play.

*   *   *

Little Bald Head liked the various games with the neighbourhood children immensely and whenever there was a chance he was always ready to join them.

One of the games he took part in had a typical Peking touch. I refer to the game known as *Ku Lu Kuo* (錮鎯鍋), or "Repairing a Pan". By way of an explanatory footnote, it may be mentioned that the cooking pans the Chinese use are made of cast iron and once in a while they get worn in spots. Then the services of the itinerant tinkers are availed of for repair work. The game is patterned after such an incident.

After a group of boys have agreed to play "Repairing a Pan", two of the bigger children are selected as the possessor of the fateful cooker and as the repairer. The possessor acts often as the referee and supervises the proceedings of the game which requires children in an odd number, no even number like 6 or 8 or 10 will do.

All except the owner and the tinker join hands and form themselves into a big ring like in a "Maypole Dance", but they are at first crowded together with their hands outstretched in the center like the spokes of a wheel from the hub. Then the tinker arrives, announcing his coming in mimicry of the real tinker by crying "pan patching and pan repairs" with a hand against his ear in the typical manner of such traders.

The possessor stops him and asks him to repair the pan.

By way of customary preliminaries, the tinker will marvel at the small size of the pan, saying "Oh, how small your pan is!"

"It could be very big, though," answers the owner, and as he says this the children walk back and form a big circle with their hands joined.

The tinker is then invited to come in "the ring" to inspect the damage and give his estimate. There ensues some bargaining as to the price. Whereupon the tinker, in the most matter-of-fact manner, starts to count how many patches there are to be made walking along the children and counting where each child's hand joins that of another as a "bad spot". While thus counting away, he suddenly gives a virtual order for the pan to collapse, repeating an old conventional phrase which may be translated as:

"Green bean and yellow bean,
With a single crack, the pan is broken!"

And at the close of this warning he, quick as a wink, selects one of the boys in the ring and holds him fast in his arms while all the children scatter and in the same manner each selects another and thus form themselves into so many pairs. All this is done in such a short time that some clumsy slow-coach type of a fellow will be left dumbfounded looking in vain for somebody to pair up with. He is conspicuous by his desperate attempts to shake off his "singularity" status by trying unsuccessfully to get a "partner". Poor fellow, he cannot do it. Amidst roaring laughter and mocking giggles, the unfortunate "left-over" is proclaimed by all to be the tinker in the next game.

*   *   *

This and similar games cannot be said to overflow with interest but they are exactly what the majority of Chinese youngsters enjoy playing when they get a chance. If not giving them undeserved credit, such games do give the children a chance to enjoy fellowship, competition and sportsmanlike companionship as well as aid to develop quick action and to acquaint them with the conception of what is fair and what is not fair, a first step toward "social justice."

THE DRAGON BOAT FESTIVAL

FOR anybody who knows anything at all about China it is not
necessary to dwell so much in detail upon the matter of
the three big *chieh* (節), or festivals, which are universally observed throughout the length and breadth of China,
but it is perhaps permissible to give a short explanation as a preamble to the description of the customs and "to do's" on the *Wu
Yueh Chieh* (五月節), or the "Fifth Moon Festival" The classical
name for this red-letter day is *Tuan Wu* (端午) which means
"Beginning of Noon", but it is better known among foreigners as
the Dragon Boat Festival.

On this festival day, it has been the custom in various river
ports to hold annual regattas, the boats used being decorated with
the dragon motif, a carving of a dragon's head being used for the
equivalent of the foreign figurehead but mounted high up on the
bow and the dragon's tail, sticking up skyward, decorating the
stern. These used to be noisy affairs with the riversides lined
thick with humanity cheering, it may be imagined, at the top of
their voices, the rows of oarsmen burning up the last gram of their
energy and the drummers thundering away and supplying encouragement. These fetes were looked forward to months ahead by
the participants as well as spectators.

Such regattas, instead of those by academic institutions, were
almost always sponsored by rich and influential business guilds
and/or religious societies, each of which had its own entry. Most
of the men engaged were so enthusiastic that for them the word
"Lose" was not in the dictionary, and if they did not win in the
boat race they would throw aside all the dictates of sportsman-
ship and proceed to save their "face" by trying to give their opponents a physical beating. The winners, of course, were not going to stand for this, and so sanguinary battles commenced.
These incidents became in due course more or less a rule, until no
dragon boat race was complete without a long-drawn out guild
fight (like tong wars) trailing months behind as its aftermath.
But we may leave the matter here.

Although there is no dragon boat racing in Peking, the Dragon
Boat Festival is observed just the same. For the Chinese have
three main settlement periods in the year, the Chinese New Year,
the Dragon Boat Festival and the Mid-Autumn Festival. As much
as they are in outward appearance periods of merry-making in
families and elsewhere, they are in cruel reality periods of acid
tests of the businessman's agility and integrity as people look
upon his ability to meet his financial obligations on these days as
a positive proof of whether or not his credit is sound. If a businessman or the financially responsible person in the family should
fail to satisfy his creditors during the account-settling periods
and turn yellow, so to speak, his name becomes mud and he is "no
go."

The Wu family fortunately was one of those few who had no
such worries (at least not to our knowledge) and all what the
Dragon Boat Festival meant to them was a general good time for
all the members of the family, some dining and wining aside from
the observances of traditional customs the same as all other
Peking families do during the festival season.

The impending arrival of the festival was first noticed some five days ahead when old Mrs. Wu made for her grandson a magnificent string of charms with bits of silk of various colours for him to wear on the fifth day of the fifth moon. While similar articles are offered for sale in the markets, orthodox Peking people like the Wus always make their own. On careful examination there are seen on the string a little red cherry, mulberries both purple and white, a spring onion, a cucumber and an eggplant in different colours. The various little silken trinkets, each not quite an inch in length and some considerably smaller, are tied together on a silken thread one above the other about half an inch apart. One small boy riding a tiger and a tiny gourd-shaped purse with yellow tassels, containing some incense powder, are attached to the end of the string.

This string of charms is known as *hu lu hua-erh* (葫蘆花兒), or "Gourd Flower." All children wear them at the Fifth Moon Festival—the girls from their braided hair, sometimes together with little chenille "geegaws" in the shape of a tiger, etc., while the boys wear them on their coat buttons.

There is also another kind of Gourd Flower entirely different from this and which old Mrs. Wu bought from a street pedlar.

*　　　*　　　*

On the Dragon Boat Festival children wear strings of silken charms and the girls and other female members of the family will also wear in their hair a number of little coloured objects such as little replicas of tigers of chenille attached to a pin and little so-called *fu* (符) or "talismans," made by cleverly folding narrow strips of red and white paper into various intricate designs of squares and triangles which, it may be imagined, represent a degenerated form of the Taoist talismans of exorcism which were once the fashion in ancient times.

Temporary yellow paper scrolls, or posters, of conventional designs are offered for sale several days before the festival is due and each family will get at least one of these to paste up high on the *chieh men* (街門), or "street door." These are wood block prints, some a foot in width and about twice as long, of crude pictures of a variety of things. Some represent the notorious *wu tu* (五毒) or "five venomous insects," the scorpion, the winged centipede (poisonous centipedes are winged in the southern regions of China), the poisonous lizard, the toad, and the snake, these being depicted as having been vanquished by a tiger which is a symbol of the great Taoist Priest, Chang, whose official title is *Tien Shih* (天師) or "Heavenly Teacher", the super authority on all things exorcistic and a sort of a "living buddha" for the Taoist sects, whose permanent hereditary headquarters here below are in the Lung Hu Shan, or Dragon and Tiger Mountains, in much-troubled Kiangsi province. Other prints would show the same five unfortunate scapegoats being overpowered by the magic vapour from a round box or a gourd and being sucked into them, like dust into an electric vacuum cleaner, where they will be imprisoned. These are all printed on yellow paper which is the official colour for all religious decorations in China.

One more popular design is a crude portrait of the Pan-erh (判兒), (pronounced as "par"), who is often represented as brandishing a magic sword and staring at a bat flying toward him, as he

A portrait of the devil-chaser with the seal of the Heavenly Teacher above him is an indispensable decoration for the Dragon Boat Festival.

literally gets "in the air" with anger with his beard sticking up like the needles of an agitated porcupine. This familiar pose is known as *Ho Fu Lai Chieh* (喝福來暹) or "reprimanding the blessings (a pun for bat) for delayed arrival." This mythological figure is pictured as garbed in a crimson court robe and jade belt, indicating high official rank and is a popular motif for Chinese artistic influence against all the evils and even the "poison gases" of bad luck in a household. Thus his portrait is everywhere to be seen.

But exactly how did the practice or belief begin?

When Emperor Ming Huang of the T'ang Dynasty (618-906 A. D.) was once suffering, of all sicknesses, from malaria, he saw in his dream or daydream a big demon catching the little elves that were bothering him and devouring them. Upon being questioned by His Majesty as to his identity, he revealed that he was a scholar from the district of Chung Nan by the name of Chung K'wei and that failing at an imperial examination he had committed suicide by knocking out his brains on the marble balustrade of the Imperial Audience Hall (he should never have been allowed there anyway). But strange as it may seem, His Majesty woke to find his malaria gone. In commemoration of this scholar he had his court artist, the famous Wu Tao Tze, paint the portrait from his description. In course of time, it became established that even a picture of this scholar will chase away all the sundry undesirable elements in the house and its use therefore was popularized and introduced into every household.

It is needless to say that the Wus procured their specimen of a picture for the festivities, one of the devil-chaser super-imposed with the seal of the Heavenly Teacher for double-sure effectiveness.

*   *   *

The Fifth Moon Festival is not only a main settlement period for all business life in China but also the time of a large scale, house-to-house, full-fledged public health movement and demonstration against the combined forces of ills and evils and epidemics, complete with emblems and posters and slogans. Though strong stress is laid on poisonous insects, including childish attempts at coercing or hoodwinking them with the counterfeited seal of the Heavenly Teacher, some realistic precautionary measures are also carried out. As we have seen in instances mentioned before, it is

Arabesque cutouts of red paper in different designs and mounted on white backgrounds are about four inches wide and six inches long. They are used as charms against insects and plagues.

useless to try to demarcate realities from superstitions in the habitual doings of the Chinese on various occasions and we will see that the same is true with the miscellaneous customs during the Fifth Moon or Dragon Boat Festival.

For in order to combat the summer plagues that may become rampant during the following months of hot weather, the Chinese make good use of a chemical which they call *Hsiung Huang* (雄黄) and which is used internally as an enhancer of resistive powers and externally as a passive defense against the onslaught of the insects by virtue of the characteristic odour of the medicine. This medicine, a yellow powder, is obtainable at a very reasonable price from all Chinese apothecaries and in terms of modern chemistry is arsenic trisulphide. In olden times a small pinch of the stuff was put into the wine consumed at the festival season but this is not so widely done any more. But it is a popular observance to mix a small quantity of the stuff with wine and use the liquid to touch up the noses, the ears, etc., of children as a preventive against "poisonous airs" or perhaps insect bites.

By carrying the practice one step farther into the domain of superstition or indeed fantasy, the Chinese also proceed to write a Chinese character "*wang*" (王) on the foreheads of the children. The character "*wang*" means of course "a king", and the tiger is the king of all animals, the Chinese say. The tiger has a sort of a natural marking on the forehead that resembles this *wang* character, which is constructed by three parallel horizontal strokes, intersected by one perpendicular. As explained before the tiger is a symbol of exorcistic authority and therefore such a marking is in itself a vanquisher of sundry bad influences. The Chinese reason that if a boy bears the mark of the tiger and the marking is done with a medicine of a great repelling property, the combination would certainly constitute a safeguard equal to any task it is confronted with and naturally will frighten away all dangerous insects including the five venomous species, the scorpion, the toad, the snake, the lizard and the winged centipede throughout the year. Hence the practice.

The various doors in the house are to be decorated with colourful touches, too.

Early in the morning on the fifth day of the fifth moon, two little bundles of cattails and branches of catnips (*artemisia vulgaris*) are inserted or nailed onto the door beams, one on each side. These will remain throughout the day and are then taken down. While the cattails are thrown away as being of no further value, the catnips are sorted out, collected together, dried in the sun, and put away, to come in handy when there is a child-birth in the family or in a neighbouring family, as they are used in the preparation of the bath for the Third Day Ceremony.

Together with these decorations there are also pasted on the various doors, and windows sometimes, little bits of carvings of red paper of such motifs as the five insects, the gourd, the box, the devil-chaser, etc., fashioned into variegated arabesques and mounted on white paper backgrounds. These are also known as *Hu Lu Hua-erh*, or Gourd Flowers. Country women make these and peddle them from door to door "for a song." They also serve as charms and, festivities over, they are torn off and thrown on the street "together with which will go the ill luck of the year."

Old Mrs. Wu arranged and attended to everything of this description, assisted by her inquisitive grandson and who button-holed her with all sorts of silly questions during the proceedings.

*　　　*　　　*

The term Dragon Boat Festival is well nigh synonymous with a feast of *ts'ung tse* (糭子), or Rice Cakes, and it is true that the festival would be robbed of much of its grandeur if these cakes were taken away from it. Rice of a special glutinous variety is used for these kinds of cakes. The rice is wrapped in little individual packages made of layers of the long leaves of reeds and boiled or cooked thoroughly to be eaten hot or cold with sugar and syrup. More often than not they are iced before serving and make a very delightful summer refreshment, a deviation from the usual pastries and things. Children like them particularly, though it is certainly more harmful to eat too much of this stuff than too much of any other stuff.

For two or three days before the Dragon Boat Festival if you stroll in the market places in Peking the odour you smell is that of rice cakes, the eyes see rice cakes, and the ears hear the rustling of the reed leaves in the preparation of the rice cakes. All shops advertise rice cakes, friends exchange rice cakes as a seasonable gift, and families make rice cakes and eat rice cakes. The garbage cans are full of the cast-away wrappings of the reed leaves. In short, they are everywhere-

Ts'ung tse of various kinds from the cent-a-piece kind which has a red date as its core to the luxurious varieties which contain the cores of a little quantity of mashed peas and sugar, or some other kinds of rare preserved fruits, or even cubes of ham, are offered for sale by a long range of sellers. The street pedlars sell them. The cheap eating-houses who cater mostly to the coolie or labourer classes sell them. The grocers sell them and even the most exclusive high-browed restaurants, the rendezvous of Peking's fashionables, are not without their special *ts'ung tse*. The custom penetrates all class or caste barriers and for hundreds of years it has known of no setback.

Devout Buddhists like the Wus who have family shrines for the various deities and a special room dedicated to the worship of ancestors usually make their own *ts'ung tse* as dishes of them are used as the season's offerings before the shrines and the scrolls of portraits of the ancestors as the religious aspect of Propriety. Confucius said, in explaining the ways of filial piety to his disciples: "When the parents are alive, serve them according to Propriety, and dead, bury them according to Propriety, and afterward, worship them according to Propriety". And in the traffic of daily life in China, be it a red or green light, jam or no jam, Propriety has the absolute right of way.

Having been prepared in the most reverent fashion, the *ts'ung tse* of the Wu family were ready early in the morning for the sacred ceremony at which old Mr. Wu officiated, supported by his wife. They had the *ts'ung tse* opened from their reedy wrappings and arranged in little dishes, five in every dish and sprinkled over with sugar. Adding another seasonal touch, they put in each dish a few cherries, and white and black mulberries, and these offerings were then put in the solemnest manner before all the various shrines. A special dish was put in front of the little shrine of the Kitchen God who is, according to Chinese belief, the Governor-General and Resident Plenipotentiary from the Great Emperor-God of Jade who lives way up on the topmost story of the Thirty-Third Heaven.

When the offerings have served their purpose, they are "withdrawn" and consumed by the members of the family.

They saw to it that Little Bald Head had all the black mulberries for there is a belief that if a child eats these on the Dragon Boat Festival, he need fear no such unpleasant happening as having a house fly come into his stomach with the food he will eat throughout the summer season. Chinese parents deliberately give these black mulberries to their children to eat for no other purpose.

*   *   *

The Wu family gathered at their annual feast on the Dragon Boat Festival, concluding the menu with a course of the famous rice cakes.

Then, in the spirit of an after-dinner speech, the family talked over the origin of the tradition of rice cakes. Young Little Bald Head listened with his mouth wide open.

The tale was laid in the period of the Warring Kingdoms, when feudal lords gained in power and robbed much of the prestige from the famous Chi family who reigned as emperors of the Chow Dynasty (1134-247 B.C.). It was roughly when Alexander the Great, King of Macedonia, conquered Egypt some 300 years before Christ when this happened. These feudal lords of the various regional governments proclaimed themselves, one after another, as independent rulers of their respective districts.

At that time the regions which are now all of Hupeh and Hunan provinces and part of Honan province were known collectively as the Kingdom of Ch'u.

There lived a young political genius, not more than thirty years of age, by the name of Ch'ui P'ing (he is better known to the Chinese as Ch'ui Yuan). Young Ch'ui hailed from a rich and influential family of nobles and before long he won the confidence of the then Ch'u emperor, Hwai Wang, and was appointed to a high administrative position. He made recommendations in lengthy memorials and advocated giving the citizens of Ch'u a new deal and a square one at that. The emperor had taken him in as his right hand man allowing him a free hand in the politico-military situation with a high-sounding title which would translates no less than Supreme Crown Adviser and Expert Consultant, and entrusted to him the important duties, on account of his diplomatic acumen, of an ambassador-at-large on a politically inspired tour of the various minor states, notably the Kingdom of Ch'i (the present Shantung province) in an attempt to negotiate some alliance of joint action in defending themselves against the expansionistic schemes of the Kingdom of Ch'in, whose domain then was roughly the present Shensi province. He almost succeeded in his mission.

The Ch'ins were not asleep either and they soon got wind of the scheme. Tracing the eruption to its pathological origin and devising a counter-measure that would surely work, they secretly commissioned one of their able statesmen to Ch'u where, according to authentic Chinese history, by silver bullets he stirred up an atmosphere in the court diagonally antagonistic to Ch'ui P'ing and anything he stood for. The plans for the "league" were frustrated. The victim of this political intrigue, Ch'ui P'ing, was relieved of his important positions and, to add insult to injury, was exiled from the capital with not even a decree to have the government finance him on a world tour on some sort of investigation to save his face. In this way, with no face or fortune or favour left and his political career shattered beyond restoration, Ch'ui became a plain citizen of the land.

Poor Ch'ui was desperate but not despondent. He appeased himself with the thought that some day fortune would surely turn again in his favour and there might yet be a chance to regain his political influence. He thought and thought and not content with idly waiting he started to write poems as a means of publicity. His endeavours were very well received and his works, filling many volumes, have been handed down among the country's best classical masterpieces. He growled, murmured, sobbed, complained, debated with himself and comforted himself much as a young person would whose love's labour is lost. But the emperor sensed a danger in the situation and chose to lend him a deaf ear.

So, finally, not receiving any word of reinstatement for a long time his hopes died within him. He became actually pessimistic in regard to everything and agreed with his goodself in mournful verses that his life was not real and not earnest and was but an empty dream and therefore not worth living. One bright early summer morning, about two thousand two hundred years ago, supposedly on the fifth day of the fifth moon, he admitted defeat, wrote his will, said good-bye to his landlord, marched out from his abode on the river Ku Lo Chiang (which is in the present Hunan province and empties into the Tung T'ing Lake), jumped into the water and succeeded in his attempt to kill himself as a protest against the bitter treatment he had received from the cold and unobliging world.

"And it is in memory of our wise and good man Ch'ui P'ing that we eat these rice cakes every year on the fifth day of the fifth moon which has developed into the Dragon Boat Festival," concluded old Mr. Wu.

*   *   *

All Chinese admit that the rice cakes eaten at the Dragon Boat Festival are in memory of a political theorist of the Kingdom of Ch'u, who committed suicide as a gesture of moral protest —the kind of gesture for which the Orientals are famous the world over. But it is not the whole story.

When the news spread that the able ex-minister Ch'ui P'ing

had drowned himself in the Ku Lo Chiang river, there was universal mourning among all his admirers and his posthumous honours were many.

And the Ch'u people in the neighbourhood district, according to one legend, started operations to reclaim the body with naturally a view to give it at least a decent burial (it may be reasonable to say that the Dragon Boats in the regattas are but an "abridged edition" of the salvage boats bearing the dragon as a royal hallmark which took part in the operations), but they obtained no results. Trying at least to save the body from being feasted upon by the river fishes, the people scattered handfuls of rice into the water in order that the hungry fishes would have something to eat and so leave the body of His Excellency unmolested and in order to make the supplies of rice last longer an ingenious device was invented whereby the rice was wrapped in little bundles with leaves of reeds and there and then the first rice cakes in history were made.

But another storyteller tells it differently. He says that the practice started with the Ch'u people offering rice thrown into the river as a sacrifice to the departed spirit of Ch'ui P'ing and which practice was carried on for some time before somebody proclaimed one day that he had, perhaps simultaneously with many others in the district as Chinese stories like to have it, seen the late Ch'ui in a dream, acknowledging the various sacrificial acts but complaining that since the rice was thrown into the water in loose handfuls, the various kinds of fishes ate it all, leaving nothing for his own personal consumption. To devise an improvement to cope with such a situation was nothing to Ch'ui and forthwith he suggested to the people in whose dreams he appeared that if it was not too much trouble, would they please have little packages made with special wrappings which would be waterproof and not easily perishable, perhaps using the leaves of riverside reeds or rushes as these would meet all the foregoing specifications and yet represent no excessive economic burden on the part of his dear friends and were specially recommended because of the simple process of preparation and the inexhaustible and self-sustaining supply of raw materials. He further suggested an equally worthy scheme of using the hollow tubings of the stalks of bamboos to encase the rice in a similar fashion. As an all-around political brain-trust all by himself, Ch'ui P'ing certainly lived up to his reputation.

The people woke up, exchanged their experiences at a conference, unanimously agreed and a resolution was passed to do exactly as His Excellency desired.

"And in the course of two thousand years, these rice cakes have come to be consumed in family platters rather than as sacrificial offerings to an ancient suicide who laid down his life that his nation might live", added old Mr. Wu.

"But offerings or no offerings. I know what I am going to do this afternoon. The Sleeping Buddha Temple will still be open today and I am going there for a look around taking Little Bald Head with me. Do you want to go, Little Bald Head?" the old man asked.

"Oh, sure, I'll go with you. When you are ready, I am ready", answered the grandson.

THE TEMPLE OUTSIDE HATA MEN

THERE are two temples in Peking known as temples of Sleeping Buddhas; one is on the main highway leading to the so-called Western Hills about twelve or fourteen miles from the city, and the other is located on the extension of the Flower Market Street outside the Hata Men. It was on this street that the makers of artificial flowers had their periodic gatherings or fairs as the majority of these people had only small family "factories" where members of the families, particularly the women and children, pursued what was a much "sweated" industry in the slums behind closed doors and all the transactions with the outside were carried on at the fairs. In those "good old days" artificial flowers used to enjoy a very regular and brisk trade as they were much in demand with the ladies, especially the young and fashionable Manchu women who used them profusely to decorate their headdresses with. Artificial flowers as an item of local manufacture have long lost at least part of their economic importance but, nevertheless, the district is still an important center for various small industries.

Almost symbolic of the collapse of the artificial flower business and as a parallel event in chronological order, perhaps more pathetic and heartrending, would be the state of neglect in which the Temple of the Sleeping Buddha, a former rendezvous for the women and children of the neighbourhood mostly engaged in the artificial flower business during the holidays, has fallen. The Sleeping Buddha, as it were, has long since given up dreaming of a day of reconstruction and revival and he has actually become more and more slumberous and from the state of a habitual sleepy head has dropped into a state of sleeping-sickness—an isolated case of the dread tropical disease—from which he does not even bother to open one of his eyes once in a long while to see if there were any sign of improved treatment coming from the surrounding humanity.

*　　　*　　　*

So when old Mr. Wu and his grandson, Little Bald Head, arrived at the temple on their holiday excursion after their Dragon Boat Festival dinner they saw few pilgrims and, indeed, only a small number of callous people on their habitual trips of "sight-seeing"; (Frequenting familiar places for sight-seeing is an old established custom for all Peking-*jen* alike). Most of the halls were without the familiar images and those that were still habitable had been rented out to some paupers attracted there by cheap rentals as well as by the prevailing low economic water level that made the tenants, who were all in about the same mendicant predicament, mutually less self-conscious.

Old Mr. Wu himself was surprised to find the last hall housing the giant sleeping image of Buddha still standing and having nothing worse than a few big holes in the roofs which were stopped by old bits of matting. Of the four walls, three and the fraction of the fourth were still standing. An old man who looked as though he were the custodian of the temple and therefore eligible for collecting cumshaw from the pilgrims burning incense before the image was in attendance. He had, by close contact with the

Buddha, gotten himself a case of slight-degreed contamination for while hoping against hope of the visit of some generous and devout visitors, he had also gone to sleep nearby. The image itself was still intact and of the many luxuriously embroidered silken coverlets donated by the believers one very shabby specimen was still in evidence covering the monstrous mud likeness to the best of its ability against the onslaught of the elements. The foundation of the thirty-foot long image, lying on his side and supporting his head with a bent arm as pillow, has stood heroically against all odds. The facial expression remained serene and contented and not without a trace of a smile with which the image was given by its maker for the Sleeping Buddha is representative of a high stage of tranquility, the fruit of immense virtue but one step short of Nirvana, the final emancipation of the soul by absorption into the divine.

Old Mr. Wu was impressed by the general dilapidated condition of the temple and felt very sad for a good many moments because the change he saw was so drastic and thoroughgoing. Conditions had not been so bad when he was there a few years back.

Little Bald Head was disappointed and suggested that they return home. And so they left.

*   *   *

On their way home from the deserted Temple of the Sleeping Buddha the mind of Little Bald Head began to wonder and finally he spoke to his grandfather.

"Grandfather, was that the old broken down temple which we have come all the way to see? It certainly was not worth the trouble considering the hot weather".

"Yes and no, my lad. I was surprised, too. Only a few years back the temple was in a much better condition and there were still a good many pilgrims and visitors during the five days when it was thrown open to the public.

"When your father was about your age we used to come here regularly every year. There were the usual little wayside shows and candy booths which were also little gambling establishments attracting crowds of children to their little games of chance, to risk and usually to lose their few treasured coppers. And that was not all. The rich people from the city used to come to race their ponies and mule carts in that vast stretch of open ground behind the temple precincts.

"Racing ponies and mule carts? Why, that must have been very interesting," Little Bald Head said, surprised.

"Yes, almost exactly like the Dragon Boat racing in the southern provinces of China. Here the rich Manchu princes and wealthy merchants used to come to the races which they sponsored as a demonstrational recreation. The grounds were first marked out and on the spot where you saw the big heaps of garbage and other city refuse used to be the main runways with mat shed "grandstands" lining the northern side against the earthen embankments. These "grandstands" were provided for invited guests as well as for the public. Weather permitting the place was literally packed with humanity, lined up many rows deep with only the thousands of human heads visible from a distance; children got on the trees from where they had vantage points and reserved seats. The crowd cheered and roared as they watched while the pedlars and tea-house managers reaped a harvest of profit."

"And they all came to watch the races in which horses and mule carts competed to see which one ran the fastest?" Little Bald Head asked.

Old Mr. Wu was amused. He smiled and went on:

"No, S-i-r, they did not really run any races but only came out one by one to show off the fine appearance of their ponies which were ridden by the owners themselves. The majority of riders were not very good horsemen to start with but only wished to show off to friends and opponents how their respective horses were smart-looking, well groomed, and how the saddles, harnesses and bridles etc. were as expensively appointed as anybody else's. The horses not only did not run any races but, on the contrary, they were not even made to run fast—the fashion then was not speed but rather the gait. Every owner-rider was his own jockey and his number one *mafoo* or groom served as valet and life insurance—for he walked beside his master and the mount, regulating the speed of the horse by holding fast to the headgear to keep the animal in check. The mule carts were entered and shown off in the same manner, each one demonstrated in turn with the owner riding in full public view. They were the hooded variety with two large wheels with iron tyres, all the wooden parts were lacquered and the other accessories and extra equipment carefully polished to look their best—even the little porcelain jugs containing the lubricating grease for the axis had to be a ceramic specimen from a famous period such as Chien Lung or even K'ang Hsi. To add a final dash of colour, little pieces of silks of gaudy hues were braided into the tails and manes of the ponies and the mules which vied with the shiny brass trimmings of the carts in points of brilliance.

"And part of the cheering was actuated not by admiration or because some stunt or any phase of horsemanship proved itself worthy of public applause. On the contrary, the cheering was often of a ridiculing or jeering sort for it often burst out if the horse suddenly acted queer while in the broad limelight of public inspection or perchance a conceited owner-rider fell off his mount which spectacle was not a very scarce happening. To save the lost face, certain types of paid bullies and *ta-shou* (打手), or professional strong men, big, husky, fierce-looking fellows, would suddenly emerge from (it seemed) nowhere and as a chastising measure to the mockers would pick quarrels and start hand-to-hand fights which proved to be more of a sight than perhaps the "racers" themselves. It is true that many a young light-headed Manchu prince could be recognized among the jockeys and amateur cartdrivers. It is also true that gangs of paid "fighters" often started to fight each other as their respective employers were jeered."

"Huh! As bad as that?" said Little Bald Head.

"Yes, but this can be seen no more", the old man said sadly.

*   *   *

The general relationship between a married daughter and her maternal family is a very delicate issue and a problem that presents many phases of appreciation.

It is a well known fact that in China the people prefer to have sons than daughters for reasons already explained. Until recent years there even existed a practice of going as far as drowning newborn girls and this was done with impunity in certain provinces in the south because girls represented too much of a burden to the family with no chance of any future remuneration which would be definitely forthcoming if the child was a boy. But there is also a sentimental problem connected with this.

It has been noticed that daughters, once married, lose all real interest in the affairs of their maternal families and also often manifest such an attitude even before they are married. Two proverbs prove such a state of affairs. One of them is "In bring-ing up daughters their faces are found to face the outside", and the other, "Daughters married away is like water thrown away". It is true that some girls find marriage a pleasant escape from the oppressive, disciplined life of a Chinese daughter. But it does not necessarily follow that from the daughters' point of view, they are considered as permanently separated from the maternal families.

An old saying goes, "A woman may live to be ninety-nine but she should always maintain contact with the maternal family for a convenient fall-back". And such friendships, except in a very few cases, usually survive all obstacles and are carried on for generations as the children and grandchildren of the married daughters become automatically related to those of their mother's brothers and sisters. This is why everybody seems to be everybody else's relative—a thing which has been surprising foreigners all along. For this is the broader sense of the word "relatives". "Relatives by marriage are connected for generations, you may smash their bones and find the muscles still unsevered" says another Chinese proverb.

From the foregoing principles there has evolved the custom of "home comings" at regular intervals which keep married daughters in contact with their maternal families as well as providing the parents with opportunities to have their daughters in their midst for at least a few days in the year. The occasions prescribed by Propriety are usually the days following each important holiday such as the Dragon Boat Festival, the fifth day of the fifth moon, others being days following the new year festivities, the Lantern Festival, and the Mid-Autumn Festival. It seems that as the daughters are required to be with their husband and their families during the holidays, the maternal families have no better days to choose than days immediately following the holidays for their family reunions. Such reunions are always accompanied by the parents doing all within their power to give the daughters a good time. Aside from the festivals, there is one particularly important occasion, especially for newly-wed daughters—the second day of the second moon, called the *Lung T'ai T'ou* (龍抬頭), or the day on which the "Dragon Lifts its Head". A little familiar song describing a parent failing to get their newly married daughter home for a reunion translates as follows:—

"On the second day of the second moon,
Everybody goes to bring home their little jewels.
And those who fail to get their jewels home,
Will shed the bitterest of bitter tears."

The custom of home-coming was carried out regularly in the

case of young Mrs. Wu and on each trip Little Bald Head was taken with her. It was a pleasant and delightful change for them because the Ho family, the maternal family of the young mother, lived in the country.

But Little Bald Head was glad to be back home after four days for he missed not only his grandparents and his young father but also the companionship of the neighbourhood children, notably the Wang brothers. He did not know that the Wang children were away with their mother on a similar trip to their grandmother's home for the custom is universally observed.

TEASHOP STORYTELLERS

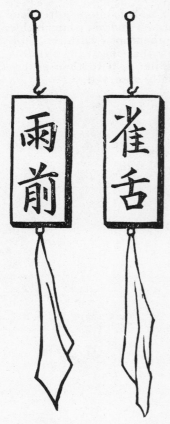

A teashop's signs are wooden boards some sixteen inches long with cloth "tails" and bearing the names of famous teas, such as "Before Rain", "Sparrow's Tongue", etc.

NO description of Peking life can leave out the teashops which dot the broad streets and narrow lanes alike, besides occupying all the desirable spots in historically famous places in and around the metropolis. It is another institution that pervades all classes of the people in its various aspects. There are the luxuriously furnished places with the wicker chairs, some inclined like steamer chairs to give the gathering fashionables more comfort. These also serve light lunches and little fancy tit-bits of dainty morsels to the "classy" patrons. These, it must be admitted, are really adaptations of something foreign although the principle of sipping hot tea to kill long summer afternoons or to enjoy breezy evenings in some scenic spot is age-old in native China. From this high level the ramifications of tea shops reach down, step by step, to the "watering places" of the labourers for whom tea is part of the menu and ranks with other items in the cheapest meals for the masses. When the range gets down to as low as the little halfgrown youngsters who balance an earthen jar full of steaming beverage made by soaking handfuls of tea "powder" or tea "dust" from the end of a stick and deal out the precious fluid in coarse pottery bowls to the rickshaw men and labourers during their hard-earned "pause that refreshes" at the price of two bowls for one big copper, it is just about where the rock bed is and as low as it can ever get.

But of the entire panorama of teashops the most fascinating would be those where the city's idle gather, where gossip of everything, from current events of assorted proportions to household scandals are exchanged, and where the pet birds these people keep as their sole companions in idleness are compared. Little wooden boards with cloth "tails" bearing the names of famous "brands" of tea serve as signboards.

Here is a place to see a phase of Peking's age-old life as the customers seat themselves on long benches set along equally long tables as if at one big invited company, some in their favourite positions and, without having to ask the attendants (who are called by some sarcastic gentlemen, the "tea doctors"—the same "doctor" as in "doctors of philosophy" and not in the medical sense), will find a pot of hot tea brewed and brought before him with the wrapper of the tea leaves inserted in the pot's handle as a voucher of accounting. The same attendants will come in at intervals with a big pot of boiling water to add as extras for each customer as the tea is consumed until there is absolutely no room for one cup more in the customer's capacity. Here only itinerant peanut and melon seed pedlars appear to add to the fare of the spendthrift few for the majority of the guests are interested in tea and nothing else.

The customers sit, engage in conversation with fellow frequenters, watch their pet birds and feed them when in season with live grasshoppers or cicadas from which the wings and the head and the legs have been pulled off and which are carried in little gauze containers. When these birds are well nourished and feel good, the proud owners will be entertained by their songsters while covetous fellow-customers cock their ears to listen and some experienced "old hand at it" will interpret or explain in a flattering manner whatever the clever lark or mocking bird or canary or whatever it is, is imitating, whether an owl, an eagle, a mountain magpie, a blue jay or (and this is absolutely true and vouched for by the writer) a wintering cricket or a cat.

From this the conversation of the customers, in small or bigger groups, will start to drift to loosely connected subjects, very much like the free association test in a laboratory of applied psychology, only the partakers in the conversation seem to be much more congenial and open-hearted and not without a degree of fine fellowship. The conversation will, for example, drift from birds in general to birds in particular, thence to the high price paid for Mr. So-and-so's robin redbreast and thence to famous "suckers" and the fancy prices paid for their pets, thence to bird-catching in the moatside swamps and the fight over a rare catch, thence to the fight at the noodle shop next door two years ago, then to comparing of notes about rumours of current happenings, and finally arriving back at the old subject of the weather—the shower the other day, and so *ad infinitum*.

Then it is here that somebody meets somebody else and his crowd regarding the negotiations on the sale of a piece of property. The negotiations will commence as the participants in the conference arrive one after another at irregular intervals at their own sweet will in the typical Chinese manner until the quorum is complete. The details of the transactions are repeated and repeated until almost everybody in the tea shop knows that everybody else knows them as clearly as the principals themselves. Meanwhile, clouds of strong tobacco smoke, cigarette aroma, and the piercing flavour of snuff fill the air while pots of hot tea are consumed.

The negotiations will give fresh impetus to the talk long after the meeting itself is over. At last the tea leaves in the individual pots in front of all but a few of the late-coming patrons are absolutely unable to give out any more colour whatever, to say nothing of flavour as water has been going in and coming out so many times. It is then that the customers will each pay the price of two or three big coppers, the price of the tea leaves additional whatever it is, two, four, or ten coppers, and start to leave in twos and threes. The time would be toward the supper hour and the teashop is temporarily empty or near-empty until the customers,

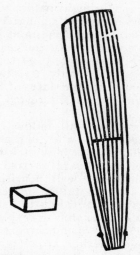

A folded fan and a little square of hard wood are the storyteller's indispensable equipment.

some the same as before, will return for their evening tea.

*   *   *

Old Mr. Wu, before his grandson came into the household, was one of such gentlemen and his attendance was almost as on schedule. Though other pastimes had been introduced into his daily program, the habit of many years' standing was not entirely removable. And it is recorded that Little Bald Head was often seen with his grandfather on such tea expeditions though the occasions became much less frequent as time went on.

*   *   *

In some of Peking's teashops, mostly in the bigger ones, there may be seen in the center of the room a raised platform made of brickwork and on which is set a small table decorated with a piece of red cloth on the side facing the public. This looks as if some preacher was to give a sermon to the idle teashop guests on utilizing their spare time in some worthy manner. This is the place which a scholarly-looking gentleman will occupy at some stated hour to give much-favoured entertainment to the customers by telling stories of ancient times.

The program is advertised by posters at the teashop door or on the glass windows if there are any. The entertainment seems to be thrown in as a premium to the guests but it is not. For though no tickets are needed to gain admittance, the storyteller will either descend from the stage himself or delegate some attendant in the establishment to pass a little round wicker tray around for a collection from the audience at intervals. The prices are by no means high, a big copper at each collection is quite acceptable as one person's contribution and only spendthrifts of a "greenhorn" type will drop in more than two or three coppers at a time. The *hsien sheng* (先生), "Mister", as the storyteller is called, brandishes a big folded Chinese fan of paper and bamboo, no matter whether it is summer or winter, in order to add emphasis by gestures or for the purpose of demonstrating in an impressionistic manner the warrior-type characters in the story who flourish their weapons in tournaments or actual clashes. He also adds exclamation points into his narration by occasionally pounding on the table with a small square of hardwood. The cracking sound of the wood would also serve as a warning for "Silence!" for it means that he is about to start the entertainment.

Such telling of stories in public by professionals is one of the popular pastimes of Peking's leisured class, old men and children alike. The Chinese call these stories *P'ing Shu* (評書), or "books criticized" which is naturally a "corking piece" of misnomer.

The stories told are daily instalments of serials and without exception are adapted from such voluminous historical fictions as "The Romance of the Three Kingdoms" and "The Popular History of the Warring Kingdoms Period''. Other stories related would be popular fictions about chivalrous ''bandits'' of the Robin Hood type.   In this class an example may be cited in the *''Shui Hu Chuan''* (水滸傳), or ''Adventures in the Water Fort''—this book has recently been translated into English by a famous American woman writer, a Nobel prize winner, under the name of ''All Men are Brethren.''   It may not be out-of-place to add here that this book has been appraised as one of the three best of China's novels, the other two being the *''San Kuo Yen Yi''* (三國演義), or ''Romance of the Three Kingdoms'' and the *''Hung Lou Meng''* (紅樓夢), ''The Dream of the Red Chamber'', all of which are available for foreign readers in different languages.

Another favourite variety of fiction being retold in this fashion to the tea-sipping public is the one known as ''court case books'' which are a sort of detective stories mingled with the doings of some heroic, gallant ''robbers'' who did their part either in protecting upright officials from antagonistic influences or in getting rid of corrupt officials by means of under-cover organizations and activities and even by assassination. The stories in this category also lay special stress on the sagacity of the magistrates in solving knotty cases of daring robberies, complicated murders, sensational court scandals and the like.   As the original writers of these novels did by pen and ink in exaggerated descriptions, the storytellers do the same by word of mouth, at times adding thrills and sensations by attributing mysterious faculties to the mandarins of reviving the dead and summoning departed spirits from the next world to stand witness at trials or to render protection to the mandarins whose life and adventures are being told.   Of this class, representative pieces are the *''Shih Kung An''* (施公案), or ''Doings of Mandarin Shih'' and *''Pao Kung An''* (包公案) or ''Cases Judged by Minister Pao.''

Still another class of stories told may be said to be of mythological origin and represents the mysterious and indeed fantastic experiences of some Taoist or Buddhist priests or some fairies and deities.   Of this the novel *'' Feng Shen Yen Yi''* (封神演義), or ''Detailed Account of the Deifications'', may be said to be a typical example.

*   *   *

There are not very many professional storytellers of the kind described for many people consider it below their dignity to learn such a trade. But the few that do follow the profession are mostly great artists in their own meaning of the word. They are invariably gifted in public speaking and capable of holding the attention of a big audience. And it is not as easy as it seems for the stories are usually of the ''thrice-told'' variety and sound like ''old friends'' to many a listener.   Besides, at least part of the gathering is actually not in the least interested in the stories.   Some may happen to be there primarily to talk over a piece of business— in other words, a conference may be going on simultaneously with the recitation of stories.   To this state of affairs should also be added the free coming and going of the public as there is no moral rule to discourage this during the performance.

Professional storytellers are expected also to imitate various dialects of the Chinese language in keeping with the characters in the fiction.   For instance if a Shantung man in the story happens to be talking to a man from Shansi the storyteller can only be sure of public approval and support if he succeeds in imitating the two distinct dialects when speaking their respective lines with at least a passable resemblance while carrying on the story with apparent ease and without any special exertion noticeable on his part or being confused in any manner. Only to those who know the Chinese language and the diversifications of the Chinese dialect, is it possible to form an idea of what kind of a headache this part of his job is. He certainly deserves many compliments, considering also the unquestionable superiority of his power of memory for he may tell a long-winded instalment of a story in two consecutive hours daily and do the "continued from yesterday" for a full two months (which is the proper "turn" or "run" of a fiction at one teashop as is agreed proper by the profession) without once consulting the "scenario" or the original book or even a written outline of the day's portion during the performance. He is not provided with a prompter to whisper to him a forgotten paragraph from behind curtains or from a concealed "box" beneath the footlights.

And this is not all for he has to figure on getting his story to arrive at small "knots" to keep his audience from dispersing while he collects his fees every ten or fifteen minutes and then to arrive at a big "knot" at the end of the day's instalment in order that his listeners will remember to come back again the next day at the proper hour to know what is to happen to a famous general who has been captured by his enemies, or to a chivalrous bandit chieftain who has been trapped in a mechanized secret chamber, or to the most admired Mandarin apparently in danger of losing his life at the hand of gangsters. The storyteller always manages to arrive at such a breath-holding junction when he announces that the time is up!

*   *   *

To listen to such storytellers is called *T'ing Shu* (聽書), or "listening to books". Of this practice young Little Bald Head became shortly a regular addict after his grandfather introduced it to him. When there was nothing doing elsewhere on long summer afternoons, he was often seen with his bearded grandfather listening most intently to the narrations as he munched watermelon seeds from the little dishes which the teashop also served.

Of the stories he heard, those which appealed to him the most were from the " *Chi Kung Chuan*" (濟公傳), or the "Life of Abbot Chi Kung," a popular fiction telling about the magical and mystical doings of a Buddhist priest in the Sung Dynasty. The stories made such an impression on the young mind that he was noticed to refer to them on many an occasion at home and abroad. It was also discovered that one of the reasons behind his industry during his first school days later was that some day he might be able to read the *"Chi Kung Chuan"* in the original.

A POPULAR FAIR

CHINESE conceptions of weather represent another phase of popular superstition. According to their idea the various phenomena of wind, rain, etc., are controlled by various departments of the deities. We have seen how the Chinese interpret thunder and lightning and it is on the same general principles that rain is controlled by the rain god and clouds by the god of clouds, wind by the god of wind, etc. To each of these a special shrine of elaborate proportions has been dedicated where the imperial families used to send a high-ranking official on specific dates for sacrificial ceremonies and to pray for "harmonized" rainfall during the year. For hailstorms there is a special god whose duty it is to destroy the crops of the farmers in various districts as a punishment by order of the Jade Emperor God. All such gods, according to popular conception, are sort of technical experts and though capable of doing big things are not authorized for free and independent function.

One of the special duties of the god of rain which is booked for annual performance is a slight shower on the 13th of each 5th moon. According to the traditional belief of the Peking-*jen*, the order allegedly received from the Jade Emperor God does not give a specified hour for this special round of duty and any hour in the day would do and, it seems, it also carries an "if" clause that should the day be scheduled for rainfalls of other categories by way of "previous engagement", then the order would automatically be considered fulfilled by that. A Chinese proverb of many years' standing says "No great drought can hold out through the 13th of the 5th moon," and judging from the persistence of this saying and the public support apparently earned by it having been proved true, the schedule must have "clicked" many times.

*   *   *

It was on account of this that certain plans for a day's outing arranged by old Mr. Wu and in which Little Bald Head was to take part were postponed.

"We cannot go out for it is going to rain this afternoon," said the old man. "For this is the 13th day of the 5th moon and there is bound to be the Sword Grinding Rain some time today though the morning has been fine."

The Sword Grinding Rain, or *Mou Tao Yu* (磨刀雨), refers to a historical anecdote of General Kuan Yu, widely known as China's War God. General Kuan was a sworn brother of Liu Pei, King of Shu of the famous Three Kingdoms period (approximately 200-220 A.D.), who, like the orthodox sworn brothers, lived through thick and thin with him in the most faithful manner. At the time of this happening, Shu was temporarily granted the mandate over the territory of Chingchow (part of present Hupei province) in the nature of a loan from the Kingdom of Wu for use as a base of action against their common enemy the Kingdom of Wei in the north. In course of time Shu occupied other territories and so plans were looming large to force the return of sovereign rights of Chingchow to the Wus. Not wishing to risk war for the scheme's materialization an invitation was addressed to General Kuan, King of Shu's right-hand-man and chief lieuten-

ant, and whose word was quite as good as the King's, to a feast
at the river port of Lukow. At this feast the Wus secretly planned to get General Kuan voluntarily to surrender the mandate in
a gentlemanly manner across the dinner table or on his failing to
do so good-humouredly soldiers concealed in the conference room,
in accordance with prearranged plans, were to emerge from ambush to kill the Shu general in cold blood. General Kuan Yu
was quite appreciative of its dangerous nature but accepted the
invitation in spite of warnings by his followers. He attended the
feast alone and by high-powered argumentations he was able to
leave the conference without consenting to the request put forward by the Wus, and furthermore, without being waylaid by
the enemy force. Throughout the trip he was armed with nothing
but a heavy, long-handled sword called by the fabulous name of
Green Dragon on the Moon, the favourite weapon of the soldier-
diplomat. The occasion is known as *Tan Tao Hui* (單刀會) or
"Single Sword Meeting," and it took place on the 13th day of the
5th moon.

In commemoration of this brave general, who has since been
deified to occupy an important shrine in the Chinese pantheon,
and the Single Sword Meeting itself, by order of the Jade Emper-
or God, rain is to fall every year on the 13th day of the 5th moon
for it is remembered that the God of War "has a sword to grind,"
referring to the famous Green Dragon on the Moon.

*　　*　　*

One of the places where Little Bald Head loved so much to
spend a summer afternoon in the company of his grandfather was
the market place and amusement center near the lotus pond of
Shih Cha Hai (十剎海), or the Sea of Ten Monasteries—a stretch
of water which was apparently designed to be used as a reservoir
for the "sea palaces" which have in recent years been thrown
open to the public as parks. The Sea of Ten Monasteries, so
named because there are ten Buddhist temples of different sizes
scattered to the north of the place, has long been famous for its
lotus flowers (water lilies) which were no doubt the original
drawing card for many of Peking's leisured and esthetic crowds.
The first visitors to the Shih Cha Hai were there primarily to
admire the lotus blossoms which to the mind of the cultured
Chinese represent a human type—that of the *chuin tze* (君子),
Superior Man. This is the model man of the Confucian school
and a golden mean between the Rich and Noble, the millionaire
type of "successful" men, represented by the tree peony, and the
so-called *yin yi* (隱逸), or Hermit type, for whom the world is not
worth a nickel, represented by the chrysanthemum. The Chinese
poets see many a beauty and virtue in the lotus flowers but even
the man in the street is not without an admiration for them for
they are beautiful to look at and certainly carry a pleasant fragrance. Acres of lotus in bloom is a breath-taking sight.

And here they are, acres of them, in a good-sized pond lined
on the four sides with willow trees centuries old and situated
next to the old pink-washed walls, topped by the yellow glazed
tiles (pulled down but a few years before) of the Imperial City,
away from the hustle and bustle of the crowded, dusty Peking
streets, though surprisingly near them. The tall backdrops
of this picturesque spot are provided by the famous Drum

Chinese water lilies have beautiful blossoms, sometimes seven or eight inches in diameter.

and Bell Towers of Peking on the north and the White Pagoda of the Winter Palace on the south. If such a place does not make an ideal spot for a "promenade deck", it would be hard to find one that does.

Here the temporary or seasonal market is held each year during the summer months, starting from the beginning of the fifth moon to the middle of the eighth. Enterprising businessmen stake out plots along the wide walk which serves also as a separating dyke and erect matshed teashops of a *de luxe* type with elevated floors for better views of everything around. Little variety shows and stalls where popular if rustic kinds of foods are sold, side by side with fruit stalls and those of a number of unexpected businesses which seem to be there more for the fun than for the profits.

Some theatrical companies are to be seen, too, giving performances in matshed theatres where the thrice blessed ones would sit in the company of their families, sipping the famous Dragon Well tea and munching away at the various edibles—candies, nuts, etc., spread out in porcelain dishes while plays are enacted by passable actors and actresses on the impromptu stages, and light, cool breezes blow carrying with them the fragrance of the blooming lotus flowers visible from the open side nearest to the pond and but a few feet away. Here the light-hearted pleasure-seekers, away from the worries of work and the scorching heat of the summer sun, laugh at their neighbours who have to stay in their homes or in some suffocating offices where "duty holds them fast."

For here is another world, a little Peitaiho Beach, a Bermuda, nay, a Coney Island in the Chinese standard of judgment. Peking people in every walk of life make excursions here, a few make it their summer resort. The characteristic noises of a Chinese gathering, the singing and playing of music from the various shows, the tea shop attendants accosting prospective customers, and shopkeepers crying out their specialties, all these mingle with the drowsy droning of the cicadas on the willow branches and supply the sound effect, while apparently prosperous restaurants and shops with the season's delicatessen, fancy-coloured toys and luscious fruits, gaily dressed children and still more gaily dressed adults combine in the endless reels of technicolour to supply the sight.

Such being the kaleidoscopic views and hues of the place, no wonder trains of rickshaws convey native visitors on Sunday afternoons to the Shih Cha Hai.

* * *

The annual summer fair at the Sea of Ten Monasteries is full of the charm that identifies itself with Old Peking. The city-builders of the early Ming started it and the Manchus kept it up and glorified it for full three hundred years. Even that august personage the Empress Dowager Tsu Hsi herself has been recorded to have viewed the lotus blossoms of the place from a vantage point on the hillocks adjoining the Winter Palace lakes on the north where she and her ladies-in-waiting, protected by the high massive walls of the Winter Palace and the Imperial City, had an unobstructed view of the willow-lined lily ponds. It can well be imagined that she viewed with a mixed feeling of satisfaction and jealousy the official residences and attached gardens of the various princes further beyond, the monstrous one-storied buildings of the quadrangles of palace proportions with roofs of yellow or green tiles, indicating the ranks of the occupant nobilities. With few exceptions all the princes had their mansions in that neighbourhood, a quiet and picturesque district conveniently near to their "jobs" in the Forbidden City—like Beverly Hills is to the movie studios of Hollywood.

Although each visit to the Shih Cha Hai fair reminded old Mr. Wu of the past glory of this historical spot all that Little Bald Head saw was nothing but fun.

Here are groups of open air wayside shows each with its domain marked off by rows of narrow benches on the four sides on which visitors may sit as they enjoy the shows. One group of men will dab themselves up like clowns in a circus and relate humorous stories interspaced with funny dialogues of the "Amos 'n' Andy" variety, invoking hilarious laughter from the audience and showers of coppers or notes of small denominations at each collection time. Here the trade is "sold on the ground" according to their own language, for the patrons toss the money on the ground to be picked up by the showmen themselves.

Another circle of spectators may be gathered around a magician who will commence his program first with simpler tricks such as the vanishing beads or the inexhaustible wine-flask. From these he will proceed to more complicated tricks as the crowd gets thicker and thicker. His young assistant will beat a brass gong and the master chants the pseudo-magical words. A little white mouse is covered with a tea cup and then, uncovering the cup in the fraction of a second, he will produce a live green frog in its place! Then from an empty can, passed around the watchers to see it is empty, and which is covered with a broken straw hat, similarly inspected, he will produce a two-foot-long tame snake, darting out its "tongue" in the vicious mannerism of its kind. Then a white rabbit, fully five pounds in weight, comes out from a coverlet put flat on the ground as he lifts it up, or else a glass bowl ten inches in diameter filled to the rim with water and holding a pair of goldfish would come out mysteriously from under a lifted cloth square. While the crowd is thus hypnotized to believe that all he says he will do he does he announces that the next piece of jugglery will be to convert a bunch of eagle feathers into a live eagle which "will dash out as I lift this straw hat here. When the eagle appears we will let loose this rabbit. The eagle seeing the rabbit, its eyes will 'grow red' and then both will engage in a fight right before your eyes, and then all you folk will say 'Hao! Hao!', or very good but I am holding this up just a few minutes while I ask you for a few coppers for my evening's bowl of rice."

This serves as a notice that it is time to pay. Spectators

will either toss some money on the ground in the enclosure or, in the case of the "thick-skinned", sneak away nonchalantly with an I-have-just-paid look on their face to conceal a guilty conscience of having "chiselled" the man of a free show. The money is collected from the ground, counted and put away in the "cash box."

In the meantime the juggler will give a lot of talk to allow the spectators to adjust themselves until but few are left from the previous gathering and still fewer who will actually wait for him to stage the promised eagle-and-rabbit fight. In this way the attention has been diverted to something else to give the men a chance to start a new series of feats and the eagle program is allowed to remain unexecuted for it was originally intended as a piece of diplomacy and nothing else.

*   *   *

Such is a manifestation cf the famous "Chinese capacity for treachery," and few people are fools enough to question it. If somebody will actually take the matter seriously and venture to ask the man where the eagle-and-rabbit fight was he promised, the chances are that half of the spectators instead of supporting him in the protest would side with the juggler and call the speaker a "trouble maker." For here is an instance of the importance of "face." It would be too cruel to make the juggler "lose face". If you understand this you understand half of the true Chinese temperament.

*   *   *

The reasons why Little Bald Head, representative of all Chinese children of Peking, found the Shih Cha Hai fair such an attractive spot were manifold and some of the phases of it, the cool shade of the willows, the carefree atmosphere, the shows and the sights have already been recorded. We will now give a brief description of the "eats" offered more or less as local specialties.

It is here that people see the first of some of the season's fruits and other produces of the farm, an outstanding example of which may be said to be the Indian corn. Although this is a staple food for an enormous percentage of North China's millions, the young corn is considered a seasonal delicacy. The corn ripens about the eighth moon each year in the natural course of things but people, the sophisticated Peking-*jen*, usually race with time and try to get the year's fresh and tender ones by the fifth moon. These, by some poetically-minded man, have been given the name of *Chen Chu Sun* (珍珠筍), or Pearl-Studded Bamboo Shoots." Whereas full grown corn of eight or ten inches length on the cob would be a cheap food for city and country labourers alike, these early specimens command a good price. Each corn-on-the-cob is offered in its original wrappings of tender husks, boiled in plain water and not buttered or salted as in the foreign way. About twenty to thirty seeds are all there are that can be obtained from one corncob.

Another timely kind of titbit would be the *Ho Hsien* (河鮮), or the "River's Fresh," referring to the fresh water caltrops and lotus seeds, fresh almonds and fresh walnuts. These are all hand-peeled and hand-picked and iced to retail at exorbitant prices to be served in the luxuriously appointed *hors d'oeuvre* dishes during Chinese cocktail hours.

In the same shops are obtainable also the lotus roots of the year's fresh growth, much sought after on account of their crisp and sweetish taste. The shapely sections are cut in symmetrical pairs and sold, wrapped for additional "local colour" in green lotus pads a foot and more in diameter. Chips of this porous root have been famous in China as a delicacy since ancient times.

The wayside restaurants have also their local novelties, advertised as "Today's Specials" on big billboards, which the visitors will enjoy. Of these honourable mention may be made of the lotus leaf porridge and lotus seed porridge.

The lotus leaf porridge is an adaptation or refinement of the everyday rice gruel in the Chinese kitchen, that is, a high grade of rice (preferably the grade known as *Hsi Kung* (西貢), or Saigon Rice) is cooked to a near paste. When the porridge is about ready a big fresh lotus leaf is put over the pan in the way of a cover. The heat will carry off the bitter-fragrant flavour of the leaf and give it to the porridge itself. By some clever trick a greenish tint is also transferred into the porridge and makes people wonder whether it is botanically possible that the little particles of chlorophyl can escape from one body into another without actual contact! Sweetened the porridge is served cold.

The lotus seed porridge is an "expensive child" for, aside from the rice congee that goes as the body of the stuff, cooked lotus seeds (old preserved ones, imported from the province of Fukien and not produced locally at the Shih Cha Hai though the shopkeeper insists they are as a propagandist aid to the sale of his wares) are added to it. An assortment of raisins, watermelon seeds, walnut meat and some other varieties of preserved berries and white and brown sugar are profusely used for the dressing. This dish is also served ice-cold. It would be easy to form an idea of how it tastes. By way of a suggestion imagine a bowl of cooked oatmeal left in the ice-box from yesterday's breakfast mixed with an ice cream Sundae from which the "cream" has been eliminated and you get the palatal impression of lotus seed porridge. Do not worry about the taste of the lotus seeds, for believe me, they have no taste whatsoever being nothing but plain starch content.

Even Little Bald Head would not order a dish of either of the two dishes unless it had been fine for several days continuously. For rainy weather means "no sale" to the restaurants and means old stock for the avaricious but fashionable gourmets.

*   *   *

A much-patronized feature at a popular Chinese fair is invariably that particular department which is occupied by the group of food-pedlars known to foreigners as "itinerant restaurants" This name they would at once rise up in unison to protest against as being entirely without reason and therefore absolutely unacceptable if they knew they had been so unjustly given such a libelous title. For they are not in permanent motion but are established at the fair with full-sized tables and benches and at least half of them are on the same spot the whole time the fair is on. The habit of local residents patronizing such food depots is in the way of an act of amusement, the satisfaction of chronic propensity unique in itself. Not one in a hundred of fair-goers approach them with an empty stomach and yet half the time the benches are fully occupied, some of the guests, quite nicely dressed, being "earnestly at it". If some day the American drug-store idea should migrate into this fair city of old Peking, all these food stalls will line up with spotlessly clean counters and with revolving stools, in imitation of the soda fountain on the other side of the ocean.

Children, except those in the family of "modern" people, follow the example of adults in this as in other trends of habit and the program for a visit, for instance, to the Shih Cha Hai fair includes automatically some such food adventures and the experience of the Wu boy may be said to be typical of that of a good many of his class.

There is the man who sells *p'ao kao* (爬糕), "buckwheat cakes", and *liang fen* (凉粉), or "cold starch-jelly." The former is made by cooking buckwheat flour into an ultra-thickened form of porridge which is then made into cakes by allowing literally hand-fuls of the stuff to stiffen and acquire a "caky" appearance as it cools. The starch-jelly has a much more presentable appearance and is made by cooking starch (made from soya beans) into a thin liquid and then allowing it to solidify into jade-white translucent blocks as it gets cold. The jelly, and the buckwheat cakes too, are iced and cut to be served in slices topped with dressings: vinegar, oya sauce, sesamum sauce and pounded garlic or mus-tard or even dried red pepper which has been fried in grease. The term "sesamum sauce" perhaps sounds a bit strange to the un-initiated. This is the residual substance obtained when sesamum oil is made by pressing the seeds in stone mills. It tastes between mayonnaise and peanut-butter yet different from either.

Others would prefer the *kuan ch'ang* (灌腸), or "stuffed sau-sage". Originally the stuff was made by filling sections of casings with a poor grade of starch mixed with bits of pig's liver and the like, cut into small slices and fried in lard. Nowadays lower manufacturing cost has been stressed at the expense of quality and only starch is used, tinted to a purplish pink to resemble the genuine stuff in colour. Fried in lard in a flat pan the *kuan ch'ang* is served hot with a dash of salt water and pounded garlic! The thin slices, browned, are conveyed to the mouth not with chopsticks but with bamboo "needles" not unlike toothpicks in appearance.

Still more people will flock to the bean-juice "joint." The bean-juice, or *to chih-erh* (豆汁), is a by-product obtained in the manufacture of vermicelli and is greenish-gray in colour. In taste it is sour like spoiled milk and about as thick too. It is served boiling hot and "drunk" accompanied by Chinese pickles which, instead of being sour, are actually salty! The more fastidious customers would get special dishes of sauced cabbage and turnips or the like as a sort of "relish" which will cost them extra, but the thoroughbreds are usually content with the finely diced salt-turnips supplied within the price of the juice itself. The turnips, cut in fine "threads," or "diced," are often mixed with fresh kohlrabi, equally treated, mixed with bits of green celery and seasoned by the indispensable red pepper which vies with the boiling bean juice in "heat". The combination is a more effective perspiratory than a goodly dose of quinine.

Little Bald Head, true to his nativity, was a pedigreed connoisseur of the bean-juice and always a "three bowler". But much as the Peking-*jen* adores it, outsiders from the provinces would not even taste the stuff as in their opinion the stuff is fed only to hogs "out their way". Many "naturalized" citizens of Peking find it the only thing that they cannot stand of all of Peking's incredible native victuals. Should we analyze the stuff, the biggest composite part, of course, will be found to be water, the "skin", and "rough parts" of the soya beans. If the bean-juice has a future and when "every bean-juice has its day," some scientist will come and tell the world that it contains, perhaps, Vitamins A,B,C...clear down to Z, and recommend it as a substitute for milk, bananas and tomato juice as a health-building food. Do not laugh at this idea as theoretically it is not impossible.

*   *   *

In so far as the wayside specialties offered to satisfy the Peking-*jen's* unbelievable appetite are concerned, perhaps those not familiar with things Pekingese would brand the items described in the preceding section as absurd and impossible. This would be thoroughly unreasonable as nothing but the pure truth has been told. Peking boasts of one and a half million in native population and at least a third of this number are carrying on the tradition wholeheartedly so there is no danger of any dwindling public support for buckwheat cakes or bean-juice. People say, it is true, that "when in Rome do as the Romans do," but nobody has said "when in Peking do as the Peking-*jen* does!"

But by way of a compromise here are some things offered at Chinese fairs that would be less difficult to appreciate.

There are the *liang kao* (涼糕) or "Cold Cakes". Glutinous rice of a high grade is ground into a fine flour, mixed into dough and then steamed for a proper duration of time. Red dates or yellow peas or red beans, mashed fine, are used as "cores". The cakes are cut into small portions and iced to serve with sugar and syrup. How does this sound to those who confess to liking Japanese *mochi* so much?

Or how about *wan tou huang-erh* (豌豆黄兒), or the "Yellow of Peas"? A quantity of dried peas are boiled and mashed and the skins taken off. Add a good quantity of white sugar, press into squares and ice.

Or Peking's own age-old version of a summer soft drink, the *suan mei t'ang* (酸梅湯), or "Tea of Sour Plums." Chinese plums are a produce of the south and are obtainable in Peking as pickled green ones or dried black ones, both from native groceries called locally the *chiang tien* (薑店), or "Ginger Shop." Get a proper quantity of the dried black variety and boil them thoroughly in water, so thoroughly that the soft pulp still loosely attached to the stones is virtually tasteless as then all the "acidity" has been transferred to the water. Put the liquid into a container and add syrup made by dissolving a generous quantity of white powder sugar, or better still, cubes or granules. Then get a small quantity of Chinese *kwei hwa mu tze* (桂花母子) or "essence of cassia" or "cinnamon tree blossoms "—a jam-like affair made in South China and obtainable from the same "ginger shops"—to the preparation, stirring it well. Add boiled water to get the suitable "strength".

Strain it through a tea-strainer or fine sieve. Bottle the stuff and put in the ice-box to serve as you would soda waters.

And this reminds me of another Three Kingdoms story.

Once Ts'ao Ts'ao was at the head of a good-sized detachment of troops on a forced march in very hot weather (I do not remember whether it was in hot pursuit during a mopping-up campaign as the aftermath of a general offensive or whether it was during a hasty retreat). His troopers became so badly scorched and thirsty that they found it beyond their ability to continue any more. From go-slowers they were actually turning into sit-downers. General Ts'ao asked his chief aide-de-camp what the big idea was of the men refusing to go on and he was informed that the soldiers were exhausted by thirst and that their energy was at a low ebb.

Ts'ao, cunning and sagacious, without pausing to think, burst out with the "discovery" that, his eyesight being very good, a forest of plum trees was not far away in the distance.

"If the men will continue only as far as the forest yonder," said Ts'ao, pointing with his horse-whip at a green wood on the distant horizon, "we shall each have a generous number of ripe, sour plums which will quench our thirst without fail."

On hearing this and seeing the hopeful signs, like the drifting pieces of wood Columbus showed to his disheartened crew, the soldiers' saliva glands, so to speak, began again to function, their thirst was gone in two seconds, and the large-scale troop movement was able to continue on the march Of course, there were no plum trees. The idea was a trick, a trick that worked.

*   *   *

This plum drink is more than popular with Peking people and still more so with the children. It is pedled everywhere and offered in the various shops. For cleanliness' sake people like the Wus preferred the home-made variety, the brewing process being so simple. It is a famous concoction and "must be good to have got where it is." Indeed, it is so famous that one decent-looking shop of many, many years' standing, situated in the very heart of Liu Li Ch'ang (琉璃廠), Peking's own culture center renowned far and wide for exclusively curio shops, throughout the year sells nothing else but *suan mei t'ang*.

*   *   *

It is a known fact that the Chinese are not a milk-consuming race. Milk-drinking was only lately introduced to this country, apparently by foreigners and their modern medical theorists. It is strange to say that cow's milk was not even used as a substitute for mother's breast milk because, it was argued, it contained excessive "fire" or "heat" that made it unsuitable to the average physical constitution of little babies. Of course milk and milk products in general have been widely used for we do not know how many generations in Mongolia and Tibet. But the fact is that the true Chinese and the Tartar tribes from the north have never been friendly long enough to make the former adapt the latter's ways of living. Not only that but the Chinese race had always thought the Mongols and other sundry northern hordes were utterly incomparable with themselves in every respect, in culture, language, manner, etc., although by sheer strength China has been subjugated by them at different times since the dim beginning of Chinese history. Although the Great Wall, which had existed in separate sections even before Emperor Shih Huang Ti of the Ch'in Dynasty consolidated them into one long bulwark 220 years before Christ was born, did not fully stop the Huns from entering China for spasmodic excursions it may be said to have been more successful in stopping milk-drinking from permeating Chinese eating habits. The Chinese of ancient times were so racially prejudiced that they coined special characters to name the various aboriginal tribes, each with a telltale "radical" for "dog" playing a part in the ideographs. If you cannot teach old dogs new tricks, certainly you do not want to learn old tricks from new dogs! It was in this lamentable state of affairs that the Chinese have been left inappreciative of the virtues of milk until Western influence in the last twenty or thirty years gradually converted a small portion of city dwellers to this "barbarian" custom. Most Chinese still cannot stand butter, to say nothing of cheese!

But Peking is curiously an exception in this respect as milk-drinking was brought here from Mongolia, as it were, *via* Manchuria by the Shanhaikwan route. The Manchu people were milk-conscious and with them, three hundred years ago, came the institution of *ta tze po po* (達子餑餑), "tartarian pastries", and *nai tze cha* (奶子茶), "milk tea."

Milk is consumed in Peking in characteristic preparations. Of these the most popular and convenient example is the *lao* (酪). Whole milk is heated and sweetened in a big pot over a brisk fire to boiling point and then a few drops of rice wine is added. Be it an organic-chemical reaction, the alcoholic content of the wine will change the density of the milk and, to a certain extent, solidify it. Bowls of this stuff are iced before being served.

The proper place to get your bowl of *lao* is at the *lao* shops which can be found scattered in various parts of the city. They are easily discernable though they display no special sign, for Peking's *lao*-makers have their dairy farms "under the same roof". Each such farm may boast of as many as ten cows and as many calves. There are no grazing grounds needed for the cows are all put on a special diet of sour dregs left over from the manufacture of Chinese vinegar by fermenting rice. During milking time the calves are first allowed to suckle and soon after the milk flow is started they are dragged away and their places taken by the insatiable milkman's pail.

Whenever Little Bald Head's father or grandfather suggested going to the *niu p'eng* (牛棚), or "cow's shed" (meaning a *lao*-shop), for a bowl of *lao*, he could always depend upon the child readily seconding the motion.

*   *   *

There are street pedlars of *lao* in Peking, too, but their goods are usually of a poorer grade, adulterated with flour or similar ingredients and often not made with whole milk but only with the whey. Parents who have an eye to the proper upbringing of their children particularly avoid these pedlars for they often resort to gambling to boost their profits. Dice are produced most mysteriously from these men's bosoms and it is then a case of three bowls of *lao* for the price of one or no *lao* at all for the price of three—more often the latter!

SUMMER PASTIMES

A CHINESE proverb says "There are buyers for everything for which there are sellers" The truth of this is proved nowhere better than in Peking for in so far as the colourful petty pedlars are concerned you can always expect the unexpected while wandering along Peking streets.

Little Bald Head and his father were on a Sunday afternoon walk along the boulevard leading from the Gate of Heavenly Peace when they ran into one of Peking's insect sellers.

There are not many insect sellers and they are an interesting and picturesque lot. A wicker-woven market basket is carried slung on the seller's arm, covered with a wet cloth and filled with the pliable green branches of a wild bushy plant known locally as "pig's tails" and which is particularly well adapted to the special requirements on account of the moisture contained in their soft and tender leaves. Another piece of wet cloth is tied crosswise to the side of the basket in which are kept lengths of green rush-weeds, the kind that grow wild in the marshes and the leaves of which we have already noted are used for making horns for children as well as for wrapping the Dragon Boat Festival rice cakes in.

The dragonflies are tied to small reeds and cost one big copper each.

The basket contains any number of insects which the seller may have caught in the countryside either with a net or by some other tricky utensils, each designed for a particular type of insect. We wish some day to corner him for a lengthy interview and make him reveal some of the tricks employed in catching such a number of beautiful specimens, but in all probability he would politely refuse to talk, at least not until he has had his patents registered.

There are concealed in his baskets a complete array of dragonflies, the yellow ones, the grey ones, the red ones (which in Chinese are called "red pepper") and the big green ones which have the lines suggestive of a racer aircraft. Also a sub-species which is distinguished by the flattened disk grown on the tail and known thereby as "old plaster." Then in a corner of the basket he stocks a treasured and rare catch of a black one, all black with four widened wings that give it a butterfly appearance, the kind known in Chinese as "old woman in black." All these have their wings flattened from their back up and held in place between layers of the "pig's tail" grass. There must be quite a number of dragonflies for every time the man searches in his basket to find a special one, the fettered fluttering of the wings of some can be heard, as though the motors of little airplanes were being warmed up in preparation for a takeoff.

He has other kinds of insects, too, the "heavenly cows," black beetles with horny wings marked with white spots covering their elongated bodies and sectioned black-and-white antennae, held fast with loops of cornstalk peelings on a piece of the same stem. They do not chirp or buzz their wings in protest but, by the movement of their powerful "iron" jaws, seem to telegraph to each other a brief message of "let us sell our lives dearly."

Another section of split sticks hold fast a few of the big butterflies whose wings are a beautiful shade of light green intersected with velvety black marks. These seem to be quite aware of their coming destiny, for the like of which most of their ancestors had been sacrificed—that of being starved to death and having the remains left to decorate milady's boudoir jewel tree! "Even that," they seem to say "would be better than remaining all one's life an ugly caterpillar crawling along a bean plant."

Personally objecting to the proposition very strongly, young Mr. Wu was influenced to get a couple of the dragonflies for his young son at the price of a copper for each dragonfly. They were tied by the tender yet fiberish "heart" of the weed, allowing them some "wing" room and restricted liberty for occasional exercise from time to time.

"What do dragonflies eat, father?" Little Bald Head asked.

"They eat mosquitoes, and . . . . but never mind what they eat. If you are my good son, I want you, after you have had them a little while, to set them free. If you will do this we may buy some others another time," said his father.

"All right, father," Little Bald Head agreed.

＊　　　　　　＊　　　　　　＊

When summer is definitely under way most Chinese families will get their icebox ready for the season's use.

The Chinese icebox is, like everything Chinese, backed by a glorious and lengthy history. It is not possible, of course, to dig into ancient volumes and find the first instance of an icebox mentioned somewhere in the chronology of China's cobwebby dynasties. But it may be interesting to note that it was known at least in the T'ang Dynasty. The famous poet Tu Fu, in one of his popular poems recording a summer holiday outing with his friends, made a note about the "gentlemen mixing the ice-water and the girls preparing the lotus-root chips." About the same period as this we have also the famous Chinese beauty, Yang Kwei Fei, the sensational imperial concubine of Emperor Ming Huang of the T'ang Dynasty, who, history definitely says, was unfortunately guilty of halitosis. In order to combat this objectionable shortcoming that almost destroyed her personal charm, she had the famous lichee fruits (a sub-tropical berry found in Kwangtung and its neighbourhood) brought to her by special mounted messengers from the southern provinces in a great daily neck-breaking speed marathon. Since these fruits are very perishable they were constantly kept in cold storage to be served to her from time to time, buried under chips of ice in luxurious trays. A modern American tooth paste magazine advertisement could easily have directed her attention to her gums and re-commended a proper brand and rendered all her trouble un-necessary but, unfortunately, times were different. Anyhow here is positive proof that iceboxes have been used in China for upward of a thousand years.

But it should not be imagined that the Chinese originally in-vented the refrigerator together with gunpowder, the printing press and the mariner's compass, for it is not so. The Chinese icebox is an "ice box" and nothing more. As a matter of fact it is not intended to "cut down the family's food bill" but is more a piece of furniture occupying a position in the *k'eh t'ing* (客廳), or "the guest parlour." It is usually a squarish box of hardwood, no less profusely trimmed with brass than a Korean cabinet, and lined inside with pewter. The cover lifts off easily and inside is a wooden stand on which a slab of natural ice rests. In points of economic upkeep, current savings and silent operation, it stands unchallenged. Moreover, it is foolproof, exceedingly portable and any child can use it!

The Wus were the possessors of just such a venerable piece and old Mr. Wu arranged to have natural ice supplied by a "contrac-tor" at so much per month. It not only air-conditioned the room to a certain extent but also helped to make iced tea and the like for all the family members. When the weather was particularly hot, little chunks of the natural ice were knocked off to be eaten. Such a practice had been allowed to go unquestioned until modern scientific knowledge came in to slowly revolutionize it.

The natural ice used in Peking for kitchen and other use is supplied by an organization of no small proportions. A certain group of "ice kings" yearly reach an arrangement with the con-servancy authorities, formerly not without a good part being played by competitive bribery, to get the officials in charge to open up the various spillways in the several dams along Peking's natural topographical waterways at different times to first clean out the water course and then release abundant water in the late fall from the Jade Fountain and Summer Palace to fill up the lakes and moats so that layers of ice sometimes two to three feet in thickness are formed during the cold weather. The ice firms build primitive underground cellars near the embankments and have the slabs, cut by manual labor in uniform sizes, put away, covered and sealed with mud! The ice is sold all the year round with the boom season naturally being in the summer months.

The ice business was not without royal favours. During the imperial dynasties, we read from reliable books that the Manchu Imperial Household Department used to distribute through the Board of Public Works, "ice-coupons" to the various govern-mental institutions and to the various mandarins throughout the *fu t'ien* (伏天), or "dog days", in the year. The coupons were redeemable at the retailing stations of the various lake-side or moat-side ice "plants" to enable the public servants in "His Majesty's Service" to fill up their iceboxes at home and in the offices.

*   *   *

In what may be called the Chinese counterpart of "A Child's Garden of Verses," a little poem designed to embody a moral for youthful scholars runs as follows:

"All people are exasperated
by the summer's heat,
I alone like summer for its
longer days.
As I concentrate in reading
the classics and practising cali-
graphy.
My mind is at ease and I
naturally feel cool."

This may sound very well but
comparatively few people would
meet the summer heat with such a
passive attitude. One of the things
with which the Chinese equip themselves against a heat wave is the
icebox described before but a still
more widely seen weapon is the fan.

The most popular fan is the
folding kind of bamboo and paper.
The general field headquarters in
Peking for paper fans are the local
paper and stationery stores which
either directly or indirectly import
them from south China, mainly from
Soochow and Hangchow, as their sign
boards always state. There are a
handful of more exclusive fan shops
(which sell also lanterns) specializing
in fans of a more aristocratic class,
of better material and workmanship.
The *shan ku* (扇骨), "fan bones" or
the "ribs", may be carved by some
famous artist, or the material may
be of a celebrated kind of bamboo,
the "Phoenix Eye," with round

This is a one-man travelling
retail and service station for
Chinese fans.

circular water-marks, or the "Concubine of River Hsiang,"
with microscopic veins on a smooth bees-wax coloured ground.
Some others may be of pure sandal wood and still others of Foo-
chow lacquer of a "chicken blood" colour.

Fans intended for use by the fair sex are even more luxurious
affairs as, besides the foregoing kinds, there are also the finely
carved ivory-ribbed ones. The paper part of the fans, known as
shan mien (扇面), or "fan face", is either of *hsuan*, or scroll
paper", or at least of Korean silk paper. The usual experience for
a person buying such a fan is a series of worries because he has to
worry about the shop where to buy it, which to choose, then what
famous artist-friend to approach to paint a picture on one side of
the fan-face and which famous calligraphical genius to approach
to write a few lines of poetry on the other side. When all this is
done the worry would be whether actually to use it or not since it
has by then become a full-fledged *object d'art*. The temptation is
to put it away in the original brocade box as a prized bric-a-brac
or a mark of good taste.

If the decision is to put it away that would end the worries.
But if on the other hand it is voted to use it there would be one
more worry. When a friend asks you to let him examine and

appreciate the painting and writing on it as a courteous ceremonial just when you need it most for fanning yourself what would
you say in order to get it back without injuring your friend's feeling in the matter?

But children like Little Bald Head have no such problems.
His fan was not of such a classy kind. He had been promised a
fan by his father since the day he first saw the immense three-
foot fan hanging outside the paper shop door advertising ''new
stock just arrived'' but he had to content himself with a cheap
one purchased from a fan pedlar passing his way one afternoon.

The itinerant fan sellers walk the streets singly and carry
their ''store'' on the elbow in a miniature Chinese bureau. From
the lee side of the case rises a musical apparatus formed by strings
of little bells stretched from a crossbar fixed on top of a stick.
The bells ring with the man's walking and announce his arrival.
On this network of bells, a little wooden pagoda with tassels or a
little banner or both are generally used as additional decorations.
These men will not only sell you a brand-new fan for fifteen or
twenty cents but will also overhaul your old ones, have a new
''face'' fitted on your old ''ribs'' or put a new axis back in commission.

There are other members in the fan family, too, such as the
palm leaf fan which are by far the most serviceable kind, being
sturdy, of a light weight and cheaply priced, the straw-woven
''ox-heart'' fan which has the shape of a heart not necessarily
that of an ox, and last but not least the feather fans. Those for
the ''poets'' and his worthy class are made with the stiff quills of
a hawk fitted on a carved ivory handle, and for the women there
are those with downy swan feathers or even those of a peacock.
For the labourer class the fan is a wooden handle with feathers of
the domestic chicken. Feathers originally designed to keep the
possessors warm are now used to keep them cool. It all depends
upon how they are used.

*   *   *

The goldfish bowl as a conventional courtyard decoration has
previously been referred to in describing the family life of the
Wus even before our hero, Little Bald Head, was introduced to
this world. The practice of keeping such a big earthen or pottery
jar in the center of the spacious courtyard garden is such an old
established institution that it has become the object of either
much admiration or ridicule, depending on the diversified opinions
of outsiders. But in course of time these outsiders gradually
changed their ideas on the matter and the first thing anybody
knew a similar goldfish jar had settled itself in their own
homesteads.

The raising of rare species of goldfish had been one of old Mr.
Wu's hobbies, in which his son, young Mr. Wu, had also taken an
interest when he was a schoolboy. After young Mr. Wu had his
attention directed to his studies more seriously, the keeping of
goldfish was discontinued and the pet birds were the only playthings old Mr. Wu had for a good many years. Not wishing to
discontinue the tradition and finding it hard to picture his typical
patio a la China going on without such a typical decoration, the
jar was kept in its place among the plants and trees of oleanders
and pomegranates. A few red fish of the variety known as ts'ao yu
(草魚), or ''grass fish'', were kept therein primarily as a precaution

against mosquitoes using the jar as a breeding ground as by the Darwin law of evolution and the survival of the fittest no gold-fish and larvae or pupae of mosquitoes can live together in per-fect harmony. The grass fish, it must be remembered, are near kin to the common river perch and closely related to the family of the carp, though by some shady manner of acquirement some may have misappropriated the three or four-branched tail that puzzles the biologists as to which family to classify them with. It was to feed these grass fish that Little Bald Head used to fetch cooked grains of rice or bits of noodles from the kitchen. In the course of time they acquired a second instinct to "rise" to such feedings and some of them even learned to eat out of the boy's hand. It was also through these grass fish that the little boy's tadpoles once passed into martyrdom.

These grass fish were robust and sturdy fellows and a "bear" for punishment in so far as rough handling on the part of the child and indifferent care given them were concerned. But the child's knowledge of goldfish did not remain confined to the grass fish for one of old Mr. Wu's friends gave him a number of baby fish of the more delicate and rare varieties.

There was a bucketful of the little ones, scarcely bigger than a phonograph needle when they came to the Wu house. This friend of old Mr. Wu's was an amateur raiser of many famous varieties. There were the ones with the pop eyes and flowing tails of four branches called the "Dragon's Eyes," and the fat ones which had a pair of freak growths on the feelers in the shape of little fluffy balls but devoid of the back fin, known by the trade terminology of "Chenille Balls." Another variety had gills grown almost inside out and thereby were known as *fan sai* (翻鰓) or "Out-Turned Gills." Still another, more fantastically named, were the *wang t'ien-erh* (望天兒), or "Sky-gazers," whose eyes were grown, instead of one on each side of the head like all fish or two on one side like the flounders, paired up on the very top of the skull which reminds one of an aviator not in action whose goggles have been pushed up on his cap, or perhaps the professor of astronomy who fell into a hole in the ground when trying to satisfy himself about the movement of a freshly discovered planet or the position of a constellation. Old Mr. Wu was invited over to this man's house and inspected his rows of mossy old jars con-taining the varieties of "queer fish" and they also exchanged their own experiences in the raising of them.

"Some of these rare ones, like the 'Duck's Eggs' (so named be-cause of their almost spherical bodies) and the 'Red Caps,' the 'Frog Heads,' etc., were given to me by the *yu pa shih* (魚把式), or 'professional goldfish caretaker' in the employ at the Chao Kung Fu or 'Duke Chao's Mansion'," explained the friend. "He gave them to me as a special favour and told me that the original parent fish for them had been presented to the Duke him-self by an eunuch who was in charge of the Emperor's own collections kept in the Imperial gardens. You do not see many of them in the open market, do you?"

"Certainly not. I used to possess but a single pair of the Red Caps," enjoined old Mr. Wu, "like these here, with the fluffy headgrowths—red like drops of fresh blood but both of them died in a single day."

Old Mr. Wu referred to the "good ones that died" and not the

A narrow but long net attached to a stick is used to catch water fleas.

"big ones that got away." He had his own "fish stories."

*   *   *

The goldfish of the rare species of "Dragon's Eyes" etc., spawn in the late spring. When the female fish begin to show expanded bellies the parent fish should be removed from the "community jars" and kept separately in small jars with bunches of the water weed of a special kind the leaves of which look much like miniature green pine needles grown on reddish stems. Thousands of little bubblish eggs will be deposited along the red stems of this special weed. The males will fertilize these eggs. Then the big fish should all be taken out. The jars containing the eggs are then kept in the sunlight to hatch. Within a few days little lively fish will appear, at first hardly visible to the naked eye. Only the professionals and those with adequate experience can expect to be successful in getting through the various processes.

Old Mr. Wu's friend gave him a lot of these little fish babies as a present for his little grandson. Being an experienced hand, old Mr. Wu was able to point out at once to his grandson the different varieties, etc., although they all looked alike to the child.

Forthwith, additional bowls were taken out from the back-yard storerooms where they had been put away. Between him and the child they cleaned the bowls and poured fresh water into them.

"We will let the water stay here in the sun for a while and then have the fish released in it," said old Mr. Wu, "for, as it is, the water is too cold and the little fish may easily be chilled to death."

Then a few eggs were boiled good and hard, the yolk taken out and made into "egg powder" for feeding the little fish—these queer fish are born with empty stomachs and a wolf's hunger.

In a few days' time they became big enough to be sorted out, and, putting each kind in a separate container, they counted five jars.

This new addition to the Wu household provided additional work and fun for the old man for it naturally fell to his lot to nurse them and take care of them in a general way. He had to hunt for the water fleas which are bread-and-butter to these carnivorous little monsters and to clean the water of the dirt deposited at the bottom by means of a special instrument built on the siphon principle and which takes out the dirty "under-current" without disturbing the peace and order of the upper realm. It also fell to his lot to prepare the sun-warmed water so his little goldfish did

not catch cold and die during the frequent acclimatizations involved in keeping the water clean and pure. All these duties he
attended to cheerfully with the off-and-on assistance of Little
Bald Head.

*   *   *

Catching water fleas for his bowls of goldfish was not an easy
job for old Mr. Wu particularly as the little fish grew not only in
size but proportionately in appetite. These water fleas are a
peculiar kind of insect and though microscopic in size are possessive of little feet like those of a shrimp and double shells
like a bi-valve. They are found in little pools of water that is
almost still and motionless but not quite for they mill around in
veritable "clouds," so massive is their numerical strength. They
are reddish in colour and are easily detected by the initiated but
a certain dexterity is required to catch only the fleas and not the
mud for they always swim in shallow water near the bank. A
special implement is also necessary—a lengthy net of fine material
fitted onto a lengthy handle. A consoling point would be that
since the fleas will not die of "thirst", except a very few, it is not
necessary to carry them home in water. They have to be revived
first in a container by themselves and only the live ones fed to the
fish. The hours for water flea catching are in the early mornings
for the fleas will take to deeper water and vanish from view with
the rising of the sun.

When Little Bald Head became tired of the expeditions on
which at first he volunteered to accompany the old man, the latter
was left alone and he soon tired of them too. Thanks to the Peking
pedlar system the fish did not starve to death for a man was
easily found to contract for the water flea supply at a very small
sum a month. These men are expert water flea catchers and get
literally pounds of the stuff from the countryside brooks and retail
them at monthly rates. He delivered the fleas daily at the door
early in the mornings as faithfully and as punctually as the milkman did his milk, rain or shine. He also threw in without extra
charge bits of advice and suggestions pertaining to the goldfish
adventure from time to time.

*   *   *

Raising the beautiful but delicate species of goldfish known
in Peking as *yu yang tze* (魚秧子), or "fish saplings", is a trying
job as the various phases of the care that must be taken require a
certain amount of experience and will keep a leisurely person constantly busy. The proud possessors are often annoyed by unexpected wholesale deaths, as if the fish had signed between themselves a suicide pact, just because of a little ignorance or lack of
attention to a small detail. But since old Mr. Wu was himself not
a novice at it, his goldfish developed very well and all his hard
labour seemed satisfactorily repaid.

From the street vendors Little Bald Head also procured some
additional fish though this was strongly objected to by his grandfather. For the old man knew from sad experience that these innocent-looking country folk (hailing almost entirely from the district of Wen-an-hsien), peddling the baby fish of the "Dragon's
Eyes" variety and other species of delicate fish, were at times in
the habit of stocking nothing but defective fish which had been

"thinned out" by professional raisers gathered in the vicinity of T'ien Chiao, or Bridge of Heaven, in a neighbourhood collectively known as Chin Yu Chih (金魚池), or Gold Fish Pond.

These pedlars parade the street announcing their wares with a charming "trade-cry" and carry the fish in tubs identical in construction to those used by the rural lads selling tadpoles and things. They sell their wares at surprising low prices—you can buy half a dozen little baby "Dragon's Eyes" for a cent. But more often than not they are the undesirables, having been thrown away by the raisers as being hopeless of developing up to standard. Not only that but sometimes goldfish which have been contaminated by certain kinds of contagious diseases peculiar to them are quickly disposed of by these travelling distributors at sacrifice prices in the few days before the fish die. Thus, buying these fish and putting them together with the healthy ones is inviting trouble for it may easily mean a clear-out *en masse*, one fish after another dying in close succession, leaving the raisers utterly helpless to check the spread of the fish epidemic. This was why the little fish newly acquired by Little Bald Head were always strictly ordered by the old man to be kept apart for a few days under observation—in quarantine, as it were—until the newcomers were able to show clean health certificates before being allowed to socialize with the others.

And in order to show the youngster what a goldfish industry Peking has, the old man arranged to take the child to visit the Goldfish Pond on one of their long walks.

This place is almost next to the northern walls of the famous Temple of Heaven where a stretch of water is unexpectedly located. The pond is divided into squares of regular fish farms. Some of the "farms" are literally crowded with the various kinds of fish. There are the rough and commonplace varieties known as "grass fish" which are visible to the visitors swimming in schools, some larger and some smaller. Other sections are devoted to the raising and temporary keeping of fresh water fish for the kitchen, such as the carp, the black fish fattened on waterweeds, etc. The delicate kinds are always kept in artificial containers, scores of them, lined up under a vast mat shade as the fish cannot stand very well too much sunshine or heat. The place is owned jointly by five or six business units who virtually monopolize the goldfish trade in North China; some of the cheap varieties are even sent overland by carriers to Inner Mongolian cities and towns where, to the Mongols, they are retailed at fabulous prices.

*   *   *

"How changed it is!" exclaimed old Mr. Wu after looking over the place.

"What has changed, Grandfather?" enquired Little Bald Head.

"When I was about your age the Goldfish Pond used to be a favourite place for crowds of permanent sight-seers, who used to come here in groups as we visit a park now. There seemed to be more trees here than there are now—ancient willows, lining the banks behind which the charming wine shop and tea gardens were found. It was here that the then fashionables used to come to "see the goldfish,", bringing their "ladies" with them. There were also wayside stands where tiny flour cakes were sold, small,

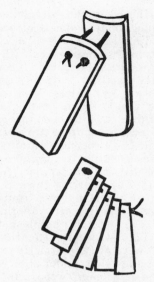

round, air-inflated affairs made to float. The visitors bought these and threw them into the ponds to see the big red grass fish rising around them making attempts to eat the food. All these, where are they now? How changed! Alas, for *Lao Pei Ching!*"

*   *   *

The original native life of the Peking-*jen* was a matter of much colour and activity. There were various kinds of sports, from the tame and softish game of kite flying to the fast and fascinating hunt of badgers in the wild prairie. Most of such recreational undertakings were indulged in by adults mostly, each to a class of patrons, and children were not encouraged to participate in these sports as they were too rough and strenuous.

Storytellers on board Peking's pleasure boats used bamboo clappers to beat time with while relating their epics.

Old Mr. Wu in spite of his advanced age was a great lover of the outdoors as we have noticed in many previously related instances. In the summer it was his habit to make excursions to the countryside, sometimes taking his pet birds with him and more often not, and spending a quiet afternoon in some *yen ch'a kuan-erh* (野茶館兒), or "rustic tea shop", listening to or participating in the conversation of farmers and rural residents as one of his ways of enjoying life's sweet idle moments so dear to people in the evening of their life. His young grandson, Little Bald Head, provided a convenient companion and, as the Chinese say, a "human walking stick" for him.

A favourite schedule was a picnic, local fashion, to the Tung Pien Men, or East Convenient Gate, one of the gates of the Peking city wall where the moat makes a turn to the east to gradually lose itself into the world-renowned Grand Canal. Here is one of Peking's coolest spots, the junction of the big stone bridge spanning the river and the overland route to the northeastern suburbs of Peking. Here an old friend of the elder Mr. Wu, a retired petty official of the former Imperial Granary Service, had established a tea house—not for the idea of money-making, but because of the fact that he loved the spot so much as he had personally taken part here during many long years in handling the traffic of rice paid to the Manchu court as tribute or tax from the southern provinces.

There was until very recent years a sort of a boat service plying between the Chao Yang Men and Tung Pien Men, covering the distance of about a mile or so on the city moat in from twenty to forty minutes, depending upon the direction of the wind and the strength of the boatmen who literally pushed the boat forward with a fifteen-foot-long pole and the two or three others who laboured ashore pulling the boat forward with lines attached to the top of the mat shed "cabin." It was a typically Chinese way of transportation and can perhaps only be seen today either in the Yangtze Rapids near Chungking or in some Sung Dynasty landscape paintings.

The boats were, even in the Wus' time, shabby things and ought almost to have been classed as "un-riverworthy" but they had certainly known brighter days in times gone by. The fare for adult passengers for the voyage used to be two coppers and for children one copper. There were no reductions for round trips and the boat averaged two stowaways per voyage.

To break the monotonous life on the boat an entertainer would board the ship in midstream and, standing on the stern next to the rudder-man, would recite some famous folklore stories in long epics beating time with pieces of bamboo strung together, one hand shaking a string of small ones and the other hand knocking together two big pieces. He got an extra copper per passenger for the service though payment was, in a way, optional. I do not know what was the agreement but may risk saying the boatman got a percentage from the gross proceeds.

The afternoons were thus spent by a quiet and peaceful boatride and then cooling and enjoying oneself at the tea shop. Here there were no tables or benches of wood but only brickwork substitutes which served the purpose well and certainly were more weather-proof and wear-proof, besides being unstealable!

When cups of tea had been consumed and the hour was about five or six o'clock p.m., the old man would decide to order a supper for himself and the child—a country supper. One of the typical fares would be noodles from the year's new wheat flour produced, nay, grown in the very locality. Sesamum sauce and salt and vinegar were the only dressing used. The foot-long jade-green cucumbers fresh from the nearby vegetable garden, selected and plucked from the vines at the customer's own choice and then rinsed with cold water from the garden well, provided the only "greens". Old Mr. Wu was a hearty eater and even the child had second and third helpings!

Soon it was sundown. The passengers would board the day's last boat for Chao Yang Men. They settled comfortably on the deck and took things easy and soon docked outside the Chao Yang gate. The cool southernly wind sped the boat and with the last twilight of the day, old Mr. Wu and his young grandson were swallowed up into the noisy dusty old city of Peking.

*   *   *

The annual season of prosperity for the so-called "rustic tea shops" in the Peking suburbs starts every year almost simultaneously with the coming of the hot weather and reaches the peak during the three *Fu* (伏) periods. The Chinese *Fu* periods are three in number, each covering a period of ten days. The word *Fu* in Chinese means "to prostrate" and is grammatically a verb, here used in a noun sense so to speak, the meaning implied being that since the weather during the periods will be so hot it is no use trying to do otherwise than "to prostrate" oneself at the advent of the heat-wave. The same word, strange as it may seem, is used also to mean "hibernation". During the *Fu* periods people are liable to lose weight as a natural physiological phenomenon, which is known in Chinese as *k'u hsia* (苦夏) and may be translated as "summer torture," and as a measure to even things up a custom was established to mark each period's beginning with a feast.

On the first day of the first ten-day period, meat dumplings are the proper feast, on the second noodles, and on the third Chinese pancakes and scra bled eggs, according to a widely known Chinese proverbial saying pertaining to the matter which is a household word.

But as we were saying, the hot weather means fine business at the rustic teashops. And a good part of the patrons at these shops are the amateur bird-keepers, the city's fortunate idlers, who find their usual urban teashops too oppressive due to the warmth. A lengthened walk out into the country would be the most interesting manner to spend long summer afternoons and besides in the countryside there are opportunities for their birds to listen to and learn songs of their kind who are free to roam the skies. Thus these pet birds are taken out to have their "vocal lessons", we may say. Another reason which seems to justify such trips all the more and gives them a seeming air of importance would be that certain kinds of insects have to be caught for their birds as a special diet during the shedding of old plumage and the growing of new which takes place annually around the "dog days". Of these insects the cicadas are the ones most often prescribed.

The bird-keepers bring long bamboo sticks with them in sections and telescoped like camera tripods to reach great heights, for the cicadas always stick to the trunks or branches of the tall poplar trees which are generally planted in Chinese graveyards and are at times twenty odd feet from the ground. A small jar holds some special glue made by rinsing away the starch from a piece of wheat flour dough until only the transparent sticky substance is left.

The cicadas in their larva stage spend long periods of time underground, according to usually dependable sources, as they have an instinct of boring downward from near the surface of the earth where the eggs are laid. When they enter the pupa stage, however, they suddenly change their mind and start boring upward. They so time their schedule that they never arrive in the open in broad daylight but always in the evenings or the dark of night. They are then ugly, wingless, six-legged crawlers for which no better name can be designed than the Chinese one of "cicada monkey". Once they are in open air they make for the nearest tree and immediately start their trip up the trunk. Overnight they graduate into adult cicadas, releasing a pair of wings from nowhere by shedding their skin and leaving it somewhere *en route* on the tree trunk. This is an authentic life history of the cicadas though to such people as old Mrs. Wu, they are believed to be converted from dung beetles (the Chinese fallacies similar to this are legion).

Singing begins with the male cicadas who use an organ concealed somewhere in the belly, thus attracting the females but not so effectively as the attention of the insect-hunting bird-keeper who searches with hawkish eyes and traces their whereabouts by experienced ears. Smearing the tip of their sticks with a little of the special mucilage, the men move their stick lightly and quietly upward. The chirping cicadas will suddenly feel something funny going on around and before their mind is made up to "bail out" the glue has reached their wings and rendered them useless. A little screened basket will be their temporary lodging until the moment comes for their honourable sacrifice.

The wings and the legs are the first parts to go. Then a sharp jackknife cuts each cicada's body lengthwise into two halves—like the big lobsters of the captain's dinner on board an ocean liner. The halves are then given to the caged birds. The red-breasted warblers need this delicacy the most and easily average fifteen cicadas a day for a three-week period.

Such proceedings were once watched by Little Bald Head. Apparently disgusted, he asked his grandfather:

"Do your birds eat these, too?"

"No, my lad. I never keep birds that require insect foods. The idea itself annoys me, to start with. That is the reason why I keep only the *Hwang Miao* (黃鳥) (Chinese Siskin) and the cross-beak."

FIRST STEPS TO KNOWLEDGE

JUDGING from the descriptions of the doings of the Wus it would seem that the life of young Little Bald Head was a continued round of amusements and entertainments, doing things and going places, and that before long the boy would be sadly spoiled from running around town with his aged grandfather who had nothing to do but enjoy himself. This was exactly what the child's ambitious young father became concerned about, particularly as his attempts to start the child on the path of knowledge were invariably turned down flat at the family conferences by the grandmother. It was when the child was about seven years old by Chinese count or five by actual time lapse that the grandfather commenced to give lessons to the boy by teaching him a few Chinese characters each day.

The characters were written on a piece of paper some two inches square in bold strokes by the old man, beginning with the simple ones of but a few strokes and going on to the more complicated ones with fifteen or twenty and more strokes. The child had a fine memory and he easily memorized each day's assignment. At first but three characters were introduced each day but later the number of new words a day was as many as ten. The child had no special difficulty with the work and in particular he easily absorbed those which are more of a hieroglyphic or emblematic nature rather than those strictly ideographic. Of this class the examples that may be cited are *ch'eh* (車) for cart, *ma* (馬) for horse, *niao* (鳥) for bird and *hsiang* (象) for elephant.

Nor was it necessary for any other member in the family to call him every day to "class" for apparently he took a personal interest in the work. The word squares, called *tze-hao-erh* (字號兒), in Chinese, he personally sorted out in the order of respective introduction into groups and wrapped up separately in packages of ten each. He soon had some two to three hundred characters in his vocabulary.

He took care of the squares himself and had the grandfather mark each package No. 1, No. 2, etc. These he carefully filed away daily after "school" in a desk specially cleared of its miscellaneous accumulated contents for the purpose.

His school sessions were daily in the morning around ten o'clock when the aged grandfather came back from his trip to the vegetable market, and again when young Mr. Wu came back from the office in the evening and when he conducted sort of a review and drill for the child. The results of the daily examinations were considered quite satisfactory and gave a good measure of happiness to the father.

*   *   *

As some of my readers may not be familiar with such things, the Chinese language is an unique example in all philological divisions. It has no alphabet and the nearest thing like an alphabet is the so-called "radical" system which takes apart the Chinese characters into 254 representative units. There are some 3,800 words which are within the sphere of say a secondary school student, at least fifty per cent of which have to be recognized by sheer memorization processes. The pronunciation of the language is difficult, too, as for all the numerous mono-syllables there are about 200 odd sounds, each possessive of four shades of tones comparable to the accents in the English language. Homonyms, therefore, are many. In forming phrases and sentences these characters come together in their "habitual" order and so it boasts of no grammar. The only Chinese grammar is more or less of a rhetoric nature which is only taught, as it were, in college. Fortunately the Chinese language has no grammatical inflections and thus saves the students a lot of headaches in this respect.

*   *   *

Starting a child on the road to education is a tedious process and a bold adventure as well. First of all the Chinese language itself is a peculiar kind of ideographs which took their first forms in picture writings very much like the ancient Egyptian, but due to later necessities it gradually became hopelessly mingled with a lot of phonetic symbols which, instead of holding faithfully to the original sounds, often transformed themselves into unrelated sounds with no binding rules. To this are added the many "borrowed" symbols, known to Chinese specialists as *chia chieh* (假借), which literally translates as "false pretense", besides a number of other irregularities which baffle even research scholars. The only way to acquire a mastery of the language is by the uncomfortable way of committing characters to memory. This is nothing less than a "feat" considering the family chores the average children are required to do in poorer Chinese families. The art being difficult to acquire, it is, like diamonds, highly priced on account of its rarity. It is no exaggeration to say that the ability to read, and still more to write, has been earmarked as the privilege of the blessed few.

To add to the difficulty the Chinese have again mixed things up with superstition, adding a touch of mystery to scholarship and placing it in a position too high even for fine mentality and favourable opportunities to reach. A Chinese proverb is indicative enough of the withdrawing tendency with which a great many people give up literary attempts when there appear handicaps which are commonplace things, traceable finally to the low economic standard throughout the land. I refer to the saying about scholarly success, "First, Virtue, second Fate, third, *Feng Shui* (風水) or Geomancy (based largely on the directional positions and geographical or topographical surroundings of a person's ancestral graveyard and the mounds therein): fourthly, Religious Merits and lastly, *Tu Shu* (讀書) or "Book Reading". This kind of a dreadful mess of hidden influences, jointly and separately, provide a strong prejudice for encouragement or discouragement on the part of parents who wish to embark their children on the hard and thorny road of study. Many families let such things so "wet-blanket" their enthusiasm that the battle is lost before the actual fighting commences. It is a common thing to hear enraged parents scolding an "unworthy" son with the saying that the child's failure at school is due to "the family not having such good virtues"! Such being the case it is easy to see why so many Chinese Buddhists worship the God of Literature so devoutly, namely with a view to winning the god's favour to put or keep their sons and grandsons among the "reading" groups.

And it was exactly this sort of thing which made the Wus so joyous about the prospects for their young Little Bald Head as he showed such remarkable progress in the pioneering period of his school days.

*   *   *

"Grandfather is taking charge of teaching the boy the 'character squares' very nicely, it seems to me," commented the elder Mrs. Wu, "and we do not need to hunt for a private tutor to do the work like we had to in the case of our son many years back."

"Yes, indeed, and very much trouble is thus avoided, too," added the old grandfather.

When young Mr. Wu was a child, it must be explained, the family put him in the charge of an old scholar who was known to the then Wu family as everybody's Hu *Lao Hsih*, or "Old Teacher Hu". Mr. Hu had been a trusted friend as well as advisor and right-hand man during old Mr. Wu's days of public life as a Mandarin in a certain government department at the end of the Manchu Dynasty. Mr. Hu was quite a few years the senior of the grandfather and came from Chekiang province where for at least three centuries most of China's legal brain-trust and secretarial geniuses found their native place. Mr. Hu had failed continually at the Imperial Examinations and having no "pull" with his acquaintances was obliged to tide himself along by clerking privately for officials or by teaching high-born children in rich families in order to finance him for further adventures at such examinations.

He never succeeded in getting even the lowest degree not because he was not learned enough but due apparently to, as the Chinese say, lack of "virtue and merits". When the examination system was entirely done away with, he lost all hope and finally left Peking for his home town a broken-hearted old man. Before he left he had been old Mr. Wu's hanger-on for a good many years and he was, even after old Mr. Wu retired, kept on the family's payroll nominally as young Mr. Wu's teacher. He drew but ten taels a year as his fees but the family provided him with board and lodging, as was the practice then. Between the highly irritable old teacher and the much petted youth there were many sad experiences recorded but even at that Old Teacher Hu was greatly revered by the family for does not the Chinese proverb say, "One day as a person's teacher, revered for life as a father?"

Hu *Lao Shih* was a typical example of a family tutor for youngsters in richer families and his counterparts are still to be found in Peking.

*   *   *

When Little Bald Head was broken in to the character-memorizing work as the beginning of his baptism at the font of Knowledge, he almost at once became fond of the work "like a duck taking to water". In the natural order of such things, his grandfather after a while introduced another phase of juvenile schoolwork in the way of Chinese penmanship exercises.

"I am going to begin to teach you the writing of Chinese characters," said the old man.

"You mean writing with a brush pen and black ink like you always do?"

"Yes, exactly."

"Not with chalk or slate pencils like my father has taught me! How interesting!" It sounded too good to be true and Little Bald Head was "tickled to death" over the idea.

The old man pulled out from a drawer from his side of the hardwood desk across from which young Little Bald Head was sitting a roll of papers. These were the so-called *hung mu-tze* (紅模子), or "red models", which the old man had bought from a Chinese stationery shop—wood-block prints of characters in red water-colour, the like of which have been in use in China for Heaven knows how many generations for giving first lessons in calligraphy to Chinese schoolboys. Then he unwrapped another small paper package and produced therefrom a brand-new brush pen and a block of ink, a dried cake of soot mixed with glue some three inches long and of the size and flattened cylindrical shape of a carpenter's pencil, and a stone ink-grinder known in Chinese as *mo hai* (墨海), or "ink sea". These he gave to the child with an air, serious and ceremonious, like a college president delivering a sheepskin to a new Bachelor of Arts. He said:

"These are called *hung mu-tze* and these characters are mostly of simple construction each with very few strokes. I have just purchased them for you as well as the pen, ink and a new ink-sea. The way to use these character models is for you to re-write the same characters over the red with black. You try to cover up the red strokes as precisely as possible without retouching. You will re-write but one sheet a day. When these are all used up, there will be new ones for you. This will not only teach you the rudiments of Chinese penmanship but also acquaint you better with the constructions of the characters.

"You are not to use the ready-made ink from my inkbox, but grind a fresh supply each time with your own ink sea with water

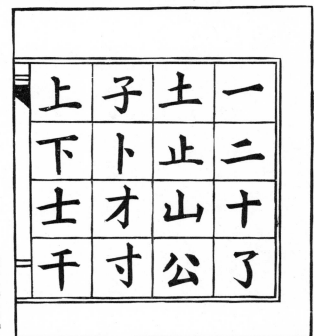

This is a facsimile of a "red model" which is used to teach a Chinese child his first characters. Each character is originally about an inch or more in size.

from this container. This will give you a chance to calm your mind as you prepare the ink and at the same time to look carefully over the red model for a preliminary idea how to start. Do you see?

"Remember also that the horizontal strokes are to be started from the left and the perpendicular strokes from the top downward. Also keep the strokes straight as the red model will guide you. Do not suck the brush pen with your mouth to get it smooth and shapely for writing, do not get your hands and clothes all messed up with the black ink. Try to keep your paper as clean as you can. I will write a few characters and you will watch how I do it and then you may go on with the rest while I watch you.

"Now, these characters are all very simple. Can you read them?" asked old Mr. Wu.

"Yes, I think so. *I erh shih liao*, (一二十了), *t'u chih shan kung* (土止山公), *tze pu ts'ai ts'un* (子卜才寸), *shang hsia shih kan* (上下士干). But they do not make sense, do they?"

"No, they are chosen for being the simplest characters for a beginner. This is writing work so do not bother about sense or no sense. When you get satisfactory results with these, I will give you more complicated ones to do."

The maiden attempts at the work were not very successful. The child's hand was not used to the proper way of holding the round bamboo pen-stem. His hand was shaky and his strokes were none too straight nor smooth.

A FISHING EXPEDITION

MUSKMELONS and watermelons are a popular group of "fruits" with all inhabitants of North China where these various members of the "gourd family" (as in the language of the botanists) are produced in large quantities and are therefore within the purchasing power of all the people. Eating melons therefore is a highlight in the life of all families during the summer season.

There are many varieties of muskmelons, each known by a special fancy name based more or less on individual taste and quality characteristics. A few examples of these names would be "Goat Horn Honey," given to the yellowish horn-shaped ones which taste invariably very sweet, and the "Frog Crisp," representing the kind with skin a delicate pastel shade of green with dark green spots like the back of the frog found in the rice paddies, and the "Three White," of which the skin, the seeds, and the pulp are all ivory white in colour. Other cheaper varieties may be the "Pumpkin's Core" and "Old Man's Delight" which has a mushy, soft, tasteless body which nobody but toothless old people would cherish. The pedlars carry them in baskets and when a bargain is struck will cut open the melons to let the customer sample it as a sort of *fait accompli*. This is done by running a regular Chinese coin, used as a knife, across the "head" end of the specimen where it is considerably sweeter than the "tail" end. The tail end may be actually very bitter! The Chinese muskmelons are always of the thin skinned kind and modern authorities on food hygiene are particularly opposed to eating them raw as evidences have been found that cholera germs easily penetrate to the very heart of the melons without apparent openings in the skin. The foreign variety of cantaloupes have appeared on China markets only in recent years.

But the Chinese watermelons are decidedly a superior article in every way. Though the Wus ate but few muskmelons, watermelons were consumed in wholesale numbers—at regular feasts. Whole melons are brought out, often *via* the family icebox, about twice every day, cut into slices and consumed to everyone's heart's content, which is the typical way for the Peking-*jen*. There are absolutely no "table manners" in so far as eating watermelons is concerned, as eating watermelons free-style is much more enjoyable than having to fight over a slice precariously balanced over a porcelain plate with a small desert spoon or fork.

*   *   *

The watermelon is known as *hsi kwa* (西瓜) in China which means "Western Melon" which, to all intents and purposes, is tantamount to a label indicating its country of origin, for from Asia Minor its kind has been introduced to China for only two thousand years which is a negligibly short time from the scientific point of view Long before Marco Polo started his journey eastward, long before even the three Magi from the East followed the star to Bethlehem, the watermelon's ancestors had started their overland travel from beyond Chinese Turkestan, following the northern route across the plateaus to the then empire capital at Loyang. This is no fiction "yarn" or groundless guesswork for Chinese historians clearly record that in the reign of

Emperor Ming Ti of the Han Dynasty the first seeds of the western melons were brought back by Pan Chao who went on a goodwill mission to the great *Hsi Yu* (西域) or Western Realms, visiting fifty odd little countries occupying then the present Samarkand, Tashkand and neighbouring districts.

In the course of time, western melons have been popularized from being rarities at the emperor's court to an inexpensive refreshment for the masses and little fruit dealers sell them in the streets in slices to the busy humanity plodding along under the hot summer sun. Though the Wus knew better than to patronize the wayside stands in view of their generally unacceptable sanitary conditions, they thought it an interesting experience to hear their trade cries:

"Come on and eat a piece of watermelon here! My melons are the size of bushel measures and the slices are as big as a sampan. The foot-high pulp melts into sugar in your mouth . . . "

*   *   *

Though the Wu family's house on Donkey Mart was each summer well equipped with an eye to the maximum of comfort during the hot weather it must be said that old Mr. Wu was not the type that would sit idle whiling away time to escape heat, rather the contrary. He was not without his daily round of duties, particularly after he had proclaimed himself the tutor-guardian of his grandchild, Little Bald Head, the details of which quickly fitted themselves among the other miscellaneous domestic duties required of him besides his hobbies of goldfish raising and taking care of his pet birds. His actual family chores were really optional and in his daily programs a good deal of spare moments were still waiting to be utilized for pleasure and enjoyment. Men struggle for a livelihood and "pursuit of happiness". For him only the latter question was to be attended to.

It was on a long summer afternoon when old Mr. Wu was sitting snugly in his wicker armchair under the mat shed, and lazily fanning himself to keep cool after a siesta that he suddenly recalled that it was the sixth day of the sixth lunar month. In the habit of his type he began to recollect the interesting bits from his past experiences and to relate them to the young boy sitting close by.

"When I was your age, Little Bald Head, the sixth day of the sixth moon used to be a great day and was looked forward to for weeks in advance. Your great grandfather, namely my father, used to take me to the Sutra-Sunning Ceremony out at the Pao Kuo Ssu, or Temple of Nation's Gratitude, the chief abbot of which monastery was a learned monk whom my father used to know and whom I was made to address as "Monk Uncle". It was more or less our rule to have a vegetarian dinner with other guests gathered at the temple. After watching the little acolytes taking out the piles and piles of holy scriptures for the annual rites of airing them, we often made our way to the canal outside Shun Chih Men to see the bathing of the elephants."

Old Mr. Wu was referring to the elephants kept in the Imperial elephant stables situated inside the southwestern corner of the Tartar City and which were yearly taken out on the sixth day of the sixth moon to have their only bath of the year. This was an annual ceremony and a spectacle attracting thousands of sight-seers. The big but under-nourished and ill-treated elephants were taken out under the custodianship of special elephant keepers officially employed for the purpose. The elephants originally came as tributes from the King of Annam, a vassal state under the "protection" of China. The practice had its beginning some time in the Ming Dynasty and lasted until the end of the reign of Emperor T'ung Chih of the Ch'ing Dynasty when the last herd of six were brought to Peking. These elephants were tamed and taught to perform certain tricks as a supposed demonstration of homage. They were employed to add to the awe-inspiring pomp and panoply of the imperial court during important state functions, such as an audience granted to the emissaries of the aboriginal tribes who came to China to present their tributes or pay their respects. Standing in pairs in front of the Wu Men (午門) or Noon Gate, the main approach to the Forbidden City, they were taught to stop people that looked suspicious or dangerous from entering the important precincts—as by the popular belief then prevailing, elephants were said to be possessive of a peculiar sense of reading human character and being able to tell good people from bad.

"But, as if foretelling the collapse of the dynasty", he went on, "one of the elephants suddenly became 'insane' and broke loose from its chains, running amuck. Near the Pailou, or Archway, on Tung Ch'ang An Chieh it claimed a toll of two human lives, two pedestrians before they could run to safety were seized in its long trunk and literally partitioned. This happened in the tenth year of Kwang Hsu, I think, when I was about eighteen years old. It marked the beginning of the term of life imprisonment for all the elephants still kept and culminated in their death within the next two or three years. With them vanished the last traces of the much-heralded elephant bathing in Peking and in all China."

Old Mr. Wu's reminiscences of the elephant baths reminded him of an old favourite pastime of his and the young grandson who had been listening absorbedly to the elephant legend was called to go with the old man to the backyard to look up his old fishing tackle.

"Come with me and let us get out my fishing rods", said the old man, "for we can go fishing though we cannot see any elephants bathe."

"Your fishing rods are not in the backyard, they are hung up on the wall in your own room", the child reminded him.

"No, I do not mean those. They are too good to use. I have some commonplace ones put away somewhere which we can use."

The old man did not wish to get the fine tackle damaged as the rods which the child referred to belonged to a very elaborate set of fishing accessories which a friend had given him. They had become a sort of mementoes as the man who gave them to him being considerably older than old Mr. Wu had long since passed from this world.

*　　*　　*

Fishing with rod and line has been an old sport in China and much indulged in by amateurs. It is still one of the hobbies of people in all walks of life. It is a slow game and therefore fits in nicely with the average tempo of the Chinese race. A proverb

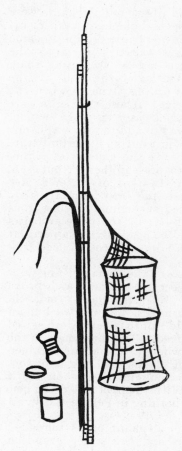

The angling kit of old Mr. Wu.

current in Peking groups the three things that require the most patience as being "Waiting for a person, fish-angling and riding an ox cart", and whoever has had the experience of one will easily form an idea of the others! It is true that this hobby knows no social castes as even Ch'ien Lung, that famous emperor of the late Ch'ing Dynasty, was fond of the sport and made annual trips in spring and autumn to the Fishing Terrace out-side of Fu Ch'eng Men where monu-mental buildings are still to be seen.

The Chinese fishing tackle is of a somewhat primitive nature, compris-ing rod, line, hooks and a net for keeping the day's catch alive in the side current of a stream and called technically a *hu* (罟). Other additional equipment would be a porcelain or pottery jar of as great age as possible for keeping the bait in, as most of the bait used is the so-called "live bait" such as earthworms, thread-like red worms, etc., which are better kept alive among moistened pieces of grass-paper in old ceramics. Little live shrimps and young frogs are used for certain species of fish. Little balls of dough are also effective in certain cases.

The proper materials for making fishing rods are bamboo and the stems of reeds, usually fitted into three sections, each smaller sec-tion being joined to a bigger section by inserting it bodily into the other. In order that the ends will not split, they are carefully bound by winding raw silk around them and then var-nished. The line used for general purposes is of raw silk in twelve or sixteen plies which would be strong enough to land even good-sized fish. The hooks are of fine and very often home-made vari-eties in ingenious designs. Imported fish-hooks from Russia have been known in Peking for many years. Modern fishing tackles, particularly the kind for deep sea, are still practically unknown to Chinese anglers. "Floats" attached to Chinese fishing lines are usually made with sections of bird quills, more often than not in the case of the more expensive and effective ones these be-ing made from peacock feathers as they have been surprisingly easy to procure—a fact accounted for by the frequent use these feathers were put to during the now defunct Manchu dynasty as official insignia or mark of official court favour for hat decoration by the Mandarins. A weight also is used to keep the hook direct-ly perpendicular from the floats by little drops of lead. These are the principal indispensable items in an angler's equipment. Other items frequently omitted would be a natural forked branch from a young elm tree which is stuck in the river bank and used for resting the rod upon so that the angler may be saved pains in the wrist from holding the rod for long periods (particularly when the absence of nibbles tends to effect a general run-down of morale) and perhaps a collapsible stool.

*   *   *

The complete kit was soon found by old Mr. Wu in the backyard storeroom as an orderly gentleman of his type always "had a place for everything and everything was in its place."

"Now all we have to do is to hunt for a few earthworms as this is the season for *chi yu* (鯽魚), or perches, which rise easily to this kind of bait", the old man explained.

So saying he brought a poker from the kitchen and digging in certain recognizable promising spots, he found quite a few usable ones, each about two inches in length.

"There will be no school for you tomorrow—which is quite permissible in this kind of weather. We are starting early in the morning on a fishing expedition. We will see what we can get," old Mr. Wu remarked.

"I hope we will get some large ones," said Little Bald Head.

"Maybe," replied his grandfather.

*   *   *

All preparatory arrangements complete and his morning's work delegated to other members of the household old Mr. Wu, with his grandson, Little Bald Head, sneaked out inconspicuously from their Donkey Mart home and without announcing it to the press started out on their fishing trip.

It must be remembered that in the time of Mr. Wu, the "sea" palaces of Peking were not yet thrown open to the public, much less allowed outsiders to fish in the forbidden grounds. Then, as it is still more or less the case now, the spots of good fishing accessible to Peking's amateur fishermen were few and far between. One of the places was the Kao Liang Bridge (高亮橋), located about ten minutes walk from the Hsi Chih Men, where the water upstream of the Imperial Canal from the Summer Palace was conserved in a sort of deeply dredged lagoon where the imperial barges of the Dowager Empress Ts'u Hsi and her predecessors were "docked". (The spot is also famous as being a fine suicide locale). An elaborately furnished landing place used to stand here named *Yi Hung T'ang* (倚虹堂), or Resting-on-the-Rainbow Pavilion, next to the covered piers where the imperial household's flat-bottomed barges were tied up while "in port" when frequent trips back and forth were made by the Manchu court between the city and the Yi Ho Yuan. Here, perch, carp and what-have-you swim in big schools.

From this scenic spot, where the Imperial Canal branches out to the south and the north, extended long endless stretches of rice-fields, irrigated by natural waterways, lying like mono-toned green carpets in geometrical designs on either side of the canal which was overshadowed by rows of weeping willows, nodding and swaying like the long sleeves of Chinese dancers. The quiet and enchanting beauty extends along the winding canal past the Five Pagoda Temple and the White Stone Bridge and beyond and gives the neighbourhood a sort of "smoke-screen" entirely unpenetrable by summer heat.

Here old Mr. Wu used to fish and chat with newly-made fishing
friends on many a long summer afternoon.. He and fellow-mem-
bers of his "poetry society" used to meet upstairs in the two-storied wine-shop, which lorded it over the surrounding country and
commanded unobstructed views of the beautiful Western Hills but
a little distance away, a beautiful mass of blue and green when
saturated with summer rain. The society convened at irregular
intervals and some members played musical instruments and sang
famous songs from the antiquated *K'un Ch'ui* (崑曲) plays, an
entirely different kind from the common theatrical stuff and characterized by emotional tunes and beauty of language and style.
Or they wrote poems at short notice on given subjects and given
metres as a literary game.

A small piece of an incense stick took the place of the modern
stop watch and was lighted as members picked up their brush
pens. The freshly composed verses were to be ready to show to the
gathering before the incense burnt out. Any member failing to do
this was penalized by having to drink as many cups of *Pai Kan*
(白乾), or "White and Dry" (Chinese wine), as had been agreed
upon beforehand. As the poetry competition went on, some members would choose to set out to hunt green frogs along the rice
paddies. A string with a little bit of meat tied at the end would
infallibly lure the hiding frogs into their hands as the frogs have a
costly obstinacy of holding fast to the meat and fighting to the
finish— their own finish.

Other members might prefer to sit along the canal and fish,
for, as we have said, fish were thick like porridge here and the
"big ones did not often get away." The freshly caught whitefish,
landed after many a hard battle, and the fat juicy legs of the frogs
were cooked by the wine-shop people into delicious dishes, "washed down ' by gallons of yellow and white wines, sometimes mixed
to enjoy the fancy name of "Snow and Sandstorm". Except when
some sudden downpours succeeded in dispersing the crowd of
"poets", driving them back to their city homes (which did not
happen often for the phrase "weather-permitting" never featured
in their agenda—more rains, more poetry), about half of the members were usually taken home, absolutely drunk, by the other half
who were by no means completely sober themselves.

*   *   *

It was to this place, Kao Liang Ch'iao, that the old Mr. Wu
had first intended to take the child a-fishing but he soon changed
his mind as the place reminded him of many happy yet sad memories, particularly as a good many of the "old familiar faces" were
to be seen no more.

*   *   *

Hailing a rickshaw old Mr. Wu and Little Bald Head, after a
hasty breakfast, started for the Yao K'eng (窰坑) pools to the east
of the ex-Blue Banner Barracks across the railway track to the
southeast of Hata Men.

The development of Peking was from the north southward and
though the northern half of the city is densely populated and fully occupied with busy streets and residential quarters, the southern portions, within city limits, have remained civilization's out-
posts as it were. The southern half of Peking's Chinese City,
barring the enclosures of the Temple of Heaven and the Temple of

Agriculture, still present a desolate, sparsely inhabited rural appearance as any one who has visited these parts will remember. To the southeast of the railway track are acres and acres of reed-covered marshlands interlocked with stretches of water.

This region, as a whole, is known as the *Yao K'eng* to the Chinese, or Kiln Holes, so called because the holes, vast excavations at one time, were man-made "craters" for the earth was removed from here to bake the bricks required for building the heavy massive walls of Peking City. Big mounds some fifteen feet high are still to be seen, they are all that is left of the original brick baking ovens, or *Yao* (窰) as they are called in Chinese. In the course of time the holes became regular lakes with accumulated rain water and perhaps more so due to some geological changes on account of the close proximity to underground "water veins". The place in all seasons except winter is the local anglers' paradise as fish of all kinds abound here. Un-walled and unfenced the place is open to the public. And at least one foreigner in Peking has been seen shooting wild ducks in the Yao K'eng marshes.

*　　*　　*

Having found a spot that looked assuring the old man and the boy seated themselves on the bank after putting up their fishing gear. An earthworm was produced from the porcelain container and knocked unconscious by putting it on the left palm of the old man's hand and clapping lightly on it with the right. The worm was attached to the hook by running the hook through the worm. Then the line was thrown clear into the blue depth.

There was some quiet waiting. Soon old Mr. Wu noticed something of a nibble.

"There it goes!" murmured the old man as he withdrew the line out of the water to find the worm gone. By experience he could

tell from the nibble that a little minnow had feasted on the worm without touching the hook!

A fresh bait was attached and the line again thrown in the water.

There was a long wait, Mr. Wu smoked his long pipe of bamboo as he waited. Then there were a few bubbles near the float and a final downward pull. Old Mr. Wu, all the time watching carefully, noticed the phenomena and with one single forceful yank and casting of the line landed a magnificent perch. This he removed from the hook and passed to the child to put away in his *hu* or "carrying-net".

"Must be some six *liangs* this one!" said the child.

"No my lad, not quite three! You have no sense of weight!" The old man was amused.

They had fairly satisfactory results in the morning's fishing and long before noon, had "packed up" and were ready to return home.

A Chinese fishing trick is to "build a nest" by clearing a spot of waterweeds by means of an anchorlike gadget and depositing there a little millet.

"We did not have any big ones," complained the child.

"Well, perch never grow to be very big though I know we have caught only small ones this morning. To catch the bigger perch it is necessary to build a trap by first removing the water-weeds in the region by means of an appliance made with four or five curved heavy wires and edged in the inside of the curve and tied together like a *mao* (錨), or ship's anchor, operated from a rod and string. Then a handful of millet should be placed in the opening by emptying a container holding the millet in the cleared spot. This in fishing language is called "building a nest". The bigger perch have a habit of being easily attracted to such a spot and people drop their lines right in the opening or trap itself. It is also necessary to sound how deep the water is as the hooks dangling about halfway in the water and clear away from the bottom will not look appetizing to the full-grown perch no matter what bait you use—they know better. Do not think I am not a good fisherman, Little Bald Head?"

"No, I rather imagine you are the way you talk!"

*   *   *

Having had their share of angling old Mr. Wu and his grandson took a walk along the shores of the Yao K'eng "lakes" watching other people engaged in the same sport.

There were some people out after blackfish, or pike, a spotted greenish black fish with sinful eyes placed at least a quarter of its

length from the tip of its head thus allowing great flexibility as to the width of the mouth. The pike is known as the fiercest fish in fresh waters and the most sporty sort in local rivers and lakes.

A thick twine of hemp is used for this fish, attached to the end of a regular bamboo pole about an inch in diameter at the thinner or top end. To the twine is fastened a hook of much greater size than the ordinary fish-hooks. The bait is a green frog some two inches in length. The frog is knocked head-first on the ground to kill it. Then the sharp hook is inserted into the frog's body from the hinder part forward. Thus the hook, sharp and unfriendly, will be concealed in the frog's mouth and hold its head up as though the frog was still alive and about to jump away. The hind legs of the little frog are tied together to the line with a thread. It is then ready for the blackfish.

The blackfish sometimes attain a length of two or three feet weighing five to six catties and have been noted as being the hardest fighters. They have also been known to bite,

The vicious-looking pikes are caught with green frog baits attached to hooks at the end of heavy hemp twine.

it seems, any time a bait is sighted. Experienced catchers let go the line from 20 to 30 feet following each bite to allow the hook to get well into the fish before trying to land them. It is then that the fight takes place and cases have been recorded in which a blackfish broke the line or even carried the bamboo pole clear out of the fisherman's hand in its desperate attempts to get away. They are provided with sharp teeth in their unbelievably wide mouths and are known to eat their own kind when smaller than themselves.

Other people were on the spot principally after the catfish for this is much sought after as a delicious dish. Old Mr. Wu could tell the men were after these without having to verify it because lying in small jars were a number of "blue" or natural-coloured earthworms which the catfish like so much. The blue colour is obtained by starving the earthworm for a time!

There were also a number of children catching tiny shrimps with the aid of small traps woven with green willow twigs. The traps are so ingeniously made that the victims can only slip in but never out. A few pieces of sheep's bones (obtainable from the mutton shops) deposited in the traps are the prerequisite "go-getters" for sure results. Those without a trap used common buckets and had but slightly inferior results so long as the proper sheep's bones were used.

Little Bald Head stopped and watched every "establishment" with interest.

*　　　*　　　*

"What places are over yonder to the east?" asked the little boy, pointing to a pavilion or kiosk perched on top of a mound and to some pink-painted temple buildings to the north of the mound.

"That pavilion is the famous K'wei Hsing Ke (魁星閣), or 'Shrine of the Star of the Foremost Scholar in the Land'. Formerly candidates from the provinces attending the imperial examinations each year used to come here to worship as this is the deity in charge of the distribution of honours or successes. He is known to have appeared in the candidates' dreams to notify them about their successes or failures before they were actually announced. That other big temple is the Hsi Chao Ssu (夕照寺) or 'Temple of the Evening Sun', in the premises of which is the famous Wan Liu T'ang (萬柳堂), or 'Hall of Ten Thousand Willows', where Emperor Shun Chih (Ch'ing Dynasty) during his youthful years before ascending the throne had his private study some two hundred odd years ago. It used to be a beautiful place and well-known to the literary classes in Peking" explained the old man.

"Let us go and look around."

"Let us not, for the place is now used for storing the dead pending interment or transportation to the native places of the dead for burial. The place is partly filled with rows of coffins containing the rotting bodies."

*　　　*　　　*

Chinese children have a kind of game which is called ch'uan (拳), or "Fist Game", and this is the childish version of that famous institution known by the same name and so much in evidence at adult drinking parties. While the drinking parties' fist game may at times be very complicated, requiring shrewd anticipation of the opponents' habitual strategies and swift decision

and changes in fraction of seconds in order not to be a loser and penalized by having to drink cups of wine (which is not fair and ought to be the other way round), the children's fist game is simply a game of chance.

One kind is the *ya ch'uan* (啞拳), or "pantomime fist". This was taught to Little Bald Head. Many heated games were played between him and either one of the Wang brothers from next door or some other boy of the Wus' acquaintance.

There are but three "gestures" indicated by the hand. A clenched fist means "stone", an open outstretched hand "water" and an upright hand with fingers sticking up a "sand bowl". The two players count "one, two, three" in their mind and at the word "Three" will simultaneously show one of the three gestures listed above.

The three "gestures" in the children's fist game. From the top, stone, water and sand bowl.

If one boy shows "water" and the other "stone", the boy showing the "stone" is the loser for water will carry the stone away. In the same way, "water" loses to the "sand bowl". A sand bowl, naturally, is a loser to "stone" for what sand bowl can stand up against a stone thrown at it? It is a game of "mutual subjugation" and two duplicates, therefore, mean "no sale".

Another similar game, equally popular, is the one of "chicken", "worm" and "stick". The "chicken" eats the "worm", the "worm" bores a hole in the "stick," and the "stick" knocks the "chicken".

*   *   *

It was from the Wang brothers next door that Little Bald Head learned Tiger Chess.

This game has sixteen pieces, one Tiger and fifteen Sheep. The board contains five large squares joined together and intersected by parallel and then diagonal lines. Thus the complete board would present the appearance of a Union Jack placed above four others.

Before the game is begun, the fifteen Sheep are put each at one junction point on the board in three rows at the bottom and the tiger in the center of the squares at top which is its ' den". The party playing the Sheep starts the game, moving any one sheep one step in any direction, and the Tiger moves also a step forward toward the Sheep. The Tiger seeks to devour the Sheep one by one by jumping clear over a sheep to alight on an empty point beyond—forward, backward or crosswise, while the Sheep will move forward in concerted action, one Sheep one step at a time, trying always to move over in double file across the field in a flanking movement to try to corner the Tiger and force it to retreat into its den. In this way, as the Sheep move forward, the Tiger will try to reduce the principal strength of the enemy by slowly cutting down their number. The person playing the Sheep resists by always trying to move in double files as the Tiger can only jump over one Sheep and never two according to the rules.

Another game Little Bald Head learned was the *lien ch'i* (連棋), or "formation chess."

A piece of paper is covered with three squares, one inside the other and then more lines are added in the eight directions straight or slanting. The game starts instantaneously with the "setting" of the men from both sides, one piece at a time in turn—there are nine or twelve pieces on each side depending on the existence or otherwise of the slanting lines at the four corners on the "board."

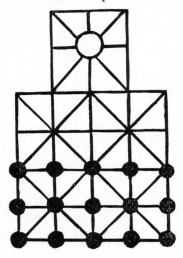

The rules provide that any formation or *lien* (連) of three men of the same side in one straight line means a "win" and a privilege to confiscate or "eat" any one man of the opposing side, except those already in formation. It is a fast game, too, particularly if plans are allowed by the enemy side to be realized to create a so-called "drawer-type" formation of a double-duty kind, with which repeated moving back and forth of but one single man will gradually but surely annihilate the enemy side in no time.

Both the chessboards and the men for the two games were purchased from the toy shops for the Wu child and he soon mastered the rules and was then approaching anybody he met.

"Come on and have a game of Tiger Chess or Formation Chess with me," he would say.

Old Mr. Wu never accepted his challenge.

"Who wants to play such foolish stuff with you!" he protested.

This is the board used for Tiger Chess. The men have been placed in position for the game to start. The pieces bear the likenesses of sheep and a tiger.

LITTLE BALD HEAD GOES TO SCHOOL

THE schoolwork of Little Bald Head at the hand of his grandfather was more or less a hit-and-miss affair. Although a schedule was at first solemnly drawn up setting two one-hour periods a day aside as his study periods, there were many reasons for calling off schoolwork for the day. A visitor in the house, some climatic extremes, a day's outing or a visit to a friend either on the part of the student or of the teacher was each an acceptable excuse for a holiday. A family school is a flexible affair, its rules elastic and as such it is not conducive to systematic progress. Little Bald Head, it was noted, had memorized roughly three hundred and fifty characters in the first two months and by the end of the sixth month, his vocabulary was somewhere between four hundred and four hundred and fifty characters, which fact bore strong evidence that old Mr. Wu's enthusiasm did not hold long and was constantly changing in a downward curve. This was, it must be admitted, no strange phenomenon as no parents can expect to teach their children with success.

In the course of time the family began considering putting Little Bald Head in a school. There was naturally another conference in the house and after some debates a resolution was passed that Little Bald Head was to attend the private school or *ssu shu*, conducted by Mr. Yung, which school the Wang boy next door was attending. They further agreed that their child and the Wang child were to go to school and come home together according to a proposal tentatively made by a member of the Wang family some time ago.

It was remarked that the scheme was virtually a decided matter before the actual conference began for old Mrs. Wu, the grandmother, was able to give off-hand a lot of information about Mr. Yung's school and sundry appertaining topics. The old woman in frequent gossips with the Wangs had gathered a lot of data in anticipation of exactly such a day and when the matter was referred to her she was already prepared for it.

"I think it would be a good plan to send our child to Mr. Yung's school, for Mr. Yung seems to be a capable teacher though I have never met him personally. The Wang child has only studied with him for a little over two years and he has already finished the *Lun Yu* (the Confucian Analects). The other day his mother showed me the boy's *fang* (倣) (penmanship exercise sheets) and they looked like pretty good work to me, full of red circles," old Mrs. Wu said. Chinese teachers draw red circles on individual characters in penmanship exercises to indicate a good specimen and as a token of his approbation. Double circles indicate "Excellent".

"How far is Mr. Yung's school?" asked young Mr. Wu.

"It is quite near here in the grounds of the Tu Ti Miao (土地廟) (Temple of the Local Guardian God on Bamboo Alley) directly beyond our lane. It is not far away at all. The Wang boy next door goes to school all by himself and needs to have nobody to take him back and forth," Old Mrs. Wu had sound deductive judgment.

"It does look like a good plan," the young father put in, "but I have been thinking about an arrangement in a friend's place. This friend keeps a private teacher for his sons in the home and he told me that he would be glad to have our child attend his family school for part of the expenses on a so-called *chuan kuan wai fu* (專館外附) (private class with outside attenders) principle. I wonder how that sounds to you. Perhaps Mr. Yung's is after all a better place, particularly as it is close to our home."

"No, no," objected the old man who had only been listening up to that time.

"I strongly object to a private teacher," he continued. "For I know just what it would mean to our child. It amounts to our absorbing part of the teacher's fees without enjoying the benefits of the matter at all. The teacher, to please his host, will never give equal attention to our child as to the host's, and our child would constantly be looked down upon by the friend's family as well as by the teacher himself. It will eventually mean trouble. I had been just such a "guest student" myself and I know exactly what that means. I would rather let Little Bald Head attend the private school at the Tu Ti Miao Temple. This would be a good transitional period for getting the boy acquainted with school life before we finally send him to a public institution. It would give him the 'feel' of the thing. The school's locational proximity suits me well for we can always be on the alert to know how things are going on and whether or not our boy is being ill-treated by his schoolmates."

*   *   *

Before education on the Western principles was little by little introduced into China, the private schools or *ssu shu* were the only kind of institutions available for the cultural advancement of Chinese boys. I say "boys" because they were intended for boys alone, for almost all Chinese were under the impression that it was no business of girls to learn even the rudiments of the written Chinese language. "Women without cultured ability are virtue itself" goes a Chinese proverb. Books were good or bad and an ability to read on the part of a girl may open the door to much vice. It is true, of course, that some girls were given chances to study but most of such cases were found in rich and cultured families which happened to be without male children or in some renegade type of families who dared to do differently from what Propriety dictated. Schools for girls were non-existent and co-education decidedly unimaginable.

There had never been schoolteachers trained for the purpose and no record of anybody ever making such an attempt as a research into pedagogical principles and practices. Teaching school was the very last thing any person would ever do and was done only as the final life line on which poor scholars had to fall back, utilizing their unmarketed classical training for a *modus vivendi* to tide them along and keep the wolves from the door. To make the matter clear, it must be added here that the express ambition of any and all scholars in China, admittedly, was to become governmental officials some day, and those who failed to make any headway in that direction and woke up to a sad disillusionment often found in teaching school a handy way to be assured of a "steady rice bowl!" Students intended for business had a very elementary education which was usually followed by serving an apprenticeship in commercial establishments. Whether later on successful or not, their education was far below a teaching standard. Farmers and craftsmen had nothing to do whatsoever with schools.

The Chinese school methods are simple and no reformation of any consequence has ever been introduced into the educational system in all the centuries. Life in a school must be said to be very harsh and at times inhuman in the fullest meaning of the words. Instead of the three R's, the Chinese school knows but two, Reading and Writing, for Arithmetic was not taught in a school (such a mean and lowly subject of vile merchants should only be taught in a shop over the famous abacus). For the first years of school work there is even but one R—Reading. Reading, however, was itself a three-act play: "Reading," "Reciting" and "Beating", or "Being Beaten" to be exact.

The lessons were never clearly explained to students neither as to the constructional usages and the idea embodied because, granting that the teachers themselves did know what they are teaching, it would actually be futile to do so as the texts contained matters incredibly far beyond the child's intelligence and any attempts at explaining them would only complicate matters. The passages from books were committed to memory by reading them out loud again and again. Thus a group of twenty or thirty pupils in a Chinese school shouting the lessons in "chorus" was a noisy affair. In due course of time, as practice made perfect, the passages would actually be fully memorized after long hours spent earnestly at it. All the while, in the natural course of things, the students did not get even the general drift of what they had been shouting except in straggling points every now and then where the diction happened to be easier to understand or the passages happened to bear a certain resemblance to the "spoken" version of the same matter. As the Chinese classical or written phraseology and the spoken language are so different from each other such points, unfortunately, were not many.

That the students were careful in their studies and exerted the proper amount of energy over the passages given them, it is logical enough, indicated by their ability to *pei* (背) or recite the lessons, with books closed, in a torrential deluge like a phonograph!

Then comes the third act of *ta* (打), or "Being Beaten," as a punishment meted out to children who fail to repeat their lessons from memory. The Chinese teachers usually chastise the students by beating with a wooden board or a rattan stick the palm of the students' left hand—the useless hand—for the right hand is the one used to write with. So that Chinese children be not spoiled, the rods are never spared.

*   *   *

It looked as though Little Bald Head was about to be plunged into a life not particularly comfortable.

*   *   *

The description of the Chinese primary school life in private schools, the only kind originally found in China, is the painting of a dark picture indeed. The orthodox methods described may be hard to believe but nevertheless are exactly what was going on. The cultural pursuit of the Chinese scholar is nowhere better represented than in the well-known phrase "ten years of *k'u* (苦) or bitterness". A Chinese proverb says "To be a man above men (meaning a "scholar"—synonymous with a 'government official' as per foregone conclusion) you must endure the bitterest of all bitternesses." Though the fundamental principle of juvenile education must be said to be very harsh and to leave much room for improvement, yet the Chinese early discovered the importance of the "expression of individuality" in the field of learning. Another Chinese proverb says "The teacher guides the students to the door, but conscientious advancement is dependent upon the student himself."

The age for the commencement of such conscientious study is a matter of much variation in different cases. Confucius said of himself that he started to concentrate on his studies when he was fifteen years old. This is the time when the catch-as-catch-can period is definitely over and the youngsters' own imaginative and reasoning power is fully developed. It is of this period that Confucius said "If the student is told the one corner is a corner and he can not reply that the other three are also corners, it is no use repeating it to him". The pedagogical characteristic for this second period is the *K'ai Chiang* (開講), or "paraphrasing and explanation", which does not begin until several years of pre-paratory labour is complete. Before that it is a matter of lead-ing a cow to water and making her drink. And it was to this disciplinary tutelage period that Little Bald Head was first introduced.

*   *   *

The classroom of Mr. Yung's school in the Local Guardian God's Temple grounds was a typical example of its kind. A sidebuilding of three rooms in the main temple courtyard was partitioned into one small single room and one big double room, the smaller one being the bed-room of the teacher and his wife and the other the school room and recep-tion room for the Yungs where they received their guests. In winter time it became also their kitchen as the school's heating stove was made to do double duty, though in summer the kitchen part of it was obligingly moved outside.

The schoolroom was devoid of any desks or benches as ordinary household furniture was utilized for such purposes. The square stools and the square Chinese tables were so arranged that the students were able to sit in groups of four or six to suit their "grades", classified naturally by the different textbooks used. A small table and a stiff-backed Chinese chair, the most uncomfortable of its kind in the world since mankind started to assume sedentary postures, made up the teacher's "Terrace of Apricot Blossoms". This term is used euphoniously to mean any teach-

A stone-rubbing portrait of Con-fucius hung on the classroom wall.

er's desk for it was at such a place that Confucius used to gather his disciples to hear his lectures. On the wall close by the teacher's desk was a mounted scroll of a portrait of Confucius, an old stone-rubbing in the present case, with his long beard and quaint, outlandish hat, no doubt in style during his time, and his sagely eyes staring down at the naughty school children below. This picture, according to the Wang boy, was hung up when the wooden tablet bearing the Sage's title of ten characters in oue long perpendicular row translating, "The Great Accomplished, Most Sage, Advanced Teacher Kung Fu Tze His Tablet" had become so "shopworn" that it had to be removed and stowed away pending repairs. It is quite permissible to say it was "shopworn" because such a school has been enjoying the ironic Chinese name of *Hsueh Fang P'u* (學房舖, or "school shop" referring to its commercial nature.

The Wang child was first requested to ask the teacher as a sort of a formality if a new student would be acceptable and then Little Bald Head was brought to the school by his grandfather for matriculation.

*   *   *

While Mr. Yung, the teacher, and old Mr. Wu were engaged in a ceremonial conversation concerning the schooling of Little Bald Head, the child had a chance to look around the schoolroom.

It was early in the morning and the students had just begun to arrive. The first boy to appear was an over-sized sort of a chap whom he later learned was the *Ta Hsueh Chang* (大學長), or head of the student body. He was followed by boys of various sizes and assorted ages, coming in twos and threes. The Wang boy next door was among the first to come, too, for he had been looking forward to the new experience of seeing his pal, Little Bald Head, in his school.

Each student unwrapped from a squarish piece of cloth his school books and from a home-made cloth bag his brush pens. Brass ink boxes or stone inkwells were also brought to school, With undertoned chatting and whispering and side glances cast at the new boy the students began to start their penmanship exercises as was the rule. Little Bald Head also noted that each student, as he came in, made a deep bow before the Confucius portrait on the wall and then an equally deep bow to the aged teacher, Mr. Yung, before he went to sit at his seat. Little Bald Head was later to do exactly the same thing.

Teacher Yung asked Little Bald Head a few questions at random, which he answered readily and clearly. The teacher, at least in appearance, showed approval of the first impressions and turning to the old man said that he felt the child was of a promising sort and was apparently of a very "high-grade talent" and of a very *lao shih* (老實) or obedient character, this in the way of a ceremonious complimentary remark.

"No, the child is both dull and naughty and will have to be put under very superb guidance such as is possible in your honourable school to save him from being ruined," answered old Mr. Wu. Chinese conversational refinements require such kinds of apparent purposely behumbling one's own self and complimenting others though each person knows exactly how the other's words must be discounted.

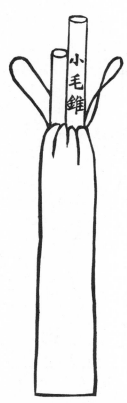

The students carried their brush pens in little cloth bags which take the place of the foreign pencil boxes.

The boy was to be taught the *San Tze Ching* (三字經) or "Tri-metrical Classic," and the *Po Chia Hsing* (百家姓) or "One Hundred Surnames", and the *Ch'ien Tze Wen* (千字文) or "Thousand Characters Essay," following the conventional manner all over China. He was to be taught three lines from each book every day without explanation or paraphrasing. He was also to have penmanship exercises every morning but not any rewriting of the "red models" as he had done before nor writing free hand as the Wang boy was already doing. It was agreed that the *ying ke* (影格) or "shadow model" method, using a black print-ed model sheet put under the ex-ercise paper and writing the same characters following the "shadow" on the paper, tracing the characters in other words, was most suitable in his case. He was to come to school every morning at eight o'clock and go home to lunch at eleven. After-noon sessions were from one to three o'clock. The first and fifteenth day of each Lunar calendar month were each a holiday. Other holidays were by advance notice from the teacher. All these things were agreed upon between the old man and the teacher in their brief talk. A matter touch-ed upon was to ask the teacher to please see that the boy comes and goes with the Wang child. The matter of school fees was not mentioned as this would not be "good form."

"If the boy should ever be found to be transgressing your rules, do not hesitate to punish him by making him kneel down, or even beating him. I will fully support all your chastisement measures and you must not feel that our child is immune to penalty only because that he is the only child in our family," the old man explained.

"I am sure the child will be a good pupil and you may set your mind at ease and leave everything to me," answered the teacher. He understood then and there that the child was, as he was told, the "only" son of the family and that corporal punish-ment was therefore not to be resorted to.

    *   *   *

The Wus prepared the necessary equipment for Little Bald Head, consisting of text-books, etc., and fixed up a square piece of blue cloth for wrapping together the various things. In one corner of the blue cloth was sewn a piece of ribbon with a big square-holed Chinese cash attached to the end. This was the con-ventional way for wrapping up schoolbooks. The round cash served as a sort of clip.

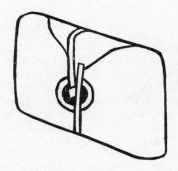

The conventional way of carrying schoolbooks is to wrap them in a piece of blue cloth which is then fastened with a ribbon and a square-holed Chinese cash.

It fell to the lot of the old grandfather to design a "school name" for the child, as once attending school he could no more go by the "milkname" of "Little Bald Head." He had to consult the family's *Chia P'u* (家譜) or "Pedigree Record" in order that the child's name might not come into conflict with that of some member of their ancestors. He finally wrote out three tentative names as he thought it would be a good thing to allow the young father the privilege of making the formal decision. They finally agreed on calling the child *Hsueh - wen* or "Learning Literature." This name implied in itself a reference to a classical passage which purported to make "learning of literature" a final touch to scholarly achievement as other ethical points were considered far more important in the making of a "superior man" and were made to take precedence over and above "Literature"— only people with the proper background of virtues therefore are fit for such unnecessary superficialities.

The family almanac was again consulted and it was discovered that the very next day was an auspicious one as the column devoted to the day mentioned a great many things as suitable undertakings for such a day. It said in plain language that the day was good not only for "Entering School", but equally felicitous for Making Sacrifices, Meeting Friends, Beginning Travels, Wedding Ceremonies and their Preceding Formalities, Adding Members to the Family Census, Bathing, Shaving, Cutting New Clothes, Commencing Building Programs, Erecting Pillars and Mounting House Beams, Consulting Doctors, Opening Granaries, Buying Properties, Burying the Dead, etc. with the particularly profitable hours indicated as the "hours of the Dragon" or between eight and ten o'clock in the morning. The almanac also gave it as being a bad day for crossing rivers and for hunting parties which, of course, did not concern the Wus.

There was no clearly understood provision made about school fees as neither the old man nor the teacher, Mr. Yung, considered it a good thing to raise such a question at their first ceremonious meeting but the family was able to find out from the Wang child next door what he had been paying. This, as a matter of fact, had long been known to the Wus. Wang's boy paid sixty cents a month in advance. Before the prices went on the silver standard it had been two hundred coppers.

Old Mr. Wu was not to be laughed at as being a person of crudity when he had the money put neatly into a red envelope and marked "*Shu Hsiu*" (束修) followed by a line of small characters indicating that it was "carefully prepared by the small, foolish pupil Wu Hsueh-wen". The phrase "*shu hsiu*" literally means "a bundle of dried, cured meats" which in ancient time, was the universally agreed present students used to bring their teachers. The phrase is still used as a time-honoured substitute for "school fees".

In another red envelope was enclosed a gift of two dollars and here the old man wrote "*Chih Ching*" (贄敬), or "commencement gift", a kind of a souvenir marking the beginning of their relationship, a sort of a "getting-acquainted premium".

"What is this *Chih Ching* for, father?" asked young Mr. Wu.

"This is a ceremonial gift to the teacher required of a new student. The word *Chih*, as you know, refers to an ancient custom. In olden times, gentlemen gave jades, silks and pet birds for a first-meeting present and ladies gave chestnuts, dried dates, and *hsiu* or cured meat strips. Money now takes the place of all these," old Mr. Wu explained.

"I thought the school fee was all."

"Oh, no, there are other sums we will be paying the teacher from time to time. The custom provides for *san chieh* (三節) and *liang shou* (兩壽) or "three annual festivals" and "two birthdays" —the teacher's and his wife's, as occasions for sending gifts of money. We shall be paying also an incense money on the days of the spring and autumn Confucian sacrifices. In winter we contribute toward maintaining the school stove, etc. Such things are never directly requested of us, but we Wus are not going to 'lose face' by exhibiting ignorance."

*   *   *

The three so-called "small books" invariably used in the first stage of a Chinese child's education were to make up Little Bald Head's curricula in Mr. Yung's school. It would not be out-of-place to give a brief review of each of them.

The first one, the "*San Tze Ching*," or "Trimetrical Classic", is an old book originally attributed to a Sung Dynasty scholar, though some recent revisions and additions must have been made. The lines are all trimetrical in construction and the rhymes, varying with different sounds, are carried clear through to the end (as also with the other two books). The book not only gives a general introduction to proper human behaviour, laying particular emphasis on the ways of a young scholar, but gives a good many bits of knowledge about various things as well as an outline of China's lengthy history with reference to each respective dynasty.

A brief reference is also contained pertaining to the various classical books, the Five *Ching* (五經) and Four *Shu* (四書). Mention is also made of various outstanding famous men of letters and anecdotes told of them in a following section and the book concludes by urging the young scholars "in the offing" to devote themselves closely to their studies. The diction itself is so difficult and so much knowledge is condensed into the 1,068 characters that make up the book it is no exaggeration to say that to give access to the ideas contained in the book a glossary of notes many times the size of the book would be necessary. For example, the first eight lines of three characters each would translate, word for word, as follows:

> Mankind its beginning
> Nature originally good
> Nature relatively near
> Habits relatively far
> If not taught
> Nature then deviate
> Teaching its way
> Valuable with concentration.

A child's first lesson at school begins like the above, it is then no wonder that nothing further than mere "shouting" and memorizing is required of the youngsters.

The next book "*Ch'ien Tze Wen,*" or "Thousand Character Essay" is yet more difficult to understand, even for adults. This little book of exactly one thousand characters is a long series of four-character lines, also rhymed, and is authentically known to be from the pen of a scholar by the name of Chow Hsing-ssu of the Liang period roughly 500-550 A.D. Emperor Wu Ti of the Liang Dynasty was himself a person of much literary accomplishment and the story goes that he personally selected one thousand characters from some calligraphical masterpieces, all different, and had Chow summoned to the imperial study to compose these one thousand characters into rhymed lines of four characters each further ordering that each of the lines was to make sense. (This is a feat possible, perhaps, only in the Chinese language. Its nearest counterpart would be the Japanese song of "*Iroha*" composed by the 47 Japanese *kana*, each one used but once in the song). Scholar Chow sweated over the task and finished it in a day. The beginning lines of the book translate (each word representing roughly one Chinese ideograph):

Heaven earth black yellow
The Universe wide barren
Sun moon full shaded
Stars planets arrange appear
Cold comes heat goes
Autumn harvest winter store
Intercalation surplus becomes year
Musical notes harmonize positive.

The scope of knowledge covered by this book is even wider than that covered by the "Trimetrical Classics." The book is adopted by the Chinese school for the reason, easily appreciated, that since there are no repetitions of characters, the students get more new words in their vocabulary than if some other book were used.

The third one is the "*Pai Chia Hsing,*" or "Hundred Family Names," and is used primarily to acquaint the students with a lot of "personal proper nouns", so to speak. The name of the book is misleading, for, by actual count, there are 472 characters, comprising 412 mono-syllabic family names and 30 bi-syllabic ones, with four additional characters at the end translating "End of Pai Chia Hsing" to fill the space.

Barring understanding of the meanings contained in the daily assignments which was not required of him Little Bald Head was able to manage beautifully with his schoolwork. The five hundred odd characters he had already learned "came in handy" too.

*   *   *

It did not take long for Little Bald Head to adapt himself to the school life at Teacher Yung's. His friend, the Wang boy next door who had been his "pal", became his study companion as well and always looked up the Wu child before going to school together. The schoolwork, though not particularly enjoyable, was not unbearable. He had always been told that the road to learning was not a comfortable one and he was inwardly disappointed to find it so uneventful.

The school rules provided no set periods for recess but the teacher often intentionally or otherwise gave the children an opportunity to relax a little from their strenuous work when he left the classroom for a while or when one boy finished his penmanship exercise sooner than the rest or when another had done his daily recitation work or when he was fully prepared for the day's examinations and thus light-heartedly was prepared for the "worst". These were sweet moments of stolen idleness, and a friendly chat with nearby students, or some little toys surreptitiously brought to school provided some fun shared with schoolmates away from the teacher's all-seeing eyes. These were interesting experiences and only people who have personally gone through them know what dear-to-the-heart moments they were.

One of the toys Little Bald Head saw in the hands of a school mate was a set of *Ch'i Ch'iac Tu* (七巧圖), or Seven "Magical Blocks", designed to help develop the child's imagination and resourcefulness. A square wooden board is divided into seven separate pieces of different shapes following a definite way of cutting. By ingenious shifting and arranging of these seven blocks a variety of designs may be formed, such as a sword, an old oil-lamp or a small boat, etc. Little Bald Head was naturally interested to have such a set for himself and he remembered to approach his father with this request. He was told by the friend who had one that the sets were sold at the bazaar.

The fifteen-piece set of "magical blocks" can produce many interesting combinations and the two examples reproduced here are typical ones.

The fifteen "magical blocks" are cut from one square piece of wood.

Many a simple design can be obtained with the seven-piece set of "magical blocks"

"I shall buy you a set of the blocks," promised his father, "but you are not going to take them to school as this schoolmate of yours has done."

Young Mr. Wu not only purchased for the child a seven-piece set but also another set of fifteen pieces, a more elaborate one with a much greater scope for possible designs. The fifteen piece set also had a book with it, printed on Chinese bamboo paper giving a collection of various arrangements discovered by a certain famous scholar who apparently had laboured intensively on the matter as the book bore witness. The set was carved from a square wooden block and there must have been some two hundred pictures of possible arrangements in the book, part of which was illustrated with famous lines from old Chinese poems or famous anecdotes. The book was not only suitable to children but was equally interesting to adults apparently.

Some of the designs were easy to do as the lines separating the blocks were clearly marked but most were not so explained and Little Bald Head had to ponder over many a difficult problem.

One of the pictures thus constructed illustrated a short poem:

Alone the fisherman in his boat clad in grass-leaf raincoat,
Fishes in the cold stream in the snowy wintry weather.

Another was the picture of a monk meditating under a clear moon, with a poem annexed:

So crystal the pool and silvery the moon,
So clear and pure art thou;
Nothing could thou be compared with except,
The empty and peaceful heart of Buddha.

OLD MR. WU'S BIRTHDAY

CHINESE polytheistic Buddhism is an interesting story all by itself and in every trade and every phase of the life of mankind there is usually to be found some sort of a god worshipped very much in the same manner as a patron saint. The various major and minor divinities were not all created in one day for we find that they were mostly humans to whom were attributed special achievements or some outstanding contribution to the particular trade which they had practised. In the same manner as honorary academic degrees are presented to living great men in modern times, the Chinese chose to confer such honours posthumously and the greatest honours thus accorded have been to deify men and put them among the gods.

The original principle, more or less as an encouragement measure for the living to aim at something worthwhile in life, must be said to be a good one. Thus a great portion of the members in the Chinese Pantheon were not purely the products of imagination but were really human creations by popular consent. While the various gods come in for collective worship and sacrificial ceremonies, each separate member is also worshipped by interested parties in individual celebrations mostly on their birthdays.

The God of Horses, according to Chinese religious artists, has three eyes, four arms and protruding teeth which. all in all, give him a grotesque appearance.

The birthday of the God of Horses and that of the God of Fire happens to fall on the same day, the 23rd of the sixth lunar month. The God of Horses is a typical one all by himself and is now worshipped only by stable-keepers, horse-dealers and Chinese veterinary doctors whose consultation offices combined with a horse pharmacy are still to be seen on Peking streets, notably on thoroughfares adjoining main roads to the country. A strongly constructed wooden frame with heavy iron rings and stout ropes stand before the door as their sign. The indisposed beasts are always tied fast to the frame while their medicine is administered to them with wooden ladles. A kicking and protesting beast taking its medicine is always a sight much more spectacular than shoeing a horse, both of which take on about the same general appearance and are done in the open street in Peking.

The God of Horses is represented as an awe-inspiring sort of divinity if the printed paper images can be depended upon to convey an acceptable portraiture. It is made to have three instead of two eyes, with the third one vertical on the forehead (symbolic of "horse sense"?) and four arms instead of the usual two, with the additional ones holding a pair of big-bladed swords. The conventional offering to the God of Horses is a big piece of mutton boiled rare, dishes of steamed breads and three cups of wine, lighted to burn during the ceremonies while the incense sticks last. It is said that the God of Horses is originally a Mohammedan which seems to be a reasonable guess as the first horses must have come to China overland from Arabia, the cradle of the Islamic religion, and its neighbourhood (some archaeobiologist ought to be able to tell us). The worship of the horse god was a household rite in Peking until modern horseless vehicles revolutionized transportation and ousted the horse and mule carts from private Chinese homesteads. In the country where horses and their cousins, the mules and donkeys, are still employed to do farm work and in the interior provinces the God of Horses is still venerated in the same old fashion.

The God of Fire, whose temporal name was Chu Jung, was a human being prior to godhood and is of an unquestionably ancient origin, for the name Chu Jung and the information that he was the God of Fire is mentioned in the "Li Chi" or "Book of Rites," a Han Dynasty volume edited from Chow Dynasty material. It is reasonable to presume that the god was originally created in commemoration of the discoverer of fire and its many good uses, but popular tradition has gradually led the people to believe, that this is the god charged with meting out punishment by setting people's houses on fire. Worshipping the God of Fire is therefore a precautionary measure to prevent the divinity from visiting the worshippers' establishments in the wake of which there is often a fire accident. The god is represented by fierce-looking eyes and "flaming" hair and is quite repulsive to look at. The way to worship the God of Fire is to make a paper shrine containing the god's paper image, send it out in a procession and then burn it.

Judging from the number of lanes bearing the names Ma Shen Miao (馬神廟) and Ho Shen Miao (火神廟) in Peking there must have been may more shrines dedicated to them than there are now.

*   *   *

No special rites marked the day in the Wu household but Master Wu Hsueh-wen, alias Little Bald Head, had a holiday from school.

*   *   *

The 24th day of the sixth moon of the lunar calendar is said to be the birthday of General Kuan Yu, one of the two "Military Sages" of China (the other one is General Yo Fei) and popularly known to foreigners as China's War God. It is an occasion for house-to-house sacrifices.

In the eyes of the four hundred million Chinese General Kuan Yu stands out prominently as a "model soldier" and a "model friend" and possessor of superhuman powers against all demons and destructive elements. Miraculous deeds have been attributed to his spiritual machination hundreds of years after he had died. His title is *Kuan Kung* (關公) or Duke Kuan and he is still more popularly called the *Lao Yeh* (老爺) (Master). He is the personification of all virtues and stands for anything that is *cheng* (正) or straight as against all things crooked. He is also revered as a great "patriot", the Chinese meaning of which word is very vague. His sumptuous posthumous title contains thirteen characters which translate as "the Prince of Military Pacification, the Adjutant to Heaven, Protector of the Realm, the Loyal and the Faithful, the Subduer of Demons, the Great King" and this title has been gradually expanded from time to time. If he manages to get but eleven more characters he will have as many as the late Empress Dowager Tsu Hsi had. Her title contained twenty-four characters.

General Kuan Yu is pictured with the eyes of a phoenix and with eyebrows that look like silkworms. His face is red in colour and he has a long beard.

General Kuan Yu was a native of Shansi Province who, as a fugitive from law and wanted by his native district authorities for manslaughter, met Liu Pei by chance near Chochow (in Hopei) while they were both scanning an official enlistment notice issued by the government. Liu Pei, a straw-sandal maker and mat-weaver, was himself a distant relative of the then reigning house of the Han Dynasty. He and Liu fell into a friendship at first sight and in a wine shop to which they repaired they met a sympathizer in the person of Chang Fei, an ex-butcher and unemployed bartender. They aired their views on current politics over the wine jugs and made hurried decisions. Forthwith they proceeded to Chang's own Peach Blossom Garden where they killed a black ox and a white horse and offering them as sacrifices to Heaven and Earth they agreed to form a tripartite sworn-brotherhood, Kuan and Chang agreeing to support Liu Pei in his attempts to "revive" the decayed Royal Han Dynasty.

There were many a sanguinary battle following the signing of the alliance, as the three "brothers" enlisted their own "guerrilla bands" during the state of chaos which ruled in the land. The three "brothers" were variously successful with their aim to "revive the Han Dynasty" until the treacherous minister Ts'ao Ts'ao usurped the throne and started his own Wei Dynasty. As a counter measure Liu Pei was forced to declare himself emperor of Shu in relativity to Wei and another kingdom of Wu. Many an interesting story is told of General Kuan Yu, showing the high lights of his character, personal integrity, high moral standard and his devotion and respect to his "brother-emperor" as well as of the great valour he showed for any righteous cause in war and in peace.

By a cunning scheme he was once kidnapped and seized by

Ts'ao Ts'ao together with the two wives of Liu Pei (Kuan remained a bachelor all his life but had one foster son) during which time attempts were made to influence him and alienate him from his sworn brother by showering on him all sorts of gifts including a fine horse, gold, silver and beautiful girls. But though he returned the kindnesses received with more than mere lip-service, his mind was always with Liu Pei. When he learned of the latter's whereabouts he made a bold attempt to join his sworn brothers in spite of the tedious thousand-mile journey. All the gifts sent to him by Ts'ao were left behind. He took only the speedy horse "Pink Rabbit" to help him escape more speedily from his kidnappers. He was so careful about his behaviour that while his "brother's" two wives were resting during the nights on their exodus, he himself refused to retire but spent many a lengthy night in reading the Spring and Autumn Annuals by candlelight.

After the re-union, there were continued services rendered to his "brother"-emperor in their ambitious campaign. He met their enemies in bloody battles and acted as the emperor's proxy on many dangerous occasions. Finally in a losing battle fought at Mai Ch'eng he fell victim to the clever military strategy of some of the Wu generals and lost his life in the cause of his sworn brother.

* * *

Needless to say Little Bald Head had another holiday in celebration of General Kuan Yu's birthday.

* * *

The Chinese make every birthday in the family a day of celebration of some sort depending on the status in the family which the person whose birthday is being celebrated occupies, and of course the style or degree of extravagance is a matter entirely restricted by the economic means of the family.

The Chinese revere age, there is no doubt about that, as it is their belief that only the "virtuous" grow to be old, as not only those whom God loves but also those whom God hates die young. The Chinese believe that the length of any person's temporal life is decided even before he or she is born but they also believe that every good deed done will add to his or her years and anything the other way will detract from the predecided "span of life". For this reason it is a very complimentary question (diagonally opposite to Western usage), indeed, to ask a newly made friend how old he is. One may ask another *"Nin kao shou?"* (您高壽),

Steamed breads in the form of peaches and a lot of noodles make conventional birthday gifts.

"Your high age?", and hear the reply *"Hai hsiao, pa shih liu"* (還小八十六), "still young, eighty-six!" (It is therefore easily seen why the Chinese make no secret of their age. The older a person is, the more esteemed and revered he is and his birthdays in the family take on about the same scale of importance.

A small child may feel that it is his own birthday but to his parents and the older members in the house it is merely "the day on which the child grows a tail". When people mature, particularly after having married, their birthdays begin to take on more importance. One of the main ceremonies after a wedding is for the wife's maternal family to send birthday presents to the young couple on their respective birthdays, their first birthdays after marriage. After that, it seems, people's birthdays begin to be noticed.

The celebrations on ordinary occasions are very simple. They naturally provide for some feasting and perhaps entertaining besides the family rites of having a round of kowtowing, beginning with the person in question kneeling down and touching his forehead three times on the ground before the ancestral tablets, and then on to all the family members above him in *pei shu* (輩數) or generation of progeny and also to those of the same generation but more advanced in age even by but a few days or a few hours for that matter. After that he receives the kowtows of all those below him in lineal rank or age in respective order. Thus in a good-sized family of fifteen, twenty or more persons (quite the rule rather than the exception in Peking), it is a long drawn out affair, picturesque yet serious, and noisy too, as there are always bound to be some good wishes expressed as each recipient acknowledges the kowtow and in certain cases there is a lot of polite "bargaining."

Close relatives and intimate well-wishers also bring a conventional gift for the person whose birthday is being celebrated on the day and who is given the temporary title of *Lao Shou Hsing* (老壽星), or Long Life God, for the day.

The commonest gifts are a lot of steamed breads each made in the shape of a peach, sprayed with some red colouring to resemble genuine ones, and a plate of fresh spaghetti or noodles. The peaches are a replica of the Magic Peaches of Immortality about which a beautiful fairy tale is told throughout the length and breadth of China; whereas the noodles, being long and ' unending", indicate long life and in colour are suggestive of the white hair of aged persons. May the person live as long a life as the noodles and live to have hair as white as their colour, too!

Little Bald Head had witnessed many a birthday in his family celebrated more or less in the above manner, with the indispensable feast of "stewed noodles" and a particularly congenial atmosphere in the family and more smiling faces than on any other day except the New Year. His father's birthday and his mother's were celebrated thus, as well as those of other persons in the house. It was on his own birthdays (tail-growing days) that he was horrified. He knew a tail would add no beauty to him and in secret fear he had at least once actually tried to feel if a tail was really going to show itself. It apparently was not and of this he was glad.

*　　　*　　　*

Of all birthdays those in each tenth year take on a greater magnanimity because, it is easily understood, they constitute more important milestones along the long journey from the cradle to the grave, and certainly are more worthy of celebration if the theory of birthday celebrations is at all sanctionable. Birthdays are not the only things counted by ten year periods, as the same scale is also used to judge human accomplishments. Of this latter an interesting example may be quoted in the case of Confucius who declared in his "Analects" that he started to concentrate on his learnings at fifteen and decided on his life's goal at thirty; his ideas on things were firmly set when he was forty; he knew definitely Heaven's will when fifty; began to accept everything heard with a compromising "ear" when sixty and at seventy found that he could do all things exactly as his mind dictated without fear of trespassing the "rules". The master was a great "ten-year period addict," for in another place in the same book he said that if you do not hear of a person after he is forty or fifty years old, such a person, in the estimation of the Master, is, well, a dud! Thus we find that the Chinese people long ago had discovered that "life begins at forty" and all the years previous to that are nothing but life's lengthy prelude.

But, as we were saying, Chinese birthdays are due for big scale celebrations with each ten year period, which in Peking is known by the term of *cheng shou* (整壽), or "whole" birthdays. These "whole" birthdays come in for more conscientious felicitations proportionately whereas the "scattered" ones are generally family affairs unless there be some diplomatic reason for "throwing" them big. And the "whole" birthdays will again begin to be more meaningful after the sixtieth anniversary, as on such a day a person is said to have completed a "cycle" of the combinations of the 12 Heavenly Stems and the 10 Earthly Branches, with combinations of which terms the Chinese mark their years.

At sixty a person's life-work is about all fixed and the period of "make or break" is over and worldly problems bother him or her no more and all the coming years, if properly prepared for, are just so much net gain in the final profit and loss account as it were. The years after this important turning point are fit to be so freely enjoyed that the Chinese have even invented the hypothesis that the God of Hades has a rule to strike out of his book of "Births and Deaths" the names of those persons who have lived through their sixtieth birthday. After that whether to live on or to die is left to the person's own discretion! If a person has managed successfully to retire and live comfortably the evening of his life, such celebrations at each ten-year period must certainly be said to be not without good reason.

*   *   *

Old Mr. Wu had by now left his sixties behind and his seventieth birthday anniversary was close at hand. Plans were soon drawn up to celebrate the occasion in good style. Young Mr. Wu was the principal power behind the entire scheme as on his shoulders fell the initiative which is the admired and coveted privilege of a proud father of an established young man as well as the fond duty of a typical pious son in China.

The main feature of the celebrations was naturally a feast and some sort of entertainment about the same as what the Wus had when Little Bald Head was a month old. The party was announced to friends and well-wishers by a red invitation card. Gifts started to come in from the Wus' numerous friends days ahead of the celebration. Some sent silk pieces with appropriate inscriptions in characters carved from gilded paper, others sent bottles of famous wines, boxes of rare teas, still others bought the old man materials for new garments, sent scrolls of congratulatory messages, etc., etc., as anything beautiful or useful made proper birthday presents.

And the old man was very happy.

*   *   *

On the day of old Mr. Wu's seventieth birthday anniversary the main middle room on the north side of the quadrangle was converted into a reception and ceremonial hall. It was arranged in the orthodox Peking fashion. A big table was placed in the center of the hall behind which was at first hung a big gilded *Shou* (Longevity) character mounted on a piece of red satin as a background. A pair of brightly polished brass candlesticks were set on the table and also a porcelain incense burner on which were painted pictures of appropriate designs. Big red candles molded in a conventional style were kept burning throughout the day and special sandalwood incense sticks were also offered in the burner as the central altar was supposed to represent the shrine of the God of Longevity. The gilded character scroll was later overhung with an expensive, elaborately embroidered portrait of the Lao Shou Hsing, or the Star of Great Age, which was a surprise gift of some of young Mr. Wu's business associates presented to the old man in commemoration of the happy occasion.

*   *   *

The likeness of the Star of Long Life is a very familiar and indeed, favourite motif for many artistic designs and is applied widely to all Chinese implements, ceramics, tapestries, etc. The star is also known as the Fairy Old Man of the South Pole (Star). In him, it is supposed, is vested authority and control over births and therefore the length of life of all mankind. He is pictured as a dear old man with a broad smile, long white beard and a big bald forehead entirely out of proportion to the face which has horizontal markings or wrinkles indicating his hoary age. He is dressed in rich, colourful robes and carries a long dragon-headed stick to which are hung some branches of *ling-chih* (靈芝), or

The God of Long Life is a popular deity in China and his familiar face and still more familiar forehead make an indelible impression on all who see his likeness.

magic long life fungus, and some other long life herbs—any human being eating these becomes immortal. From his belt hangs a gourd containing the famous elixir of life. A stag is also pictured accompanying him (sometimes ridden on) or perhaps also red bats, tokens of "blessings."

It is also said that the stag has the instinct of recognizing the long life fungus from all the mountain flora and which human beings pass by unnoticing. The old man also carries a magic peach in his hand. The magic peaches, or *p'an t'ao* (蟠桃), according to Chinese mythology, grow in the legendary mountains of Kun Lun in the western regions where only superhumans live. The trees blossom once every three thousand years and the fruits ripen in another three thousand years and lowly human beings eating such a peach will attain immortality.

At birthday parties in honour of a woman the portrait of the Star of Long Life is replaced by that of *Ma Ku* (麻姑), or Aunt Ma, a beautiful young deity with the same stag, the same peaches, etc. The goddess was first mentioned in the "*Shen Hsien Chuan*" (神仙傳), or "Biographies of the Gods," a book written in the second century. The book says, *inter alias*, that Ma Ku once appeared in the temple of a Taoist priest as a good-looking girl some eighteen or nineteen years of age but she had claws like those of a bird on her hands (sic). She declared to the gathering there, continued the book, that she had three times witnessed the seas changed into mulberry farms and *vise versa* during her life. We wonder if that was before or after the Dinosaurs roamed the Gobi desert and to what geological periods that would correspond.

*   *   *

In the main reception room at old Mr. Wu's birthday party was a gorgeously decorated altar in front of which was placed a big crimson red carpet where all the guests were to see the old man and offer him in person their best wishes for many happy returns of the day and where the old man's juniors were to kneel down and show their respect by kowtowing three times before the old septuagenarian. But in accordance with Propriety old Mr. Wu was not actually to receive these felicitations ostentatiously. A big chair was placed near the impromptu altar where old Mr. Wu was supposed to sit and receive the kowtows but the old man was seen most of the time standing close by unless the guest happened to be a close relative and a considerably younger person and which made it proper for the old man to sit for the ceremony. All the others, after some polite bargainings, were requested to kowtow to the portrait or image of the Star of Long Life hanging behind the table as though the guests were worshipping the Star to give added years to the old man.

Old Mr. Wu thanked every guest with some auspicious words in token of his acknowledgment of the ritual acts. It was a strenuous day for young Mr. Wu as he was required, again by Propriety, to kneel down and to kowtow to each of the guests at precisely the same moment each kowtow was done by them to the old man as the bounden duty of a filial son to thank the guests for the good wishes expressed to the father. He kowtowed as many times on that day as did all the guests combined. At noon when the guests were coming in crowds he did not have time even to stand up much. As to the family rites they had been performed early

in the morning before the outside guests started to arrive. One of
the Wu family members was also required to appear before each
table to which guests had seated themselves to thank the guests
for the favour of feasting with them by appropriate words of
gratitude and to request them not to stand on ceremony but drink
heartily the old man's health. For gentlemen guests young Mr.
Wu poured wine into each cup, and his wife did the same for the
lady callers.

The feast was ordered from a renowned establishment which
specialized in culinary arts and which had its headquarters in the
West City of Peking.   Young Mr. Wu's business associates, looking forward to the feast, had requested or suggested that it be a
typically Peking feast as distinguished from the Cantonese and
southern varieties. As it was a summer day no excessively greasy
dishes were desirable and the particular kind chosen with an
abundant variety of delicious *hors d'oeuvres* was heartily enjoyed.
Some additional dishes in season, such as crystal ham, bamboo
shoot chicken (young chicken) and some sweet dishes like the almond bean curd, fresh nuts, etc., were added attractions.

The entertainment program started toward the afternoon on
a small stage erected for the occasion and a group of performers
came to give a variety show throughout the day.   There were
musical storytellers who related fairy tales suitable to the occasion, and jesters, fancy diabolo players, fancy jar-balancers and
the tricky shuttle-cock players.   A party of Eight-Corner Drum
singers, very fashionable at the time, was also on the program.
These are thus called because their drum is octagonal in shape
and supposed to be originally a kind of victory war drum of the
Manchu hordes during the heyday of the Manchu conquest; the
eight corners of the drum being symbolic of the eight imperial
banners.   The singing of some little girls was also part of the program as also some acrobatic and trapeze shows by some trained
young boys.   Some little theatrical pieces were also presented
toward the late afternoon for these were very much in demand by
the female guests in the audience.   It may be added here as an
explanation that at that time lady patrons were only beginning to
be allowed in public theatres.   Prior to that the old fashioned
women were only permitted to attend family performances in private residences as invited guests.   Though a handful of actresses
were at times incorporated into the theatrical companies women
were never seen in theatres for such was "bad form".

All this was a new experience for Little Bald Head for this
was the first time that this had taken place in the house.   He was
the proud host to a number of his schoolmates who came to offer
their congratulations.   His teacher, Mr. Yung, came also and was
a sort of a guest of honour as both the old man and his son managed to sit with him at the feast to say nothing of Little Bald
Head himself.   Mr. Yung had not been specially invited but he
came as an unexpected guest after he had learned of the occasion
when the child requested a day's leave.   He gave a little sum of
money as a present as most of the others, who did not bring gifts,
also did.

*   *   *

The "variety show", as an entertainment for the benefit of the
guests gathered at old Mr. Wu's birthday feast, was not paid for
by the Wus but was arranged by a certain Mr. Chao, previously

introduced as Little Bald Head's "father-in-faith", who donated it as his present. Young Mr. Chao had always been desirous to please the old man as in times gone by old Mr. Wu had done something very nice for him though very few people knew exactly what it was. He might have found him a job in which he made good or something but we do not know. The gift was kept a secret from the old man until the morning of the day, for he knew that the old man would not allow him to do it if there was time to stop him. The program was not a long one and was brought to a close shortly after the evening feast when most of the guests left though ordinarily the show would be kept going till midnight. But the stage was not allowed to be left vacant. A group of amateurs, belonging to a dramatic club of which young Mr. Wu was a member and the members of which were mostly his ex-schoolmates and business friends, offered to come in full force to give a short evening performance expressly for the amusement of the old man.

It must be explained here that Chinese theatre fans have a habit of learning amateur theatricals as a very highly esteemed recreation and amusement. These people usually get together and organize themselves into a club, known by the name of *p'iao fang* (票房) by the sound of which it might easily be mistaken for "a ticket office". The amateur actors or actresses are known as *p'iao yo* (票友), or "ticket friends". These amateurs, naturally, accept no remuneration for their performances which go by the name of *wan p'iao* (玩票) or "playing tickets". A group of friends, all "*hsi mi*" (戲迷) or theatre enthusiasts, collectively donate a complete set of the equipment necessary for the teaching and practice of the Chinese dramatic art, comprising mostly musical instruments such as the indispensable *hu ch'in* (胡琴), or Chinese violin, and the *yueh ch'in* (月琴), or Chinese banjo, the castanets and gongs and drums, etc., and some copies of the original plays in book form, privately circulated by making hand-made copies of them which people, the amateurs, treasure so much for being some famous professionals' "genuine lines".

Some unlucky professionals who had gone through the years of intensive training in some theatrical school but who, on account of some unfortunate reason, are not prosperously engaged in the show business, are easily engaged (there are a good number of them, the supply is entirely too great for the demand) to guide the club members in their research work in a general way, or to give them instructions in the niceties of certain particular plays. The teachers receive a very meagre monthly fee toward the payment of which and other maintenance expenses members pay club dues. The club always has its headquarters in a member's house, very often that of the head of the club, who is the biggest contributor of money and time indicative of his particularly zealous interest in the club. As the amateur's only one ambition is often some day to appear on the stage like a regular professional, it is a common thing for him to be so eager in his "career" and allow himself to be so exploited that in consideration of his being drafted for a stage appearance, besides performing for absolutely nothing, he would consent even to pay for the privilege, pay for a violinist's service to accompany him in the singing, pay for the rental of the gaudy expensive theatre robes, pay for all the other supporting characters in the play......all these arranged through the good offices of the "teacher" himself, his manager and advisor. Besides being a "greenhorn" and not commanding much attention on the part of the public, the performing amateur must often guarantee the day's program as a commercial success which is very easily done. On him then falls the lot of one of the general ticket agents, bound to sell one hundred, two hundred or still more tickets to his friends and friends' friends, very often actually giving away the tickets bought with his own good money in order to assure himself a full house. And a full house he gets, too, provided the weatherman favoured the project for nobody will bother to brave a snowstorm to hear such a performance!

Thus it may mean a lot of outlay for the experience but some have found the result worth every cent of the cost, being instrumental in acid-testing his own stage-worthiness, breaking all his stage fright and self-consciousness as a preparation toward that eventual future day when he may decide to "go down to the sea", or *hsia hai* (下海), by which term the process of any amateur turning professional is called. It is surprising how many current double-stars are ex-amateurs who "went down to the sea."

*   *   *

The amateur theatrical rehearsal in honour of old Mr. Wu's seventieth birthday anniversary, lasting from early evening to midnight was a great success though it was only of a so-called *ch'ing ch'ang* (清唱), or "pure singing," variety. There was no acting either as the members of the club merely sat around a big round table and sang their parts with "between acts" sips of tea and puffs of cigarettes. The singing itself, including the dialogue parts, was superbly rendered and all the Wus and their guests listened attentively for some of the amateurs were quite well-polished artists. This kind of a rehearsal is more thoroughly enjoyed and appreciated than the actual acting as the high points in Chinese plays are really the singing pieces in their tone quality and expressional rhythm and emotional shadings of voices, rather than in the bizarre showy effects and rich, colourful stage settings which are not half as important in the judgment of good Chinese play-goers. Of course, *ch'ing ch'ang*, or "pure singing", has its main drawback in that the acrobatics or mimicry fighting are naturally impossible and with them are forfeited the so-called *wu hsi* (武戲) or "military" plays. There were many well-rendered pieces and Little Bald Head watched curiously and absorbedly. He felt it strange indeed to see his father singing a female impersonator's part which was his specialty. He was still more tickled when his aged grandfather, amusedly forced, took a part in the performance of a famous play called "Pearl-Screened Fort."

*   *   *

It was a cool evening as the day happened to fall on the festival of *Li Ch'iu* (立秋), or "Commencement of Autumn," when the year's hottest days are due to come to an end and the first taste of the ideal autumn weather (a famous Peking asset) is ushered in. The evening was particularly pleasant and breezy for in that year the festival hour had come in the early morning. A Chinese saying goes "*Tsao li ch'iu, leng sou sou, wan li ch'iu, jeh ssu niu,*" (早立秋冷颼颼晚立秋熱死牛) "If the *Li Ch'iu* festival falls on an early morning hour the forthcoming autumn will be a cool one whereas if it comes in at a late hour in the day there are bound to be additional hot days to expect, so hot as to kill a cow." On this subject the Chinese almanac is in a position, by clever astronomical

"Pushing the Card Nine", played with 32 small ebony blocks
and two dice, is a favourite
gambling game at birthday and
other parties.

and meteorological forecasts, to fix
the festival hour exactly to the
minute. It is also said, subject to
verification, that at the exact minute
of *Li Ch'iu*, one single leaf, no more,
is due to fall off from each *wu t'ung*
(梧桐) (of Tung oil fame) tree!

Such being the case the weather
was certainly ideal for the celebration and as it was suitable for the
theatrical performance, it was more
so for some other guests who chose
gambling as their entertainment.
There were two groups of guests
engaged in this pastime. One group
of gentlemen were gathered in the
southern rooms around a table where
a game of *t'ui p'ai chiu* (推牌九), or
"pushing the card-nine", was going
on briskly, a fast game played with
32 pieces of ebony blocks, each bearing from two to twelve points and
a couple of dice. It was a lively
game and was specially adapted to
accommodate an indefinite and irregular number of participants.
In the inner rooms to the north a group of ladies were engaged in "eight rounds" of mahjong—the Chinese national
game which needs no introduction. The former group was an off-and-
on affair which lasted well into the small hours of the morning and
the latter was apparently an all-night arrangement as intimate
friends are expected to stay long at such parties. The participants
at the mahjong table were familiar persons and family friends of
the Wus. Madame Ho, Little Bald Head's maternal grandmother,
and Mrs. Wang from next door, whose son was the Wu child's
schoolmate, were the two winners at the last count and young
Mrs. Chao, the child's mother-in-faith, was a heavy loser.

*   *   *

Gambling as a feature at a Chinese social gathering applying
equally to so-called "red" parties (marriages, birthdays, "full-
months", etc.) and "white" affairs ("mourning parties") is another old deep-rooted Chinese institution which originated most
probably from having to provide something to do for people required by necessity to "sit through" the nights. Thus no Peking party
in a small family nowadays is complete without some gambling
going on for two or three days before and after each "party" and
the practice has such a great influence that even the police rules
give it the right of way and refrain from raiding such gatherings.
It is also a commonplace thing for a poor family to finance a wedding or even a funeral from the contributions donated by the participating guests in the "party gambling" from each person's winnings, this is called *to-erh* (頭兒), or "head money."

The Wus, of course, were not interested in this "head money"
though their only maidservant and Liu Ma, Madame Ho's "lady-
in-waiting," each received a present of money from the gambler-
guests.

THE SEVENTH DAY OF THE SEVENTH MONTH

OF THE various insects which receive the attention of Peking families, none receive a bigger measure than those of the orthopterous or straight-winged families and of these there are many.

The *kuo-kuo-erh*, or katydid, is a constant singer and is sold in a corn stalk cage which allows it little elbow room.

There are the locusts which roam the North China plains and are such a destructive force for all farm plants that they are likened in China to an epidemic for clouds of them render green fields stem-bare as quick as a wink as if by the deliberate will of the gods antagonistically directed against the peasants although they (the locusts) are really doing their legitimate part in the struggle for existence. This common locust is known as *ma cha* (螞蚱). It is considered a delicacy by the peasant population. Thousands of them are caught, roasted or fried and rolled up in big flat flexible Chinese cakes, eaten and enjoyed with smacking lips. The locusts eat the people's crops and people eat them in turn. This practice is nowhere more enthusiastically carried out than in Tientsin and its vicinity where the locusts, like popcorn and peanuts, are peddled in the main streets. Perhaps some psychologist of the "symbolism" school will be able to tell us what kind of an emotional compensation this stands for.

Then there are also the various kinds of insects which come under the never-clearly-defined names of grasshoppers and katydids and for which it is hard to give specific or easily-recognized titles. A beautiful variety with a pinkish belly and a pointed head with short flat antennae is known as *ma cha pien-erh* (螞蚱扁兒), or "locust flattened". These are usually caught for children to play with in Peking, a favour also proffered to the "locust proper", with a passive sanction from parents as they are well-known as being collectively harmful to mankind. The common katydids go by the poetic nomenclature of *fang chih niang* (紡織娘), or "spinning and weaving girl", on account of the buzzing sound they make which resembles or suggests a Chinese spinning wheel, though because of its queer shape, it is also called *lui chui tze* (驢駒子), or "baby donkey".

The prize member in the class of katydids is the sort known as a *kuo-kuo-erh* (蟈蟈兒) in Peking. This is a magnificent two-inch specimen with an oily black body, strong legs, bright green stubby wings and long feelers. It is found in the fields and in the mountainsides (the mountainside variety is bigger in size and easily reaches over three inches from tip to tip). The catching and distribution of *kuo-kuo-erh* is an industry by itself and there must be quite a number of people engaged in the trade. Women and children are employed to make individual cages measuring no more than four inches each way with corn stalks in which each *kuo-kuo-erh* is imprisoned for life. It may be imagined that the entire family is mobilized to search the wilds for them, mother and sister and daughter make the cages and father carries them in tiers in big baskets and makes for the city where the last stage of distribution is carried out.

The *kuo kuo-erh* are great singers and seem to be interested in nothing else; the singing, a continuous volley for hours with a nerve-racking audio-frequency, of course, is made by rasping certain thin portions of one of the wings against the file-like area on the other. They eat any plant food; pieces of cabbage leaf or the "tails" of cucumbers—kitchen wastes—serve them nicely, although, as Little Bald Head was told, their most preferred diet is one composed of the flower petals of the pumpkins. It is hard, not being *kuo-kuo-erh* ourselves, to understand how in the world they can be so loud in their songs of praise or contentment (?) while imprisoned in a cage that gives them not even antenna room, nor why, since they have such strong mandibles, they do not start a jail-break.

The Wus, like many another Peking family, understood environment hygiene for the *kuo-kuo-erh* most thoroughly and had theirs hung, cages and all, in the shade of their morning glories and among other thickly foliaged plants, for in this way they also will "get plenty of dew-drops to drink" which they need for subsistence.

The *kuo-kuo-erh* being such indefatigable songsters they are good for one thing. For people like old Mrs. Wu believed that so long as a singing *kuo-kuo-erh* is kept in the house, there is no fear of the children and babies in the house getting fits of "frights" at night. This, as an advertising slogan, doubtlessly was instrumental in boosting the trade to its present popularity. It would be more reasonable to say that with a constant chirping in their ears babies never really fall sound asleep which is a negative precaution against "sleeping sickness."

*   *   *

The seventh day of the seventh moon of the lunar calendar is a day of great mythological significance and is looked forward to with great reverence (or amusement, as the case may be) by the Peking-*jen*.

First of all this is the day celebrated in honour of *Tou Mu* (斗母), or Mother Bushel, referring to the two star constellations of the Southern and Northern Bushels, which correspond to the Ursa Minor and Ursa Major (or the Little Dipper and the Big Dipper) respectively. The Chinese have a myth concerning these two constellations of seven stars each represented by two *hsing chuns* (星君), or star gods, who are supposed to be two brothers between whom the job of fixing each human being's life span is entrusted. The south pole star, a seven-in-one deity of the Little Dipper, is in charge of births and is represented by an old man, the God of Long Life, and his younger brother, the north pole star, is in charge of deaths. These two work in constant consultation with each other. There is no question raised as to who their father was though all devout Chinese Buddhists know they were the sons of a female deity known by the name of Mother Bushel. Mother Bushel's birthday is the seventh day of the seventh moon.

Little Bald Head, on several occasions, had been to the *Tou Mu Kung* (斗母宮), or Mother Bushel's Palace, on a narrow lane not far from their home on Donkey Mart. And so when old Mrs.

Wu told him it was Mother Bushel's birthday and there was to be burning of incense sticks no further explanation was necessary.

Mother Bushel is represented as a kindly-looking woman wearing a five-sectioned Buddhist crown and sitting on a lotus flower stand mounted on a two-wheeled chariot. She has eight arms (a sign of omnipotence derived no doubt from Tibetan influence in image making), with the two "original" ones in a typical Buddhist pose and the other six extending out each carrying a so-called "precious article". Two disks carried in the uppermost hands represent the Sun and the Moon; other hands carry the bottle of holy water, the lotus flower (symbolic of purity), a flaming "wheel of doctrine" and a sacred banner with which she is supposed to guide the spirits of the dead. Little is known about the rites in worshipping this famous goddess except that people who expect to enjoy her blissful protection are required to abstain from eating all meat.

Little Bald Head was referred to the picture scroll hanging in their parlour depicting two old men playing a game of chess under some pine trees with a little boy kneeling close by with a tray holding some foods and a flask of wine. The story of the picture old Mrs. Wu explained to him thus.

"There was once a young man whose name was Chao Yen (趙彥) and who was nineteen years old. He was one day plowing in his father's field when a Taoist priest saw him. This Taoist priest was no other person than the famous astrologer Kuan Lo (管輅) (about 200 A.D.) who had learned to know about the doings of superhuman beings. The priest asked him a few questions and told him that he was due to die in three days. At this the boy was greatly astonished. He ran directly home and described what had happened to his father. His father, equally dumbfounded by the alarming prophecy, ran and caught up with the priest, wept bitter tears and entreated the priest to design a way to help matters as the boy was, like you Little Bald Head, the father's only child!

"The Taoist priest was moved by their sad case and tearful sincerity and told them to prepare a flask of the best wine and some venison and told the boy to take these to the South Mountains early the next morning where he would find two old men playing a game of chess under some pine trees, one red-robed, very benevolent in countenance, and the other white-robed with a cruel face. The boy was told to watch for an opportune moment when the two old men seemed to be entirely absorbed in their game to offer the wine and venison to them, and after they had partaken of the things to cry to them bitterly and persistently and beg them to have pity on him, explaining to them his request, and the gods (for that was what they were) would not disappoint the pleader and would have his life span extended.

"The boy did as he was told and found the place, the very men at the very game and did exactly as he had been told.

"The two men were surprised and guessed instantly that it must be Kuan Lo who had revealed "celestial secrets", but having enjoyed the boy's hospitality they could not very well refuse his request.

"So out from somewhere they produced a big book and found the boy's entry where it said he was due to die when nineteen years old. The red-robed, good-looking old man produced a pen and had the word "nineteen" crossed out and the word "ninety" substituted. The boy thanked them and went home. He lived to be ninety years old.

"Mother Bushel, you will remember, is the mother of the two brothers, who are the God of Births and God of Deaths respectively," the old woman concluded her tale.

*   *   *

On the seventh day of the seventh moon the Chinese also commemorate the day of the happy meeting of Niu Lang (牛郎), the cowherd, and Chih Nui (織女), the weaver-maid, and refer again to the clear autumnal sky and the twinkling stars symbolic of continued fine weather.

The Wus had prepared the bowl of water by which each of the family members, the women primarily, were to tell the future. This is known as *ch'i ch'iao* (乞巧), or "begging for cleverness", in Chinese. A full bowl of water was left out in the open court-yard throughout the previous night in order "to catch the dew-drops" and by noon on the seventh, each person was to place gently and lightly a very fine embroidering needle on the surface of the water in the bowl and could than tell about his prospects for the future, basing his judgment on the shapely, or otherwise, shadow of the needle cast on the bottom of the bowl.

By the law of surface viscosity and the law of surface tension for liquids the water will actually keep the needles afloat before the surface film is broken, and by the dispersion of light through the microscopically affected surface the shadows take on irregular shapes. Of course, the telling of how each shadow is shaped like a utensil, a pair of scissors, a hammer, a thread, or an iron, etc., must be left to childish imaginations.

*   *   *

It was a fine evening on the seventh, and the Wus, gathering in their courtyard scented by the evening primroses and plantain lilies which were giving out puffs of delicate fragrance, scanned the sky for their own share of astronomy. There was many an inter-esting thing explained to Little Bald Head by members of his fami-ly which represented the notions of the average Chinese about stars.

There is first the misty cloud of stars, the Milky Way, which the Chinese call the *T'ien Ho* (天河) or *Yin Ho* (銀河), "heavenly river" or "silver river" respectively, in which water is always full to the brim but never spilled as a few drops spilled from the Hea-venly River would mean monstrous floods on our world. Then there is the Great White Star of Gold (Venus) which, if it appears, would be symbolic of heaven's warning of forthcoming wars and bloodsheds in the world, as also the Water Star (Mercury) which heralds coming floods. There are twenty-eight *su* (宿) or important planets according to the Chinese and they take on the names of various animals from dragon through to earthworm, and which give an interesting coincidence of the foreign practice of naming stars, the scorpion, the sea goat, the swan, etc. All these planets are brave generals serving in the Celestial Empire and are on duty by shifts as are the officers-of-the-day in the armies.

The nebula, a cluster of small stars arranged in a veritable circle as it appears to the naked eye, is known to the Chinese as the *Pa Chiao Liu Li Ching* (八角琉璃井), or "Eight Cornered Glazed

(Brick) Well," which is the main water source for the heavens. "There were originally eight stars but only seven are now visible, as the Western Queen Mother, while drawing water from the well, inadvertently stepped on the eighth one and rendered it dormant."

But all the Chinese can tell the Northern and Southern Bushels and by observing in which direction the Bushel's handle points (corresponding to the foreign Bear's tail in the Major Ursa and Minor Ursa) the Chinese can check with themselves what month of the year it is, for the handle makes a complete revolution each year and comes to point to the northeast (the segmental position of the hour of the Tiger) when the New Year starts. The Northern Bushel is also the Star of Governmental Good Omen by the brightness or dimness of which the world's administrative and political equilibrium is foretold, as they always shine the brightest when the world is at peace, say the Chinese, by which the emperors of the Middle Kingdom used to read Heaven's approval or otherwise of their administrations. Comets are known as "broom stars" in China and are also considered signs of warning from Heaven foretelling some calamity in the Flowery Realm and when one appears the Emperor would be made very uneasy. The central observatory (an old established institution in China) would locate the respective position of the "broom star" on their instrument, the celestial globe, and burn the spot with a grease lamp (the grease being obtained from dog's "lard") until the comet disappeared from the sky. This is what tradition says.

It was then that the Wus pointed out to each other the stars of the cowherd and the weaver-maid and old Mr. Wu, in his habitual poetic mood, murmured to himself lines from an old poem:
"The autumn light shines like silver candles
    on a pictured screen;
And waving my silken fan, I try to catch the fireflies.
The nights in the capital are cool,
    cool like water
And lying on my couch,
I watch the stars of the cowherd and the weaver-maid."

*   *   *

According to Chinese folklore and mythology the stars of the cowherd and the weaver-maid have a beautiful story. The story, with slight variations in different localities, is a household word and is as follows:

Once upon a time there was a simple-hearted young man who was without parents and who was ill-treated by his brother and his brother's wife. He was given the humble task of looking after the cow kept in the home. The cow in course of time became his only friend in the world but it was well for the cow was a magic cow. One day the cow spoke in human language to him.

"Young man," said the cow, "go to the side of the brook tomorrow morning and you will find seven beautiful girls bathing there. They are the daughters of the Sun God and of them all the youngest one is the prettiest. While they are bathing in the brook, go and seize the clothes of the seventh daughter, which is a red dress and white skirt of sheerest silk, lying on the bank. And when they get through bathing the seventh will miss her clothes and come to ask you to return them to her. You will ask her to promise to be your wife and you are not to give back her clothes until she has consented, for thus you will gain immortality. The seventh girl is the weaver-maid in the upper realms and is in charge of weaving the beautiful materials from which the heavenly beings make their robes.''

The young cowherd did as he was told and was greatly impressed by the matchless beauty of the youngest daughter and he hid her clothes and when she requested their return he advanced the proposal as he had been told to do by his cow. The girl accepted. So while her six sisters went back to Heaven riding on the backs of snow-white storks, she was left with the cowherd, her lover and her lord.

They lived happily together for three years during which time two children were born to them. At last, the gods, their stock of brocades and silks exhausted and the weaver-maid's services not being available, became angry and having located her, forced her to leave at once and to return to her old job at the looms and shuttles. She had a heart-breaking parting with the cowherd.

The cowherd was very sad and the magic cow again offered its services. It requested the cowherd to kill it and use the skin as a magic carpet with which he would be able to ascend to the heavens where he would be able to be near his wife and sweetheart.

The cowherd did so.

But as he was about to join the weaver-maid the Celestial Mother, exasperated and jealous of her daughter, drew a line on the ground with her hairpin and created thereby a river which stopped him from coming close to his beloved. Thus the two were separated by the heavenly river but in sight of each other.

The case was reported to the Jade Emperor of Heaven who had mercy on the poor lovers but fearing their co-habitation might be conducive to poor work or neglected duty on the part of the weaving-maid, decided to allow them a happy reunion only once every year, in the evening of the seventh day of the seventh moon! On this evening the cowherd will be allowed to cross the heavenly river on a bridge, built by the combined efforts of the world's magpies who volunter their services by joining together their wings to form a temporary bridge.

The Chinese *Niu Lang Hsing* (牛郎星), or Star of the Cowherd, is the Aquila and the *Chih Nui Hsing* (織女星), or the Star of the Weaver-Maid, is the Vega, both being ''stars of great magnitude in the firmament'' close to the Milky Way. The Aquila has two minor stars or satellites nearby which the Chinese call the two children of the ill-fated couple.

The legend is very popular with the women and has been dramatized and presented on the Chinese stage as the play *''T'ien Ho P'ei,''* (天河配) or ''The Matrimony at the Heavenly River,'' which almost all theatres play as a seasonal feature on the seventh day of the seventh moon.

Chinese children, more often little four or five-year-old girls, are also told to gather in the shade of the garden shrubs or under the grape vines in the evenings on the proper day to listen intently trying to detect and pick up the feeble signals of the weepings and the tête-à-tête of the pair during their annual meeting.

Even Little Bald Head could tell the story in his own vivid fashion after the style of his grandmother from whom he had learnt it.

There are certain species of insects which enjoy much greater attention and esteem from the leisured classes in Peking, and a great part of China for that matter, the raisers of which devote so much time and money to them that their mere mentioning will silence the city's proudest singing katydids. All these, jointly or separately, come under the category of crickets. The keeping of crickets is a great fad in which not only children but also adults are interested. It found a ready patronizer in our hero Little Bald Head as representative of all Peking youngsters.

One particular species of the crickets, of very minute size and hardly larger than certain kinds of house flies, are known by the name *Chin Chung Erh* (金鐘兒), or Golden Bells, and are a famed special product of the Northern Mountains near the Ming Tombs some thirty miles north of Peking. They appear in the Peking market at the very beginning of the autumn season and their admirers buy and keep them in big porcelain vases, nourished on moistened tea leaves for the sole purpose of listening to their delicate metallic chirps. The vases have been known to magnify and improve the singing tome.

Another kind of cricket is of a much bigger size and measures an inch or more in length, is plumply built and goes by the name of *Yu Hu Lu* (油葫蘆), or Oil Gourd. These are not only good for their songs, which sentimentally-minded people such as the many Chinese poets like so much in the autumn evenings, but also serve the double purpose of feeding certain pet birds which have been known to require them for their body-building qualities. Their chirping is very long-winded and suggestive of the quivering and shaking of a poorly clad person in a cold stormy night.

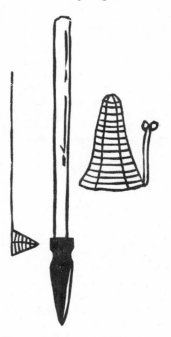

There is also another variety characterized by its ungainly, curiously shaped head which has the contours of that of an owl and is known by its peculiar rattling songs as *Pang-erh-t'ou* (梆兒頭), or Rattler-Head (the head, of course, does not rattle, it is the wings that do). For those persons who keep these as pets they either get handfuls of them and put them in a small-mouthed vat or else release them in the courtyard to give them pseudo-natural surroundings and enjoy their singing without hampering their liberty which is a very sensible way provided no cats are kept in the house or in the neighbouring houses. Country people are often seen plodding along the streets carrying big baskets with baggy cloth tops and sell them as a seasonal rural avocation.

But it is the particular kind called *Hsi Shuai* (蟋蟀), or more colloquially, *Ch'ui-ch'ui-erh* (蛐蛐兒), that come to be so greatly valued by the Chinese people, and strange as it may seem, all on account of its

The cricket hunter's equipment includes wire nets and an iron "digger" fighting qualities which the Peking-*jen* has exploited to the satisfaction of all parties concerned.

The crickets are collected by professionals who launch regular expeditions to the Western and Northern Hills in parties of three or four, very often to points so far off the beaten paths that it is necessary to provision themselves for the journey to make it possible to remain afield for ten or more days. A specially made spear with a wooden handle will dig loose the earth around the nest or hole of a fine promising specimen after it has been tracked to its dwelling by making a direction finder of its singing from a distance. Pouring water into the hole is another effectvie technique. The hunters will recognize from afar and almost infallibly judge without seeing it, what type of an insect is liable to be "bagged".

They have some special tools, including wire nets of different sizes, conical in shape, with long or short handles each well adapted for a special use, for as much as possible the hands should not touch the insects for fear of doing bodily harm to them. Good specimens are kept in separate jars, each one by itself to prevent unwarranted skirmishes with the others whereas the common and mediocre ones—the *hoi polloi* are kept in a concentration basket subject to classification and appraisal at the expedition. The crickets are judged by weight, by size and by colour, as well as by the proportions of the body, all of which have to do with the original breed and surroundings of its habitat. Some particularly good specimens are responsible for a small fortune to their captors both from the point of arena winnings and the market value they would command in the cricket exchange.

*   *   *

Little Bald Head and his pal Wang and many another pupil at Mr. Yung's school were cricket-keepers. Nobody dared to bring their crickets to school but gossips on their respective specimens were freely exchanged during off-class time—that is, when the teacher was not around.

The crickets kept by Little Bald Head were mostly bought from a dealer who had his "place" on the street leading to the Temple Fair not 'far from his home, for during the cricket season there are annual cricket markets in at least half a dozen places in the city of Peking. Each of the dealers has a number of individual jars of glazed clay each housing a cricket and a big basket from which the buyers may choose at "wholesale" prices, as the great unwashed may contain certain potentially formidable fighters that have escaped the attention of the dealers and who may be spotted by an experienced buyer.

The crickets selected are placed in individual paper tubes, stopped at the ends by folding in a special manner, for convenient carrying home. The Wang boy next door was Little Bald Head's experienced advisor and though he could not really tell with certainty whether one would fight or not nor the intrinsic value or characteristics of each of the high priced ones, nevertheless he could tell whether one had *lao-mi-tsueh* (老米嘴), or "old rice mouth" (characterized by brownish mandibles) which would never fight, or at least to enlighten the uninitiated Wu child that the ones with three "tails" instead of two, with the "big javelin" by which they referred to the egg placers, in between the two others, would neither fight nor sing for they were females.

The child also bought with the help of young Wang a number of clay jars with fitted massive covers and some little dishes for water and food and a little bricken *kuo-lung-erh* (過籠兒), or "passing corridor", which were to be put in each cricket home to eat and drink from and to "sleep" in respectively.

Little Bald Head had the jars thoroughly washed with the help of his pal, had the "bottoms" pounded in using a mixture of yellow earth, black earth and old lime, and forthwith had the crickets safely deposited into the jars. Fresh water and green beans were put in the little troughs. The boy was also advised to have the jars rinsed with clear water every day and to put fresh beans in the dishes. A wire net was also purchased in order to catch the unruly, jumpy specimens which still showed occasional preference for the freedom outside to the secluded life in the jars.

"Keep them in the jars for two or three days and they will start to fight afterwards", the Wang child said.

*   *   *

The cricket fights take place in a bigger, flatter jar and two crickets are put in the jar each time. In order to start a fight more speedily a small "tickler" is used. This is made by tying two or three strong rat-whiskers to the end of a little bamboo stick and with this the fighters are taunted toward one another until they meet face to face—some crickets are very reluctant in deciding to take up a belligerent attitude though scientists have attributed this phenomenon to the crickets' poor eyesight. If fighting still does not start the instrument is applied to the hinder part of the crickets until they are irritated. The crickets react to this technique almost invariably except when there happens to be a true-to-the-bone pacifist, such as the Old Rice Mouth mentioned before.

The cricket's jar is a veritable home with all the comforts desirable. The food dish, water basin and the "passing corridor" are indispensable.

The fighting starts without a preliminary "calling of names" and is always an exciting affair in its own way for the combatants will chase, circle, corner and hop, clamp their jaws and bite with an intensive fighting urge entirely out of proportion to their size. The fight may be kept on for as long as two full minutes until one of them definitely cannot keep it up a second longer and ducks away in utter defeat, while the winner proudly strikes an attitude of victory, congratulates himself and announces his win with a triumphant chirrup "Drrrrrrrrrrrrrrrr". It is often a desperate battle and a cruel one, too, as the loser, if not at once removed from the arena, will be set upon again and again until he is virtually half-dead or one or both of the big hind legs have been twitched off in the course of hostilities.

*   *   *

Some of Little Bald Head's crickets turned out to be acceptable fighters though most of them could do no more than sing.

*   *   *

Cricket fights in China take on about the same prestige and interest as bullfights or cockfights in certain foreign countries, and the possessors of fine specimens and their opponent friends bet heavily on such fights. For this type of cricket-keepers, there is very much ado about the caring for the insects and even the utensils used, the rules of the fight and so on which would fill a book—there are really books on the subject, of modern as well as ancient authorship. Compared to the descriptions contained in these books, Little Bald Head's own technique was, as it actually was, childish play. Cricket fighting in the old dignified manner is still being enthusiastically carried on in Peking and some special organizations are sponsored by famed members of the local Chinese intelligentsia of the old school.

Invitations are always sent out by the chief organizer of cricket fights to people known to be interested. A spacious guest parlour is usually the locale of such a picturesque affair. The proud possessors bring their crickets, often in wooden cases carried by a coolie from a pole in the typical Chinese fashion, as many entries may be registered by each participating fan. Rich cricket keepers bring their "advisor"—a professional— with them. The crickets are given identifying titles by their proud masters such as "The Big General with a Silver Head", "The Golden-winged Constant Winner," etc. The fighting is preceded by weighing each fighter on a set of fine "druggist's scales", as only those of similar weight can be slated for each battle in fairness to all concerned. The stake for each fight may be a couple of dollars or as much as may be agreed upon on the spot.

The prize fighters offered in the Peking market come from various distant regions even from as far as certain districts in Shantung province. The prices vary considerably with the fluctuation of the supply and demand, current prices are around thirty or forty dollars for a good "thoroughbred."

The best cricket jars are the old ones, made some two hundred years or so ago and bearing the hallmark of an exclusive maker by the name of Chao Tze Yu (趙子玉), such jars are still obtainable from curio shops in Peking though most of them are clever, and acceptable, counterfeits. The originals are made of "silted earth" and seem to bear certain "watermarks. The fine specimens for the champions to ride in to the meetings bear ornate designs of exquisite carving.

The crickets are put on special diets, too, although their average life span is only about four or five months at the most. No cricket can survive the *Ta Hsueh* (大雪) or Big Snow festival in January. The peace time rations for the crickets contain such items as steamed rice, fresh green beans, chestnut meats, etc., but during the fighting season, sheep's liver, crab meat, etc., should be given them in small portions. A type of water spider is given to crickets to eat as a tonic and ant eggs are their most effective stimulants. The experts also take good care of the domestic life of the crickets by allowing them to associate with the females at proper intervals and this requires much care and attentive insight into cricket physiology on the part of the keepers.

The climax of the cricket fight season is toward the end of autumn when the constantly changing weather is a problem for the experts who have to move the jars containing the crickets from the shade to the sunlight and so on, or heat them by a hot water pot placed in their midst and moving them indoors. When going to a fight the jars should be protected from the cold by putting a cotton-padded wrapper around each jar.

*   *   *

Cricket-keeping is an old hobby in China. It enjoyed patronage in the old imperial days. An interesting Ming Dynasty cricket story is found in the *"Liao Chai Chih Yi"*, "Strange Stories from a Chinese Studio." The sport is still popular.

ANCESTOR WORSHIP

FROM the first to the fifteenth of the seventh lunar month is a period devoted by the Peking-*jen* to the special religious observance of ancestor worship. Primarily it is a family rite but it has been extended to a much wider scope to become a universal day of remembrance by which the fifteenth day, the principal day, has been known to foreign residents as China's "All Souls Day". It is a period of prayers, or Buddhist masses, and "burning of paper" as a gift or offering to the dead in the next world, very solemn in nature and touching in effect yet picturesque and charming and even colourful in its general observance.

The Chinese bury their dead "with appropriate ceremonies" as has been taught since the time of Confucius and all families who have the means possess their own family graveyards. Only the poor resort to burying their dead in the community graveyards which incidentally also serve as temporary interment grounds for the bodies of residents whose old homesteads are in some other districts or provinces. Residents from certain provinces or important cities have their own community graveyards, known euphemistically as *Yi Yuan* (義園), or "Garden of Chivalry," usually administered by the respective district guilds or *Hwei Kwan* (會館) (meeting houses) where members pay annual dues to keep their burial grounds in good condition.

Apart from these the other public burial grounds are far from being tidily kept and very few mounds are marked with anything in the way of a decent epitaph. A slab of stone bearing the name of the dead person or even a narrow wooden board is all the means of identification there is and most of the mounds are even without that. New coffins are superimposed on old ones before the decomposition process is complete with no consideration whatever for anything except for the little money accompanying each burial which is paid to the owner of the land who looks upon it as sort of an income. Here burials are mostly done in a slipshod fashion as they more often are intended as a *modus vivendi* pending transportation of the remains to the home town, hundreds or perhaps thousands of miles away for permanent and formal interment. Certain reasons though, may tend to convert the *status quo* into a *fait accompli* until "to dust they shall return".

The Wus had their own family graveyard out in the eastern suburbs of Peking at a small village called the Stone Gate, as an old landmark there was a marble arch which was also what had been left of a former pompous and stylish graveyard. Like all typical Peking graveyards theirs was a spacious piece of land many acres in size, though only a small part of the land was actually used as the burial ground, surrounded and thickly shaded with rows of tall poplar trees and old cypresses and cedars planted several generations back and dating from the very days when the Wus' ancestors had acquired the land for that purpose.

There were several groups of gravemounds as the original "first settlers" of the Wus were three brothers whose sons established their own respective graveyard localities, burying each of the three brothers as the "first ancestor" of the group. From the mounds of these extended the *hsueh* (穴), or "holes", for the sons and grandsons in a theoretically unending "V" formation until the tract of land is exhausted as staked out at the recommendation of professional geomancers whose services and advice determined the details of such things as has been done for centuries in China.

In this country the superstitious believe that the proper burial and directional details and topographical elements of a burial tract are of primary importance not only for the prosperity or otherwise of posterity but also as a sort of measure or counter-measure in the secret "warfare" between the branches of the immense Chinese family in competing for the lion's share of the family's good fortune at the expense of another or all the other family branches. The Wu family graveyard was a living (yet dead) record of but five or six generations beyond which the family history was not easily traced for that was in the dim, dim past.

The rest of the land, acres of it, was used as *Yang Shen Ti* (養身地), or "sustenance fields", for the caretakers and their families who, as local small farmers, were entrusted with the job of looking after the graveyards in a general manner, seeing to it that the mounds were kept in good and big conical shape, that the weeds did not grow wild in the burial tracts and that no neighbourhood ruffians stole or destroyed the magnificent trees or, indeed, violated the graves themselves in their quest for "buried treasures."

In consideration of the *bona fide* performance of this service the caretaker planted the remaining fields for their own benefit absolutely free of all land rentals as a sort of a permanent lease and as a typical remuneration. Of course, the Wus had the right any time to convert any of these fields into burial tracts whenever the need arose.

A brick house had also been built on the grounds, expressly intended for the Wus' use when there was, say, a burial in the family. This stood close by the farmer's own hut—a lowly, yellow adobe building of the kind familiarly seen in a typical North China farmscape.

*   *   *

There are three main "decoration days" observed in China, they are at the *Ch'ing Ming* (clear and bright) festival about thirty days after Chinese new year, on the fifteenth of the seventh moon and on the first of the Chinese October. Of the three the most important, it seems, would be the fifteenth of the seventh moon, perhaps originally intended to see if the summer floods had not affected the gravemounds.

Visiting family graveyards is technically *sao mu*, or "sweeping the tombs," but the actual clean-up is often attended to by the caretaking family in anticipation of the family's visit as a measure to please them as well as the basis for expecting a little monetary gift. The rites performed at the graveside consist principally of burning a lot of good, white paper, which is purchased from shops by the ream (that is unless the family cannot afford but a few sheets) and has the markings of a Chinese cash chopped with special crescent-shaped and square chisels in rows. This process converts the paper into legal tender in the next world when burned.

Strings of paper ingots, made of silver and gilt tinsel-paper, are also burned at the graveside for to the dwellers of the other world they become the respective articles in hard species. Of late the currency problem in the next world, apparently, has gone

Sheets of paper bearing the imprint of a Chinese cash and strings of tinselled paper ingots constitute proper offerings to be burned before the mounds in the family graveyard.

through some reformation and modern banking practice has been introduced to supplement the metal coins, for the shops which sell the paper "cash sheets" and the imitation papery ingots have designed and put on the market lithographed banknotes of various denominations bearing the name of an imaginary banking concern. It must have enjoyed wide circulation in the spiritual world, judging from the inflation policy perceivable at the paper shops.

Little Bald Head was now for the first time in his life brought to the family graveyard for it was felt that the youngster should be impressed with the past grandeurs of the Wus at an early date as an encouragement to him—to make him feel that it was something by itself to be a member of the Wu family. The suggestion was made by the aged grandfather and young Mr. Wu agreed it was a good idea. The trio made the trip together, representing three generations of the Wus.

Donkeys were rented for the round trip at the city gate for that was the only means of transportation suitable for the journey as no wheeled traffic could negotiate the narrow farmland paths. A good quantity of paper was purchased at a paper store near the city gate and they waited as the clerks chopped on the markings, sinking the "dies" with a heavy wooden hammer.

The ceremonials consisted of burning the paper offerings at each of the gravemounds and of the trio kowtowing before each grave. The graves contained two persons each and some contained three or more as each husband is buried close to his wife and some of the dead had had second wives and third wives or had had "legalized" concubines, this necessitated repeated kowtowings on the part of the three Wus. None of the graves in the formations contained single bodies because those who had died before attaining majority or before marriage were not "admitted" there but interred in a separate lot where they were buried with the children who died at a small age (young Mr. Wu's two baby daughters were buried here). It was not a comfortable day what with the frequent kneelings and kowtowings but Little Bald Head, having been taught to revere ancestors according to Propriety, had no complaint to make. The paper offerings were carried in baskets by the caretakers as an unquestioned duty since they bore the relationship of servants toward the Wus. A free-handed distribution was made as no counting was feasible.

There was a rural lunch consisting of things produced on the farm, fresh eggs, corn cakes and millet porridge prepared in their honour which is another established custom in Peking. The graveyard caretaking farmers are also required to present some small sample quantities of these products to the master's family as a token of courtesy and respect.

At the lunch table the old man impressed on his son and grandson the highlights of the Wu family's past history in the persons of some bright men who had distinguished themselves in officialdom, referring to some gravemounds which had just been visited.

Visiting family graveyards is always a sad experience but, nevertheless, is a typical episode in Chinese family life.

*   *   *

The fifteenth day of the seventh moon is a Ghost Festival.

According to the Chinese version of Buddhism, all human beings become *k'wei* (鬼), or "ghosts, after death and are said to roam the universe like gusts of wind or clouds of vapour. There are those who have the peculiar faculty of being able to see these ghosts and Chinese folklore contains many tales of such persons. The spirits take on near-human forms although variegated in appearance—"big head ghosts", "small head ghosts", "headed ghosts" and "headless ghosts", *ad infinitum*. At least one Chinese scholar artist has been able to record in pictures the likenesses of the transformations of departed souls.

Most of the good people, or "legitimately-deceased" people, when put through their trials in the court of the King of Hades are sentenced to be reincarnated as human beings or other baser kinds of animals, etc., but there are the suicide ghosts and those who have died violent deaths, such as on bloody battlefields, in hazardous conflagrations or torrential floods, or through criminal executions and the like, whose spirits "the big temples do not receive and small temples refuse to accept" as the Chinese saying goes.

Then there is another category covering those people who have died while on a worldly pursuit in strange lands with no acquaintances to burn paper money or offer sacrifices to their spirits, or of those who have left no sons or daughters to take care of their "spiritual comforts" in the next world. All these, according to Chinese "ghostology" are what may be termed "vagrant ghosts", wandering from place to place like tramps looking for some charity. For these there is no New Deal lending or breadline relief, and compared to the other souls, such as the Wus' ancestors, they are a miserable lot and their needs are many.

Nor are these vagrant ghosts a harmless group for they have

This is an artist's conception of the vagrant ghost of a person who hanged himself. It is dressed entirely in white and carries a fan and a "stick of mourning".

their patented mischiefs by which they play havoc with human beings as befits their malevolent nature and violent temper borne out by the manner of their deaths, coupled with their exasperating ghost life. The spirits will haunt children and give them sicknesses or enter into the weakened systems of the sick and coerce them into giving Buddhist masses for their delivery, or worse still, join together into teams and bring the world what is known as epidemics! These beliefs are unshakeable in the mind of the average Chinese, clear as two and two make four. The suicide ghosts, it is also firmly believed, have a habit of "pulling a proxy" to die in the same fashion corresponding to their own experience in order to release themselves to appear before the judges in the next world in preparation for reincarnation. Thus many a boatman or river passenger falls overboard not because of his own carelessness or because he has the intention to take his life, but because some vagrant ghost, lurking in the darkness or the invisible, has pulled him in "by the leg", so to speak. Thus these ghosts, if not appeased, would certainly constitute a serious problem.

Hence the compassionately inclined populace has organized co-called *Shui Lu Tao Ch'ang* (水陸道場) (Water and Land Masses), inviting a number of Buddhist monks to perform a ceremony, characterized by the chanting of the world's most effective soul-reclaiming volumes of the Diamond and other sutras, the holiest of all holy scriptures, in a monastery or by the side of a river or in some other fitting and proper location, and recommend these nameless, numberless groups of spirits—vagrant ghosts—to a large scale, wholesale amnesty and thus to save their souls from eternal suffering in the ghostly, ghastly life of permanent vagrancy. For this noble undertaking the Chinese have found no better date than the fifteenth day of the seventh moon when all the families remember their own ancestors and their spirits and this kind of a ceremony has come to be known as *Yu Lan Hui* (盂藍會), or "The Meeting of Ullambana," which word, in Sanskrit, has a meaning something like "liberating the suffering souls".

The Ullambara Meetings have come to be colourful affairs and Little Bald Head Wu remembered having been at some with his grandfather who, as a charitable old gentleman, never failed to receive an invitation to attend and to contribute a small sum of money toward covering the expenses.

*　　　*　　　*

The All Souls Day Buddhist prayer meetings, called *Yu Lan Hui*, have annually been held in certain spots in Peking. Some urban locations have been the famous monastery of Kwang Chi Ssu (廣濟寺), or Temple of Boundless Salvation, in the northern part of the Tartar City and the Ch'eng Hwang Miao (城隍廟), or City Guardian God's Temple, out in the southern section of the metropolis adjoining Peking's most extensive public burial grounds, and in years gone by, believe it or not, near the present Water Gate (Legation Quarter) on the southern section of the famous Jade Canal now a covered underground waterway. A suburban spot famous for the same reason in those good old days was the *Erh Cha* (二閘), or Second Lock, on the Grand Canal about a mile to the east of the Peking wall, due east from the famed Fox Tower. The greatest crowd of spectators and sightseers usually gathered at the last mentioned place.

It was then a booming village, particularly in the summer season, as barges and junks loaded with tribute rice from south China came Pekingward by way of this man-made water system. It was a great assembling and distributing point as the rice was thence despatched to the different storehouses in and out of the city. It was a busy, prosperous town then and restaurants and amusement houses were established catering to the patronage of the immense number of labourers, stevedores and members of boat crews, besides the always over-sized government staff the granary department had on duty in that region. It was also a rendezvous for Peking idlers and "nature-lovers."

Little Bald Head remembered having been taken there time and time again by his grandfather and, perhaps, his father on excursions when they viewed the man-made waterfall at the lock spilling noisily away as they seated themselves in the shaded courtyard of a teashop and restaurant occupying a vantage point. Coppers were often tossed into the whirling foamy currents right beneath the spillway for the nude beggar-boys to dive after and fight over much in the same way as the natives crowd about passenger liners in the harbours of certain ports in warm tropical waters.

Erh Cha was a small place (it is almost off the map now) but a rich place then and the Buddhist Prayer Meetings there were the most elaborately appointed as the contributing sponsors were numerous and generous. The affair used to last three days with a continuous chanting of *Yen K'o* (焰口), or "Flaming Mouth", sutras "in rotation"—it must have been a rotation of chanting to keep going so long—with the priests throwing bits of food into the water from time to time while they made certain symbolic finger and hand movements supposed to bear an exorcistic importance and render the bits of food even more effective in their ghost-appeasing faculty.

Typical religious documents written on yellow pieces of paper in the form of applications entered in behalf of the ghosts were prepared by the priests and sent, in ceremonious processions with Buddhist music playing, to the side of the river and burned—a post-haste special delivery to the gods who would answer these prayers unreservedly in the manner solicited.

Near by the prayer hall, a temporary mat shed erected for the purpose where the drums and cymbals and the drowsy chorus sung by the monks proceeded in full strength interparagraphed by the ringing of the sacred bell for the assembling of the vagrant ghosts, was seen the typical *Fah Ch'uan* (法船), or Boat of Doctrine, "lying in state" close to a big flag bearing seven white discs joined together like the stars in an astronomical sky chart. This was a sign of the God of Birth and was used to announce to the ghosts the gospel meeting. The Doctrine Boat was not anchored at the pier but rather tied to some poles in order to avoid being capsized by the chance blowing of a northwestern gust of wind for the enormous colourful boat was made of paper on a frame constructed of kaoliang stalks.

The builders of the Doctrine Boats know no specifications as to the sizes and designs of such a boat as the elaboration and dimensions depend solely on the pecuniary strength of the sponsors but thirty odd feet is an acceptable over-all length. That part of the keel under the waterline is not represented though the upper portions of the sides are profusely decorated with a design of lotus flowers and waves and surfs drawn on the paper in water colours. The superstructure is made to resemble a temple with paper images, etc., while the main deck is crowded with life-sized grotesque members of the out-door staff of the deities enshrined inside the boat's central quarters.

There are the ox-headed and horse-faced ushers, the white and black spirits of the self-strangulated suicides, who are said by some to have been given jobs in the next world's bureaucracy as they had no further interests in reincarnations having been so pessimistic about things in previous existences, and other unnamed and unnamable members of the coterie, including last but not the least the monstrous giant called *Yeh Ch'a Kwei* (夜叉鬼), who is made to gaze down into the "water" course, standing on one leg at the bowsprit and brandishing a three-branched pitch fork as if he has already located some concealed ghosts in the black depths of the water and is ready to dive overboard to salvage it with the pitchfork!

The idea of such a boat, it may be gathered, was to give the spirits of the drowned further chances of salvation by providing them with an itinerant circuit court of appeal on board this paper boat which, of course, is converted into a real magnificent junk when burned, carrying around the entire court in working order and dealing justice or leniency to the suffering and the oppressed.

The burning of the *Fah Ch'uan* is the climactic finale to the prayer meeting.

                    *   *   *

Still another feature of a Buddhist Prayer Meeting for the Ghost Festival is the so-called *ho teng* (河燈), or river lanterns, calculated to bring the spirits of the drowned to the light of Buddhist salvation. Pumpkins and eggplants are cut into halves and quarters and little candles fixed onto each piece. The floating lamps are lighted in the evening and put adrift in the canals and waterways. As a religiously meritous rite, combined with earthly royal pleasure, it was recorded in a Chinese book written in the seventeenth century that Emperor Shun Chih of the Manchu Dynasty used to sponsor imperial Ullambana meetings during the Ghost Festivals at which a famous priest officiated with headquarters at the Wan Shan Tien (萬善殿), or Temple of Ten Thousand Mercies, in the sea palaces for three consecutive evenings. At these functions river lanterns were set adrift, thousands of them, equipped with glass floats and decorated as lotus blossoms while a thousand young eunuchs lined the banks each holding a candle light fixed to a long-stemmed lotus leaf. His Majesty boarded the dragon pleasure barge at the Ying T'ai (瀛臺), or Sea Terrace (where Emperor Kwang Hsu, some two hundred years later, was imprisoned by order of the Dowager Empress) where Buddhist music and prayers were being performed. Setting the course northward they used to cruise through the Nan Hai, or South Lake, passing under the three-arched bridge to enter the Pei Hai, or North Lake, visiting the Five Dragon Pavilions on the northern shore before returning to the Forbidden City in the moonlight. This custom has not been so elaborately observed in recent years as in the good old days.

*   *   *

But the markets for days ahead are colourfully touched up with the stalls selling lotus flower lanterns for what Chinese youngster could bear the idea of passing the Ghost Festival without a lotus flower lantern of some kind to participate in the parades of children in the evening of the fifteenth! There are all sorts of designs and shapes, in various degrees of elaboration and expensiveness. Miniature boats, small paper theatrical figures, flower baskets and even airplanes and war tanks designed to hold candles and executed by skilled workmen sell at fancy prices. All these are mainly pasted over with pieces of paper made to represent the petals of the lotus flowers, tinted in all the colours of the rainbow. Children whose parents could ill afford an extravagant specimen are content with simpler varieties such as a single lotus flower mounted on top of a kaoliang stalk with little green leaves surrounding it, or a lonely blossom set on a branch of lotus root, each bearing but a single candle. But somehow or other the superstitious Chinese never wish to keep the lanterns after the ghost festival. Children parading the streets with their favourite lanterns all sing together:

"Lotus Flower Lanterns!
Lotus Flower Lanterns! Today we light thee and tomorrow
we throw thee away!"

Poorer people also utilize the "stubs" of the incense sticks left over from Buddhist rites and paste them in pairs to the ends of narrow paper strips. These are lighted and tossed to fall and catch onto the branches of the *Hao Tze* (蒿子) or artemisia (wormwood?) plants, collected from the countryside for the purpose. (Burning *hao tze* plants is China's own mosquito expulsive). Children parading the streets carrying these *hao tze* "lanterns" present an effect of clouds of fireflies moving about in the dark, nothing else being visible. Watermelons, after the "inside" has been "spooned" out through a hole at the top and the skin left intact, are carved with eyes, noses and mouths, etc., to represent the heads of ghosts. A candle is lighted and placed inside each melon and the greenish tinge, shining through the half-transparency, gives a dreary appearance like the pumpkin of Halloween nights and sends many a cold shiver clear through the spinal cord! It is the ghosts' night, and they are in every nook and corner!

A Ch'ing Dynasty poet has written:—

"On either side of the Jade Canal
The crowds gather to see the river lanterns,
Where the sacred drums and cymbals,
The Buddhist benevolence enhance.
The Boat of Doctrine is burned and so
No more straggling ghosts are left wandering about.
Only the moonlight is clear and humanity quietens,
While the murmuring stream flows on peaceful and
serene."

*   *   *

Like the rest of his kind Little Bald Head had his lotus lanterns. Twilight found "the gang all there" awaiting him for the parade. It was a hilarious, uproarious evening and the fun was shared by the adults as well.

END OF VOLUME ONE

WATER PLANTS AND DRAGONS

WE already have noted that Peking families are very fond of lotus roots and lotus seeds as dainty titbits, particularly the fresh and tender kinds available in summer time. But there are also other varieties of water plants equally sought after by the children as well as the adults while they are in season. The *pi ch'i* (荸薺), or water chestnuts, are not really nuts but are the starchy bulbish part of the underground stems of a perennial grass with a blackish brown skin. Eaten raw they are sweet and crisp and when cooked they form a very palatable part and enhance the taste of many a meaty dish.

The Chinese believe that this water chestnut, though quite agreeable and friendly in appearance and in every way else, is a positively irreconcilable enemy of brass utensils. The juice of the water chestnuts smeared on a brass article, they believe, will crack it in no time. Hence children who have inadvertently swallowed brass tacks, etc., are given a quantity of raw *pi ch'i* to eat as these should dissolve the brass objects in the stomach and prevent them from doing harm in the body.

Then there are the *ts'u ku* (茲菇), or arrowroots, the underground stems of which are also edible, steamed and sugared or used as an accompaniment to stewed Peking ducks! The Chinese have a superstition with this plant, too, on account of which

The Old Hen's Head is a thorny sort of an affair, unlike the water caltrops the prickly tips of which are easily cut off with a special pair of scissors.

few families keep them for courtyard or garden decoration even though the luxurious foliage of the plant shaped like arrowheads is highly ornamental in effect and it is easily grown in a jar with plenty of water and mud.

The arrowroots have a very beautiful three-petaled blossom, snow-white like the narcissus but which, in so far as the plants themselves are concerned, are nothing but a fruitless development as the plants apparently propagate through their underground stems and the flowers really do not help matters any. They seldom grow the degenerated flowers at all except once in a while and that for some particular reason which nobody knows except perhaps the arrowroots themselves. But this irregular appearance of the blossoms has given rise to suspicions. If the arrowroots planted in a family jar blossoms, the Chinese say it is a bad omen indeed for this prophesies that a daughter or some other female member in the family is soon to die!

Both the foregoing kinds are obtainable in the spring but autumn has its own specialities in the *Ling Chiao* (菱角), or water caltrops, and the *Lao Chi T'ou* (老鷄頭), or "Old Hen's Head", which make their debut about the time of the Ghost Festival.

Water caltrops are of several species. Those from South China grow three or four inches in length (or width rather) but the Peking variety is usually not much bigger than an inch. The young ones are eaten raw and the old ones are usually first boiled. The pedlars sort and wrap them in packages of big lotus leaves which have become a conventionalized wrapper in the trade and sell them at so much per package. A peculiarly shaped pair of scissors are used to cut off the prickly tips of the shells and by another operation each water caltrop is sliced in two for easy peeling.

The Old Hen's Head, so named because of its shape which much resembles the head of a hen, is the seed pot of a renegade member of the lotus family (*Euryale feroz, Salisb*). The leaves are big and round and barely float on the surface of the water as they plainly do not believe in having long stems. The flowers are provided with an enlarged swollen sort of a sepal very much like that of a fig. The flowers, though a charming shade of wistaria, never blossom and the seeds ripen in the fleshy "fruit" by themselves, with the fertilizing process most likely facilitated by the water. They are thorny, prickly objects with a tapering end where the flower is permanently encased. The round seeds are hermetically sealed in a thick hard shell, each wrapped in another sticky, slippery sort of skin inside the fleshy Old Hen's Head itself. Boiled and cracked, the kernels are nutty in flavour by virtue of their starchy content and are eaten like peanuts.

Not only children but also adults are fond of these waterplant seeds as it is believed that they contain certain elements good for the human body—a statement backed by the "*Pen Ts'ao*" (本草), the supreme authority on "origins of the grasses", which is, as the name implies, China's infallible and unquestioned guide for native medical principles and practice.

*   *   *

It was often the pleasure of old Mrs. Wu or some other member of the family to get either of the two kinds of plants, while they were in season, to give to Little Bald Head after school. Munching these served as good accompaniment to his "home work."

*   *   *

The mystic dragon or *Lung* (龍) occupies a unique position in the mind of the Chinese, no less prominent than is its position in Chinese art and even children are early acquainted with the doings of the dragons. The word is frequently seen in Chinese school books. (It is a surname, too, though not as commonplace as "Chang" or "Wang".)

Little Bald Head had his first inkling of dragons when he peeped into the pages of the family almanac, on the first page of which was a picture of a number of these fantastic animals curled among clouds over a stretch of "sea water" and bearing the caption "*Wu Lung Chih Shui*" (五龍治水), "Five dragons control the water.'' He was told that the dragons on duty each year exerted a great influence on rainfall, water sources and floods. He wondered how the number of dragons operating during the year could ever be revealed to mankind through the almanac but his inquisitiveness was soon satisfied when he was told that it all depended upon whether the first ''dragon day'' (in the twelve animal cycles) fell on the first, or the second and so on up to the eleventh day in the first moon, as this system was used as the basis for such calculations!

Not only that, but he learned early also that dragons were gods, for was not there the small shrine situated close to the well in the courtyard of the temple in which Mr. Yung's school was housed? The importance of this god was also the more deeply impressed in the child's young mind because of a decorative couplet on the little doors (quite within his reading ability) saying: ''The master of the nine rivers and eight streams; the god of five lakes and four seas''.

Nobody could enlighten him as to what rivers, streams, lakes and seas were referred to, just as there was no chance, under the watchful eyes of the august Mr. Yung, to peep through the closed doors into the shrine to find out what the dragon god looked like. He knew, however, that the dragon god controlled the water supply in the well and should never be offended by the water pedlars for fear of a sudden stoppage of the supply.

He often heard people complain about the mischievous doings of the dragon king when there was a scarcity or overabundance of rainfall in the year. On the second day of the second Lunar moon, he had heard people mention ''the dragon lifting its head'' and on this day the noodles people ate were dragon's whiskers, the flat cakes dragon's scales, and so forth, and that on the twenty-third of the fifth moon, the dragons hold military conferences regarding the despatch of soldiers for the summer's rainy season ''duty''. The soldiers whom the dragons commanded, he learned, were all sorts of water animals such as turtles, shrimps, fish and even crabs which carried out the orders of the Dragon King in distributing the desired rainfall or the undesired floods.

''The dragon had nine sons,'' said Teacher Yung, referring to a story in an old Chinese book, ''and each of them was different from the others.''

While the students listened, he went on:

''They were all about the same in appearance but not quite, and all were allotted some work to do that was suited to their individuality. The first son liked to bear heavy burdens on his back and so he was appointed to carry the heavy marble monuments in the temples. The second was told to mount guard on the roofs of the temples for he loved so much to gaze into the distance. The third son liked to roar and so was appointed to be on the ''handle'' of the big hanging bells in the monasteries. The fourth stood at the prison door for he was a ferocious and watchful sort of a chap. The fifth, a gourmet, is seen on the covers of ancient cooking tripods. The sixth liked water very much and so his likeness is often carved on a bridge. The seventh son was a bloodthirsty killer and he left his image on the sword handle. The eighth loved fire and the best place for him was found on an incense burner. The ninth, the youngest, preferred to confine himself indoors, hence his portrait is often painted on gates."

But the most dreaded stories about dragons he heard were connected with the repairs or construction work on the dragon palaces, for the dragon king has his palaces somewhere under the sea and at intervals messengers are sent to this world to purchase building materials, lumber, bricks, stones and so on for shipment to the submarine site of a new palace. The dragon king's purchasing agents conclude the supply contracts with dealers in this world and often propose to buy whole stocks, paying cash for them but never mentioning how and where delivery is to be made. While the dealers are thus left wondering about the unusual customers, mountain torrents suddenly descend in monstrous proportions and wash off all the purchased materials in devastating floods as that is apparently the only means of transportation known to the dragon.

There have not been convincing verifications but the Chinese, particularly the old people, insist on the existence of such a thing called *Lung Fa Mu* (龍發木), or "dragon delivering lumber", *Lung Fa Shih* (龍發石), or "dragon delivering stones", and so on. In other words, when there is a building program going on in the submarine palaces there is a big flood in our world, the Chinese say.

*   *   *

The legend of "dragons delivering lumber", etc., is firmly believed in by superstitious Chinese and rumours of such happenings prevail every time there is a flood. People give all sorts of descriptive details about such an affair, for example when it is a *Lung Fa Mu*, all the lumber, big heavy beams and pillars, travel down the muddy current in a perpendicular position and in perfect order, piece by piece, with a goodly portion of the logs showing above the surface of the water like periscopes of submerged underwater craft. Besides, at night, each of the pieces would bear a red light on the top clearly visible to the naked eye.

*   *   *

The rivers around Peking are liable often to overflow their banks and one of the rivers, the Yung Ting Ho (永定河) or "Permanently Fixed River", has a habit of changing its course of its own free will. That is how it got its present name, an expression of the public wish, as formerly it was known as Wu Ting Ho (無定河) or "Never Fixed River." But no matter what great proportions the floods should assume in nearby districts and no matter how near the inundation should approach the Peking city wall, Peking itself will never be affected by the floods for in the early days when the city was built insurance against floods was carefully attended to, Peking folklore explains and tells many an assuring narrative of which the following are typical.

Not long after the plan of Peking's construction was laid out a dragon was discovered in the northeastern part of the city. This dragon had, by virtue of his great magical power, taken on human form. He was found out, however, and caught by the priests assisting in the pioneering work. The dragon, it must be explained, was not without his own official and recognizable identification being a representative of the dragon king and so he protested against the action taken towards him, for this dragon, like all dragons, was authorized to start floods if and when orders were received from his superiors. To make a long story short, the priests succeeded in overpowering him and imprisoned him, as befitted his watery disposition, in a well by using some miraculous process.

A bridge was just then being built in the vicinity.

The dragon protested against the treatment being meted out to him and demanded to know when he was going to be released.

"Oh, when this bridge becomes old," answered the priests, and so saying they laid a heavy slab of stone over the well and constructed a temple above the spot.

To hold the dragon in the well and to do so without breaking the promise made by them, the priests named the bridge *Pei Hsin Ch'iao*(北新橋), "Northern New Bridge," lest the dragon should learn that the bridge had become old and demand his release.

At or about the same time this dragon was jailed in the East City, another water terrorist was apprehended in the West City and the priests, the only persons capable of doing such things, discovered and imprisoned him in the same manner as his brother was, in a well, and built a heavy pagoda over the spot after sealing the well by some magical talismans. So while this big pagoda at the Pai Ta Ssu Temple (shaped like a bottle and known thereby to foreign residents as the Bottle Pagoda) lasts there will be no fear of the dragon escaping and starting to convert the city into a lake. And it was in order to double-insure the "workability" of the scheme that the gods often send mystic workmen to this world to repair the pagoda, patching it with heavy iron work every time there is a sign of a possible collapse. "No human craftsmen could tackle such a job as putting iron joiners on the structure which bears witness to superhuman activity."

Such stories have been handed down for generations and people like old Mrs. Wu would insist wholeheartedly on their authenticity, although others may give more rational reasons for the fact that floods have never seriously damaged the old capital.

"The top of the thirteen-storied pagoda located in the northern portion of the Tung-hsien city is on the same level as the square stone on the ground under the arch of the Ch'ao Yang Men of Peking," others point out. "And when the pagoda of Tung-hsien is entirely submerged, that would be high time for the Peking-jen to seek refuge from floods."

The minds of the Wus were at ease though floods threatened nearby districts.

THE WAYS OF PEKING PIGEONS

IT was in the early fall of the year in which Little Bald Head or Wu Hsueh-wen (it is not good form to address him by any other name than "Hsueh-wen" now, although his parents and grandparents found it hard to make the change as the milk name of "Little Bald Head" sounded much more affectionate) was eight years old that he was transplanted from Mr. Yung's school to a public institution in another lane not far from their own house. This was a big place and contained well furnished classrooms and a spacious playground with certain items of gymnastic instruments and fixtures in evidence. These all struck Little Bald Head as something very strange for nothing like them had been seen at Mr. Yung's.

He was puzzled to hear that the new school, many times bigger than Mr. Yung's was *hsiao hsueh* (小學), "small school", for he did not know that elementary schools are known as *hsiao hsueh*, secondary schools as *chung hsueh* (中學), "middle schools", and universities are *ta hsueh* (大學), "big schools". He was still more perplexed to learn that the students all go through the small and the middle schools and then study in the *ta hsueh*, which term sounded to him like a Confucian classic his pal Wang was already studying at Mr. Yung's "school shop" at the "temple".

The change was a very welcome one for Little Wu, indeed, and even the big white signboard bearing a long string of black Chinese characters looked good to him and he was secretly proud to belong to such a magnificent place. All the school work, too, was a whole lot easier and more agreeable to him, and his schoolmates in soldierish uniforms certainly looked more cheerful than his companions at the old place. But nothing pleased him better than the assurance here, which he took pains to verify with his new friends, that no matter how poor your school work proved to be, there was no chance of the pupils being beaten as he had seen them at Mr. Yung's. Out there though he had never run into corporeal punishment himself, the frequently enacted scene of a schoolmate suffering such a fate was enough to make him form an opinion about the school bordering on antagonism.

"Tell me, is it true that no beating is given in this school?" he asked his new schoolmates.

"Yes, but you get bad *fen shui* (分數) (marks) if your studies are not well done. The teacher gives you marks to show how good you are at school and whether you are a well-behaved child or not."

He was thankful to his father that he had arranged to effect the change.

* * *

The school work here was a lot more friendly, too, and no more reciting, parrot fashion, was required of him. There was more play than study in his judgment. In Mr. Yung's school, a boy got a sound spanking when the teacher found him drawing a picture on a piece of paper but here drawing pictures was an openly encouraged "lesson" in which all the children competed. Absentmindedly humming a song in class used to cost a schoolmate many an hour's kneeling before the Confucius portrait hanging on the wall and a lot of scolding from Mr. Yung, but here singing was a daily "lesson". And just when there was a faint feeling of nastiness about a thing and children craved a change, a bell rang calling them out to play! Even that was a *kung ke* (功課) or "lesson". "Anything passes as a lesson here," he thought.

Besides, the teacher only urged him to try better and never frightened the pupils with such dreadful stories as he had learned from his "Trimetrical Classic". These told how a diligent scholar used to study in the evening with his head attached by the hair to a rope hanging from the ceiling in order that his noddings during the study hours at night would pull his hair so painfully that he would be cured of sleepiness. Or how another scholar, to keep from going to sleep over his book, used to prick his legs with a sharp spindle when he began to feel too tired to go on.

Here in his new school, too, there was more spare time left in the daytime so that it was not necessary to study much under lamplight, much less to do as another story suggested in the same book about the scholar, too poor to buy oil for his lamp, who used to catch a number of fireflies and put them in a cellophane, no, I mean thin paper bag, using the little shimmering light to study by! Still another used to read books by the side of winter snow for lack of other lighting arrangements in his humble home.

All these stories, as you probably already know, were mentioned in the first children's book, the "Trimetrical or Three-character Classic" although no teacher ever bothered to explain fully the stories alluded to by the few characters. In the case of Little Wu, he learned about them from his father.

*   *   *

Little Bald Head Wu did not take long to accustom himself to life at the public school and soon learned really to enjoy school life. In the course of time he showed himself to be amongst the first pupils in his class, distinguishing himself to a certain extent from his schoolmates in many ways. His reports of the public school spread fast in his neighbourhood and his pal Wang came also to study here for his parents had been moved to let him discontinue attendance at old Mr. Yung's school.

New friends were soon made amongst his classmates. In his class there was one boy whose name was Chin. He was from a family of the near-nobility of the late Manchu house. He was what people called a *Hwang Tai Tze* (黃帶子), "Yellow Belt", as a traditional yellow belt had always been worn by the distant relatives of the reigning house during the heyday of the Ch'ing Dynasty. This belt, of an imperial yellow, was always exhibited ostentatiously because it was representative of an exalted social standing which distinguished the wearers as a particularly privileged class until the overthrow of the dynasty. This boy Chin was not well known by his profficiency in his school work but rather the contrary was the case, for he was a typical example of a number of such "spoiled" children of parents who had known no adversity and hardship in their life.

Chin was a very clever and sociable fellow about five years too old for his grade, judged Little Wu. His school marks were never anywhere nearly as good as those of the latter, a fact which coupled nicely with the truth that he had stayed where he was in school for three years and could point to a class graduating that very summer as his original class when he had first come. But the old slowcoach was improving for he did manage that term to escape "sitting on a red chair" as the Chinese students dub the poorest scholar in a class. In the list of school marks the names of all the students in a class are given in order of school "credits" received, and a red mark like a big "check mark" is put at the end of each such list hence the last scholar is said to "sit on a red chair", but in many a course he still featured a number of "eggs" by which the zero mark is generally referred to by school children.

Strictly speaking, it was really not the fault of Chin alone for his mind was constantly preoccupied with a big flock of domesticated pigeons kept in his house. During classes his mind would, for example, drift away from the arithmetic exercises on the blackboard and wander to his spacious courtyard on Bitter Water Well Lane to be with the new pair of "Tiger Caps" lately purchased from Li No. Six at the last temple fair. For Chin was a pigeon-fancier, like a good many Peking natives. Half the time when he talked with his comrades in school the conversation concerned his pigeons in some way. Little Wu and his pal Wang had been asked many times to visit him and see his pigeons and at last Chin was able to have their company.

Chin's house was a veritable mansion although a goodly portion of it was left vacant and another goodly portion was rented out by some arrangement of which even Chin himself was not really clear—nor even his father, the sickly master in the compound. The courtyard which Chin occupied was good sized, but the southern portion was entirely taken up by a pigeon-house, nay, a pigeon apartment, constructed with rows and rows of pigeon-holes in typical Peking fashion with a shallow straw basket for each pair of pigeons. The entire structure, and the ground in front of it, were netted in by a fence work of doubled sticks of reeds, woven with diamond-shaped meshes of, as in Chin's language, "four-finger-mesh", measured by the joint width of four adult fingers for that was the proper density of a pigeon fence. There were many pairs of beautiful pigeons (they were quite a pleasing sight!) some sitting leisurely in pairs in their individual baskets and cooing affectionately and intimately with his or her spouse. Some were seen coming down to the ground to peck away at the dishes containing food—kaoliang grains and dried green beans—or drinking from a covered basin through some holes about two inches in diameter carved in the wooden cover.

Scattered about in the courtyard and free to mill around were more groups of pigeons. A number also loitered on the house tops. Some pieces of green and yellow glazed tiles were perceivable, mounted on the top of the curved roofs. These were, as Chin explained, for the purpose of guiding his pigeons during the flying exercises and maneuvers as otherwise the roof tops of rows and rows of houses in the neighbourhood would look all alike to the birds from a high altitude.

* * *

Keeping pigeons is one of the orthodox hobbies of Peking people and it is one of the favourite pastimes indulged in by the cultured as well as leisured classes. It is considered quite permissible as a "casual occupation of otherwise unoccupied sentiments," as the Chinese scholars love to put it. The attachment of men to feathered friends is an old institution in this country. Authentic stories are told about a famous official and calligraphical artist of the Chin period (265—419 A.D.), Wang Hsi-chih (王羲之), who was very fond of keeping geese in his garden. His calligraphical masterpieces were very hard to get and were greatly prized by his contemporaries (they are priceless curios now) but he seldom wrote for his admirers until people discovered his weakness. After that no applicant who sent a pair of white geese to him as gifts was ever disappointed.

Another bird that has featured itself so outstandingly in history is the stork, or so-called red-crested whooping crane. The poet Lin Ho-ching (林和靖) (Sung Dynasty, 960-1276 A.D.) contented himself with a quiet retreat on the shores of the famous West Lake where in his own words, "a plum tree was his wife and a stork his son". But so far nobody has duplicated the folly of King Yi Kung of Wei (衛懿公) (of the Warring Kingdoms period about three centuries before Christ) who loved storks more than he did his own subjects. In his court more officials were appointed to take care of his pet storks than for the administration of his kingdom. A greater part of the revenue was spent on his storks than on all the branches of the government combined. As a result when his kingdom was being attacked by the northern aborigines there was hardly any response to his conscription notices as the people were disillusioned about their king who had levied special taxes to maintain his birds. "Why does he not send his storks to the front to fight for him?" they all asked. His kingdom was soon at an end.

* * *

Coming back to where we left off, the domesticated pigeons are distinguishable from the wild species by their shorter, more blunt beaks, a bunch of small feathers on the "nose"—called technically *feng t'ou* (鳳頭) or "phoenix head" and abbreviated to *feng* (鳳) in the trade nomenclature—and some minute erruptions on certain parts of the eyelids. The plumage is black, purple (a rust brown), grey or blue, more often than not combined with white. The Chinese have coined fancy names, all based on the colour schemes and colour combinations of the plumage. It would be hard to give an exhaustive list of such names, but let it suffice to give a few examples.

A pigeon with a white body but black tail is known as a *Hei Tien Tze* (黑點子) or "Black Spot", and one with a purple tail is known as a *Tze Tien Tze* (紫點子) or "Purple Spot". Any pigeon with a snow white body is a *Tien Tze* (點子) or "Spot" and one with a black body is a *Wu* (烏) or "Crow". One with a coloured body but white tail is known as *Tao Ch'a-erh* (倒插兒) or "Struck Up-side-down", referring to the unusual arrange-

ments.   One with black wings is a *Tieh Ch'ih* (鐵翅) or "Iron
Wings", and by *T'ung Ch'ih* (銅翅) or "Copper Wings" is meant
one with brown wings.   *Hsueh Hua* (雪花) or "Snow Flower" is
one with finely mixed plumage of "salt and pepper".   A "Tiger
Cap" or *Lao Hu Mao* (老虎帽) is one with a white body, a
black tail and a brown or blue crest.   An "Ink Ring" or *Mou
Huan erh* (墨環兒) is one with a black circle around the neck.
One with a white body and a reddish brown crest is known by
the name of *Hsueh Shung Mei* (雪上梅) or "Plum Flower on
Snow".   A white pigeon with a black head, black *feng* (i.e.,
"nose feathers"), a black tail and a pair of black wings, is known
as *Hei Ssu K'uai Yu* (黑四塊玉) or "Four Pieces of Black Jade",
and one with similar brown parts, "Four Pieces of Brown Jade".

*   *   *

All the foregoing were represented in Master Chin's dove-
cote and were pointed out to Little Wu.

*   *   *

Keeping pigeons is a much more costly affair than it would
appear, for their keepers following man's collection instinct
never know where to stop once an earnest start has been made.
The pigeons are great lovers and are strictly monogamous in
habit and pairs are so devoted to each other that no "hubby"
deserts his "wifey" and goes searching for romance elsewhere
and the wife too is inflexibly faithful to her male. Except when
a death or loss occurs, no pigeon ever peeps around and tries to
push into another pair's company under any circumstances, so
their married life is generally bounteously blissful with a pro-
fuse measure of balanced life of co-habitation, whatever that
includes.   A pigeon is happy with a spouse of his or her own
plumage, and match-making therefore is a constant and bounden
duty of a pigeon fancier.   The females are about a size smaller
than the males and the expert can also tell the sex by feeling
certain parts of the body as also by watching the winkings of
the eyes when a pinch is made somewhere on the neck—a sort of
"necking" as it were.   A female's wink is more sheepish than
that of a male, according to the experts.

The amateur pigeon-raisers' "stock" is usually added to by
new procurements purchased at the various markets—temple
fairs generally, held on certain days in the month at the Lung
Fu Ssu (隆福寺), Hu Kuo Ssu (護國寺), Pai Ta Ssu (白塔寺), and
T'u Ti Miao (土地廟) temples, with another popular market
place at the Flower Market Street outside Hatamen.   Here the
amateur raisers gather in the afternoons as also the professionals
from various parts of the city.   In the midst of the cooings of
birds, arguments and bargainings mostly in "trade phraseology", pigeons and money change hands.   The birds are brought
home by the new possessors wrapped in handkerchiefs, or in
portable cages if there is a bigger transaction.

The professionals are a bunch of smart people and they not
only conduct an above-board pigeon exchange and supply service
but are also known to be very capable of "doctoring" the
pigeons in such a way that more expensive specimens are
"produced" from less expensive ones, or to sell a female pigeon
as a male or a male as a female with high voltage sales-talk to
fill a specific bill.   All but the real *au fait* fall easy victims to

their tricks.   Tails not black enough are dyed with a mixture of colour pigments using iron rust to good advantage, or cutting or weeding out black feathers from a white area or white feathers from a black area and so on with a pair of scissors with usually undetectable results, so well done is the operation. Good pigeon curves require a short, blunt beak, and the pigeon dealers in the manner of a beauty treatment can miraculously make a beak blunter by filing off the surplus portion by means of a piece of sandpaper.   All trades have tricks, you would say!

Not only these but the professional pigeon raisers are said to have a trick to so train a pair of pigeons that no matter what fine treatment is received in the house of the new host, they will fly back to the raiser's as soon as there is a chance.   In this way, one pair of pigeons serves as three or four pairs in so far as reselling profits are concerned.   To combat this, the new possessors tie up the wings and keep the newly acquired birds under vigilance for a long time until the impressions of their first homes are blurred and then there will be no further chance for their decamping in favour of their original homestead.   It is an exasperating experience, as Master Chin told Little Wu, to find a pair of pigeons paid for in good money fly back to the original keepers and more so to find the same man offering the same pair again at the fair.   Some people having thus fallen prey in order to put the treacherous dealers in an awkward position— make them "lose face"—would again buy and pay for the same pair and after broadcasting his sad experience would, right in front of the dealers' eyes, have the pigeons' brains dashed out on the ground, thus implying "let us see how you can use them for pulling further tricks!"   It is a cruel way of doing things, you might say, but no genuine Peking pigeon fancier could put up with such kind of humiliation without giving the devil his due.

"See that pair of Tiger Caps over there, Wu? I have bought them three times already!" remarked Master Chin.

*   *   *

Master Chin, Little Bald Head's pigeon-fancier schoolmate, was well versed in all such matters, mostly learned after he had been "stung proper".

*   *

*

Besides adding new members to their collections from time to time by purchasing pigeons at the various fairs the keepers also find a source of joy in watching their own multiply.

Domesticated pigeons reproduce with marvellous rapidity and many a pigeon-rearing family find it much too fast for comfort, and the first thing they know their feeding bills have taken on a grave outlook as a large measure of grain is consumed by their flocks of rather hearty eaters.   They are also a bunch of mischief-makers in that they have a habit of pecking away listlessly at the masonry on the house-top or at the foot of the walls as they find the little bits of lime to be a very desirable food, particularly for the females before laying eggs for reasons easily understood. Such an operation of course does not agree too well with economic house upkeep.   They are a naughty lot, too, at the drinking fountain for unless preventive measures are taken, they will often jump bodily in and bathe themselves where only drinking is legitimate.

The females lay eggs, usually two, every ten days or thereabout. Hatching takes place right after that until the little ones pop out their ugly heads from the cracked shells in about eighteen days. Sometimes, the little ones are so weak that outside help is needed to break the shells. They require, however, little attention from the raisers as the male and the female take equal interest in the matter and take turns in nursing their children, the duty shifts always taking place about ten o'clock in the morning and about four o'clock in the afternoon with surprising punctuality. The mother pigeons have a sort of milky juice exuding from the gizzard with which the young are fed, from mouth to mouth, for about two weeks after birth. After that, millet, thoroughly soaked in water, should be fed to them with human assistance. Pigeon eggs are considered a delicacy in the Chinese culinary art and are a tonic during the winter months. They sell at fancy prices, constituting a side income for professional pigeon raisers. The pigeons have their enemies, too, as eagles and owls and cats are very fond of them and a certain type of parasitic worms are also known to be a constant problem to Mr. and Mrs. Pigeon and their children as they bite mercilessly at the quills and live on pigeon blood besides.

The fun of pigeon rearing does not end with the fencing in of the dove-cote and watching them as we would goldfish, or allowing them to roam around in the courtyard like the familiar white doves of the Italian cities or the Asakusa temples in Tokyo. During the Ch'ing dynasty there used to be a group of people whose infamous trade it was to keep a flock or flocks of trained pigeons for the purpose of releasing them every morning to allow them to steal into the imperial granaries then operating outside the eastern wall of Peking, beyond the region of the Peking Observatory. This establishment was the T'ai P'ing Ts'ang (太平倉), or "Peacetime Grain Depot". These pigeons would make daily trips to the granaries and eat from the barns to the capacity of their gizzard and then make a flight back home before twilight. There they were made to retch up the rice, as the cormorants surrender their catch of fish, which represented a very profitable enterprise for their masters. It was said that the practice averaged about 50 pounds of rice per flock of 100 pigeons! Whether this is wholly true or partly true or not true at all, let bygones be bygones, for such a thing is non-existent and impossible now, as the last of the granaries disappeared some twenty odd years ago and not even their ruins can now be traced!

One of the practices now is based on the pigeon's so-called homing-instinct, for the trained birds will fly back direct after it is released from even a long distance. This is the culmination of long periods of training the distances being gradually increased from the "base". Chinese native pigeons are not so renowned for superiority in this respect, of course, as the foreign species which have been introduced in this country in recent years. Of course in so far as putting this homing instinct to any utilitarian purpose is concerned, the Chinese have apparently never given it any serious consideration. It would not be a Chinese way of doing things, anyway.

* * *

The exercising of the pigeon's homing instinct by setting them on solo homeward flights is in reality the initiative stage of a pigeon fancier's adventures and is not without a certain competitive nature embodied in the undertaking. It is another phase of the exhibitive showing of the finer specimens so dear to the heart of the possessors. A frequently seen sight is the owner of rare and high-priced specimens bringing them to the fair or to a tea shop close by to be admired by their friends and then releasing them one by one, with hand-pitching assisting the birds in their take-off, while people watch them vanish on their homeward dash. The main point in such an undertaking, of course, it to impress on the envious fellow raisers the proud possession of such expensive specimens and the risk the man is willing to run in setting them free on their own wings and depending on no concrete guarantee that they would actually reach home. What a "pigeon story" he will have to tell the enthusiastic friends and ill-wishing "foes" the next time they meet as to the result of the flights! Whatever the individual feeling about the matter, much gossip is to go on after the man has left as to what a fine, or poor, trainer he is or whether or not he has not boldly overconfided in his newly acquired birds, and so on. As to the owner himself, his knowing that he is just one step higher than the rest of them is satisfaction enough for himself, it is the fulfilment of a sweet ambition.

The next step toward pigeon enjoyment is to set them flying in so-called *pan-erhs* (盤兒), or "plates", as an irregularly shaped pigeon formation is called As a healthy recreation for the keepers, it ought not to be condemned, particularly as it requires very much outdoor activity and early rising for better results. The program consists of setting flocks of trained pigeons flying and wheeling and darting in the sky, the famous Peking spring or autumn sky if you know what that means, circling around the "headquarters" on the ground.

The pigeons when properly trained do not have to be chased out from the dove-cotes as the master only points at each one chosen for the manoeuvre with a small stick and as though touched by a magic wand, the call is answered by a hurrying out of the fencework at the narrow opening of the door—the door is not left ajar as volunteers are often too numerous to be easily controlled. The chosen bird will first mount the roof and stop there for a few seconds as though to hear the latest weather report and to check up on the fuel supply and then it takes off gracefully. Gaining the proper altitude, it circles overhead and awaits the others drafted for the flight in the same manner, who "zoom" skyward one after another to form the flying patrol. Twenty-one is the minimum number in a proper *pan-erh*, and forty to fifty would be a good-sized formation. There may be some lazy or slow starters still milling around in the courtyard or lounging on the roof, and these are hastened off with a long bamboo pole to the top of which is fastened a bunch of red cloth pieces. (In pigeon traffic red is "Go".)

When the human ground commander is satisfied with the manoeuvre he gives an order for the squadron above to land by sending some birds to the roof-tops, perhaps some known to be regular landlubbers or stayhomers, in order to influence the squadron to make for the headquarters below marked by the coloured tiles. Tiles of all colours but common grey make proper landing marks but not red—the sign of "Go". The pigeon raiser must not send his entire collection aflying as in such a case he would lose the above-mentioned remote control and be unable to land them at his will, and some, known to be less air-minded, must be reserved in the dove-cote to ensure the safe return of the squadron. Sometimes the pigeons may get tired from wheeling above in the sky and may choose by a majority vote among themselves to make attempts to land before the human ground commander is ready to "call it a day". Then he resorts to more brandishing of the stick with the red cloth pieces until they take to the air once more.

It is during these exercises that the pigeon fanciers attach the famous pigeon whistles to the root of the tail feathers of certain dependable (!) members of the squadron, which supplement the familiar charming and "unearthly" sound effect heard nowhere else but in Peking. These are made with bulbs and tubes of bamboo carved to egg-shell thickness and lighter-than-air weight, beautifully lacquered. The slender ones are known as *shao-tze* (哨子), or "whistles," and the fat ones *hu-lu* (葫蘆), or "gourds", both with obstructed openings in the tubes working on the principle of the diabolo and producing many shades of tones during the pigeon's flying hours.

*   *   *

The pigeon whistles are a rather costly item of outfit for the enjoyment of pigeon-culture. There were formerly four or five families who made it their trade to manufacture them and nowadays no more than two or three attend the pigeon markets where their showcases are seen among the cages and cages of pigeons. They are there, it seems, just for the "effect", for they do not make sales very often and actually about one sale a day is all that they expect. It is of course no fault of theirs considering the expensive prices which hamper the whistles from being popularized. Real good ones are not even made now, and whatever perchance appears in the second-hand stores quickly finds its way to some collectors who are willing to pay the exorbitant prices asked. Master Chin possessed only a few but one had thirteen tones, called the "Thirteen Princes" design and was worth more than twenty dollars.

But whether whistles are high or low it does not make much difference for the pigeon fans' enthusiasm does not stop there but finds its climax in pigeon warfare.

The stratagems of pigeon warfare are very complicated though to the laymen they appear rather simple. Briefly it is a matter of sending a group of pigeons into the air when an enemy force, a neighbour's flock, is seen patrolling the sky. By using trained birds to purposely mingle and stampede into the enemy group and getting your own flock down at the proper moments causes pigeons in the enemy flock to be captured during the general mix-up. It is an exciting sport and requires good eyesight and sound judgment and a certain amount of insight into ornithological mob psychology. The result may be very gratifying or exasperating depending on the outcome of the war.

In case a new bird has been rounded up and forced down with your own flock, the first thing to do is to open the door of your dove-cote fence and try to get him to follow your own birds inside. Luring by food and company appeal does not always work and such a bird is usually suspicious and so utterly perplexed that it takes a long time for his "pigeonish" brain to make a decision. If it refuses to alight on the ground after all stones have been turned, then the *tan-kung* (彈弓) or "bullet crossbow" is taken out and trained on it. A round ball of yellow earth, about 15 millimeter caliber, is quite capable of dealing death to a persistently negative-minded bird of a cheap variety such as a "Black Spot". In the case of a rarer specimen like a "Four Pieces of Purple Jade," a more lenient attitude is taken. A skillfully aimed bullet will knock the pigeon from its perch by tearing open the front breast where the gizzard is located, as such a wound has been found to be usually not fatal. Surgical attention is immediately given the bird by sewing up the opening of the gizzard with human hair. After that the bird is fed only kaoliang grains and no water and with proper nursing the wound will heal in about ten days. It is a delicate operation from start to finish and requires the most immaculate marksmanship on the part of the shooter and quick skilled action afterwards—all of which are included in the qualifications of an accomplished pigeon-fancier.

There are certain hard and fast rules governing pigeon warfare, mutually understood in advance between pigeon raisers. The raisers are not very numerous in each neighbourhood and it does not take long to bring them together, often meeting one another across the pigeon cages at the market. A verbal agreement will be reached, concluding, as it were, a friendly war pact, the only clause of which provides that each high contracting party agrees to a free, willing, and unrestricted exchange of prisoners captured from the other party. This arrangement is technically termed *kuo hou ti* (過活的), meaning "passing live ones" as against *kuo ssu ti* (過死的) which means "passing dead ones", though strictly speaking only the "live ones" can ever be passed as the "dead ones" are dead from the "feet up" and no passing is necessary. In the usual course of things two raisers who are first on a friendly agreement eventually become hostile to each other as it is often hard to part with a good captured specimen and ceremoniously return it to its owner when it is so much easier and more agreeable to cheat and deny having any knowledge about the disputed bird. Pigeon warfare does not provide for a search of an enemy's ranks and files, neither of the prison camps and whatever is known as conscience just does not always work!

*　　　*　　　*

It was not long after Little Wu's visit to Master Chin's that the latter left school. It was rumoured afterward that he turned professional pigeon-raiser. There was no way to confirm the rumour.

THE IMPORTANCE OF FRIENDSHIP

LITTLE Wu's schoolmates were not all like Master Chin who paid more attention to his pets than to his studies and aside from still another boy who habitually went to sleep at his desk about once in every three study periods and who had the pleasure of staying behind to join a new class coming up the summer after Little Wu entered public school all the rest were quite industrious scholars.

Of the best lads in the class there were four outstanding ones and the five pupils, including Little Wu, became an inseparable set. Out of school they were dear friends and formed a sort of study club among themselves. It was their habit to arrange for after-school get-togethers at their homes, and the southern rooms used as a study and guest parlour in the Wu house on Donkey Mart were often chosen for their meetings. This was, as may easily be guessed, a scheme devised by the elder Wus to see that their child kept proper company and paid due attention to his schoolwork, as nowhere could such supervision be possible except "right under their nose". Of these boys the Wang boy next door, Little Bald Head's old pal, needless to say, was one. Before long the boys won the full approbation of their parents for their mutual friendship and were told to become sworn brothers.

Friendship has rightly been considered in China as one of the five principal *lun* (倫), or "human relations", since ancient times and beautiful stories concerning friendly devotion have been told in all ages. There is for instance the story of Tze Po-t'ao (左伯桃) and Yang Chueh-ai (羊角哀)—a three-thousand-year-old story now still thoroughly enjoyed as a famous Chinese play.

Tso Po-t'ao was a poor scholar on a trip to the Ch'u (楚) capital to seek an official appointment. He met Yang Chueh-ai at the latter's house where he sought shelter for the night when caught in a snowstorm. The two quickly developed a friend-mania and the next morning decided to make the trip together as they agreed that there were possible opportunities for both of them at the capital.

Two days out they were marooned in the thick of a prolonged cold wave, a blizzard thoroughly drenched their heavy winter garments and the provisions they carried fell low. The region was a mountainous wilderness and the howling of hungry wild beasts was clearly audible.

It was still a long way to the Ch'u capital and they soon saw to their utter dismay that their ambitious scheme was gravely threatened. Ere long Tso Po-t'ao, being of inferior physique, lost confidence in himself (he got "cold feet" so to speak) and suggested that Yang Chueh-ai go on alone as the provisions while not enough for two might serve for one. Yang Chueh-ai, like the true and faithful friend he was, was not willing to comply with such a request and told him so. Purposely he sent Tso Po-t'ao to fetch some dry twigs to make a fire with which to warm themselves. When the latter returned with the wood, he found that his friend had taken off his clothes and was lying naked in a hollow tree, offering his own clothes for his friend's added warmth. Surprised, Tso Po-t'ao asked what the idea was. His friend told him then that he had decided to freeze and starve to death in order that Tso Po-t'ao might have a better chance to bring his journey to a successful end.

While the two argued Yang Chueh-ai breathed his last. Tso Po-t'ao buried his friend's body in the snow-covered ground and with tears continued on his way. He was successful in getting a job in the capital and the first thing he did was to look up his friend's remains and bury them at the proper place in his family graveyard. According to the book in which this story is found the two were sworn brothers, the oaths being performed during their overnight first meeting in Yang Chueh-ai's house.

Duke Kuan Yu, China's "War God" and a Han Dynasty deputy generalissimo, and his two sworn brothers are well known in this country and their example is admired and revered by all those who thirst for friendship. Their joint oath sworn to at their brother-making ceremony was:

"Now that we have not been born on the same day in the same month of the same year, let us seek to die on the same day in the same month of the same year", meaning, in the Oriental circumlocutory way of saying things, that they valued their friendship above the pleasures of life itself. Their sworn-brotherhood was also of a twenty-four hour rapid-production variety. The three died about two years apart.

*   *   *

When the youngsters were offered the suggestion to become sworn brothers they were unanimously "sold" on the idea. Little Wu had often heard the expression, for were there not *pa tze ta yeh* (把子大爺), or "sworn older uncles," and *pa tze shu shu* (把子叔叔), or "sworn younger uncles," his father's own sworn brothers to whom he had been introduced? His grandfather had his sworn brothers, too, though only a straggling few were still alive and he called each of them a "grandfather." These were all "friends" he was told and this checked with the lesson on "making friends" which his teacher at school had just taught.

He learned that Confucius believed "people should not befriend persons who are inferior to themselves," and also that there were three good friends: "he who is straight, he who is forgiving and he who knows much" and three bad ones: "the queer, the soft and the 'chatterbox' ". Bamboo, plum and the pine tree were known as "the three plant friends who thrive in the cold weather," forming a favourite subject of Chinese painters, and the harp, wine and poems are collectively known as the scholar's three friends. Mo Tze (墨子), a contemporary of Mencius, Little Wu read in his books, was greatly impressed with the dyeing processes at a filature where "white silk placed in vats containing green dye turned green and that placed in the vats containing yellow dye turned yellow" and which phenomenon the great philosopher likened to the effect of friendship.

In his lessons on character building, called in Chinese *Hsiu Shen* (修身), most probably a school subject unique in itself as being strictly Oriental, Little Wu remembered the passage

A printed brochure, called "Gold Orchid Register", is used to record a sworn-brotherhood. In it is written each member's family record for three generations. A copy is given to each signatory.

which said; one who befriends good people may be likened to a man who has entered a room in which are kept orchid flowers for after he has stayed for some time in the midst of the flowers, to him their fragrance will be less and less noticeable. Likewise whoever befriends bad people may be likened to lingering in the fish market where the vile odours, at first so offending, seem to get less and less objectionable. "A person gets so used to his surroundings that he quickly loses himself in their midst and his character changes for the better or the worse corresponding to the sort of friends he keeps."

*   *   *

There were certain preliminary steps in the preparation for the establishment of the sworn brotherhood, beginning with referring matters to their respective parents for approval. (A swornbrotherhood pact is ratified before signatures are affixed thereto.)

An auspicious day was selected for the noble ceremonials by Little Wu's grandfather who, as the promoter of the scheme, was instrumental in seeing everything through. He also selected the small Kuan Ti Miao (關帝廟) or Kuan Yu's Shrine on the western side immediately outside of the Chien Men arch as the most suitable place for a simple religious rite, considered indispensable, consisting of burning bundles of incense before the image of the famous "War God" who personifies the zenith of faithful friendship. The five youngsters were told to kowtow before the god, swearing cooperative assistance in time of need.

A set of papers, made out in five identical copies, were also exchanged between them, each of the five boys keeping one copy. This contained a brief list of each of the children's genealogical record for the last three generations and each of the five parties' age, birthday and so on, prefaced by a foreword reiterating their common intention of entering into the alliance and recording in black and white their irreversible commitment in the most-high-sounding phrases, such as "the sea may become dry and stones rot but our friendship shall remain everlastingly unchanged!"

To this agreement they, on that very day, set their hand and seal, each one witnessing the signature of the other four. This paper is known in Chinese as a *Chin Lan P'u* (金蘭譜) which literally translates as "Gold Orchid Register" and refers to a passage in the ancient classic, "Book of Changes" where it is said, "Two people with the same mind can sever solid gold and the words from similar hearts are sweet like orchids!"

After this a round of calls was made and a series of kowtowing to the elders of each family, beginning from that of the "first brother, the second brother, the third brother," and so on. Thus they acknowledged in theory each others' parents as their own parents. Following this a feast brought the ceremony to a complete and successful end.

"Now that you are *ju hsuing ti* (如兄弟) (quasi-brothers)" old Mr. Wu advised the youngsters, "you must consider yourselves real brothers. As the old saying goes, *yu fan ta chia chih, yu tsueh ta chia shou* (有飯大家吃, 有罪大家受) (having rice all eat, having misfortune all share) and under no condition should you 'uproot the bundle of incense stick butts' "(Which colloquially indicates a breaking off of such an agreement.)

*　　*　　*

In the long run most sworn brothers "having rice all eat but having misfortune all do not share," for "laugh and the world laughs with you, weep and you weep alone," seems to be the rule and few bundles of incense butts, as it were, remain in the pot.

*　　*　　*

Early autumn is the season for another typical Peking fruit, the date, which is known as one of the three famous "D's" of Peking: dates, ducks and dust!

The Chinese dates are not really dates but jujubes as dates are, strictly speaking, the fruits of the famous Arabian date palms (*phoenix dactylifera*), the life line of so many native tribes of northern Africa and Asia Minor. The Chinese native jujubes, though surprisingly similar in flavour and texture and shape to the dates, are really the fruits of a member of the buckthorn family (genus *zizyphus*), growing on a tree as distinct from a palm as the willow or the elm in your courtyard.

There are a great many kinds of jujubes, each one distinguished from the rest by its shape and taste and all of them find a lasting place in the local markets throughout the month of September. There are the olive-shaped ones which are by far the commonest and therefore the most inexpensive variety, and the almost round ones known by the name of *ying lo tsao* (櫻絡棗) or "tassel knob jujubes", and the famous egg-shaped ones known by the name of *Lang Chia Yuan* (郎家園), or "Lang Family's Garden", which have gotten their name from a garden

The Chinese jujubes are of the backthorn family and do not grow on palms like their Arabian namesakes.

belonging to some people of this name situated some distance to the east of Peking.

The Langs' dates are still adjudged by jujube connoisseurs as the city's best though there is no way to prove it as the Langs do not sell their crop and so exactly what a "Lang Family's Garden" tastes like still remains a question mark. The egg-shaped jujubes obtainable in the markets which go by this name are by far the most delicious. There are also the "lotus seeds" and the "tiger's eyes" which are known for their sour taste, and the mountainous jujubes which are thick-skinned and taste-less and are sweetened to sell as a confection. The seedless jujubes which are not a native of this region complete the list.

The jujubes are not only eaten raw but are also used for making the jammy stuffings of many a Chinese pastry specialty, such as the famous moon-cakes. Preserved with a little *samshu* wine and therefore called *tsueh tsao* (醉棗), "intoxicated jujubes", they remain juicy and will keep for a long time.

The itinerant pedlars threading Peking's hutungs sell jujubes in conjunction with grapes as the latter appear in the market about the same time. Some of the latter are also given strange local names of which the most interesting should be "rabbit's dung", given to a small pearly variety which is seed-less and very sweet in taste. The highest mark for grapes goes to the "crystal grapes", in shape elongated like an American cucumber, and a wee bit less than two inches in length, jade green with a tinge of waxy yellow. These go most agreeably with iced Chinese yellow wine!

*   *   *

The Wus had some jujube trees in their backyard and exactly which kind of fruits they yielded is unknown. Little Wu and his schoolmates were often seen climbing to the upper branches to get the red ripe ones—an undertaking done without proper authority from his parents and grandparents whose idea about proper jujube-collecting was to stand beneath the trees and knock the fruits off with a long bamboo pole, a procedure decidedly too tame for the youngsters. Chinese "jujubing" is comparable to American "nutting", the more dangerously collected the better the fruits taste!

*   *   *

Speaking of "nutting" reminds one of chestnuts. Chestnuts are not grown within the city limits but Peking annually con-sumes tons of them. They are produced in the mountainous regions to the northwest. The Chinese, true to their epicurean reputation, have discovered that by roasting their chestnuts in black sand and pouring honey in the roasting pot during the process enhances the taste of the nuts and gives them a sweeten-ed flavour.

Schoolboys welcome the appearance of the season's new jujubes and nuts and enjoy listening to the long, shivering cries of the jujube-and-grape pedlars piercing the clear autumnal air of the season's first chilly evenings, or waiting for a catty of hot chestnuts while watching the roasting pot with the shiny brown chestnuts rolling up and down, "surfboard riding in the black current" with every movement of the stirring shovel.

The sagacious shopkeepers have found that roasting chestnuts in public is a good advertising stunt and means more sales besides affording bystanders a chance to see for themselves whose paws are used for pulling out the hot nuts!

But to the multitudinous poor Peking-*jen*, all these activities serve as a timely warning that it is time to pick out the proper ones from the many pawn-shop tickets at home, to start making arrangements to redeem their old padded jackets and see if, with some more patching, they will still do for another winter! Oh, for the life of poor Peking-*jen*!

THE COMING OF AUTUMN

ON the third day of the eighth lunar moon the birthday of the Chinese Kitchen God is celebrated.

The Kitchen God, or Tsao Wang Yeh (竈王爺), occupies an important position in the Chinese home as a liaison officer between the celestial regime and the resident observer of the activity of each family. His image, painted in multichrome, is seen in the kitchen of every Chinese home, almost always above or near the cooking stove as the Chinese name Tsao Wang actually means "King of the Stove."

The cooking stove unquestionably is considered the most important equipment in the home, as the prerequisite of a Chinese house running to schedule is that the pot be kept boiling and the advancement of family welfare follows and not precedes a full stomach. There is so far no indication of any drastic change

The Chinese Kitchen God is represented as a benevolent old gentleman but his sense of "Good" and "Evil" is not easily influenced as he registers the family's actions in two differently-marked jars.

in the formula before the Chinese learn to habitually "eat out" at the corner cafeteria. When the Chinese have learned to warm up their canned soups over an alcohol burner or an electric cooker the paper Kitchen God image will be pasted on such an appliance—there is no doubt about that.

The Chinese Kitchen God is an old deity, dating from about the same time as eating cooked foods originated in this country. Some say the Kitchen God is nobody but the Yellow Emperor himself who ruled China for 100 years beginning from 2697 B.C., and who invented the cooking stove. Still others identify him as Chu Jung (祝融), the God of Fire.

The Kitchen God is mentioned in the Confucian "Analects," too. One of his disciples asked the Sage why people would rather worship the god of his kitchen than the god of the Sacred Corner (Japanese *tokonoma*?). Confucius, for once in his sagely career, was outquestioned for his disjointed answer was: "Not so. He who offends against Heaven has none to whom he can pray!"

Tsao Wang Yeh, according to a T'ang Dynasty book, is a Mr. Chang, who had a wife and seven daughters in his immediate family circle. He, the legend says, was the head of a big Chinese family of many members in which were counted nine living generations, all living in one big-sized compound somewhere in Shantung. He managed the big family so well that there was scarcely a single quarrel in the house.   His feat of personality adjustment and harmonizing family relations was such a great success that even the many cats and dogs in the house ate together and would refuse to commence eating if one of their number was found to be absent from their midst.

, An emperor happened to be touring his kingdom and honoured the Chang family with a visit.   His Majesty was greatly impressed with the congenial atmosphere.   By imperial decree Chang was deified (!), after his death, to become the family or kitchen god.   He is represented as a very good-looking black-bearded gentleman with a red halo, who registers the good and evil thoughts and actions of the family to which he is accredited by slipping tokens into two jars marked *Shan* (善) for "Good" and *Ou* (惡) for "Evil" respectively.   All of these tokens are data from which his annual report to the Jade Emperor is prepared.   This is submitted in person to the high-ups, strictly confidential, at the New Year.

Mr. Chang's birthday was on the 3rd day of the 8th moon and so on this day he gets a special offering in the shape of a bowl of noodles, for using human practice as a premise the Chinese construe that it would be equally agreeable to the god to celebrate his birthday with a noodle feast!   The noodles are not served with stew in the typical Peking fashion or with soya sauce and bean sprouts like the famous "chow mien" in your old chop suey joint but are only relished with some sugar.   Whether this was originally intended as a false pretense in order to impress the god with an affected virtue of family frugality or because Mr. Chang had a sweet tooth nobody can tell.   It has been done this way in the past and is done this way now.

*   *   *

Outside Hata Men on the bustling Flower Street is a temple dedicated to the Kitchen God where a fair is held annually on the god's birthday and neighbourhood residents flock there to burn incense and do obeisance before the god's image.

Unfortunately, Little Wu's plan to make an excursion there to see the *jen nao* (熱鬧) or "busy sight" was frustrated for his school apparently did not take note of the day's importance whereas in the private school of Mr. Yung such an occasion would be a good reason for taking a day off from school work.

*   *

At the beginning of the eighth Lunar moon Peking's summer has taken French leave and the autumn has duly come in to stay. The Almanac says it is the season of the White Dew and of the Autumn Equinox and ere long it will be Cold Dew, until Frost-Fall rolls along and ushers in the long dreary winter. The season is described in the preamble to a popular Chinese song:

> "In the eighth moon, the autumnal wind gets
>   colder and colder with each gust,
> And a day of cold dews is followed by another of
>   frost.
> The cruel frost, as if intentionally, strikes first
>   at the rootless grass,
> And the grasshoppers lay their eggs beneath the
>   maturing buckwheat plants."

The mercury makes a few phenomenal high jumps daily for the mid-day is still warm but the blue autumnal sky is easily covered with thin but evenly spread formations of grey clouds and persistent "goose-feather" rains convert the narrow dusty hutungs of Peking to quagmires so thoroughly saturated and so churned by the feet of pedestrians and rickshaw traffic that picking your way through them is like walking in a dish of photographer's paste! All looks entirely too disheartening and when you think of the poor Peking working people who will be kept indoors from their labours, you may say to yourself, "If the drizzling rain continues another day, well, it will be just too bad"!

Which conception is all right and yet all wrong. For behind the tightly latched and weather-beaten door of a tenant house where an all-weather hero's, the rickshaw man's, family is quartered in one tiny room, the members uncomplainingly pursue their happiness while trying to help matters by earning a few coppers by pasting match-boxes together or finishing machine-made socks. The big sister takes care of the little brother while her overstrained eyes follow the tiny needle in her deft fingers in the dark room made darker than usual by the "weather".

The big brother does not work much for on him the family pin their hopes of a brighter future. The family has managed to put him in school and after he has been to the shop to purchase and bring back the evening's supply of corn-flour or corn-meal, two full catties of the precious stuff in a little old newspaper bag, his day's labour is done and sitting Japanese fashion close to the little glass-paned window, size roughly twelve by sixteen inches, he bends almost double over a small k'ang table (known to foreigners as a "chow bench") and concentrates on his penmanship exercises.

Mother has just made the wo-wo-t'ou (窩窩頭), sarcastically called by those who do not know how good they taste the huang chin t'ah, (黃金塔) "yellow golden pagoda", or conical-shaped corn-flour cakes with a big hole beneath to insure quicker and more thorough steaming. When the neighbour's time-worn alarm clock strikes seven the food is ready, for it takes approximately an hour to cook it and fully that long for the steaming utensil is made of bamboo and matting and is not without some leaky spots through which the heat escapes. Besides, as their year-round experience has taught, wo-wo-t'ou "rarely-done" are never as palatable as when they are "well-done"!

The rickshawman's wife has just bought a few coppers' worth of ch'ou-to-fu (臭豆腐), or "stinky bean curds", little flat cubes hardly two inches square of regular bean curds salted and fermented, actually very disagreeable in odour, which go in team with Chinese raw onions. This delicacy, which makes its appearance in early autumn decidedly of and for the poor, is sold at the house door by little pedlars about as poor as the rickshawman's family. They make a 10% commission retailing the cubes in a small jar carried in a basket hanging from the elbow. The pedlar also sells as a side-line the salty pickled hsiao ts'ai (小菜), or "small vegetable", a mixture of bits of string beans and celery, green hot peppers and p'ei-la (苤蘭), or kohlrabi, cut into diamond-shaped chips, heavily salted, to which a dash of shrimp-sauce oil has been added. All these will be so tasty to eat with hot, gold-yellow *wo-wo-t'ou* particularly if made from the year's fresh corn, served piping hot direct from the steaming utensil where they are kept warm for some time with the residual heat even after they have been taken off the little stove. The stove has a story to tell, too, for the muddy body is built inside a salvaged 5-gallon tin that has carried oil for the lamps of China from distant America.

Father will be back soon as his physique although still "can do" would never stand a prolonged evening's work in this kind of weather without having to take a forced holiday recuperating afterward and father just must not take a holiday. He will be happy to be back in the little warm room after returning in good shape the vehicle he rents from the rich rickshaw company, and after paying fairly and squarely the day's rickshaw rent, he will still have fifty, sixty, seventy cents left, perhaps a dollar who knows! He needs more calories and vitamins than the other members of his family and so mother has bought for him twenty coppers' worth of cooked *yang-t'ou-jo* (羊頭肉). "meat from a sheep's head", as part of his fare from the itinerant specialist. This is his hard-earned privilege which only the eldest son will share with the father as he, studying so hard, needs some good nourishment also.

The rickshawman's home was but a few doors away from Little Wu's home and his son studied in the same public school as Little Wu. It is characteristic of Peking that the homes of the rich and the poor are not separated by deliberate demarcations and a rich man may have a poor man living next door.

*   *   *

As the cool western winds herald the advent of autumn, river crabs make their annual debut in the Peking market and are a welcome contribution to the long list of seasonal morsels for the Peking gourmet. To these, autumn is the logical time to bring their energy up to a new high standard as it has been seriously impaired during the hot summer when lighter foods have been a rule rather than an exception. Such a nutrimental rehabilitation is indeed a source of joy and delight, with new and tasty effectives to boost up the variety.

The Chinese river crabs have a more spherical body to distinguish them from their maritime cousins. On the under side of the body may be seen, folded back, a part of the degenerated abdomen and appendages covered with a jointed shell. By the shape of this jointed shell covering the abdomen, erroneous-

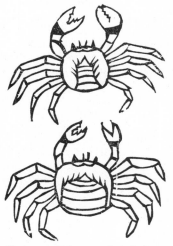

The rounded or pointed shape of the abdominal shell of the river crabs reveal their sex. The males also have bigger pincer claws than the females.

ly known by the Chinese to be their *ch'i* (臍), or "navel", the sexes can be easily distinguished as the abdomen of the female is a great deal larger and is rounded while that of the male is smaller and rather pointed. The average Peking-*jen* is not a born biologist and so it would never, upon my honour, have been his habit to examine these abdominal differentiations were it not for the fact that it represents a reason for his selection, for the males called the "pointed navel" ones, though they have more massive "pincer claws" and richer meats in them, are never so welcome as the female or "rounded navel" ones with their large chunk of yellow substance (eggs?) encased in the body, so tasty and much sought after. This is called the "crab yellow" and a dish of "crab yellow" is twice the price of a dish of mere crab meat at the restaurant.

The river crabs in the Peking market are advertised under the slogan of "Big Crabs from Shengfang", referring to a busy water-town in the Wen-an district to the southwest of Tientsin. The crabs are supposed to fatten on ripening rice and Shengfang and its vicinity are the only places in North China where rice to any appreciable quantity is cultivated. That crabs live on rice may be as true as it is false until it can be established with scientific support for biology teaches that they are scavengers and "live on small living organisms crushed in their huge claws."

The crab crop is ready to harvest when rice is. The way to catch river crabs is easy and all that is required is to hang a little lamp on the bank of rice paddies. The crabs, attracted by the light and probably thinking it an interesting change from the pitch dark nights in their cave-dwellings in the rice fields, make a crosswise dash, crab-fashion, to the shore *en masse*. The men, waiting on land have only to pick them up one by one as a child would gather pebbles on the sea shore and each wicker container is soon full. Then a fast mule cart caravan, nowadays a fast freight train, whisks them packed solid in matting baskets to the big cities. The crabs are a sort of amphibian and have a marvellous reserve energy for keeping alive without food and drink, for not only can they subsist on their inner savings but they also find spare water which they blow out continually in masses of bubbles with which they supposedly kill their idle moments en route.

The way to cook river crabs is as simple as A.B.C. and consists of steaming them alive in the famous *lung t'i* (籠屜), steaming case, found in every rich or poor kitchen alike. The steaming is preceded by a bath in clean water which is more or less a luxury and a surprise to the crabs. The crabs, after being deposited in the steaming case, will crawl about in the company of their "fellow passengers to the graves," until the heat rising from the basement makes it more and more uncomfortable for them. With a strange feeling, never experienced before, their former green shells are now converted into a pretty shade of orange.

The feast begins by shelling the crabs and segregating the meat, relished with a little vinegar and some ginger chopped super-fine. No other ingredients are necessary as the considerate crabs have already seasoned their meats to a tasteful perfec-

tion which humans can hardly add to or lessen. Culinary refinements are certainly quite superficial in so far as doing full justice to crab meat is concerned.

This is the way crab feasts are conducted in the average Peking family where only a kitchen roller and a knife assist the
fingers in the "carving" of the meat, But in the fashionable
down-town restaurants outside Chien Men, where the Wus sometimes entertained their friends, Little Bald Head remembered the
restaurants supply a number of classy utensils such as a midget
hardwood hammer and anvil set for cracking the pincer claws
and legs and silver-tipped chopsticks and silver spoons to test
the presence or otherwise of suspected crab poison, and a small
finger bowl with tea leaves and chrysanthemum petals for de-
odorizing the fingers afterwards.

*　　*　　*

About the time river crabs appear on the Peking market, the
season for the year's best mutton is also at hand.

Mutton to be of the best has to come off the bodies of the
Hsi K'uo T'a Yang (西口大羊), "Big Sheep from the Western
Pass", as the mutton shop sign indicates. The "Western Pass"
is Kalgan as relative to *Tung K'uo* (東口) the "Eastern Pass" by
which is known the Jehol and Kupeikow route. With the advent
of cooler weather, the sheep-dealers close their sizable deals of
live sheep with the Mongolian ranchers in the grasslands beyond the mountainous regions where the nomadic Mongols count
part of their wealth by so many flocks of sheep. Forthwith the
sheep are entrusted to the transportation organizations who
undertake to deliver them two hundred miles or so to the Sheep
Market about a mile north of Peking's Teh Sheng Men, one of the
northern gates.

Expert herdsmen are contracted to escort the living cargo
which travels the entire route on foot and part of their duty it is
to see that the sheep fatten on the way on the tender green
grass and drink water from the clear mountain streams. A proper
amount of exercise is taken care of by just so much leisurely
travelling every day but without losing time en route so that
they arrive in A-I shape and weight and with the guaranteed
fine meaty body but minus excessive fat and with a clean, fluffy,
heavy-bodied sheepskin to boot.

It is understood that these sheep will give the best mutton
with the faintest trace or no trace at all of the offensive
"muttonish" flavour. When these sheep arrive on schedule,
not only are the herdsmen glad for their accomplishment and
the money earned, but the mutton sellers themselves are also
happy for all summer their business has been conducted in a
restricted manner, suffering from adverse merchandising conditions as well as poor "appetites" on the part of the consumers.

The sheep and mutton business of Peking and indeed of the entire country is in the hands of Mohammedans as if it represented a
special concession granted to their race which quite likely is
the case. But one way or the other the fact remains that they
still monopolize the mutton situation and will continue to do
so indefinitely. The Mohammedans are known to be a clean people

as their always cleanly scrubbed counters and the equipment of
their mutton shops bear witness.

Modern concentrated slaughter-house projects were introduced in Peking only in recent years and with their establishment there vanished from Peking streets the pathetic but picturesque sights of sheep butchery seen for so many past centuries.
In Peking, people say, anyone standing at a busy street corner
and gazing intently at the sky for a few minutes will soon and
with certainty attract a group of passers-by who will forget all
about their business (if they have any) and stop and gaze into
space in order to see what the first person sees. The urge for
watching something spectacular or getting fun out of seeing
everyday happenings is an inherited instinct in the average
Peking-*jen*. Such being the case, it is no wonder if idlers on their
morning walks and children (like Wu, the Little Bald Head) on
the way to school will stop for a few minutes and form a small
crowd around sheep-slaughtering in front of a mutton shop where
a life-and-death pantomime is enacted free for the public's enjoyment.

The mutton-shop proprietors have discovered long ago that
their business, to be profitably conducted, must be housed under
one roof and the maximum amount of profit is assured only to
those who do their own manufacturing from raw materials to
finished products. And so only the very small mutton shops get
their daily stock in halves and quarters from a bigger establishment. In this respect mutton differs from the pork trade in
which the sellers are never the killers.

But because of religious considerations the mutton shop
managers are not allowed to do the killing themselves. This is
done by a number of Islamic priests who make the daily rounds of
the mutton shops and do the killing for a fee, so much money for
each sheep killed. The money thus earned is used for certain
religiously permissible purposes as the Islamic people are not
given to wanton killing and they kill the sheep, so to speak, with
strong regret. Before applying the sharp knife to the neck of a
meek, bleating sheep, tied "four-legs-in-one," the priest murmurs
a prayer and blesses the soul of the sheep with a solemn and
serious air decidedly bespeaking of no encouragement to the
"unkind" practice.

The killing done, the priest wipes his knife and sheathing it
makes off for another engagement and still another until his
day's work is finished, sticking a voucher at every place for
services rendered and leaving the sheep bleeding to death into a
wooden tub with their sheepish eyes turning quickly from a clear
brown to emerald green.

After the ceremony is completed the shop assistants will step
forward to skin the sheep and hang it on shiny brass hooks,
polished to a Brasso brilliance, where they cut up the body and
put the pieces on the counters ready for sale still warm and
trembling!

As the morning sun ascends, the richer Peking-*jen*, some sending their cooks, will come for their "legs of mutton." Poorer people will come for their dime or quarter's worth, and so forth,
while the bird fanciers, slowly and leisurely, their pets carried on
a perching stick or in a cage, call in turn for their three coppers'

worth of "tender and lean" for their warblers.

*   *   *

Peking's mutton in autumn and winter is about the very best there ever can be and there are a good many characteristic ways to cook this meat. The most interesting ways are more or less of nomadic origin. One of these is by open-air roasting, popularly known as *K'ao Yang Jo* (烤羊肉). Roasting mutton in this fashion is known in the Japanese language as *chinjisuhan nabe* or "cooker of the Great Ghenghis Khan", a picturesque name that bespeaks its decidedly Mongolis origin. In a way it is the privilege of the northern people to enjoy roast mutton for not only is the fare disagreeable to the usually delicate digestive organs of the southerners but even the mutton itself changes its flavour in the south. Roast mutton is such a popular dish that it enjoys equal patronage with the delicious river crabs which two, as the season's "double specials", are featured side by side in all of Peking's restaurants, particularly in the Mohammedan establishments.

There are for "the men in the street" also wayside roast mutton places where the roasting is done in full public view with the cooking handled by each customer himself. Standing in a typical pose, with one leg resting by "knee action" on the bench set beside the table where the roasting outfit is mounted, your Peking-*jen*, a funnel-shaped wine flask in the left hand, roasts his mutton in single slices on the red-hot "grill" sizzling with the hot grease drippling into the fire beneath. The mutton slices are held by extra-long chopsticks, eighteen or twenty inches in length, an invention that has been born from necessity. Like eating Japanese *sukiyaki*, it is never proper to have your roast mutton brought to you in a platter to the table for part of the fun is in handling the stuff and watching the pinkish meat turn into a juicy mouthful. Any other way would be too tame in the desired effect.

*   *   *

A day had been fixed for the Wus to have their grilled mutton feast for although not an expensive business the average Peking family do not get it more than three or four times each season for it represents a lot of trouble in preparation.

The proper location for the feast was found in the center of the courtyard for it was to be a smoky affair and would be impossible indoors. Even in the open air the family's flower pots had to be temporarily moved away particularly old Mrs. Wu's favourite begonias. A small pit was dug in the ground about ten inches deep after lifting temporarily a few pieces of bricks from the pavement. The iron "grill" a rounded framework of flattened cast-iron bars, each about half an inch wide and bolted about a quarter of an inch apart, was brought out from the storeroom in the back-yard. It had not been used for more than six months and the maidservant spent a solid hour polishing it with a piece of new brick until it became reasonably shiny and clean. Another piece of the "detachable stove" was also brought out and forthwith the roasting equipment was set up in three minutes ready for immediate service.

It was old Mrs. Wu's pleasure to purchase the proper ingredients for the feast and the onions and other vegetables were soon prepared. The ingredients included also the indispensable soya sauce and a special concoction of sugar-cured garlic and some shrimp-sauce oil which most of the family liked for the delicate sea-food flavour it gave to the meat. The dressing was individually mixed to suit each person's taste and the meat was thoroughly soaked in it before the roasting process. Mutton from the hind legs, solid but tender meat of fine, juicy histological construction, was ordered the day before and delivered in the morning. The slicing was performed by the skillful hands of young Mrs. Wu who laboured half the morning for the Wus had found that while the mutton shops would offer to do the slicing at no extra charge yet it was not always desirable to let them do so for the shop assistants to demonstrate their skill would often slice over-thin with the result that the meat often charred in the hands of the amateurish chefs during the fire-side adventure.

Everything was ready when scholar Wu came back from school hungry as a wolf. The feast then started in full earnest. The family sat around a low table set on the ground, surrounded by little flat stools to insure comfort and easy accessibility to the "spits". The fire underneath was fed with specially selected pine cones brought from Madame Ho's country estate. Pine wood is always used for this purpose for its alleged flavour-improving properties. After the red hot iron "spits" had been smeared with mutton fat, the roasting started as the flames darted about and smoke whirled skyward like a miniature volcano in eruption. For an hour or so, watering mouths and burned fingers were the fashion!

There was meat enough for everybody and so no other food was prepared except some sesamum cakes and "ox-tongues" (a sort of oval Chinese hot roll) bought from the corner "bakery". Old Mr. Wu, of course, had his flask.

THE MID-AUTUMN FESTIVAL

THE eighth Lunar moon is the happiest month for China's immense agricultural population as the year's most important crops are harvested at this time. A stroll in the countryside will reveal scenes of the contentment of those who live on the good earth, where the simple rhythm of the flail resounding on the hard-surfaced threshing floor and the creak of the stone roller-mill operated by blind-folded donkey power mingle with the farmer's song in praise of a year's assured livelihood.

The Mid-Autumn Festival, the fifteenth of the eighth moon, is usually accompanied by fine weather for at this time the moon shines brightest, the sky is clear and often free from all atmospheric interferences. Gathering under the moonlight it is often the family's pleasure to recount legends about the moon and its imaginary inhabitants. Such mythical stories based no doubt on the black spots on the "face" of the moon are legion. One such is the one about the beautiful Ch'ang-O (嫦娥) who fled to the moon, a favourite Chinese fairy tale enacted on the stage by all theatrical companies during the mid-autumn festival period under the name of "Ch'ang-O Pen Yueh" (嫦娥奔月).

In the early days of the creation of the Universe, the story goes, there were ten suns—one genuine and nine false. A famous bow-and-arrow sharpshooter by the name of Ho Yi (后羿) was responsible for shooting off the false ones and for this meritorious feat he was given in marriage the hand of the daughter of Ho Po, the River God, a beautiful young lady by the name of Ch'ang-O.

Now Ho Yi was merely a "terrestrial being" and so craved for immortality. The Western Queen Mother very kindly gave him a pill of elixir and told him to take it in order to realize his ambition after fasting for a certain period of time. In the meanwhile he put away the pill high up on the house beam and proceeded to get himself in shape for the important transformation.

Ho Yi, like all faithful husbands, probably made no secret of the matter to his pretty wife and told her all about his scheme. His wife, apprehensive of the possibility of being left behind by an immortalized husband, became restless and hit upon a timely counter-measure. While her husband was looking in another direction she reached to the house beam and snatching the pill swallowed it before her husband noticed what had taken place.

After swallowing the pill (a bitter pill?) she found that her body became as light as vapour and like a toy-balloon with the cord cut she began to float skyward. Her husband, waking up too late to his wife's mischief, tried to run after her but she made a dash for the moon where far beyond the radius of her husband's fine archery, Ch'ang-O became an immortal all right but her solitary life was predestined and could not be helped.

Another story concerns the scholar Wu Kang (吳剛), a sophomore majoring in Immortalogy in the college of the fairies (for that was practically what Wu was, according to popular legend). Wu Kang was found guilty of certain "mistakes" and so by order of the administrative committee of the college was sent to the Moon where he was told to cut down a big cassia tree to be found there. Wu Kang has ever since been whacking away energetically at the cassia tree and should still be doing so today as the tree is a magic one and has the peculiar faculty of healing every axe-wound as soon as it is made. Wu Kang has not awakened to the fact yet that the faulty sophomore's work is never to be finished!

Emperor Ming Hwang of the T'ang Dynasty paid a visit to the moon accompanied by a Taoist priest and was taken to meet again his favourite concubine, Yang Kwei-fei, forced to hang herself in compliance to the demand made by a mutinous battalion of the emperor's bodyguards who refused to accord the fleeing court protection unless the death penalty be meted out to the woman who had been the cause of all the nation's troubles. Emperor Ming Hwang was able to return to his capital intact to live out the balance of his life lamenting the sad fate of his late sweetheart, a victim of circumstances. The Taoist priest was able to establish contact and arrange the sensational reunion with the parted soul resident in the Palace of Kwang Han Kung (廣寒宮) in the Lunar paradise.

*   *   *

In the primitive folklore of Chinese history heaven and earth were one and it was up to a mythical personage, known as P'an Ku Shih (盤古氏) to create the world by chiseling apart heaven and earth. P'an Ku Shih, it is said, came out of the combination heaven and earth in the manner of a small chick from an egg shell. He lived to be eighteen thousand years old and when he died his limbs became high mountains. His left eye became the sun and the right eye the moon.

Another story says that in the sun is a three-legged crow. The three-legged crow became a "golden rooster" and the story became ameliorated with the handing down from generation to generation. The sun god is worshipped on the second day of the second moon, the typical offering being a group of round, flat, rice-flour cakes, each one smaller than the other, set like a midget tower in a dish and surmounted by a rooster made of coloured dough. But the moon contains something else, a rabbit, a white rabbit, nay, a jade rabbit, represented as standing on its hind legs and engaged in pounding the famous medicine of long life, the elixir of immortality, with a jade pestle held in the front legs and a jade mortar. Whatever is made of stone or marble in this world is made of jade in the "moonland". Jade must be dirt cheap up there.

Although there might be a moon paradise and moon palaces and beautiful Ch'ang-O and romantic Yang Kwei-fei, "the most famous beauty of China", living in the moon, the lot of the Jade Rabbit must be very monotonous and none-too-enjoyable for it is no fun standing all year long and pestling in the one-man apothecary as he is represented doing in Chinese mythology.

The Jade Rabbit, in the peculiar Chinese way of deification, has also taken on the status of a god—a Rabbit God—T'u-erh Yeh (兔兒爺) in Chinese. The Chinese Rabbit God is a favourite

Clever craftsmen in Peking elaborate on the Rabbit God images which, as toys, sell at fancy prizes when in season. The one depicted here is a version of the "hundred baby" motif.

toy (!) in the minds of youngsters and appears punctually on the market shelves immediately the lotus lanterns beat a hasty retreat after the ghost festival. And while they last, until the fifteenth day of the eighth moon, they command fancy prices. Elaborate ones have an empty mud body all hand-painted in gaudy colours and profusely gilded, fully three feet high with the typical rabbit-lip and two big ears sticking up as if the sound of a hunter's threatening rifle has just been heard! In most cases the clever craftsmen have fashioned the bases of the rabbit gods with various typical designs and scenes, or portrayed the god as riding on a horse, a camel, an unicorn or a donkey.

The rabbit gods look very amusing and are often seen clad in fighting robes and armour which give them a sort of dignified air contrasting diagonall y with their playful countenance as clothes not only make the men but also make the rabbit gods. Rich people buy them for their children or as "exchange presents" for their equally high-born friends. But except in a very few cases mostly with the copper-a-piece varieties catering to deflated purses and niggardly spenders, they are unanimously represented as holding their all-important pestles as if labour is really holy and work a constant joy to them.

The youngsters (from amongst whom our hero Wu had already graduated) make mimicry worshipping ceremonies and from the same people who sell the rabbit gods they also get miniature temple altar paraphernalia, such as a diminutive incense burner and a pair of lilliputian candlesticks. A set of little dishes containing some peanuts and things, children's own titbits, as offerings complete the "properties" at the altar where children mockingly kowtow to the image.

The hare in the moon is a famous legend well-known in Buddhist lands such as India and Tibet where the hare is symbolic of great self-sacrifice. The hare presented his own body to a hungry pilgrim in contrast to other animals like the jackal and the otter, who presented their day's catch. The hungry pilgrim was a transformation of Buddha himself who greatly approved the hare's way of doing things and forthwith gave it a coveted place in the moon.

If proper trails are followed in rabbit god research, the Chinese *T'u-erh Yeh* might be found to be originally "made in India".

*   *   *

The Mid-Autumn Festival is the time for moon-cakes as it comes exactly a hundred days after the Dragon Boat Festival of the *tsung-tse*, boiled rice cakes wrapped in reed leaves. The moon-cakes are of different kinds and even more popular than the rice cakes.

In the interior districts of China

The family moon-cake, weighing many pounds, serves a special purpose. The famous rabbit design decorates the big cake. Under the famous cassia tree facing the Kwang Han Kung Palace, it stands and labours energetically, "keeping its nose to the mortar stone."

frugal housewives make their own moon-cakes, using common yeast dough and white or black sugar filling, steamed in the same way as the familiar *man-to*. But in Peking, where everything is elaborated and extravagantly represented, the moon-cakes are of different kinds. Fundamentally they are divided into two main classes: the *su* (素), or vegetarian, kind and the *hun* (暈), or "meaty", variety, the former being prepared with sesame oil and the latter with lard, both mixed into the dough itself.

It is on account of this main difference that the original Peking moon-cakes are known by the names of *tse-lai-hung* (自來紅), or "naturally-red", and *tse-lai-pai* (自來白), or "naturally white", respectively whereas the "white ones" are the original colour of the flour, the "red ones" are a sort of greasy brown colour and on the top a reddish circle is always put as a marking. In the same way as B.V.D. for underwears and Victrola for a talking machine, Peking's moon-cakes have come to be known as "naturally white" and "naturally red", which terms have to a great extent overshadowed the name of "moon-cakes", more prominently so across the pastry shop counter.

Other names given to special makes of moon-cakes are the *Fan Mao* (翻毛), or "Upturned Feather", no doubt referring to the brittle, thin, multi-layered "crust" produced by a delicate technique in the baking process. Then there is the *T'i Chiang* (提漿), or "Extracted Juice", kind made with the minimum of water contents in the cakes so that they take on the flavour of foreign biscuits. Of all moon-cakes, experience will tell that the "Upturned Feather" with nuts-and-honey stuffing are by far the most delicious, being unfortunately also the most expensive.

China is a big country and so the baking of moon-cakes has

become variously tinted with locative characteristics but in Peking, the "melting pot" of people from all regions, there are obtainable the Shansi moon-cake, the Tientsin moon-cake, the Szechuan moon-cake. . .clear across the country to the Canton moon-cake. Each of these kinds has its typical shape and texture as different from each other as the dialects spoken by the people of the various regions. As to the fillings, they may be counted from the commonplace white and crystal sugar, jujube jam, mashed peas, mashed black beans, *Shan-ch'a* (山查) (solidified jelly made of sugared haws), salt and sugar, to chips of turnips, bits of ham, and indeed coconut meat. Moon-cake prices range from a-cent-a-piece to half a dollar a piece.

Beginning from the day on which the red posters of moon-cakes sales are pasted on the shop fronts, the average Peking-*jen* calls at the pastry stores and loads up with the stuff for his family "cookie jar" where he draws from occasionally as moon-cakes are made to keep for a reasonable length of time. Peking moon-cakes are really quite good to eat and not merely to gloat over—an impression absorbed by many a foreign resident on account of their seemingly indigestible appearance.

The Wus, following the tradition of the family as of all Peking families, annually also bought their big moon-cakes for sacrificial purposes. These are known by the name of *T'uan Yuang Ping* (團圓餅), or the "Cake of Happy Reunion", and are to be offered to the moon in a picturesque ceremony. *T'uan Yuang Ping* are invariably of the *su*, vegetarian, variety, weighing from half a catty to five catties or more each to meet the requirements corresponding to the size of the various families, for no matter how many members are in a family but one such cake is permissible. Such a cake is later divided into as many slices as there are members in the family who join in "eating the big cake" as a good omen for the unification of the house. To add a seasonal touch the likeness of the rabbit god pounding the famous elixir in the moon is always moulded onto such a cake as a fitting and proper decoration.

*   *   *

Being one of the three important gift-sending seasons in the year, the Mid-Autumn Festival is looked forward to with very much enthusiasm by the various shops specializing in the gift trade. Chinese gift senders, barring special cases, add an intimate touch to their considerateness and resort to sending various kinds of food, known by the name of *kuan-li* (官禮), "legitimate gifts" or *shui li* (水禮), "water gifts", in opposite to *kan li* (乾禮), "dry gifts", meaning sending a sum of money. This system of sending food has incidentally saved a lot of headaches for late shoppers in trying to show personal good taste or "rugged individuality" in gift selections. The autumn season is also marked by an abundance of attractive foods with new supplies of fruits and things shipped to the big cities from the various producing centers.

The average Chinese gift shopper prepares no list before setting out on his gift hunt and the "sets" of gifts are quickly assembled in the shopping districts where the store attendants make most of the decisions on behalf of their customers. A "set" of gifts may contain two, four or six items of things and the sender may easily be confident of at least one item among them to please the recipients—if Mr. Chang does not like Chinese preserved duck, he probably will appreciate the fruits. Mr. Li does not smoke but his tobacco-conscious wife will adore the "Three Castles", but Mr. Li does drink a little so the "Bamboo Leaf Green" will make him smack his lips in approbation and his children will like the moon-cakes.

But the biggest troops of shoppers with loosened purse strings whether preparing for gift-sending or shopping "for domestic consumption" invariably make for the fruit markets.

The principal wholesale fruit markets in Peking are two in number and are located respectively one outside Chien Men close by the "Market Street" and "Central Avenue" and the other inside Teh Sheng Men in the North City. The latter originally was founded there to accommodate the fruit growers from the Northern and Western Hills. These are noisy and interesting places during the festival days for the orchard owners, to command better prices, have so timed the picking of their fruits that the majority of the crops arrive in Peking just in time for the most lucrative prospects in distribution. Here may be seen the rustically dressed country-gentlemen with long trains of pack animals, donkeys, horses, mules, each loaded to capacity with baskets heavily and solidly packed with familiar local fruits. Others bring their goods to the city in mule carts or on wheel-barrows. The tall and dignified camels are also to be seen for they convey the grapes and persimmons from distant regions. These squat down at the order of the camel-drivers to have their heavy baskets taken off their backs, each basket being handled by two husky, sinewy coolies.

It is very hard to out-manoeuvre the fruit brokers at the market for they form the brain trust of the rural growers who depend upon them to get the day's best prices for their produce. As a link between the sagacious fruiterers purchasing their stock and the growers who have been cheated often enough to trust no new faces they are indispensable. The shrewd fruit brokers meet every mule caravan or camel train and ask for a verbal manifest of their cargo while renewing an old friendship, and will then take the owners to their establishments where they will be made at home, and their animals will be made at home, too. Then with an expert glance they will judge each for himself whether the merchandise is good enough for A or only good enough for B, and in a jiffy, a "little bird" brings the message to the prospective customer who comes for a brief inspection and after exchanging opinions whispered back and forth the deal is closed.

The service costs the buyer a ten per cent commission (no more, no less) and the sellers pay nothing with the good offices of an appraiser and weighmaster thrown in for only a "yours truly", for it is clearly understood that as a Chinese saying goes, "the wool comes off the back of the sheep" and all the terms of the contracts have been reduced to almost nothing. In the days of the old Octroi when anything sold in the Peking market paid a tax of three per cent, called the Hatamen Tax (because the tax office was situated near this famous Peking gate), the fruit brokers were also tax-brokers and they operated on licenses obtained by competitive arrangements, paying a lump sum of so much for the year's tax on peanuts, haws, and so forth, then collecting the legalized three per cent, from the trade with the surplus over their outlay as their own profit. (This is a typical example of Chinese bureaucracy since time immemorial.) The wholesale markets conduct their business in the early mornings but on the days preceding the Festival, they work all day and all night, the trade being so tremendous.

It was here that the youthful scholar of the Wu family, taking advantage of a school holiday in the company of his grandparents, baskets in hand, loaded up with luxurious fruits, for although some gift baskets had been received they wanted certain special kinds for their moon sacrifice. Combining business with pleasure, they found it an interesting pilgrimage to attend the fruit market.

* * *

The Mid-Autumn Festival is the second important settlement period in the year. There are three such periods which, as safety valves for the otherwise unrestricted credit extended all along, are considered of great significance in the economic life of the country. To hasten operations to meet obligations and the various technicalities directly or indirectly connected with such schemes, men are kept busy for weeks ahead and their energies and resources taxed to the limit but in the home women and children are seen keyed up for nothing but enjoyments and pleasantries, a veritable heaven for the tired husband or father after battling the "high seas".

For in the minds of Chinese women, this is the *T'uan Yuan Chieh* (團圓節), or the "Festival of Reunions". These two words, *T'uan* and *Yuan* are somewhat synonymous, both meaning "round". The full moon of Mid-Autumn is round and symbolizes a happy, complete family "circle", and to keep a family "circle" round, that is without sad partings and unwarranted absences of members, is a woman's duty, her cherished desire and fond hope. Hence to her is assigned the task of the day's celebration and ceremonial undertakings.

To avoid discouraging the moon worshippers, the day must be as fine as the Weatherman can make it, for much of the enthusiasm is dampened, the preparations wasted and the joy killed if it proves to be a cloudy or rainy night. Weather permitting, the Chinese family would cheerfully watch for the clear bright moon, three or four times the ordinary size (the Harvest Moon, in other words) rising bashfully and silently from under the eastern horizon as preparations are made for the moon rites, whereas foul weather will spoil everything. Besides, the Chinese believe that if the moon is obscured at the Mid-Autumn Festival, exactly five months later snowflakes will "strike the lanterns," at the New Year lantern festivities.

A simple religious ceremony is conducted in the Peking family in honour of the moon. This is held in the open courtyard, the proper time being when the moon has skimmed over the tree top skyline and assumed a suitable position so that the altar table can be set at a vantage point. On one side of the altar table is fastened a special paper effigy of the moon, called *Yueh Kwang Ma-erh* (月光禡兒), or "Moonlight Nimbus", a bizarrely-coloured affair some two feet wide and four feet high, with the moon rabbit occupying the position of the *primus inter pares* surrounded and superimposed with the various deities and Buddhisatvas. Such an effigy is obtainable during the season at the corner grocery store. Mounted on a framework of corn stalks, it is easily fastened to the table.

On the table are spread the familiar candlesticks and incense burners and various paper offerings. The big family moon-cake is put on a platter and placed nearest to the effigy, while five other plates hold five kinds of fruits—the proper varieties being pears, apples, pomegranates, persimmons and grapes, all the best, biggest and most unblemished ones obtainable. Some families would also require that stems of red cockscomb blossoms be used as an offering as also branches of beanstalks complete with the green, hairy soya beans. Cockscomb is called a *Kuan* (冠) in Chinese, which has the same sound as the word for "officialdom", hence the flower is a good omen. As to the beans, what rabbits do not love beans? Still other families would further expand the idea to cover everything in the vegetable kingdom as suitable offerings for the moon rabbit, and so turnips, cabbages, radishes, in fact everything, find a place on the altar, giving the overladen table the general appearance of a Thanksgiving display or a farm product exhibition.

The paper nimbus of the Rabbit God is mounted on a corn-stalk frame and is obtainable from grocery stores for the annual Mid-Autumn sacrifice to the moon. Above the moon disc are the tandem Gods of Wealth before whom are seen the silver bullion and the flaming pearl.

There are some superstitions too. For instance, if a water melon is used as an offering it must be cut with a saw-tooth edge and carved in the shape of a lotus flower, as a cut-up melon suggests "partition" and as such is a self-defeating, anti-climactic addition directly opposite to the original central theme of the ceremony.

At the Wu family's moon sacrifice, old Mrs. Wu officiated, ably assisted by her daughter-in-law. Even Little Bald Head

was obliged to watch the sight from indoors. Worshipping the
moon is a job for the fair sex alone. A Chinese saying goes:
"Men do not worship the moon; women, not the Kitchen God".

*   *   *

When young and ambitious Mr. Wu, father of our hero
Little Bald Head, was able to leave his work later than usual
and pulled away from his office on the day of the Mid-Autumn
Festival it was late in the evening. A fast rickshaw brought
him to his home and hearth at the Donkey Mart. He had allowed himself to be starved a little in order to attend the festival
feast of Happy Reunion in the home to which he had keenly
looked forward; he knew his family would be anxiously awaiting
his return.

It was a superb night and the round moon, with a broad
smile like that of a Santa Claus, shone proudly on the family
gathering at the big feasting table which an hour ago had been
the altar of moon sacrifice. The entire family sat around the
table on which were spread delicious dishes cooked by the
skilled family chefs, the mother and grandmother, and bowls
holding lustrous fruits. Wine was freely enjoyed, even the
little youngster had his cup of rose-liqueur!

So the feast went on merrily.

"Let us have some music," suggested the grandfather, "and
sing me, Little Bald Head, that Autumn Night Song you learned
so well at school."

The child rose and sang while his father, bringing out his
bamboo flute, accompanied him.

> "The summer heat is entirely gone, clouds are
>   light and the sky clearer and higher.
> Leisurely, the day's work done, I stroll about
>   in the courtyard.
> See, how the Silver Stream, hanging slantingly
>   across the heavens, the stars does belittle!
> So clear a full moon, bright and serene, as it
>   is tonight. How seldom do we have it in
>   a lifetime!
> Who ever plucked the Cassia Tree from
>   yonder Moon Paradise,
> Where the seeds of the tree their fragrance cast
>   far beyond the clouds?
> Or ever overheard the chattering of the Im-
>   mortals, talking about Great Riches, Great
>   Happiness, and Great Longevity?
> I ask ye, where are the Palaces of Jade and
>   Jasper,
> And where have the divinities betaken
>   themselves?
> Seeking for fame, seeking for pleasures,
> All such labours are lost, and so, Scholar,
> Keep your mind on your books and forget
>   everything else."

A clapping of hands applauded the youngster as he finished the song triumphantly.

"Will you sing, too, that old song from the Poet Li T'ai Pai, which you used to like so much? We have not heard you sing for a long time. Come on, father, I will play the flute for you," young Mr. Wu urged. The old man accepted the challenge.

"A clear full moon, when do we have it?
A wine cup in my hand, I ask the blue heaven.
'Cause I do not know what night is this, what
    year is this, in the Celestial Realm.
How I wish to get up there with the drift of the
    wind, though how I fear being unapt to the
    cold up there in the Jade Palaces.

"You shine on the dancers here below and
    their shadows you enliven;
Across the boudoir with crimson-lacquered
    pillars, and through the silken windows,
You annoy the tortured sleepless.
Whatever makes you so disgusted,
That you choose to be round just when humans
    are so sadly parted?

"O, the moon is round, or deficient, and the
    heavens bright or clouded,
Like humans, separated or gathered, with sor-
    row or mirth,
These things, since ancient times, cannot be just
    as we want.
So let us hope that forever and ever,
We be allowed to be near our loved ones."

"*Hao, Hao chi la*!" (good, extremely good) cried the family in unison, as the old man slowly and beautifully rendered the old song with complete success.

"Oh, this reminds me, what is the name of the other song, which starts: 'The evening breezes of autumn. . .'?"

"Yes, I remember," said the aged grandfather, "let me try once more at it—you go ahead and play."

"The evening breezes of autumn,
Blow and blow, moving the curtain cords;
As I sit utterly alone, listless, thoughtless, how
    sentimental,
While the tiny light of my oil lamp dances in
    the wind.

"Hark! Whence comes this music from a jade
    flute,
Playing mercilessly on and on, so touching,
That my heart aches with each note!
How am I to stand the hissing and rustling of the
    leaves of the *T'ung* trees in the courtyard

Coupled with the tinkling of the little bells
 hanging on the eaves of my room,
As the harsh autumnal winds drive ruthlessly
 past them?
All these cruel sounds, how dreary, how dismal
 and how dreadfully disheartening!

"Each year its trains of beautiful sights does
 bring,
Each day the precious time—speeding, flowing
 and gone!
As the autumn moon and the spring blossoms,
 mock so apathetically,
The hurrying humanity, busy, but what for!
Tell me not about success or renown,
These are little more than dreams to me.
How I fear tomorrow, as I lift the mirror and
 look,
Alas! to discover a fresh layer of frost on my
 hair."

"Oh, do be cheerful, this song is very *pu hao* (no good)"
commented the grandmother. "Though I could not follow your
words, it sounded to me like weeping!"
"More wine, father?" urged young Mr. Wu.
"Yes, my lad, give me plenty!"

IN SEARCH OF A PEKINGESE

THE busy festival season was soon over and the Wus embarked on a fresh adventure—hunting for a new pet, a Pekingese dog.

The Wus always kept a dog. During his younger days, old Mr. Wu had kept Chinese hunting dogs for in those days it was a fashionable sport to keep such dogs and take them on cross-country hunting trips. Chinese hobbies and amusements are classified under the four words: "Sounds, Colours, Dogs and Horses" and by these words they are contemptuously referred to. Of course, but few can afford horses while dogs are much more within the average means. As to the sounds and colours, the meanings are so vaguely defined and so subject to each person's own interpretation that no general condemnation, or otherwise, is possible.

"Little Black," the misnomer of a big brown mastif kept by the Wus, had been their faithful watchdog for many years until it died suddenly one winter night. Regarding the death of the dog, there were different opinions expressed. To old Mr. and Mrs. Wu, the dog died of old age. Young Mr. Wu thought differently for he had eye-witnessed the maid-servant striking the dog for no good reason, and he therefore suspected the servant had a hand in the dog's death somehow or other. The maidservant, on her part, was sure that something very bad was behind the incident for some dog-thief, she feared, having been favourably impressed with the fluffy brown winter coat of the animal, might have poisoned it when it chanced to be outside the home with a view to coming back later to secure the carcass for skinning. If that had indeed been the case, the man was sorely disappointed for the Wus dug a hole in their back yard and had the remains of their faithful dog buried. There was another thought on the matter: that some burglar, perhaps, had schemed thus to get rid of the barking dog that might bite, in preparation to steal into the house by night and commit some petty thefts. The family felt bad for a good many days and, the burglar idea was in the air for a week until it died down when nothing happened.

There was a chance to get a dog from a neighbour's but the offer was politely refused with thanks after a hurried inspection in which it was revealed that the dog in question was a lowly, ugly sort of a so-called *pan t'eng kou* (板櫈狗), a "bench dog", built on the dachshund principle. Old Mr. Wu did not like it at all for he had planned to get a beautiful Pekingese. There were thought to be several possible sources among his friends for a desirable young pup of good breed, failing all of which he was decided to buy one.

He went to the dog market, accompanied by his grandson, at the temple fair at Lung Fu Ssu which was held in the narrow alley running along the east wall of the famous but delapidated Lama monastery where Peking's "professional" breeders habitually market their dogs. These professionals are mostly women of poorer families who carry their dogs and litters of pups to the fair in little baskets, protected with a cotton-padded coverlet in winter, and part with their dearly-reared pets with tears in their eyes. To all intents and purposes, there may actually be some real professionals counting on the breeding of dogs as a productive industry, but the general appearance of the dog market does not seem to indicate such a possibility. The only commercialized branch of the trade still seems to be in the accessories, collars, bells, tassels and so forth.

The dog market might have seen better days in years gone by, but of late it is a forlorn business and might even completely vanish from the picture. For it is well known that the keeping of these dogs was originally a more or less aristocratic pastime and not without bounteous imperial patronage, and Peking's most famous dog-fanciers were the eunuchs who exchanged or bought and sold between themselves, seldom if ever permitting their fine specimens to be possessed by outsiders. Now-a-days, more so than ever, the "gold buyers do not often meet the gold sellers" and so very few remarkable dogs are ever available for a patron at the Peking dog markets.

*   *   *

No doubt the dog has always shared man's home in China as in many other lands. In Chinese myths the *T'ien Kou* (天狗), or Heavenly Dog, is responsible for the eclipses of the moon as he is supposed to be desirous of gobbling up the luminary and so makes attempts at it every once so often. During the eclipses the Chinese used to beat brass and copper gongs and similar utensils that may be handy in order to produce a din to scare off the Heavenly Dog, which efforts have always been successful as the moon has always survived the eclipses. In certain Chinese families where children are rare or where the infant death rate has been high, a small scroll can always be found hung up in the nursery depicting a bearded gentleman in a blue gown, with bow and arrow in hand, shooting or attempting to shoot at a winged black dog on a cloud. This is the *Chang Hsien Yeh* (張仙爺), the Immortal Grandfather Chang, whose presence will be a guarantee that the Heavenly Dog will not invade the nursery and bite the small inmates to death. Chang Hsien Yeh's offerings are a group of seven little balls of dough to be replaced with seven new ones every seventh day.

Many virtues have been attributed to man's canine partner in this country and that most often used word is *yi* (義), "faithful". A Chinese proverb says: "A son never thinks his mother ugly, or a dog his master poor", for the dog has always adhered to its master long after his former human friends have deserted him.

There was once in the district of Chow Tsun a merchant who went to trade in Wuhu and made a fortune and was coming home after having chartered a junk for the journey when he saw a butcher about to kill a dog. He was greatly moved and paid the butcher double the price of the dog and kept it as his own pet. The boat crew, entirely unsuspected, turned out to be a group of river pirates and midway on the journey, they tied up the merchant and were about to kill him as they had learned of the great riches in silver and gold he was carrying in his baggage. The merchant begged to remain a "whole corpse", to which the pirates agreed, and so they wrapped him up in a piece of matting and threw him overboard. The dog, seeing what had happened to his master, jumped in and followed the package for some distance. He finally retrieved it and dragged it to a shallow spot. Barking loudly he soon attracted a group of people and with their help the merchant was saved.

The merchant not being contented at thus losing his hard-earned money returned to Wuhu to await the return of the pirate boat for prosecution purposes. At this time the dog disappeared and for three or four days the forlorn merchant could find no trace of the pirate junk, as many similar vessels had tied up at the wharves. At his wits' end he was about to let a fellow-townsman take him back to Chow Tsun. At this junction the dog appeared from it seemed nowhere and, barking loudly at his master, led him to a junk. Once on board the dog made directly for a deckhand, bit his leg severely and refused to let go in spite of a heavy beating—they then discovered that this was the pirate junk. The case was brought before the magistrate and the lost fortune was returned to the merchant.

A man of Lu An, whose father having been involved in an important law-suit was imprisoned through no fault of his own and dying, was able to get together one hundred taels in little pieces of silver and with this money he was hoping to bribe his father out of jail. Hastily he packed up and mounted his mule and set out on the journey. Anxious and ill-humoured, he was annoyed to find his own black mastiff dogging the mule's every step. He whipped the dog again and again but it followed him persistently. Thus they went about fifteen or twenty miles from home. Finally he dismounted and picking up a big stone, hurled it at the dog. But once more on his mule the dog came up again and this time kept on biting the tail of the mule and even jumped to reach its head with the apparent intention of blocking their way. Thinking it a bad omen prophetic of failure in his mission, he was all the more enraged. So turning back he gave the dog a hot chase and then again galloped on his way.

At sundown he was at the city's gate but how great was his shock and grief when feeling for his money he found about half of the silver gone! He put up at an inn although he could hardly get a single wink of sleep. It suddenly dawned upon him that perhaps the dog's strange behaviour the previous day had something to do with it. Early next morning he set out, back on the previous days's trail, to see if any trace could be found of the money on the road. He was reduced almost to desperate despondency as on the way the passers-by were so numerous that he could imagine of no reason why the lost silver could still be found intact.

At last he reached the spot where he had alighted the day before. Here, in the thick grass, lay his faithful dog. He found the lost silver assembled neatly together and hidden by the dog with his dead body.

       *   *   *

It is hard to say exactly when the Pekingese began to be so

The long-haired Pekingese, called "lion dog", has such an abundant hair growth that its eyes are often obscured. To clear its field of vision the Chinese braid the hair into little queues in front of its face.

highly esteemed in China. A Sung Dynasty writer in a book called "*T'ung K'ao*" (通考), or "General References", mentioned that the emperor of the Turkoman country once sent an envoy to the court of Emperor Kao Tsu of the T'ang Dynasty (618-906 A. D.), bringing two dogs, one male and one female. Their height was about six Chinese *ts'un* (7-1/2) inches and their length about one Chinese *ch'ih* (1 foot). These dogs were of great intelligence. They could lead horses by the reins and each was trained to light His Majesty's path at night by carrying a small torch in its mouth.

In another book of a similar nature written about the same period is found another reference to the Pekingese dog. Emperor T'ai Tsung of the Sung Dynasty, it is said, received as tribute from an official in Szechuan a little dog called *T'ao Hwa erh* (桃花兒), or "Peach Flower". It was extremely small and very intelligent. It followed the emperor everywhere. When there was an audience the dog preceded him, and by its barking announced its imperial master's arrival. When the Emperor T'ai Tsung fell ill, it refused to eat. When the Emperor died, the dog manifested its sorrow with tears and whining.

The palace eunuchs endeavoured to train the dog to precede the new emperor but without success. The emperor caused to be made an iron cage with white cushions (for mourning) and this cage, containing the dog, was carried in the imperial sedan to his master's tomb. There the dog died. Emperor Chen Tsung, the new ruler, issued a decree, ordering the dog to be wrapped in the cloth of an imperial umbrella and to be buried alongside its master.

Her Majesty the Empress Dowager Tsu Hsi was a great dog fancier and her fondness for the Pekingese breed is well known. She had at one time about one hundred such dogs, and the feeding and caring for them was under her personal supervision. When she died in the year 1911, at her funeral a yellow-and-white Pekingese dog named "Peony" with a white spot on its forehead was led by the famous Eunuch Li Lien-ying in about the same manner as the Sung Dynasty dog had set the precedent. Thus the world was made to understand that the dog died at the side of the Empress' tomb. "Peony" however, did not die for by the clever hand of one of the big eunuchs, by previous arrangement, it was sold outside for a handsome sum!

The esteem for the Pekingese dog was not without a religious significance, which was even more aggrandized by the relations of the Chinese with the Lama priests. The Lamas brought to Peking the famous white Lhasa dogs but these dogs unfortunately were not warmly received on account of their colour which is the colour of mourning in China. But, at the hands of the Lama priests, the Pekingese dogs found great favour. Its appearance, to the devout Buddhists, suggested the lion ridden by the Buddha of Wisdom, Manjusri. In the original Buddhist legends, of Indian origin, the lions, five in number, were symbolic of Buddha's omnipotence and stories about his fingers changing themselves into five lions and conquering a herd of trumpeting, charging elephants, and another tale of the vanquishing of a stampede of infuriated water buffaloes, were well known to the Lama priests. And these Pekingese dogs, so astonishingly tallying with the traditional sacred lions in almost every detail as represented by their own religious artists, soon became valued by Lamas. It cemented the relationship with the Chinese court, too, as the Chinese emperor had always been represented—deliberately and maliciously misrepresented, as the reincarnated Manjusri Buddha to the simple-minded inhabitants of the Tibetan highlands.

*   *   *

At present, the Pekingese, called locally the *pa-kuo-erh* (叭狗兒), are divided into two kinds: the long-haired and the short-haired, the latter goes by the name of "pugs". The kind with particularly long hair is known by the name of *shih tze kuo* (獅子狗) or "lion dogs". In colour it is white, black and yellow mostly partly-coloured, with the yellow commanding the highest prices. The dogs eat steamed rice, mixed with sheep's liver, cooked and chopped fine, two or three times a day, and for between meal snacks they get anything their master or mistress gets, that is, if the food seems to suit their taste. A small basket with cotton-padded cushions serves as the home for the average Pekingese which is kept indoors, but most of the highly favoured ones have a place on the brick bed with the master and mistress. The dogs have very clean habits, and being so clever are easily taught where to go to "wash its hands".

*   *   *

It took young scholar Wu and his grandfather many a trip to the dog market at Lung Fu Ssu and elsewhere in order gra-

A Pekingese like the one shown here is known as a "black clouds on white snow" type. It has admirable proportions, "leopard" eyes and "tortoise" mouth with the tip of its tongue showing, as it should, towards the left.

dually to acquaint themselves with the important points of Pekingese dogs. The way the talkative professionals talked, almost every dog they offered had some valuable characteristic in one way or another, such as in colour arrangement of the coat or its shape and angle or certain parts of the body.

The best liked Pekingese dogs are those of a yellow colour or apricot colour, shading from golden yellow to orange as the well-known term *chin ssu ha pa* (金絲哈叭) indicates, which translates as the "golden silk Pekingese." A dog with a tri-coloured coat, mixed up somewhat thoroughly, is known as a "tortoise shell". A black dog with white legs is known as "black clouds over snow." By the arrangements of the coloured spots, obtained by careful cross-breeding, they have been given various fancy names.

There are many points on which to judge a good Pekingese besides the colour of its coat. Firstly, the head must be rec-tangular in shape and not snouted or roundish. The eyes are to be as far apart as possible. They must be big and "popped out" in appearance like those of a "dragon-eyed" goldfish. Some insist that the iris should be broad and dark and prominent, deserving the term of "waterchestnut eyes" while others say more white should be shown, calling such eyes "leopard eyes." There must be a black circle around them called *ssu yen-erh* (四眼兒) or "four eyes", which incidentally is a nickname often jokingly given to a person who wears spectacles. The nose must be short and broad. The mouth has to have the sides slightly lobed and depressed, adhering tightly to the jawbones, but not oversized—these are called *kwi tsueh-erh* (龜嘴兒) or "tortoise mouth."

The ears must be large and thick and squarish in shape and not narrow and pointed and are known to the trade as "sesamum ears". They should be located as far back on the head as possi-ble, drooping down heavily. The chin must be well-developed and not "like that of a frog." The tongue is to be long and when the mouth is closed must show its tip a little bit between the lips, but it should not project right in the center of the mouth, although either to the left or to the right would be equally permissible. It is felt that the tongue dropping from the middle of the mouth suggests the ghost of hanged persons and as such is not desirable. The desired effect is produced by artificially pulling the tongues of the pups until they are much oversized.

Second only to the head in importance would be the points governing development. The waist must be well-shaped, the back slightly fallen-in and compared to the shape of a Chinese silver ingot. The body as a whole must be as short as possible and the shorter the better. The front legs are to be short and the hind legs long and bowed and bent in a special way thus giving them a rolling and shaking sort of a gait. The tail is of importance too and should be raised in a special way and should not drop or curl between the legs. To produce the de-sired effect there is a special technique.

The tail of the Pekingese is docked as follows: The process is to cut off a little piece from the tip of the tail of the young pup and using human teeth as a pair of forceps, to draw out a white tissue from the tail bones and cut it off about an inch or so. Thus when the wound heals, the tail stops growing in length and would naturally bend upward, producing the desired effect simulating the tail of the famous Buddhist lion. The nose is also often operated upon to secure the desired shape and also by long-term rubbing and pressing with the hand. The curved back is obtainable by constantly stroking and patting from puphood. Peking families have also a way to deodorized their dogs. This is by a thorough bathing not long after birth with the fluid obtained by cooking the twigs of the locust tree and the catnip plants, much as a newborn baby is bathed in the Third Day Bath ceremony. It is said and insisted on that a dog thus bathed will be deodorized for life. To keep the dogs from healthful physical development which might easily render them too big for the desired proportions, their growth is often cruelly checked by keeping the pups in a wire net, leaving only the head to grow freely, as in the eyes of Chinese connoisseurs the head should be as big as possible.

* * *

Finally, at the dog market, old Mr. Wu found a dog that he really liked. It was a comparatively young dog, only four or five months old, a beautiful specimen with medium long hair, a combination of yellow and white, with yellow predominating, a good deep tone of golden yellow and the pattern so arranged on the back that according to experts it was what should be called *an tze hua-erh* (鞍子花兒), or "saddle markings," with a wider band around the waist than the *tai tze hua-erh* (帶子花兒), or "sash markings." It had a very shapely skull and a tail that had been properly operated on. It was not particularly small-sized, being somewhat larger than the conventionally desirable measurement, as the woman who sold the dog to old Mr. Wu said she had not been severe enough in "stunting" its growth when it was a pup. There were two faults with the dog, mutually acknowledged and discovered before the transaction was made. One was that the dog's nose was just a little bit too domed in shape and not flat enough to suit the most fastidious connoisseurs and the other fault was that where it should be pure white a few small coloured spots appeared on the legs immediately above the paws which in the trade phraseology is known as *hwa t'i-erh* (花蹄兒), or "flowered hooves", and this is a rather bad point.

The sales woman told old Mr. Wu that if he wanted to he could improve on the shape of the dog's nose by nailing a piece or raw pig-skin on a wooden board with the flesh side showing and having the dog lick from the skin when it was hungry. This, if done often enough, should be productive of the desired effect. As to the spotted legs, it was immediately considered as *mei yu fah tze*—something that cannot be helped. There was no way to find out exactly how much was paid for the dog, but the price was somewhere between eight and nine dollars for it was on this difference that the two parties concerned were seen arguing back and forth in the last stage of the bargaining. It was most likely the latter figure for the woman threw in extra a silken leash and

Small, cone-shaped dog-houses woven of hay are peddled in the streets of Peking at the same time as grass mats by itinerant sellers just before the severe winter weather sets in. In shape the "house" suggests an Eskimo's igloo.

a whip that she had brought with her—nor did she take off the collar that was on the dog's neck.

* * *

"*Yeh Yeh* (Grandfather) has bought his dog at last," cried Little Bald Head as soon as they arrived home. Upon this all the folk gathered around to watch the dog, unanimously declaring it a very beautiful creature.

"What is the dog's name, grandfather?"

"Oh........I forgot to ask ....no, I did too...the woman told me ...*Hsiang-erh* (香兒) (Fragrant), that is it. Is it not, Little Bald Head?"

* * *

Hsiang-erh was said to be able to do many tricks, such as to stand erect and sit on its hind legs and folding its front paws shake them up and down in the way of a Chinese woman's salute. It had also learned to roll itself on the ground at a word of command.

"I have always preferred a dog like that to one of a black colour for the Pekingese dogs have a habit of following people's foot-steps and in the dark, a black dog is easily stumbled upon and may cause trouble", remarked old Mrs. Wu as they all gathered to watch it eat its first meal in the Wu house.

"When I was in my mother's family, we used to have a dog like that, only somewhat bigger, called *Ting-erh* (頂兒) (Button) because on its head was a white spot like the Chinese hat button. It was a very clever dog and used to fetch for my grandfather his pipe and tobacco pouch, also his flint-stone and tinder box —there were no matches then," continued old Mrs. Wu.

"A neighbour of ours had a lion-dog, who used to buy its own liver from the butcher shop every morning," said young Mrs. Wu.

"Well, that is very interesting, but how?" asked the grandmother.

"Every morning the mistress would wrap three coppers in a handkerchief and the dog would hold the parcel in its mouth and make for the village butcher shop, two streets away—that was in the country you know, and bring back the liver which the butchery people wrapped in the handkerchief for it. It was taught to do so, little by little, and the butcher shop people all knew the family and the dog, too."

"Now, let us listen for the hawker of grass-mats and the dog-house pedlar. It is a bit early for the season, but we want to get him a dog-house as soon as possible," concluded old Mrs. Wu.

YELLOW WINE AND WHITE WINE

THERE are many kinds of Chinese wines and principally they come under two names, "yellow wine" and "white wine". The yellow wine is itself of two kinds, the Shantung yellow and Shaohsing yellow. Shantung yellow is manufactured in Peking while Shaohsing yellow is supposed to come only from the district of Shaohsing in Chekiang province from where it is distributed all over China, in like manner perhaps as the Japanese *nada-no-sake*. This Shaohsing wine is packed and shipped in the original crude earthen, small-mouthed demijohns of a typical shape and sealed with a big heavy cake of yellow mud. It may be ten, twenty, fifty or more years old with the "vintage" year clearly marked by a date stamp—the older the better and the more costly.

It is said that in Shaohsing when a daughter is born to a family, the family makes a certain quantity of yellow wine and has it "demijohned" and stored away. When the daughter is ready to marry, say around twenty years of age, the wine originally produced at a small cost, is sold at a high price and the money realized will be enough to finance the girl's nuptials with a very handsome equipage—a sort of a self-endowment wedding expense insurance and dowry foundation with compound interest. Shaohsing yellow wine tastes like good beer to the uninitiated and Shantung yellow wine tastes like spoiled sour beer!

The other kind is that which goes by the name of *samshu*, a naturalized Chinese word in the English language which came originally from the Cantonese dialect for *san shao* (三燒), or "three burn" or "thrice distilled". This is a wine with a high alcoholic content made principally from kaoliang grain, and known in Peking as *pai kan* (白乾), or "white and dry". When "wine" is mentioned here, it almost always refers to this kind.

White wine itself is subdivided into many kinds as it is variously scented with certain medical herbs, rose petals, bamboo leaves, young sprouts of the wormwood plant and so on. One special kind is supposed to be manufactured with tiger's bones as an essence and is said to be an effective relief to chronic rheumatism of the aged.

Those who are regular consumers and appreciative of good quality wine deal with the wholesale establishments whose depots are located in a cluster outside the Hata Men, about ten or twelve houses all told, established long, long ago by special permission of the government. These houses import the liquor from the breweries in the country south of Peking in big consignments by mule cart caravans and distribute to all the sub-wholesale and retail shops, operating besides a revenue-collecting service for the government. Their minimum sale is a *kuan* (罐), "jug", of sixteen local catties, delivered with a govern-

The yellow wine from Shao-hsing is "bottled" in typical containers with a big cake of mud on top to insure airtightness. In such jars it is transported and sold all over China, and abroad wherever Chinese are found.

ment duty memo, bearing a big red chop or stamp, signifying the stuff's legal standing and no order smaller than a *kuan* is filled. It was not the habit of the Wu family to buy their wine in this manner as old Mr. Wu was the only person who drank regularly. The rest of the family, though not professedly teetotalers, were not interested in the matter except every now and then when parties were on to sip just a little. As a matter of fact, they never had to buy their own wine for friends always kept them well-supplied the year round. With their demand so little, a few bottles accepted as gifts at the festivals went a long way.

But old Mr. Wu used to be a hearty drinker in his youthful days when social functions were numerous. He was called by his comrades a *hai liang* (海量), or "sea capacity", by which term anyone who can hold much liquor is known. At least once he lost his way *en route* from his family's private mule cart between a restaurant and his home. It was midnight on that occasion. The driver had stopped the cart to go to the sidewalk public lavatory and resuming the journey drove the empty cart to the Wu home. Lifting the cart curtain, the driver found his master gone. Terrified, he drove back on the road and found his young master asleep on the bridge of the Imperial Canal.

Old Mr. Wu later often recalled the experience with a "silent smile."

That old Mr. Wu used to get drunk was not solely his own fault because drinking was openly encouraged by the Chinese "poets" to whom getting drunk meant one of life's chief joys. Even Confucius was not a die-hard prohibitionist, for did he not say that in a game of competitive archery a person should assume his position with a ceremonious gesture by shaking his own hands put together and then after shooting, "drink the wine and withdraw." It is easily suspected that Master Confucius might have kept a miniature still in his own basement and made his own moon-shine, for he said that he "never drank liquors from a bar." So exactly how he laid his fingers on a drink, we cannot tell. Confucius had a rule though, a very sympathetic rule, as recorded in the "Analects," where he said: "Though wine be without measure, do not get to the point of confusing." How smartly said this! The sage apparently meant it to be subject to diverse interpretations with plenty of leeway.

Besides, in the way of Chinese parties, in order to produce the good-natured hub-bub and noise in the desired hilarious and friendly spirit, it is considered only proper to force a person to drink beyond his capacity. For a person to decline a helping of wine at a Chinese feast has been described as *mien pi* (面壁) or "facing the wall"—it is easy to picture such an awkward situation by visualizing a guest sitting with his face to the wall while the rest dine and wine. Old Mr. Wu was a "regular good fellow", and so always left a feast tipsy if not "mud drunk" which is the Chinese equivalent to "completely passed out."

Later in life, certain friends persuaded old Mr. Wu to join the Li Men (理門) Society, the "door of reason", a religious union for the advancement of temperance.

He was introduced to a *Tang Chia-ti* (當家的) (house-runner) or "head promoter" in the local chapter, a long-bearded venerable man always dressed in grey, by a friend who with a many years membership standing was a *P'ei Ts'o Ti* (陪座的) (assistant sitter) in the institution. Here in the small shrine situated in the side-wing of a small temple, they burned incense and kowtowed to the image of Kwan Yin, the Goddess of Mercy, pledging absolute abstainment from strong drinks and all forms of tobacco, for it was discovered long ago that humans needed religious zeal to reinforce their will power. After the simple initiation ceremony, lectures were given him in semi-privacy and certain things explained to old Mr. Wu, then a young man, to help overcome his desire for drinks and help him with his courage to do things well. A short phrase, supposed to be most influential in aiding him when facing temptations of all kinds which outsiders proclaimed was to be kept a secret amongst the members and not even "leaked" to their immediate relatives was taught the new member. It is said that this so-called *chen yen* (眞言) or "true word," was nothing but *Nan-Wu-ah-mi t'o fo* (南無阿彌陀佛), or "Oh! My Amita Buddha", a sort of a short prayer calling upon the Buddha for courage.

A certain kind of black medical concoction, a mysterious black paste like prepared opium in appearance, was also blessed at the shrine of the goddess and given to the members. This stuff, called *ch'a kao* (茶膏) or "tea plaster", is to be boiled and drunk as a substitute for wine until the habit is entirely gotten rid of and is regarded as an agent for breaking the tobacco urge. Old Mr. Wu used snuff then, which was also prohibited, and in its place a certain kind of "smelling medicine" was supplied by the Society.

For a time old Mr. Wu did "ride the water wagon" and stopped smoking and using snuff but he, bless his old soul, was not to be bound by the rules of this famous institution and it was not long before he began to allow himself little liberties every now and then, particularly as his friends were not willing to lose him from their midst. He quit the "anti-saloon league" in less time than it took his friend to enroll him.

*　　　*　　　*

In his fifties and sixties old Mr. Wu gradually stopped excessive drinking. But he often frequented the little bar around the corner not far from his home, a favourite rendezvous for many of the "wets" living in the neighborhood. This type of place is known locally as a *Ta Chiu Kang* (大酒缸), or "Big

Wine Vat". A Chinese proverb says, "one person must not drink wine (alone) and two persons must not gamble," but old Mr. Wu paid no heed to this taboo and silently he would sit in the wine shop, sipping little mouthfuls of the burning white wine and but seldom did he engage in conversation with any of the other customers although he knew most of them and of at least half of them he could write a biography. Between the tea shop and the "big wine vat" he spent a good portion of his idle moments. With some of those who were more than nodding acquaintances, a laconic exchange of courtesy was often offered and acknowledged with a "this time on me?" and "no thanks, *liang-pien*" (兩便), meaning mutually convenient!

The "big wine vat" is so called because although the shop is equipped with a regular Chinese full-length counter where much of the trade is conducted, it is also provided with a number of big heavy vats, half sunk into the ground, leaving just so much of the height also to serve the purpose of acting as the "legs" of tables. These vats—a number of them— are lined up against the walls, with heavy wooden covers serving as "tops", and a number of little stools around them seat by twos and threes the customers coming in groups for their daily ritual. On these big wine jars, glazed a shiny black, are pasted squares of red paper bearing any one of a group of four-charactered conventionalized phrases in praise of the precious liquors, such as *Chiu Kuo Ch'ang Ch'un* (酒國長春), "Wine Country Always Spring", or *Wen Hsiang Hsia Ma* (聞香下馬), "Smelling Fragrance Dismount Horse", and so forth. The shop owners apparently had some spare red paper left after making these squares, for scattered all over the walls were little stickers, reading *Mo T'an Kuo Shih* (莫談國事), meaning "Do Not Talk Politics," and others which would translate as "No Credit", "Cash Only", and "Please Do Not Open Your Honourable Mouth"!

On the counters are arranged the wine jars with glowing pewter covers decorated with pieces of red and green, cloth, and the long-handled measuring ladles made of bamboo. Here wine is sold by the cup, either cold or warmed over the fire in a conical copper utensil. Shops of this kind also maintain a mutually co-operative buffet service offered by a semi-portable restaurant, featuring principally the meat dumplings and other ready-made foods (hot dogs, quick lunches, you would say) which enjoy considerable patronage.

A long line of miscellaneous edibles are also provided which constitute an inseparable part of a *ta chiu kang* adventure. Examples of these may be fried Chinese crackers, sweet or salted, nuts and confections, little dishes of jellyfish and gelatin salad, dried shrimps and pickled baby crabs, and so forth. Certain itinerant food pedlars may also stop itinerating here and establish themselves temporarily outside the shop as the customers provide unlimited sales opportunities. Besides, the pedlars may need a cup or two themselves to carry on "spiritedly" the balance of the day's trade. Among such pedlars may be mentioned the seller of donkey's meat and salted beef, all ready to serve in five or ten-cent portions, their wheelbarrows or baskets set next to the case of the seller of "smoked fish" which is an euphemistic title given to a kind of pig-head meat, pig's liver, pig's heart, eggs, and thus like, all dyed a brilliant red after cooking and smoked over a fire of sawdust.

Often did little Wu find his grandfather here, and he always was delighted to come and call the old man home to supper. Grandfather also bought him titbits and sweets here which the child liked so much.

The "big wine vats" are genuinely democratic outfits and here, like in the public rooms of world cruise boats "you meet such interesting people."

*   *   *

Little Bald Head came home from school one day with the news that it was going to be a holiday the next day, the twenty-seventh of the eighth moon, for this was to be the day of the "Autumn *Ting*" (丁) sacrifices, a day for the worship of Confucius, and there was going to be a ceremony at the public school.

So the next morning, at school, a solemn ceremony was held, presided over by the schoolmaster and the students, according to a pre-announced program, gathered in the central courtyard in the school compound. The students stood in rows led by their teachers and bowed three times to the portrait of the great sage hung up for the occasion and then listened to a speech given by a special teacher, a Mr. Hu, who taught Confucian classics. Mr. Hu was an expert on things Confucian and was himself a Shantung man, a native of Ch'uifu where the Master himself had lived. An impressive speech was delivered by Mr. Hu, characterized by his own Shantung dialect and his "all the world is wrong" attitude toward all things, for without these points he would not have made a good teacher of the classics. Mr. Hu never said anything without referring to the "Four Books" and the "Five Classics," for which he had earned for himself the nickname of "Confucius."

*   *   *

The spring and autumn sacrifices to Confucius are an old custom and date back to imperial days. The days chosen were and still are the second *Ting* days in the second moon, called *Ch'un Ting* (春丁) or "Spring *Ting*", and in the eighth moon, called *Ch'iu Ting* (秋丁) or "Autumn *Ting*" respectively. *Ting* is itself the fourth of the so-called Ten Heavenly Stems (cyclical signs). These two days were chosen for this important purpose because during the time of Confucius, they were the days on which the State Colleges were annually opened by a minister by order of the emperor.

Up to the end of the Manchu Dynasty, the reigning Chinese Emperor was obliged by Propriety to visit the Confucian Temple, situated inside Anting Men, twice a year to do obeisance before the tablet of the "Supreme Teacher". This was a state function, for Confucian teaching has kept China from "going to the dogs" it was felt. It was an early morning affair and the emperor, after "fasting" and "purifying" himself the previous night, used to come to the holy precincts of the temple in a special coach over streets specially covered with yellow earth and sprinkled with "clean" water for the occasion. The sacrificial performances and the offerings, wine and a whole ox, and so on were all conducted or offered in identically the same manner in identically the same kind of vessels as were used in the Chow Dynasty (1122-222 B.C.). A number of musicians, donning court robes and hats of the period, and trained specially to play Chow Dynasty tunes and belonging to the Board of Rites, played on quaint instruments as the elaborate program was carried out by the emperor and the ministers assisting him. The ceremonies lasted for several hours and finished about sunrise. There was not only music but also dancing. A group of special dancers were also kept on the government payroll for the sole purpose of performing antiquated "steps" while brandishing certain curious objects such as pheasant feathers mounted on long handles, short three-holed flutes, battle axes, pointed shields and other implements.

The Confucian canon mentioned the old music and dancing in many places. The master was also responsible for a novel way of government—government by "string-instrument music and songs"—and having apparently a musical talent and being something of a composer also "rectified music after he returned to his native kingdom of Lu". The dancing was a more serious matter, for over the number of feather-bearing dancers employed by a certain feudal lord he raised a great fuss. The matter was considered to be a grave incident, inexcusably violating the rules of propriety and gave the old Master a "pain in the neck" as is registered in the third chapter of the "Analects". "Whoever can stand such an outrage will stand for anything", was his angry remark.

HUNTING IN ANCIENT CHINA

The "big wine vats" or Chinese bars and the famous tea houses, both previously described, are places where all types of people can be met and studied from convenient angles. It was often the pleasure of the youthful scholar of the Wu family to appear with his leisurely grandfather and listen to the stories and yarns of the customers seen regularly at these establishments. There were, for example, the group of idle bird-fanciers who turned also amateur hunters during the autumn and winter months. Though these hunters, apparently belonging to a past generation, are "as rare as the stars in the morning sky" now-a-days, they were then still much in evidence with their last flickering traces of glory.

*   *   *

Hunting as a royal sport has been so closely inter-woven with important historical happenings in China that it is mentioned in all the chronological works of the country. At the very beginning of the practice, it may be gathered, this was really used as a pretext for the ancient Chinese emperors to make a wide-scoped inspection tour of the land over which they ruled, to demonstrate their martial spirit in an agreeable manner and to let it be known to the public that they had not become soft and weakly in spite of confinement in the palaces.

It was then provided that the emperors were to make hunting trips once in each of the four seasons of the year, designated by various names. But in the course of time, the Chinese monarchs began to develop a personal liking in the matter and artificial hunting grounds were prepared for them not far from their palaces even before the time of Confucius. In these hunting parks vegetation was allowed to grow wild and all sorts of game and wild life multiplied therein for the sole purpose of the royal enjoyment.

According to a usually reliable source of information, the works of Mencius, King Wen Wang of Chow had a private hunting park seventy square *li* in area—about seven-tenths the size of the Tartar City of Peking. Emperor Hsuan Wang of Ch'i (Western Shantung) had one of forty square *li*, being but a *chu hou* (諸侯) or feudal lord himself. These imperial hunting parks were so closely guarded that no poachers dared steal into the grounds. In a way King Wen Wang's park was less strictly controlled for the same book said that people were perfectly welcome to drop in there and gather some dried grasses for their kitchen fire or even catch two or three rabbits there but in the case of Ch'i Hsuan Wang, a Department of State notice was displayed prominently on the barricaded door saying that whosoever dared to kill a deer from the flocks found in the hunting park would be punished in the same manner as if he had committed first degree murder, which in the then existing criminal code was to have the man's irreplaceable head cut off. Mencius, in his spicy and saucy manner of speech, was bold enough to tell the emperor right to his face that he might as well have dug a forty square *li* pitfall where the park stood!

Until as recently as the beginning of the Republic, the imperial hunting parks had been kept at Hsiang Shan in the Westerly Hills and at Nanyuan in the southern suburb of Peking, both walled in and properly taken care of by a special detachment of imperial bodyguard. The hunting was done mostly with hawks and dogs, and seldom were fire arms used, and even on such rare occasions the old fashioned native flintlocks were the only kind in the imperial hunting ordnance. Bows and arrows were used at times and the biggest game kept there were deer of various kinds. A group of professional soldiers were also trained in order to "assist" the royal parties, and were composed of "strong men" selected from the rank and file of the Manchu soldiery of the Left Wing and the Right Wing, between which two regiments the garrison of the Peking city was divided, the east city and the west city in the order named.

To keep themselves in shape for their "duties", these hunters were always required to keep their own trained hawks and dogs, and naturally they would wish to enlarge the scope and make it pay in so far as personal pleasure was also concerned. The friends and neighbours and admirers would also get themselves interested in the sport and so amateur hunting by hawks and dogs became an old institution.

It was in this respect alone that some of these Manchu bannermen or soldiers preserved the martial character of their ancestors although elsewhere, their fighting spirits were, as a whole, hopelessly demoralized.

*   *   *

Of the trained birds of prey closely associated with the Chinese amateur hunting indulged in by the Peking-*jen* of a certain type and responsible for an important part of this interesting pastime, there are three main classifications.

There is the so-called sparrow-hawk, which is the smallest-sized of the entire family, being about seven inches from tip to tip, in colour grey, shading to green and brown, and known locally as a *hu-ba-la* (虎伯劳) which is said to be a word of Mongolian origin. Hu-ba-la's are the easiest to train and are used to catch sparrows and other small birds with and are often seen carried on a branched twig the shape of an inverted "L". Bigger than the sparrow-hawk and about ten inches in height are the small eagles, a blackish grey bird with yellow bare legs. The big eagles or prairie falcons, regularly engaged in countryside hunting are of immense size, heroically built and standing fully twenty odd inches high with a wing spread of about four feet and with shanks heavily feathered. These are fierce looking things, and perch on the keeper's strong left arm.

According to those well versed in the identification of various prairie falcons there are various species in the group, and each is given a proper name based on certain characteristics. A falcon of light creamy colour considered to be the strongest and most formidable is known as a *su ying* (素鷹)—by the word *su* is indicated anything that is soberly coloured and should not be confused with the *su* for "vegetarian" as naturally no birds of prey live on vegetable foods. Another high-priced variety is the "Clear White", a snow-white bird said to be very common in Tibet and Chinese Turkestan but rarely seen in North China, whose portrait is often seen in the Ming paintings, particularly those credited to the pen of Emperor Hsuan Ho. Other kinds also well known but not so valuable are the "Apple Green", the "Grey Head," the *San Seh* (三色) or "Three Colours" with white parts on the wings like those of a jay; the commonest variety is the *T'u Hu-erh* (兔虎兒) or "Rabbit-Tiger". A *T'u Hu-erh* is easily procured at the bird market around the latter part of the eighth moon and the beginning of the ninth and costs about five dollars.

Groups of these prairie falcons or Rabbit Tigers are often seen, perhaps on their annual migrations, hovering in the sky and milling around over the wilderness of the mountainside to the west of the Peking plains, reconnoitering and searching for little rodents and small domestic animals on the ground, and it is at this time that they are caught for the local market. A large net, many feet in length and width with cleverly concealed mechanisms and closed from above the victims, is spread on the ground in a cleared spot near some cliffs. All the ropes and gadgets are camouflaged and operators are also hidden under cover. A stuffed falcon and some small birds tied with strings long enough to permit hopping about serve as baits to lure the "king of birds" to the spot and, before he discovers that what looked like one of his cousins thousands of feet on the ground

No keeper of falcons wishes to run the risk of ugly gashes inflicted by the birds' powerful claws and heavy leather gloves are a necessity.

A lot of silken cord is wound round a piece of wood and is protected by a weaving of rattan bark. The "perch" is fastened to the eagle-keeper's wrist. The black eagle drinks frequently and a little gourd with an opening holds its water supply.

was only a taxidermist's specimen, the net closes in and he is bagged. It is said that at each "pulling" of the net, four to six falcons are usually caught, though constant shifting of the location is necessary. These are then taken from the net by the trappers whose hands are heavily protected as a mere scratch by the claws is always an ugly wound and a serious matter and the falcons fight bitterly during such critical moments. Forthwith they are blindfolded with a strong leather cap and both legs tightly secured with twine. Perched on bundles of straw they are transported to the market, still untamed and capable of doing considerable damage.

From thence onward, their having been bought and sold notwithstanding, the falcons have a hard time for by nature they are ferocious and hard to manage and in the beginning of their captivity they literally refuse to eat. This attitude is said to be not necessarily due to a hunger strike but rather because of the fact that they are rich in reserve energy and certain fattish matters in their system they can carry on for a long time without food.

*   *   *

The smaller black eagles are very easy to train and are used for catching small birds. Though common sparrows are usually caught in this way the main object in keeping these eagles is for the purpose of obtaining other more valuable specimens, very often the pet birds that have succeeded in "jail-breaking" from cages. For this purpose the birds are trained to give only a single blow to their victims enabling the keeper to capture them alive. Such an eagle is always attached to the end of a silken twine, wound on a wooden bar called a *ying-bang-tse* (鷹棒子) or "eagle rod", and protected from entangling the feet of the eagle by a woven work of rattan. During the chase the rod and protecting cover are fastened about a man's wrist with a leather belt buckled like a wrist watch. The eagle proudly delivers a live bird to the keeper in exchange for a dead sparrow, its previous catch, kept in a box hung from the man's girdle.

The big falcons are very hard to train.

After a raw specimen is obtained, its original fighting spirits are first broken down by its own hunger strike and a special dose of cabbage-water is administered to it to further knock down its "inside" reserve. This water is obtained by wringing the fat portions of leaves of the North China cabbage in a piece of coarse cloth. During this time, the falcon is kept awake day and night under the watchful eyes of a two-man team, one taking charge of the left and another taking charge of the right eye. It is a very tense watch, indeed, for it has been noticed that a single wink of the eye will restore the reserve of the bird and will necessitate further artificial wasting of its energy. For three whole days and nights two men and a bird stay awake, the men constantly hitting the bird with a small stick to prevent it from trying to take a nap. After such a prolonged endurance test, the birds are literally at their energy's end and the experts will then abandon the vigilance.

By this time the bird will be actually very hungry and will not object to taking nourishment and then follows another cruel process.

Little bits of mutton or beef are now washed to a "dead white" and given to the falcon to eat, but with human hair (some say raw hemp) wound around each mouthful. These are placed at the bird's feet for it to pick up which it actually does with its strong beak and swallows instantly. The mutton or beef thus treated will not be digestible and so in a short while it will be forced up from the stomach and thrown out of the mouth again. This continues for three more days. It must be a very unpleasant experience for the bird and chastising in effect for after that the bird will learn to eat from out of a man's hand. Later whenever the falcon should turn "funny" and show his original non co-operative attitude the same treatment is repeated.

The bird is now ready for his lessons which are taught after each purposeful period of starvation, using a dead cat or a dead rabbit as the quarry. At first the bird is tied to a strong cord of raw silk, made still stronger by soaking it in brine, and the length of the cord, or the distance of "leap", is lengthened from ten to say fifty feet. The claws of the falcon are so sharp that once it has caught a small animal, usually striking at the hinder portion, they will be so deeply sunk into the flesh that to dis-lodge them the keeper has to render assistance. A properly train-ed falcon will catch a rabbit or other rodent with one foot and holding fast the animal's head with the other, bend it back with such a forceful stroke that the animal is instantly killed.

During the chase falcons are always blindfolded and once a game is sighted, the cap is lifted and the birds are set loose from the chains attached to their feet. Quick like a flash of lightning, it takes off and attains a high altitude and dives down after its prey, catching it, and waits for its master to claim it and then be rechained back to the arm. Unlike when in training, the birds are not tied with long strings.

It is said that during the later years of the Manchu Dynasty when there was a royal hunt hundreds of these giant falcons were in evidence, those belonging to the imperial household were blindfolded with finely decorated caps and a red tassel made of yak hair hung on each bird's breast. The legs were chained with leglets of solid gold.

*   *   *

Another important participant in amateur hunting is the Chinese dog.

The original dogs kept in China for hunting purposes were a kind of greyhound which were bred in the western provinces and known as *Kan su Hsi Ko* (甘肅細狗) or "slender dogs from Kansu province." These are seldom seen now-a-days except in the elaborate funeral procession of certain Mongolian princes and ex-Manchu-superlords. Funerals of such personages were represented to be their hunting trips and their processions used to contain a full-sized hunting retinue.

The dogs kept by the local people for hunting purposes are of the ordinary breed, mostly heavily-built mastiffs which have been put through a rigid training course.

The keepers of hunting dogs usually look for their prospective animals from among those dogs in the neighbourhood which have been known to be ferocious guard-dogs, known to mean business and to be good, conscientious biters, and to procure them by open negotiations or, more often, by foul measures, stealing mostly. The dog thus obtained is first knocked unconscious by a hard blow on the forehead and while the dog lies in a state of coma, the ears are sheared off to the proper length. This is said to be effective in developing further the dog's sensitivity. Forthwith it is revived by pouring cold water over its head. Following this operation the dog is given a new name to which it will answer henceforth, forgetting entirely the old name and its former memories and everything connected with them. Only male dogs are used for hunting purposes.

These dogs are then chained in a convenient place in the house and given very rich foods to eat and at the same time their exercises are curtailed to a minimum. After a certain period of seclusion and fattening, they will be buoyant with new energy and with an impulse for activity. Then a period of training starts, first by daily promenades in the mornings and evenings, and gradually shifting the hours to late in the night through to two or three o'clock in the morning. Much of the promenading would be conducted in the woods to give the dogs a first taste of their future career.

Such dogs which are intended for further development of their senses and eyesight, during the daily rounds are tightly fastened to the end of strong ropes and while the vitality in the dogs urges them forward they are held back forcefully by the keepers, strong men themselves, and thus gradually the dogs' "go-getting" habit is fostered and brought up to the "boiling point". Thereafter, the neighbours' cats and dogs will provide abundant objectives for "target practice" as the dogs will have learned by then to charge and engage an opponent when the master whistles to them. Further weeks of training will be required before the dogs are put into the field.

The field practices of hunting dogs are always carried out in old graveyards and ruined country temples where raccoons are noticed by knowing eyes to roam about and where the dogs are taken in the dead of night. The dogs will then be able to pick up and follow a trace invariably to the raccoon's finish. In general, the dogs are used mostly for hares and raccoons, as the hares are a very tasty game much liked by the Peking-*jen* and the raccoons are the only other kind of animals easily accessible in the Peking district the hunting of which is legally permissible.

There are two special uses attributed to raccoons; one being that its grease is a good ointment for burns and another that a stool with raccoon skin mounted on the top is a good cure for sufferers from piles; directions for use in the latter case being for the patient to sit constantly on such a stool. Whether or not this is a lot of "hot air" is not stated. Nevertheless, these merits, even if imaginary, are capable of giving more weight to the publicity due to an amateur hunter who has a raccoon or two to his credit.

Little Bald Head remembered having seen such a raccoon exhibited at the wine shop, with the proud hunter relating graphically his experience of the chase and the bystanders gaping in admiration of the hunter.

THE FESTIVAL OF THE DOUBLE YANG

THE ninth moon is the month of the chrysanthemum and in almost all Peking families may be found this seasonal flower. The flower markets are filled with them and flower hawkers peddle them in the streets. Amateur gardeners show their new specimens in the public parks as each year their painstaking work in crossing the various kinds is rewarded with novel varieties, and friends gather in parties for "viewing" them.

The purely commercial florists reap a rich harvest in profits as the chrysanthemum craze is universal and few people would permit the season to go by without getting at least a few plants just to keep up with the style. The Wus naturally had their chrysanthemums planted in their old porcelain and pottery pots lined up in their courtyard as they are such an important part in the esthetic life of the Peking-*jen*.

The principal at young scholar Wu's school was an admirer of flowers too and a chrysanthemum pageant was sponsored by him. Each class was requested to enter their own flowers brought to the "show" which was held in the school garden. A prize was given to the class entering the rarest and most beautiful specimens, for chrysanthemum raising has always been of a competitive nature. Master Wu's class won highest honour by virtue of some specimens from the Wu family collection.

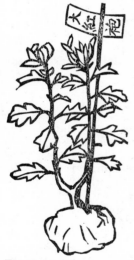

The chrysanthemums are sold in a ball of earth and to save tho salesmen many a head-scratching the fancy name of each specimen is indicated on a paper tag fastened to a little stick thrust into the earth ball.

*   *   *

Before its adaptability to artificial pollination and cross-breeding was discovered, the chrysanthemum had already been a favourite flower with the Chinese. A poet, T'ao Yuan-ming, of the Chin period (265-419 B.C.) took the lead and proclaimed its nature to be symbolic of the hermit. It was his own pet version of happiness to drink wine and look at chrysanthemums no doubt because he saw in them an image of himself, for then chrysanthemums were not so much noticed by the flower lovers in spite of its "frost resisting" and "unretouched beauty" (chrysanthemums were then mostly of yellow and white hues).

T'ao was a queer fellow with certain abnormal psychological tendencies that made it hard for him to adjust his relations harmoniously with his fellow-beings. When he was serving as the magistrate of the district of P'eng Tseh, he was once asked to dress up in his official robe to meet a petty courier from the governor's *yamen*. He protested, saying that he was not going to "bend his back" or bow to a person like that just on account of the "five bushels of rice" which was his allowance and resigned his office.   Later he distinguished himself as a great poet, writing on rural subjects and singing the praises of the greatness of nature and the sweet freedom of retired life.   As a mandarin he was an out and out failure.   His name and the word "chryanthemum" are now so co-related that one thinks of the other when either one of the two is mentioned.

Another Chinese poet, Fan Ch'eng-ta of the Sung Dynasty, was also a lover of chrysanthemums and wrote a short treatise on them, naming thirty-five fine varieties most of which were of a yellow colour.   Some of the names he gave to his favourite specimens were "Dragon's Brain" (as it had the flavour of a famous Chinese incense by this name), "New Silk," "Jade Bells", "Silver Terrace," and so forth. With clever and elaborate cultivations there are said to be more than two hundred kinds obtainable today, each with its own characteristics in the petals, ligulate, or ray flowers, each different in shape or size, some broad and others tubular and still others hairy and long, curved or twisted, and in colour all the shades of the rainbow are represented.

Fancy names given to the flowers include "Peach Flower Fan", "White Goose Quills" "Phoenix," "Spring Morning in the Han Palace", "Yellow Stork of the Immortals", "Coral Hooks", and "The Drunken Danseuse". Some of these are so minutely different from other similar varieties that only experts can tell which is which, particularly when the flowers are still in the "budding stage."   To save the florist many a baffling moment, each plant has a label inserted on a stick stuck in the soil to show its identity.

*   *   *

The chrysanthemums obtainable in the Peking markets are divided by cultural characteristics into three main classes: the *yuan ken* (原根) or "original root", the *chieh ken* (接根) or "jointed root", and the *fu ch'ien* (伏扦) or "*Fu* (hot weather) period saplings."   The first named is the kind grown in the natural way and the second is grown by grafting the stems of the chrysanthemums to the more sturdy and energetic roots of the wormwood.

Most of the plants offered by the florists are of the jointed-root variety which can be distinguished from the others by its typical bulby, swollen joint, marking the place where the operation was made during the rainy season.   The *Fu* saplings, being branches cut off and immediately planted in rich soils during the prolonged rainy summer of the three *Fu* periods, are often responsible for magnificent blossoms though, on account of their physical drawbacks, they do not grow high and usually bloom late in the season.

Another trick in chrysanthemum culture is to grow the so-called layers, branches pressed down from the parent plant and covered with earth and afterwards severed from the parent plant to grow independently after the stems have grown roots.   All these kinds were experimented on with success by old Mr. Wu in his own backyard garden.

To get the best results in developing the most luxurious blossoms, the buds of the chrysanthemums have to be cultivated. These buds are always seen sprouting from the base of each "original root" plant after the flowering season is about over in late autumn. They are cut off with a pair of sharp scissors and temporarily inserted in a flat basin of soft, rich mud, kept moist constantly and also agreeably warm under cover with plenty of sunshine throughout the long winter. Thus the buds will be kept alive until spring of the next year when they are transplanted into the ground, nursed and fertilized.

In this way, at the next chrysanthemum season, each of these plants will attain a height of seven or eight feet, a solitary flag-pole stem having a single flower of immense size and fine colouring. This is often an outstanding example of the fantastic variety it represents, as the side branches and the undesired buds have been eliminated and only the central or top flower is reared to perfection. Flowers of this type, often the chief attractions at shows, require rings to support the flower particularly the pompom variety which may reach ten inches or more in diameter.

The grafting of the chrysanthemums to the root (really the stem) of the wormwood is a delicate operation and only a person with much experience in plant surgery can expect to be successful. Specially raised wormwood plants are used and during the transitional period the joined parts are bandaged for a week or ten days with layers of the leaves of a kind of iris. The "saddle graftage" is the usual technique. After the healing process is complete, the plants will be so doctored that the few flowers expected to blossom, the rest are "weeded out", will grow parallel and in proportion and actually blossom about the same time.

Another variety known to the trade as *chi ching* (集錦) or "gathered brocade" is composed of a number of stems with flowers of many different colours and varieties joined to one robust stalk in the same process described above. These are not really much valued but for decorative purposes they are certainly masterpieces. At recent exhibitions in Peking, plants each with fifty and up to more than two hundred blossoms, timed to bloom with equal strength simultaneously, have been noticed. This, it seems, is achieved by retarding the fast-growing branches by inflicting small wounds on them and allowing the slow-coming branches to catch up while the wounded branches heal. The various branches are also bent and twisted to give the plant a shapely contour.

The most difficult method of chrysanthemum culture is by the planting of tiny seeds. The seeds mature late in winter and rearing and gathering them require a lot of care. Dyeing the seeds with colouring materials dissolved in a solution of raw opium has been found to impart new colourings to the future plants, but the new colour will keep only for one generation, and the next generation will revert to its original colour.

The petals of chrysanthemums are edible and stylish restaurants in Peking offer the "chrysanthemum samovar". Dried chrysanthemum flowers are used in Chinese medicine and are considered to be good for the eyes. They also serve as a substitute for tea.

*   *   *

The double ninth is also the annual season for eating the *hua kao* (花糕) or "flower cake". Following in the wake of the moon cakes, these make their appearance in the local pastry shops and shop-keepers hang out the advertising poster for *Po Kuo Hua Kao* (百果花糕), "Flower Cakes with a Hundred Fruits."

They are small round cakes about three inches across made on the sandwich principle with various nuts and dried fruits as fillings. The average Peking-*jen* usually finds them a strong temptation and few refuse to buy them and be thereby not "in fashion".

In past centuries the flower cakes were made in different manner. One writer records: "The people in the capital make chrysanthemum cakes filled with pomegranate seeds and chestnuts, pine weeds and dates, and decorated with small flags of coloured silks which they give to their friends as seasonable gifts."

Another historian says that at early dawn on the double ninth a thin slice of this cake was formerly placed on the head of each youngster in the house, to be an omen that everything would grow "high" with the child, "go over big" in other words, as in Chinese the word for "cake" has the same sound as that for "high", and this curious act served as a blessing and a prayer.

At one time in the past, too, the cakes were actually made in the shape of chrysanthemum blossoms and a meat core was also an important feature. But in spite of the colourful family history of the cakes, they are traceable only to the T'ang Dynasty and before this period the cakes were unknown. A famous poet in this dynasty thought to write an "ode to the flower cakes" but he had to give up the idea when be found that the word "cakes" *kao*, had never been used in the ancient classics. This story is according to a Chinese "Sketch Book".

The ninth day of the ninth moon is known as the *Ch'ung Yang Chieh* (重陽節) or the "festival of Double Yang," as the figure nine, being the highest of the odd numbers, is considered representative of the fullest force of the *Yang* or positive elements. Besides being a day for feasting it is also a day for making excursions to the countryside and to climb some lofty spot is particularly encouraged for which the phrase is *teng kao* (登高), "climbing high".

The custom of climbing some high places brings to mind the story of Fei Ch'ang-fang (費長房) and Huan Ching (桓景) of the Eastern Han Dynasty(25-220 A.D.). Fei was a scholar who specialized in divination and other similar mystical subjects. He served an apprenticeship with a famous magician of his time. From this magician, named Hu Kung(壺公) or Master Kettle, after a lengthy period of study he learned to foretell future happenings. Legend says that from his teacher he received as a graduation present a bamboo stick. Riding astride this bamboo stick he was able to get speedily to whatever place he wanted to go for the stick was the transformation of an enchanted dragon.

Besides, being in possession of a talisman of strange attributes, he was able to make the spirits of the dead run errands for him and even the petty local guardian gods bowed to his command. Riding about on the bamboo stick distances meant nothing to him and he was seen at various places a thousand miles apart on the same day.

Huan Ching was a friend of his and one day, said to be the ninth of the ninth moon, he told Huan Ching that if he really trusted him he should climb up the high mountains this day and take his family with him for an immense disaster was to come to his home. Huan Ching did as he was told and returning to his home the next morning found all his dogs and chickens dead. He was told by Fei that these domestic animals had suffered this fate in place of the Huan family.

The news soon spread in the neighbourhood and ere long it became an established custom for people to vacate their homes and seek refuge in the mountains on the Ch'ung Yang festival.

*   *   *

Of the many favourite places visited by the Peking-*jen* on the occasion of *Teng Kao*, or "Climbing the High Places" on the festival of the Double Ninth, the Western Hills of course is the ideal place and in the fairyland of the Imperial Hunting Park or in the woods and the templed hills to the west picnic parties were often held on such a day. It was at one time the vogue for people to bring their portable grilling utensils and hold an open-air feast and drinking party to which friends were invited.

Young Master Wu remembered having been on many such excursions with his parents and their friends and though too young to thoroughly appreciate the fun and significance of the occasion, yet it never failed to be an interesting experience to him. In the course of years he had been to many a historical spot in and around Peking, famous for being "lofty" places and therefore suitable for the purpose.

He was among the first visitors to the Coal Hill, right in the "backyard" of the Forbidden City, as then it was not yet thrown open to the public. He braved ascending the hill, pass-ing the spot where, as was explained to him by other members of the party, the last Ming Emperor hanged himself with a belt from a small tree in the face of an approaching rebellious army. From the summit of the hill he cast his eyes around for a panoramic view of the fair old city. Since that day he grew proud of Peking. There was then a school housed in the precincts of the Coal Hill enclosure and it was by specially arranging with the school authorities that they had gained admittance.

Another place he visited on a similar pilgrimage was the Fa T'a Ssu (法塔寺) or the Temple of the Pagoda of the Doctrine, situated near to the spot where he and his grandfather used to go fishing in summer. The seven-storied pagoda had been built with staircases in the inside and until shortly before young Wu's time it was possible for visitors to climb to the top and look out through the windows. But the police had to block the door with masonry after unpleasant incidents had marred many a happy day of recreation. An annual fair was also then held on the Double Ninth Festival although the bare pagoda, like a solitary lighthouse on a desolate island or an untiring sentry on first line duty, now remains alone to impress on passers-by the vanished glory of the old monastery.

On another occasion Young Wu was taken to the T'ao Jan T'ing (陶然亭) near to the narrow lane known as the Factory of the Black Kiln, where in the dim past of Peking's history bricks and tiles, glazed black and used for Tibetan or Lamaistic architecture, were baked. The T'ao Jan T'ing is the name given to n small pavilion perched precariously on top of a small hillock ia the midst of many Buddhist structures. The name *T'ao Jan* literally meaning "merrily" is a reference to a line by the famous poet Pai Chu-yi, which translates as:

"We shall date for a get-together
When the Chrysanthemums are yellow,
When merrily, merrily, you and I will drink,
My own home-made brew."

It is a lofty spot and actually a few feet higher than the old city wall encircling it on the south and the west. It is an adequate place for the festival's purpose.

The neighbourhood of T'ao Jan T'ing is also famous for being the location of several famous graves. There is one called the Fragrant Grave, where some say a disappointed scholar who had failed at the imperial examinations buried all his manuscripts and where others say a famous sing-song girl is buried. All who visit the grave seek out and read the weather-beaten tombstone on which is carved the famous lines, so romantic and touching and to a higher degree enigmatic and ambiguous, signed by the *nom de plume* "Scholar from East of the Bridge".

And close by is the Grave of the Parrot. A Mandarin serving a term in Canton had his parrot brought to the capital. A snow-white bird, it was no common parrot being definitely of super-parrot intelligence. It was so clever that it learned to recite lines from famous poems and sing short songs from memory. When it died the Mandarin had it buried here.

A few steps away is the grave of Tsueh Kuo (醉郭) or Kuo, the Drunkard, who was renowned far and near as an important popularizing genius standing supreme during the pioneering days of journalism in China. Kuo, a disillusioned patriot and under the influence of wine most of the time, used to lecture about current events to crowds gathered in the streets. An amateur press conference and headline commentator, he served the newspaper "audience" as a self-appointed "town-crier" and indirectly changed the reading habit of the immense populace to a certain extent until he died a pauper. This was in the declining years of the Manchu regime.

*   *   *

In late fall and winter it is the fashion of the Peking-*jen* to enjoy the *huo-kuo* (火鍋), "fire cooker," which is the name of an utensil, similar in principle to the Russian Samovar, used to serve a Chinese counterpart of the Japanese *sukiyaki*. It seems of Mongolian origin, perhaps an immigrant from Russian Siberia *via* the Ulanbator and Chita route, and has firmly rooted itself in the Chinese eating habits of ithe northern provinces. It is a pleasant informal deviation from the usual eating fashion and a very tasty gastronomical pastime. Being inexpensive and devoid

A Chinese *huo kuo* is a fast cooker, it burns charcoal and is usually made of copper. It is of Mongolian or even Russian origin.

of any waste, a *huo kuo* meal is well suited to the domestic house-keeping principle of frugality and most houses of the well-to-do families keep a *huo kuo* in their kitchen. It is also the season's *piece de resistance* in the restaurants, particularly in the so-called Mutton Restaurants run by Mohammedans.

The *huo kuo*, or samovar, is a copper utensil about ten inches high with a miniature charcoal stove built in the center around which is set a ring-shaped pan of proper depth. Live charcoals, burning briskly, are inserted into the stove and the rich soup stock is kept constantly at the boiling point in the surrounding pan during "performance". Like the *nabe* in the sukiyaki feast, the samovar is placed in the center of the dinner table and all the partakers attend to their own cooking.

The principal fare at such a meal is dishes and dishes of tender and juicy mutton, sliced thin, and which is taken up with chopsticks, placed in the boiling soup, kept there for a few seconds and then eaten with proper seasonings added afterward. The Chinese verb for cooking meats in this fashion is *shuan* (涮) which literally means "to rinse", and from this fact alone it is easy to understand the technique used. Thus the meat is cooked very rare, only the outside surface of each slice has changed colour and the inside is still a delicate pink for over-cooked meat would be tough and tasteless.

Soya sauce of a high grade is an important contributing factor to such a meal and each chopstick load of cooked meat is dipped in the sauce before being eaten. This also serves the purpose of cooling the meat off a little the same function as the bowl of beaten raw egg performs in the *sukiyaki* and no blowing is necessary!

Though mutton is the most important ingredient in the samovar recipe, there are many other things going with it. The most important vegetable in accompaniment is the Chinese sour cabbage, made by preserving half-boiled cabbage in a warm room for three or four days when it acquires the appearance and flavour of German *sauerkraut*. Then there are also the vermicelli made with bean starch and the frozen bean curds—regular bean curds frozen into an icy block and then de-iced with the texture changed into a porous, sponge-like matter. It is also common to cook a special kind of noodles prepared with the flour made from a local kind of small beans.

The soup used in the samovar is a rich pork soup and when this is not obtainable, as is usually the case in the average Chinese kitchen, certain kinds of cooked pork are used to produce substitutes by boiling them in water.

The Wus had their own samovar but it was often their

habit to order a specially filled samovar from the shops which, though costing a little higher, is properly filled with various fancy foods solidly packed in the ring-shaped pan, such as shrimps and oyster meats and ham and slices of fish and other kinds of sea foods, shark's fins, for example. Such an order, delivered at the house, also included a big complimentary pot of rich clear soup for refill purposes.

Old Mrs. Wu, of all the members in the family, was particularly fond of "rinsed mutton", and whenever during the wintry season there was a reason for a feast in the house, a guest staying for dinner, a small celebration or any other kind of an excuse, she would invariably suggest the use of the samovar.

*   *   *

In naming the chief delights of the Peking gourmet, one must never fail to mention the famous Peking duck. It is true that few formal and well-prepared menus could ever achieve the desired success without taking this famous dish into serious consideration. Ducks, like everything else in the Chinese kitchen, are cooked in a hundred and one ways and by "Peking duck" is always meant the roast duck. Of course, it is a sad mistake to list Peking duck as a family dish for it is rarely if ever included in the average family's food budget and if it ever appears in a budget it would be under "Entertainments." It took even the Wus a very good reason to order a duck from the shop though every morning's walk old Mr. Wu made was past the door of exactly such a place.

To enjoy Peking duck in a restaurant is a comparatively new practice grown out of modern tourism and the orthodox way was really to eat it in the home where it was delivered from the *lu p'u* (爐舖) or "oven shop", which specializes in the preparation of roast ducks and roast young pigs. An oven shop is also a Chinese delicatessen shop for here all the fancy ramifications of prepared meats are obtainable and an affiliated department is the Chinese sausage factory. Most of these oven shops have been named *Pien Yi Fang* (便宜坊) or "The Shop of Convenience," and a *Pien Yi Fang* is found in every important shopping district. One of them at least, to distinguish itself from its numerous namesakes, has prefixed to its name the word *Lao* (老) meaning "Old" or "the Original". This, it must be understood, is a typical example of a famous practice of commercial competition commonly seen in China—all over China.

Another well-known example is found in the scissors and knife trade. In one neighbourhood on the so-called Brass Street in Peking there are about seven or eight cutlery shops, crowded solidly together shoulder to shoulder, all displaying signs of *Wang Ma Tze* (王麻子), or "The Shop of Wang the Pockmarked", for it was once noticed by the critical buying public that one man with such markings on his face and going by the name of Wang sold the best pairs of scissors in town. To keep themselves "in the money", these shops unanimously adopted the same name and to avoid friction with a view to harmony and co-existence, each of them has affixed a word before the name and side by side stand the shops of *Wang Ma Tze*, and *Lao* (老) (Old) *Wang Ma Tze*, *Chen* (眞) (Genuine) *Wang Ma Tze*, *Chen*

Cheng (眞正) (Genuine and Straight) *Wang Ma Tze,* and *Chen Cheng Lao* (眞正老) (Genuine Straight and Old) *Wang Ma Tze,* and so on and so forth and Mr. Customer is the only one ever puzzled by these names. Ironically enough, none of the crowd would sue or ever think of suing another or all the others for patented name infringement for, none of them knows exactly whether his shop was really the original one and whether he has any right therefore to monopolize the beautiful name himself!

It was in this same way that *Pien Yi Fang,* or the Shop of Convenience, has become synonymous with an oven shop and by oven shop is meant a roast duck establishment.

Ducks intended for roasting are raised in a typical manner and it is interesting to look into the life story of a duck though it represents a short span of but seventy or eighty days from egg to oven. The duck is a strangely stupid bird and it is true that most of the drakes do not even know how to hatch their eggs and so a great part of the work is delegated to the motherly hens. Young ducklings fresh from the shells are fed with water weeds (the cartloads of water weeds from the Sea Palace lakes often seen on Peking streets are all used for this purpose alone), and after they have attained the desired size they are fattened with "bullets" of duckfood, each about the size of a man's thumb made with a mixture of kaoliang and bran and a certain kind of buck-wheat paste.

The ducks are well attended in a way and are fed by the raisers with these "bullets" which are forced unceremoniously down their throats accompanied by a poking with the finger to keep the food on the move and a gentle massage of the neck in order to allow each attendant to serve as many ducks as possible. About ten "bullets" constitute a meal and a duck gets three meals a day. The ducks are not allowed to exercise much as to do so would mean a waste of food and some quacking and an occasional flapping of the wings are about all the controlled physical exertion they are permitted.

The oven for roasting ducks is an open fire place burning heavy logs or other substitute fuels and a slow process is responsible for the thorough-going job and the most delicious flavours. During the roasting process the duck, first emptied inside, is filled with a rich soup and hung in the oven with iron hooks, carefully watched by an expert chef with constant shifting of the position to avoid burning. When the first Japanese farmer roasted his chicken on a plowshare and so invented the *tori-nabe,* he probably did it with similar vigilance!

Peking duck is served with little round flat-cakes and, breaking all rules of good form, raw garlic and raw onion are freely used even by the most fastidious persons. The enjoyment is not in the fattened meat but in the crisp golden-brown skins with a very small amount of fat attached thereto. Even a good-sized duck will have only so many square inches of skin and so a duck feast is always an expensive matter.

* * *

In the late fall Peking's famous multitude of bird-lovers again crowd the market place in search of the season's new additions to their collection for it is at this time that the various

kinds of migratory birds pass through North China on their annual trips to the warm southern regions in their escape from the
bitter, biting, frozen north.   A stopover is made by the flocks
either in the neighbourhood of the Eastern Tombs or the Western Tombs, the Manchu Mausolea, where thick pine groves and
clear streams offer abundant feeding and watering and it is then
and there that they are caught in the ingeniously placed "pull-
nets" and therefore "lost in the shovel" to the migrating
flocks.

Collectively speaking these little birds are locally known as
Hawa Niao-erh (花鳥兒) or "miscellaneous birds", and amongst
these the expert long-timer and the novel "freshman" would
find suitable little companions to keep them company and help
spend the forthcoming dreary winter and on whom the men
will lavish tender care.   Trick birds are not kept long and their
last days come at the season of the "Small Snow" and "Big
Snow". Such birds very seldom live through the winter season.

The common pet birds in cages, such as the canary, the
"Yellow Bird" (Siskin), the "Hundred Clever" (Mongolian lark),
the *Tze-tze-hei-erh* (自自黑兒) (Tit) and the *Tien-k'e-erh* (靛脦兒)
(Ruby-throat) are famous for their songs and live for many
years (Old Mr. Wu once had a yellow siskin which was with him
for eight years) no doubt on account of their being natives of
this region and well adapted to the climatic conditions.   The
passing migrants are never impressive in their singing and are
never expected to live long.   This is a sad yet true statement
and a fact put up as "unavoidable" by bird-lovers in this
country.

Young scholar Wu was not openly encouraged to keep such
birds though many of his schoolmates had their trick birds for,
in the opinion of his parents, his time was to be devoted to his
studies alone.   But his grandfather once did promise him a bird
and in search of such a bird they made frequent trips to the bird
market at the Lung Fu Ssu Temple Fair.

The trick birds are kept perched on a stick.   First of all
they must get absolutely used to frequent handling and the first
lesson in their education is to eat from their master's hand.
Around each bird's neck is worn a wire collar with a short chain
and by a specially made hook it is then attached to a length of
string tied to a branched stick.   The string is often put through
a hole in the stick and weighted at the other end with a suitable
drop to prevent the bird from hanging itself after entanglement
with the superfluous string when the bird is standing on the
perch.   During the performance of tricks the birds are detached
from the hook and if a bird loved freedom it could get away
easily at such a time but well-behaved birds usually do not
cherish such dangerous thoughts.

The season's first comers are the *Chu tien-erh* (祝點兒) or
redpolls (*Acanthis linaria*), a greyish white bird with streaks of
brown and greenish black with a little indistinctly marked red
crown and a similarly coloured region on the throat.   This bird
is taught to fly to its master from a distance, which trick is
known as *chiao yuan* (叫遠) or "calling afar", and to catch a
bird seed thrown in the air.   This is termed *chih fei-shih*
(吃飛食) or "eating flying food".   The redpoll is also taught to

fetch little paper flags from a piece of cardboard to which the flags are loosely clipped. Another kind of bird that makes its annual appearance about this same time is the *Yen chiao-erh* (雁雀兒) or brambling, which is also taught to do the same tricks.

Other trick birds to follow immediately are the *Chiao-tsueh* (交嘴) or crossbill (*Loxia curvirostra japonica*), the *Lao hsi-erh* (老西兒) or hawfinch (*Cocco thraustes japonicus*), and the *Wu-t'ung* (梧桐) or masked grosbeak (*Eophona pervonata magnirostris*). And another commonly seen bird at this time is the *Tai-p'ing-niao* (太平鳥) or waxwing (*Bombycilla garrulus centralasiae*). Young Wu was allowed to choose one amongst these for his own pet.

*　　　*　　　*

The most interesting member of the trick bird class must be said to be the crossbill with its typically twisted and crossed mandibles. Most of the crossbills are rather good-sized, averaging about five or six inches from tip to tip but the bird-fanciers seem to value the smaller ones more highly. It is said that the plumage of this bird changes with age; starting with a greyish yellow during infancy the males gradually turn red as they grow older and the females a dirty green. The Chinese believe that if the crossing of the bill is with the upper mandible turned to the left, it is a male and if to the right, a female.

In general appearance they are very good looking and suggest a small parrot, as they do also in their habits. Though the curious bills seem to be a handicap for the poor little birds, this conception must be a personal prejudice for you do not need to feel sorry for them at all. Such bills are very useful in cracking the woody seed coverings of the coniferous trees on which, in the wild state, they depend for their food supply.

The crossbills are taught the most interesting tricks and one of these is to fetch a small empty walnut shell with many holes bored in it which they catch and hold with their bill and hand to the master *par avion* after flying a distance to reach him. These birds are fed with the seeds of a kind of flax which are given to almost all pet birds in North China. Another often seen crossbill trick is opening a small miniature trunk and fetching from therein various trinkets. The bird flies to the trunk from a distance and, pulling a bolt with its bill, unlocks the trunk which opens with a concealed spring. It then conveys to its master any one of a number of little miniature weapons, mason's or carpenter's tools and similar things, all carved of bamboo and very light in weight. There may be ten or fifteen things in the box and the crossbill makes as many trips to fetch them one by one, each time, opening the trunk by the bolt.

The hawfinch and the grosbeak are taught to do an entirely different type of tricks and the most characteristic of these is the *tah-tan-erh* (打彈兒) or "shooting the balls". It is a very difficult trick apparently and takes many days of intensive training for the bird to gain any real proficiency. There are usually two balls, one called the *ti-tan-erh* (底彈兒) or "bottom ball", and the other a *kai-tan-erh* (蓋彈兒) or "cover ball". The former is small and about four millimeters in diameter and the latter is up to ten millimeters. Some birds can handle three balls. The balls are made of bone or ivory. A hawfinch is a heavily-built bird about five inches from tip to tip and generally of a buff and plain brown while the grosbeak is a grey bird with black wings and tail feathers and a bright yellow beak, and it is a much larger bird, too, easily measuring seven inches in length.

As preliminary training the birds must be taught to recognize their master and to develop an attachment to him. After this is achieved they are taught to catch the little balls which are dropped literally into their open mandibles from a distance of but a few inches and then little by little the altitude is increased finally reaching forty or fifty or even more feet in the air, and the birds will fly up and catch them in mid-air at a distance so far away from the ground that the balls are practically invisible to the naked human eye.

The bottom ball, the smaller one, is first tossed into the air and the larger one follows afterward so that the bird will first manage to catch the bottom one and then make another sky-rocket dash to catch the bigger one—very often the two balls are thrown in two different directions! The hawfinch and the grosbeak are both equipped with rather strong and conically shaped bills which make it possible to do this trick. These balls are then returned to the master in token of which success, they are fed a few grains of their food. They eat a kind of seed known locally as *hsiao mah tze* (小蔴子) or "small flax seed". In order to reach still higher altitudes these balls may also be tossed mechanically. In this case use is made of a longhandled thrower with a tubular socket for holding the balls. This is an old pastime and very popularly indulged in. It was much favoured by the former eunuchs during the imperial days. Old Mr. Wu used to know a man, an eunuch, who had a grosbeak which was trained to circle around its master seventeen times, somersault-ing and looping-the-loop as it wheeled about after catching the bottom ball and before soaring skyward again to catch the cover ball. This, of course, was a record so to speak and ordinarily those doing about eight or nine rounds would be considered acceptable performers.

The waxwing is a beautiful grey bird with silken plumage and a good-looking crest with the wing-tips decorated with bright wax-red and yellow tips. These are a rather sluggish lot and good only for catching things thrown to them as food, notably the Chinese black dates. It is said that in the wild state, the waxwings live on the berries of the mistletoe alone.

*　　　*　　　*

Young Master Wu was not disappointed for his grandfather bought for him a trained crossbill with many tricks in its repertoire and a set of five "properties" and so, losing no time in the training process, there was fun ready for the enjoying.

OLD MR. WU BECOMES ILL

LITTLE Bald Head, later named Wu Hsueh-wen, attended the public school for six years and in due course graduated with high honours from the institution and was transferred to a secondary school through a matriculation examination which he passed without difficulty. He was then fourteen years of age. The Wus were very happy. This was on the whole a good year for the Wus because certain business in which the old man was interested in partnership with others had a prosperous year and Master Wu's father also received a promotion in the bank where he had been working for many years.

But as misfortunes come to all families they must be expected to fall on the Wus too. Old Mr. Wu had begun to note a general decline in his health. For a long time there was always something the matter with him and he became much less active, got suddenly much thinner and his old wife, his son, and the grandson, too felt very concerned. Young Mr. Wu was particularly worried and bought all sorts of tonics and various kinds of dainty things for him to eat with the expectation of whipping up a fresh appetite, for old Mr. Wu was noted to be taking much less food than he had been in the habit of doing.

At different times young Mr. Wu invited doctors to come and visit his father. These doctors, like all Chinese doctors who never fail to find something wrong with any person—even an entirely healthy person—always had prescriptions to write out and pills and herbs to offer, all had medicines to recommend. The old man took the medicines faithfully but they were of little help.

One doctor, an old man with much experience who had been introduced to them by a family friend, was frank enough to declare that there was really nothing the matter with the old man for his "six pulses were peaceful and harmonious", and he had nothing to recommend in the way of medicines except the advice that the old man take a little opium, just a little. At this idea old Mr. Wu smiled. He thought the suggestion absurd.

That same evening, after office, young Mr. Wu went to visit the doctor at his residence and anxiously enquired of him:

"What do you imagine is the matter with my father?"

"My good old nephew (this was the conventional way for an elderly man to address a young person) there is really nothing that medicine will do for your father. Believe me, medicines though we Chinese say *yung tang t'ung shen* (用當通神) (administered properly, they compare with Creation) will do no good for your father. The proverb says: Fine health with the aged, cold spell in spring and heat wave after the Autumn Solstice, which means that these three things are not to be expected to last long. Your father, I must say, has managed very well indeed, and it would be hardly possible to expect his health to pick up much— yes, he is thin and pale and I would suggest, since he does not favour taking opium, giving him few medicines but good nourishing foods and to take good care of him. Then he might be

with you a few more years. Do all you can to make him eat,
do you understand? Man is iron but food is steel, goes the saying. How old is he, anyway?"

"Seventy-six, at his last birthday", said young Mr. Wu.

"No wonder. That is not a bad age at all, is it not? Remember my suggestions—there is no point in giving him the 'bitter
fluids,' not because I do not wish to help him."

      *   *   *

Young Mr. Wu was suddenly awakened to the grave outlook
to which he was only faintly prepared—rather he was unprepar-
ed. And after he got home that day he wept bitter tears.

That autumn the old man became rather sickly and oftentimes as he came into the open to enjoy the morning for a few
minutes, not satisfied with being confined in his room all the
time, he caught a cold. And a cold meant coughs for him, and
sleepless nights. His old wife kept awake too and helped him
pass the long nights for, more so here in China than in other
countries, the wife is an old husband's nurse. The old couple
often kept awake for hours.

"Perhaps a little food may help you to sleep a little while?"
the old wife would suggest. And forthwith she would light up
the alcohol burner and over the fire cook for him a little *ou fen*
(藕粉) (lotus-root starch) or *hsing jen fen* (杏仁粉) (almond
powder starch) which take the place of the foreign Ovaltine or
Ovomaltine.

Sometimes it helped and sometimes it failed to help.

The young couple living in the western side wing of the
quadrangle of the house were often disturbed, too, and young
Mr. Wu, seeing the light in his parents' bedroom, often rose
and came over in the cold of the night just to see the old man
but he invariably returned, after being persuaded to do so by
his parents, feeling an unnamable blank.

Little Wu who slept in the next room was also disturbed and
awakened, he would ask his father in an undertone, "What if
Yeh-yeh is going to die?"

"Go to sleep and ask no questions. You have to be in school
early in the morning, do you not?" or something like this was
usually the annoyed remarks yelled at him. Young Mr. Wu was
really worried.

      *   *   *

Old Mr. Wu had not been well for a long time but thanks to
the careful nursing of his aged wife and the attention constantly paid by his son he was able to carry on for some time without any serious development for the worse but there was very
little, if any, appreciable improvement in his condition. Young
Mr. Wu understood the old physician's advice very thoroughly
and no more medicines were given to his father, which incidentally agreed with the old man's idea very well for of all the things
in the world he hated nothing more than having to take medicines.

But old Mrs. Wu was of a superstitious turn of mind and
often thought that there must be something the matter somewhere and one day, taking out the family almanac for the year,

she found the section where it said that sickness in the family is always due to some ghost or spirit being offended. It depends on which day of the month a person falls sick on to find the proper ghost to seek relief from. Calling her grandson to her side she had him read out a column from the book, wherefrom she hoped to learn something to help the old man's indisposition.

"Perhaps this might work," said the old lady. "Your grandfather got sick last month on the fourteenth and this column here is therefore the proper answer to it."

Youthful Master Wu did not believe in such things but nevertheless read to her:

"If a person becomes sick on the fourteenth of the month, this is on account of a female spirit, a former member in the immediate family circle, who is doing all the mischief Such a victim is liable to show spells of cold and an ache in the head. The limbs are heavy and stiff. The spirit is hiding somewhere on the patient's back. Instant relief is assured if five sheets of the white ghost-money paper are burned twenty-five paces to the east of the door of the house, and a talisman is written with cinnabar on a yellow piece of paper and worn on the person and a duplicate one is pasted onto the bedroom door."

This mysterious-looking calligrapher's nightmare and etymological enigma is a Taoist talisman which, if written in red cinnabar and worn on the person, is a certain remedy for any person who has fallen ill on the fourteen day of any month.

"So it must be," said the old lady. "And where is the specimen of the talisman to be prepared? Let me get the paper and things ready and you will write the talisman for your grandfather. You can do it very nicely."

They did exactly as the almanac dictated, without telling the old man about it. They noted no effect whatsoever afterward.

*   *   *

In the same book there was also another section where a simple way of fortune-telling was explained. There are sixty-four formulas or explanations, each represented by a combination of six Chinese cash, showing either a "tail" or a "head" with each composite cash. Sixty-four combinations, which are all the possible formations, are the keys to sixty-four explanations. The technique is very simple. Take six coins and shake them in the closed hands, praying in the meantime for the heavenly spirits to give the person an inkling of an answer for the question being asked. Then these six cash are set down one by one in a line as they come out from the hand. By the combination, like in a telegraph code of dots and dashes, the proper item of explanation will be located in the book, which would give an alarmingly interesting answer to the question being asked.

Old Mrs. Wu, secretly praying and begging for a revelation of her husband's future, particularly stressed whether or not he could be expected to recover. The cash, duly rattled, were laid on a table and they were in order: head, tail, head, tail, head, head. Searching the almanac pages with a beating heart, she found the entry: No. 61. She knew most of the characters but had her grandson read to her the divination:

> "As if caught in a big rain or snow-storm,
> The traveller, how bitter and cold!
> Drenched with water and feet in the thick mud,
> Things do not suit your hope, and so be careful."

and further on it said:

> "Sickness: prolonged.
> Chances for Wealth: meager.
> Court Suit: very unlucky.
> Marriage: hopeless."

"It sounds very bad, does it not?"

"Yes, but grandmother, these are all such foolish things. I wish you would not believe in them", exclaimed young Master Wu.

* * *

Old Mr. Wu was a much beloved person in the Wu family and his sickness was causing all the family a lot of uneasiness. Nor did the concern stop with their own people for all the old friends and relatives hearing of the old man's illness came in parties of twos and threes to see him and offer their best wishes. Chinese people do not stay in hospital under ordinary circumstances and the more serious their sickness becomes the less willing are they to move away from their dear homestead. These well-wishers also brought various kinds of gifts as a matter of ceremony, amongst which were noted the famous bird's nest and the white fungi from Szechuan province, both considered important tonics, and also medicated pear syrup, which is a popular remedy for coughs. These people came invariably in the early afternoons for in the Chinese way of doing things a seriously unwell person must not be visited in the evenings for fear evil spirits roaming in the dark may follow the strangers into the sick room and cause trouble!

Madame Ho, young Mr. Wu's mother-in-law, was a frequent caller during these days and she, though reluctant at first, was bold enough at last to recommend a witch doctor, an elderly woman who lived near her country estate and was known "far and wide" as a very good witch doctor, having many cases of cure on her record.

In the usual course of things such a recommendation is rarely made for not all people believe in such exorcistic therapy and in the case of the Wu family opinion was so clearly divided between the believers and the unbelievers that it was a very delicate question to raise. Not only that but there were also other things to be taken into consideration. One of these was represented by a prevalent maxim that "one may recommend a fortune-teller but never a physician", for the Chinese do not wish to be involved with any unnecessary controversy liable to give rise to serious consequences. But in the present case, it was, as another Chinese proverb goes, "trying to cure a dead horse as if it were a live one." Besides, Madame Ho had been approached by young Mr. Wu on the question many times and she was clearly given to understand that even if the scheme she might suggest did not work out satisfactorily she would not be to blame.

*   *   *

It must be understood that in spite of all that native and foreign medical practice has been able to demonstrate, there are still a good number of people in Peking and elsewhere in China who believe that these witch doctors can actually do things. Witch doctors are known as *ch'iao-hsiang-ti* (瞧香的) in Chinese, or "incense watchers", because they base their prospects of each case upon how the incense offered burns at the shrine—whether very briskly or otherwise.

If the incense burns briskly enough and the flame is high the spirits are said to be pleased and success is but a matter of course. But a witch doctor would consider a case hopeless if the incense refuses to burn with vigour! It must also be understood that sometimes faith does cure certain maladies and the witch doctors are usually thoroughly versed in the art of mind reading and human psychology and are able to give soothing advice as we shall see in the case of our old Mr. Wu. They practice, of course, without official permission and theirs is, as it were, a "shady" business.

To make a long story not so long, young Mr. Wu, desperate to do everything to bring his father back to his good old self, was (as might be expected) perfectly willing to give the witch doctor a chance and one early morning he was taken to the house of the renowned Sun Nai Nai (孫奶奶) (Grandmother Sun) out in a little village adjacent to the main highway leading outside Hsi Chih Men. Sun Nai Nai had her own prestige to protect and was not to be summoned by a hasty informal call; she always required that somebody responsible for the patient call on her in person and beg her ardently to do so before she would agree to condescend to exert herself on any "philanthropic" missions.

Sun Nai Nai was a witch doctor by inheritance, her late mother-in-law figured gallantly in the trade in her day and survived many a police raid and government ban. Her house was patently decorated, as young Mr. Wu saw, with oblong squares of cloths of different shades of yellow and orange on which were mostly inscribed the hackneyed phrase "*Yo Ch'iu Pi Ying*" (有求必應). "Where there is a prayer there is an answer", with other slightly modified versions of the same phrase. Others bore the positive indorsement of *Chen Ling* (眞靈) or "Truly Marvellous".

All of these were nailed to the walls inside and out, in many tiers, some even doubled over others. Each one of these had been presented to her in acknowledgment of her good work and was a dated document and bore a signature. Some of these were faded in colour but others were apparently newer additions. Young Mr. Wu, originally somewhat half-hearted, was now definitely sure that if she could do such wonders for others, she could no doubt be able to do just one more miracle in the case of his sick father.

*   *   *

The Chinese witch doctor's trade is built on a foundation of a peculiar sect of paganism, nay, of animal-worship.

There are four important branches of animal-worship, known to the Chinese as the *Ssu Ta Men* (四大門) or "Four Big Doors (Divisions)", referring to the fox, the mink, the hedgehog and the snake. The fox and the mink are primarily worshipped as family gods of fortune and, if properly worshipped, are quite capable of bringing prosperity and other kinds of good luck to the worshippers. Stories of incredible intercourses of men with them are legion. It is a commonplace to find a small shrine devoid of any images, in every detail a miniature temple in a spacious garden or in the backyard or some other desolate spot in the compound where offerings of eggs and wine are placed so many times in the year. These shrines are built for the benefit of the fox and the mink.

As to the hedgehogs and snakes, these are mostly considered as evil spirits and to be shunned as much as possible. So much is this belief so that to see a hedgehog, even by accident, foretells bad luck, and as to snakes, the very word suggests destruction and bankruptcy. Snakes of one sort or another are said to dwell in every Chinese house and are often concealed above the papered Chinese ceilings which by right is also the dominion of the rats. These snakes are called *chia sheh* (家蛇), "domestic snakes", and these domestic snakes simply must not be seen for then they would be an omen of impending catastrophe of great proportions coming to the family of the person who has seen them. This may be a tragic death, repeated deaths, some major mishap or a fire.

During the troubled days of the Han Dynasty there were simultaneous insurrections of various assorted sizes and designs and famines in the land answering to every conceivable description which were followed immediately by a collapse of the ruling house, and this series of misfortunes was foretold, it is said, by a reptile falling on the emperor's audience throne when the emperor was just about to sit down. This happened on the fifteenth day of the fourth moon of the second year of the reign of Chien Ning, as is set down in Chinese history. If the emperor had been diligent enough with his state affairs and, instead of getting himself preoccupied with other interests, had held his audiences oftener and not once every six months the snakes might have known better and taken a seat elsewhere.

Not all snakes and things are possessive of magical influence but only those are which have undergone a course of *hsiu lien* (修煉) or "practice of the austerities of asceticism" of various durations from 200, 300, 500 or even 1,000 or more years with merits proportionate and per scale. Exactly what kind of curriculum a course of *hsiu lien* includes must be left to those who have practiced such to explain but suffice it to say that after such a lengthy period of *hsiu lien* they would be possessed of miraculous faculties which, if demonstrated to Alladin himself, would make him feel so ashamed of his lamp that he would halt the first rubbish man that passed along and sell it for "scrap".

One of these faculties enables sanctified animals to take possession of some human beings, known to be of a benevolent type, and through them worshippers are advised what to do and how to deal with a sickness or some other misfortune. They are always women who are thus possessed. A woman who has been possessed by a fox is said to *ting* (頂) a fox, by a mink to *ting* a mink and so forth. *Ting* itself means, "to carry something on top of the head" and a corollary meaning of the word is "to act as a proxy", particularly "substituting something good with something not quite as good."

Sun Nai Nai, the witch doctor whom young Mr. Wu went to entreat for the benefit of his aged father, was said to *ting* a mink though nobody dared in her presence to breathe the word mink as this would be a first-class insult and would bring disastrous consequences. There the word is represented by the phrase *Ta Hsien Yeh* (大仙爺) meaning the "First Fairy Grandfather". The portrait of "First Fairy Grandfather", a smiling white-bearded old mandarin in Manchu court garb, carefully painted by an artist, was ceremoniously hung on the wall in Sun Nai Nai's shrine room, beside a big carved wooden shrine housing, as all who had eyes could see, an image of the Goddess of Mercy. In front of both these images were to be seen dishes holding "fruits in season" and cakes and things all presented by the benefited clientele.

Young Mr. Wu reverently (he had not been so reverent for many years before this) lighted the incense bundles and set them in the burner, kowtowing three times to the Goddess of Mercy, aggregating nine bows.

In the meantime old Sun Nai Nai assumed her position beside the shrine with her legs bent *a la* Buddha fashion. As if hypnotized, if not under mild anaesthetic, she became sleepy and yawning three times she definitely fell asleep. In her sleep she began to talk and gave a vivid description of her instantaneous call at the Wu residence. She then dictated a simple prescription for the old man to take. An elderly man sitting in a corner of the room jotted it down on a piece of paper. He was apparently Sun Nai Nai's private secretary. She did not speak very fast so her secretary did not seem to need stenographic training.

*   *   *

By a casual conversation briefly exchanged with Madame Ho, who introduced young Mr. Wu to the witch doctor Sun Nai Nai, a circumstantial background was quickly formed in the mind of the self-proclaimed medium with the superhuman beings and she was able to construct a picture of the Wu house and the general condition of the patient, with which she was able graphically to impress the somewhat skeptical applicant.

"*Ta Hsien Yeh* and I have just been to make a rapid inspection of your house as is usual with the doings of the *hsien chia* (仙家) (super-humans). *Ta Hsien Yeh* says there is nothing critical about your father's sickness although it is not something that can stand neglect. *Ta Hsien Yeh* knows your father very well. He says your mother is even a more devout Buddhist. We must all rely upon the Buddha . . . There is something wrong in your honourable residence, something like a female ghost looking for worldly offerings having taken advantage of the occasion as a pretext—for there is a gust of *yin-ch'i* (陰氣) ("negative air") in the sickroom. Your father should move to another room to avoid the evil *yin-chi*. Why do you not do so? There are several vacant and unoccupied rooms in your compound... Your father must have been sleeping then and your mother was sitting in a chair near the bed, perhaps trying to take a nap... that must have been your mother, is it not? About sixty-odd years old, with whitish hair, wearing a dark-coloured gown of blue or something. We were there only a few moments and so did not see very clearly. There is something very shiny which projects a beam of light in the outer part of your father's room, perhaps a mirror or a picture-frame. *Hsien Chia* do not like mirrors as you know and *Ta Hsien Yeh* and I quickly withdrew."

Young Wu was somewhat mystified for outside his father's bedroom was a full length mirror, a dressing mirror. Perhaps *Ta Hsien Yeh* had really been to inspect the place he thought to himself.

"Give the old man a dose of medicine and some of the *hsien yao* (仙藥) (super-human medicine) to take," Sun Nai Nai went on with the prescription. "Use a vehicle for the medicine, consisting of seven walnuts, baked in the shell and then cracked, and seven big nutmegs, boiled thoroughly in three cupfuls of rootless water (fresh well water caught at the fountainhead without touching the ground or bottom of the reservoir is called *wu-ken-shueh* (無根水) cr rootless water), and add while boiling a small pinch of salt and seven large pinches of tea leaves. Pour into the sieved liquid the *hsien yao*. Give him fifteen small packages, use five packages a time. Drink the fluid only, though it would be much more effective to wash down also the residual matter in the cup for it has all been blessed by *Ta Hsien Yeh* and is therefore good medicine."

Young Mr. Wu received fifteen small packages of incense ashes gathered fresh from the incense burner, about three grams in each package. This is the *hsien yao* dispensed universally at the witch doctors' almost anywhere in China.

Yawning again, Sun Nai Nai came to herself again looking awfully tired and her secretary and assistant quickly brought her a hot towel with which she wiped off the sweat from her forehead.

"You live so far away from here: it was hard for me to follow, the *Ta Hsien Yeh* goes so fast!" said the witch doctor, panting heavily as a novice runner at the end of his first hundred yard dash.

*   *   *

Sensing that the interview was at an end young Mr. Wu in his business mind realized that it was time to pay and suddenly recalled that in their rush trip out he forgot to ask his mother-in-law how much it was going to cost him. So in a brief phrase he whispered the question to her but before she got the message and filed back the answer, witch doctor Sun burst out:

"No, no, do not give us money, for this is all charity work on our part. There will be further trips, for *hsien chia*, unlike your worldly physicians, do not count upon instant cure. We will accept only some money with which we will buy incense and so on. We shall also see if it will be necessary for me to visit your house and try to appease any possible evil spirits that might be tormenting your father. Such a thing must be carefully done and in your house."

Sun Nai Nai prefers to settle a local issue on the spot preceded by an investigation commission.

Young Mr. Wu pocketed the prescription and the small packages of incense ashes and leaving a dollar on the shrine table bade good-bye to the witch doctor, his mother-in-law following behind.

"I will come with my mule cart if we find we need your visit to our son-in-law's house."

"Very glad to go, this is all *hsien chia's* charitable duties."

Sun Nai Nai was waiting for exactly such an invitation.

*   *   *

It was not without much trouble that the Wus induced the old man to take the "super-human medicine," for old Mr. Wu represented a type of person who was amongst the first to "rebel" against the superstitious beliefs of the old school. He took the medicine with tears of gratitude in his eyes for he saw from the fact that his son's usually sound judgment was being affected by emotional influences that his condition must be very serious and his dear boy was doing everything to save him.

The "super-human medicine" was not without some effects, for the family (if not the patient himself) was able to see a slight improvement in the old man's condition. There were two or three more visits to the witch doctor. The improvement, however, was not to last long, for about a week later old Mr. Wu developed new complications. He was either sleepy or unconscious most of the time and took still less nourishment than usual. He was sinking slowly but surely.

The routine life of the family was paralyzed. Young Mr. Wu had to ask for more leaves of absence from work and scholar Wu was also told to stop going to school for the time being. Scholar Wu was not sorry to do so though it had certainly not been his habit to ask for leave from school. He wanted to be near his sick grandfather and he had found it hard to concentrate on his lessons anyway.

"Perhaps there really is a need for Sun Nai Nai to come to our house and look things over," suggested young Mr. Wu. "Let us get her."

*   *   *

Sun Nai Nai came with Madame Ho in her mule cart.

She talked with the Wus for a while (gathering more data for reference) and asked that a table and incense burner be put in the central courtyard. Out of a yellow cloth bundle she produced a number of round paper discs, yellow in colour, some four inches across, overprinted with magic words in the Tibetan and Chinese languages arranged in circles. Kowtowing in the four directions and burning bundles of incense she lit the paper discs on the incense flame one by one and cast them about her on the ground.

"What is she doing?" asked scholar Wu of his grandmother, who were both watching through the glass windows.

"She is burning the *Wang Sheng Ch'ien* (往生錢) (Cash of Deliverance)", answered the old lady. "*Wang Sheng Ch'ien* are of great merits for the person on whose behalf they are burned. They bear sacred words from the Diamond Sutra and other holy books and are good for saving the souls of all from peril. Do you not see that Sun Nai Nai is murmuring as she lights each one of the discs? She is speaking to the *Ta Hsien Yeh* for whose benefit they are intended."

Sun Nai Nai then asked to be shown the patient.

Fortunately for her old Mr. Wu was just then resting himself with closed eyes. For had he been awake it would have been a very doubtful matter whether or not she would have been allowed to come in to see him.

Sun Nai Nai made a hurried inspection of the room and then made for the Wus' backyard where she was led by young Mr. Wu and Madame Ho. There again she knelt on the ground and kowtowed in the four directions. Scholar Wu was with them, filled with curiosity as to what the woman was going to do there.

"A child's eyes are *ching* (淨) (pure) eyes," said Sun Nai Nai, accosting the child, "and you can see there is a cloud of black smoke on top of that big elm tree over there. You can see but they, the others, can't."

Everybody looked up but saw nothing.

"I will ask *Ta Hsien Yeh* to drive it away for it is a bad sign and if that cloud of black air can not be driven off, it will be just a case of *t'ien shu* (天數) (will of heaven)."

*　　　*　　　*

The next morning witch doctor Sun Nai Nai sent word by Madame Ho that she was sorry she could do nothing for the old man, not even the omnipotent *Ta Hsien Yeh* who had admitted his helplessness to her.

"Sun Nai Nai says that she has asked *Ta Hsien Yeh* to consult the records of births and deaths at the *Kwei Men Kwan* (鬼門關) (the Pass of the Ghost Gate) kept in the office of the archivists, one of which is *Ta Hsien Yeh's lao p'eng yu* (old friend) and through him he was able to learn of good news.

"According to him, there is a vacant position in the local Guardian God's temple in a certain village in Yunnan, and the deity in charge of such appointments having been favourably impressed by the fine virtues and upright character of the old man, has nominated him to be appointed to this position in the next world. They are going to send for him within the next few days as soon as the proposal, now before the Jade Emperor God, has been formally ratified."

DEATH PROCEDURES

WITCH doctor Sun Nai Nai, an expert rumour-monger, set up a smoke screen with the farcical news that old Mr. Wu had been nominated to an official position in the next world and, thus cleverly covered, effected a strategic retreat in perfect order and per pre-arranged plan having earned all possible money from the Wus. Though not all people believed what she said, such a piece of good news was quite effective in taking away a part of the bitter sting from the impending death of the old man who was but four years short of being an octogenarian.

*　　*　　*

During the last days of old Mr. Wu there were a number of things to be done which were not within the knowledge and experience of his family members but the Wus being such nice people not a few amongst their old friends and neighbours volunteered their services in rendering the much-needed help. Of these people one man stood out eminently, one of old Mr. Wu's sworn brothers, one of the few still living, a certain Mr. Liu, young Mr. Wu's "Seventh Uncle".

Seventh Uncle had more leisure than he could find use for and was always the friend in need whenever there was something to be done in the families of his acquaintances. He stayed with the Wus at their invitation as an extra handy man around the house. Being an experienced hand with everything, to render such timely assistance was his amateur specialty and fond pleasure.

"Perhaps it is not inopportune now for me to suggest getting Old Brother's clothes and things ready. He may not go yet but again he may and we Chinese have a tradition which is to scare off the evil spirits with such preparations as you must have heard about," Seventh Uncle said one day soon after his arrival.

"Yes, I suppose father will prefer to don his old Manchu court garb for he always felt it an honour to have served as a government official during his younger days. The things are all well kept and my mother will know exactly where to lay her hands on them," young Mr. Wu replied.

"You have at least to get a special pair of boots from the Shou Yi P'u (壽衣舖) (store specializing in funeral clothes) in front of which shop a monstrous-sized wooden Chinese boot, lacquered black, stands as a signboard. It is not proper for a dead man to wear satin boots. Satin is called *tuan tze* (緞子) in Chinese which sound-combination, represented by different characters, would also mean "discontinued sons" and it is not a good omen for posterity. This is all *mi-hsin* (迷信) (superstition) though. You must get a pair made with soft thin *silk* called *ling-tze* (綾子) and which are proper."

"That reminds me," enjoined old Mrs. Wu who had been listening to them, "your Old Brother mentioned to me the advisability of making his funeral clothes last year, for it was then a leap year. We did not pay much attention to his request and thought it was just one of his silly jokes. Now we are left to regret not having done so!"

"No use talking that way now," said Seventh Uncle, "for you should believe in such things as well as not".

It was understood by them that there is a superstition in China if funeral clothes are prepared for an old person in a leap year this is an auspicious omen and the old person may be able to "leap" over a few more years and his life be lengthened that way. Of course, looking at the idea from the practical angle it is reasonable to say that this is not a bad suggestion in order that very old people get such things done while there is yet ample time and thus avoid a last minute rush. Even if the "leaping" did not come out right there is no harm done.

Young Mr. Wu, taking the Seventh Uncle with him, also made another inspection of the coffin he had bought for the old man several years before and which had been stored away in a small temple in their neighbourhood under the custody of the monks. It was a magnificent coffin made of fine Kiangsi cedar, strong and reddish in colour with very fine grains. They had bought it in the manner usual with the richer Chinese people in Peking. Young Mr. Wu had had it painted with a layer of black lacquer every year and it now wore a thick shiny black paint and rang more like metal than wood when knocked with a knuckle.

"It is a very good thing indeed to have a fine son like you" remarked Seventh Uncle. "Now we do not need to find a suitable coffin for your father at the *wei ch'ang* (桅廠)!"

A *wei ch'ang*, meaning a "mast factory", is in no way connected with the shipbuilding trade in China but is really a coffin factory. A coffin is known as *shou mu* (壽木) or "woodware of longevity". The common word *kuan ts'ai* (棺材) should be avoided in cultured conversation as just another Chinese custom.

*   *   *

The twenty-four *chieh ch'i* (節氣), or festival dates, two in each month and noted in the almanac as being fixed annually by the astrologers since they do not fall on the same days each year, are not only useful in China's agricultural life but are also used to foretell the immediate turn of aged or sick persons. Such dates as "Rain Water", "Great Heat", "Frost Fall" and "Big Snow" are important hurdles, as it were, as these periods never fail to coincide with a severe change in weather and atmosphere which has such a great effect on a serious and bedridden patient. It is common to hear people say that so-and-so will find it hard to pass the coming "Rain Water," or to say that if he could manage to clear the "Frost Fall" he might be expected to live, and so forth.

It was in this very way that the condition of old Mr. Wu was judged, for the "Beginning of Winter" was drawing cruelly near and it was feared that this period would be difficult for him to live through.

*   *   *

"Seventh Uncle, I am afraid the last fateful moment is near at hand," said young Mr. Wu to old Mr. Liu. "My father passed a very uncomfortable night last night and we noted that his hands and feet were very cold at times. He seems to see my late grandfather or my late grandmother smiling at him or else some other old friends who have long been dead, though he says he is not afraid."

"Oh yes, as I thought," answered Seventh Uncle. "Such, phenomenon is a very common thing with people about to pass away and is known as *hwei chia ch'in* (會家親) (meeting family relatives) and is the first sign that an aged person is about to leave our midst. But did he say he wanted to see any particular person?"

"No, he did not ask to see any person in particular," young Mr. Wu said. "Yesterday when I mentioned that you have been with us for several days, he nodded his head or tried to nod his head but said nothing. I asked: 'Do you want Little Bald Head to sit beside you?' He said he did not. Little Bald Head was sitting right behind him but he did not know."

"If such is the case, you had better take the first opportunity to ask him if he has not something special to tell your family. But now. . .there you go, Good Old Nephew, be calm and do not get excited. This is bound to come. . .No parent will stay with his children throughout life." Young Mr. Wu was weeping bitterly.

"Little Bald Head has nothing to do; send him to me as I want him to do something. You go and get a little rest while you can. You did not sleep last night, nor did your wife. I saw the light burning in your room throughout the night, you were probably not in your own room anyway. I stayed awake most of the night myself as with an old head like mine I do not expect to sleep much."

*   *   *

Little Bald Head was told to get some sheets of white paper and cut them into pieces about four inches wide and ten inches long, each one bearing a small red paper label pasted onto the left hand top corner. Having brought the ink and pen, he was told to make many copies of a small "express" with only the date and time left blank. Seventh Uncle, far-sighted of eye but hard of writing, made a draft copy and the youngster copied the announcement on the sheets which he had prepared. It read:

"Old Mr. Wu, residing in Donkey Mart
Hutung, adjacent to Tung Ssu P'ailou, passed
away at.........o'clock.........noon on the day of
the.........moon. Respectfully this notice. To
be reported verbally by the gatekeeper."

Seventh Uncle was systematic and he would lose no time notifying the Wus' relatives and friends with the news as soon as "the last bulletin" had been issued. Though never having been a press agent, he believed in efficiency and speed. A man servant from his own house was ordered to stand by for immediate action to send these "expresses" according to an old custom in Peking. The name and address of each intended recipient of the message was written on the red label. It would be considered very disrespectful not to do so, the same as to omit making the notation that the message be delivered by word of mouth though the recipient may not have a gatekeeper.

There were about forty families to be thus notified and to
the remaining less intimate friends, as well as their families, a
formal *Fu Wen* (訃聞), or death notice, an interesting document
that was to be printed, would be sent as soon as they came off
the press.

Seventh Uncle was not expected to know the who's who of
the Wu family's many, many friends but with a former record
book of gifts received at old Mr. Wu's seventieth birthday celebrations and the help of Little Bald Head to make a new list did
not take long.

                    *   *   *

And so old Mr. Wu died.

His death was not unexpected and thanks to the methodical
advisorship of Seventh Uncle many a last minute rush was
avoided.

Before the old man breathed his last he was dressed in the
robes and garments representing the best days of his short official
life during the Manchu Dynasty. This was in compliance with
the suggestion of the old man himself and they, the Wus, had
obtained his approval at a proper moment. While he was thus
being dressed by his wife and son, an order was sent for a *ch'uang*
(牀), a special kind of a bed, by old Seventh Uncle to the *kang
fang* (槓房), or "catafalque store", which is the equivalent of the
foreign undertaker. The *kang fang* specialize in renting biers
and other funeral equipment as well as supplying the labour
employed in processions and so forth. A death-bed as was
ordered is the proper place for the body of the deceased to lie in
state before being encoffined. It is painted all in red. On this
bed the Wus moved the body. It lay on several heavy cotton
mattresses, all new and just sewn by an urgent order placed with
the tailor shop on the main street.

Old Mr. Wu was "attended to" in proper style and there
were three big mattresses and as many heavy coverlets or quilts,
all of good silken materials and thickly padded with cotton. A
mirror was placed on the old man's chest following an old belief
that such a mirror is supposed to be protection from evil spirits.
A small paper package containing a small pinch of tea leaves and
a pearl was placed between his lips. The paper and tea leaves
were to be thrown away the moment the body was placed in the
casket but the pearl was to be inserted into the mouth according
to another old custom. A pearl, it is said, is of use in protecting
the remains from dust!

From the *Shou Yi P'u*, or store for clothes for the dead
where a pair of special boots were purchased, a particular pillow
was also bought, shaped like a cock. The cock, crowing regularly in the mornings and evenings, would serve as a timepiece to
the old man bound for eternity (another design is lotus flowers
which are also a favourite Buddhist motif). The old man's legs
were tied loosely together with a hemp string. This was the so-
called "foot-entangling rope", designed to prevent the corpse
from getting up and chasing the people in the house should some
evil spirits take possession of the remains and play havoc. This
"rope", as explained in an earlier chapter would be carried on

to the next incarnation of the spirit and be responsible for a future child's tottering steps. It had to be cut with a meat chopper in the imagination.

The Wus had been cautioned not to cry until the remains were well taken care of in the manner described but then crying and wailing started in earnest. This lasted for fully half an hour. The family were told by Seventh Uncle not to stand too near the corpse for should tear drops stain the "shrouds" it would be a very bad thing for the deceased and each tear drop mark would be counted as a bad point in the "judgment".

In the meantime the announcement of the death had been filled out and given to a servant to deliver to the family friends and the *Yin Yang Sheng* (陰陽生), the Scholar of the Positive and the Negative or in a word, the "diviner", was also sent for. Nearby the hutung, on the Southern Small Street, was the office of such a diviner bearing the business title *Teh An T'ang* (德安堂), or the Hall of Virtuous Peace, where a man by the name of Chang had his general headquarters and consulting office.

Mr. Chang was a combination diviner and geomancer as is usually the case with such people. Besides "divining" at a death their job is also to serve as advisors on *Feng Shui* (風水) (Wind and Water) or topographical influences and geomancy, and people who want to chart out a new graveyard or who suspect the directional environment characteristics of their houses are not bringing them the maximum of prosperity and happiness consult and invite them to make surveys and suggestions. Their cult is somewhat connected with Taoist beliefs but not always so.

There are not very many such diviners in Peking but as all families having deaths must consult them as an official formality more or less, theirs is a prosperous trade. Boiled down, their work is ninety per cent. pure superstition and the other ten per cent. additional alloyed superstition, but in spite of that their position in the social structure of the Chinese is not to be defied and they certainly operate with the fullest co-operation from the police administrations which sounds very queer, but is not. *Yin Yang Sheng* are put through police examinations and are allowed to practice only after a permit has been issued to them and on condition they promise to bring to the attention of the police force even the faintest trace of foul-play in connection with a death in the course of their business. It is a fact that through this branch of "non-commissioned" detectives and disguised coroners, cases of murder by poisoning are brought to the attention of the proper authorities from time to time.

*   *   *

A *Yin Yang Sheng* never knocks at the door of a family by whom he has been invited to render his services. This is an old custom which no doubt originated because of some awkward incident, perhaps an absent-minded diviner once knocked at a wrong door and asked if there were a death in the family and if he had been sent for! Such a thing, naturally, would not be welcome. As a substitute measure for door-knocking, Peking's death diviners announce their arrival by calling in a reasonably loud voice for the people in the house to watch their dogs!

Mr. Chang, the *Yin Yang Sheng*, was invited to name the most suitable hours for the funeral and other death ceremonies, and he proceeded to inspect the dead body of old Mr. Wu immediately on his arrival as men of his profession are never in the habit of engaging their clients in friendly conversations because families to whom they go are not in a mood to do so and their business is far too serious for such a practice.

He picked up the old man's hand and looked at the fingers (and incidentally at the fingernails; poisoned people show black nails after death). Then, lifting the red silk square covering the old man's face, he quickly examined the general appearance of the corpse and in less time than it takes to describe, he ascertained that old Mr. Wu had only died, that was all, and had not been killed! They do also have a way of telling what hour the death took place allegedly by noticing how the fingers rest and so forth, and do not need to be told when death actually came.

"About six o'clock this morning?" Mr. Chang said.

"Yes, almost, about five forty-five by our clocks" was the answer.

Mr. Chang then sat down at a table and took out from his pocket a dog-eared almanac, almost worn out from constant handling. He reckoned silently a while, and then spread out a piece of paper he had brought with him. In five minutes he wrote out an important document and delivered it to the Wus. This was, as a matter of fact, a rather important document for it served as an official death certificate and a passport in a way, for no funerals are permitted to pass the city gate on their way to the countryside burial grounds without such a document. The police and census officers work with the diviners in constant checks on the population.

Mr. Chang put down on the paper the name and age of the dead man, the day and hour of the death and also gave the most auspicious hours for encoffining and starting the funeral. The former was given as the hour of the Monkey or between four and six o'clock in the afternoon, and the latter was stated to be the hour of the Snake or between ten and twelve in the morning.

The document also indicated that during the encoffining, persons bearing birth symbols of the hours of the Cock, the Rabbit, the Dog and the Dragon were to be barred from the ceremony, with the phrase *Ch'in Ting Pu Chi* (親丁不忌) inserted, meaning "Close Relatives not Barred". Further he wrote that the last part of the "lingering spirits" of the dead would stay in the house until the fifteenth day after the death when they, the spirits, known as *yang* (殃), would take the shape of a gust of blue air and travelling twelve feet above the surface of the ground would make their way to the west.

This was considered very lucky for only good spirits "take" the blue colour and travel to the west where the Buddisatvas live, other colours and directions are not considered so good. At the bottom of the paper he put his chop or stamp and then wrote in four big characters another conventional phrase, *Hsiao Hsin Huo Chu* (小心火燭) or "Take Care of Fire and Candles." This caution has always been inserted in this way and is appreciated for it is considered a family's biggest misfortune should there be a fire and the coffin with the body be consumed in an accidental cremation.

Finishing, the diviner took his fee and left. This document was then placed under the mirror on the breast of the deceased after its contents had been duly noted. Mr. Chang also left a small yellow paper label bearing his "trade mark" which was to be pasted at the gate on the left side (a female death would be indicated by pasting the label on the right side).

There were sundry small rites performed. With pieces of white paper the doors where the red spring scrolls were pasted at the new year were covered. A small oil lamp burning sesamum oil with a grass wick was immediately lighted and placed beside the dead body to be of use in serving as the old man's "guiding light" on his way to the next world and which would be kept burning until the coffin was moved away for burial. Some paper joss-money, similar to the kind burned at the graves during the annual visits to the graveyards but only about one sixth as big were bought and burned a few pieces at a time at regular intervals of an hour or so. These were to serve as old Mr. Wu's petty cash or pocket money to meet sundry expenses en route. After encoffining the regular kind would be burned.

A barber was also sent for and young Mr. Wu's and the grandson's heads were shaved for such is a mark of mourning and young Mr. Wu would be obliged to go without a shave or a hair-cut for one hundred days and his son for sixty days. As to the female members of the house, they were required to use white in place of red ribbons for their hair for one year and then use black ones for two more years. During these periods only silver and enameled blue jewelry, respectively, would be permissible. Nor could they use cosmetics.

*   *   *

Having had their heads clean shaven and the ribbons in their hair changed to white cotton ones respectively the male and female members of the Wu family put on their mourning gowns and accessories which had been quickly prepared.

Such mourning clothes and accessories are of very ancient origin and are made of coarse white cotton materials and in degree of coarseness are proportionate to the closeness of relation of each wearer to the deceased. Those of old Mrs. Wu and young Mrs. Wu were, for instance, of the coarsest kind, a sort of rough unbleached muslin. These mourning clothes are in general cut and sewn with the fewest tailored lines, are loosely draped around the body and tied with little unfinished cloth slips in place of buttons of any sort. The collar line is made like that of a monk's robe, following an ancient style. A sash of the same material is tied about the waist, knotted but once in front and gives the wearer the most sloppy and untidy appearance imaginable. This is exactly the impression such a costume is intended to give, it is to show that the wearers are so deeply absorbed with their bereavement that they have no time to think of the cut and fit of their gowns or to care for their personal appearance—the cloth ties are used in place of the buttons because theoretically the mourners are so paralyzed by grief that their fingers become too stiff to use buttons!

The male members of a household also wear mourning caps of the same material as their gowns and made in one piece of cloth folded and sewn along simple lines. A small Chinese square-holed brass cash is sewn to the front of the hat crown of a son and a red chenille ball to that of a grandson. A small cloth badge, cut in the shape of a small bat or a small peach, about two inches across, is sewn to the shoulder of a grandson, the left shoulder for the grandfather's death and the right for a grandmother's. A great grandson will have two such badges and a great great grandson, three and so on. Children of the married daughters, if any, and if they come for the ceremonies, use blue badges. Their gowns are of a finer material and are bleached instead of their natural colour. Coarse cloth shoes are worn and covered entirely with white cloth. The son and daughter-in-law, and the surviving wife, too, put a black piece of cloth at the heels and the grandson a piece of red cloth.

The female married members of the family also wear *pao t'ou* (包頭), or "turbans" These are also of coarse white cloth folded into a long belt about three inches in width. A surviving wife's turban is made with a belt thirteen feet in length and a daughter-in-law's eleven feet in length with all the surplus belting twisted into a solid mass and worn sticking out from the forehead after being wound around the coiffure. Thus by the way a person wears his or her mourning clothes, known in Chinese as *hsiao yi* (孝衣), or "filial clothes", it is possible to tell at a glance what relationship he or she bears to the deceased.

The customs above described are typical of Peking. People from the southern provinces will also wear hanks of raw hemp on their hats and around their waist. They also wear their mourning caps with a veil in front made of hemp netting (very much like tailor's "stiffening" and which combination might have inspired the creation of a famous milliner) but the Wus did not wear this kind.

Thus dressed up in full regalia in accordance with the provisions of Propriety; the Wus took up their respective positions beside the bed where the body of old Mr. Wu was lying in state, and knelt on flat cushions also covered with white cloth. There they were required to remain the whole time, eating and sleeping, and wailing with any friends or relatives who came to offer their condolences.

The visitors being close relations, intimate friends and recipients of the "express" notice, it fell to their lot to come and pay their respects to the corpse before the encoffining. Each one besides bringing presents in the form of paper-money or joss-money, bundles of incense, pairs of big white candles, etc., was also required by good form to cry loudly and to shed tears to which the family responded.

A female visitor should be joined in crying by the female members of the family and a male by the male members, for all this is provided by *Li* (禮) or ceremony. Also, the proper way to greet an arrival and to thank him or her is by a kowtow on the ground and the fact that a guest may happen to be a younger person or an inferior in family relationship makes no exception to the rule. This procedure is based on an old custom whereby the members of the bereaved family should attempt silently to confess or admit that it is all due to their own sins and their misdemeanors and not the fault of the deceased that a death has taken place in the family. Such an attitude is expressed in words in the formal death notice. As to the practice of kneeling beside the corpse, this might be said to have originated from ancient times when members of some rival family or tribe occasionally came and violated the remains held sacred by deceased's family. It was a close watch, too, as no dogs or cats are allowed to come into the room where a dead person lies in state for which rule a reason is not far to seek.

People with a death in their family are not permitted to argue or fight with others no matter how wronged or insulted they are, for to do so is not good form. Theoretically they are supposed to be so grieved and perplexed that the state of their mind borders on mental paralysis all the time, and they should be denied all comforts and left "sleeping on grass and using a block of earth as a pillow", as the old saying goes.

FUNERAL CEREMONIES

A FUNERAL is known in China as a *pai shih* (白事) or "white affair" and a wedding, a *hung shih* (紅事) or "red affair", because such are the predominating colours used in connection with these events. Red is the colour of happiness and white that of sorrow. That a bride should wear a white gown with white blossoms and a groom be dressed in black is terribly in contradiction to the traditional colour-consciousness of the race. In Western countries, the Chinese are told, white is symbolic of happiness and black that of mourning but they cannot find a good reason why the bride and groom should be so differently attired!

Invitations for happy events are printed on red paper and funeral notices and invitations to the ceremonies are printed now-a-days on white paper, though orthodox Peking families still use a kind of yellow or light brown paper like that known as Manila paper for though a death is a sad event to the family it is not to their friends, and how should you dare to put a piece of white paper before them? Even their names should be written on a red slip and pasted on.

Such a funeral invitation is an interestingly worded affair and was formerly prepared in off-set wood-block printing (some stylish ones still are) to insure prompt delivery off the crude hand press. China's first official newspaper, the "Peking Gazette" or "*Kung Men Ch'ao*" (宮門抄) (literally translated as "Copied at the Palace Gate") began to appear some three centuries ago and flourished for a long time. It was printed by the same technique.

Nor was the old funeral notice a monotone impression, for the words representing the name of the current dynasty, the official titles and scholastic honours and those stating the relationship of the person notified to the deceased's family, etc., were required to be printed in red and the rest of the text in black. These humble old wood-block printers should get first honours in craftsmanship and at least an honourable mention should be made of them when a complete history of the art of printing is written. They deserve honour, in no lesser proportion than that conferred for the discovery of the modern orthochrome colour-photogravure.

The Chinese funeral notice also commands respect for its prompt local circulation. The copies are turned off the press, then hand-addressed one by one and distributed, generally on foot, throughout the town in record time considering that all the recipients are required to appear on the Third Day Ceremony which may, according to the advice of the geomancers, actually be fixed as early as forty-eight hours after death has taken place. Funeral notices, like newspaper extras, cannot wait.

The *fu wen* or "funeral notice" for old Mr. Wu was turned out, as expected, in almost no time and the final proof was shown to young Mr. Wu for his O.K., after having been prepared in the "rough" by Seventh Uncle himself who consulted the Wus from time to time. Young Mr. Wu thanked Seventh Uncle for his efforts with many kowtows.

Translated, the funeral notice read:

"The unfilial son, Kwang Tsung, whose sins are most profound and whose retributions should be of the heaviest and yet not trying to do things to reconciliate such misdemeanors, calamity has diverted from its course and attacked his 'distinguished accomplished' (Any dead father is known ceremoniously as a *k'ao* (考) which means 'accomplished', and if he has served during his life as a government official he should be called *hsien k'ao* (顯考) or 'distinguished accomplished'. A mere Mr. Average Citizen should be termed *hsien k'ao* (先考) too, but with the other character for *hsien* (which means only 'the late'). Shih-jen Wu Esquire (This way of putting the family name behind the personal name, the only approved manner for funeral notices, has been used for many years and has got nothing to do with the foreign custom), has died in the 'central sleeping chamber' (A male person dies in the central chamber and a female in the inside chamber, according to funeral notice propriety), in the hour of the Tiger on the.. day of the.... month in the... year of the Republic. He was born in the hour of the....on the....day of the....month in the....year of the reign of Emperor Hsien Feng of the Ch'ing Dynasty and enjoyed the age of seventy-six. The unfilial son, having personally witnessed the death and seen to it that the body has been encoffined with a pearl in its mouth, and have put on their mourning clothes in accordance with propriety, and since you (the recipient of this notice) are, as a favour to the deceased and his family, an acquaintance in the category of a fellow-townsman, a fellow candidate at the Imperial Examinations, a relative by marriage, an associate in official life, a friend by inheritance, and old friend (the Chinese do not strike out the inappropriate provisions or mark the proper one with an "x" but leave the recipient to use his own good judgment as to which class he belongs in), stricken with grief, he brings to you this sad news."

Here the word *wen* (聞) for "news" is printed in extra large type, at least forty-eight points Gothic, to use printer's language.

Then follows the schedule of the ceremonies, in small type, which in the case of old Mr. Wu's funeral, translated as follows:—

"Have been carefully selected. The seventh day of the tenth moon for Third Day Ceremony;

"The eleventh, the twelfth, and the thirteenth for Sutra chanting by Buddhist monks, Taoist priests and Lama priests.

"The thirteenth for Night Accompanying and sending off the Warehouses (meaning the last service and the burning of paper houses).

"The fourteenth, in the hour of the Snake, funeral procession to start."

And underneath this was printed:

"The Orphaned Son Wu Kwang Tsung, crying so bitterly with his eyes bleeding and knocking his forehead forcefully on the ground.

"The One-Year-Mourning Grandson, Hsueh Wen, crying and kowtowing......"

Following these were several other names and the status of some other distant family members but who, having not been previously introduced, we will not bother with. It must be explained, however, that a person without a father is a *ku tze* (孤子) or "orphaned son" and one without a mother is an *ai tze* (哀子) or "grieved son." A person with neither is *ku ai tze* (孤哀子) or "an orphaned and grieved son."

*　　　　　*　　　　　*

In the famous Confucian Classic of "Filial Piety" or *Hsiao Ching* (孝經) (known in Japanese as "Kokio" and used in China as well as in Japan as a textbook in primary schools before modern education found its way into these countries) there are given rules and explanations for this famous Oriental teaching. There is an Eighteenth Chapter on how to behave on a parent's death. It says, roughly, that when a filial son loses one of his parents he cries but without "posing" and talks without refinement of speech. He feels uneasy if clad in fine clothes and is never noted to be happy even listening to gay music. He may be given to eat very nice foods but he does not notice their taste. In such ways the feeling of grief is expressed. He will eat on the third day (implying that he has refused to eat for that many days already), for the sages teach that people should not harm their life because of a parent's death. He may deny himself many things but may not alter his instincts—which is the fundamental policy approved by the sages.

The period of mourning in the case of a son, the book says, is set at three years, to show people that there is an end to everything. The son makes for his dead parent the inside coffin and the outside coffin to contain the body; he arranges the sacrificial dishes of food and offers them before the coffin; he sends the remains to the graveyard with loud crying and wailing and constant beating of the breast and stamping of the feet; he finds the luckiest spot and buries the remains there; he puts his parent's name (on a tablet) in the family shrine and worships the ghost and in the spring and autumn he offers sacrifices and remembers him or her at the proper time. It is interesting to note that after almost three thousand years these rules are still being followed in very much the same way in almost all parts of China.

*　　　　　*　　　　　*

There was much crying and wailing on old Mr. Wu's death

but the Wus were told not to cry too much because it was a case of *hsi sang* (喜喪) or "happy death" by which a natural death at an advanced age is distinguished in the conception of the Pe-king-*jen*. And many callers at the house comforted the family with this thought after offering their condolences with bitter tears themselves.

At the hour of the Monkey, set by the geomancer as the most auspicious time, the heavy casket made of solid cedar planks full five inches in thickness was conveyed by a group of professional bearers to the house on a bier. It weighed more than three hundred pounds and was quite a load for the sixteen coolies who carried it on a framework of heavy wooden posts on their shoulders. Under the supervision of Seventh Uncle it had been quickly lined with silk and cotton inside.

The windows and doors of the central portion of the northern or principal rooms in the Wu home had been temporarily knock-ed down and removed to make room for the ceremonial "dis-play" and the coffin was conveniently placed in the central opening, resting on two benches which the undertakers had brought with them.

The coffin was placed on the benches in the direction north to south and its inside was spread with sawdust which is the Peking custom. Packages of lime take the place of sawdust when the casket is to be transported to a distant region or remains unburied for a long time as in a temple. The body of the old man was then conveyed from the temporary "bed" to the coffin with young Mr. Wu himself taking care of the end where the old man's head was and the grandson where the feet were, in strict-ly traditional manner, with the other members and old friends helping. The body was placed in the coffin and all saw to it that the old man was placed "snug and comfortable" and was proof against shaking and rolling.

The red silk piece covering the old man's face had been removed as was also the paper package containing tea leaves earlier placed in the mouth. The pearl contained in the package was inserted into the mouth and the "foot-entangling rope" was removed. Old Mrs. Wu also took a cup of clear water and wetting a plug of cotton wiped clean the old man's eyes, silently praying that he might have good eye-sight in the next world. Three extra quilts, good and thick, were then laid on the body and tucked in at the sides and corners. The thinner inside cover and the heavy top one were then laid in place and the encoffin-ing was pronounced complete, leaving only certain concealed locking devices to be "set" at a later day.

The job was neatly accomplished in good order under the expert superintendance of Seventh Uncle, who saw to each detail including the forceful upsetting of the wooden "bed" with a loud bang calculated frighten away the evil spirits that might be lurking about invisible. The encoffining was followed by loud wailing on the part of all present. Many relatives were barred from the ceremony in accordance with the advice of the geomancer or diviner. It was also seen to that no "four-eyed" person stood close to the coffin for the Chinese superstition has it that "four-eyed" persons, meaning women in a state of pregnancy, are liable to miscarry the baby if their body or clothes should touch a coffin!

It was a busy afternoon for Seventh Uncle. He also was asked to negotiate with the *p'eng p'u* (棚舖) or mat-shed renting establishment to have the entire courtyard covered with a shed with proper decorations for the occasion as it was here that the multitude of guests were to sit at the ceremonial feasts. There was soon erected, too, before the coffin a so-called *yueh t'ai* (月臺) or "moon platform", with decorative railings and wooden steps for ceremonial purposes. A *ching t'ai* (經臺) or sutra chanting stand, which in this case was a three-in one affair to accommodate three different groups of priests, was also erected. This was a two-storied stand and was hung with gaudy decorations when in use. A fitting decoration was also erected at the main gate entrance with paper flowers and cloth bunting.

Outside on the wall near the gate was also posted a simplified program of the coming ceremonies, written on strips of paper for the benefit of neighbourhood friends who might like to come but might not happen to have been invited.

*   *   *

Old Mr. Wu's remains having been carefully encoffined, the casket was loosely draped over with a tent-like covering of red silk with proper designs (bats and the Chinese character for "Long Life") embroidered in gilt letters, leaving only part of the front portion visible. A professional artist was on hand and using golden lacquer he quickly painted the conventional design of the rounded character of the word *Shou* for "Longevity" in the conventional seal-carvers' style on the front of the casket.

Before the coffin was placed a big square table on which was put a pair of candlesticks, an incense burner, a pair of flower vases with a pair of paper flower bouquets of snow-white lotus and green leaves which Seventh Uncle thought was better than the white peonies which he ruled out.

These ritual utensils, of shining pewter, were all rented from the undertakers as was also a pewter kiosk-like affair about two feet high called a *men teng* (悶燈) or "dim lantern" into which

A square table is set before the coffin and many sacrificial utensils are placed on it. The kiosk-like object contains the "dim lantern" which throws a faint light constantly on the black lacquered coffin in which old Mr. Wu had been "put to sleep permanently".

the sesamum oil lamp was placed. The lantern had a small opening which was turned to face that part of the coffin left uncovered and the flickering light of the lamp was directed to shed its "dim" light there. In front of the table on the temporary platform was also put a set of brass wine-sacrificing utensils resting on a small short-legged bench. Four sticks of incense were then tied together with blue paper ribbons and put into the incense burner in the center. This was not to be burned but used for the ceremonials when the guests later on came to pay their last respects.

Beside the tent-covered coffin and on either side of it were laid the flat cushions one behind the other, marking the places where the Wus were to kneel to receive the visitors. Young Mr. Wu knelt on the first cushion nearest to the guests and his son, Little Bald Head, on the one behind his, both of them on the left side. Old Mrs. Wu and her daughter-in-law occupied similar positions on the right. There they were obliged to kneel or sit tailor fashion to rest their sore legs when no visitors were nearby to stare at them for taking such a liberty!

A temporary financing office and accounting department was set up in a side room where Seventh Uncle had his desk. He had been asked to take care of the "business end" of the ceremonies, receiving and registering the gifts and paying the expenses of this, that and the other. Another gentleman was invited to assist him. Young Mr. Wu advanced a sum of money to them for which the pair were held responsible and a set of books was quickly prepared. They had a busy time of it then and afterwards for the funeral was quite elaborate.

As is proper with families of means, it is a filial son's duty to spend much money in funeral ceremonies for a dead parent as an expression of the esteem the son had of the deceased. It is a fact that many Peking families incur debts that take them a long time to repay just to give a showy funeral for their parents. It is a matter of "face" and whenever "face" comes in, sound economy goes out!

Little Bald Head also had his work to do and it consisted of burning joss-money offerings during the various daily rites at the crowing of the cock in the morning, at twilight and again at the meal-time sacrifices after the Third Day Ceremony. No food offerings were presented before this.

On the second day as the mat-shed people completed hanging their mattings on the wood work, part of which the Wus already had, and as the furniture men moved in cartloads of tables, benches and chairs, the gift bearers also made their appearance at the Wu house. Most of the latter were servants of the sender's family, some sending a card with the gifts and others reporting the sender's name only verbally. Seventh Uncle and his assistant registered each entry duly in the gift book and issued a receipt on a printed form with the names of the Wu family members shown in the same order as in the funeral notice. It was also their duty to give each gift-bearing servant a small tip called *li chien* (力錢) or "strength money." Strength money is a flexible matter and is proportionate to the value of the gift received.

There were many gifts received. Some were of the *Kuan*

Tiao (官吊) or "conventional condolence gift" kind, comprising incense sticks, candles, paper ingots, etc., which had begun to pour in even before the old man's remains were encoffined. Others brought cloth pieces with proper phrases of condolence or of appreciation of the deceased "in memoriam", touching on the fine virtues of the old man and his "model" citizenship, etc., all in big characters cut from gilt paper as were also the old man's and the sender's names (Chinese seal carvers prepare these carved characters at small price). Grey, blue or black cotton cloths in length from eight to eighteen feet were the most numerous, being the most appropriate although many others sent silken pieces. But all were of sober colours; the gaudy reds and pinks are good only for congratulatory purposes. Some of the phrases read:

"Happiness and Longevity All Belong (to him)".
"A Perfect Man of the Age".
"A Bright Star Has Fallen".
"A Wise Man Has Withered".

Others also brought *wan tien* (輓聯) or "condolence couplets", or paired phrases, of laudatory expressions eulogizing the old man's high moral standards, brilliant career, etc., mostly from business associates. These were, like the cloth pieces, hung out in the mat-shed one by one for the visitors to see and to read.

*　　　*　　　*

It has been the custom for the Chinese dead to be kept in the house after encoffining for a certain period of time, ranging from five days for the poor to seven times seven or forty-nine days for the very rich. The most common period is seven or nine days. During this time priests of various sects are invited to hold masses for the dead which daily last from, say, nine in the morning till about five in the afternoon, with irregularly inserted recess periods—Chinese monks work roughly eight hours a day.

Not all the priests are paid by the family as some of the masses are contributed by friends and relatives as a sort of gift. A period of chanting of scriptures lasting three days is called *yi p'eng ching* (一棚經) or "one shed of sutras", and requires from eleven to fifteen priests all working as in a choir. Such a gift would cost the sender quite a sum of money, more so if the priests are from some famous monastery in Peking as Peking's monks are notoriously expensive. At old Mr. Wu's death there were three groups of priests conducting services simultaneously. The Taoist service was a gift from young Mr. Wu's friends and the Lama service was from another source; only the Buddhist monks were planned and arranged for by the family.

On the third day after the death there was a ceremony the like of which is known as *Chieh San* (接三) or "Third Day Reception." This is a noisy affair lasting well into the small hours of the next morning as nocturnal sutra chanting is one of its important features.

A group of funeral musicians were negotiated for. These brought their equipment early in the morning and established themselves at the front and the inner gate. Outside the gate they put up a heavy wooden stand on which was hung a big drum some five feet in height with skin stretched on both ends, each "beating" face some three feet across, and also similar stands from which big brass gongs were suspended. At a table nearby sat other musicians who played various instruments, such as the long and short trumpets and the cymbals.

At the "second gate" were placed two small flat drums and small gongs. The big drum and gongs outside were used to report the arrival of guests, gentleman guests by beating four or five times the big drum and lady guests by an additional short blare of the small trumpets. These signals were then picked up and relayed by the small drums and carried to the ears of the mourning family so that if they had had to leave their proper kneeling position at the coffin they might return there to acknowledge the coming condolences.

In the evening, after dusk, a mule cart and trunks, etc., all made of paper over a framework of corn-stalks were to be burned with all the male members of the mourning family and the guests seeing off the departed spirit in the "covered wagon" some distance from the house, and the musicians would be used as vanguards in the procession.

These musicians are always dressed in green native uniforms with crudely stenciled designs on them in colours and they wear strangely shaped hats very much like those worn by officials during the late Manchu Dynasty. The musical instruments and the big drum stands, are mostly painted a bright gilt lacquer with designs of dragons and phoenixes. Just what a picturesque set of people they are can easily be imagined.

At noon old Mr. Wu's spirit was to have his first food offerings which, according to the local custom, must be served by a married daughter whose family is also required to furnish a "table" of foods (a complete multi-coursed feast) to be offered as a duty and a privilege. That the old Wus had no daughter presented a situation that puzzled the family quite a bit until the resourceful old Mrs. Wu suggested that Mrs. Chao, Little Bald Head's "Mother-in-faith," whose husband was the old man's favourite, be given this particular honour which she was very eager to accept and the foods were quickly ordered from a famous restaurant. They were brought to the Wus' house and arranged on the big square table before the coffin.

Young Mrs. Chao, properly clad in snow-white mourning clothes of a finer material than those worn by the Wus, knelt on a cushion in front of the table facing the coffin, with the hot foods a-steaming and the candles a-burning, and offered wine in the appropriate manner, using the special brass utensils supplied by the undertakers. A woman servant knelt at the side of the table and poured water (taking the place of real wine) into the brass cup held in a brass saucer and passed it to Mrs. Chao. She lifted the cup and saucer high above her head with both hands, then took the cup and poured a little of the water into the big brass basin and followed this immediately with another lifting of the cup and saucer. She then returned the set to the servant. She kowtowed once. This ceremony was repeated three times at the end of which she started to weep and the mourning family, kneeling solemnly at the sides of the casket, joined her until some guests came forward and persuaded all to stop. During the wine offering the musicians played appropriate numbers outside at a signal given by the "bandmaster". The ceremony was brought to a close in about ten minutes.

This wine ceremony was also performed by most of the guests during the receptions.

* * *

It was a fine day on which the first reception was held in memory of old Mr. Wu—the third day after his death. All the guests and the neighbours thought it was no mere accident but was due to Mr. Wu having been such a good man in his life that it was such fine weather on this day. Some of them even risked the prophecy that it would be an equally fine day for the other reception yet five days ahead and for the day of the funeral as well.

There was no feast at noon but a dinner was arranged for all the guests in the evening. At midday they sat down to a feast of noodles and other light dishes. All who gathered for this reception were intimate friends. The guests who sent no presents brought little sums of money in yellow envelopes with a blue label on them. These were marked *cheh chi* (折祭) or "substitute for funeral presents."

The custom in Peking requires two monetary gifts—the other called *tien ching* (奠敬) or "sacrificial present", which is also popularly known as *fen tze* (份資) or "portion money". "Portion money" is sent on weddings as well as funerals and other celebrations, and perhaps is a survival from the ancient custom of collecting money amongst friends to finance a burial or a wedding. As to the "substitute for gifts" category this may amount to very little or very much depending on the degree of friendship and the rate at which gifts had been exchanged in the past. Thirty years ago the minimum used to be twenty coppers or a bit more than four cents in local currency at the present exchange rate

The affair became more and more noisy as the afternoon advanced and at about four o'clock the effigy shop people brought the private travelling outfit for the old man's spirit and exhibited to public view at the gate for, according to Buddhist tradition prevalent in Peking, this was the time when the journey to the next world was to start in proper style. Had old Mr. Wu been from some other part of China such paper things would have been burned as soon as he breathed his last.

The set ordered for old Mr. Wu consisted principally of full-sized paper mulecart with proper fittings and wheels that actually turned. A servant riding on a horse was also prepared in paper to lead the mule cart. The paper-made driver and mounted footmen were represented in the clothings of a Mandarin's servants for old Mr. Wu was not going to travel incognito. There were also four paper trunks filled with paper ingots and sealed with paper labels in keeping with an age old custom, although no space apparently was provided for them in the "rolling stock". Around these interesting objects quickly gathered a number of spectators, notably the neighbourhood children, who had waited for them as well as the forthcoming procession in the evening when they were to be sent to a big open space and burned. Some of these urchins were suspected of being belligerent in nature and definitely out to damage the paper things and so a couple of beggars were hired for a consideration to watch over the paraphernalia.

The monks arrived at dusk and took up their positions in the sutra chanting grandstand where their layman temple assistants had preceded them and had spread out the religious paraphernalia after hanging a number of embroidered canopies at the proper locations in the matshed courtyard. Candles were then lighted and the sacred books opened at the suitable chapter. The nine monks, including the abbot, distinguished from the rest by a folded crown of five leaves on which were drawn the images of the buddhas, were all dressed in black robes. The monks had their own musical instruments, too, which their assistants arranged in order. These consisted of drums, flutes, fifes and cymbals, and so forth.

The program opened with two musical selections, the first being of the nature of a "brass band" piece and the second of the "wind instruments". Immediately following the chanting in chorus of a particularly meritorious section from the Diamond Sutra, the monks were ready for the "send-off".

In the meantime, young Mr. Wu and his son had been told to kneel in front of the sacrificial table and when the order for the procession to start was given, they burst into loud wailing and those of the guests who were intimate enough for it joined them in crying. The participants formed themselves into a long procession as they made for the gate. It was a full-fledged procession in which Seventh Uncle's genius of organization demonstrated itself most methodically, for as the monks went on with their music and chanting, Seventh Uncle, having donned his white mourning clothes, arranged the guests, and he and his assistant of the accounting department stuck a bundle of burning incense sticks or a lit cheap white-paper lantern into the hand of each one of them and also into the hands of a large crowd of neighbourhood children as they moved on to the street and formed themselves into lines on both sides of the hutung.

The procession was headed by the musicians in the green garb, followed by the guests and "friends" carrying the incense sticks, now blazing torches, and the paper lanterns. Then the paper mulecart rolled on gloriously on its papier mâché wheels held up by the shafts by four strong-armed coolies. Two big lanterns carried by servants heralded the chief mourners. Young Mr. Wu was assisted at his side by a young man dressed in white mourning gown, his wife's brother, on whose lot fell this duty, and Little Bald Head followed immediately behind. The nine monks playing the musical instruments brought up the rear.

The procession moved slowly and made for the big street. It was brought to a halt at the plaza in front of the Lung Fu Ssu Temple, where the paper objects were burned in a magnificent bonfire amidst the noise and uproar supplied by the "cheering" neighbourhood children.

Young Mr. Wu and his son knelt on the ground and as the old man's spirit boarded the mulecart converted into the real thing after burning, they kowtowed to each guest who came up to bid them good-bye.

The procession was a success. Seventh Uncle was glad of it. His old friend Wu had deserved such a noisy send-off.

*　　　　　*　　　　　*

It is the custom in Peking for guests, who are intimate friends of the family in which there is a death, to wear a certain mark of mourning supplied by the bereaved family in the form of a white cloth belt (of a fine bleached material) which is loosely tied around the waist over the ordinary clothes. In some families a white paper chrysanthemum is used in place of the belt. These are laid ceremoniously on a brass tray and are presented to each guest as he or she approaches the kneeling mourners to deliver the monetary gifts after having paid homage to the dead man on the so-called "moon platform". This the arrivals did some by kowtowing and others by merely shaking their own hands, placed together, in an up-and-down direction and holding the incense sticks found in the burner in the hands in a perpendicular position in the meantime and lifting them high above the head.

The mourners always present the belt or paper flower with the request that the guest be kind enough to wear it "so that the sins of the dead would be lightened" as they have no right to force a guest to wear mourning. Some close friends may also come dressed in mourning gowns befitting the rank or status of each individual. If a person happens to be a sworn brother of the mourning son or grandson, he would be required by propriety to wear full mourning dress as he is allied equal in status to the son or grandson himself, being looked upon as a true brother. Young Mr. Wu's sworn brothers, for instance, wore coarse muslin gowns and Little Bald Head's sworn brothers (of whom there were four) wore white gowns with a red mark on their left shoulders. But even in such cases the belts are supplied by the mourning family. Such friends, of course, are not required to wear mourning shoes and mourning caps.

*　　　　　*　　　　　*

There was a temporary lull in the house as the procession of the Third Day Ceremony left to send off the old man's spirit in the paper mulecart. The female members of the family and the female guests were not required to take part in the procession but they, in keeping with good form, did their crying in the house which died down in about a quarter of an hour. When young Mr. Wu and Little Bald Head returned most of the guests had gone and only a few intimate friends remained.

The monks, however, returned at nine o'clock for there was to be a long service of sutra chanting and religious music that very night. Such a service is known as *Yen K'o* (焰口) or "Flaming Mouth". This name has its origin in an ancient Buddhist legend.

There was once an old woman who had been a devoted Buddhist most of her life but who, finding that no apparent blessings came therefrom, changed her ways and began to do exactly as she had been told not to do. She had always given alms cheerfully to poor pilgrim monks and Taoist priests and had burned vegetable oils in the lamps at her family shrine, all of which were the proper things to do. Lately, however, she began to turn away such mendicant ex-fellow-believers with angry words and used animal fats for the lamps.

When she died her spirit was imprisoned in the darkest dungeons of the Eighteen Departments of Hell and tortured in a hundred and one ways for having deserted her religious belief. She had a son who was given away in childhood by her to be a monk and who had kept on with his religious work, in due course becoming a Buddhisatva with a high religious record and the possessor of great magic power.

He learned of the sad fate of his dead mother in purgatory and made up his mind to save her. The guardian ghosts refused to let him enter purgatory and closed the big iron-bound doors as he approached but he knocked the doors down with his powerful "pilgrim's wand", and found his mother in the custody of a ferocious demon jailor, who made her uncomfortable in every way in spite of her words of repentance.

His mother had become blind but Monk Mu Lien (目蓮) (for that was his name) licked her eyes and her eyesight was restored. She asked him for food, for she had been starved, which he at once produced for her but on account of her past sins, the food turned into flame at her lips and she could not get the benefit of it. The monk then chanted some paragraphs from the Holy Books; the flames disappeared and she was able to eat the food he gave her. Monk Mu Lien was able also to save his mother's soul from further sufferings for his great filial devotion to his mother was considered enough reason for the gods to grant her release.

*   *   *

The nocturnal Buddhist service for the benefit of the departed soul of old Mr. Wu was an interesting ceremony.

It started about ten o'clock in the evening when the monks had gathered at the grandstand erected for this and other similar purposes. While the monks went on with the preliminary chantings a number of documents were prepared giving the details of old Mr. Wu's name, age, etc., and the names of the monks acting as officiating priests together with the name of young Mr. Wu who, in the capacity of a "filial son," had applied to the monks to use their magical influences in seeing to the welfare of his father's spirit. These documents were burned at the proper moment with the Wus kneeling in front of the coffin. The service continued until well after midnight with religious music interspersed with sutra chantings.

After midnight there was also performed a ghost-appeasing rite similar to the kind seen annually at the Lotus Lantern Festival. The monks read the sutras and then called upon the vagrant ghosts to take advantage of the service, naming groups of likely prospective beneficiaries one by one and following it with a chorus of ".. all these straggling ghosts, and all the unnamed others, let them depend on the influence of the Three Precious Ones and the omnipotent words of the Buddhas, this very night and here come and enjoy the boundless foods of the

The chief abbot dons a crown composed of five "leaves", each bearing the image of a Buddha. He shakes the magic bell with his right hand while assuming a symbolic position with his left. Thus he summons the spirit of the dead person to the "assemblage of all souls". This is a touching spectacle under the flickering candle light and with incense sticks burning low.

Doctrine of the Sweet Dew".

A number of steamed little puddings, piled high in a big plate and painted green and red and decorated with paper flags, which had been brought to the Wu house the previous afternoon and placed before the coffin, were then taken to the head priest who broke them into tiny pieces and cast them down from the sutra chanting stand together with handfuls of different grains. The children brought by the guests, who had struggled to remain awake expressly for this occasion, ran forward and gathered up the pieces of pudding, for to eat such sacred foods would give them valour and make them unafraid of ghosts.

There are many superstitions about this mystic service and one of them is that the chief abbot wearing the Buddhist crown is able actually to see all the ghosts that gather at such a moment, their variegated features clearly visible to his eyes although even the other monks may not see them. It is also said that a very young boy (but not a girl) with "pure" eyes can also get a glimpse of the spirits provided he is bold enough to get behind the seat of the chief abbot and peep into a mirror held in his hand. It is further said that during certain parts of the chanting the spirit of the newly dead in whose behalf the service is being conducted will also make his or her appearance before the monks in the clothes in which he or she has been encoffined, and invariably will appear kneeling' for the monks to all intents and purposes represent the divinities themselves. This is why the family mourners are required to kneel before the coffin at a sign from the monks' layman assistants.

The moment of the assemblage of vagrant ghosts is also accompanied by the burning of a great quantity of paper joss-money for it is said that as the hungry ghosts are engaged in fighting for the sacred foods thrown by the monks, the spirit of the dead person may find it an opportune moment to gather the money and put it away in his own pocket-book free from interference. This sensational and climactical moment always comes at the very end of the service at the chilly hour before dawn and is a dreary and melancholy spectacle, indeed, with much crying, for if the mourners do not cry, it is also said, the spirit of the dead may not know what the whole thing is all about.

In such a service the monks also describe, by chanting in

unison, the journey after death and the passing of the various legendary landmarks on the road to the Yellow Spring on which road "there is no differentiation between the young and the old". One of these places is the Wang Hsiang T'ai (望鄉臺) or "Home-Viewing Terrace" which every spirit is permitted to mount and from it to see at a distance the heart-breaking scene of the widowed wife and the orphaned sons crying bitterly around the coffin and lamenting the sad departure! To this famous spot the spirit of the dead arrives on the third day, according to schedule.

The daily adventures and experiences after death are graphically described together with phrases of warning intended for the living more than for the dead. These include "...now you see you can never bring here with you ten thousand ounces of yellow gold and all that comes with you are the accumulated sins of a lifetime and their lamentable and unbearable repercussions, each item of which represents a torture in the next world," and "having lived a human's life here below but without having chanted the sacred words of Buddha, you have certainly travelled through the world in vain," etc. All these are calculated to bring the living to the fold of the Buddhists after waking up from the follies of the hustling, bustling life of the world!

The monks were then served an "after-show" supper and left shortly before daybreak.

*   *
*

Following the Third Day Ceremony, which culminated in an all night Buddhist service designed for the comfort of the spirit of old Mr. Wu, there was comparative quiet in the Wu house for two days. No special rites were performed but the family saw to it that the corpse was offered three meals a day of the same foods the family ate. These were placed on the table before the coffin with the family doing homage during the sacrifices. They also burned joss-money in the morning and the evening for the deceased must be well provided with funds in his spiritual travels.

It was on one of these quiet days that young Mr. Wu made a trip to the family graveyard where at the proper location in the family burial ground a deep hole was ordered dug about five feet wide, eight feet long and ten feet deep. The peasant family who acted as the Wus' graveyard caretakers had been notified of the impending burial and, assisted by "recruited labour", had dug the grave in time for the burial, erecting a simple matshed over it to prevent the possible gathering of rain water in the hole. For this work young Mr. Wu once again had the good

The Chinese geomancer uses a round compass with which to find his directions and bases his geometrical calculations on this instrument. The "surveying" is done mainly by the naked eye and no scientic instruments are needed to insure accuracy as the chief interest in this procedure pertains to the "Feng Shui" or "Wind and Water" influences.

services of the geomancer, Mr. Chang, for although the spot where the grave was to be located had been previously charted out, expert advice had to be sought and acted upon as to the direction which should be taken by the coffin, whether it was to be due south and north or by so many degrees slanting to the east or the west, etc.

The true straight line pointing to the Poles was first to be found with the aid of a compass and based on this, the other relative points for the coffin's position after burial were calculated with geometrical accuracy. Such considerations are believed by the Chinese to be a serious matter, having a great bearing on the family's good fortune in the future. If the Wus wanted to have their good fortune kept at the high level they had been enjoying or still to improve on it, such specifications were certainly not to be neglected.

A survey was made on the spot.

In that year the "God of Happiness" or *Hsi Shen* (喜神) was located in the north, as per necromantic predictions, and good luck was due to come from that direction like a search-light, straight to the point of the element of Fire which was the south side and a 45-degree angle would be reflected from an oblique row of tall trees in the neighbourhood graveyard of some other family, at the high earthen mount to the northwest, to turn back in a beam of good luck to the position of the coffin. There was a pagoda in that direction which, after careful surveying with one eye closed, Mr. Chang found to be fortunately just a fraction of a degree "off course" and therefore not a particularly formidable obstacle. "Pagodas, even at a distance, are usually harmful objects as far as *Feng Shui* is concerned, for they tend to absorb all the auspicious influences of the terrain," Mr. Chang declared.

In order to adhere to the "safety first" principle he advised that the coffin be buried with the head pointing to the southeast and about two degrees to the other side of the pagoda, thus "if the old man sat up in his coffin he would meet the good luck influence face to face and so bring great prosperity to posterity without fail". By thus avoiding the southern element of the Fire, symbolic of destruction, explained Mr. Chang, there would be a stronger possibility for the Wus to have more numerical strength in their offspring, which factor was particularly important considering at what great risk of discontinuance of the genealogical line they had been "operating" in two generations with one male offspring each.

With such advice the geomancer convinced young Mr. Wu not only that he knew his business but also that he was doing his best for the good of the Wu family. The proper points were pegged out after further checking and the digging started. As to the depth of the grave this was also for the geomancer to decide. Such a decision was not made hastily and was finally fixed at ten feet. "The deeper you dig the grave for the dead, the wiser the future generations of descendants will be," said geomancer Chang, "for that would be nearer and nearer to the element of subterranean water which symbolizes wisdom!"

Chinese geomancers are fully capable of giving such advice in which young Mr. Wu showed a "nodding" interest.

"Though it falls to our lot to give the maximum of wise counsel to our clients," added geomancer Chang, "we usually do not do that—seldom do we reveal so much as I do to you in this case."

"Why is that?" asked young Mr. Wu.

"Because if we tell too much, we would be punished by losing our own eyesight", answered Chang relating a traditional fear of his profession.

Young Mr. Wu again showed "nodding interest."

THE FUNERAL IS HELD

AS young Mr. Wu went to the family graveyard to see about digging the grave for old Mr. Wu's remains, Seventh Uncle had his busy day, too, for there were many things to be attended to in the short period of time available. He spent a long time with the caterers over the menu for the forthcoming reception which was to be held in full style prior to the burial day.

This grand reception is known in the vernacular as *Pan Su* (伴宿) or "Accompanying Overnight", as theoretically all the guests are to stay with the mourning family during their last night with the deceased "at home". It was going to be an expensive affair and the purchases of the things needed and all the payments had to be authorized by Seventh Uncle who was entrusted by young Mr. Wu to handle this angle.

He also summoned the representative of the undertakers' establishment and negotiated with him about the procession, about the labour force to be employed, the route to be taken for the funeral, etc. Amongst other things he stipulated that thirty-two people were to carry the coffin on a heavy catafalque of wooden beams and posts which, he pointed out, was to be of a bright, newly-painted red colour and the ropes and accessories were to be covered with red cloth. The coffin was to be covered by a wooden frame-work mounted on the catafalque, draped over with a beautifully embroidered canopy and topped with a "flaming pearl" of gild-lacquered wood. All the coolies carrying the catafalque were to be dressed in green uniforms and feathered caps, their heads cleanly shaven and they were to wear boots of black cloth.

In order to allow the beautiful black lacquered coffin to be viewed and admired by the neighbours, he ordered that a smaller and simpler bier of but sixteen men was to carry the coffin and transfer it to the big catafalque on the main street. The big catafalque, too, properly draped and "roped", was to be exhibited on the main street for three days before use, following an old custom. Instead of only one overseer of the professional pall bearers, beating time with teakwood "timing sticks" for the men's steps, two were to be used for the procession, both clad in white mourning gowns. In the procession was to be also a "spirit chair" carried by four men and a red sun-shade carried by another man was to go with it.

Music was to be supplied by the group of men described before as well as by a seven-piece band of "light music" and a juvenile drum and gong corps, accompanied by a group of children bearing small Chinese umbrellas. All of these were to wear embroidered costumes and fancy hats—decorated fishermen's strawhats. Another group of youngsters were to carry a number of "snow willows" which are bunches of bamboo splits pasted entirely over with white paper strips shaped like big brooms and said to be symbolic of the mourning family's tears.

The custom of sending paper articles and paper servants for the comfort of the spirit of a dead person dates back to the dim past. Human sacrifices were practised in China before figures of "straw and paper" took their place. The skillful Peking artists who make these objects hang wall-paper when they have no orders on hand. The above sketch is of the so-called "gold and silver mountain".

Eight tall footmen were to be the old man's "guard of honour", carrying the conventional official weapons of "the melon, the axe, the stirrup and the hand", all carved in wood, mounted on long wooden handles, gilded and painted red as old Mr. Wu had been an official in his life. A suitable number of flag and banner bearers were also called for, as well as a man to walk in the procession and throw handfuls of paper money, round paper discs some four inches in diameter with a square hole in the center, intended to pacify the evil spirits that might be lurking in the "invisible" to molest the procession.

Besides, there were to be a large number of "extras" who were to carry the flower wreaths, the paper scrolls and eulogies received and also the paper articles which were sent by the Wu family's many friends. The general terms were fixed in a verbal contract accompanied by a written list of details. Roughly figured, about eighty people were to be employed not counting the "extras", the number of which was to be fixed as soon as the needs were known.

Seventh Uncle made no mistake about the "extras" for paper articles soon began to arrive from friends. Some sent paper pots with wooden stands containing "four seasons' plants", others sent "gold mountain and silver mountain", miniature fairy mountains of gold and silver paper mounted on paper tables with suitable decorations, presenting the general appearance of the famous Japanese "potted sceneries"(*hakoniua*), etc.

Friends with "modernish tendencies" sent flower wreaths of paper and those of the old school sent paper servants, full-sized effigies of the cook, carrying a market basket and a cut of meat, and the maidservant with a face-basin and a towel and a dish containing a cake of soap, etc., all made of paper and each bearing on the back a paper label with a name written on it, so that the spirit of old Mr. Wu would be able to address them by their names instead of calling them "No. 1 Cook" and "Sew-sew Amah"!

Each gift received was acknowledged with a formal receipt issued by the "accounts division" and then put on display on the "moon platform" so that it would be in public view at the final reception.

*   *   *

The three-day Sutra Chanting period started on the sixth

day after the demise of old Mr. Wu.

The grandstand erected for the three groups of priests was elaborately decorated with silk bunting and paper flowers and the attendants of each group of priests came early and made the proper preparations.

The grandstand was divided into three sections, the left-hand side was for the Taoist priests, the right-hand side for the Buddhist monks and the central section for the Lamas or Mongolian priests. These spaces were quickly allotted and the interior furnishing at once began, starting with the hanging up of the painted images of the divinities.

The Taoists hung up the portraits of the "Three Pure Ones" including the full-bearded Lao Tze (老子) or "Old Boy," whose family name was Li and who founded the Taoist faith. Li is said to have been born in 604 B.C. after a legendary period of gestation of 70 years (!). Taoist priests do not shave their heads like the Buddhists and the Lamas do but knot their hair in the center of the skull and wear a black cap with a hole in the center for the knot. A Taoist mass is characterized by the low and almost inaudible chanting from the holy books, principally the *Hwang T'ing Ching* (黃庭經), or "Book of the Yellow Courtyard," and also by the frequent changing of gaudy embroidered robes during the services which give the laymen an idea that they are the best dressed of all with the richest wardrobes.

They also burn certain paper communications commending the spirit of the dead to the mercy of their deity, the First Creator of the Universe, the Heavenly Honour, Ultra-Supreme Old Lord, who would save the soul by helping it to evade transmigration and reincarnation. For exactly this purpose the Taoists practice self-denial and cultivate a "humble and weak" innate self-subsistence and self-sufficiency in the *tan tien* (丹田) or the "Field of the Elixir," abstaining from all temporal foods, so that their spirit would "fly to the sky" and convert itself into an "immortal" after shedding the corporeal "skin bag." This, they explain, is possible only through a clear understanding of the futility of worldly ambition and the subjugation of all desires for fullness in this present life.

The Buddhist monks also hung out their three-in-one portrait of the Buddhas of the Present, the Past and the Future, as also the painted image of Mitreya, the next Buddha to be born

Lama priests always sit tailor fashion and read the scriptures in a monotonous canting voice. All the scriptures of the Lama faith are in the Tibetan language and to the average Chinese are "closed books". With such services, not fully intelligible to the Mongolian priests themselves, they administer to the spiritual comfort of the Chinese dead.

in this world after Cyakamuni, who would escort the spirit of the dead to the Western Region after bringing a pardon from the King of Hades, and then make for Nirvana, the state of spiritual accomplishment.

But the central section where the Lamaist priests made their shrine was the most interesting and, not willing to let the others get all the honours for exhibition of religious art, they put up their own hair-raising, awe-inspiring group of image scrolls, painted on silk, called in Tibetan the *tancha*. Their scrolls depicted Tibetan gods and goddesses, some with the head of an ox and all with flaming hair and hairbands and necklaces of human skulls, treading on all forms of animal life. These Tibetan divinities have also multi-faced heads and any number of extra arms and hands carrying symbolic religious attributes and tokens of authority.

The Lama priests dressed in yellow, the official colour of the new Yellow Sect as advocated by the great reformer Tsong-kaba, sat tailor fashion on yellow cushions and did their chanting of the sacred books from printed cardboard sheets in the Tibetan language. They chanted in a low, deep-toned voice, described by some to be similar to the lowing of the cows, with the details and meanings decidedly not available for outsiders to understand or appreciate. The noise was enhanced by the din of the particularly voluminous sounds of Mongolian and Tibetan music played on big copper twelve-foot trumpets and drums mounted on a handle erected beside the priest and beaten with a curved drumstick. A pagoda-shaped object made of dough was brought by the priests, filled with melted butter and kept burning throughout the chantings. It was placed on a tray before the seat of the high-priest who is called a *Dumchi*.

This chanting continued for three days including the day of the Last Reception and kept the Wus busy with sacrificials here and there and the burning of religious documents at the door as required by each of the three priest groups. Old Mrs. Wu was glad, though, that everything was being done for the spiritual welfare of her husband's soul.

*   *   *

As some hyper-sensitive friends had anticipated it was a fine day on which the Wus held the final reception in honour of the deceased Mr. Wu. This was a noisy affair indeed and of much bigger proportions than the Third Day Memorial Service. The same musicians were in attendance as well as the three groups of priests as this was also the third and final day of the sutra-chanting period.

All of the guests who had come for the previous reception again came to do obeisance before the spirit of old Mr. Wu and to sit at either the morning or the evening feast, or at both. A good number of others who had been prevented from coming "by previous engagement" to the Third Day Ceremonial also presented themselves. The courtyard, covered with matting, was filled to capacity with guests who were served tea and introduced to each other.

They took their seats, six people per table, the men and women seated at separate tables in 'shifts, and partook of the feast. As the hosts, the mourners, were obliged to kneel beside the coffin most of the time and only went to each group of guests after the latter had seated themselves to thank them for their kindness by a single kowtow, kneeling on a white cushion, the guests were left to "help themselves" and did full justice to the elaborate menu. It is a peculiar custom of the Chinese race that a person offering condolences at a funeral ceremony can sit down and enjoy a feast, often right after the ceremonious wailing before the coffin. It is nothing short of a fine art, which no novice should expect to master.

The ceremony went on in the accepted triumphant manner as each guest was announced by the musicians and ushered to the "moon platform" by family friends. Here candles were kept burning all day long and an endless list of rites were performed both on the part of the guests and on the part of the mourning family itself.

Some of the guests also sent "sacrificial" feasts. It was therefore considered the proper thing to have each of these feasts actually offered to the spirit of the departed on this

This honest-looking young man is the person to whom is entrusted the custodianship of gold and silver hoardings. He lives and dies, so to speak, with the cash register and the storehouse key in his hands. Made of paper, as is also the house under whose roof he stands, he stays there rain or sun on duty twenty-four hours a day, a veritable Good Man Friday.

particular day and old Mr. Wu's spirit was presented with about ten dinners in the short period of four or five hours. This was accompanied by as many periods of wailing and all the other formalities connected with it. For, in the estimation of the Chinese, it would be considered a great "loss of face" to both the sender and the mourning family if such a presentation were inadvertently omitted. Such an honour is most valuable, as the Chinese proverb says "though boundless money you may have you can never buy a guest sacrificing before the coffin", and at least in this respect equality should be meted out to all gift-senders.

Much had to be done on this particular day and even the priests chanting on the grandstand had to hurry in order to finish the day's program in time for the burning of the paper houses before sundown.

*   *   *

Though a Chinese may spend all his life struggling economically to keep his head above water, it is an easy matter to make a dead person a millionaire in the next world or at least make him look like one as filial sons and well-wishing friends, their means permitting, would not fail to furnish him with a group of storehouses for the hoarding of possessions of the dead, made of painted and coloured paper on frameworks of kao-liang stalks. A conventional group is a three-piece set of three paper houses, a two-storied building placed between two others, in all the glories of Chinese architecture with painted beam, curved roofs and marble balustrades.

They are masterpieces of craftsmanship, towering fully twelve feet high in the case of the center piece and but slightly lower in the wings. Here the spirit of the dead will keep his valuables in safety. Each of the paper houses is barred and locked and the keys are placed in the hand of some paper figures standing on the steps who also carry an account book showing the debit and credit entries made from time to time as the master adds to and subtracts from the balance brought forward day by day.

The doors are also sealed with dated strips of paper in the typical Chinese manner and as an insurance against burglary and pilferage and, perhaps, infidelity on the part of the custodians, a Buddhist priest is invited to set his hand and seal on these paper strips so that no vagrant spirits or any other unauthorized parties will dare to tamper with the contents—a quantity of paper ingots prepared by the family or given by friends. Though all these paper things, on the whole, look so flimsy and deceiving to us, the living, they will become the real things in the next world after being burned.

*   *   *

Paper houses answering to the foregoing description were ordered by Seventh Uncle. They were first exhibited at the Wu house and then sent to be burned in the late afternoon.

*   *   *

The procession for burning the paper things for the use of old Mr. Wu in the next world started from the house on Donkey Mart in full pomp and wound slowly *via* the main street to the same spot where they had burned the old man's mule cart a few days before. In general appearance the procession was a duplicate of the previous one except that, it being still broad daylight, the incense torches and paper lanterns were absent. The paper things had been transported to the appointed place half an hour or so before the procession was due to start and did not form a part of the procession itself. In spite of these drawbacks it was a no less colourful pageant, for all the priests were engaged to parade in full regalia.

The Taoists, true to their religious credo, moved along in their typical leisurely fashion as though to indicate thereby that it made no difference whether people saw them or not. Then followed the Mongolian priests beating vehemently on their peculiarly shaped instruments, the monstrous cymbals, and blowing the curved horns and the pair of big trumpets fully ten feet long, each of these last were carried at the far end by a coolie while a Lama blew two characteristic low notes, long drawn out and a tribute to the lung capacity of the priest, at intervals of ten seconds each, like the steam sirens of the delapidated coastal freighters caught in a dense fog in rugged and treacherous inland seas.

The many guests formed the principal part of the procession and everybody saw everybody else, for it is something of an honour to be seen as a participant in one of these processions, because anybody who has a friend rich enough to stage such an expensive funeral wants to keep it no secret. Young Mr. Wu was seen bearing with both hands the brass tray in which was placed the dough lamp which had been blessed by the Lama priests and his son, following immediately behind, carried the yellow paper offerings with a similar gesture as they moved slowly and reverently along, each of their steps a geometrically correct square.

The Buddhist monks, with embroidered capes thrown over their shoulders tied with a jade hook in front and gorgeously wrought in gold tinsel on a ground of red satin, trooped behind everyone. Not willing to resign their position due to the overwhelming noise produced by the Lamas, they were doing their very best to play their music loudly enough so that although to compare with the din of their Mongolian comrades was out of the question, at least their presence could not be denied.

The burning of the dough-lamp and the paper documents as well as the paper houses and "gold and silver mountains" was soon over, and of all the colourful pile still intact but five minutes ago, only a smouldering heap of ashes and debris remained. However, it would not be right to say that the entire thing was consumed in flames for a few paper heads of the effigy bookkeepers were saved from the conflagration by some poor children of the neighbourhood. They had been lying in wait for the opportune moment to jump out from ambush, dart for exactly these souvenirs which they quickly "salvaged" in defiance of the bamboo poles of the attending servants. To the children any such ceremony meant paper heads "salvaged" and paper heads thus procured bore a reselling value of five big coppers each! For them the colourful procession was only a sideshow of no importance.

*   *   *

After the procession a few minor rites were held in the Wu house. Appearing in order of precedence, the mourning family and close relatives knelt one by one before the coffin and paid final homage, concluding a series of kowtows with crying, for this was the *Ts'u Ling* (辭靈) ceremony or "bidding farewell to the remains." This done, a man from the coffin shop set the locking devices of the coffin with little pieces of wood and tightly blocked the holes from the inside of which the mechanism of the lock was worked. He pounded in the wedge-shaped stoppers with a heavy hammer.

This was accompanied by more weeping and wailing as is required by good form. The man also swept clean the imaginary dust from the coffin top and deposited it in a pan in young Mr. Wu's bedroom for, in this way, the spirit of old Mr. Wu would

This jar, containing bits of food, is sealed with a cake and an apple and buried with the Chinese dead. Though no argument in support of this practice can be said to "hold water", it is nevertheless an old and established custom.

be sure to bestow a further legacy of imaginary wealth in the future. He also lifted the coffin a little from one of the supporting benches and placed a coin underneath to serve as another superstitious formality to give the old man notice of his forthcoming removal. It might have been devised for certain practical reasons though exactly for which is not known.

In the evening the family gathered to prepare the jar containing bits of food which was to be buried with the coffin. This is a pottery jar about ten inches high into which, when the sacrificial feast was spread on the table, each family member placed some food gathered from the various dishes. When full, the jar is closed with a flat cake which is, per custom, nibbled off the edge by the head mourner to fit the size of the jar's mouth. An apple is then placed on top of the cover of cake and sealed with a flapping piece of red cloth and bound with five-coloured threads.

The son's wife is required to carry this jar in her bosom all the way to the graveyard where it is placed near the coffin's "head" and buried with it. This jar of food would give strength to the dead should he come back to life, enough strength to make it possible for him to make his resurrection known in some effective manner. At least this is the explanation given for such a custom.

*   *   *

One of the sights frequently seen on Peking streets are the elaborate funeral processions of rich families, and to the leisured classes such processions are looked forward to with considerable interest. Expecting a big funeral in Peking is like expecting the circus to come to town in, say, the United States. Although no coloured posters herald the impending procession, such sensational news goes from house to house and on the proper day, hours before the procession is due to pass a certain point, eager sight-seers line the streets to feast their eyes on the parade.

Of these spectators women and children form the majority, as to go to the big street to see a funeral is, or at least used to be, one of the accepted excuses for the secluded women to appear in public. As a matter of fact, it would be a most deplorable thing indeed for a big Chinese funeral to go along entirely unnoticed by the people in the streets. Moreover, such a happening would be an economic waste, considering the money spent for this colourful parade.

It is the opinion unanimously held by all Peking-*jen* that really big funerals are rarely seen now-a-days, for the people have either changed their respective importance or else do not spend their money so lavishly as they used to. The pomp and splendour of such a parade is almost extinct, gone with the last rays of the twilight of feudalism and imperial favours. There are still to be seen the funerals of rich merchants and maybe some big officials and warlords, either incumbent or retired, who in their life-time had been in the limelight of republican officialdom. But such funerals would include at most the giant paper gods and demons, some fifteen or eighteen feet high, and others mounted on little chariots pushed by a coolie and revolved by a mechanism. They brandish a many-sectioned weapon to clear the path of evil spirits for the procession to pass, and perhaps one, two or three modern brass bands "in field marshals' uniforms" playing in turn anything that goes as foreign music except the proper pieces to be played at a funeral.

In the costly funerals of former Mandarins big wooden boards, shaped like a Japanese shuttlecock bat (hak ita), were paraded through the streets. On each board is a phrase commemorating the bright spots of the dead official's career and the receipt of sundry court favours The board illustrated says that the deceased was given moon-cakes to eat by the Emperor. The bearers are beggars and their own rags are visible beneath the colourful costumes lent them for the occasion For them, with reference to their garb, "beauty is only skin deep".

There may also be a latest model paper automobile or two, even a squad of paper bodyguards armed with small weapons made also of paper carried by liveried coolies marching ironically in the midst of the real bodyguards armed to the teeth provided for the safety of the mourning heirs, rich and important, bearing mute evidence to the secret plots and possible designs that might already be brewing at home. These funerals may feature also big lion-dogs, made of the twigs of cypress, and various kinds of paper figures of nymphs riding on fabulous birds of gaudy plumage, the real specimens of which are never seen this side of Paradise. But this would be about all.

In olden days, however, a big mandarin's funeral would be preceded by a tall pillar of bamboo and cloth, called a *ming ching* (銘旌), towering forty feet high and carried by a number of coolies, on which would be inscribed the titles and ranks of the deceased in gilt letters. Then would follow the complete coterie of courtiers in colourful costumes, including the executioners and punishment-meters fully equipped to cope with and torture any offending "evil spirits" as in the corrupted lawcourts of the past.

Then would follow rows of

long handled yellow sign-boards each carried on the shoulder of a coolie, commemorating imperial favours, ranging from permission to wear peacock feathers with two "eyes", to wearing a "yellow jacket" or to riding a pony within the Forbidden City . . . special appointments to represent the Emperor in certain state functions, down to the small royal favours as having been given to eat moon-cakes or tribute venison from Mongolia. If the deceased happened to be a Manchu "banner-man" his procession would of necessity include a number of banner-carriers, whether the All White or Bordered White, etc., and a special flag-staff mounted on a heavy wooden stand carried on the shoulders of coolies in a perpendicular position. Indispensable would be also the so-called professional mourners, dressed in coarse white robes, twenty or thirty of them in two rows, single file, carrying trays hung from their necks containing bric a-brac, either the real objects or paper imitations, which the deceased used to be fond of. Still more picturesque would be the so-called *Ch'ien Hu* (前扈) and *Huo Yung* (後擁) or "front and rear guards", groups of men in warrior robes riding on horseback, arranged eight in a crosswise row in four, six or eight rows before the catafalque itself and an equal number behind, carrying wooden spears or javelins, each held by a trooper, erect like a flagpole, and joined together with yellow silk bunting fastened near the tips of the weapons and set about three feet apart so that none of the bearers could stray away or drop off from the others in his row without destroying the ceremonious effect. Such a catafalque might be carried by as many as eighty people and all the equipment and accessories would be in yellow in the case of a member of the nobility. A touch of lively zoological interest, again as in a circus, would be added by camel and horse teams and the falcon and dog hunters in grey uniform, the animals all real and quite alike and the men carrying real old-fashioned flintlocks on their shoulders, and then effigies and things such as may still be seen now. Processions literally miles in length thus moved slowly along the main streets. That was, of course, before the coming of tram-car wires made most of these undertakings impossible.

At important street junctions, friends used also to erect way-side sacrificial halls of de luxe mat-sheds in which were displayed a complete set of the ceremonial paraphernalia and where musicians played while the coffin made temporary short halts nearby so the mourners could repair inside these halls and accept the homage of such friends. This attracted immense gatherings of "rubberneck" sight-seers and "side-walkers" who peeped through the sides of the matting.

All these extravagant shows of colour and action cost the Peking-*jen* nothing but the time and the trouble of attendance. The crowds were good-natured and must be said to constitute an important factor in such a big show, adding prestige to the dead and his family.

* * *

Old Mr. Wu's funeral was nowhere near so elaborate but nevertheless a small crowd began to appear near the Wu residence on the morning of the procession.

*　　　　*　　　　*

Even as the guests who were required by good form and friendship to accompany the funeral began to arrive at the Wu residence and the final details were checked over under the able management of Seventh Uncle inside the compound, appointing the labour force of domestics to attend to various things before and after the procession left the house, the coolies and youngsters who were enlisted by the undertakers to take part in the procession began to present themselves in crowds bringing along the equipment supplied them by the undertakers' establishment.

In a short time everything was rigged up, they were ready to stand by and Seventh Uncle was notified to that effect. Meanwhile the coolies and youngsters, mostly beggars picked up from the streets except perhaps those who were assigned to carry the heavy catafalque and who, of necessity, must be experienced hands and trained to do flawless multiplex team-work, were quickly garbed in green garments with stencilled designs.

The men were sitting and "taking it easy" near the north walls where there was sunshine, relaxed in preparation for the strenuous work before them. Having been paid part of their day's earning, some of them ("most of them" would be more accurate) formed themselves into little gambling groups for, with the exception of what had already been spent to get a hearty meal, all the rest of their day's earning was good capital. Bamboo dominoes and paper playing-cards, portable and handy, were produced mysteriously and the games started. These went on until the beating of the big gongs by the headmen sounded the call for "immediate formation." This decided the fate of the gamblers, the winners smiled over their doubled or trebled income and the losers felt "down" but not "out" for the "show must go on"!

Inside the Wu house the moon platform was reduced to its bare original self for the paper articles had either been burned the previous day or taken outside for the coolies to carry in the procession. The coffin drapery had been taken off and the ropes had been coiled ready for removal, all presented something like pre-sailing orderlessness—even the dim oil lamp was permitted to burn itself out after trying its best to continue with the last drops of sesamum oil which had been placed in it the night before.

The shop making paper objects brought two more items of their creative productions, a spirit banner with appropriate designs of the lotus flower motif on a stick and a small paper shrine, a foot and a half high. Young Mr. Wu was to carry the spirit banner in his hand in the procession. On it was inscribed his late father's name and the date and hour of his birth and death, for this was going to serve as a beacon for guiding the spirit along a peaceful course and to a safe landing at the graveyard.

Little Bald Head, as the second-in-mourning, was to carry the shrine which was used for similar purposes. His mother, who would be travelling behind the coffin in a Peking cart, the blue hood covered with white cloth, was to carry the food jar already described and her cart was to follow behind that of her mother-in-law's, which was also covered with white cloth. The other women who decided to go with the procession as a courtesy were to ride in similar carts but which were not covered with white cloths, trailing behind and in order of relational precedence. There were some ten or twelve carts and Seventh Uncle and his assistant had hired them three days before.

The all-important geomancer was again called upon to do an exorcistic house-cleaning immediately following the start of the funeral procession. This was to follow the traditional methods consisting of the burning of incense, the chanting of magic words in all the rooms and in the courtyard, nooks and corners of the house, the throwing of handfuls of miscellaneous grains and beans and the pasting of a sacred charm or talisman at the street gate. For the same purpose, the pillow which the old man had used was to be emptied of its contents of grain husks (Chinese pillows are filled with either the husks of millet or of buckwheat) onto the street and the geomancer's burning bundle of incense was to be placed on the heap for both to burn together.

The guests had by then all arrived and they sat down to a simplified feast, for nobody should accompany a funeral with an empty stomach, as the old saying goes. It was soon time for the procession to start. According to the geomancer's adivce, it was to be the hour of the Snake or between ten and twelve in the morning.

*   *   *

At the proper hour for old Mr. Wu's funeral to start, the mourning members of the family knelt at their respective positions in front of the coffin. The musicians came in and played suitable pieces and when these were concluded the professional pall-bearers, clad in green uniforms and wearing feathered caps, came into the courtyard and began to move the coffin under the supervision of the two overseers who were dressed in white mourning gowns as specified by Seventh Uncle. As the music started anew the coffin was moved slowly out through the street gate and was placed on the smaller catafalque from which it was later to be transferred to the more elaborate one on the main street.

Young Mr. Wu, his eyes overflowing with tears, watched the entire proceedings and on the street, before the men shouldered the catafalque to set off, performed another small

The chief mourner at a funeral carries a paper gadget, some five feet in length, hung from a stick. In the central panel is written the name of the dead person, the date of his birth and death, etc. Guiding the spirit of a dead parent to the grave with such a thing is an important duty of a son.

ceremony—that of "breaking the mourning bowl."

As we have had an occasion to explain before, the spirit of the Chinese dead after going through all the trials and formalities in Purgatory will be conducted to the "wheel of incarnation" to be born into a rich mansion or a beggar's hut, or to be an animal, a reptile or an insect, etc., depending on how it had behaved in the previous "life". Before such a change is to take place the spirit must be disarmed of all the wisdom and faculties acquired in the preceding "life" in order that its past history and experience will not leak out from the lips of a talkative dog or a loquacious water buffalo! According to the Buddhist belief, this is taken care of by an old woman, known as Wang Ma Ma, or "Mother Wang" who, at a small wayside counter, deals out to the unsuspecting thirsty spirits bowls and bowls of a liquid called *mi hun t'ang* (迷魂湯) which serves exactly the purpose for which it is intended.

A filial son naturally does not want his parent to be victimized in this manner and so he offers him or her a bowl with a hole in the bottom so that this liquid will run out through the hole while the spirit pretends to drink the stuff. Such a private drinking bowl is a device guaranteed to be effective. Wang Ma Ma is said to offer no objection to her guests bringing their own bowls, having been sold on the idea of individual personal hygiene. For guests who bring no bowls with them she uses her own—which have no holes!

Such a bowl as described is made of pottery and about four inches across. The filial son picks it up as the procession starts and smashes it into pieces on a piece of brick, pasted with coloured paper to look like a volume of the famous Chinese "Classic of Filial Piety".

Young Mr. Wu attended to this while in a kneeling position facing the coffin and followed it with further kowtows. Meanwhile the procession started on its way and the catafalque coolies gathered enough courage (!) by crying out certain traditional phrases while the overseers beat time on their "timing sticks" to keep the men in step. Such loud shouts usually announce to all that certain gratuities have been promised by the mourning family or their friends and these cries will be repeated on the way, as they changed their shoulder in unison, or at certain important street crossings. They sound more like "three good cheers" than anything else. The Chinese are a noisy people and the harder they work the louder the noise they make—noise in this country takes the place of variety as the spice of life!

Paper offerings were burned on the way notably where there was a well or a bridge or a temple by the wayside. Handfuls of paper disks were also tossed into the air. It is believed that the higher these disks

A pottery bowl is smashed to pieces on a piece of brick made up to look like a set of the famous Chinese "Classic of Filial Piety".

fly in the air the better their merits will be and so rich people employ specialists for this work for so much per "trip". Good paper disk throwers are very scarce as the technique is not easily mastered. The quantity of paper disks thrown is also in direct proportion to the extravagance of the funeral, and it is a common sight to see a mule cart in a funeral procession carrying nothing but solid strings of these paper disks to be used for throwing about.

On the streets there was many an impromptu "tea table" put up in front of the shops which old Mr. Wu had patronized or where the Wus had a friend. These were little square tables on which hot tea was offered, as the procession arrived at each place, for the benefit of the guests as well as the mourning family. Young Mr. Wu and his son knelt down before each place to thank the friends sponsoring these tea tables though drinking was optional. Servants bearing cups of tea on brass trays also went to the women riding in the mule carts behind the catafalque to offer them a drink. These tea tables, in the funerals of plain citizens, take the place of the elaborate wayside sacrificial stations and the mourning family's "business manager" sees to it that a small sum of money is deposited at each table as a tip for the sponsors' help as well as a "certificate of thanks" formally acknowledging the favour rendered.

*   *   *

Old Mr. Wu's funeral procession paraded the main streets in its full grandeur with the various component parts described before attracting many a passer-by to stop, look and read the eulogistic couplets friends had given, hanging from bamboo poles carried by hired youngsters.

Near the Hata Men most of the friends dropped out from the procession after asking young Mr. Wu to pardon them for their inability to accompany him further. Acquaintances are required by custom to go with the funeral only part of the way and solely the intimate friends present themselves at the interment ceremony.

The procession was finally broken up at Kwang An Men, the "city limit", for further on the narrow country roads did not permit the heavy catafalque, carried by the thirty-two men, to travel with ease. The number of men at the bier was reduced to a practical minimum. The mulecarts in which the women travelled had to go by a different route and the friends who wished to see the burial were requested to board the carts and make for the destination in a more comfortable manner.

And so in the bleak wintry weather of late November, along the narrow beaten paths winding through long fields of the frost-bitten wheat of next year's crop and patches of early spring spinach, protected by crude wind-breakers of tall rushes, young Mr. Wu and his son, Little Bald Head, were the only persons who walked all the way with the coffin borne on the shoulders of the coolies looking like a gaudy-coloured tropical giant spider making speedily for the family graveyard at the village of the Stone Gate.

The musicians had preceded the coffin and as the catafalque with the reduced force of carriers appeared they played a mourning air which was carried through the clear air to a great distance. The guests and the female family members who had arrived some time earlier and had been resting in the caretakers' farmhouse, heard the music and made ready for the last rites, appearing by the side of the hole dug to receive the coffin. A group of hired labourers were standing by, shovels in hand, ready to cover up the pit when the order was given.

The bottom of the pit was first strewn over with a lot of the paper disks left over from the "expensive" tossing on the way. Then the coffin was taken from the catafalque and using two heavy beams as supports, it was lowered with ropes, working on the pulley principle, by the skillful professional pall-bearers with great precision and dexterity. The head of the coffin was pointed to the southeast according to the advice of the geomancer. The direction was accurately adjusted by surveying with a long red string to the ends of which were tied two Chinese coins as plumbs. The jar containing bits of food was taken from young Mrs. Wu's hand and placed before the coffin. All this was done solemnly under the watchful eyes of young Mr. Wu who assumed a kneeling position at the edge of the pit. He pronounced himself satisfied with the work and the burying began.

A shovel, which had been laid aside containing the original first shovelful of earth picked up when the digging of the hole started, was handed over to young Mr. Wu, and he threw the earth back into the pit, signifying thereby that he had himself dug the hole and buried his dead father. Then the hired men followed up and in half an hour a new grave mound was formed on the ground some three feet high. Into this the stick of the paper spirit-guiding banner was inserted as the banner itself was torn off and burned with other paper offerings at the graveside, paper flower wreaths, paper servants, etc.

There was also a brief sacrificial immediately following. A complete feast had been transported to the graveyard by a coolie and a cook warmed the foods up and spread them out on a low table before the new grave. Everybody present did homage in proper order and all wept bitter tears. Young Mr. Wu and his son were among the last ones to stop weeping. Then the guests and family members left to rest at the reception rooms located close by which the forefathers of the Wus had built, following an old custom in China, especially for such and similar occasions. After refreshments had been served, the party broke up and made for their respective homes in the city.

At the gate of the Wu house, a servant had been posted in

Returning from a family burial, the Chinese observe a series of petty superstitions at the front door. A knife is ground against a basin to frighten off evil spirits, their absence is verified by looking into a mirror, and a piece of sugar will take away the "bitterness" of the recent bereavement.

anticipation of the family's return and at about five o'clock in the afternoon the rattling of the springless Peking carts announced their arrival. The servant brought out a glazed pottery basin in which a meat-chopper was placed. A bowl containing pieces of crystallized sugar and a hand-mirror were also prepared. Each person was told to take up the meat-chopper and grind it two or three times across the edge of the basin, then take up the mirror, look at it in a perfunctory manner and then place a piece of sugar in his or her mouth. All this was in strict compliance with local superstition.

Needless to say, there was a further shedding of tears when the Wus saw their home restored to its normal condition and missed the good old grandfather for the first time.

* * *

On the third day after his father's funeral, young Mr. Wu and his son again made a trip to the graveyard to perform what is known locally as the *Yuan Fen* (圓墳) ceremony or "rounding up the grave." Most families leave this small detail to the graveyard caretakers but the Wus preferred to do it themselves.

This ceremony no doubt evolved from the ancient custom of the mourners staying for a certain period of time at the side of a new grave as a gesture of devotion to the deceased. They denied to themselves all the refinements of life and called a stop to all their worldly pursuits during such a period which ranged from a few months to as long as several years. When Confucius died Tze Kung, one of his seventy-two famous disciples, built himself a little hut by the side of the sage's tomb and spent six solid years in hermitage there. So far as is known Tze Kung's record has never been shattered.

For "rounding up the grave", the Wus brought with them two round cakes made of wheat flour and splitting them, inserted in each pieces of a kind of edible lichen or fungi. The two cakes were then buried in the earth to the left and right of the grave mound. Next they erected a rough arch on the ground with a kaoliang stalk where the coffin's "head" was, all in the traditional manner. Edible lichen is known as *mu erh* (木耳) in Chinese which means "the tree's ears" by reason of their shape. That these "ears" would give the buried dead a chance to hear what was going on outside seems to be the best explanation ever given for their use.

Another three days later, on the fifteenth day counting from the day on which old Mr. Wu had died, the family also arranged to offer a sacrifice before the *yang* or "lingering spirits" of the old man which, according to the geomancer, were due to leave their old haunt on that very day at the hour of the Monkey or between five and seven in the afternoon. The preparations were made according to local practice and a long while before the *yang* were due to start, the family told everybody to stay away from the room as it was too serious a matter to risk being stricken by the *yang*.

To explain what the *yang* are, or are supposed to be, it must be clearly understood first that the Chinese believe every human being has three *hun* (魂) or "souls", and these three souls are interdependent of each other in the make-up of the "spiritual bloc" in an offensive and defensive alliance on the "united we live and divided we die" formula. When a person is dead, however, the three souls are scattered and one of them goes with the demons who are sent by the King of Hades to arrest him for appearance in Purgatory. The second soul stays with the corpse and follows it into the grave, while the third stays in the man's dwelling, being somewhat unwilling to leave the ones dear to him.

On a certain day, divined by the geomancer, the second soul comes back to join the third soul and the two then make for some regions never as yet discovered as the geomancer's art has not yet been developed to such a stage of perfection! Thus the spirits of a dead person cannot be said to have left his house until after the particular day on which the *yang*, the last lingering spirits, depart.

Although a living person may be benevolent and affectionate to his family members and friends, once he is dead his spirits will lose all the emotional characteristics of a human being and the social and relational ties are utterly broken. The "lingering spirits" are said to be a dreadful lot and whoever stands in their way at their departure will be stricken by them and rendered at least unwell or given bad luck for a long period of time. Stories of people having been "knocked" down and killed by a gust of *yang* are often referred to with apprehension. When a person looks "queer" or "seems to have the blues" a Chinese colloquialism says: "So-and-so looks as though he has been stricken by some *yang*"! That *yang* should not be kidded or petted is a foregone conclusion and there is no room for arguments.

*   *   *

The matting and felt covering of the brick bed on which old Mr. Wu used to sleep was rolled up from one side exposing a bare space of masonry some three feet wide. Three dishes of meat dumplings were prepared and arranged on the bed. Care was taken that these dumplings be with but a little meat filling though the why and wherefore of this has never been explained.

The old man's wine flask and cup were also in evidence. Next in place were put a face basin with warm water as well as a cake of soap and a towel, as even the "lingering spirits" prefer to go about with a clean face. The paper of some of the latticed windows was also removed to facilitate an unhandicapped "take-off".

Little Bald Head was particularly bidden not to peep in at the windows to see what might have been taking place as he was known to be inquisitive by nature. Not until late evening did the Wus venture into the room as by then the entire pantomime had been given plenty of time to be enacted, that is if there had been any.

*   *   *

It took the Wus some days to adjust themselves to the absence of the old man, for habitually, when the family was in doubt on anything it was a matter of "ask grandfather." Grandfather had been the center of gravity, the center of the very Solar system. Such an adjustment was particularly hard for Little Bald Head as he and his grandfather had been regular pals.

Three weeks after the day on which the old man had died, they arranged to feast his ghost at what is known as the *San ch'i* (三七), or "Third Seventh," ceremony.

Old Mrs. Wu personally prepared some dainty dishes of food which had been specially liked by her late husband and bought some of the city's best wine. She spread these out in the morning on a square table on the brick bed on which, behind

The spirits of the dead, it is believed in China, have to go long distances in the regions where the courts of Purgatory are located. To protect the spirits from the burning sun, family members burn paper parasols for their benefit. This is done on the thirty-fifth day after a death. Paper offerings, wrapped in paper and pinned with red paper flowers, are "sent off" with the parasol.

the table, they placed a beautiful cushion where the spirit of the old man was to sit while enjoying the family reunion. Three little white paper packages about a foot square were prepared, in which were wrapped a lot of paper joss-money, each sheet of which was rolled into a ball and placed behind the cushion, for it behooves a good son or a faithful wife to remember the dead by sending him paper money from time to time so that he shall not be in want in the other world. This was a sad party, though, for all who knelt to do homage to the spirit of old Mr. Wu found it hard to keep their tears from flowing as only a comparatively short time ago his cheerful personality had been among them.

At sundown the three paper packages were taken out into the street and burned, for the ghost must leave the house before nightfall. Old Mrs. Wu ordered her grandson also to take a few extra sheets of joss-money and burn them separately from the paper packages, to get a bowl of water and throw little bits of the food offerings on the ground while the paper packages burned for in this way, Little Bald Head learned, the hungry ghosts who might happen to be around would also be appeased.

A fortnight later, they again feasted the spirit at another family reunion. This, in accordance with local custom, was more elaborate.

A paper figure of a handsome boy, almost life-size, wearing a red gown with flower-designed laces, a little cap and a big red paper sunshade, an exact replica of the kind formerly used to shade the mandarins from the sun during their official outings and the like of which are used now-a-days only as a salutatory token of gratitude presented by thankful people to a governing magistrate, was ordered made by Mrs. Chao and sent over to the Wu residence. The old Wus had no daughter of their own so Mrs. Chao acted in the capacity of one as tradition requires such a gift of a paper parasol to be donated by a married daughter. Mrs. Chao also came to do obeisance as befitted her "acting" rank.

The Chinese believe that the spirit of the dead is bound on a long and tedious journey along a road entirely unshaded by any trees and on which the fierce sunlight pours its hottest rays (this is what is known as the Road of the Yellow Spring). Whoever has been survived by a daughter would receive a gift parasol from her to save him from possible sunstroke. Poorer people burn only a sunshade but richer families also send a paper boy to carry it for the dead one and to keep him company so that he will not be lonely on the road. A feast similar to the one held on the twenty-first day was prepared but instead of three packages of paper joss-money five were used, each of them this time being pinned together with imitation pomegranate blossoms of paper, deep red in colour. According to old Mrs. Wu these flowers were to serve a special purpose.

"The Chief Justice of the Fifth Court in the Eighteen Departments of Hell is nobody but the august personage Pao Kung, or Duke Pao," explained the old woman. "Duke Pao has been holding this important post since he died some seven hundred years ago in the Sung Dynasty. Duke Pao is as severe a judge and as enthusiastic an advocate of judicial integrity as has ever lived. His sense or justice has never been influenced by personal feelings or bribery. Spirits of the dead who are all made to go through the Fifth Court for hearings are invariably in for a thorough boiling down."

The knowledge of this procedure in time leaked out to this world. Whoever brought this revelation also brought the news that if the family of the dead one should send some paper flowers with their paper offerings on the "Fifth Seventh Day", the deceased can send them as a little "door opener" to Duke Pao's young daughter. Duke Pao's young daughter who lives together with her dad at the official residence is fond of flowers. "If she is pleased, the sentences her father might pass on the sender will be much ameliorated," old Mrs. Wu concluded.

At sundown the sunshade, the paper boy and the paper offerings were taken out into the street and burned.

*   *   *

On the sixtieth day after old Mr. Wu's death the family solemnized the occasion with another simple ceremony in the home, offering food in the same way as on the two previous occasions. This was also the date on which the coarse mourning gowns of white muslin were to be discarded as were also the heavy cloth turbans which had been worn by the women since the day of the old man's death and for the balance of the three years of mourning, ordinary clothes of cotton materials of sober colours would be permissible for the family members.

At the end of the sixtieth day ceremony the Wus, who had put on their mourning attire while doing obeisance, actually cut off some corners of their gowns to symbolize the formal change. As a matter of fact, however, young Mr. Wu and his son had effected a compromise long before this day as, having to attend to business and to go to school, it was not feasible to wear mourning clothes nor to go without a shave for so long as dictated by propriety. Grey and black, however, were the only colours used for their clothes.

The Sixtieth Day memorial service ended with the burning of a paper barge and a pair of paper bridges, allegedly for the purpose of aiding the spirit of old Mr. Wu to cross the Nai Ho (奈河) River in the "lower region." It is a trying business to cross this fabulous river, if the legendary description of the river is to be credited, for it is said that the water is the domain of ferocious water demons as well as various poisonous creatures, such as venomous snakes and stinging scorpions, who are found in good numbers in the water. Those spirits who are not well-equipped for the journey fall victim to these tormentors.

It is also said that this Nai Ho River is formed by the streams of blood flowing from the various departments of hell and it is a nauseating experience to cross it as sinners are often pushed bodily into the "pool" of blood and their cries for help are loud and unending. To the spirits of those who have done good on earth, the heavenly gods provide a sort of escort, a convoy system, carrying paper banners to direct the spirits to the otherwise invisible sacred bridges or to aid them to board the divine ferry-boat for a safe trip across. To be certain of proper accommodation the family of a dead person are in the

To enable the spirit of a dead person to cross a certain river in the next world with ease, the family burn a paper barge and a pair of paper bridges on the sixtieth day after the death. Paper banner-bearers provide spiritual guidance. The water design is an artistic touch to this seven-foot example of the paper craftman's skill.

habit of burning such articles of paper. This at least makes for the survivors' peace of mind.

The paper barge burned on such an occasion is a magnificent piece of craftsmanship and the living quarters in the middle of the deck contain all the furniture and fixtures for the comfort of the occupant: tables, chairs, regular beds and not berths, all the articles of interior decorations made of paper and a complete crew of many members, including a team of oarsmen and a pilot at the head of the boat. The latter is there to beat a big gong to frighten away the evil-dealing denizens of the deep while a handsome boy acts as helmsman and navigator.

With such a private yacht what might have been a dreadful journey becomes a joy-ride. The bridges are also made of paper varying in size, as is also the barge, in accordance with the family budget. One of them is white in colour symbolizing silver and the other yellow symbolizing gold. The bridges are also provided with paper figures carrying spirit banners. That it is very costly to maintain such a big group of ship and land forces is fully appreciated by the donating family and so little strings of paper ingots are hung around the neck of each of these paper figures as is also a wheat-flour cake from the end of a thread. This is the custom in Peking.

*   *   *

Burning the paper barge and the bridges marked the very last rite in connection with old Mr. Wu's death and after this nothing further commemorated the event except a temporary sad spell in the house when anyone happened to mention the late grandfather. And the long period of mourning of three years was soon at an end.

In China some people also solemnize the first and third anniversaries of a death, sometimes even the tenth, with Buddhist services and feasts to which friends are again invited but the Wus only held family ceremonies on these occasions at which their own folks gathered to remember the old man.

For was it not amongst the sayings of Ts'eng Tze, a talented student of Confucius: "Let there be great attention in performing the last rites for parents and let these rites be followed for long afterward, with the reverent memory, then the virtue of the people will revert to their original excellence." The young Mr. Wu, well versed in Confucian classics, also recalled that he had learned in the Confucian Analects: "While a man's father is alive, look to the bent of his will; when his father is dead, look to his past conduct. If for three years he does not stray from the path of his father, he may be called filial."

He agreed with the famous saying, also by Ts'eng Tze: "To see to the comforts of living parents, for instance by occasionally buying them a chicken or some pork, is much more desirable than to kill a fatted calf for sacrifice on the grave of the dead".

Young Mr. Wu was satisfied that he had loved and revered his father while his father was alive. As to old Mrs. Wu, she had no regrets whatsoever. She firmly believed that her husband had been appointed to serve as an official in the next world, as witch-doctor Sun Nai Nai had assured her, and for her to join him was only a matter of time.

SKATES, CHESS AND PORRIDGE

DURING the lengthy period of mourning following the passing of old Mr. Wu, the family life of the Wus took on a dull atmosphere for members of a mourning family in China are not supposed to enjoy themselves with any amusements, particularly not with entertainments of a public nature. Going to a theatre, for instance, has been ruled a breach of etiquette, as also is participation in dinner parties, especially being a host. Occasions of celebrations are of necessity disregarded as such and even a hearty laugh is considered bad form. A son or a grandson in mourning is not even to marry before the expiration of the nominal three year period which, in certain Peking families, is actually observed for twenty-seven months only, a sort of a twenty-five per cent discount.

In this typically quiet manner the Wus spent their mourning period. But Scholar Wu Hsueh-wen had not much to lose as he was thus enabled to concentrate still more on his school work which by then had become rather of a serious kind. On Sundays and holidays he often made excursions to the countryside with his father. They took long hikes or visited famous historical spots in and around Peking as mourning custom does not prevent people from recreations of a non mirthful character.

During the winter months they would also go to the moats or the nearby lakes for ice-skating which they soon learned to do very well.

Skating on natural ice is an old recreation in North China and is much indulged in by children and grown-ups alike. Chinese skates are a very simple appliance and consist of little pieces of wooden boards cut to rectangular shape a size bigger than the sole of the shoe, mounted below with pieces of iron wire and strapped onto the shoe with leather bands. It is a fact that what may be called fancy skating and figure skating have also been the ambition of many a native sportsman but what really receives the most attention is long-distance racing and the development of speed.

It was not a rare case for a man to glide on these native skates of the board-and-wire design from the city moat outside the eastern Peking wall along the Grand Canal to the town of Tungchow to the east, passing the various canal locks on the way, in a great solo marathon. While in Tungchow the skaters loaded up with certain local souvenirs (to show unbelieving friends that the destination had been attained) and then skated back "upstream" to Peking within say an hour and a half in actual skating time. It was a wonderful stunt indeed and certainly far from being a tame exercise as natural ice in a canal is different from a man-made skating rink and a constant vigilance must be paid for possible ice-holes on the way, often made by peasants living in nearby villages to draw water or to catch fish from. The distance itself is considerable, being about eighty Chinese *li* or roughly twenty-six miles the round trip. An acid test for strength and a daring attempt it must have been for no ambulance service or first-aid kit were available for any possible untoward incident.

Or else the Wus would go sledging in the lake districts to the west of the Drum Tower where during winter the neighbourhood labourers conduct an ice transport service covering a distance of about a mile and a half, offering sledge rides from the Silver Ingot Bridge to the Teh Sheng Men which cost the passenger on a "community sledge" only a very small sum of money.

A Chinese sledge is a simple, even a primitive, affair and probably retains all of the constructional details that the inventor, Emperor Yu Wang, specified two thousand years before Christ. It is a roughly constructed table-and-bed combination with the two side legs joined together with a long piece of wood in which are attached iron band "rails". A strong belt is attached to the sledge and "hitched" to the puller who supplies the motive power. The journey starts with conscientious pulling but once the sledge has gathered enough momentum the puller will permit himself to "drop" back, sit on the sledge and "free wheel" for a certain distance before again applying the "high gear", running to accelerate the dwindling velocity. A sledge-puller wears straw shoes of Manchurian design and origin and little iron hooks fastened to the soles to prevent slipping. Notwithstanding the fact that they are crudely made, the sledges are rather practical.

Board-and-wire skating and sledging are a fast vanishing sight from the frozen winter water-ways of Peking and the last of them will probably be seen shortly. Thirty years ago, skating native style was encouraged by the Manchus as a national sport. To add to the zeal of the fans, imperial favours were showered on certain demonstrative performers and a reliable historical record describes a sort of ice-football with annual tournaments played on the Forbidden City lakes at which the royal family and nobles were distinguished spectators. It is also recorded that sledges were often made use of by the Man-

The primitive Chinese sledge, pulled by strong labourers, has been an ancient winter institution in Peking. Not many are still to been seen in operation.

chu royalty on the palace ice and sledges used for the emperors were said to have been elaborately-appointed affairs with a hood mounted on top of them, lined inside with sable furs and covered outside with satins of yellow colour.

To commemorate a sledge trip, Emperor Ch'ien Lung wrote the following poem:

In the twelfth moon, every day new sights
parade.
The palace lakes frozen are like pieces of dust-
less jade.
Snow and frost, cold to those waiting for a
ferry-boat, are unknown to me,
As sitting warmly on the "ice bed" (*i.e.* a
sledge) I float
On the silvery sea.
On the Tai Yeh Lake, a man's each step leaves
a tiny flower on the ice,
While I try to locate the Chin Ao Arch under
heavily clouded skies.
A pleasureable jaunt, it ended not in the Pei
Hsi Island, where we sojourned,
For the crowing of evening ravens in the trees
greeted us as to the palace we returned.

*   *   *

During long winter evenings at home young Wu Hsueh-wen sometimes played Chinese chess with his father.

The Chinese *Hsiang Ch'i* (象棋) or Elephant Chess, is almost an exact counterpart of the foreign chess; both are patterned after mimic warfare and both are played with sixteen pieces on each side. The chessboard used in the Chinese game represents the territories of two countries divided by a "river."

The King and the Queen in foreign chess have their places taken by a mere General in the Chinese game, as the "conflict" is more or less in the nature of a border incident. The foreign Castle is represented by a Chariot in Elephant Chess. The Bishops are sadly wanting and their places are taken by the Aides-de-camp and the Elephants, one of each kind on either side of the General as the game starts.

Chinese chess has a weaker man-force than the foreign game as each side has but five Soldiers and before the game commences these are deployed along the front line, supported behind by two formidable Cannons. Instead of Knights, Chinese chess has two Horses on each side. Another difference between the two games is that whereas the foreign chess pieces are placed in the squares on the board, the Chinese pieces are placed on the intersecting points of the lines.

Chinese chess pieces are not carved ornately like their foreign counterparts but are usually little round pieces of wood on which a character denoting the identity of each is indicated in red or black for the two sides. The principal operation in the Chinese game is to checkmate the General of the opposing faction to do which all the pieces are used, each in its own way, except the Aides-de-camp and the Elephants who are confined to only a few movements near or inside the "headquarters" which occupies four squares in the central "background" on the chessboard and is marked with diagonal lines. Some pieces are called Elephants because elephants must have been important in ancient Cathay's warfare.

The following is a brief outline of Chinese chess rules:

(1) The General stays in the headquarters and only moves one step, straight only, in order to avoid being checkmated by an enemy piece. The Aides-de-camp travel in single steps along diagonal lines alone to afford the General needed protection from time to time as necessity arises. They, too, are not allowed outside of headquarters under any circumstances.

(2) The Cannon and the Chariot move in straight lines of as many steps, forward, backward or crosswise, as seen fit to achieve their purpose in enemy territory or in their own field. The Horse jumps in a characteristic manner from one position to another in the pattern of a Chinese *jih* (日) (day) character, or in other words, from the corner of one square to the farthest corner of an adjacent square. The Elephant jumps in the pattern of a Chinese *tien* (田) (field) character, or in other words, from the corner of one square to the opposite corner of another square diagonally connected to the first. As the Elephants are not permitted to cross the river into enemy territory their possible

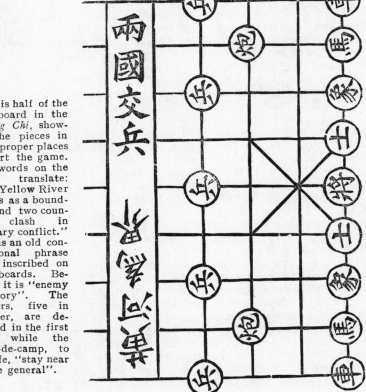

This is half of the chessboard in the *Hsiang Chi*, showing the pieces in their proper places to start the game. The words on the left translate: "The Yellow River serves as a boundary and two countries clash in military conflict." This is an old conventional phrase often inscribed on chessboards. Beyond it is "enemy territory". The soldiers, five in number, are deployed in the first line while the aides-de-camp, to be safe, "stay near the general".

steps are numbered but under their heavy legs imprudent enemy pieces come to grief. The Soldiers are moved one step at a time, are allowed only to go forward and not to retreat nor to move crosswise while in their own field. But once in enemy country they can go in any direction they please but yet only one step at a time.

(3) Each piece has the ability of "eating" or capturing any enemy piece by the proper steps described above and captured pieces are removed from the chessboard and their places taken by the capturing pieces, thus reducing the strength of the losing faction. The Cannons have a peculiarity in their operation of "eating" enemy pieces in that they must have something (whether of their own side or of the enemy's side) lying between themselves and the objective in the straight line in order to be at all effective——they do not shoot from point blank.

(4) The main operation consists of trying to attack or checkmate the opposing General, counting on the effective operations of one's own side, as well as in defending one's own General by proper strategy. There are many possibilities by which a General can be checkmated or escape being checkmated and so a single game may take from a few minutes to as long as one or two hours, depending upon the "strategic" skill of each player in relation to that of his opponent.

*   *   *

The younger Wu proved to be a better player than his father and he was always in a position to score a *san p'an liang sheng* (三盤兩勝) (winning two games out of three) which is the Chinese rule in chess playing.

*   *   *

Chess is a very popular game in China and many treatises have been written on the subject as the varieties of the operational niceties are diverse and highly absorbing to devotees. A good player is known as a *kuo shou* (國手), or "the Nation's Champion". In China, anywhere and everywhere, shop assistants and office clerks and tradespeople and students come into friendly conflicts as they "steal" an idle moment in the day's work. Outside Chien Men in Peking, at the so-called Bridge of Heaven amusement districts, open-air chessboard clubs are busy places where accommodations are offered to enthusiasts for a small charge. It is an open secret that little stakes of money, mutually agreed upon before "hostilities break out", are often won or lost with each game. Here future *kuo shou* are no doubt always in the making.

Chess playing is known also as "the Game in the Orange", which refers to an old legend.

In a certain Szechuan garden an orange grew to an enormous size to the surprise of the owner of the garden. At long last the man picked it off and cut it open to see what could be inside when, lo and behold, he found two old men inside busy over a game of Elephant Chess! This legend was recorded in the book *Yu Kwai Lu* (幽怪錄), or "Collection of Wonder Stories", by an anonymous author.

*   *   *

Just as the hot season of thirty days in the year is called the *San Fu* period, the cold season of eighty-one days is known by the name of *Chiu Chiu* (九九) or "Nine-Nine". The Chinese saying goes, *jeh tsai chung fu leng tsai san chiu* (熱在中伏，冷在三九) meaning, "the hottest days are in the Middle *Fu* period and the coldest days are in the Third *Chiu* period." Another Chinese weather expert left the saying *chiu chin wu leng ssu, fan tung shih pa tien* (九盡無冷絲，反凍十八天) "when the *Chiu* are through not a thread of cold will be left, but returning a cold wave will be experienced for eighteen more days." We cannot but admit that the wintry weather of North China is cold and we cannot but admit, either, that the Chinese weather expert when he said the above did think "safety first" and took no chances.

The counting of the eighty-one days starts with the day of the Winter Solstice and is called *Tung Chih* (冬至) in Chinese which means "Winter Arrives." Christmas, known properly as the *Sheng Tan Chieh* (聖誕節) or "Day of the Birth of the Holy," is colloquially called, on account of its proximity to the *Tung Chih* festival, the *Yang Tung Chih* (洋冬至) or "Foreign Winter Solstice" and by this name this important Christian holiday is often referred to by heathens and the uninitiated.

The period of eighty-one days begins with the Winter Solstice. Witness the local Chinese doggerel:

First *Chiu* and Second *Chiu* can hardly be called *Chiu* (being not so cold);

Third *Chiu* and Fourth *Chiu* are so cold even dogs and cats are frozen to death;

Fifth *Chiu* and Sixth *Chiu*, we look at the branches of the willow-trees (to notice the colour of the twigs changing into a fresh yellowish green);

Seventh *Chiu*, the river ice melts and Eighth *Chiu*, the teals come back (from the warm south whither they migrate in winter);

Ninth *Chiu*, up to the eighty-first day, foods are cooked in the home and eaten in the field (farm hands would be busy tilling the good earth).

The nine Chinese characters shown above contain nine strokes each and, strange as it may seem, make a line of Chinese poetry. Blackened with Chinese ink one stroke a day they constitute a chart with which scholars "count the days."

To record the weather condition in an amateurish fashion, the Peking-*jen* prepares what is known as a *chiu chiu hsiao han t'u* (九九消寒圖) or "Nine-Nine Passing Cold Chart". Nine groups of round circles, totaling eighty-one circles, are drawn on a piece of paper and each circle is divided into five segments by drawing a square inside. This chart is pasted on the wall and every day one circle is inked black in one segment, recording whether it has been a fine day, a windy day, etc., following a rule which reads:

The upper segment, a cloudy day;
The lower segment, a bright day;
The left segment, a windy day;
The right segment, a rainy day;
The central square, a snowy day.

Another type of the Nine-Nine Chart has been invented by a certain Chinese scholar by using nine Chinese characters of nine strokes each which are first traced on a piece of paper showing only the outlines and as each day passes a stroke is blackened with ink, thus converting the outlined characters into solid black ones in eighty-one days. The commonest phrase used is *Ting Ch'ien Ch'ui Liu Chen Chung Tai Ch'un Feng* (庭前垂柳珍重待春風), which translates as: "The drooping willows in front of the courtyard gracefully await the spring winds".

There is another interesting way to record the Nine-Nine period, and this is often resorted to by Chinese girls of the old school who are not, as a rule, so well acquainted with Chinese characters. In their little boudoirs hangs the sketch of a branch of plum blossoms drawn with Chinese ink, only the outlines of the petals (the Chinese plum or *mei hwa* (梅花) blossoms before it grows leaves), which are eighty-one in number, are traced. And each day as they finish their labours at the dressing table, they would use their Chinese rouge to colour one of the petals a delicate pink. This is easily done as the Chinese rouge is nothing but little pads of cotton richly saturated with red colouring. A little piece at a time is torn from the cotton pad for daily use. In this way when the cold season is over the branch of white blossoms will be a beautiful bouquet of pink.

In the course of years all the schemes described above were made use of by our youthful scholar Wu. He liked the one using the nine Chinese characters best and though busy with his homework in the evenings he never neglected "inking in" the day's stroke on the chart before going to bed even during the busy New Year periods. New Year periods, incidentally, fall due about the end of the Fifth *Chiu* or the beginning of the Sixth *Chiu*.

*   *   *

The celebrations and festivities of the Chinese New Year actually start with the advent of the twelfth moon of the old year which is known as the *la yueh* (臘月), meaning originally "the moon of the ceremony for the chasing of the plague". On the eighth day of the twelfth moon, called *La Pa-erh* (臘八兒), the Peking-*jen* observes the ancient practice of preparing the *La Pa-erh Chow* (臘八兒粥), or "the Porridge of the Eighth Day of the Twelfth Moon." Such a custom has been universally

observed and in the Buddhist families takes on a special significance as bowls of this porridge are offered before the shrines
of the gods and the ancestral tablets. In the Wu family the day
was observed with a vegetarian diet.

To prepare *La Pa-erh* porridge, a Chinese family has a
special cooking pot of copper which is used only on this annual
occasion. The composite parts going in to the *La Pa-erh*
porridge are many and may be roughly divided into two groups,
grains and nuts (including certain kinds of dried fruits). To the
former group belong the various kinds of grains: millet, ordinary
and sticky rice, barley, wheat and all kinds of beans, red beans,
kidney beans, black beans, "small beans" (every kind except
soya beans) which are added to the porridge at different stages
of the cooking in order to assure the proper result, an art in
which most housewives of the old school are expert.

As to the latter category, these consist of dried red dates
and seedless raisins, peanuts, walnuts, chestnuts, hazelnuts,
pine seeds, lotus seeds, almonds and the kernels of the water
caltrops, pumpkin and water melon seeds, which go into the
porridge either during the cooking process or else are arranged
on top of each thick bowl of the stuff, in clever patterns of bats,
flowers, birds, etc., an important decorative touch to each
portion of the porridge distributed amongst friends or offered
on the family altars.

It is needless to say that all children cherish the famous
La Pa-erh porridge which is eaten with a generous amount of
white and black sugar. As a seasonal present exchanged by
friends, bowls of the stuff are sent out early in the morning on
the eighth day of the twelfth moon and to be properly appreciated
must be delivered before noon as otherwise it may be suspected
that the sender perhaps did not actually cook his own porridge
and only made use of that received from other friends for
"redistribution".

It is also the local custom to cook an unbelievably large
quantity of the porridge as it is so cold in the *Chiu* period that
the stuff will freeze into regular "porridge ice" and keep for a
long time. Cutting a block of the "porridge ice" and heating
it piping hot to serve to casual visitors throughout the twelfth
moon and up to the Chinese New Year holidays is considered
a token of hospitality supreme and a sign of prosperity in the
house as well. Economically speaking, *La Pa-erh* porridge is an

The eighth day of the twelfth moon
is the day for the exchange of gifts
in the form of a special thick porridge
prepared with a number of cereals and
nuts in commemoration of a Buddhist
miracle. The rich use the conventional
"porridge jar" here depicted though
recipients take only the porridge and
return the jar with many thanks.

extravagance, a waste and a costly family observance, but for a family to discontinue preparing *La Pa-erh* porridge is like for an American family to go without the habitual turkey at Thanksgiving and in effect would be quite as devastating to the family morale.

According to Chinese folklore, *La Pa-erh* porridge originated in Taiyuanfu, the capital of Shansi province. Many, many years ago, during a cold winter, a Buddhist monastery in that city with a large number of inmates suddenly found to its dismay that its stores of grains were reduced to the last bushel and donations from laymen supporters of the city were not forthcoming. This was a serious matter as hundreds of monks had to be fed. The head priests were at their wits' end, as the Chinese proverb goes "even a clever wife cannot prepare porridge without rice".

But faith was strong and "in their gods they trusted". On the next morning, said to be the eighth day of the twelfth moon, entirely unexpectedly, mule vans loaded with bags of assorted grains and nuts and dried fruits; all mixed beyond sorting, arrived at the temple gate. The drivers stated that the foods were transported to the temple for the use of the monks and were donations from certain rich people whose names had been entirely unknown to the priests. In their usual fashion they accepted the foods, for in China "monks eat from the ten directions".

Investigating into the mysterious godsend later, they finally found that the image of the *Wei T'ou* (韋馱) or "Guardian God of the Faith" of the temple was sweating all over its muddy body, from which phenomenon they concluded that the "Guardian God" had volunteered silently his service as a food administrator and had secretly passed the collection bag from family to family during the previous night for the benefit of the faithful. Buddhist organizations in Peking still send out gifts of *La Pa-erh* porridge to their supporters in acknowledgment of past donations and in anticipation of future ones.

Not only is *La Pa-erh* porridge prepared on this day but also the *La Pa-erh Ts'u* (臘八兒醋) and the *La Pa-erh Suan* (臘八兒蒜), vinegar and garlic respectively, are made in a "killing of two birds with one stone" manner by soaking the famous Chinese garlic in a sealed jar of Chinese vinegar. The jar is kept in a warm place and opened on New Year's day, twenty-two days afterward. Garlic bulbs, originally white in colour, would be turned green and the vinegar would have acquired the taste of the garlic. The majority of the Peking-*jen* seem to like both the sour garlic and the hot vinegar thus obtained, particularly as a "sauce" to go with the meats and the meat dumplings at the New Year feasts. The mere mention of the subject to certain other people, though, would be enough to make them feel in their pocket for a chewing gum or dash hurriedly for their gas-mask.

PREPARING FOR THE NEW YEAR

THE days toward the end of the old year and before the coming of the new are known in China collectively as the period of *Suei mu* (歲暮), meaning the "evening of the year." This period lasting about three weeks is a busy season for the Peking-*jen* and parading through the Peking streets may be seen a group of country people who, not profitably engaged on the farms, turn their attention to the urban districts for business opportunities in order to earn some extra money for their expensive winter house-keeping or for certain things to make their own new year a happy one, to help pay for holiday luxuries and incidentals not provided for in the budget.

Some of these bring to town the peasant pastimes and amusements much in demand as family entertainments during the Chinese equivalent of the Japanese *Oshiogatzu*, but the pedlars appearing before new year's day are more or less small merchants (although they may turn show-men overnight for all I know), peddling certain kinds of seasonal merchandise. It is hard to list all the things they offer but a few stand out as worthy of special mention.

There are for instance the picture pedlars selling a kind of wood-block

Before the New Year picture-pedlars go through the hu-tungs with their collections in a straw-album thrown over the shoulder. Each crying of his ware is accompanied by capping his ear with one of his hands and is then followed by a cocking of his ears to try and detect if anyone is not bidding him come and ask for a glance over his goods.

print pictures intended for decorating the rooms of Peking families. The Chinese do their spring cleaning before the new year, usually before preparations for the festivities are made in earnest and almost always following the dictates of the almanac, choosing a day of the element of *tu* (土) or "Earth" for such an undertaking. Cleaning at an end; their attention invariably is directed to discovering the shabby condition of the wall-paper. Now, the walls of Chinese homes are mostly pasted with a kind of white paper printed with floral designs in shiny cheap white paint made with the fine powder of mussel shells, and though the smoke and soot of the cooking or heating stoves of the Chinese pipeless variety are quite capable of rendering such wall paper a perfect disgrace in no time, not all families have the means to redecorate their rooms with new paper every year. But the new year being the time for a Chinese family's "at home" period, when social calls are exchanged freely and, indeed, compulsorily, to allow friends to see the sloppy appearance of one's home interiors is something that must, as far as possible, be avoided. The

Chinese believe as their proverb says, that "People laugh at the broken but not at the patched", and the cheap pictures for sale go a long way to serve a double purpose and their virtue stops not with adding splashes of colour to a drab interior.

These wood-block pictures, it is sadly true, have in recent years been replaced almost entirely by modern lithographed outrages, harbour scenes of Shanghai or of Hongkong, air battles fought over a park with planes of all models from the latest Lockheed and Douglas and Clippers to the first models of the Wright brothers, with giant dirigibles threading their way in the great air traffic jam, and so forth.

The original Chinese new year pictures were quite presentable and their manufacture used to be monopolized by a group of mass-production artists living in the village of Yang Liu Ch'ing (楊柳青) a watertown not far from Tientsin. Yang Liu Ch'ing people were, and perhaps still are, renowned as good artists and it is even said that most of the pictures were executed by young women and girls as a family industry. Printed with wood-blocks in black and white each picture was then coloured by hand, though not without some economy of lines and strokes due to the cheap prices at which they were sold to the public— one picture say 24 by 40 inches used to cost the equivalent of two cents in current Chinese money and a smaller-sized variety actually retailed at a copper a piece.

The favourite subjects of new year pictures used to be family panoramas of Chinese new year celebrations, or a busy harvest scene depicting all the family engaged in agricultural pursuit, or the visit of the God of Fortune to the family with his assistants hauling into the courtyard little carts laden with silver and gold sycees and all kinds of jewels, and with boys gathering strings of Chinese cash from a tree which yields them in profusion.

Other types of pictures catered to clientele of a different taste. These portrayed scenes from Chinese historical dramas with the colourful costumes exactly as seen on the stage. For the benefit of those who might not be well-acquainted with theatricals, each part had its name shown clearly in Chinese characters beside him or her. Still another type would be those intended for the nursery (which in most Chinese homes is nothing but the parents' bedroom). Of this kind the *Ta P'ang Hsiao Tze* (大胖小子) pictures, or those of The Big Fat Boy engaged in different games or posed with his pets in happy and playful roles, were most in demand.

The Wu home did not really need these pictures for practical purposes but, nevertheless, the family habitually called in the itinerant picture pedlars and selected a few pieces as they were spread out on the ground. This was such an interesting adventure into the land of fine arts that young Wu was always delighted when he heard the cries: "Pictures ... have .....come! Buy .... your ...... p-i-c-t-u-r-e-s!"

*   *   *

Standing at one's door in Peking during the days before the Chinese new year one sees a number of seasonal traders, besides the new year picture man already described, selling their wares from door to door such as the seller of spruce of cypress branches and stalks of the sesamum plant, the seller of paper decorations for new year's food offerings and the seller of the "door god", paper hangings, etc.

On four important occasions during the new year festivities, the green branches of spruce and cypress and bundles of sesame stalks are used when the paper images of the divinities are burned in bonfires in the courtyard after the proper ceremonies have been held for the worship of each respective deity. The paper images, joss-money etc., are laid on a stand made by erecting three bundles of the sesame stalks leaning together and overlaid with the branches of the ever-greens. Then, using the remainder of the incense sticks, still burning, the whole thing is lighted and burned "to the ground".

The reason why they are used is that the spruce or cypress branches, and the sesame stalks as well, burn wtih vigour and their "seeds" and seedpots respectively crack during the burning and produce a sound resembling miniature firecrackers which is a fitting feature for such a send-off. The sesame stalks ordinarily serve as fire-wood in peasant homes and are very cheap, but at new year they are tied into bundles of eight or ten stalks each and, brought to town, they are sold as a "luxury". It must be a profitable business to deal in them this way and it is only unfortunate that the quantity so consumed is necessarily limited.

As to the spruce and cypress branches, each sale of these represents a net gain for although the sellers never explain openly how these have come to be their stock-in-trade we all know that the evergreens planted in the Chinese graveyards come in for a generous surreptitious pruning annually, possibly with the permission of the graveyard caretakers but certainly without proper authority from tree surgeons! That the farmers have deliberately planted the young trees in order to cut the branches to sell at the new year is a lot of "hot air" which fools no one, but nobody bothers to dig into the real facts. So these country people continue to bring into the city daily consignments of them for two weeks each year, carrying

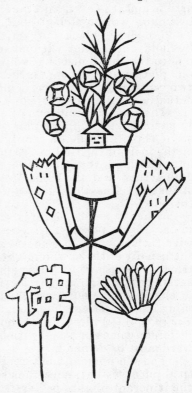

The annual display of food offerings before the family shrines is an old Peking custom and lasts some fifteen days during the new year festivities. To please the gods these offerings are decorated with paper ornaments in the manufacture of which certain peasants find their avocation. Those shown above are typical examples of such decorations.

Red paper strips bearing goodwill or congratulatory messages are posted on house doors at New Year. This custom provides a business opportunity for wayside poets and holiday-ing school-boys. To keep up with the demand the artist-trader often prepares his wares in public, attracting a crowd of appreciative onlookers. To keep his ink pot from freezing a small charcoal burner is placed under the ink container. The burner also keeps his fingers from becoming numb which might prevent a proper demonstration of his calligraphical talent.

them about in baskets and managing to sell their entire stock every day, sometimes even selling at a "sacrifice" towards evening.

The next pedlar to arrive would be the seller of decorations for food offerings. These are usually articles in gaudy colours made of stiff paper with little bits of gold tinsel. At the Chinese new year, quantities of offerings are placed before the family shrines and elsewhere, mostly in sets of five dishes of each kind. Five dishes of the season's fruits, particularly red apples; five dishes of moon cakes, in towering piles, each one smaller than the one below it and surmounted at the top with a peach also made of dough; five dishes of *Mi Kung* (蜜供) or "honey offerings" of Mongolian origin, made by piling one above the other of a quantity of thin oblong cakes fried in vegetable oil, all uniform in size, about half an inch wide and thrice that long, arranged in a regular brick-laying technique but with openings and the whole covered with a coating of honey—one foot, two feet or three feet high with a Washington Monument top; or five dishes containing big squares of sticky cakes of a yellow and white colour with layers of dates; or even five dishes of steamed round breads; all these make legitimate offerings and all are to be embellished with the paper decorations.

In design these may be the familiar *Pa Hsien Jen* (八仙人) or "Eight Immortals", Taoist saints, each with his or her emblem of the magic fan, the flute, the gourd etc., or various other good-omen figures, the trinity of the gods of Wealth, Happiness and Longevity, or the fairy Liu Hai, with his skipping rope strung with gold coins, mounted on a paper facsimile of gold ingots, or merely pomegranate flowers and gold-paper *Fu* (福) characters for "Happiness" or *Fo* (佛) characters for "Buddha", mounted with wire pins by which the decorations are attached to the food offerings. The shrewd housewife usually knows beforehand how many dishes of offerings would be used the coming season and she never buys too many nor too few of these decorations. Such offerings are an annual family tradition and the quantity is not subject to minor fluctuations on account of

the economic outlook of the family although naturally it is
affected as to elaborateness or otherwise.

The seller of "door gods," who may next stroll along, also
deals in various kinds of paper images of the sundry divinities
and a kind of paper hanging called *Kua Ch'ien* (掛錢) or "hanging
money", attached to walls and to eaves throughout the festival
season. These are carved from a thin but strong native paper dyed
in various colours with red, of course, being the most popular.
They bear certain popular designs and often include in arabesque
certain phrases of good wishes, such as *Fu Kwei Yu Yui* (富貴
有餘), meaning "Riches Enough and To Spare", or *T'ien Hsia
T'ai P'ing* (天下太平), translating as "Peace Throughout the
World".

*   *   *

During the new year festivities, known in Chinese as *kuo
nien* (過年) or "passing the year", the doors of most Chinese
houses are posted with certain paper decorations and the door
gods peddled along the streets are only a part of these.

Almost all Chinese street doors are composed of two heavy
sides opening in the center and so the door gods are also two in
number, two warrior-type figures pasted facing each other on
the two door-leaves. One of these has a very handsome face, a
fair complexion and a flowing black beard while the other has a
reddish biown face with an exuberant growth of porcupine
whiskers and round eyes that seem to pop out from the eye-lids.
Both are clad in heavy coats-of-mail, are equipped with a bow
and a quiver of arrows hanging from the belt and hold long-
handled weapons in their hands. With these two personages
standing guard at the door, the family need fear no evil spirits
who might otherwise sneak into the courtyard.

The one with the fair complexion is General Ch'in Ch'uing
(秦瓊) and the other, General Yu-Ch'ih Ching Teh (尉遲敬德).
They are traced to another T'ang Dynasty legend, very much
alike in plot to the tale of the devil-chaser whose portrait is
hung out during the annual Dragon Boat Festival. According
to the popular romance of *Hsi Yu Chi* (西游記) or "The Trip to
the West", Emperor T'ai Tsung of the T'ang Dynasty once
suffered from a nervous disturbance and every night as he closed
his eyes, he saw visions and dreamed dreadful dreams. Only
when his brave generals Ch'in Ch'uing and Yu-Ch'ih Ching Teh
stood outside of his palace could he obtain some much-needed
sleep. Not wishing to trouble his brave generals with such
humble and tedious tasks, he had their portraits painted and
hung them at his palace door which proved to be equally effective. In the same manner the devil-chaser came to be a popular
deity, these two generals' portraits have been made door gods
for the public. Door gods of various degrees of elaboration are
also sold in the Chinese stationery stores and some people paint
them in colours on their door fronts for permanency.

Another kind of decoration for the door is the spring couplets
or pairs of red paper strips of various widths, bearing phrases
mostly in praise of the coming spring weather although some may
imply conventional good wishes or purport to beseech blessings
for the family during the year. They are so called because the
two strips bear an equal number of characters and are gram-

matically balanced phrases or sentences, written in vertical lines which are possible only in the Chinese ideographic language. For example, a popular example of these reads:

Yu shih yi nien fang ts'ao lui (又是一年芳草綠);
Yi jan shih li hsing hwa hung (依然十里杏花紅).

which translates:

"Again is one year's fragrant grass green;
"Same as (before) ten miles apricot blossoms red."

Another equally popular example is:

"Heaven increase its years and humans, their age;
"Spring fills the Universe and blessings, the door."

A short phrase of four characters indicating good wishes is also written on a shorter piece of paper horizontally and a paper square bearing the "Happiness" character goes with each pair of couplets. These are pasted on the upper part of the door frame. As not only the street doors but also the "inside doors" are decorated with these paper strips and as the value of good calligraphical execution and poetic compositional merit is esteemed by cultured patrons, sales are brisk and competition keen.

It requires a certain cultural foundation to conduct such a business successfully and it falls to the lot of poor scholars and youthful students to meet this literary demand. Yearly the god-forgotten literati and wayside poets who try to make a little money and the school boys who wish to take advantage of the new year holidays to demonstrate their calligraphical achievement put up temporary stands along down-town streets and hang out these paper strips, properly executed, for sale. Prices for these decorations are never fixed, nor even asked, and the illiterate as well as the truly appreciative are both glad to pay well to encourage this culture trade. Bargaining does not occur here.

Advertising posters reading *Shu Ch'uan* (書春), "Writing Spring", *Chieh Chih Hsueh Shu* (借紙學書), "Borrowing Paper to Practice Writing". appear days ahead of the business season for these unique traders, marking the location of each appearing and disappearing establishment.

*　　　*　　　*

As a public school pupil, youthful Wu managed to pool with some of his classmates and ran a spring-couplet stand for several seasons but the net profit earned was negligible. A few bundles of big firecrackers were all that could be bought with the money.

*　　　*　　　*

In the evening of the twenty-third day of the twelfth moon, the Peking-*jen* send off their Kitchen God in a picturesque ceremony. It is said that the Kitchen God makes annual visits to the Jade Emperor God, the supreme authority of the heavens, to make a report in his capacity as resident plenipotentiary and general supervisor in the family to which he has been accredited. The Kitchen God is a sort of liaison officer and on his recommendation the worldly happiness of the family depends. Regarding the legendary life history of the Chinese Kitchen God we have had an occasion to explain before and so there is no point in dwelling again on the subject.

For days ahead the Peking market has been flooded with a kind of candy, the making of which is a somewhat technical problem but suffice it to say that this consists of cooking millet into a paste and then mixing into it sprouting wheat. By some natural reaction the starch content of the paste is converted into what is probably called a "sugar" in organic chemistry. Candy made by this process is formed into oblong blocks and is ivory white in colour. This is locally known as "Kwantung Candy" (關東糖) or "East-of-the-Pass Candy" referring in all probability to the Shanhaikwan Pass and to the fact that it is equally popular in Manchuria.

Clever manufacturers shape this candy into various forms, such as melons, ducks, gourds etc., but only the oblong candy bars are used for the ceremonial purpose. There is a special grade made, it is said, with rice which is particularly favoured by the Peking-*jen* for offering to their Kitchen God and this kind is sold as a seasonal feature in the Chinese pastry shops. The pastry shops also offer a kind of so-called *Nan T'ang* (南糖) or "Southern Candy", an assortment of little pieces of sweetmeats, some mixed with sesamum seeds and others having cores made of various nuts or mashed black beans. "Southern Candy" is also used as an offering to the Kitchen God and is, frankly speaking, even more delicious than the mere candy bars. For the average Peking-*jen*, well-known as having a sweet tooth, spending money for candies to serve the gods is a delight, for it must be remembered that Chinese food offerings are not to be thrown away after their purpose is achieved. No, never! Humans eat them afterward!

The hour for the ceremony is usually fixed at nine o'clock in the evening when the shrine of the Kitchen God is moved from the original place of honour near the family cooking stove and placed on a table before which the offerings of candies are placed as well as a small plate of hay and fodder and a round

Candy gourds and candy melons are the children's delight but for the ceremonial offering to the august person of the Kitchen God only the oblong candy bars are proper.

cake of wheat flour. The Kitchen God travels on his trips to the celestial regions on a divine horse, the likeness of which can be seen on the more elaborately prepared paper images of the Kitchen God, and its feed is served to the horse once a year at this time.

As to the flour cake, it is provided for the God's retinue who must also be looked after. From the table also hangs a string of paper ingots and several sheets of joss-money which come into play whenever there is a more formal occasion of incense-burning. The male members of the family will then light the incense and candles and kowtow to the image in proper order. After a while the image is torn from the shrine, onto which it was pasted, taken to the courtyard together with the paper offerings and burned on the stand of sesamum stalks and cypress branches.

The candy offering is not without its purpose. It is used as a kind of bribery to the Kitchen God so that he will avoid mentioning things which the family has done during the past year which may be detrimental to its interest. These may include family quarrels or domestic extravagance and various other "dirty linens which should not be washed in public" but which may trail behind as an appendix to the lengthy report the Kitchen God will submit in his attempt to solicit heavenly bliss for an otherwise well-behaved family. To influence the Kitchen God to talk "sweet", custom provides that the family "put some sugar into his mouth".

In the Wu family it had always been the duty of the late Old Mr. Wu to officiate at this important ceremony but now it passed on to his son to do so, for the worshipping of the Kitchen God is a man's job in which women should not meddle.

The Kitchen God will be gone for seven days until new year's eve and during his absence the family lives free of serveillance and may do as they please with impunity. When the cat is away the mice enjoy more liberty and it is up to them to play to their heart's content.

*   *   *

New year holidays begin roughly a week or ten days before new year's day and last virtually until the middle of the first moon of the new year. This, of course, refers to the old Lunar calendar new year and not the Solar new year or Gregorian new year.

In the old days the schools dismissed for new year holidays invariably on the nineteenth of the twelfth moon as did also the Chinese theatres. In the latter case it is known as *Feng T'ai* (封臺) or "Sealing the Stage"—a fairly understandable arrangement as in the so-called "evening of the year" people would be too busy with various other things to have time to sit through the long performances in the Chinese theatres and so, instead of running at a sure loss, they take this opportunity to rest for ten days in order to be in good condition to cash in on the new year spending of the holidaying public. This custom of the Chinese theatres is still adhered to but one interesting custom for new year holidaying must be said to be gone forever—that of the *Feng Yin* (封印) "Sealing of the Official Seals."

Until the end of the Manchu Dynasty, it was the habit of all officials in the various branches of the government service to enjoy the same lengthy new year vacations, as they were anxious to stop work and seek amusement or family reunions. It sounds very strange but nevertheless is as true as true can be that even the garrison forces, then serving in lieu of the present police system, were to go on in a more or less hail-fellow-well-met manner during the holidays and it was no isolated happening to have beggars and mendicants snatching food or money in broad daylight from busy shoppers or promenading citizens. These petty law-breakers did such things practically unpunished except for public resentment that might be in evidence against them for they knew that even the magistrates, who acted as district judges, had their "seals sealed away" and had gone home to enjoy a happy new year with their own family!

Following the "sealing of the seals," on or about the nineteenth of the twelfth moon, there used to be also a boom season for the fashionable restaurants as high government officials were in the habit of giving expensive dinner parties at this time, entertaining amongst themselves in the most extravagant and hilarious manner, until new year's day when a red paper slip on the doors of restaurants announcing "Closed temporarily for kitchen-stove repairs" excused them for their own holidays.

Within the grey walls of the Chinese house, family life takes on a holiday spirit. Although the master of the house might be away in the office sweating over his account books, if he was a businessman, trying to see by how close a shave he could get by with his creditors as the Lunar new year is the most important settlement period in the year, or in the case of a mandarin out with friends entertaining and being entertained as a good sport, the mistress has to arrange the various details for the new year period. She usually had many problems to solve, such as getting new clothes made for every member of the household, buying the children new hats, new shoes etc., and figuring on what to put on their backs and her own back, too, when they would come out to visit famous temples or amusement places, without which much of the new year enjoyment would be ruined.

Then she must also figure on laying in food supplies, meats, vegetables and sundry daily necessities as beginning from new year's day for five days no shops will be open for business from the big million-dollar concerns to the corner grocery stores. She was also to attend to the preparation of the new year dishes of cooked food which must be ready to put away by new year's eve to be eaten during the festival period as a good omen of overflowing abundance in the family and also because it would not be good form to do much cooking in the first five days of the new year as doing so would be very unlucky. Even if the superstitious factor be annulled it must be taken into consideration that during these days there would be so many callers who would demand to see the mistress to offer their best wishes that no time would be available for cooking. Besides, any time available should be reserved for theatre going or other amusements and it would be a cruel thing to tell the women to return to the kitchen while all neighbourhood friends go out visiting.

The children in the house are about the happiest of all for

there is no school to go to and no home work to ponder over but plenty of loose money in the pocket and prospects for fun and still more fun close at hand, particularly as the parents will be too busy with their own work to be very strict about the children's doings.

Chinese new year holidays represent an old institution and even though the Republican government proclaims it a national policy to use only the solar calendar still the Lunar new year seems to be possessive of greater significance. Even the public schools, like the one young Wu attended, give only three days on the Solar new year but three weeks for the "spring vacation" around February. That the Chinese new year comes perchance during this period is officially a mere coincidence.

*   *   *

One of the important features of Chinese new year festivities is the shooting off of firecrackers and fireworks of various kinds for which Peking is unexcelled. Gunpowder is a Chinese invention but the native use of it seems to have gone no farther than the making of firecrackers.

Making firecrackers is an important industry in China and small family factories are found in all the suburbs of Peking. And of all the devices designed to chase off evil spirits, including various kinds of plagues, none compares more favourably with firecrackers in so far as popularity and nationwide utility is concerned. Firecrackers are known as *pao chu* (爆竹) in literary Chinese, meaning "Exploding Bamboo", as the first firecrackers were made by filling the hollow sections of bamboo stalks with powder which were then used by the highland dwellers to scare away mountain ghosts.

To make the powder used for firecrackers is very simple: add an equal amount of charcoal ground fine to an equal amount of saltpetre, thoroughly mixing the compounds. This will produce fairly good results. The formula is well-known to most youngsters in Peking and they are often to be seen scraping off the white crystallized matter off whitewashed walls, looking forward keenly to the fascinating result. Saltpetre in commercial quantities is obtained by boiling the "ore containing" surface soil scraped from the ground and this, on a large scale, is a govern-

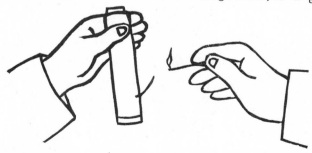

The "Double Reports" are innocent-looking seventh-inchers but capable of produing deafening detonations. The proper way to set off these two-tone fire erackers is to hold one in the left hand, light it with the right and let go at the right time. Any other way is considered too tame.

ment monopoly in China and, it seems, an auxiliary of the Chinese department of war.

The best firecrackers of North China come from the Shu Lu (束鹿) prefecture in southern Hopei province and it is as Shu Lu products that all firecrackers are advertised. Kiangsi and Fukien are also famous firecracker provinces and their products are exported to foreign countries in both hemispheres. In America, most of the firecrackers used for the Fourth of July celebrations are made in China. All Chinese children, at least all the boys, adore firecrackers and many grown-ups do too. In such Peking families as the Wus, shooting off firecrackers is a favourite holiday pastime.

The Chinese firecrackers are well known for their deep detonation and loud reports. The biggest single firecrackers, five odd inches long, are known as "Hemped Thunder" and are made with solid layers of hemp tightly packing the black powder and capable of a detonation comparable to thunder. The most popular kind is the *Shuang Hsiang* (雙響) or "Double Reports". These are made to contain two units in each piece and are lighted by a fuse from the side instead of from the top as is the case with "Hemped Thunder".

The first section is exploded directly after the fuse is lighted and then the entire firecracker is shot bodily into the air, forty, fifty, or even a hundred and more feet high. When the concealed fuse ignites the second unit it explodes in the air, rending it literally into pieces. To light one of these tandem firecrackers, the proper way is to hold it lightly between the fingers which is entirely harmless if you know when to let go and if the firecrackers are well made. Built on the same principle are the ones which carry a group of little firecrackers inside instead of the second unit. These in trade terminology, are called "The Five Elves and the Devil-chaser."

Small firecrackers of less than an inch to more than three inches in length and braided together by the powder-loaded fuses are known as *pien* (鞭), and a string of *pien* may contain any number of rounds up to say fifty thousand. Such strings are set off after a sacrifice before the God of Wealth and for a sending off and welcoming back the Kitchen God, and like ceremonies. It is principally, though not necessarily always, for these purposes that thousands of dollars worth of firecrackers are set off throughout the new year festivities. Setting off of *pien* is also intimately a part of the commercial life of the Chinese people as strings of them must be set off in front of a store when it opens for business after the new year holidays in order to chase away the year's bad luck.

Firecrackers are symbolic of juvenile new year joys and are an important item of expenditure for the children. Into buying firecrackers is blown a good portion of their savings. Itinerant toy-sellers make them their specialty and not satisfied children will make for the tea stores on the main streets which carry them as a customary side-line. Certain kinds of firecrackers used to be the famous product of southern provinces and the tea dealers of Anhwei and Fukien probably were the first promoters of the firecracker business.

*   *   *

Although the shooting off of firecrackers may be said to be part of the ceremonial acts in connection with religious functions, setting off of fireworks is intended wholly for the amusement of men.

Chinese fireworks may be said to be divisible into three main classes: the *teng* (燈) or "flames", the *hwa* (花) or "sparks", and the *p'ao* (炮) which covers the firecrackers. The powder used for the making of these three is about the same but different results are obtained by different techniques. Briefly speaking, when the powder is pounded solidly into a container, tightly sealed and the ignition is by a fuse, a sound is produced as in the case of the firecrackers.

When the powder is loosely contained and not lighted by a fuse the internal combustion will force a stream of sparks into the air, letting fall a shower of sparks which is called a *hwa*. The *teng* is made by shooting little tablets of powder into the air where they burst into flames. The making of Chinese fireworks is based on these three points and various colour effects are produced by using different chemicals containing manganese or magnesium. Sulphur is also freely used in the making of Chinese fireworks.

The most popular kinds of fireworks in Peking are the "Flower Pots", with each blossom a concealed "tubeful" of potential sparks connected by built-in fuses; the "Eight Corners," an octagonal block of mud containing eight "tubefuls" of "sparks" interspersed with pairs of "flames". The sparks of this latter kind might shoot to a height of twenty or fifty feet which is a conservative estimate of the possible altitude reached by the "flames". Still another kind is the "Bombardment of the City of Hsiang Yang," which in appearance is a mud cake about a foot or so across with a soft paper hood. When lighted, a monstrous "tree of fire with silver blossoms" shoots into the air and is followed by a wholesale

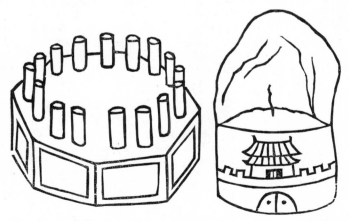

This is not a birthday cake for a sixteen year old but a Chinese firework known as an "Eight Corners." The other is a kind known as "Bombardment of the City of Hsiang Yang". Chinese sky rockets are mounted on long reeds and are dangerous playthings; being under a constant police ban they are practically non-existent.

shooting of "flames", hundreds of them. The "Bombardment of the City of Hsiang Yang" is an age-old firework specimen in China and when it is burnt out nothing is left but a piece of scorched earth.

The most outstanding kind of native firework is what is known as a *Hwa Ho* (花盒) or a "Flower Box." "Flower Boxes" are made in assorted sizes and the big ones may measure five feet across and be two feet in height, either round or polygonal in shape. To set off such a big "Flower Box," a scaffolding of many feet is a necessity as the contents of the box, magic strings of firework lanterns, grape vines with bunches of purple flaming grapes produced by the burning of manganese balls, etc., may trail many feet from the bottom of the case which is burned off when the fuse is lighted.

A "Flower Box" may contain many layers and each layer is a firework masterpiece cleverly packed in the paper box. Not only that but as the "Flower Boxes" are set off at public gatherings, often as an advertising stunt by some prosperous shops, the appreciation of the multitudes of spectators attracted to such an entertainment must be obtained at all cost and merely allowing the first-rowers to get the benefit of the show is not enough.

Fireworks of the more expensive kinds are sold wholesale in one or two shops alone in Peking which are found, strangely enough, right in the center of Peking's famous cultural market of Liu Li Ch'ang, where curio stores and bookshops dealing in antique editions are gathered. Stranger still is the fact that although they have been operating in the district with a heavy stock of "highly risky" goods, for which most underwriters probably would refuse to issue a fire policy, no accidents have occurred, at least not in the last thirty years.

Little children have their own fireworks, too, the little *ti ti chin* (滴滴金) or "Drops of Gold", powder wrapped in sheets of paper rolled into little sticks, and the *hsien chuan mu tan* (線穿牡丹) or "Threaded Peonies", tiny twin tubes of powder mounted together and hung on a string, spinning round and round while shooting out sparks when lighted, and the *Ch'i Hwa* (起花), or sky rockets. Big rockets are capable of reaching unbelievably high altitudes, are entirely uncontrollable as to where they may drop with their burning "shells" and so are really very dangerous playthings.

Though our hero young Wu Hsueh-wen had long outgrown his childish stage, he found it hard to part with his firecrackers and fireworks. The Wus' friends habitually bought them such things as new year presents and to set them off was naturally Schoolboy Wu's privilege. He also invited his classmates to enjoy the fun.

*　　　　*　　　　*

Another sport that is popular at and around the Chinese new year period and is even more colourful than firecrackers and fireworks is that of flying kites. For this Peking justly enjoys the fame of being the country's, indeed, the world's foremost city.

Whereas foreign kites are more or less built on the prin-

Built of a bamboo framework and paper, a Chinese kite may take a hundred and one shapes of which the "Sand Swallow", depicted above, is the most popular. Heavier than air and hard to control, it habitually somersaults while in flight. To counteract this constructional defect Chinese children tie paper tassels to the proper "leg".

ciple of being a square-shaped matter with or without a long tail or string or tassels like the Japanese *tako*, or the diamond shaped ones of other countries, the Chinese kites are made in a hundred and one different designs. The most common kind is the so-called "Sand Swallow" which is by far the easiest to fly, but fancy shapes and designs include human figures or famous legendary characters such as the "Fairy Monkey," well-known in Chinese folklore. Another popular design is the gold fish with big goggly eyes mounted on bamboo sticks that roll and spin while the kite is in full flight, and with a big flexible tail of paper that flutters and waves with very realistic motions.

Examining casually the wares of a Peking kite-seller, a great many other kinds will be seen including some which are constructed in such seemingly ridiculous ways that you would question fundamentally whether they can really be flown in the air as some are made so entirely out of keeping with the rules in a book of physics. Expert flyers, however, will tell you that remarkable altitudes are usually attainable with them if you know how.

Among these may be mentioned the ones shaped like a pair of water pails, or the Chinese corridor lantern, cylindrical in shape. Anyone who has had any experience at all in flying the Chinese kite will not deny that those shaped like a dragon or like a long centipede with many, many sections joined together with strings are by far the most difficult to handle. Another specimen that taxes the player's nerves and tries his temper to the limit is the grey hawk with "soft" wings, which is the most interesting to watch, and rather realistic in effect when properly flown several hundred feet up with the string nearly indiscernible.

The Peking kites, so fantastic in shape, are also made in incredible sizes and although the usual ones seldom reach beyond a dimension of say four feet, some large kites are actually seven or eight feet high and as many feet wide. Bamboo splits and a strong native paper, called Korean paper, well-known for its durability are ordinarily used for kite-making and certain big ones are made with cheap thin silk but all are beautifully coloured. The strings used differ with the various sizes of kites and range from the common sewing thread to a fine gut string, the same kind as used on Chinese violins.

Formerly the *Ta Nei* (大內), the "Big Inside" by which the imperial family used to be referred to, used to buy the most expensive kites and of late, it seems, the rich actors are by far the best customers in the kite business. Many important Chinese stage stars are known to be enthusiastic patrons. As a famous amateur kite-flier (there are really no professional ones), Dr. Mei Lan-fang used to be reputed the first in the land, if I am not mistaken.

Early spring is the best time for kite-flying as at this period the wind in the upper air strata is stiff and constant in direction and therefore most favourable to good results. Before the advance of the electrical age into Peking bringing with it the network of wires to the streets, kite-flying parties formed here and there around the street corners whenever a steady breeze was blowing, but now-a-days to select a location is the pre-requisite on which depends whether the kite breaks an altitude record or comes pitifully to grief. To dislodge a kite entangled in electric wires sounds easy but is really difficult if not impossible.

Youngsters like young Wu are encouraged to fly kites as a healthful recreation and it is said to give the children exercise beneficial to the eye-sight and the lung capacity. But few have been encouraged to make their own kites which would give the sport additional virtues.

The humble Chinese kite is traced back to certain chapters of ancient Chinese history. During the Confucian period Mo Tze (墨子) made a "wooden kite" that actually flew and on which he had laboured three years. Kung Shu Tze (公輸子) of the state of Lu (魯) of the same period invented a kite-like machine with which he was able to reach a goodly height to reconnoitre over a city of the state of Sung (宋) with which Lu was apparently at war. In the ninth century A.D., when the city of Liang T'ai (梁臺) of the state of Liang (梁) was besieged by rebels, a minister named Huo Ching (侯景) was able to communicate with the outside relief columns by virtue of messages tied to kites which they flew from inside the walled city.

Flying kites became a peace-time sport in the Five Dynasties period and it was at this time that people began to mount certain musical instruments on the kites to be played with mechanisms set in motion by the wind—this is still being done by the kitewise Peking-*jen*. A small paper lantern or a long strip of paper of many colours may also be carried to a great height by the lines of the kites simultaneously as the kites are flown. These are more recent additions to this interesting sport.

THE LUNAR NEW YEAR

NEW Year's eve finds the Peking family at their busiest period of the year. In the shop and in the office they also work their hardest as each person has many important functions to attend to. The last day of the old year is the only time, since the Mid-autumn festival four and a half months before, when a creditor may press for payment of various debts which have been allowed to roll along getting bigger and bigger like a snow-ball. A statement is rendered to each customer who has had a "charge" account and shop clerks, mostly junior accountants and the original salesmen who have attended to the customers, make rounds of calls on all customers to deliver these notices.

Most of the people who think anything of their names at all will immediately, or as soon as they have collected their own bills, call and fulfil the obligations and few will wait until a second notice is served toward the evening of this "one day in the long calendar of the year." All day long and all night too, the streets are thick with people attending to this important financial operation. Before street lights were popularized in Peking, these people "running after" their debtors used to carry paper lanterns with the names of their shops inscribed on them. For these bill collectors the dead line is nominally fixed for midnight but practically any time before dawn is a proper time to call on anybody for this purpose.

It all seems as though some of the shops will certainly have to write off many items of bad debts from their books, judging from the desperate way in which they debate and harangue with their clients but most commercial houses are really successful enough to start with clean slates when they open for business after the holidays. To facilitate a last minute realization of resources even the native pawnshops which daily close up cold-facedly at dusk, will extend their hours to mid-night, to which effect an announcement appears at their doors. There are many things said against the habits and rules of Chinese pawnshops but this particular nocturnal service is worthy of much praise.

Not only must money be obtained at this special loan department to meet the demand of some unconciliating Shylock of a bill collector but also certain items of "Sunday best" clothes, which have been obliged to go involuntarily into storage, must be taken out by timely last minute redemptions so that when the owners go out on their new year calls they can put on a more presentable plumage. In these two respects, the pawnshops meet some crying needs!

Everything was in good shape for the new year celebrations at the Wus and in this particular year the Wus were more anxious than ever before to enjoy their new year festivities. For three years after the death of old Mr. Wu they had been going on with the least of new year enjoyments, for being still in mourning according to the Chinese conception all celebrations were ruled out. They had pasted no spring couplets at their doors and used blue paper instead which bore special phrases befitting the bereaved outlook in the house.

They had had few if any new year callers and had called on nobody—their new year social calls have had to be postponed each year a month or so behind schedule. Being an orthodox old Peking family they were not to be laughed at. A small paper strip of a blue colour pasted at the door at new year explained to the public that they were in a state of *shou chih* (守制), or "Observance of Rules", and declared also that "No new year greeting cards will be acknowledged and no return calls paid".

To the lot of young Wu naturally fell the work of preparing the spring couplets and little ones were also pasted at the shrines of the Goddess of Mercy and of the Kitchen God. Those for the Kitchen God read:

> "Going to Heaven, report only our fine deeds:
>
> "Returning to the shrine bestow good fortune."

A brand new Kitchen God, purchased from the stationery store, was pasted onto the little shrine. The god looks exactly the same each year but a small condensed calendar for the coming year, printed over the image, adds the needed touch of chronological correctness to the otherwise unidentifiable image.

Resembling a Christmas tree or the Japanese *kadomaisu*, door pine' is the Chinese *Nien Fan* tree. Hung with nuts and things it occupies a place of honour in the drawing room during the new year festivities. A dried persimon at the base prevents the top-heavy "tree" from toppling over.

A big bowl of freshly prepared rice was placed on a table in a prominent position in the central room. This was their *nien fan* (年飯), or "New Year Rice", in which a green branch of cypress was inserted. On this was laid a small string of loosely tied old cash and a paper decoration was attached to the cypress branch. An assortment of dried nuts was strewn over the rice. This would be displayed until the sixth day of the first moon of the new year. It is a sign of abundance and an embodiment of prayers tantamount to saying: "Give us this day our daily rice."

*   *   *

The religious doings of Peking families on new year's eve vary considerably in each case and in certain respects the racial or provincial origin of the family has much influence on the details of the observances. The big families usually move out their ancestral tablets from the individual wooden cases in which they are kept and offer a feast before these tablets. Others would hang out their ancestral portraits mounted on scrolls, ordinarily rolled up and stored away in a box, and conduct a ceremony with many kowtows. Burning special kind of incense before the scrolls is also a part of the rites to be carried out in connection with ancestral worship. Other customs require a visit to the family graveyard to burn a lot of paper joss-money before the grave mounds as is also done at the Ghost Festival.

To those for whom such an undertaking is not feasible paper packages about 2 feet square and printed with passages from sacred Buddhist scriptures are bought from the stationery store and filled up to bursting point with paper joss-money. These are burned before the house gate after having been given much religious reverence including offerings of foods and kowtows. This really is the most universally observed custom in Peking as it is not always convenient to make a hurried trip to the countryside to visit the family graveyard and allow various other important worldly affairs to take care of themselves at a time when the winter daylight hours are so short.

This was the way the Wus habitually worshipped their ancestors. The paper packages are known as *pao fu* (包袱), or "Cloth Packages", and propriety provided one such package for each namable ancestor and his wife or wives as the case might be. Old Mr. Wu's spirit was provided with such a package only the third year after his death. Before that, as a "new ghost", he was worshipped separately in his own ex-bedroom and a plain white

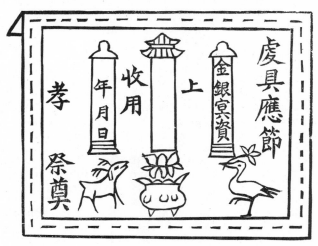

Burning packages of paper offerings saves many a Peking-*jen* from a hurried trip to his family graveyard during busy new year's eve. The paper bags are bought at the stationery store and spaces are left for the insertation of the names of sender and recipient. The contents are declared to be "Gold and silver and joss-money". Another blank space is for the date. A passage from the Buddhist scriptures is used as a border, This system was invented in China long before the modern parcel post came to this country.

package with a blue label bearing his name was used.

Evening soon came, heralded by the shooting of firecrackers and the lighting of the red lanterns under the eaves each bearing a phrase of good omen. On new year's eve all heavenly divinities are supposed to descend to tour and inspect the world and a proper demonstration should be carried out to please them. It is for this purpose that certain Peking families erect a high pole in their courtyard and hang a red lantern from the top. This lantern is known as *t'ien teng* (天燈) or "Heavenly Lantern".

At this time there also come to the doors of each house groups of youngsters, mostly from poor families in the neighbourhood, with dozens of printed likenesses of the God of Fortune in their arms. Knocking feverishly at the door they cry at the top of their voices: "We have come to send you the God of Fortune. Will you take one?" Anyone who hears such a call will not fail to hasten to the door, answer in the affirmative and with a broad smile on his face will receive an image sheet from a youngster, paying a price at least five or six times higher than what is legitimate at the stationery store.

But people are glad to pay it for who would turn away the God of Fortune at the new year when a few coppers will welcome him into one's own courtyard! The youngsters comb the hutungs in record time and "make a lot of hay while the sun shines"; buying the God of Fortune at the door is like buying your newspaper extras, though everyone is glad to pay highly for the first one to come nobody wants to buy it a second time.

Schoolboy Wu bought his own God of Fortune and put it ceremoniously above the family shrine under the reverent supervision of old Mrs. Wu who always thought that her family ought to be grateful to this divinity for, to use her own language, "The God of Fortune always smiles on our family and we have good reason to be thankful to him."

This paper image, it must be explained, is to be used as the object of worship on the second day of the first moon in the new year.

*   *   *

Ancestor worship ended, the impromptu altar table in the main sitting room of the Wu residence was cleared away and in its place a big round table was quickly brought up for the family to enjoy their new year's eve dinner. Though there were no family members rushing home from distant cities to sit at this important reunion, as is very often the case, the Wus always made it a point to seat all the family members at this hearthside function. A local Chinese proverb says of the ill-treated daughter-in-law that "A thousand beatings and ten thousand scoldings, yet on new year's eve she is seated at the feast of the round table." It is also to be noted that no matter how intimate some friends may be, they are never really welcome at such family gatherings.

The family waited until young Mr. Wu was able to leave his work late in the evening to sit at the feast where elaborately prepared dishes of expensive foods were served. There were meats and fowl of all kinds and certain kinds of fresh vegetables, such as green cucumbers, string beans and even green eggplants, the natural season to eat which being really the summer.

Their availability was the result of the hothouse cultivation conducted by native-method specialists with their headquarters in the Fengtai district who were able to offer the vegetables in the wrong season at fancy prices.

These same people also raise certain kinds of expensive varieties of plants, such as the tree peony, peach blossoms and dwarfed trees of citrous fruits, to serve as a magnificent display during the new year holidays. All command exorbitant prices as decorations for stylish homes. The Wus' dinner, however, had no beef dishes for in the old Buddhist families of Peking and in all China beef is not eaten. In the judgment of the Chinese, cows having done their share of service in helping plough the fields and so forth, to eat their flesh is decidedly against "conscience". For a similar reason is the eating of dog's meat forbidden.

After the feast the family gathered to say good-bye to the out-going year by a round of kowtows from all the junior members to the seniors. This ceremony is known as *t'su sueh* (辭歲) or "Farewell to the Year". Scholar Wu received from his grandmother and his parents little sums of money wrapped in red paper as *Ya Sueh Ch'ien* (壓歲錢), or "Money for Weighing down the Age". He was quite big at this time but still being the youngest person in the family he was much coddled. Gratuities were also given to their woman servant.

Then the family busied itself with the preparation of the new year dumplings which had to be offered to the Kitchen God when he was welcomed back officially into the house. Dumplings with cores of various kinds of meats and vegetables were to be fundamentally their daily fare for five days beginning on new year's day following an old custom. These dumplings are shaped like so many little silver ingots and therefore are symbolic of great riches though from the second day on it is the habit of most Peking families to break away occasionally from this monotonous habit in favour of other tasty foods prepared beforehand and warmed to serve.

Dumplings for the Kitchen God and those eaten on new year's day, however, were made to contain vegetable cores and no meat whatever was allowed as it is believed that to abstain from eating meat on new year's day, as a religious gesture against "killing for the sake of the mouth and the stomach", is highly meritorious. These vegetarian dumplings are made with an assortment of ingredients, such as fried bean-curd, mushroom, edible fungus and dried blossoms of the tiger lilies (called "golden needles"), chips of carrots and so forth, mixed with seasonings. They taste rather unlike what one would expect them to.

By twelve o'clock fresh volleys of firecrackers testify to the ushering in of the Kitchen God from his annual trip to Heaven. The details of such a ceremony are generally the same as for the sending off seven days earlier, except that the above-mentioned dumplings, and later other food offerings, take the place of the candies and, of course, the image is not burned with the other paper offerings.

A Chinese custom, called *shou sueh* (守歲) or "Watching the Year", is generally observed. This requires all people to stay awake throughout the night as going early to bed on new year's eve is considered a bad omen and certainly will deprive one of any happiness worthy of the word. In order to stay awake people resort to gambling and similar pastimes or sit together in pleasant conversation around the heating stove, partaking of sweetmeats and eating dainty fruits and nuts and with an occasional braving into the cold night to shoot off a few fire-crackers.

Most people do not feel like sleeping on new year's eve anyway and those who do want to sleep find it a hard job to do so for here and there in the city firecrackers make an almost continuous din, amidst which sleeping is practically impossible. Toward dawn a short lull on the firecracker front permits people to take a nap from which they have to wake up early in order to attend to certain duties.

*   *   *

On new year's day the Peking-*jen* dress up in their best clothes and call on their friends and relatives to wish them a happy and prosperous new year. The first time any one meets any one else they exchange greetings by saying *Hsin Hsi, Hsin Hsi* (新禧, 新禧), meaning "New Happiness", accompanied by proper ceremonial acts. Very often this is followed by phrases of good omen, such as *To To Fa Tsai* (多多發財) (Much prosperity be yours) and *I Shun Po Shun* (一順百順) which translates word for word as "One Smooth Hundred Smooth". This is a con-traction of "wishing you a hundred things to develop smoothly to your satisfaction as unanimously as one", for there is a belief that the first word spoken or heard on new year's day in-dicates the general trend of events for the entire year and ex-changing such kind wishes is a mutual obligation rather than a unilateral expression of individual desire.

The new year calls are universally paid to all friends whether the people have been seen every day or have never been seen since the last new year and this is known as *Pai Nien* (拜年). *Pai Nien* in many cases serves as the sole link by which friendships are kept "in force" and by which the remissness of a scarcity of social calls during the last twelve months is excused. Neglecting to call on a friend for a whole year is nothing, but to omit the new year call is equal to a silent notice of discon-tinuance of a friendly alliance which, once broken, will be hard to revive.

Such new year calls are not as simple as they sound. Custom requires all junior persons to kowtow three times to each and every one of the senior members in the house they are visiting no matter whether there are only two such senior members or two dozen and even if some of these happen to be out when the call is made this does not serve as a good reason to omit doing obeisance for it is still required of the callers to kowtow to an empty seat. This is accompanied, before and after, with polite bargaining and kind remarks of thanks, all of which are carried out with proper phrases that no person other than a clever conversationalist can expect to master much less use with immaculate judgment.

Besides it is also necessary for each caller to bear in mind how many people eligible for such honours belong to the house and to miss one is considered a breach of good form. This requires a good memory, indeed, as the family being called upon do not remind the caller that any person or persons have been neglected for fear of making the caller "lose face".

There is also a scale of estimation for such calls depending upon whether a call is made on new year's day or the day after or on still a later date and in proportion to such facts the caller's valuation of the friendship is based. Often there are so many families that come under this category of first importance that it takes a sociable person a good portion of, if not all, the day to finish these calls and each call being equal to so many kowtows by the time his obligations are finished he is tired out and his legs and neck are sore. This business of paying new year calls is an ordeal, indeed, and whoever started the system of "saying it with kowtows" started hell as it were.

Fortunately one person from each family is usually considered enough and so the list of the "must be visited" can be divided among the members of the house as was done in the case of young Mr. Wu and his son. Women do not pay new year calls before the sixth day as from the first to the fifth day of the first moon outside women are banned from entering a house. In order to receive callers some important family members are also required to stay home. Children, however, love to pay new year calls and love to have callers as they are entitled to a gift of money from every elder visitor as well as from anyone to whom they have kowtowed new year greetings.

There are also petty superstitions in the house on the first or the first five days in the year varying with different families. On general principles edged tools of all description are banned from use for at least one day and even the dough for making the dumplings is separated by hand. No baking or frying of any food is allowed and where steaming and boiling fail to serve the purpose in preparing certain foods, the eating of them is postponed rather than that the rule be broken. Brooms, dust pans and feather dusters are not to be used at least before noon on new year's day for gathering and throwing away dust is compared to gathering and throwing away gold!

Ask the Peking-*jen* on new year's day what he has been doing and in nine cases out of ten you will hear the reply, "Oh, making new year calls!"

VISITING THE TEMPLES

ALMOST quite as important in the schedules of the Peking-*jne* as making new year calls is visiting the Buddhist and Taoist temples during the festivities. Of these temples the most outstanding ones are the Tung Yueh Miao or "Temple of the Eastern Sacred Mountain", where old Mrs. Wu often went for her religious devotions and which is open for one day at the new year, the Wu Hsien Ts'ai Shen Miao (五顯財神廟) or the "Temple of the Five Distinguished Gods of Wealth," situated some three miles outside of the Kwang An Men (廣安門), open on the second day of the first moon, and the Temple of the Local Guardian God open on the third day.

This last is located on a narrow lane inside the Kwang An Men and to the west of the old Vegetable Market, well known as the place where capital punishment used to be meted out, at the executions some of the prisoners were literally cut into pieces and most of them by the oriental method of beheading in which way ended the life cycle of many criminal offenders including many a "Public Enemy No. One" of ancient Cathay.

Besides these three temples the Temple of the Big Bell and the Temple of White Clouds, situated to the northwest of the city and immediately outside of the Hsi Pien Men (西便門) respectively, are also famous shrines to be visited. The temple of the Big Bell keeps open for fifteen days beginning from new year's day and the Temple of White Clouds will remain open for four more days, closing for the season on the nineteenth. To these temples the Peking-*jen* go to do obeisance before the deities or just for the fun of it, taking advantage of the new year holidays.

The Temple of the Eastern Sacred Mountain is the most important of all and people come from different parts of the city to worship there on new year's day. Some come on foot and others on various vehicles or on donkeys to await the opening of the Chao Yang Men (朝陽門) at dawn and when the gate is opened the vast murmuring, rumbling tide of humanity dashes out in dusty stampede for this holy place, each person trying to be the one to burn the first bundle of incense sticks before the Emperor God of the Tai Mountains. But all console themselves with the thought that though he has not himself done so, at least none of the others has really achieved this purpose for the Taoist priests living in the temple have all the pilgrims beaten, for to burn the first bundle of incense sticks is naturally their "chartered privilege".

Here then, before the images of the gods and goddesses of Buddhistic and Taoistic Pantheon, the Peking-*jen* kowtow and pray for the realization of their fond desires, for health, wealth, marriage and so on as new year's day is an important day to begin a new page of life and devotion and in order to keep to their resolutions the masses call upon the divinities to "give them strength".

In the spacious temple courtyards a big fair is held where there are found all kinds of small merchants with their special

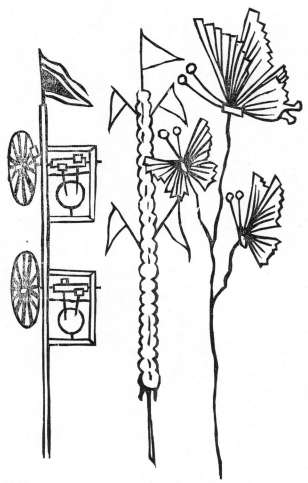

At the new year temple fairs many seasonal attractions
are offered. The "sticks" of candied haws, the wind-
mills and paper butterflies seem to be the most popular.

stalls selling different varieties of seasonal toys and souvenirs
and which activity overshadows all the rest of the business life
in the temple premises except perhaps the collection of donations
from pilgrims.

The most popular souvenirs are naturally the little charms
made of red chenille which each visitor to the temple buys and
fastens to the hat or in the hair in the case of a woman. The
red paper carps, crudely shaped affairs with gilt designs of
auspicious phrases, each attached by a fine thread to the end of
small stick, are also the outward signs with which every returning pilgrim announces to all that he has accomplished the sacred
mission.

Red hawthorns, strung onto wicker sticks some three feet
to five feet long and smeared over with sugar, are the edible
specialty of a few stalls here and paper butterflies coloured with
weird effects and mounted on bare branches of willow are

offered by others. While still another group of pedlars offers the wind-wheels made of coloured paper and mounted on a framework of cornstalks. These operate a mechanism by which little drums made of paper and mud are beaten as well as little gongs made of the tops of cigarette tins. These wind-wheels are attached to frameworks of various kinds and each combination may contain from one to as many as thirty or forty wind-wheels, arranged in geometrical patterns and all mounted in the same direction. When a steady breeze is blowing the little drums create an earpiercing rattle.

Then there are other kinds of toys which appear during the new year holidays but the above-described ones are the most widely distributed at the Tung Yueh Miao.

Old Mrs. Wu, in the year in question, was amongst the first persons to arrive at the temple for she had a special prayer to make which was known to all the Wus except our young scholar, for it concerned a serious matter still being kept from his knowledge.

* * *

The Temple of the Five Distinguished Gods of Wealth is open for one day only on the second day of the first moon each year and attracts the greatest number of visitors, pilgrims and sightseers alike. Here the Peking-*jen* come in great numbers to wish themselves prosperity throughout the new year.

This old temple is said to date from the Ming Dynasty and though quite disappointing to those who expect to find a palatial institution, the deities worshipped in this wayside shrine are in a class by themselves. We are told that the Five Distinguished Gods, otherwise known as the Five (Sworn) Brothers,

The Gold Colt, a souvenir sold at the Temple of the Five Distinguished, is not valued for its intrinsic worth or artistic execution but purely on account of its symbolic significance. It carries a big flaming pearl on its back and imitation ingots. A string of mud and gilt paper ingots serves as another memento of a trip of devotion.

used to be interesting figures during their lifetime.

They were men of great physical strength and athletic accomplishments, knowing all the fine arts of "flying the eaves and walking the walls," and they were endowed with chivalrous natural tendencies. They were also fond of befriending the brave and the daring and appropriated wealth from the unrighteous rich to give to the deserving poor. They were what the Chinese call "heroes of the green forests" or free-booters. Highwaymen, that is the word.

It is said that the eldest of the five was General Ts'ao, an Assistant Garrison Commander at the Chiayui Pass (嘉峪關), Kansu, during the Ming Dynasty, who was equally distinguished as a soldier as he was a bandit chieftain. In the rear court of the temple is also found the store room of these Gods of Wealth under the divine supervision of another deified person named Chang who in his lifetime was a trusted henchman of General Ts'ao's and as such was entrusted with this important portfolio when General Ts'ao was made God of Wealth after death.

Those who come annually for the purpose of doing obeisance to these gods will burn the indispensable incense and then make for the back court to appear in the store-room. There each borrows from the attending temple assistants a pair of paper ingots, one silver and one golden in colour, as a loan from the gods. The gods of course are very glad to accommodate their devout believers in a generous manner but the human clerical force at this unique department must be paid and so twenty cents in real currency is set as the proper handling fee for each loan of two ingots. There are no special instruments signed for this loan, not even the borrower's name is asked, but it is understood that if the paper ingots prove to have served in "attracting prosperity to the possessors" in the following year or years (which they never fail to do as Faith works wonders) the benefited borrowers will return to square up with the gods by donating any number of similar paper ingots, paying ten or twenty cents for each piece. These they then hand to the temple assistants to dump on the great piles of unnumbered and uncounted paper sycees with which the storeroom is filled.

Thus paper ingots received "in quantities" are sold to the borrowing public at the price of two for twenty cents at a minimum, which represents a net profit for the resident priests and the layman assistants who annually run the service for one day with enough dividends declared by early afternoon of the day to last them for a year's livelihood, for the devout followers always manage to arrive early in the day at this important temple as coming leisurely in a halfhearted manner is decidedly sacrilegious. There is no way for outsiders to find out exactly what the attendants' annual income amounts to but judging from the throngs of people literally fighting to buy their paper ingots who line up outside the wide windows eight or ten deep most of the operating hours without an idle moment allowed to the dispensing staff the business done must be considerable.

Here, too, is sold the Golden Colt, a miniature horse made of mud and covered with gilt paper bearing little mud facsimiles of the silver and gold ingots. The pilgrims buy them from certain "licensed" sellers at fancy prices. They bring them home as good luck charms for the Golden Colt is believed to be capable of bringing to its owner fabulous wealth. Little imitation ingots tied with silken threads are also sold as a characteristic souvenir commemorating a trip to this temple.

On the same day at home a sacrificial ceremony is held before the paper image of the God of Fortune bought at the door from poor children on new year's eve. The original God of Fortune is said to be a Mohammedan from Arabia or somewhere around there and so the proper things offered before his image include a big chunk of mutton, slightly boiled before offering and in which is thrust a sharp knife in conformity with his outlandish eating manners. Three cups of wine, lighted to burn with blue flames and as many dishes of steamed breads are also set beside the mutton.

The Wus made a visit to the Temple of the Five Distinguished Gods of Wealth but for nothing more than to see the sights there. The traditional family rite before the God of Fortune, however, was always carried out with proper reverence. In coping with the God of Fortune nobody can afford to take chances.

*　　　*　　　*

The Temple of White Clouds not far from the Hsi Pien Men is the most influential Taoist monastery in Peking and its existence is traceable to the T'ang Dynasty. A famous Taoist priest, named Ch'iu Ch'u-chi (邱處機), from the P'eng Lai (蓬萊) district of Shantung (whence hailed also the late Marshal Wu Pei-fu) was well known for his great learning and was called to appear before the Great Khublai Khan or Emperor Shih Tsu of the Yuan Dynasty (1277-1367). His wise counsels against war and in favour of peace were so much appreciated by the emperor that he was appointed Chief Taoist Abbot of the Land with his headquarters in this very temple where he lived until his death some years later. This famous temple is said to occupy a central location in the Yuan Capital of Kambaluc. The slight removal eastwards of the city to its present location in the Ming Dynasty isolated the temple in the western suburbs.

The temple is of great proportions, exceedingly well kept and houses a hundred or more Taoist priests. During the new year holidays an "open house" is observed for all visitors who are welcome to inspect the living quarters, the various ceremonial and image halls and even the vast kitchen and dining saloon to which the priests are called at dinner time by a loud banging on a big wooden fish some five feet long and suspended from a stand.

The priests here, including a number of young novices, devote their time to the reading of their holy books and enjoy very meagre worldly gratifications. They raise their own food on the patches of land adjacent to the temple grounds, including a few acres of vegetable garden. The Taoists do not allow themselves refinements and luxuries and the less they require the nearer they are to their ideal "perfection". Such a colony of priests, therefore, has no important economic ties with the outside world and boasts self-sufficiency.

There are only a small number of visitors who come here for the purpose of religious worship while the majority of them do

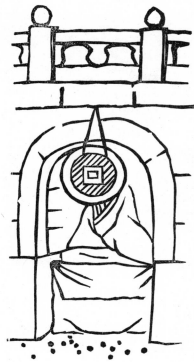

In an effort to register hits on the bell to foretell the new year's fortune, visitors to the Pai Yun Kwan Temple throw handfuls of copper coins into the arena. The priest, sitting in stony silence behind the hanging disc, probably sees to it that no coins are retrieved by the enthusiastic public.

not even bother to find out what kind of images are worshipped or what their histories are but they would rather see the Hall of the Old Men where on brick beds are seen the figures of some old priests, sitting peacefully and silently like sedentary statues. Some of these actually look like nothing else but animated skulls wrapped in cellophane and stuck onto heaps of blue cloth which are their robes. A small basket placed in front of them receives little sums of money from the admiring (?) visitors, and a priest, not quite so old and standing by, points out which one is a hundred and twenty-five years old and which one is still young, being barely ninety-eight.

It seems that even the ninety-eight-year specimen is already too callous or too weak to engage the visitors in even an exchange of greetings and as to the one-century-and-a-quarter venerable, he is nothing less than a living fossil. He does not even bother to open his eyes to a narrow slit to see how fast the money is accumulating in the little basket—he probably is no more interested in it as a paying enterprise.

The lecturing priest is always the only one who has anything to say at all and he makes repeated requests to the passing visitors to "tie a knot of friendship with the old men", though "reading between the lines" you seem to hear him declare that already he is tired of the miserable and desolate life in the Taoist monastery!

Close to the Hall of the Old Men are the animal pens where pigs and sheep are kept, having been delivered to the monastery by the temple's laymen patrons as an act symbolic of the "sparing of life" and these barnyard animals are allowed to live the length of their natural life spared the terror of the slaughter house. Some of these animals look quite old. Here the visitors invariably make a hurried inspection.

Immediately inside the temple's arched entrance is the place which attracts the biggest number of visitors for here is where they test their luck for the year. What originally was intended to be a little goldfish pond spanned by a marble-balustraded bridge, a familiar item of Chinese landscape gardening, is now utilized by the invention of some provident priests to serve a noble cause. In the semi-circular arch on either side of the bridge, like a hermit in a grotto, a nonchalant priest sits quietly and motionless from morning till night without even taking time out for his lunch. (Taoists strive to go without food as a preliminary step toward the state of immortality and to go without lunch is nothing marvellous.)

Right before the face of each priest is hung a wooden disc made with a square hole in the center to resemble ancient Chinese coins and in the hole itself is hung a shiny brass bell. The visitors surrounding the small waterless pond "elbow" for the privilege of throwing copper coins to strike at the bell. If one succeeds in hitting the bell and making it ring that would be extremely efficacious and to him a full measure of good luck throughout the year is assured. If he misses it, which is much more likely, his year's prospects are not so good. But whether the visitor's luck is good or not there is one thing certain and that is the coins thrown are not to be retrieved and right into the botton of the pond they fall where the floor is already carpeted with them—an income for the priests!

*   *   *

At the main entrance to the Temple of the White Clouds is a piece of marble carving forming the border of the masonry of the doorway and here is found a small monkey some five inches high carved out in arabesque pattern. The visitors to this famous Taoist monastery during the new year festivities will always remember to touch or pat the stone monkey for it is said that to pat the monkey on any part of its anatomy will relieve the toucher's pain or affliction on the corresponding part of his body. To this monkey there is a counterpart in the Temple of the Eastern Sacred Mountain, where in a big hall in the rear of the temple stands a full-sized bronze mule, said to be also possessed of curative properties. Certain parts of it shine brightly indicating where the most contacts are received the year round. It is also said that if a healthy person touches the marble monkey he will be hale and hearty throughout the year and blessed with good fortune from time to time.

Here at the Temple of White Clouds are held annual feasts in the night of the eighteenth day of the first moon in honour of the famous Taoist personality Sh'iu Ch'u-chi. It is said that some immortals descend to the temple on this night, disguised in some undisclosed fashion, to meet the lucky ones amongst the visitors. So the devout believers arrange to stay at the temple overnight in order not to miss such a golden opportunity. This is known as *hwei shen hsien* (會神仙) or "Meeting the Immortals."

Another strange ceremony at this temple is that of the annual washing of the mortal remains of the priest Ch'iu, although this is a somewhat closely guarded secret not often explained to outsiders. It is said that a small pottery jar contains the bones of this great Abbot of the Land, suspended by a rope into a well in a tiny room built behind the Taoist sage's own statue which occupies an exalted position in one of the main halls. On the second day of the first moon, in the early morning, this jar is taken from the well and its contents of white bones removed with great reverence and thoroughly cleansed with water. Then they are put back into the jar and this is returned to its original position in the well. It is also said that such a ceremony is accompanied with a full day's chanting of the holy books.

There are also some interesting anecdotes connected with the Temple of White Clouds. One of these refers to a certain abbot in the temple some years back, a man of refinement named Kao, who was a great favourite with all the courtiers and the eunuchs of the Manchu court. Many of these registered their names with him as his "honourary students". By associating with the powerful eunuchs, such as the notorious Li Lien-ying (李蓮英) he was able to exercise great influence in court affairs especially with regard to the appointments and dismissals of the personnel for the lucrative official positions which were openly bought and sold after competitive biddings in regular business procedure. During the heyday of this corruption and bribery the temple was compared to a busy "position exchange". A famous restaurant outside the Hsuan Wu Men (宣武門) was the abbot's city agent for making arrangements on behalf of ambitious mandarins to meet him and his powerful associates and from these the restauranteur harvested a rich profit for "brokerage". Kao was one day brought back to the temple from the home of a woman of bad reputation, terribly sick, and died the next day.

Another famous anecdote also refers to Abbot Kao and says that it was through him and the Eunuch Li Lien-ying that the Russian emissary to the Court of the Manchus, who rented a villa in the temple's gardens as a summer home, succeeded in convincing the Empress Dowager Ts'u Hsi, then reigning, that Czarist Russia was the only nation in the world that really had any goodwill toward the Manchu Court. It was as the result of this *pourparler* that Li Hung-chang, as representative of the Chinese court at a Russian coronation, was authorized to sign certain secret treaties in regard to railroad construction in Siberia that later virtually started the Russo-Japanese War.

Year after year the Peking-*jen* make these trips to the Temple of White Clouds to see the sights and enjoy the rustic outing away from the busy city, or to try to foretell their own fortune. But how many of them realize that here the partial ruin of a dynasty was spelled and a chapter of history made?

*   *   *

Though our schoolboy Wu and his schoolmates made new year excursions to the Temple of Gods of Wealth and the Temple of White Clouds and in each case enjoyed themselves heartily, their trip to the Temple of the Local Guardian God was very much of a disillusionment for here they saw no spectacular sights. Rustic crowds of villagers from the south-western suburbs came here to do their shopping for cheap house hold utensils and farming implements for even in the new year season dealers in these things were by far the most numerous in the temple precincts.

This temple is not so well preserved and most of the buildings in the compound are rented to cloth weavers and spinners of coarse woolen yarns which are required in enormous quantities by the makers of the famous Peking rugs. This temple being situated in a somewhat urban surroundings to reach it not even a donkey ride is available, whereas to the other temples youngsters indulge in donkey racing en route which fact in itself is a drawing-card.

At the Hsuan Wu Men is a narrow lane known as the *Kan Lui Shih-erh* (趕驢市兒), or "Market of the Donkey Transport", which is the city terminus of a popular service with the other termini at the various important temple fairs during the festival seasons. Here men with their donkeys meet the holiday-makers for possible custom and after negotiating for the trips these donkey "liners" are delivered to the customers, symbolized by the handing over of the whips. Mounting the donkeys, the riders dash off in a cloud of choking Peking dust, galloping the fastest the donkeys know how along the north bank of the city moat in the shade of the ancient willow trees (their twigs showing a pale yellow with the advent of the warmer Fifth and Sixth Nine day Periods of cold weather).

These donkeys have been trained to serve only these lines and so back and forth they go without the "owner drivers" following behind them. At the end of the journey some other members of the "donkey combine" will attend to the details of the discharge including the collection of riding charges. There are usually no arguments about the terms regarding prices, for they are generally set at an uniform tariff and when there is any deviation from the understood rules such information is brought to the destination agents by a secret code word represented by typical knots tied on a piece of string that dangles as part of the harness or is hidden under the saddle bags. There was no fear of some ill-designing customer misleading the animals as the donkeys protest noisily if the customers desert them halfway and no matter how hard they may be beaten or otherwise intimidated they will not budge an inch if the customers should try to take them off the beaten track, but will create a scene that will spoil the scheme of any potential donkey-thief. The donkey drivers are bound by mutual covenant to look after each other's interest, saving much unnecessary labour running back and forth with the animals and the unending trains of holidaying excursionists on the road provide added insurance.

Besides this interesting system of "stage-donkeys" and for the benefit of those who are not inclined to "equestrianism", there are also the "stage-carts" as the suburban farmers, taking advantage of the holiday seasons, habitually put their heavy two-wheeled wagons on the holiday run and by crudely equipping them with little cushions and things transform them from vegetable or grain freighters to regular passenger coaches. From the city limit junctions to an important temple these wagons, pulled by a donkey, a mule, a horse or even an ox, will carry excursionists back and forth for a little sum of money per person. And, frugality being the watchword of Chinese domestic economy, in spite of the shaking and rocking and the long waiting at the starting point to get a full quorum or a paying load, these bone-rattlers are never without their joyous riders and merrily, merrily on the flagstoned highways they go.

The niggardly passengers seem to enjoy the community atmosphere on the wagons and their low fares much too much to think of the discomfort which attends such a ride. And so since heaven only knows how long ago these wagons with the colourful pilgrims—men, women and children—in their holiday best of dazzling colours have paraded in front of a backdrop of the yellowish grey monotony of the countryside's desert-like terrain. Particularly colourful are the return trips from the temples when the pilgrims invariably are loaded with toys and things which, being gaudy in themselves, furnish another dash of holiday splendour.

Riding one of these wagons, the Wus made a trip to the Temple of the Big Bell about four miles to the northwest of the Hsi Chih Men (西直門). To get some privacy they charted their own wagon which cost them the sum of one hundred coppers the round trip, with enough time allowed for sight-seeing in the temple grounds. The Wus were not tight-fisted but, for local colour, voted for and selected the farmer's wagon.

*   *   *

The Temple of the Big Bell is situated on a narrow byway, cut deep by the summer rains and the narrow wheels of the North China farming wagons, not far off the main road from Peking to the Summer Palace. The temple has several main prayer halls and houses in a cylindrical tower a gigantic bell which according to some reliable data is 21 feet and eight inches high, ten feet and five inches across at the bottom by inner measurement and eight and half inches thick. It weighs 84,000 catties or 105,000 pounds, being one solid mass of cast bronze. It is hung inside the two-storied tower by a strong wooden beam some three feet square in thickness.

The bell is said to be more than 500 years old and was first installed in the Temple of Ten Thousand Merits, some three miles to the south of its present location from where it was transported by a specially prepared ice-way one winter during the reign of Emperor Ch'ien Lung of the Ch'ing Dynasty. The

The farmer's wagon put on a holiday run is Peking's own version of the tourist third class. Its community atmosphere and the low fare is its greatest attraction. Apart from rocking, bone-rattling and long waits at the starting points there are no other short-comings. Returning from a temple fair, passengers are loaded with new year toys and souvenirs.

entire surface of the bell is engraved with the complete versions of three volumes of important Buddhist sutras and certain other Buddhist quotations in bold relief, the original manuscript being prepared by a famous scholar in flawless handwriting.

The Wus followed the crowds of visitors to admire the big bell and climbed to the second floor by some narrow stairways inside the tower. They viewed the bell from vantage points on the narrow circular gallery protected by rails for the spectators, safety. Visible from here and some six feet away from the spectators is a hole, about a foot in diameter, in the top of the bell underneath which is suspended a single brass cymbal. Here, too, like what is done at the bridge in the Temple of White Clouds, visitors try to hit the cymbal with copper coins through the hole to foretell their year's luck and thus contribute incidentally to the exchequer of the resident monks.

In recent years, to combat the scarcity of copper coins which threatened the income of the temple in this annual exploitation, some money changers put up their stalls, apparently by express permission or in a "joint stock company" with the monks, and for the benefit of the crowds anxious to have their fortune tested in the conventional fashion provided these with copper coins, so many coppers for a dime in paper money, their change being about forty per cent. less than the legitimate exchange rate.

Outside the tower in the spacious courtyards of the temple are the outfits of a number of keepers of diversified games of chance, each with its own specialty attracting a group of spectators and adventurers trying their luck and skill.

There is the "Hill of Nails", a miniature hill made of wooden boards studded with rows of nails. On the top of this "hill," in a little pavilion, a customer places a little glass ball after paying a copper for it and this rolls down, picking its way between the nails to stop at any of the various parts of the base marked "five pieces of candy", "three pieces of candy", "one big candy figure" and so forth. Most of the prizes are marked "one piece of candy" which is less than what that same copper can buy at a strictly business place. This is the penalty for "expecting too much" on the part of the customer.

Another place allows customers to shoot a toy cannon with a cork mounted on a needle at a revolving disc which is divided into many segments of varying widths, marked with various prizes (the bigger the prizes the narrower the segments). This game costs also one copper a try. Another place is roped in as a shooting gallery where with toy rifles, discharging corks, customers shoot at various premiums, packages of cigarettes and so on, for so much per try. Here the prizes are entirely out of proportion to the cost and the "blanks" are not even rewarded with a consolation prize of two tiny pieces of candy.

The most popular game is "Tossing the Rings", with the various "possibilities" arranged on the ground. The prizes are cheap mud dolls and the like in the more easily won front rows and tea cups or rice bowls and tea pots and magnificent toy figures in the more and more distant positions in the "arena"— the farther the distance, the bigger the bounty. One copper buys six rings which the customer tosses, trying to encircle his objectives and often registering no hit for handfuls of rings bought.

Once in a while he may actually succeed in achieving an objective by "looping" it and claiming the prize. The rings are made either of thin wire or pieces of rattan and they have a habit of deviating from the intended course by the action of the wind or of bouncing about like rubber balls after hitting an objective by which erratic actions the owners of the outfit are saved from bankruptcy.

A good loser at these games, sportsman-like, never growls and a winner is rewarded with the prizes as well as the moral effect of a divine promise that similar lucky happenings are in store for him during the year.

"Around the corners" groups of "flying gamblers" form themselves into itinerant casinos where the stakes are much bigger and chances of winning for the patrons still less. These regular prowling sharpers are a formidable gang and to watch for a police raider some of the members stand vigilance while the rest are busy outwitting their customers in the most "black-faced" manner which is the local colloquialism for "merciless gambling engagements."

At the Temple of the Big Bell, the gambling atmosphere reigns supreme—much more so than at any other temple fair.

"Tossing the rings" is a typical new year pastime—a mild form of gambling. "Mary" who goes to the fair with her father has spent her money on a kite. Her father has registered "no hit" with two of his wire rings but "steady your hand you may win the pot yet."

THE CHANG TIEN-ERH FAIR

BY THE *Ch'ang Tien-erh* (廠甸兒), or "Factory Suburb", is
generally meant the district of *Liu Li Ch'ang* (琉璃廠), or
Factory of the Glazed Wares, principally the busy street
east and west running almost the entire distance from the Chien
Men Street to the Hsuan Wu Men boulevard and known throughout the country as Peking's cultural market. In ancient times
this must have been somewhat of a wilderness as the development of Peking was from the Tartar City southward and what is
now one of the important shopping centers was until the latter
part of the Manchu Dynasty a deserted region marking the place
where once upon a time the baking of bricks and tiles for the
construction of the golden yellow roofs of the Imperial Palaces
had been carried out during the period of Emperor Yung Lo in
the beginning of the Ming Dynasty. The manufacturing plants
had long since gone down under the scythe of Time and only the
buildings housing the supervisory departments remained to be
seen until, say, the time of Emperors Tung Chih and Kwang
Hsu of the Ch'ing Dynasty when these, too, vanished as
landmarks.

Part of the site is now a small park known officially as the
Park of the Village of the King of the Seas. During the new
year holidays an immense bazaar is held for fifteen days with the
adjacent streets completely lined with booths and stalls belonging to various kinds of merchants, displaying their various wares
some of which are traceable literally to the corners of the earth
and thus do full justice to the name *Hai Wang Ts'un* (海王村),
which may also be translated as "Neptune's Market". Here the
Peking-*jen*, enjoying their happy new year, come in full force
and often entire families, after their new year feasts, arrive *en
masse* to take part in forming the carefree crowds of humanity,
milling shoulder to shoulder and at least looking prosperous
even if not really out to spend. Such big crowds are often seen
during the fair season that vehicular traffic is diverted by police
order to neighbouring thoroughfares to ensure the safety of the
holiday makers.

Part of Ch'ang Tien-erh is a children's "treasure island" for
here is a full representation of Peking's own and imported
toycraft, from the cheap native jack-in-the-box made of
paper and mud to the expensive clockwork toy train or toy
airplanes, *papier-mache* theatre masks complete with beards
of white or black horse hair, life size wooden replicas of ancient
war weapons familiarly seen in the hands of the military heroes
of the Chinese stage, little motorboats with oil burners that spin
about in a face basin filled with water, and midget movies
shaped by the clever hands of the makers from the tinsmith's
cast away pieces of tin and from pieces of old films cut into
"stills". Paper butterflies operated by a rubber band propeller
that actually soar into the sky are sold after demonstration and
trial. The toy-balloon sellers bring their chemical laboratories
with them including little pieces of galvanized iron with the
indispensable zinc coating and bottles, of sulphuric acid, with

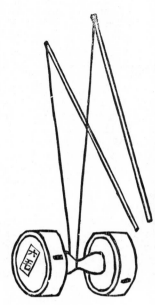

Of all the toys sold at the Chang Tien-erh fair the diabolo is every Chinese child's desire. To spin it requires a pair of strong arms and considerable skill as well.

which in a flask hydrogen is "brewed" and balloons are filled right under the eyes of the watchful and waiting customers.

Near by are the stalls of the new year specialties which are seen also at the temple fairs including the omnipresent self-advertising wind-wheels side by side with the stalls of the lantern-maker's cheap paper lanterns of all shapes and designs and all loudly coloured.

There are also certain kinds of toys which are typical at Ch'ang Tien-erh and other new year fairs, such as the *K'ung Chu* (空竹), the "Empty Bamboo" or diabolos, a circular pair of slitted cylinders made of bamboo, hollow inside, attached to an axle of strong wood and looking very much like an athlete's dumb-bell, which is spun with a piece of cord tied to the ends of a pair of sticks. This produces a whirring noise.

There are the aristocratic varieties of shuttlecocks made of swan feathers and the famous *P'u P'u Teng* (撲撲燈), the gourd-shaped sounding bottle of blown glass a vicious colour of dark red with the bottom end not much thicker than the film on your teeth which Pepsodent toothpaste destroys and which are played by alternately blowing and inhaling to produce the characteristic sound from which their name is derived. The same men who sell these glass gourds also sell the long glass trumpet about three feet long and as thin as or even thinner than your small finger. These require a strong and capacious lung to blow and produce a shrill sound audible for miles. The men who deal in these dangerous toys offer also blown glass fruits, brightly coloured on the inside and so thin and fragile are they that a person's sustained stare at them would be enough to crack and shatter them into pieces.

*   *   *

A few steps from the toy department on a narrow lane reached by a side-door of "Neptune's Market" is the food vendor's domain where wayside specialties are dealt out to those of the promenaders who might feel like pausing for some refreshments. Crowded around the stalls sit the customers some in family groups, to enjoy a bowl of steaming "bean juice" or a hot bowl of sugared black peas cooked into a porridge. The food stalls are in certain locations so near to the establishments of some other merchants that the very system furnishes a chance to the customers while eating to think a second time about whether or not to go back and make another bid in order to get that pigeon-fancier's cross-bow or to forfeit the joy of possessing a violin or a banjo of the mass-production quality by definitely refusing to go back to offer more, while the merchants within whispering distances would cast sidelong glances at their would-be customers who could still be called back to close the deal should it be thought inadvisable to hold out any longer for a better price.

Extending a long distance to the south on either side of the extension of the New Glory Road are the stalls of the sellers of quasi-curios and similar articles. These are known collectively as "Canton goods dealers" and to some as "tiger shops" indicating their not-so-highly commendable business methods. Their wares include attractive arrays of things, beautiful and useful, such as old pieces of cut-glass vases and plates from Hamburg or brass samovars from Tomsk, hardwood boxes and trays with inlay work of mother-of-pearl, and a thousand and one articles utterly impossible to list on account of their endless variety.

Here the more practical-minded spend long hours trying to procure some heirlooms of some other families recently fallen into insolvency to embellish their own sitting rooms and parlours. Here also perfectly good articles of older vintage are offered second hand at a mere fraction of what the same articles must have cost a few years back and a knowing customer can find just what he has been looking for, be it an old camera, a gramophone, binoculars or, indeed, some antiquated radio parts, a transformer or condenser costing the price of a couple of brand new screws.

Still another type of people would make for the Temple of the God of Fire, a little inconspicuous shrine of great fame situated to the east of the main fair grounds, which is annually converted for fifteen days into Peking's No. One showplace. A visit to this veritable exposition is an education in itself.

In the temple courtyards, protected from the dust by mat sheds, are rows and rows of stalls of the famous jewel traders. Under the light of electric lamps, wired only for the duration of the show and kept burning all day long, may be met all the members or their representatives of the curio and jade guilds of Peking. Each, beside his own tiny concession, spreads out his dazzling wares of precious and semi-precious and not-so-precious stones, brilliant green and white jade carvings of intricate design and jars of agate and crystal with tricky carvings of floral designs, antique figures of ivory in the likenesses of the Goddess of Mercy, the Eighteen Lohans (Buddha's disciples), various other legendary figures and all sorts of little ornaments including little elephants and camels and other animals and birds carved in rose quartz, turquoise or lapis lazuli.

In more prominent places is displayed a toy-sized jade pagoda of thirteen stories but only two feet high or a tall tea jar the cover of which is connected to the jar itself at one of the "ears" with a many-linked chain all of which, the jar, cover and the chain, are carved from a single piece of green jade representing the zenith of Peking's jade carvers' art or some similar specimen that dazes the admiring visitors and cause them to whistle with wonder. "Similar specimens", they whisper in agreement, "have only been seen in some renowned museums or in the Forbidden City palace exhibits." These rarities of rarities are labeled "For Exhibition Only" or "Not For Sale,"and are the proud possessions of some million-dollar firms whose permanent headquarters are found amongst the little unassuming shops on Lang Fang Erh T'iao Hutung (廊房二條 胡同) known to the globe-trotting tourists and foreign residents of Peking as "Jade Street." As a matter of fact these signs are used for the sole purpose of barring casual and irresponsible visitors from asking about the prices or entering into fruitless negotiations that lead absolutely nowhere but cost the owners or their assistants much loss of time.

The rich collectors comment on the pieces, the cream of the year's production, give expert opinions and acquire new additions to their private museums if there are suitable pieces available while their wives and daughters, powdered and perfumed, examine with a veteran's eyes pearls, diamonds, rubies and alexandrites for new rings and bracelets as calmly and unexcitedly as in a five-and-ten store. The sagacious stall-keepers practice methodically the national game of "talking prices" in an affected undertone until a bargain is struck and so much paid for a piece of "spinach green" jade or a sea-blue sapphire that reflects a perfect golden star in it.

The jeweller's emporium here is a quieter place and unlike the other noisy and hustling sections of the Ch'ang Tien-erh fair.

*　　　*　　　*

Still another section of the famous Ch'ang Tien-erh Fair is devoted to the display and sale of second-hand books and old and new paintings. This occupies the entire length of the main street leading south from the Ho P'ing Men (和平門), the Gate of Peace, where a section of the Tartar City wall was pulled down and a twin-arched gateway constructed in commemoration of a historic armistice in Republican China's internecine warfare.

Those who frequent these districts are what may be called, or pretend to be, Peking's intelligentsia, from young scholars who thirst for after school reading to the collectors of old editions. Temporary stalls are erected by these book sellers, some bringing their books in roughly made sectional book cases containing old editions of Chinese books, all in rice paper, yellowed with age, bound in paper cover, sewed together with silken threads and protected or decorated by a cloth-protected card-board cover that fastens on the side with little clips made of bone attached to cloth ribbons.

All these books are printed by wood blocks including the famous *Tien Pan* (殿版) or "Palace Blocks Editions" indicating royal favours in the past when emperors found time to take part in the literary enterprise of book publications—the first comprehensive Chinese lexicon was compiled in the reign of Emperor K'ang Hsi by famous scholars by appointment to His Majesty and the book is known as "K'ang Hsi Dictionary", still the unquestioned authority on Chinese etymology. Bespectacled old gentlemen (who may have one or more degrees of Imperial Examinations to their credit) would look around here, examining the shelves of books and some voluminous works boxed in camphorwood chests for protection against moths.

Silent and careful, they seem to be entirely absorbed in their hunt for rare books, checking over with their own collections.

These are the regular book-worms and "oracles on points of learning" who are not only well versed in the bibliographical aspect of the affair but also equally well acquainted with their contents. The cream of five thousand years of thinking in this country is theirs for keeps. Some of these people are known to be rapid readers and it is said that while they bargain with the booksellers about the prices, they would, by what seems to be a mere fingering of the pages, memorize all that is worth while in some lesser volumes and when this is done they would have no more need to buy the books except for the purpose of adding them to their collections.

Other booksellers actually deal in foreign books in all the modern languages although they may not know what they are really selling, at least not all what they are selling. In their stock are seen big bulky volumes of the sciences and arts and even old incomplete sets of such famous works as the Encyclopaedia Britannica or Historian's History of the World in de luxe bindings standing with their glittering letters on the back beside some equally bulky volumes of some old export catalogs of railway locomotives and plumbing or electric fixtures or even some hoary, old editions of commercial directories of London or Antwerp, older than the booksellers themselves.

Side by side may be another place selling China's own dime novels and popular editions of famous works in newsprint so full of typographical mistakes that they provide good practice for an understudy proof-reader but kill all the fun and benefit to be derived from reading them.

Temporary mat-sheds mark the "shops" of the sellers of Chinese paintings, some of whom may be frank enough to say that their pictures are only copies of genuine old ones but most of them sell their pictures by shameless misrepresentation that fools no one but the really uninitiated. Most of the pictures they sell are on fine paper or thin silk, mounted on beautiful scrolls with redwood rollers and silken ribbons. Some are even doctored to look like old masterpieces by smoking the paper before and after the execution of the pictures.

Really good specimens of "guaranteed" authenticity by famous masters are exhibited in certain exclusive places, for instance, in a small temple on this main thoroughfare where contemporary artists often exhibit their paintings for the admiring public to see or buy. Calligraphical masterpieces are also exhibited here for this is as important a fine art as painting, for Chinese art is not appreciated as an "art for art's sake" but rather as the demonstration and expression of inspirational delights and scholarly achievement of a wide scope and a thorough appreciation and enjoyment of each is a pre-requisite of the other.

Hung by wooden clips on the street walls and spread on the ground or bound into brocaded volumes are also the rubbings of inscriptions on certain kinds of Chinese stone monuments which are often from the brushes of famous scholars. Most of these are sold at very reasonable prices to be used as models for Chinese penmanship. These are known as *T'ieh* (帖)

in Chinese. Early impressions of famous specimens fetch high prices, too, and at the Ch'ang Tien-erh Fair are found all kinds and as many poor ones are sold as good ones, or the other way around, all depending upon the acumen of the sellers as compared to that of the buyers.

Ch'ang Tien-erh's book market is an old institution dating back to the imperial dynasties when scholars from all over China gathered in Peking for the court examinations and here, too, were the results of these examinations made known to the public through some publicity agents of the government. Our scholar Wu was early introduced to this readers' happy hunting ground and here he went to spend long hours during the new year festivities and each time came home loaded with second-hand books, each volume bought for little more than a song. In this cultural hobby his father encouraged him.

*   *   *

Although the new year festivities cannot be said to be over until several more days later, all shops open for business on the early morning of the sixth day of the first moon. The morning of the sixth is also the proper time for the important annual occasion of *Shuo Kwan Hwa* (說官話) or "Talking the Official Language", which is the expression used to embody the making of all formal statements in the business houses. These may cover, *inter alia*, the continuation or otherwise of the contracts for the employees. The management of the firms, large and small, will review and comment in each one's presence, privately, on the employee's record for the past year if their services are still desired. In case the employees are discharged, which is also announced at this time, usually there is no more criticism.

Promotions and increases of pay are announced as well as the declaration of bonuses for employees which is known as the *Hung Li* (紅利), or "Red Profit". The net earnings are clearly listed on a statement showing the year's business and showing in big letters the amount of money due to the owners of the firms. These lists are known as *Hung Tan* (紅單), or "Red Lists", for they are always written on pieces of red paper—the sign of prosperity.

From the sixth day on there will be no further felicitations in the shops and clerks and apprentices who have been dining and wining and playing various musical instruments behind closed shop-fronts at the firm's expense and who have been going out by turns in twos or threes to the theatres and elsewhere are once more confined behind the "wooden skirts" (meaning the counters) until another holiday, on the Lantern Festival, gives them a further chance to do some visiting or to attend some amusements. But since business goes on as usual the rest of the year such a holiday is more or less a nominal matter.

Young Mr. Wu was no longer young and, now a man past forty, was an important staff member of many years' standing in a Chinese bank. On his shoulders rested great responsibilities and so his holidays were of necessity much curtailed. He went to the office for important conferences before his bank opened for business on the sixth day of the new year.

On the eighth day, in the early evening, the Wu family following the custom of the Peking-*jen* sacrificed to the stars with much reverence in a typical and picturesque ceremony.

The Chinese, as we have seen earlier, revere the stars in much the same way as the foreigners do their patron saints. There are certain important stars which are really deities responsible for the happiness or otherwise of various groups of persons classified according to age. There are nine such stars which remind of the Eight Planets of the Solar System. Seven of them are of good omen and two of bad but all must be worshipped equally to insure a full measure of blessings or lucky escapes from harmful influences in each respective case.

It is also a Chinese belief that for every person in this world there shines a star in the sky, the bigger stars for important personages and the little ones for common people. Comets or meteors represent the death of important personages and the common people's stars, at their deaths, merely fade out unobserved. Proper rites are said to be capable of keeping the stars from dropping

Lighting little lamps for the worship of the stars to avoid calamity is an old mystic custom in China. Each so-called "lamp flower" rests on a small cake of earth. One hundred and eight small ones and a single big one are the required number.

and stories are told of such mystic performances. It is for such a purpose that the stars are worshipped.

The nimbus of the important stars encircled by the twelve animal symbols each representing one year of the cycle of twelve years, somewhat similar in appearance to the foreign zodiac surrounded by the mystic names of various constellations, and a separate paper image of the God of Longevity are inserted on a wooden stand and set on a big table in the center of the courtyard.

Before this are placed one hundred and eight little mud dishes some two inches across and one extra-sized one, on each of which is placed a little so-called "lamp flower" which has been prepared by cutting and twisting together yellow and white paper strips with a circular base to stand upright on the mud dishes. These "lamp flowers" are made beforehand by the families and are thoroughly saturated in sesamum oil.

The small mud dishes are arranged on the table in the pattern of the Chinese character *Shun* (順) ("smooth" or "agreeable") by which is meant all lucky turn of affairs. The single big one is the lamp of the God of Longevity. All the "lamps" are then lighted one by one while five bowls of a special kind of pudding are offered as the proper sacrifice and incense is burned. The ceremony is concluded by the burning of the paper things in a bonfire of cypress branches.

The ceremony over the pudding is eaten by the family members.

To make this pudding involves a special technique. Sugar with flavouring ingredients is first pounded into a solid slab and then cut into dice about half an inch square. These are then slightly watered and placed on big flat baskets containing the flour of glutinous rice. Forceful rolling and shaking of these baskets will give the sugar cubes a coating of flour. These are again bathed in water and then placed back in the flour for further rolling. When this process has been repeated about half a dozen times, the dice will have become spherical in shape and more than an inch in diameter. These are boiled in big pans of water until thoroughly soft. The sugar cores will have melted into a syrup and the bales are served hot in the "soup".

Rice pudding made this way is known as *Yuan Hsiao* (元宵) and is widely sold at the Lantern Festival, being quite as popular as the moon cakes at the Mid-Autumn Festival.

* * *

The Lantern Festival covers a period of seven days from the thirteenth to the seventeenth of the first moon of the Lunar calendar, a period of hilarious good time for all classes of Peking-*jen* which literally assumes riotous proportions. It is an old custom and marks the climax of the new year festivities.

There are a great number of lanterns which contribute to the colourful pageant of this festival and these are roughly divided into two main classes; those for the homes and those for public use. The former cover the kinds which are more or

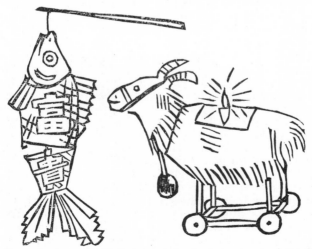

Fancy lanterns of all designs and shapes cater to juvenile customers. The sheep lantern has a big ball of earth attached to the neck with a stick and when the lantern is moved the sheep seems to nod its head. A red carp also contains a candle in its belly and designs of good omen are written all over its scales.

less playthings for children. Some of these are cheap things offered at the wayside stalls lining the main streets of Peking or crowded into the busy bazaars for this seasonal trade. There are those made of paper, perforated and carved with fancy designs pasted on a bamboo framework, such as the red carp and gold fish and the "lantern of good luck", a multi-faced lamp with many pointed spines of red or green paper, like gigantic caltrops. The Chinese word for "caltrop" has exactly the same sound as the word for "Good Luck".

Then there are the sheep lanterns, which are also equally liked by Chinese families for the word for ' sheep" has the same sound as that for "Good Auspices". The famous "running horse lanterns", with revolving paper figures that throw shadows on a midget screen when lighted by a candle inside, are also much in demand. In certain shops are also sold the *Wei Teng* (衛燈), or "Tientsin Lanterns", the name no doubt referring to the place where they were originally made. These are cleverly shaped with bamboo and paper, oiled for transparency and beautifully coloured. They are in all conceivable shapes, such as fruits, melons, animals and human figures and are made to contain the candle light inside as are all the other varieties mentioned above.

All the lanterns are light in weight and convenient in size and make ideal lanterns for parading purposes. The Tientsin lanterns used to be distributed by the so-called stores of "summer goods" (meaning umbrellas, fans, raincoats etc.) as a filler for the slack trade in the cold months. These same shops also distribute "sand lanterns" which are really no lanterns at all but a kind of mechanized toy which takes the shape of a wall lantern. Made like a clock, the faces are painted with scenes which include a number of little figures cut out from cardboard and fitted into the background all finely painted and coloured.

These figures are so made that certain parts of them are movable, the heads, the legs or the arms, depending upon the scheme of the picture's general make-up, be it a theatrical picture or a rural landscape. They are operated by concealed mechanism which is set into motion by the gradual leaking of a quantity of very fine sand contained in a paper bag with a small opening at the bottom. One takes the entire affair in the hands and gives it a slow twist and the sand will be gathered into the bag. Then the lantern is hung on the wall and the mechanism is set in motion by the movement of the sand, working all the movable parts on the face while little bells inside ring at intervals to give this animated cartoon its sound effect. All ceases when the sand has run out. Lanterns of this kind and many others are freely exchanged as gifts amongst families with children or are bought as favours to the youngsters from their seniors.

Lanterns for the amusement of the public are either displayed in the stores or in the various temples. The original kinds are in the shape of the so-called palace lanterns or what goes by the name of wall lanterns, both made of hardwood frames mounted with thin silk and elaborately painted with scenes from the famous Chinese storybooks, one scene on each face with proper captions. The palace lanterns, decorated with silken tassels of bright red or green, are hung from the ceilings in the empty space in front of the old-type wooden counters of the shops and the wall lanterns are hung like mural paintings on the temple walls, tiers and tiers of them.

In the evenings they are lighted with candles in the inside so that visitors can appreciate the artistic highpoints of the drawings as they trace chapter after chapter of legends and stories which are depicted on them. It is the rule for each store or temple to have its own feature but the principle seems to be for the stores to have the illustrations from famous novels and so on, while the temples would confine themselves more or less to the historical or mythological records of the respective principal deities worshipped in each shrine.

Thus the stores put up series of pictures from episodes of the "Dream of the Red Chamber" or "Strange Stories From a Chinese Studio" and so forth, while the Temple of White Clouds devotes its lantern faces to the graphic descriptions of their Taoist Sage, Ch'iu Ch'ang Ch'un, and the Temple of Kwan Kung has a complete collection of the life and anecdotes of its famous War God which is identical to the entire volume of the Romance of the Three Kingdoms.

It is the custom* in Peking to display* in public a "voluminous" series of picture lanterns at the stores and temples as an

Painstakingly prepared icemen are cousins to the snowmen and give caricatural representations of folklore figures. They are a sight which attracts many enthusiastic sightseers to the shops sponsoring them. The weatherman's practical joke at their expense soon reveals the straw skeletons.

attraction during the Lantern Festival. Unhappily, however, it has not been so enthusiastically observed in recent years partly because the stores, the old shops following the almost obsolete trades of Manchu pastries, Chinese cosmetics and so on, are themselves left pitifully behind in the progressive buying habits of the public. It has become too expensive for them to keep up the good work. Besides, modern fancy electrical lighting, with which certain fashionable stores do their festival lighting, has gradually sidetracked the advertising significance of the ancient stunt, and the appreciation of the public to these eighteenth-century pageants has lost its force as an aesthetic demand.

Such displays had their best days during the late Ch'ing Dynasty when according to reliable sources, even the important ministries of the imperial government had their own respective features. The Board of Public Works boasted of the best picture lanterns in Peking, closely followed by those of the Board of War. The lantern display of the Board of War was the last "government project" to vanish in the ninth year of Emperor Kwang Hsu (1883), at the recommendation of a certain minister named Yen. The next few years from today will see the disappearance of the last displays under the onslaught of neon and other modern luminous signs.

Certain other types of festive lanterns are, however, still being encouraged, such as the ice lanterns of some grocery stores. Bundles of straw are first formed and tied together to represent rough human skeletons or groups of human figures and other objects. Many days in advance water is poured on the "skeletons" from time to time and so by the time the Lantern Festival comes along they have become solid ice pillars. Cutting and hewing of the sculpture work converts these into the desired statuary shapes and designs and then final additions are made with coloured paper and the like. Candlesticks are mounted in certain hollow portions in convenient places so that the gathering sightseers can recognize in these man-made icicles groups of legendary and lifelike figures such as Scholar Hsu Hsien and his snake wife and her snake maid, the God of Fortune or the Laughing Buddha.

Another type equally popular is the wheat lantern: wheat dragons, wheat phoenixes and so on. A quantity of wheat is first spread on a trough in which is placed a thin layer of cotton. Then the trough is kept in a warm room and frequently watered so that in about a fortnight the wheat will sprout into pleasing "needles" of delicate green. In the meantime the growths of the roots would also weave themselves into a veritable green carpet. This is then severed into pieces of the desired sizes and shapes and mounted on frameworks of bamboo and wood to create grostesque animals and things. Bright-coloured papers and candles will add the final touch of splendour.

One more kind of funny character must be said to be the *Huo P'an-erh* (火判兒), or the "Flaming God of Judgment", which is annually prepared as a festival attraction at the Temple of the City God out in the north city of Peking. In one of the spacious courtyards is yearly erected the statue of the god of judgment in a sitting posture, constructed of hollow masonry work fully twenty feet high, with holes representing the eyes, the nostrils, the mouth, the ears and, indeed, the navel of the big bare abdomen. A big fire of coal balls is made to burn in the hollow statue so that by night, when visitors arrive in good numbers to favour this deity with an inspection, tongues of flames will dart out from all the holes. As a matter of fact, this is about all there is to it, but a surprisingly big number of visitors are annually attracted to this spot, year after year, to see this big practical joke at the expense of the god.

On Lantern Festival nights everybody goes out to see the lanterns and the various sights and the streets are literally thick with people, particularly at the places of chief attractions where there are such vast throngs of humanity that it is indeed hard to move about and it is just as difficult for one to get near the lanterns as it is to back out from them. Men, women and children push each other about, and certain types of people would also add to the turmoil by stupid mischiefs of all sorts while pickpockets are given a golden opportunity to operate with fine results.

While going from one place to another to inspect the lanterns the people will also inevitably stop here and there in the crowded and brightly lighted streets to see a free show of fireworks, some staged by prosperous firms and others only being the fireworks shops clearing up their surplus stock as by now the new year festivities are about over and the public's "buying fad" is at a low ebb. Instead of stowing away the fire-crackers for the next new year period's trade, by which time they would almost certainly become "duds" on account of the atmospheric changes, they rather prefer to set off all that is left for the public to enjoy, free of all charge, as a swan song to the season's successful business. These displays would block up the street traffic in many a hopeless jam while the show lasts. Meanwhile, crude amateurish music on the drums and gongs, coming from behind closed doors here and there adds still more noise and good-natured cheers to the enjoyment of the Lantern Festival.

*   *   *

It is true that the Lantern Festival of Peking used to be the year's happiest occasion for the fun-loving grown-ups, children as well as women. Judged by present-day standards the street attractions then were really nothing extraordinary and certainly nothing to rave about but comparatively few years back they had been habitually looked forward to by people of all ages and in all walks of life, as the Chinese people's fondness for noisy festivities is proverbial.

There were several reasons contributing to the fun of the Lantern Festival but the fact that women were allowed to take part is the main factor, for it must be remembered that on general principles the Chinese woman's place was behind the grey walls and the devil screens and going out for recreation (barring combined "shopping" and devotional visits to the temple) was not allowed—even the pleasure of going to the theatres was categorically denied to the women—to say nothing of going out to see the sights of the streets at night.

Poor street lighting made it all the more impracticable.

Around the Lantern Festival these restrictions were relaxed and young women and girls were allowed to see the nocturnal street sights to which the lanterns were only additional attractions. They come out in parties mostly chaperoned by older women or accompanied by women-servants, all dressed up in their best clothes. They visit the various showplaces in town on foot or in mule carts for their thrills of the year, concluding their adventures with purchases of the festive *Yuan Hsiao* or rice puddings to bring home to cook and eat.

There were then also certain current superstitions in connection with the outings on the nights of the Lantern Festivals. One was that if a person went out to take a walk in the moonlight on the Lantern Festival, he or she would be insured against all illnesses in the coming year particularly if they would walk over the Bridge of the Noon Hour Sun, by which is known the bridge on the city moat immediately outside the Chien Men to the north of the five sectioned archway. And so the holiday promenaders purposely routed their itinerary to include this spot "for the sake of good health."

Another superstition claimed that if a young married woman, on Lantern Festival night, should go past the Chien Men and rub her hand on some of the big round nails or tacks on the heavy iron-clad doors she would be able to give birth to a male child that same year. This rubbing, it was also claimed, should be done without people detecting her at it in order to bear surer results. It must have been an interesting sight and a captivating experience for the young women, indeed, considering the heavy traffic on such a night at the Chien Men when we bear in mind that this was before the gate was reconstructed and, instead of the present five, there was only one arch leading to the Bridge of the Noon Hour Sun past the two side-arches which stood where the two railway stations now stand on a circular extension of the city battlement.

Another thing that was also partly responsible for the festive fun was that the city officials were away from their duties and they would not return to their offices until the eighteenth day of the first moon, after the Lantern Festival was over, and so during this period of "anarchism", minor offences were not even noticed by the peace-and-order authorities, much less prosecuted according to law and so everybody, so to speak, had things his own way. In the most unrestricted fashion imaginable people crowded the streets, milling around after supper hardly ever thinking of going home before the small hours of the morning, going from one part of the city to another in order to "cover" as many attractions as possible and stopping at wayside wine shops and restaurants (open all night) for refreshments.

To discourage the waves of humanity from lingering on the streets, older Peking-*jen* will recollect, night-watchmen beating their heavy wooden rattlers as they went about to announce the hours of the night were purposely instructed to report the wrong hours, beating five times, the sign of the "fifth watch", when they ought to beat only three for the "third watch" but even this did not appreciably break up the street crowds. They petered out of their own sweet will and then each holiday-maker turned homeward his or her weary feet.

* * *

Scholar Wu had vivid memories of trips made for viewing the lanterns in the company of his family when he was a child as their home on Donkey Mart was not far from the busy shopping centers of the east city of Peking. Since then, however, much of the clamouring fun still in evidence in those days has disappeared from this colourful pageant of old Peking.

* * *

On the eighteenth day of the first moon new year festivities end and even in the homes the holiday atmosphere is at an end. The children are told that on the night of the eighteenth the mice get married and that failing to find suitable sedan chairs for their bridal parties they are liable to take possession of the children's new shoes for such purposes. And under this fictitious excuse the children are made to go to bed earlier than usual and their new shoes are then hidden away by the parents for, with no more places to go to and no visits to make, the old shoes would be quite good enough for the youngsters.

The last day of the first lunar moon is the day for the Devil Dance at the Lama Temple, the very last chapter of the Peking-*jen's* new year fun.

The Devil Dance is known locally as *Ta Kwei* (打鬼), or "Fighting the Devil", and is annually staged at this famous temple in the northeastern city of Peking. Similar functions used also to be held at the Yellow Temple outside An Ting Men (安定門) and at the Black Temple outside of Teh Sheng Men (德勝門). The Yellow Temple which people visit to see the elaborately sculptured marble monumental stupa marking the spot where the remains of a Living Buddha, supreme religious and temporal authority of Tibet, are buried has seen days of wanton destruction when in the past Chinese soldiers of various politico-military factions were quartered here at different times, as well as systematic embezzlement and fraudulent misappropriation of the temple's priceless paraphernalia at the hands of ill-famed priests. The resident monks or lamas have mostly left for other better-sustained monasteries (for that is the nomadic way with the lamas). As to the Black Temple nothing but a few buildings in the very last stage of decay mark the former objective of much imperial patronage where favours were lavished on a group of aboriginal priests for the sake of political support.

The Lama Temple is itself a bit of transplanted Tibet enshrined *in toto* in Chinese architectural surroundings and, retaining all its own ways and habits, is decidedly foreign to Peking in many respects. Until converted into a Lama monastery in the year 1736, it was used as the residence of a Manchu crown prince who left the palace to be Emperor Ch'ien Lung.

Here the curiosity-seeking local residents and tourists alike come to see the multitude of fantastic images of the Tibetan sect of Buddhism and demon worship, including the towering sixty-foot image of Matreya carved from one single trunk of cedar and the various mystic gods known in Chinese as the *Huan*

Hsi Fo (歡喜佛), or "Gods of Happiness", or to watch Lama services in the various halls but invariably they come away with the impression of having been in a foreign country.

For some distance to the Lama Temple, on Devil Dance day, the streets are packed with eager sight-seers and, taking advantage of the situation, toy stalls and food-vendors gather here for a day's trade the same as they would anywhere else where there are such prospects. Some of the new year specialties are still to be seen here as are also masks, shaped in weird shapes which represent near-replicas of those worn by the priests at the dance.

The front court of the temple would be crowded to capacity with sight-seers from early morning. To prevent mobbing of the inner precincts, where most of the temple's images and various religious and sacrificial attributes are kept, including certain temple treasures and gifts from the Imperial Manchu court, these are forbidden to the visitors for the day. By noon the dance party would come out to the front court for their mystic antics, performed in full public view.

To get to a vantage point to watch a Devil Dance is not an easy matter for the crowds are thick and each person is intent to catch a glimpse of the curious sight but it is highly worth the trouble if one can make it. (Some "reserved seats" are on the walls or in the trees where Tarzan-the-Apeman youngsters perch.) In the center of the courtyard the attendant priests with the help of the police manage to make a clearing with the help of long whips and the tossing of handfuls of lime powder and within the cordon thus thrown are seen the various characters of this colourful paganistic show, all clad in conventional garbs of rich embroideries though shabby from age and wearing big, top-heavy masks of various kinds, some representing the various Lamaist deities and others the devilish members with ugly faces, some with their hats decorated

Weirdly masked and embroidery-clad Mongolian priests of the Tibetan Buddhist religion hold a Devil Dance every year at Lama Temple in Peking What looks like the *oni* of the Japanese fable is really the Diamond Guardian of the Faith, the three human skulls on the top of his mask indicate destructive power, Deer-head will cut up the buttered dough-figure, symbolic of bad luck, at the end of the dance.

with facsimiles of human skulls and others brandishing short religious weapons and others wearing the heads of cows and deer.

In the center is the figure of buttered dough painted red and carried ceremoniously on a small wooden stand—the embodiment of the devil. Chanting of Tibetan scriptures and playing of religious music, echoing drums and horns, accompany the mimicry subduing processes. A few minutes later the entire group form into a procession and make for the gate of the temple where the dough figure is cut into pieces and burned, thus ending the Devil Dance.

There are various explanations given for this mystic undertaking but few know exactly which one is correct. The Lamas do not know it intelligently themselves but do it just as a matter of precedence. Briefly, it is a symbolic getting rid of the year's bad luck. In Tibet and Mongolia such mystic rites are held from time to time, sponsored by rich laymen patrons of the monasteries. In Peking, it is just another "sight", which people come from far and near to see, like Scholar Wu and his classmates did.

THE BETROTHAL OF YOUNG WU

IN THE fourth year after old Mr. Wu's death, Scholar Wu Hsueh-wen graduated from the secondary school and the Wus had to decide then whether he was to continue with his studies or be started in business life at an early date. It was in favour of the latter course that the family, including young Wu, decided finally and following the footsteps of his father, conforming to the business tradition of this country, he was recommended to start as a clerk in a banking house. His father having been reputably established in such circles, it was no trouble at all to get him a suitable position and soon heproved himself, in the eyes of his employers and superiors, to be a hard-working, energetic young man definitely headed for success. Of this everybody was glad but no one was surprised.

It was at this time that the Wus started to talk about his getting married. There were certain family conferences, mostly held without his knowledge, to consider the matter for to see a son or a daughter happily married is not the duty of the youths themselves but rather that of the parents. Here in China parents arrange everything for their children's marriage from the selection of the future wife or future husband to the financing of the ceremonies and the various details and often including the support of the sons' wives until the sons are well established. Merely offering advice is not enough and most young people are glad to be able to depend upon their parents who are naturally anxious to do their very best in their children's behalf.

In recent years modern social habits have made it possible for young people to seek their own lifetime partners as co-education and the so-called "emancipation of the fair sex" have contributed much to this great change which is eventually to revolutionize the time-honoured practice. Of course there are pros and cons to this important question of the times but that such a change should not and could not be averted is considered by most to be a foregone conclusion. Unfortunately, during this transitional period certain tragic happenings occur either from the fact that unwilling parents obstruct the plans and ambitions of their children or from a misinterpretation of this right or from extremistic utilization and enjoyment of this newly acquired privilege by the parties concerned. Exactly how should people manage their affairs so that propriety and happiness are both assured is not our concern and only time will see an ideal solution of the problem.

As to young Wu, having been brought up in an orthodox Peking family and being able to depend on his parents to do their best for his own happiness, he was not found to be inspired to be an example of social reform. As a matter of fact, whether he had either pondered seriously over the matter and decided in favour of the old practice or whether he had not even begun to think of it, nobody knew but from what could be observed it seemed he just took the whole procedure as a matter of course when he was told of the arrangements his family had made for him, saying that he was glad he did not have to venture out for himself in the "treacherous seas" which characterize the introduction of a new principle and a radical change for which he was not prepared.

On the other hand, however, he was fortunate not to have fallen victim to certain marital tragedies of the old system; for this the credit went to his wise parents and grandparents. Strange as it may seem there had been talk about his marriage before he was born. They had a family friend about the same age as his father whose wife was also expecting to have a baby the same time his mother was expecting him. They were rather intimate friends and so it was suggested that the two families agree to a *Chih Fu Wei Hun* (指腹爲婚), or "concluding a betrothal while pointing at the stomachs". This is a much-practiced custom in China with which people seek to unite more closely friendship ties between families, promising an irrevocable marital alliance should the children born be of different sexes, no matter which one is a boy and which a girl. But much opposition was expressed by young Mr. Wu and the scheme was dropped. As a matter of fact the scheme, even if agreed upon, would have died a natural death for this friend's wife also gave birth to a boy.

Another occasion came up when he was only about twelve years old. Some well-wishing friends suggested getting the child a so-called *T'ung Yang Hsi Fu* (童養媳婦), or "wife brought up since childhood in the husband's family", in which case the "lady-elect" was a very beautiful young maiden about his own age who had lost both her parents. The grandmother opposed the project and explained vehemently that since no one could be certain whether or not young Little Bald Head (this was how he was referred to then) could be expected to make good, it would be unfair to the girl to enter into such an agreement.

"If he turned out to be a fine young man, well and good. If he grew to be a worthless youth, how could we expect the girl to be happy?" she argued. What she had actually believed, however, was that since the girl belonged to such a "bitter-fated" class of "life pattern" that had caused the death of both of her parents when she was so young and if she had been "taken on" as a *T'ung Yang Hsi Fu*, living in the Wu family, she might bring bad luck with her, resulting in untoward happenings in the Wu family to the regret of all.

From then on there were also other propositions made to the Wus in regard to the child's marriage but these were unanimously turned down.

"Our child is still young and it is no time to get him engaged. Once he is engaged we would too easily think of getting him married which is harmful to our child who ought to devote his time and attention to his studies. When schooling is over and he has a job and earns enough to support a wife, we shall give the matter proper consideration," it was proclaimed.

*   *   *

Speaking of marriage as a family adventure in China it must

be said that very often boys are married at an early age to girls many years older than they and this is the rule rather than the exception in the interior of China. Boys ten or eleven years old, entirely undeveloped physically and mentally, are provided with wives of eighteen or twenty. Why? Because the families need some help in the home or on the farm. It may serve nicely to alleviate a labour shortage or rid the wives' maternal families of an economic burden but the resultant tragic consequences surely to follow—are often unavoidable. City families, however, are more rational in their ways and usually insist on younger wives for their sons who are almost never married before twenty.

It the Wu family Old Mrs. Wu was, indeed, the most concerned about her grandson's marriage for she was anxious to experience the satisfaction of another family problem being solved more or less according to her own idea. She had invited a blind fortune-teller to offer his advice on the subject and she was happy when he divulged that according to the young man's "eight characters" of "life pattern", his Star of the Red Phoenix was in an active mood for the year. Questioned as to further details he was also able to predict that the bride would come from a northwestern direction.

And in pursuance of this same aim she made a devout pilgrimage on new year's day to the Temple of the Sacred Eastern Mountain where, as she had done before for her own son, she "borrowed a piece of red thread from the Old Man under the Moon," half of which she stretched across a door in their house. In the evening, entirely unawares, the youth broke it in two as he entered the room. The other half she had her daughter-in-law sew into one of the youth's garments. After the "breaking of the thread" the family became all the more convinced that it would not be long now before an engagement would be announced, for this was an aditional way of foretelling the prospects for a person's marriage as controlled and arranged by the Old Man Under the Moon. But exactly who is this interesting personage whose kind-faced image is so reverently worshipped in the side court of the temple? The Chinese have a beautiful legend.

Once in the T'ang Dynasty there lived a scholar whose name was Wei Ku (韋固). He was one evening staying in an inn in the southern outskirts of Sung Ch'eng (宋城) when he was going to the capital city to seek an official appointment. Here he saw an old man perusing a thick record book under the bright moonlight. Curious, he asked the old man about the book he was examining and was told that it was the complete register of the world's matrimonial unions.

After a while he met the same old man again while promenading in the Rice Market and the old man, pointing at an old woman, blind in one eye and carrying a small girl about three years old in her arms, said to him:

"See that girl over there in the woman's arms? She is going to be your honourable wife."

Wei Ku was annoyed and returning to the inn he sharpened a pocket knife and gave it to his serf-boy and told him to try to stab the girl with it. This serf-boy did so hurriedly, and escaped into the crowd in the turmoil that followed.

Fourteen years later a young Mandarin now, Wei Ku was married to the daughter of the Governor of Hsiang Chow (相州). She was a very beautiful and charming woman but close to one of her "spring mountain" eye-brows she always wore a floral decoration. He questioned her and was told that she had a tiny scar on her temple left from a wound received at the hand of a crazy ruffian who attacked her with a knife when she was but a wee bit of a child in the arms of Chen Ma (陳媽), a maidservant. She was then three years old and living with her father who was serving at Sung Ch'eng as the district magistrate.

"Was the maidservant not blind in one eye?" asked Wei Ku.

"Exactly," answered his pretty wife.

Wei Ku then related the happening at the Sung Ch'eng inn and the attempt he had his serf-boy make and they both agreed that the Old Man Under the Moon was really the god in charge of marital relations and that couples registered in his record book were not to be separated by any force whatever.

The Old Man Under the Moon, it is said, ties a boy to one end and a girl to the other end of a piece of invisible red thread and people thus united are bound to be husband and wife in this world and no matter how far apart they may live from each other Fate will bring them together for a life-long partnership. Hence the Chinese proverb: *Ch'ien li yin yuan yi hsien ch'uan* (千里姻緣一線穿), or "Destined to be united in marriage, a thousand miles apart one single thread ties the two together".

*   *   *

In the old-school Peking families women are supposed to know the importance of "Three Dependences" and "Four Virtues", the former covering "Dependence on father before marriage, dependence on husband after marriage and dependence on son, or sons, if left a widow", and the latter refers to "Character, appearance, speech and work." By "work" is meant proper housekeeping and everything connected with it. Most Chinese girls of the old school were not well-known for their education in the sense of literary achievement or in what may be termed "executive ability" for they were permanently to be a follower and not a leader in all phases of life.

It may also be mentioned that under the heading of "Character" was included a liberal attitude toward the husband in so far as his own personal affairs were concerned. For instance, a Chinese husband is permitted to keep concubines in the house and the wife, as a respectful consort, must neither raise any objection to such things nor seek to monopolize the husband's attention in any manner. If she fails in this, she is ridiculed as a "vinegar bucket" as any expression of jealousy is called *chih ts'u* (吃醋) or "eating vinegar" in Chinese colloquialism.

A Chinese proverb says: "A good woman should not be wed to two husbands for who has seen a single horse carry two saddles?" There is no provision for divorcing a husband but there are many acceptable grounds for divorcing a wife. In the ancient Classic of Rites are mentioned the seven "outs" which constitute good reasons for getting rid of a wife: not giving birth to a son; impure desire; lack of respect for husband's parents; gossip and quarrels (chronic nagging); stealing and jealousy. A husband, on the other hand, is not restricted by any such rules and, besides, he does not have to think of the problem of alimony payable after divorcing a wife for theoretically he is never in the wrong.

Marriage propositions are always indirectly put before the opposite faction not by the parents of the parties concerned but by their mutual friends. These may be carried out either voluntarily or actually be prevailed upon to act as a friendly obligation, serving as go-betweens or match-makers. These people ordinarily would be very glad to help materialize a scheme if in their judgment the match is suitable as a Chinese superstition has it that any person having helped in arranging three happy marital unions will be immune to the after-death tortures in Purgatory. If they do not wish to obtain such an immunity after death at the above-mentioned attractive price, they, of course, need not bother seeking to be match-makers, for there is no moral or legal condemnation against any one who does not feel like rendering help in this manner. But under no circumstances should he oppose a suggested match or try to dissuade the tentative proposers to labour for the solemnization of the union or to prevent the project from making healthy progress, except when there is really a good reason to do so. A Chinese saying cautions: "Rather destroy a Buddhist temple than purposely break up a hopeful marital negotiation."

These amateur match-makers are known in the Chinese classical language as icemen, referring to an old legend. A man once dreamed that he stood on ice in a frozen river and wondered what meaning the dream had. His friends explained that it indicated he was going to be a marriage go-between because he was, in the dream, standing between the positive and the negative elements, air and water.

There are also certain professional match-makers who mediate between the high contracting parties for a monetary consideration, but their services are not always welcome nor desired except in the case of procuring a concubine who is, more often than not, bought for a sum of money and the go-between gets, as it were, a buying commission.

There are also certain provisions which are so commonly believed in that they constitute an important chapter in the family almanac book. Based upon the animal cycle of the twelve years there is a verse reading:

> The White Horse dreads the Black Ox,
> The Sheep and the Rat, one day and they
> part.
> The Snake and the Tiger are like swords to
> each other,
> And Rabbit and Dragon, if united, will see
> tears flow.
> A Golden Cock a Jade Dog does fear,
> As Pig and Monkey will never see a happy
> end.

According to the same source, Rat and Ox, Tiger and Pig, Dragon and Cock, Snake and Monkey, Horse and Sheep, Rabbit and Dog are pairs with the most promising futures.

There is also a belief that a girl whose animal cycle pattern is Tiger is bound to prove a termagant wife and a harmful addition to the family as the Tiger is man-eating in habit. Girls born in the year of the Sheep are even more to be shunned, particularly if born in the twelfth moon, although there seems to be no explanation for this superstitious fear. In order that one-sixth of the female population of the land may not live to be old spinsters, when girls of these patterns are proposed for marriage deliberate misrepresentation of their age is widely practiced in order to detour from the curse.

In Scholar Wu's case, the same as in most cases, these matters of first importance were given careful consideration and for this reason only confidential persons were relied upon in order to avoid a tragic catastrophe that might be brought to the happy Wu family.

*　　　*　　　*

Although the Wu family were somewhat anxious to get young Wu married they were careful in getting a proper match for him and were not prepared to make any hasty decisions. Many a proposition was turned down in various stages of preliminary negotiation. The Wus were well established financially, owned properties in town and had interests in certain business enterprises. Yet in the eyes of the judicious and far-sighted parents who had daughters to marry off these did not constitute all the attractive points as most parents wisely emphasize that a promising young man is the thing of first importance, rather than the family's social or financial background at the time of marriage.

The family history of the Wus was an honourable one and their habits or traditions were decidedly of an admirable type, which facts were well-known to their friends and acquaintances. As to young Wu himself, there was nothing to be said against him except that he could be said to be too young to marry. All who knew the Wus knew that the youth was well-behaved, self-respectful and ambitious. Physically well-developed, fairly well-educated and, under the capable guidance of his parents, a bright future was but a matter of course. Everything taken into consideration he was as good a prospective husband as any young man would make and the Wus were therefore confident of a suitable party eventually if not right then and "quality was not to be sacrificed for speed."

As would be expected under the circumstances the honour of suggesting the proposition that developed into an engagement and then into a brilliant wedding fell at last to Mr. and Mrs. Chao, the "parents-in-faith" of the young man.

The girl in question was from another old Peking family which was well known to the Chaos and lived in the West City. The eldest of a group of five children, she was then sixteen years of age. Her family's name was Ch'i. The Ch'is were quite well-to-do. Being a typical Peking family they allowed young Miss Ch'i to have only a few years' schooling in a public college for girls, after which period her father acted as her private tutor at home and taught her certain rudiments of Chinese literature.

Her mother instructed her in sewing and needlework and various other branches of domestic economics by allowing her to get a practical mastery of such matters. It was thought that she ought to be well acquainted with all the duties of a house-wife and was well-equipped with knowledge and experience to handle housekeeping as her parents expected her to be married at a proper age which they thought would be when she was twenty years old.

She was a bright girl and in a way wrote fairly beautiful Chinese characters and did sums rather intelligently. "She wrote so nicely that her family friends often asked her, through her father, to copy some famous Chinese poems on paper fans used in summer," said Mrs. Chao in the boastful manner that is often noted in the art of match-making, "and she painted fairly good free-hand pictures in the Chinese style, for at school drawing lessons were greatly liked by her."

It was also mentioned that she was made to keep the family's account books of daily expenses, besides assisting her busy mother by taking care of the endless chores in the house. She was not bad to look at, too, as shown by a number of photographs brought by Mrs. Chao at the beginning of the nego-tiations. One of these photographs was purposely taken for the Wus although this was not so explained to the girl.

According to Mrs Chao, Mr. and Mrs. Ch'i had mentioned several times to her that they expected her to be on the lookout for a suitable "home" (this is exactly how the Chinese say it) for their daughter, as it was their knowledge that Mrs. Chao had been successful in making, or helped to make, certain other matrimonial arrangements that proved to be rather happy. And so when it was made known that she intended to bring to their consideration the case of young Wu, Mr. and Mrs. Ch'i were quite agreeably inclined, not only because the prospect sounded interesting to them in the first place but also since they knew they could rely on the Chaos in the matter.

"Our daughter is the same as your daughter and we will depend upon your doing your best to help materialize the scheme," said Mrs Ch'i.

"Yes, that is the idea", answered Mrs. Chao. "You see, the young man in question is our son-in-faith and a highly promis-ing young man and theWus are our old worthy friends and we are duty-bound to them to get them a good daughter-in-law. Theirs is an old Peking family, the same as yours is. Mr. Chao and I seldom meddle in other people's affairs unless we are under obligation to all the parties concerned You know how few people ever praise the match-makers responsible for their happy mar-riages and how often you see a match-maker in hot water after the matrimony proves to be unhappy!"

It is true that match-makers are unjustly blamed for unhap-py marriages while for all the good work of China's sagacious go-betweens, the credit goes to the Old Man Under the Moon.

*　　*　　*

Mr. and Mrs. Chao being so intimately acquainted with the Wu family when they came to see the Wus formally and ex-plained to them their desire to place before the Wus for their consideration the case of Miss Ch'i as a suitable girl to be young Wu's bride, they found ready attention.

A detailed description of the Ch'i family in general and of the girl in particular was given first to Old Mrs. Wu, the grandmother, and then to her daughter-in-law, young Wu's mother. They both seemed to be favourably impressed. After being told that the case would be referred to the young man's father for his approval before going on with the negotiations, the Chaos departed. Ordinarily they would have stayed longer but with such an important problem that called for unbiased judgment they did not wish to be thought that they wanted to force matters.

Taking advantage of young Wu's absence from home, the Wus gathered together in a conference to talk the matter over as they have so often when there was anything important to discuss. The case of Miss Ch'i, based upon the description given by the Chaos and the photographs which they left with them for ready reference as to the girl's appearance, was carefully considered. At this conference old Mrs. Wu served more or less in an advisory capacity and her son and her daughter-in-law were naturally the principal participants.

Opinions were freely exchanged and even the maid-servant of the house, an aged and experienced woman, was called in to listen and was asked to draw their attention to anything that sounded disagreeable. The conference was over in an hour and it was agreed that Mr. and Mrs. Chao were to be requested to do their good work to secure, as the first step in the negotiations, the Ch'i family's *Men Hu T'ieh* (門戶帖) or "genealogical memorandum" in exchange for their own which they quickly prepared. The memorandum gave a brief outline of the family pedigree for the last three generations, together with a reference to their respective calling as such a process used to be looked upon as a very important matter considering how racial differences and what may be called a "caste system" played important parts in marriages.

As a resume of the opinions expressed at this important conference it was interesting to note that the Wus did look at the matter from different angles according to each of the participants although in general they agreed beautifully. Young Wu's father liked the idea because he always felt his son ought to get a wife who could read and write, if only fairly well, and he preferred to have her come from a cultured family. His wife thought it a good thing that the girl was a first child as in such a case she could be expected to be of a tender nature, cultivated by living amongst younger brothers and sisters. That the girl was described to be very capable in household affairs was another point that won her approbation. Old Mrs. Wu liked the idea because the girl looked very pretty to her!

Busy days followed as investigations were made all around, both families instituting inquiries. A week later, all being satisfied, the *Hsiao Tieh-erh* (小帖兒), or "Small Slips," were exchanged. On the so-called "Small Slips" the Wus wrote the date and hour of birth of the young man and from Mr. and Mrs. Chao obtained in exchange a similar slip bearing the same information about the girl.

These slips, after being exchanged, were carefully placed in the shrine of the family Kitchen God for three days following receipt to see if the Kitchen God was equally well disposed to the project which was indicated by three peaceful days in the household. It was understood that had anything untoward happened during the three days, such as a quarrel in the family or some other unlucky incident or mishap in the home or even to the family members outside of the home itself, the proposition would have been considered to be inauspicious, opposed to by the gods, and therefore the best thing to do was to end it before it began. This decision could be conveyed to the opposite faction by returning the slip to them, indicating the party's unwillingness to go on with the negotiations.

Afterwards the two slips are given to an astrologer to compare to see if any conflict was to be expected. If in his opinion the match was indicative of happiness the families concerned would put their minds at ease and get on with the next step. If he shook his head, well, it would be a case of "just too bad."

* * *

On a narrow lane leading from the busy thoroughfare directly in front of the famous Drum Tower of Peking was the shop (or should it be called a consulting office?) of a well-known professional horoscope reader and marriage astrologer, whose signboard could be seen at a distance from different directions according to whether his clients approached the place either from the narrow lane mentioned above or from a crooked alleyway branching out from the Oblique Street of the Pipe-sellers. The signboard listed the man's specialties: Minute Examination of Eight Characters of Birth; Comparing Birth Patterns for Betrothals; Selection of Auspicious Dates; Forecasting the Current Year's Fortune; and so forth. This was the place of old Mr. Liu, who was respected as Peking's unimpeachable authority on such matters as mentioned above, being eminently well qualified to advise on these important subjects. The Wus were his regular customers.

It was true his place was a humble shack unlike certain others who rent expensive hotel rooms in the down town sections of Peking and who cater more to the trade of office-seekers. But Liu's slogan was *Chih Yen Wu Yin* (直言無隱) (Straight Words Without Reserve) and he was known always to live up to it. He spoke nothing but the truth and in case there were unlucky signs in the propositions brought up by his clients he was perfectly frank in saying so without trying to "smooth the corners".

It was well known that there had been many cases in which the parties concerned had gone against his advise and lived to regret it. These alarming truths that seemed stranger than fiction the wise man recounted in detail to his clients, case by case, during the friendly chats preceding and succeeding professional conversations. That he was not mealy mouthed was what he was trying to put across to the customers even if his predictions might spoil a prospective engagement.

So while the Ch'i family sought for advice from a similar place in some other part of the city, young Wu's mother called at Astrologer Liu's and left with him the two red paper slips on which the fundamental information was clearly given. Using this as a basis of calculation Liu was requested to look over the combination thoroughly even if it did require two or three days.

On the agreed day the good woman again called at Mr. Liu's and a written statement was delivered to her together with Mr. Liu's congratulations, written on the folded document in clear language and with accuracy. The betrothal was predicted to be exceedingly auspicious and therefore highly recommended for further negotiations. Among things which the wise man revealed after scrupulous scrutiny and rigorous research deep into his volumes and checked again and again were that not only was the union devoid of any bad influence whatever to either person immediately concerned but, indeed, it was good for both families. The signs were indicative of abundance and prosperity for the couple as well as of prolonged happiness for three generations of their posterity. The husband's life pattern was that of Wood (a blind fortune-teller once said so when Wu was a baby) which agreed very well with that of the wife's which was that of Water. Their animal symbols were correctly matched and in so far their future harmony was concerned this, in the opinion of the astrologer, was absolutely guaranteed as their individual Eight Character Combinations were of a very good omen, independent of each other and which Liu separately examined as a lateral reference.

"Such a union is," explained the astrologer, "according to the books, a *Shang Teng Fu Teh Hun* (上等福德婚), (High Class Betrothal of Happiness and Virtue) and almost the best to be expected. The books provide, of course, also the *Sheng Ch'i Hun* (生氣婚) (Betrothal of Vigorous Air) and the *T'ien Yi Hun* (天醫婚) (Betrothal of Heavenly Doctor) but we common people could hardly expect either of these. I have never met a single case corresponding to either of the two kinds in all the thirty years of my practice. You know, of course, that the worst kinds are the *Chueh Ming Hun* (絕命婚) (Betrothal of Interrupted Life) and the *Wu Kwei Hun* (五鬼婚) (Betrothal of the Five Ghosts!) which should not end in marriage under any circumstances whatever."

The old man chopped a red seal on the document showing his responsibility and delivered it to young Wu's mother after reading over and paraphrasing the contents rather carefully so that she could better understand their meaning. The paper also pronounced that the first and the seventh moons were to be the best months for the wedding and the next best would be the third and the ninth, though Mr. Liu added verbally that as a matter of fact, a "High class Betrothal of Happiness and Virtue" may have the wedding in any month in the year as "One major auspicious point counteracts all minor ill omens", as the Chinese say.

The usual charge for such an analysis was two dollars The astrologer refused to accept anything less than four in this case. He gave as his reason, "since such a happy combination does not happen often it is worth a double fee".

Mrs. Wu gladly paid the extra charge.

*   *   *

The horoscopic influences of the girl Ch'i and that of young Wu having been considered favourable to each other as per the advice obtained independently from different sources, the betrothal was considered to have made an important headway. Naturally Mr. and Mrs. Chao were glad to notify each faction of the other's findings.

The next step to be taken was an inspection of the Wu house and an observation of the future husband which was smoothly carried out as both the Ch'i family and the Wus were of a straight-forward nature and both had confidence in the go-betweens, Mr. and Mrs. Chao. A pre-betrothal inspection of the home of the groom is known locally as *Hsiang Chia* (相家) or "Examination of the Home" and is of great importance to the bride-to-be's people in getting a general idea of the family tradition of the future home.

A wise parent can easily gather from the atmosphere prevailing, even if only sectional (as it is bound to be), whether or not the family is rationally organized and running on a sound economic principle. The inspection also serves as a valuable opportunity to feel by personal interviews whether the future "in-laws" are of a reasonable character and not too harsh and fastidious for on this depends the happiness or otherwise of the marriage. This is of great significance in China as the Chinese young man does not have a home of his own after marriage and Chinese "in-laws", particularly the husband's mother, are well-known for their strict discipline of the son's wife, which is a deep rooted tradition in this country.

It is only too true that many a husband's mother "takes it out" on the son's wife for the unfortunate experiences she has had when she was merely a "son's wife" herself. She has many good reasons and a legitimate moral support to be strict with the youthful newcomer and to expect the young woman to show talents in every turn of the day's work in the house, for "a son's wife" is expected to carry on the family "way" which often is found to be more or less reactionary to the younger generation. Even if the newcomer is willing enough to compromise her own ideas with those of the husband's mother and even if the mother is good enough not to abuse her authority, still there are bound to be minor differences to be noticed in housekeeping, to say nothing of social and ceremonial functions, though fortunately a daughter-in-law is not required to take any initiatives.

It does take a clever girl to be able to make the necessary adjustments without necessarily being literally "whipped into line" and in case she fails to see her position objectively and to stand ready to "follow the leader" her days will be full of agony until in the course of years she becomes the logical survivor, which is a slow and distressing process, indeed, as may be imagined. For a son and his bride to crave a small home of their own is socially condemned as a dangerous idea and a sinful act and is often referred to as a "family revolution."

Of course, there was no reason to be apprehensive on the

part of the Wus in so far as such a home inspection was concerned. A day was set for the purpose and on that day young
Wu was made to stay home as also was his father. Besides the
girl's parents there were some others who came to take part in
the visitation. These, as previously notified through the go-
betweens, were the girl's uncles and aunts who were requested
by her parents to help out as the opinions of these people were
considered to be highly valuable. Young Wu was somewhat
surprised to meet these many new people who were introduced
to him as Mr. and Mrs. Chao's cousins. One gentleman with a
mustache, who looked like he had seen him somewhere before
made him self-conscious. The man's many questions bored him
considerably and made him rather uncomfortable. He seemed to
recollect having met the same gentleman a few days before,
across the counter at the bank where he worked, as a man with
similar features had called at the bank and obtained some information on business matters from him. He little realized that
that also was done purposely as another way to check up on
him for an important purpose.

The Wus soon learned from the Chaos that the Ch'i family
were entirely satisfied and ready to allow them to repay the
visit.

*   *   *

The Ch'i family let it be known to the Wu family that they
declared themselves satisfied with what they had seen at the
Wu house and that they accepted young Wu on general principles as their daughter's future husband in so far as their
opinion was concerned and they made it known through the go-
betweens that they were prepared to allow the Wus (young Wu
excepted) to see the girl.

Under usual circumstances such a thing is often done outside the girl's home and a meeting is usually arranged to take
place "unexpectedly" at an amusement place or a temple fair as
the average Chinese girl is more apt to welcome the idea of
making a trip outside the home looking her best in every way.
This makes her more readily approvable and such an arrangement is a safer way to inspect without arousing her suspicions,
whereas to ask her to dress up just to meet certain strangers in
the house is certainly not in keeping with the domestic habits of
most families. In recent years a shopping trip to the bazaar or
attending a theatrical performance would also serve such a
purpose.

In such cases the girl always goes in the company of her
parents and the go-betweens who can easily identify the girl
from a gathering of people particularly when a description of
her clothes worn on the occasion is previously given to the
inspection party. Mr. and Mrs. Ch'i thought it better to invite
the Wus to come to the house for this important mission as
their daughter was not in the habit of frequenting noisy outside places. The Wus favoured the idea, too, for a visit to the
girl's house would also help not only in acquainting themselves
with the general condition of the Ch'i house but also in seeing
the girl as her real self.

The Wus showed great prudence in making such an inspec-

Tho Chinese solemnize an egagement with conventional mementoes —a pair of heart-shaped pouches, each holding a pair of good luck *Ju Yi* of precious metals. *Ju Yi* translates "As Wished". Richer families would use a family heirloom for future identification purpose·. This is valuable in cases where a wedding is delayed for many years after the engagement.

tion and they finally agreed that besides young Wu's parents, his grandmother and the maidservant were also to go, for there is the Chinese superstition that some mischievous spirits, lurking invisible, might blind the eyes of the inspectors and allow some important defects to escape notice. Such a spirit is known as *Meng Yen Sha*(蒙眼煞), or the "Eye-Blindfolding Ghost", and is always mentioned with apprehension. Anyhow, eight eyes are better than four.

On the pre-arranged day, the Wu's arrived at the Ch'i house and were courteously ushered into the inner part of the home and found the Chaos already there. The girl was formally introduced to the family of her father's "rare friends", the Wus. Thus opportunities were provided for them to meet the girl personally and engage her in conversation. It was clearly noticeable that the Wus were immediately impressed by the girl's unaffected and courteous manners and cultured speech. As to her personal appearance they all agreed that she was good-looking though she used no cosmetics and wore only an ordinary dress of blue coolie cloth.

That same afternoon Mr. and Mrs. Chao called on the Wus to hear their decision which was gladly conveyed to the Ch'i family on the same day and the betrothal was definitely solemnized by the sending to the Ch'i family of a group of mementoes which served as a token of the validity of the engagement. These were wrapped in a piece of red silk and delivered to the girl's parents without letting the girl get knowledge of them. Congratulations were happily exchanged afterwards and the Wus marked the day with a feast in their home at which the news was broken to young Wu, asan accomplished fact, with an air of jubilation.

The enagement mementoes which Mr. and Mrs. Chao delivered to the Ch'i family were of a conventional kind and while not of any great commercial value were typical of an old custom. They consisted of a pair of little heart-shaped embroidered pouches with silken tassels in each of which were placed a pair of miniature silver *Ju Yi* (如意), or "Good-Luck Scepters," one pair of which was gold-plated. There was also an old pendant of mutton-fat jade, beautifully carved in a design of *Fu Shou*

San To (福壽三多), represented by the three magic fruits of good omens with a long-life character and a bat. This beautiful gem was one of the Wus' old heirlooms and had been used in tying many matrimonial knots in the family and was a valuable possession, dear to the hearts of many generations of Wus. It was said that the girl's father and mother, though quite ready for the glad news that her daughter was thus engaged to the promising scion of an old and decent family, burst into tears at the receipt of these mementoes as they were warned that their dear daughter would soon be taken away from their tender care to embark on a new phase of life with a young man a virtual stranger to her!

Such a ceremony is known locally as the *Hsiao Ting* (小定) or "Minor Engagement" as compared to the *Ta Ting* (大定), or "Major Engagement" later on. The engagement mementoes, it must be explained, serve as the embodiment of the sacred, unbreakable promise and are to be sent back to the groom's family together with the girl's trousseau immediately before the wedding rites.

*   *   *

A wedding ceremony in China may not be solemnized until a year, two years or even ten or fifteen years after the betrothal is definitely announced by the placing of the "Minor Engagement" mementoes, which is more often the case in the country. During such a long wait there may be some drastic changes in the social or economic standing of either or both families and often Fate may indeed dictate such changes in two opposite directions resulting in controversies of various kinds. Such examples are legion in fact as well as in fiction. But even they are not considered reason enough to wish to cancel a betrothal. The majority of people consider such engagements far too sacred to make any alterations in them, as breaking one intentionally is considered a great loss of prestige all around and is seldom resorted to except when there are really serious reasons. City people are usually married not long after the betrothal.

And so not many days after the "Minor Engagement" tokens had been delivered ceremoniously to the Ch'i family, the Wus sent word by the go-betweens Mr. and Mrs. Chao, conveying their intention to have the wedding take place in the seventh moon of the year which was but roughly sixty days after the engagement was announced. This was in keeping with the advice given by the astrologer, Mr. Liu, when he was consulted to match the couple's Eight Character Combinations. To this Mr. and Mrs. Ch'i were of course quite willing to agree although personally they would have preferred the wedding to be put off at least until the first moon of the next year which time was said to be equally auspicious. It is the common thing for a girl's parents to try to keep her in the family longer but such an effort is always doomed to failure because of the insistence of the opposite faction.

And besides, all parents know it too well that once the girl is engaged she does not belong to her parental home any longer and it is just as well to get her married off at the first opportunity. This is more true when there are disturbances in the land as may be witnessed by the numerous weddings during troubled times.

While the month for the wedding is settled by the bridegroom's family, that is about all they can decide for themselves in so far as the exact date of the nuptial ceremony is concerned. For as the Chaos visited the Ch'i people to announce the intention of the Wus they also were requested to ask for the "small date" by which is meant whether the wedding should take place in the first, the second or the third ten day period of the month. This depended upon something very intimate and known only to the girl and her parents, nay, indeed, only to herself. To be straightforward, such a thing had to do with the situation of the girl's being "unwell". To have a bride arrive at the groom's family during her "unwell" period is considered a very unlucky matter and an omen for *Chia Pai Jen Wang* (家敗人亡) or "collapse of the home or a death in the family." Such a thing must be avoided by all means.

Nor were the bride's parents in a position to fix the date for all they could say was the wedding should take place in the latter half of the month. The final decision, strange as it may seem, actually depended upon the astrologer, for he was relied upon to find the most likely auspicious day in the half-month period. For this purpose Scholar Wu's mother again visited the astrologer.

The astrologer prepared for the Wus the *T'ung Shu* (通書), a formal notice of the forthcoming wedding. This is a big document of red paper folded into a pamphlet and encased in a big red envelope. Both the document and the envelope are printed in gold with a beautiful design of dragon and phoenix. In this the principle clause was naturally the date of the marriage ceremony as this document served as the formal communication to the Ch'i family and was to be delivered to them in proper style. It also contained some mystic information.

Before the introduction of the marriage license system in China this famous *T'ung Shu* served a double purpose, for it was considered the official certificate of the union; to issue them all astrologers were responsible for a report to the government. And for this the law provided a revenue stamp of forty cents.

*　　　*　　　*

The special document called *T'ung Shu* which the astrologer prepared for the Wus contained a formal notification of the date of the forthcoming wedding as well as the date for the delivery of the document itself which the astrologer took great pains to select as the one with the best auspices. The document is always despatched to the bride's family approximately a month before the wedding date.

This document also gave the most propitious hour for mounting or dismounting the bridal sedan chair (*i.e.*, if it is not feasible to arrange mounting the chair at the given hour, try arranging a timely dismounting then), in which direction the couple should kneel when worshipping Heaven and Earth immediately upon arrival at the bridegroom's home, and similar provisions of a superstitious nature. It also warned the Wus to route the wedding procession so that all wayside wells and temples be avoided or at least as many as possible, because these are the favourite rendezvous of evil spirits and vagrant ghosts which might cause an unfortunate happening to the bride on the way.

Small boys and young girls were not to be permitted in the room when the bride entered the marriage chamber. Widows and women "in the family way" were also cautioned not to appear until after the bride was properly dressed to meet the family members and their friends. This also applied to people with animal cycle symbols of the Pig, the Rabbit and the Sheep, which varies with each year.

Before the notice was officially served to the Ch'i family, the gist of the information was made known through the go-betweens so that the Ch'i family could be prepared to expect the ceremonial party of "messengers". This important visitation is known as *T'ung Hsin* (通信), or "Sending the Message," and is otherwise known as *Kuo Li* (過禮), "Passing the Presents", although it is commonly referred to as *Tah Ting* or "Major Engagement".

There were a number of things to be sent as betrothal gifts to the Ch'i family and the Wus spent many a busy day of preparation. There were firstly a complete wardrobe of four season's wearing apparel for the bride, all made with the best silken materials procurable and following the specifications supplied by the Ch'i family through the go-betweens in order to assure a proper fit. There were also proper materials for making the bedclothes though, in accordance with an old local custom, the making of these was left to the girl's family and a sum of money went with the cloth to defray the "thread and needle expenses."

A complete set of beautiful jewelry in silver and gold, placed in a glass case decorated with proper design was another important item. A pair of domesticated geese of snow-white colour but painted a pinkish red were purchased and kept in the Wu family for a few days before sending. These geese are a noisy lot and with their high-pitched voices broadcast the glad tidings to the immediate neighbours of both families. (This is all that

Many kinds of gifts accompany the official document, announcing the date of an impending wedding. The Dragon and Phoenix Cakes are an indispensable item.

remains from an ancient custom of many hundred years' standing and the original birds used were the wild geese, perhaps an evidence of the bridegroom's skill in hunting.). A quantity of wine was also prepared as well as a hundred pieces of big pastry shop cakes with sugar cores, called *Lung Feng Pin* (龍鳳餅), or "Dragon and Phoenix Cakes", so-called from the pattern of the molds with which they are made. Also many big, ripe, red apples.

Another set of gifts was also prepared, consisting of many interesting objects: a quantity of pork and a quantity of mutton (rich families use live pigs and live sheep), a pair of live golden carps tied together with a red string by the back fins, a pair of lotus roots and a pair of hairy yams, also similarly tied, a lot of Chinese cosmetics (say, a hundred packages of Chinese face powder and as many round sheets of rouge cotton, each about three inches across), and an assortment of nuts and things called "fruits of happiness". There were also a few catties of white and a few catties of black sugar. In certain families all the things mentioned in this paragraph may be omitted.

Some Peking families also require a pair of hams and two legs of mutton as part of the betrothal gifts and these are to be presented to the go-betweens after having been received by the bride's family for the purpose of "helping the go-between's sore legs, fatigued and stiff from the many trips back and forth"! Most families, however, think this is nothing but a joke.

YOUNG WU IS MARRIED

A N AMATEUR matchmaker is referred to locally as the person "who drinks the pumpkin soup". This expression is widely known and almost universally understood by all Peking-*jen* but few can give the exact origin of this interesting metaphor. It is really very simple as any person who drinks a hot bowl of pumpkin soup (which is a familiar Peking family dish) will exude just about as much perspiration as an amateur matchmaker must expect to exude on account of his self-imposed exertion. The matchmaker's good work is never pronounced complete until the wedding is over and, as in the orthodox Peking families, the bride's high moral standing is definitely proved by the girl's purity. This is known as *Pao Kung Mei* (保紅媒), or "Guaranteeing the Red Match". Should there be anything wrong, the matchmaker will be the first to be blamed in the great commotion that always follows such an unfortunate incident. A clear and objective insight into the girl's family, uninfluenced by emotional like or dislike, and a sagacious observation on the part of the intending matchmakers are therefore an absolute necessity before even suggesting a match, considering how great an importance the Chinese place on the purity of a bride.

When the betrothal gifts had been duly prepared by the Wus, they invited Mrs. Chao to go formally to introduce the Wu family's official representatives on the forthcoming important mission to the house of the Ch'is. These representatives were to be two in number as two is an auspicious number and tradition required them to send two married women whose husbands were living. Widows must never be sent for this important visitation. Gentlemen are not eligible either.

The morning of the proper day found the Wus in a joyous mood, putting the final touches to the various gifts and by ten o'clock the headman and a number of coolies arrived from a store which rents wedding equipment and who had been engaged by the Wu family. Each of them wore a feathered hat and a gaudy-coloured robe over his own clothes, bringing with them the red and gild-lacquered gift boxes and wooden poles, painted red. In a few minutes the gifts were properly placed in the various containers. The geese were placed in a wooden container with a caged top and two lacquered jars of pewter were filled with wine and placed in similar carriers. The various other gifts were also placed in gild-lacquered trays and placed in conventional gift boxes made of heavy woodwork, lacquered and painted with beautiful designs.

The official *T'ung Shu*, the document notifying the bride's family of the impending wedding, was placed in a small box of red lacquer and together with the glass case containing the jewelry was mounted on a gift stand similar in shape to a table with a large tray on top, also properly coloured. The bride's wearing apparel, neatly folded, was carried on another such table.

Each of these units was carried by two coolies and the group of twenty-four were supervised by one headman. They formed a colourful procession. Mrs. Chao, young Wu's mother and another lady, all "dressed up", brought up the rear in a horse carriage and the procession slowly wended its way to the Ch'i residence on Pine Tree Lane in the west city. It is needless to add that all the Wu neighbours who saw the procession start were filled with admiration for it and many passers-by cast envious eyes on the stylish gift-bearing caravan as the big golden-crested geese announced triumphantly their progress by noisy cries.

On arrival at the destination the procession was welcomed inside the Ch'i house with a courteous reception and the gifts were placed on a big table in the main sitting room where there were a handful of women guests who had gathered to witness the ceremony. The geese were released in the courtyard. These, in the usual course of things, are not to be killed, cooked and eaten, nor kept as pets in the house as they have very naughty habits and the average Peking-*jen* finds no better thing to do but carry them to the market and sell them some days after their arrival, their part having been played!

The bride, who had by then been told of her betrothal, was asked to sit on the brick bed after having put on some of the clothing brought and then the lady representatives went forward and placed on her fingers the rings and on her arms the bracelets and in her hair the pins and other items of jewelry, while her young heart beat fast with the novel experience and her face blushed in fast flashes of red and white at the emissaries' murmured phrases of good luck. Congratulations, complimentary remarks and happy giggles filled the rooms.

A perfunctory conversation concluded the ceremony of

The betrothal presents are carried to the home of the bride with exaggerated pomp and panoply. The gifts are purposely spread out to require as many carriers as possible and a procession of twelve or sixteen units carried by twice that number of coolies is the typical Peking fashion. The above sketch shows a goose being carried in a special container.

"Major Engagement" and the official gift-bearing messengers bid the Ch'i family good-bye.

*   *   *

Immediately after the betrothal gifts were received by the Ch'i family they were distributed amongst their relatives and friends with the exception of the wearing apparel and jewelry. Everyone received a few Dragon and Phoenix Cakes, two or four packages of face powder and as many pads of rouge, and so forth which Mrs. Ch'i, the girl's mother, delivered when she called on each family in person to announce her daughter's engagement. As there were many such families to be notified, each family could get but a very small share of these gifts but small as each share was it served an important purpose. For, as is well known to the Peking-*jen* to receive such a share of the betrothal gifts is tantamount to receiving a requisition to send a present to form part of the girl's *Chia Chuang* (嫁粧), trousseau or dowry.

The conventional gift to a Chinese bride includes a set of China with a lucky design. Such a set includes a big vase in which to put feather dusters. A couple of imitation millet stalks with proper decorations are also inserted as lucky charms.

By *Chia Chuang* is meant the entire collection of gifts received and those of the family's own preparation which go to the bridegroom's family prior to the wedding to "stock up" the future home. The principal items of *Chia Chuang* are, of course, for the girl's family to donate, but friends and relatives are welcome and, indeed, are required to add to the collection and this is known as *T'ien Hsiang* (添箱) or "adding to (the contents of) the boxes."

The quality and quantity of the bride's trousseau depends naturally upon the financial means of the family, but it is a common thing for a father to run into debt in order to give his daughter a magnificent amount of presents, particularly when the bridegroom belongs to a rich family and even at that the bride's father has to be very courteous and apologize before and after sending the presents for "having given practically nothing." Some Peking families give their daughters at marriage a complete kit for housekeeping, including all furnitures and fixtures and the bridegroom's family will have no trouble filling up with these things their living quarters. Tables, desks, chairs, chests and bureaus, dressers, anything and everything, which may come under the heading of "household effects" as understood in the language of a customs examiner. It is a common practice to send a couple of maidservants, or little servant girls, as part of the bride's equipage, to stay with the bride in the new home for a month, two months or longer or even for life.

The Ch'i family did not have as many friends as the Wus had. Yet, nevertheless, there were many visitors from that day on and each visitor brought "additions" to the family's own gifts. Some sent a box of handkerchiefs of beautiful floral designs and others sent bottles of perfume and jars of face cream. A box of luxurious toilet soaps formed the gift of one and two pair of embroidered shoes formed that of another. The girl's father provided a collection of things following the conventional pattern. He did not wish to spend foolishly as he had other daughters to marry off yet and must not set an extravagant precedent. He bought her four pairs of camphor-wood chests, two pairs of big ones to store her clothes in and two pairs of small ones to contain her various other trinkets and jewelry and things, all bound with shining brass trimmings engraved with good-luck designs.

He bought her the indispensable dressing box (popularly known to foreigners as a "missey box") of beautiful hand-polished ebony with fine mother-of-pearl inlay work in gorgeous intricate designs. A pair of jewel trees in glass cases and a complete set of china of the conventional *Chia Chuang* style, including the big fruit bowl, the hat stands, flower vases, tea service and the big vase for putting the feather-dusters in. Even the feather-dusters were selected from the shop's best and embellished with proper symbolic decorations, a pair of paper fish dangling from the ends of the replica of a *Ch'ing* (磬) (a musical instrument originally made of jade) attached to a pair of imitation millet stalks complete with green leaves and golden-yellow ears, for these are symbolic of two phrases of good omens. The set of china had the same design on each of the pieces, that of the *Fu Kwei Po T'ou* (富貴白頭) or "Prosperity and Fame and Heads White" (*i.e.* may the couple be rich and distinguished and live together to be white-haired) which is represented by the tree peonies and the white-crested cuckoo.

As to clothes, there were enough to last her two years, the assortment being particularly strong in underwears and such things. Mr. Ch'i also bought her a pair of candlesticks and an oil lamp, made of sterling pewter that would not easily tarnish, although he knew they would hardly be of use in his daughter's new home. According to an old custom, however, a pair of big red candles must be kept burning throughout the evening of the wedding day and an oil lamp with a grass wick kept lighted throughout the first night. The latter is called the *Ch'ang Ming Teng* (長命燈) or "Long Life Lamp".

Miss Ch'i had a busy time, too, between then and her wedding as many of her schoolmates and family friends all wished to invite her to spend a day with them following another old local custom.

*   *   *

On the day before the wedding ceremony was to take place all the items that made up Miss Ch'i's dowry were assembled and the clothings and similar things were packed away in the camphor-wood chests at which four elderly married women whose husbands were living were invited to assist. After this little pieces of silk yarn of a bright red and green were tied to all the trimmings and to various other convenient places, such as the stems of the candlesticks and so on. There were several mirrors and each was covered with an embroidered "curtain" or handkerchief. A number of red paper decorations cleverly shaped with a pair of scissors were prepared and pasted on the

The Wus' housedoor was properly decorated on the occasion of young Wu's wedding. Four "Joy" characters were pasted on the brickwork beside the door. The colourful arch was heavily bedecked with silk hangings and paper flowers. The central part of the arch bore a phrase of four characters in shiny gild paper: *Tien Tso Chih Ho*, meaning "A Heaven-made Match"

boxes where they opened to serve as sealing labels. Some of these were of the famous endless knot design and others of the *Shuang Hsi* (雙喜) or "Double Joy" character.

The shiny brass locks were then closed and the keys given to the girl to keep in a purse in which the girl's father also put a sum of money as a symbol of good fortune. A pair of round lacquer boxes were filled with Chinese cookies, with auspicious designs on them, bought from the pastry shop. In tea jars were put a number of packages of fragrant jasmine tea and a number of red apples were piled into the fruit bowl. All these will be distributed to children and youngsters the guests might bring to the Wu house upon arrival of the gift-bearing procession. According to local custom everybody had a free hand there and then to take possession of a few from each kind as a legitimate privilege belonging to pre-wedding congratulators.

The Ch'i family had issued invitations to their friends asking their presence on the proper day for happy wine-drinking, at the same time the Wus invited their friends to witness the nuptial ceremony. The majority of friends were notified by messenger and others living far away were notified by mail but some of the important families and close relatives were paid formal calls. The invitations the two families sent out were both printed on red paper, enclosed in big red envelopes and were delivered more than a week before the day set for the wedding.

The Ch'i family had their house covered with a mat-shed (had the season been winter a covering of blue cloth would have been proper) and this was put up promptly. The Wus had their own summer shed still up and so had only to arrange for some proper decorations such as tiers of detachable glass windows each pane bearing the big red character *Hsi* (喜) for "Joy". At their door was put up a gay arch of colourful silks and paper flowers while over the door of the Ch'i family only some red and green silk buntings were hung. This is the local custom for a family marrying off a daughter and the simplicity does not mean that the family cannot afford a more showy decoration. Both families had big red paper squares bearing the *Hsi* character pasted on the sides of their doors, obliquely positioned in the conventional manner. Two would be quite enough but the Wus used four. It was rumoured that they were executed by young Wu himself. If this was true his handwriting must be said to be very good indeed, considering his youth.

An inner room in the Ch'i family was fixed up to be used as the *Hsi Fang* (喜房) or "Joy Room" where the girl sits the whole day on the brick bed, amidst callers who feel it a great favour to stay with the lucky girl. Here soft chatting is heard continually. Certain intimate information about certain things was whispered and explained to the girl by an elderly and affectionate aunt of hers, taking advantage of moments when they were alone in the room.

At the Wus, the three-roomed wing on the eastern side of their main courtyard quadrangle was fixed up properly, as here young Wu and his bride were to live from then on. All the furnishings were removed from the rooms and only some woodware was left as it was expected that the girl's dowry would fill up the rooms in so far as interior decoration was concerned. The rooms had been repapered snow-white and on the corners of the walls was pasted the same "Joy" character. The original white lace window curtains were taken off and ones of red silk took their place.

This was the happy couple's *Tung Fang* (洞房), literally translating "Cave Room" which is the proper phrase in the Chinese language by which a marriage chamber is referred to, particularly the bedroom.

*   *   *

The feast contractors with whom arrangements had been made brought their equipment and had a big stove built in the backyard of the Wu house. As the materials and ingredients were brought in the cooks started to busy themselves in their temporary headquarters there. Additional chairs and tables were also delivered by a furniture-renting establishment and set up in the courtyard, bearing embroidered chair covers and so forth.

Certain groups of guests had already begun to arrive with presents. Some brought red silk hangings with good-omen phrases in gold paper, such as "The Dragon and the Phoenix Present Good Auspices," "A Heaven-Made Match" and so on. Some brought red paper couplets with congratulatory messages, properly mounted. A friend of the Wus was again requested to act as bookkeeper to record the gifts received and to take charge of the expense account on the day of the wedding ceremony.

The most common form of wedding present, required to be given by each guest representing his or her family, is a sum of money placed in a red envelope and marked by a red label carrying the sender's name and address, the amount contained therein and the words *Hsi Ching* (喜敬), or "Congratulatory Gift". Those who are intimate enough to stay till the religious ceremony is over to meet the bride and to receive ceremonial kowtows from the newlywed couple are also required to give to them another present: a pair of earrings, a silk handkerchief, or some such thing. But the Peking-*jen* have found it a great convenience to give a sum of money with which the bride may buy herself anything she wants. Such a sum of money is also enclosed in a red envelope and this is called *Pai Li* (拜禮), or "Greeting Gift". These monetary presents are to be handed in on the day of the ceremony. Other gifts are more preferably delivered on the preceding day as thus they may be conveniently exhibited for the other guests to admire.

By four o'clock in the afternoon the bride's trousseau arrived—a long procession of sixteen parts forming the entire collection, each lot on a decorated table carried with poles by two uniformed coolies and all forming a picturesque spectacle. At the head of the procession were two well-dressed old gentlemen who were sent by the Ch'i family to be their representatives. These gentlemen were met by the Wus and ushered into their main sitting room. Congratulatory messages and polite words were exchanged, the two gentlemen apologizing for the poor dowry that the Ch'i family were able to give. The various things were then dismantled from the carrier-tables and in half an hour's time had all been properly placed in the room of the bride and her groom.

The two honorary escorts produced a list from their pocket and checked over the various items with the Wus. They found everything in order and left to tell the Ch'i family to that effect. It was interesting to note that the very first lot of things brought in was the important document of "Marriage Notification" or *Tung Shu* and the jewelry and clothes which had been originally sent by the Wu family. The bedclothes made in the Ch'i home with materials supplied by the Wus were also brought. Some married women with husbands living had been employed to sew the bedclothes and in the four corners of each piece of cotton-padded quilt or mattress were placed a few nuts and things, previously introduced as "the fruits of happiness". These consisted of dates, peanuts, a kind of dried berries called *Kwei Yuan* (桂圓) and walnuts. Collectively these names abbreviate to *Tsao Sheng Kwei Tze* (早生貴子) or "Speedily giving birth to a noble son" which, in the Chinese estimation, is the best of all good wishes for the occasion. The apples and eatables which were in the bride's boxes, or course, disappeared in no time and found their way into the hands of the youngsters who were on hand to do a faithful job of dividing them amongst themselves.

The main sitting room of the Wu family was again properly fixed up as a ceremonial hall and all those who came to offer their felicitations were ushered in where they were presented to the joyous Wu family. Young people also kowtowed to young Wu's grandmother and his parents. This was required by etiquette as being the proper way to show their respect and tender their congratulations. Most of them, however, actually kowtowed to the "Upper Side" where, behind a big table with brilliantly burning red candles, hung a scroll with a big "Joy" character.

Feasting began separately at the houses of the two families with a marriage supper and these were attended by many close friends and relatives happily wine-drinking till a late hour. Recently, however, instead of having the feasts in their own houses, people often hold their wedding receptions in some fashionable restaurant. This system has many conveniences, indeed, but in such cases there is usually no pre-wedding supper.

* * *

It was a bright day on which young Wu was to be married. Since early morning the men from the store that supplied the wedding equipment had presented themselves bringing with them the required paraphernalia including three sedan chairs, one red in colour and the other two green, all beautifully embroidered in festive designs of the dragon, the phoenix, the tree peonies and other floral motifs. A Chinese sedan chair is a closed affair squarish in shape with a top that simulates the curved roofs of a Chinese kiosk, surmounted by a ball-shaped top of shiny pewter. From the extending corners of the top hang strings of red tassels while little tassels of assorted colours line the edges and form pretty fringes.

Long-handled horn lanterns bearing the "Joy" character are carried by coolies in gala garb to form part of the wedding procession. This brings to mind the ancient custom of holding the marriage rites during the nigh .

Each of these sedan-chairs was to be carried by eight bearers in livery and tasseled hats. The chairs were at once rigged up in full style and then placed for exhibition on special stands of gild-lacquered woodwork, looking somewhat like stilted benches. By the side of the chairs were the stands on which rested the flags and wooden replicas of ancient war weapons which were to be carried by a number of coolies in gala garb to form a sort of "guard of honour" before the chairs when the procession went to and returned from the bride's home. There were the tiger flags, dragon flags and phoenix flags, and longhandled swords and spears all in gild-lacquered wood. Pairs of embroidered canopies in red silks and ultra-sized wooden fans painted green were also in evidence as well as a pair of "the sun and moon symbols" mounted on long handles.

These "symbols" were made by painting bamboo sieves about three feet across in red and hanging a round mirror on one side of each and decorating them with silk pieces tied into balls with the ends fluttering in the breeze. On another such stand were displayed the twelve pairs of lanterns made of water-buffalo horns also mounted on handles. These were also to be borne by pairs of coolies. Once upon a time marriage processions used to fetch the bride at night and these lanterns then served a useful purpose, but nowadays they are there just for the effect. One pair of square flags on shorter handles bore the characters K'ai Tao (開道), meaning "Clear the Way (for the procession to pass)". Two men with conical-shaped red hats will bear them on their shoulders rifle fashion and from the end of the flag-rods will hang the big brass gongs beaten for the same purpose.

Three or four horse carriages were also awaiting orders for immediate action. The musicians, very much similar to those employed at a funeral, had also arrived and besides the other instruments ten pairs of big kettle drums were brought and placed on individual drum stands draped with panels of embroidery. Even the No. 1 beggar of the district had presented himself in a decent-looking blue gown and reported to the Wus, declaring himself ready to lend a helping hand.

It was a busy day for the Wus, indeed, for guests soon arrived in good numbers and they had only time enough to say but a few words to each guest, acknowledging their "bestowing upon them their face", but the guests had no trouble engaging in conversation between themselves as is the usual fashion in such big gatherings, especially as most of them had met each other before in the Wu house and no introductions were necessary. They were served tea and cigarettes by the professional ushers and then grouped themselves to sit at the marriage feast.

At the proper hour suggested by the astrologer everything was in shape for the procession to start for the Ch'i residence to fetch the bride.

*　　　　　*　　　　　*

According to the custom in Peking a woman who has given birth to a boy or boys and whose husband is living should be sent by the bridegroom's family as the *Ch'ui Ch'in T'ai T'ai* (娶親太太), or "Lady to Fetch the Bride". Another woman answering to above qualifications should also be sent by the bride's family and she is called the *Sung Ch'in T'ai T'ai* (送親太太), or "Lady to Escort the Bride".

These two personages play important parts in the wedding ceremony. The former is entrusted with the work which the title indicates as well as carry to the bride's home a red silk hood with which the girl's face will be veiled until it is taken off by the bridegroom after her arrival at her new home. She is also to take to the bride the so-called "Chair-Mounting Robe", a loose garment of red silk to be worn by the bride en route. Such a robe is not possessed or prepared by each family as marriages in a single family are necessarily few and far between but any family who has such a robe will be only too glad to lend it to friends and relatives as there is a superstition that the more weddings such a robe has been used for the more auspicious it will be to the next bride who wears it.

There were also to be four gentlemen guests who would be sent to the bride's home nominally to see that the girl is "fetched" and on whom rests also the responsibility to steal the pair of "Bowls of Posterity" from the bride's home. As a matter of fact they do not really need to sneak into the kitchen, identify the proper pieces from the family's crokery and secretly decamp with them back to the groom's family undiscovered as the things, tied together with red string to two pairs of chopsticks, will be delivered to them by the professional ushers at the bride's home.

An aunt of young Wu kindly consented to act as the "Lady to Fetch the Bride" and a group of his friends agreed to be the gentlemen representatives and they pinned red silk flowers on their robes as a badge. The "Lady to Fetch the Bride" was also asked to sit at a "table" at the feast all by herself where she received three kowtows from the groom. She did not really eat as this was just a ceremonial act.

On that day young Wu wore a brand new ensemble composed of a gorgeous long gown of blue satin with a medallion design and a black jacket of the same design and material On his breast was pinned a big red peony of red silk, fully nine inches in diameter with beautiful green leaves. This was one of a pair, the other was to be worn by his bride.

*　　　　　*　　　　　*

At the proper hour the wedding procession started off fn

full style.

Under the direction of the procession leader, the chair-bearers manned the sedans and the coolies with the various flags and things formed themselves into two lines. A professional master-of-ceremonies took a brass tray holding a copy of the Almanac, a mirror and an apple as well as a small oil lamp and made the rounds of the three sedan chairs to satisfy himself that there were no evil spirits hidden away in them. The flickering light and the almighty Almanac would be quite effective for this check-up. The musicians, notably those carrying the big drums slung from their neck, took up their positions in two rows in front of the marriage chamber and awaited a signal from inside to strike up the proper joyous air.

Inside the marriage chamber the "Lady to Fetch the Bride" lighted a bundle of incense sticks before the God of Happiness, kowtowing three times, then she left with the maidservant who was to assist her and seated herself in the red sedan chair with the front open. The servant carrying the "Chair-Mounting Robe" and the red silk hood or veil was to go in a carriage behind the sedan chairs. Four women of the proper qualifications were invited to "make the bed", *i e.*, to spread the mattresses and so on. Four small boys were selected from those brought by the guests and told to sit one on each of the four corners of the big brick bed. Another small boy was told to stand in the room holding a big brass gong borrowed from the musicians on which he beat three times. This was the signal for the procession to

Before a wedding procession starts off to fetch the bride, the sedan chairs are inspected to see if any evil spirits might be lurking in them. The all-reflecting mirror, the almighty Almanac and an oil lamp will do the trick. An apple is also used as the Chinese word for "apple" has the same sound as that for "peaceful".

start and the signal was immediately picked up by the waiting musicians in the courtyard.

Young Wu, the bridegroom, was not to wait idly for his bride to arrive for he had an important duty to perform. In the company of Mr. Chao, his father-in-faith and the chief match-maker, he entered one of the horse carriages and started a few minutes later for the Ch'i residence. In another carriage rode the four gentlemen representatives for the same destination, their pockets full of little red paper packages, some containing pinches of tea leaves and others containing small coins. One man was equipped also with a good handful of small coins. In the meantime a couple of coolies in livery carrying a gaudy gift box containing a complete multi-coursed feast was also des-patched to the bride's family for this was the *Li Niang Fan* (離娘飯), or "Farewell Dinner to Mother". A similar feast was despatched to the Chao residence as a proper token acknowledg-ing the good offices of the honorary go-betweens.

*   *   *

The house of the Ch'i family on Pine Tree Lane was also a busy place on this day as feasting was going on briskly for many guests called to offer their congratulations. These also brought sums of money as a *Lien Ching* (奩敬), or "Dowry Gift", but in reality this money did not go to the bride herself but rather to her family. Gifts "in kind" were not to be brought at such a late moment. A group of four women were invited to "assist" the girl to mount the sedan chair. These included a married cousin of the girl who was to serve as the "Lady to Escort the Bride".

About noon the colourful procession with the three sedan chairs arrived at the door of the Ch'i residence and the red sedan chair was lowered to the ground and the "Lady to Fetch the Bride", who alighted therefrom assisted by the servant woman, was welcomed into the compound. She was ushered to the bride's room whom she found sitting on the brick bed. She and the other women helped the bride to don the red robe and on her head was placed the silken hood or veil.

Following in the footsteps of the "Lady to Fetch the Bride" were the four gentlemen representatives who came in a carriage and who wished also to gain admittance into the Ch'i house but their fate was different. They found the gate shut tight in their faces! This was not at all unexpected and was quite in keeping with an ancient custom.

There was then a staged conference at the door between the four gentleman representatives on the outside and some men and children, members from the "guest body" in the bride's family, on the inside. They bargained with the door barred tight between the two parties. There was some make-believe arguments, the representatives, requesting humbly for the opposite faction to please open the door but all to no purpose. There were demands made from inside. First the musicians waiting outside were to play them a piece of music known as "The Beetle Creeping on a Bamboo" and then another piece called "Chao K'uang-yin Beating the Date Tree," the former with typical short pauses between the cantos of the music and the latter characterized by rattling with drum-sticks on the wooden edges of the drums. All these requests were gladly complied with but still the door was not opened. The men outside then decided to resort to bribery.

A small package containing some tea leaves was pushed under the door, followed by another and still another. The opposite faction were apparently delighted as the children could be heard fighting noisily over them. These were followed by the little packages containing money over which the children fought even more feverishly. The "ice" having thus been broken, the representatives in a soft-toned and humble manner, begged that the auspicious hour should not be allowed to elapse at which the faction inside showed a fellow-feeling and so a *Ho Yueh* (和約) or "reconciliation" was declared and the door was opened wide to allow all to enter. To mark their triumphant entry the handful of coins were tossed to the children as a good omen by the four gentleman representatives as they entered the courtyard.

*   *   *

The red sedan chair occupied by the "Lady to Fetch the Bride" on the way to the bride's home was dismantled from the carrying poles and moved inside the courtyard of the Ch'i residence where a number of drum-stands had already been brought by some coolies from the Wu home and set up. As the sedan chair was placed against the open door of the room where the bride was the drummers and other musicians began to play. The four gentleman representatives who had been entertained more or less half-heartedly in the shed-covered courtyard saw to it silently that the bride mounted the chair without a "hitch", "stole" the so-called "Bowls of Posterity", took a hurried leave, more or less in a "French" fashion, and returned to the Wu house.

The bride was helped to enter the sedan chair by the "Lady

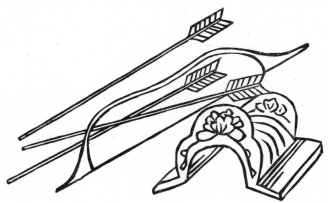

A bride steps over a saddle when she alights from her sedan chair, while the bridegroom shoots three headless arrows through the door of the "Cave Room" at some imaginary evil spirits. These acts are merely a symbolic procedure now but must be said to be reminiscent of some savage customs in the dim primitive past.

to Fetch the Bride'' and the ''Lady to Escort the Bride.'' She wept audibly and shed tears as she was actually faced with the cruel reality of having to leave ''by force'' her dear parents. As a matter of fact, to weep when a bride leaves her parental home is not only permissible but actually encouraged for there is a belief in Peking that for a bride not to weep indicates trouble ahead. Parents are proud of their daughter's weeping as this shows not only her maiden helplessness but also is a reflection on the happy relationship that had existed between parents and daughter. In certain families there is the custom of having the girl carried and deposited bodily in the sedan chair by the girl's father or an uncle or by a brother of hers but this was not followed in the case of Miss Ch'i as such a custom is not universally observed. Both her parents had tears in their eyes, too, as they watched the sedan chair being carried away with their daughter.

Meanwhile the two matrons, to fetch and to escort the bride respectively, walked out of the house and mounted the two green chairs waiting for them in the street. Two younger brothers of the bride took up their positions beside the red sedan chair as, by rule of propriety, they were required to walk with the sedan chair as a sort of bodyguard to their sister (still weeping inside) all the way to the family of the groom, thus to demonstrate their brotherly affection in a fitting manner. And so the entire procession started on the journey Wuward.

Young Wu, who had by then arrived in a horse carriage, was for the first time presented formally to his wife's parents by Mr. Chao, the chief match-maker, who had come with him. In the main sitting room of the Ch'i family under the curious, staring eyes of a multitude of admiring guests, ladies and gentlemen alike, he, silent and indeed somewhat dumbfounded, was told to kneel and kowtow three times to the father and then three more times to the mother who sat in a chair to receive the obeisance. Then, as though by an invisible rope fastened to his nose he was led away. This is an important duty on the part of a son-in-law to thank the bride's parents for giving the girl away to be his wife and it is a trying experience for a bashful young bridegroom indeed.

*   *   *

The triumphant music of the procession announced to the Wus the arrival of the bridal party. Young Wu, who had arrived home some minutes ahead, was told to stay in the ''Cave Room'' or marriage chamber to where the ''Lady to Escort the Bride'' and the ''Lady to Fetch the Bride'', who had dismounted from the two green chairs, also went and there they stood by the side of the open door. A brazier containing burning charcoals was placed in the courtyard and over this the red sedan chair was carried as a sort of exorcistic measure.

Young Wu's happy and proud father was also in the room ''by appointment'' to light another bundle of incense sticks before the paper images of the Gods of Heaven and Earth. And when the sedan chair was placed tightly against the door, he placed a saddle of gild-lacquered wood on the threshold. He also handed his son a bow and three pointless arrows which

One of the formalities immediately following the arrival of the bride in her new home is the ceremonial wine drinking from the "Interchanged Cups". Both pots and cups are tied together with red string. The couple silently toast each other.

the latter shot through the door crack "in order to scare away the evil spirits that might have been there." The "Lady to Fetch the Bride" had taken in her hand a lacquered vase containing some "five kinds of grains" and two small ingots, one of silver and the other of gold, as well as the midget Good Luck Scepters of silver which had been used as betrothal mementoes and had since been brought back with the girl's dowry.

In less time than it takes to describe it the bride was assisted to alight from the sedan chair by the two matrons and stepping over the saddle was for the first time in the bridegroom's domain. In that very minute an apple was held out by one of the matrons to the bride's mouth and she was told to bite off a mouthful from it. This she did and the apple was then thrown on the brick bed. The Good Luck Scepters were also placed in the bride's hands for a symbolic moment and then taken away from her. The lacquered vase called *Pao P'ing* (寶瓶) or "Treasure Vase" was handed to her and she carried it against her bosom as she walked, or rather as she was moved, to the right side of her bridegroom. Both knelt down together and kowtowed three times before the Gods of Heaven and Earth. Then the bride was taken to the inner room where the matrons assisting her took the Treasure Vase from her and she was helped to sit on the brick bed near the edge with her legs folded and draped over with the long flowing red ceremonial robe. Young Wu was given an old-fashioned Chinese steelyard (minus the weight) and with this he lifted the hood or veil, which had covered her face all the time since she left her parental home, off the bride's head. And so for the very first time the young couple were brought face to face.

She was too bashful to look up, as can easily be imagined, but from what he was able to discern by a hurried glance young Wu saw for himself that his young bride was not bad to look at!

*   *   *

On the trip from the bride's home to that of the groom the wedding procession was accompanied by four gentlemen selected from the many guests who had gathered at the Ch'i family's reception. These came in a carriage provided by the Ch'i family and they were briefly entertained by the Wus after the arrival of the procession. The two younger brothers of the bride, who had walked all the way by the side of the red sedan chair, however, were specially invited to come inside the marriage chamber to see that "their sister had had a peaceful journey" as riding in an air-tight sedan chair for the long trip,

particularly on such a warm summer afternoon as it was in the
present case, was a tedious experience. The two boys were glad
that their sister was none the worse in spite of the trip and they
left to tell their folks back home to that effect. The four gentlemen also left.

Meanwhile there went on another series of semi-farcical
doings in the marriage chamber.

The first thing was to stick in the hair of the bride a pair
of chenille ornaments in the form of two miniature young men
riding on the legendary animal *Ch'i Lin* (麒麟) or "Unicorn".
Then the matrons attending the bride and groom took a pair of
gild-lacquered wine pots which were tied together with a long
piece of red string at the handles and poured from each pot
some wine into two small cups also tied together in the same
fashion. The cups were handed to the bride and the groom respectively and each of them was told to drink a small mouthful.

Then the cups were exchanged, the bride to drink from the
groom's cup and the groom from the bride's. thus performing
the ceremony of *Chiao Pei* (交杯) or "Interchanged Cups" each
toasting in silence his or her spouse. The "Bowls of Posterity"
were now brought into play. In these were placed thirty-two
small meat dumplings of a halfmoon shape and four round ones,
some of them tied together with red strings by pairs. These are
called the "Son and Grandson Dumplings" and by custom are
to be supplied by the bride's family and brought with
the "Lady to Escort the Bride" by her servant and delivered to
the cooks at the bridegroom's family, together with a small
sum of money enclosed in red paper as a "tip" to the cooks, so
they will remember to cook the dumplings only "half-done"!

These dumplings were brought in the "Bowls of Posterity"
quite raw, and were taken to the bride and the groom to eat.
Being raw they were not good to eat, so the bits bitten off were
taken out of the mouth and, tradition faithfully followed, were
placed under the mat covering the brick bed. While this was
done some children anxiously waiting to see the bride questioned from outside the room in a playful manner whether they
were not raw. Some one inside the room answered that they
were. In this humourous way a good wish was expressed to the
new couple, for the Chinese word for "raw" (*Sheng*) (生) has
the same sound as the word meaning "Giving birth to children"
and this good wish is therefore expressed in unison by different
well-wishing groups of guests for the benefit of and also at the
expense of the bashful new couple. By now a group of musicians
who had been playing certain smaller instruments in the
courtyard also withdrew, for the duty of the procession men
was at an end.

The bride was given a short time to rest herself. An elderly
woman with threads of five colours went to her and applied
them lightly to the girl's forehead pretending to remove by
twisting the threads some of the hairs on that part of her head
for the purpose of trimming the hair to a clear squarish front.
This is called *K'ai Lien* (開臉), or "Opening the Face", as all
married women according to the old rules must have the forehead cleared of the hair in a neat line. Pulling out the hair to

get the proper effect would be done earnestly some other day but the ceremonial beginning was made at this time.

Then the matrons helped her to do her hair properly, applied cosmetics and dressed her up in a brand new gown of fine material (this must be originally from the groom's family, no matter how poor and no matter how many better ones her parents gave her in her dowry) and on her head was placed a "Phoenix Hat", a headdress of chenille flowers, with nine phoenixes arranged around the front rim and on the crown. The big red silk peony was pinned on her dress.

Thus properly dressed the young couple were made to sit shoulder to shoulder on the brick bed and before them a complete feast was spread. The women in turn offered them helpings of the food. With each helping a good wish was expressed. This was just another formality for the bride and her groom certainly could not eat.

*   *   *

After young Wu and his bride had been exclusively "feasted" in their marriage chamber, which ceremony is known as *Yuan Fan* (圓飯) or "Feast of Harmony", they were taken by their parents to worship the family Kitchen God, as well as the family shrine of the Goddess of Mercy and other deities. They also kowtowed to the ancestral tablets kept in a separate room. The new couple were then taken to the main sitting room where all the women guests were waiting for them to appear. Gentleman guests were either grouped in the outside guest parlour or in the big courtyard and were all equally anxious to meet the bride and the groom in the formal way, which is known locally as *Fen Ta Hsiao* (分大小), "Designating Big or Small", as the relationship between the bride and each of the family members and the many relatives and friends gathered there must be verified at this time. The ceremony started from the eldest member of the immediate family circle and went on down in the order of precedence.

A big chair was moved to the centre of the sitting room. Young Wu's grandmother was naturally the first person to be honoured and she sat in the chair while the bride and the groom knelt on a piece of red carpet and kowtowed three times to her. She acknowledged the obeisance with good wishes and gave the bride a small present wrapped in a piece of red paper. Exactly what was inside nobody knew. Some said it contained a gold hair pin.

The next to receive kowtows were Wu's father and mother who sat in the chair one after another for the purpose. Then followed some near and far relatives, men and women and children, and each person bargained politely before sitting in the chair of honour but no one actually withdrew from this important function. An elderly woman who knew most of the Wu family's relatives and friends was urged to be "Mistress of Ceremonies" and she arranged the order for each person to be presented so that the nearest proper order of precedence was able to be followed in a way satisfactory to the entire gathering. Guests are liable to feel offended in case an oversight occurs and may express their annoyance in a noisy fashion, resulting in loss of face to all concerned. To sum up, all the guests who were senior to the bride and her groom either in age or in genealogical order received ceremonial *Shuang Li* (雙禮), or "Paired Kow-tows", from them and handed them gifts of different kinds as a token of thanks, mostly sums of money. All who were their juniors were also called before them one by one to wish them happiness by saluting them in some fitting manner. There were many people to whom they kowtowed and the ordeal took fully two hours.

By five o'clock in the afternoon the professional ushers (con-currently waiters at the feast tables), called *Ch'a Shih Fu* (茶師付), or "Tea Masters", announced by a typical call the arrival of the *Ch'ih Chiu Ti* (吃酒的), or "Wine Eaters", two ladies sent by the bride's family for this particular purpose in a carriage. They were invited to sit at a table at which four women selected from among the guests in the Wu house also sat and a complete feast was spread out before them. At this nobody actually ate but in a congenial way conversation was carried on in a hushed undertone, the callers expressing the Ch'i family's gratitude in a general way and apologizing on their behalf for their ignorance about the niceties of good manners. The feast which was not started, however, ended by the Tea Master bringing a bowl of clear soup on a brass tray, and serving it to the guests, signified that the ceremony was at an end. The two guests tipped him with a red envelope containing some money by placing it in the brass tray. They left after the bridegroom had thanked them for coming by kowtowing to them.

Supper had by then commenced and every caller was again entertained at a luxurious feast, everybody drinking happily to the full of their capacity.

In the main sitting room guests were formally served with tea and cigarettes or tobacco by the bride with her own dainty hands. She poured and brought tea to each person and lighted the cigarettes or pipes. Meanwhile talkative guests, mostly women, button-holed her with little questions about her own family which she answered briefly in a near-whisper as it would be considered bad manners for her, a "new wife", to speak loudly.

Everybody eulogized her for her good manners and fine appearance Some old women openly talked about her beauti-ful features. Old Mrs. Wu, the grandmother, was overwhelmed with joy. Tottering forward to the bride, she lifted the small tassels on her headdress to see if her hair was good and black. It was quite black, she found.

*   *   *

A popular Chinese doggerel gives the four happiest incidents in life as being a heavy downpour after a long period of drought; meeting unexpectedly an old friend in a foreign land; seeing one's name in the announcement of successful candidates' at the Imperial Examinations; and the "Night of the Floral Candle" in the "Cave Room". The Chinese have a way of listing many things of a similar nature with the most positive one at the end and it is only natural that the "Night of the Floral Candle" comes as the last item in the list. By "Night of the Floral Candle" is understood the first night of a happy wedding.

*   *   *

By ten o'clock in the evening of the day of the happy event, young Wu's grandmother bade him and his bride leave the main sitting room to go and have some rest for "they had a busy day and must be quite tired." Thus excused, they made for their own room, accompanied by a group of women at the head of which were young Wu's mother and the young person who had acted as the "Lady to Fetch the Bride". The bed was made by these women with the new bedclothes and a big padded coverlet of red satin was spread out for both to use.

Before the newly-weds retired they were made to sit shoulder to shoulder on the edge of the bed and eat the "Long Life Noodles". This, as a sort of light supper at the bed-side, consisted of some noodles cooked in broth and placed in the "Bowls of Posterity". It was fed to the bride and the groom by the matrons who had prepared the bed. There were good wishes said as they ate, such as "May you live to have hair as white as the noodles and may your happiness be as endless," and so forth. Young Wu finished his bowl but his young bride only nibbled a little mouthful. "People must not go to bed on their first night with an empty stomach", the matrons explained.

After the noodles had been eaten it was time for all to withdraw from the bedroom. All the lights were put out except the small flickering lamp of sesamum oil which was to be kept burning until the next morning.

*   *   *

Early the next morning the bride's mother called in person in a carriage to congratulate the Wus and to take her daughter and her husband to her home for their first visit together. This is locally known as *Hwei Men* (回門), or "Returning to the Door" of the maiden home. Young Wu and his beautiful bride who had risen very early in the morning and had hurriedly dressed in proper style were soon triumphantly on their way.

At the Ch'i residence young Wu was naturally the "man of the day" and very much "in the limelight" and all the Ch'i folks and their friends greeted him with suitable congratulatory remarks. His wife was also warmly received by the gathering of people there, who had stayed overnight in order to meet her home coming husband. A full-coursed dinner was served in their honour and much happy wine-drinking was again indulged in. Before noon the couple were escorted to their own home by the proud mother-in-law. She was happy beyond description for everybody who saw young Wu said that in matrimony her daughter had got a "bargain."

On the morning of the third day the young couple performed the rite of "Emptying the Treasure Vase." Young Wu and his bride were made to sit tailor fashion, facing each other, on the brick bed with their garments lapped over their knees. The vase was emptied of its contents of grains and silver ingots and so on into their laps, thus symbolizing an abundance of food and money. It was said that into whose lap fell the most of everything was adjudged the future prosperity of the two families (that of the bride or of the groom) thus united by their marriage.

Not long after this ceremony, on a properly selected date, the bride was taken in the company of her groom to the Wu family's graveyard where she was presented to the spirits of the Wus who had gone on to the next world. Later a round of calls were made on all friends and relatives who had either presented themselves at the wedding or else sent gifts. Before all seniors they kowtowed together in the same way as they had done on the day of the ceremony in their home. This, of course, did not apply in cases where such a rite had been performed before.

The young wife was accustomed to the domestic work in the home and her ability was not without its due admirers. It was true that she was careful in everything and tried successfully to please everybody in the family, particularly the old grandmother, to whom particular respect was requested of her by her husband in their private moments.

*   *   *

There were frequent exchanges of visits between the Wu and the Ch'i family during the first month after the wedding. On the fourth day and the sixth day the visitors were confined to people from the Ch'i family alone but on the ninth and the eighteenth day, as local custom decrees, the Ch'i family brought also their friends and relatives who were desirous of being presented to the Wu family as a token of their wishing to be considered also relations to the Wus. The Wus were really glad of this and they hastily repaid the calls at the different houses to confirm their willingness.

On the fifteenth day the bride was taken to her maiden home for the day but much as the Ch'is wished to keep her overnight they had to send her back before sun-down, for a newly married couple must not be separated even for a single night in the first month and the absence of either the bride or the groom during the month is considered a bad omen. In this respect it is similar in principle to the foreign honeymoon except that the Chinese do not travel about during the month but stay in their home.

Young Wu loved his bride dearly although he had not met her before the afternoon of the wedding day which sounds rather amusing but it must be admitted that marriage in this conventional way is responsible for many happy unions in China. In this country courting begins after marriage which, instead of being the grave of Love, is rather its cradle. "Chinese marriage", declares a famous scholar, "does require much adjustment on the part of the husband as well as that of the wife but they always do their best at such efforts with the understanding that they both are in for it and must make the best of the situation from which there is no turning away and no back-door for a convenient exit."

On the day the marriage was exactly a month old, the bride's mother came to take her daughter home for the customary "time

away"—an occasion of family reunion much looked forward to
by the entire Ch'i family·   Mrs. Ch'i brought up the question in
the typical Peking manner before young Wu's grandmother, she
being the eldest female member in the household it was up to
her to decide how many days the bride should be allowed to stay
away or whether she should go at all.   Such an application is
never refused for to refuse it would mean controversy of one sort
or another. Young Mrs. Wu got permission to stay away six days
but she came back on the fourth, for it is considered disrespectful to stay away the full length of the permitted period.

*   *   *

About a year later, it was disclosed that young Wu's wife
was an expectant mother.   She thought that she was sick but
her observant mother-in-law thought differently and it soon was
confirmed that the latter was right.

The white-haired grandmother was particularly glad to hear
of the tidings. Often she had secretly watched the young woman
while she was about to cross the threshold.   She noticed that
every time she crossed it she used her left foot.   Of this she was
glad, for it indicated to her superstitious way of calculation
that the baby to come was to be a boy. . .And that would begin
the life cycle of another Peking man.

THE END

INDEX

This Index is the work of Mme. Elena Vetch, widow of the late Henri Vetch, considerably supplemented by Derk Bodde. Under each entry, the book's Volume I or Volume II are respectively indicated by an italicized 1 or 2, followed by a period, in turn followed by the relevant paginations. Thus "Drum Tower, *1*.160; *2*.198," indicates that references to this structure occur both in Volume I, page 160 and Volume II, page 198.

The main text of the book contains such an abundance of names and terms, both in Chinese and English, as to preclude the inclusion of all of them here. For example, the book quotes twenty-nine proverbial sayings and names eleven varieties of pigeons, but none of these is individually listed in the Index. Nonetheless, all of them can in fact be readily located by referring to the pages listed in the Index under its two general relevant headings, "proverbial sayings" and "pigeons, varieties." Similarly, although the Index itself provides no Chinese characters for its Chinese names and terms, the characters will nevertheless almost invariably be found on the same pages of main text indicated by the Index for these names and terms.

The book's major technical weakness is its occasional failure to romanize Chinese names and terms strictly according to the standard Wade-Giles system. Most such errors result from the author's changing of Wade-Giles initial *hu-* and *ku-* into his own *hw-* and *kw-*, or of Wade-Giles *tzu* into his own *tse* or *tze*, or yet again because he omits all umlauts over *u*, thereby producing such oddities as *ch'ui* and *lui* for Wade-Giles *ch'ü* and *lü*. These and other romanization errors have been systematically corrected throughout the Index, whose romanizations, therefore, should be accepted as accurate even when they differ from those in the main text. In a few individual instances, cross references from the wrong romanizations to the corrected forms have been included in the Index. In a more general way, warnings of *group* misromanizations have also been inserted at the places alphabetically appropriate for them, as, for example, in the caption: "*kwang/kwei*, errors for *kuang/kuei*."

ERRATA

Page	Paragraph	Line	Correction

VOLUME I

Page	Paragraph	Line	Correction
19	bottom	2	for *K'ang* read *Ch'uang* (twice)
23	4	3	for *tsueh chin* read *tsui chin*
29	2	1	for *Ko Sheng-erh* read *Kou Sheng-erh*
41		23	*for* ortures *read* tortures
43	3	5	*for* tonque *read* tongue
61	bottom	6	for *to* read *tou*
69	6	8	*for* elearly *read* clearly
116	4	3	*for* 厶 *read* 光 (second character for 光 Shan Kuang Niang Niang)
159	bottom	1	for *Mou Tao Yu* read *Mo Tao Yü*
165	3	11	*for* oya *read* soya
181	bottom	3	for *Hwang Miao* read *Huang Niao*
181		bottom	*for* cross-beak *read* grosbeak
184		13	for *Lao Hsih* read *Lao Shih*
220		5 from bottom	for *to-erh* read *t'ou-erh*

VOLUME II

Page	Paragraph	Line	Correction
vi	under "Preparing for the New Year"		*for* b anches *read* branches
6	5	1	for *fen shui* read *fen shu*
7	bottom	11	*for* profficiency *read* proficiency
10		9	for *Hsueh Shung Mei* read *Hsüeh Shang Mei*
13		14	*for* it to impress *read* is to impress
16	3	4	*for* Tze Po-t'ao *read* Tso Po-t'ao
19	2	1	for *ju hsuing ti* read *ju hsiung ti*
19	2	4	for *tsueh* read *tsui*
20	2	4	for *tsueh tsao* read *tsui tsao*
23		15	for *Ou* 蒙 read *o* 惡
23	5	2	for *jen nao* read *je nao*
31	3, 4, 5		*for* Ho Yi *read* Hou Yi (three times)
34	3	9	*for* 暈 *read* 葷
35	3	4, 5	for *Yuang Ping* read *Yüan Ping* (twice)
46	middle	1	for *pa-kuo-erh* read *pa-kou-erh*
46	middle	3	for *shih tze kuo* read *shih tzu kou*
47	3	bottom	for *kwi tsueh-erh* read *kuei tsui-erh*
52		3	*for* 璧 *read* 壁
57	bottom	4, 5	for *hu-ba-la* read *ho-po-lao* (twice)
58		9	*for* Ming paintings *read* Sung paintings
63	picture caption	3	*for* tho *read* the
64		8	*for* chryanthemum *read* chrysanthemum
65	4	1	for *chi ching* read *chi chin*

Page	Paragraph	Line	Correction
66	middle	7	*for* when be found *read* when he found
68		7	*for* to n *read* to a
68		8	*for* hillock ia *read* hillock in
68	bottom	7	*for* ithe northern *read* the northern
72	2	2	for *Hawa* read *Hua*
100	3	1	for *wan tien* read *wan lien*
119		18	for *Huo Yung* read *Hou Yung*
129	picture caption	1	*for* riyer *read* river
144	4	1, 10	*for* Ch'in Ch'uing *read* Ch'in Ch'iung (twice)
144		10	*for* Yu-Ch'ih Ching Teh *read* Yü-ch'ih Ching-te
154		11 from bottom	*for* Huo Ching *read* Hou Ching
162		1	for *-jne* read *-jen*
168	4	3	*for* Sh'iu Ch'u-chi *read* Ch'iu Ch'u-chi
192	2	1	*for* It *read* In
202	3	12	*for* asan *read* as an
202	bottom	1	*for* enagement *read* engagement
205		11 from bottom	for *Lung Feng Pin* read *Lung Feng Ping*
207		12-13	for *Pao Kung Mei* read *Pao Hung Mei*
216		bottom	*for* off fn *read* off in